중학 영문법

COOL grammar

Book 3

Happy House

About This Book

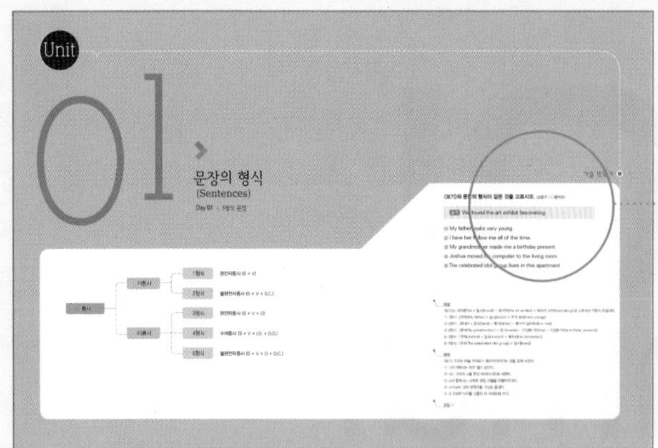

기출 맛보기

실제 중학교 내신 기출을 응용한 문제를 통해
해당 Unit에서 배울 내용을 간단하게 확인할 수 있습니다.

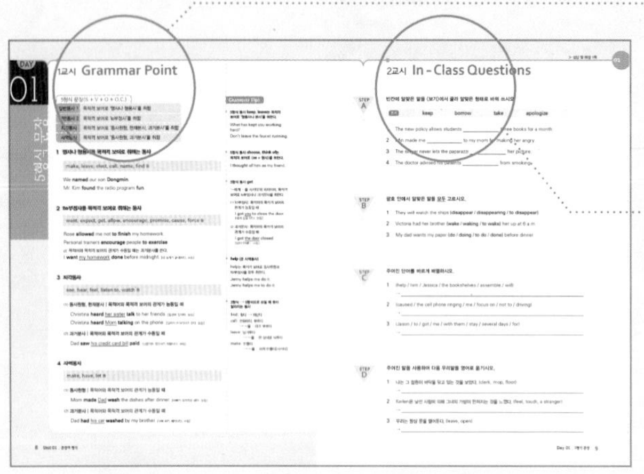

1교시 Grammar Point

해당 DAY에서 배워야 할 핵심 문법들을
간단하고 명확하게 체계적으로 정리했습니다.

2교시 In-Class Questions

1교시 Grammar Point에서 배운 내용을 확인할 수 있는
문항을 통해 간단하게 핵심 부분을 확인할 수 있습니다.

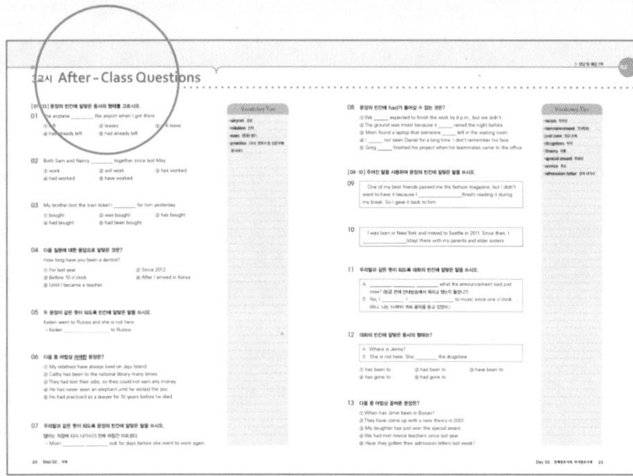

3교시 After-Class Questions (25문항)

다양하고 풍부한 주관식과 객관식 문항을 통해서
1교시에서 공부한 내용을 자연스럽게 이해하고
습득할 수 있습니다.

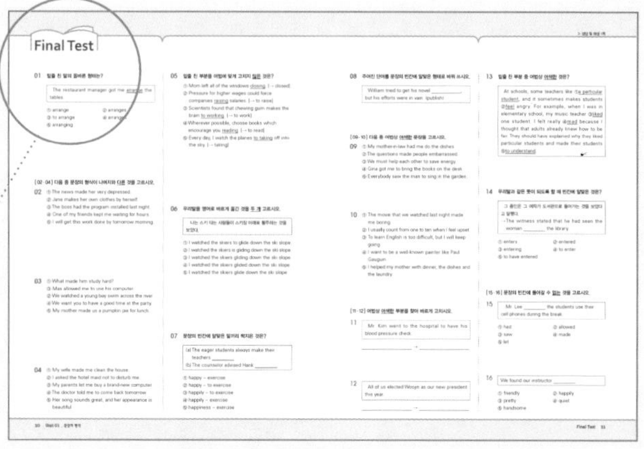

Final Test (30문항)

Unit에서 학습한 내용을 총괄하여
좀 더 다양한 유형의 문항을 추가로 풀어 봄으로써
완벽하게 익힐 수 있습니다.

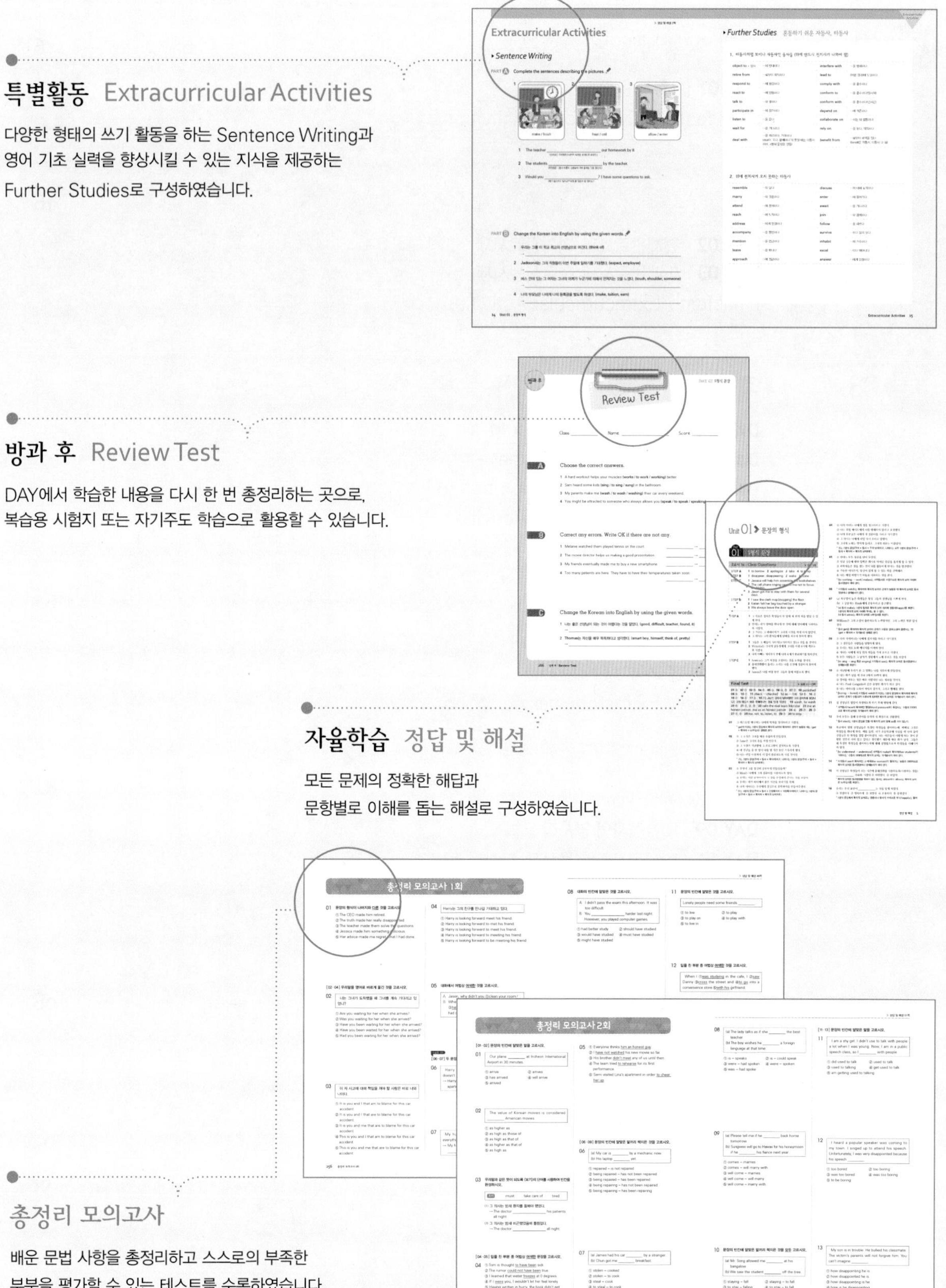

특별활동 Extracurricular Activities

다양한 형태의 쓰기 활동을 하는 Sentence Writing과 영어 기초 실력을 향상시킬 수 있는 지식을 제공하는 Further Studies로 구성하였습니다.

방과 후 Review Test

DAY에서 학습한 내용을 다시 한 번 총정리하는 곳으로, 복습용 시험지 또는 자기주도 학습으로 활용할 수 있습니다.

자율학습 정답 및 해설

모든 문제의 정확한 해답과 문항별로 이해를 돕는 해설로 구성하였습니다.

총정리 모의고사

배운 문법 사항을 총정리하고 스스로의 부족한 부분을 평가할 수 있는 테스트를 수록하였습니다.

Contents

문장의 형식 (Sentences)

Day 01 | 5형식 문장

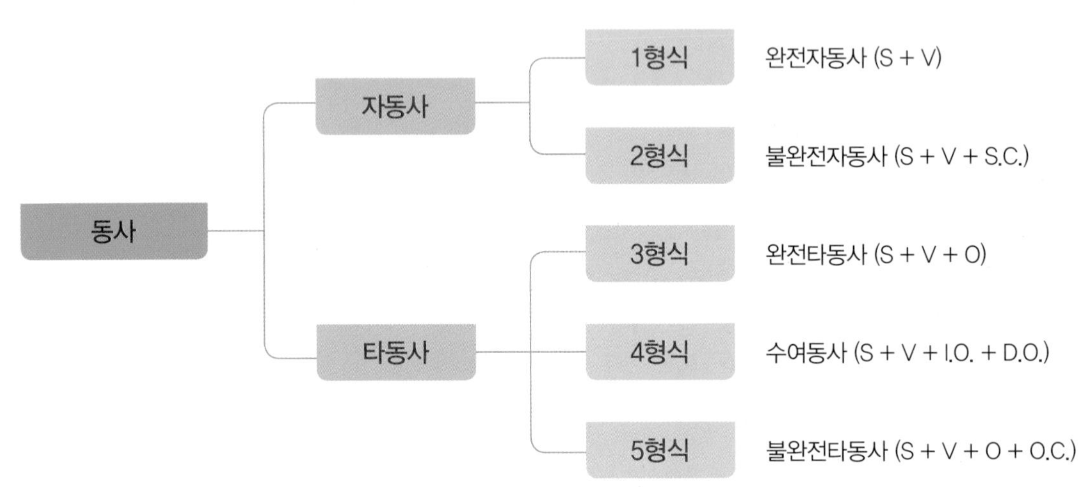

기출 맛보기

〈보기〉와 문장의 형식이 같은 것을 고르시오. (강동구 ○○중학교)

보기 We found the art exhibit fascinating.

① My father looks very young.
② I have her follow me all of the time.
③ My grandmother made me a birthday present.
④ Joshua moved his computer to the living room.
⑤ The celebrated idol group lives in this apartment.

해설
〈보기〉는 〈주어(We) + 동사(found) + 목적어(the art exhibit) + 목적격 보어(fascinating)〉로 이루어진 5형식 문장이다.
① 2형식: 〈주어(My father) + 동사(looks) + 주격 보어(very young)〉
② 5형식: 〈주어(I) + 동사(have) + 목적어(her) + 목적격 보어(follow me)〉
③ 4형식: 〈주어(My grandmother) + 동사(made) + 간접목적어(me) + 직접목적어(a birthday present)〉
④ 3형식: 〈주어(Joshua) + 동사(moved) + 목적어(his computer)〉
⑤ 1형식: 〈주어(The celebrated idol group) + 동사(lives)〉

해석
〈보기〉 우리는 미술 전시회가 흥미진진하다는 것을 알게 되었다.
① 나의 아버지는 매우 젊어 보인다.
② 나는 그녀가 나를 항상 따라다니도록 하였다.
③ 나의 할머니는 나에게 생일 선물을 만들어주셨다.
④ Joshua는 그의 컴퓨터를 거실로 옮겼다.
⑤ 그 유명한 아이돌 그룹이 이 아파트에 산다.

정답 ②

DAY 01

5형식 문장

1교시 Grammar Point

5형식 문장(S + V + O + O.C.)

일반동사 1	목적격 보어로 '명사나 형용사'를 취함
일반동사 2	목적격 보어로 'to부정사'를 취함
지각동사	목적격 보어로 '동사원형, 현재분사, 과거분사'를 취함
사역동사	목적격 보어로 '동사원형, 과거분사'를 취함

1 명사나 형용사를 목적격 보어로 취하는 동사

make, leave, elect, call, name, find 등

We **named** our son **Dongmin**.

Mr. Kim **found** the radio program **fun**.

2 to부정사를 목적격 보어로 취하는 동사

want, expect, get, allow, encourage, promise, cause, force, advise 등

Rose **allowed** me not **to finish** my homework.

Personal trainers **encourage** people **to exercise**.

cf. 목적어와 목적격 보어의 관계가 수동일 때는 과거분사를 쓴다.

I **want** my homework **done** before midnight. [내 숙제가 끝내지다: 수동]

3 지각동사

see, hear, feel, listen to, watch 등

(1) **동사원형, 현재분사 | 목적어와 목적격 보어의 관계가 능동일 때**

Christina **heard** her sister **talk** to her friends. [동생이 말하다: 능동]

Christina **heard** Mom **talking** on the phone. [엄마가 이야기하고 있다: 능동]

(2) **과거분사 | 목적어와 목적격 보어의 관계가 수동일 때**

Dad **saw** his credit card bill **paid**. [신용카드 청구서가 지불되다: 수동]

4 사역동사

make, have, let 등

(1) **동사원형 | 목적어와 목적격 보어의 관계가 능동일 때**

Mom **made** Dad **wash** the dishes after dinner. [아빠가 설거지를 하다: 능동]

(2) **과거분사 | 목적어와 목적격 보어의 관계가 수동일 때**

Dad **had** his car **washed** by my brother. [아빠 차가 세차되다: 수동]

Grammar Tips

- **5형식 동사 keep, leave는 목적격 보어로 '형용사나 분사'를 취한다.**

  What has **kept** you **working** hard?

  Don't **leave** the faucet **running**.

- **5형식 동사 choose, think of는 목적격 보어로 〈as + 명사〉를 취한다.**

  I **thought of** him **as** my friend.

- **5형식 동사 get**

  '~에게 …를 시키다'의 의미이며, 목적격 보어로 to부정사나 과거분사를 취한다.

  (1) to부정사: 목적어와 목적격 보어의 관계가 능동일 때

  I **got** you **to close** the door. [네가 문을 닫다: 능동]

  (2) 과거분사: 목적어와 목적격 보어의 관계가 수동일 때

  I **got** the door **closed**. [문이 닫히다: 수동]

- **help (준 사역동사)**

  help는 목적격 보어로 동사원형과 to부정사를 모두 취한다.

  Jenny **helps** me **do** it.

  Jenny **helps** me **to do** it.

- **3형식 → 5형식으로 쓰일 때 뜻이 달라지는 동사**

  find: 찾다 → 깨닫다

  call: 전화하다, 부르다 → ~을 …라고 부르다

  leave: 남겨두다 → ~를 …한 상태로 놔두다

  make: 만들다 → ~를 …하게 만들다[시키다]

2교시 In - Class Questions

빈칸에 알맞은 말을 〈보기〉에서 골라 알맞은 형태로 바꿔 쓰시오.

보기 keep borrow take apologize

1 The new policy allows students ______________ three books for a month.

2 Min made me ______________ to my mom for making her angry.

3 The singer never lets the paparazzi ______________ her picture.

4 The doctor advised his patients ______________ from smoking.

괄호 안에서 알맞은 말을 모두 고르시오.

1 They will watch the ships **(disappear / disappearing / to disappear)**.

2 Victoria had her brother **(wake / waking / to wake)** her up at 6 a.m.

3 My dad wants my paper **(do / doing / to do / done)** before dinner.

STEP C

주어진 단어를 바르게 배열하시오.

1 (help / him / Jessica / the bookshelves / assemble / will)
→ ______________________________

2 (caused / the cell phone ringing / me / focus on / not to / driving)
→ ______________________________

3 (Jason / to / got / me / with them / stay / several days / for)
→ ______________________________

주어진 말을 사용하여 다음 우리말을 영어로 옮기시오,

1 나는 그 점원이 바닥을 닦고 있는 것을 보았다. (clerk, mop, floor)
→ ______________________________

2 Keilen은 낯선 사람에 의해 그녀의 가방이 만져지는 것을 느꼈다. (feel, touch, a stranger)
→ ______________________________

3 우리는 항상 문을 열어둔다. (leave, open)
→ ______________________________

Final Test

01 밑줄 친 말의 올바른 형태는?

The restaurant manager got me arrange the tables.

① arrange ② arranges
③ to arrange ④ arranged
⑤ arranging

[02-04] 다음 중 문장의 형식이 나머지와 다른 것을 고르시오.

02 ① The news made her very depressed.
② Jane makes her own clothes by herself.
③ The boss had the program installed last night.
④ One of my friends kept me waiting for hours.
⑤ I will get this work done by tomorrow morning.

03 ① What made him study hard?
② Max allowed me to use his computer.
③ We watched a young boy swim across the river.
④ We want you to have a good time at the party.
⑤ My mother made us a pumpkin pie for lunch.

04 ① My wife made me clean the house.
② I asked the hotel maid not to disturb me.
③ My parents let me buy a brand-new computer.
④ The doctor told me to come back tomorrow.
⑤ Her song sounds great, and her appearance is beautiful.

05 밑줄 친 부분을 어법에 맞게 고치지 않은 것은?

① Mom left all of the windows closing. [→ closed]
② Pressure for higher wages could force companies raising salaries. [→ to raise]
③ Scientists found that chewing gum makes the brain to working. [→ to work]
④ Wherever possible, choose books which encourage you reading. [→ to read]
⑤ Every day, I watch the planes to taking off into the sky. [→ taking]

06 우리말을 영어로 바르게 옮긴 것을 두 개 고르시오.

나는 스키 타는 사람들이 스키장 아래로 활주하는 것을 보았다.

① I watched the skiers to glide down the ski slope.
② I watched the skiers is gliding down the ski slope.
③ I watched the skiers gliding down the ski slope.
④ I watched the skiers glided down the ski slope.
⑤ I watched the skiers glide down the ski slope.

07 문장의 빈칸에 알맞은 말끼리 짝지은 것은?

(a) The eager students always make their teachers ________. (b) The counselor advised Hank ________.

① happy – exercise
② happy – to exercise
③ happily – to exercise
④ happily – exercise
⑤ happiness – exercise

08 주어진 단어를 문장의 빈칸에 알맞은 형태로 바꿔 쓰시오.

William tried to get his novel ____________, but his efforts were in vain. (publish)

[09-10] 다음 중 어법상 어색한 문장을 고르시오.

09 ① My mother-in-law had me do the dishes.
② The questions made people embarrassed.
③ We must help each other to save energy.
④ Gina got me to bring the books on the desk.
⑤ Everybody saw the man to sing in the garden.

10 ① The movie that we watched last night made me boring.
② I usually count from one to ten when I feel upset.
③ To learn English is too difficult, but I will keep going.
④ I want to be a well-known painter like Paul Gauguin.
⑤ I helped my mother with dinner, the dishes and the laundry.

[11-12] 어법상 어색한 부분을 찾아 바르게 고치시오.

11

Mr. Kim went to the hospital to have his blood pressure check.

________________ → ________________

12

All of us elected Woojin as our new president this year.

________________ → ________________

13 밑줄 친 부분 중 어법상 어색한 것은?

At schools, some teachers like ①a particular student, and it sometimes makes students ②feel angry. For example, when I was in elementary school, my music teacher ③liked one student. I felt really ④mad because I thought that adults already knew how to be fair. They should have explained why they liked particular students and made their students ⑤to understand.

14 우리말과 같은 뜻이 되도록 할 때 빈칸에 알맞은 것은?

그 증인은 그 여자가 도서관으로 들어가는 것을 보았다고 말했다.
→The witness stated that he had seen the woman ________ the library.

① enters
② entered
③ entering
④ to enter
⑤ to have entered

[15-16] 문장의 빈칸에 들어갈 수 없는 것을 고르시오.

15

Mr. Lee ________ the students use their cell phones during the break.

① had
② allowed
③ saw
④ made
⑤ let

16

We found our instructor ________.

① friendly
② happily
③ pretty
④ quiet
⑤ handsome

17 문장의 빈칸에 들어갈 수 있는 것은?

> Mr. Kim ________ me as the leader of this team.

① thought ② named
③ chose ④ called
⑤ consisted

18 밑줄 친 동사에 유의하여 다음 문장을 우리말로 옮기시오.

(1) Fortunately, Jay found his lost dog on the street.
→ 다행히, ______________________________.

(2) The executives found his attitude too rude.
→ 그 임원들은 ______________________________.

19 두 문장이 같은 의미가 되도록 주어진 동사를 알맞은 형태로 바꿔 쓰시오.

> Tim had me __________ my hands before dinner. (wash)
> → Tim got me __________ my hands before dinner.

20 다음 중 어법상 올바른 문장은?

① Mom had my old suit alter.
② Danny let us arranged the chairs.
③ Mason made us to dig in the ground.
④ Sera made her students wasting their time.
⑤ He won't leave his baby alone for an hour.

21 밑줄 친 부분 중 어법상 올바른 것을 모두 고르시오.

① They heard us shout at them.
② Jin had his notebook to steal from his bag.
③ She won't get you watch that movie.
④ My mom made the children pleased.
⑤ Jinhee listens to the man playing the violin.

22 주어진 단어를 바르게 배열하시오.

> Monster / calls / the rival team

→ My team ______________________________.

23 우리말과 같은 뜻이 되도록 빈칸에 알맞은 말을 쓰시오.

> 그들 모두는 나를 정직한 사람이라고 생각한다.
> → They all think ______________________________.
> → They all think of ______________________________.

24 대화의 빈칸에 알맞은 것은?

> A: Hey, did you close this window? It's too hot in here.
> B: No, I asked Mom to leave it ________.

① opened ② to open
③ opening ④ open
⑤ opens

25 글의 빈칸에 알맞은 말끼리 짝지은 것은?

In 2060, people will have a new means of visiting their friends. They'll be able to buy their own wings. They will let people ________ freely. So the wings will help people ________ some time. To keep flying ________, new rules might be needed.

① move – to save – safely
② move – save – safe
③ to move – save – safe
④ to move – saving – safely
⑤ moving – save – safely

26 다음 중 목적격 보어가 있는 문장은?

① Nicole wants something delicious.
② Billy doesn't want to play pool with Noah.
③ Brian wants his father to play with him.
④ The boss wanted all of the employees at the meeting.
⑤ All of the students wanted some time to solve the math problem.

27 문장의 빈칸에 알맞은 말을 모두 고르시오.

Most Koreans saw the Korean national baseball team ________ a gold medal for the first time.

① win ② won
③ wins ④ to win
⑤ winning

서술형 대비

28 우리말과 같은 뜻이 되도록 빈칸에 알맞은 말을 쓰시오.

나의 어머니는 내게 공부할 때는 음악을 듣지 말라고 항상 말씀하신다.
→ My mother always tells ________ ________ ________ ________ ________ music when I am studying.

29 문장의 빈칸에 알맞은 것은?

In order to make my dream ________ true, I decided to save money.

① come ② came
③ to come ④ coming
⑤ comes

30 주어진 말을 빈칸에 공통으로 알맞은 형태로 바꿔 쓰시오.

(a) My girlfriend helped me ________ smoking. (stop)
(b) The police officer ordered my dad ________ the car. (stop)

≫ 정답 및 해설 2쪽

Extracurricular Activities

▸ Sentence Writing

PART A Complete the sentences describing the pictures.

1

make / finish

2

hear / call

3

allow / enter

1 The teacher ____________________ our homework by 8.
(선생님은 우리에게 8시까지 숙제를 끝내도록 하셨다.)

2 The students ____________________ by the teacher.
(학생들은 그들의 이름이 선생님에 의해 불리는 것을 들었다.)

3 Would you ____________________? I have some questions to ask.
(제가 들어가도 될까요? 여쭤 볼 질문이 좀 있어요.)

PART B Change the Korean into English by using the given words.

1 우리는 그를 이 학교 최고의 선생님으로 여긴다. (think of)
→ ____________________

2 Jackson씨는 그의 직원들이 이번 주말에 일하기를 기대했다. (expect, employee)
→ ____________________

3 버스 안에 있는 그 여자는 그녀의 어깨가 누군가에 의해서 만져지는 것을 느꼈다. (touch, shoulder, someone)
→ ____________________

4 나의 부모님은 나에게 나의 등록금을 벌도록 하셨다. (make, tuition, earn)
→ ____________________

▸ *Further Studies* 혼동하기 쉬운 자동사, 타동사

1. 타동사처럼 보이나 자동사인 동사들 (뒤에 반드시 전치사가 나와야 함)

object to + 명사	~에 반대하다	interfere with	~을 방해하다
retire from	~로부터 퇴직하다	lead to	(어떤 결과)에 도달하다
respond to	~에 응답하다	comply with	~을 준수하다
react to	~에 반응하다	conform to	~을 준수하다(일시적)
talk to	~와 말하다	conform with	~을 준수하다(긴시간)
participate in	~에 참가하다	depend on	~에 의존하다
listen to	~을 듣다	collaborate on	~하는 데 협동하다
wait for	~을 기다리다	rely on	~을 믿다, 의지하다
deal with	~을 처리하다, 거래하다 (deal이 '주다, 분배하다'의 뜻일 때는 타동사이며, 4형식 문장을 만듦)	benefit from	~로부터 혜택을 입다 (benefit은 자동사, 타동사 다 됨)

2. 뒤에 전치사가 오지 못하는 타동사

resemble	~와 닮다	discuss	~에 대해 토의하다
marry	~와 결혼하다	enter	~에 들어가다
attend	~에 참석하다	await	~을 기다리다
reach	~에 도착하다	join	~와 함께하다
address	~에게 연설하다	follow	~을 따르다
accompany	~을 동반하다	survive	~보다 오래 살다
mention	~을 언급하다	inhabit	~에 거주하다
leave	~을 떠나다	excel	~보다 뛰어나다
approach	~에 접근하다	answer	~에게 답장하다

시제
(Tenses)

Day 02 | 현재완료시제, 과거완료시제
Day 03 | 미래완료시제, 완료진행시제

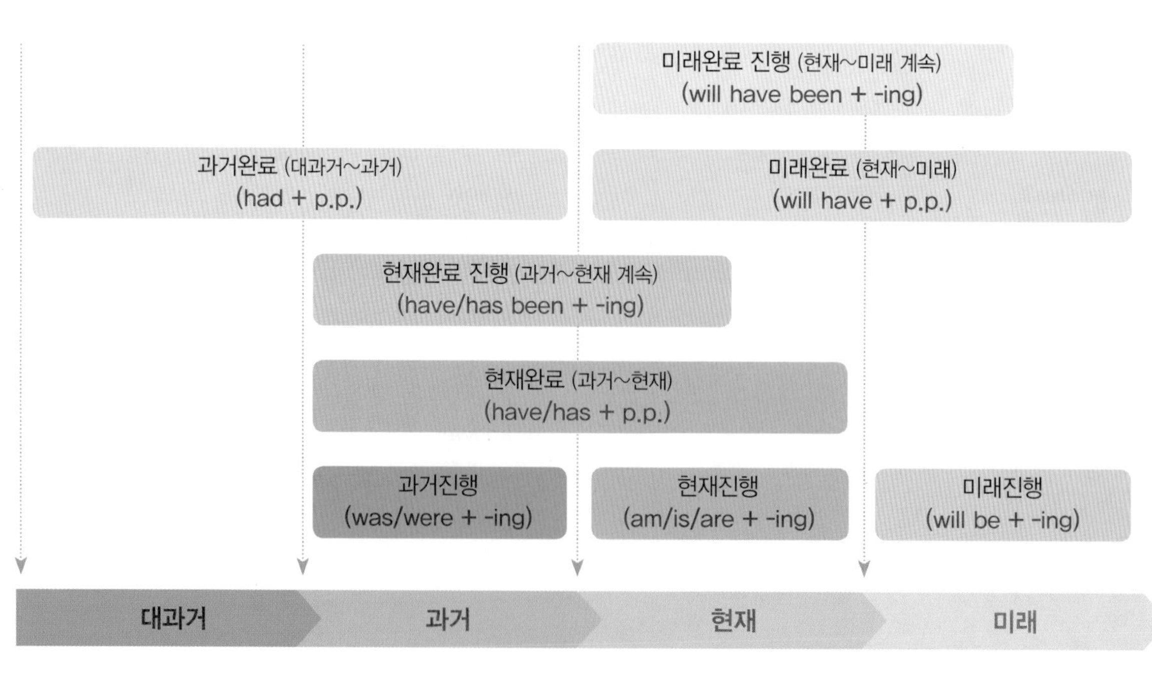

기출 맛보기

괄호 안의 동사를 문맥에 맞게 고친 것끼리 짝지은 것을 고르시오. (양천구 ○○중학교)

(a) Kyle **(teach)** English at a university for fifteen years.
(b) Park's family **(live)** on Jeju Island a long time ago.
(c) I **(play)** baseball games since this morning.

① taught – have lived – have playing
② taught – lived – is playing
③ has taught – have lived – have played
④ has taught – lived – have been playing
⑤ have taught – have lived – have played

해설

(a) for fifteen years라는 시간의 길이를 나타내는 말이 있고, 그때부터 지금까지 영어를 가르치고 있다는 내용이 되어야 하므로 현재완료시제(have/has + 과거분사)로 표현해야 한다.
(b) 과거를 나타내는 부사구 a long time ago가 있으므로 과거시제로 표현해야 한다. 현재완료시제는 과거를 나타내는 부사(구)와 함께 쓰일 수 없다.
(c) 현재완료 진행시제(have/has + been + -ing)는 계속의 의미를 가지며 for, since와 함께 쓴다.

해석

(a) Kyle은 15년째 대학교에서 영어를 가르치고 있다.
(b) 박가네 가족은 오래 전에 제주도에서 살았다.
(c) 나는 오늘 아침부터 야구경기를 하고 있다.

정답 ④

DAY 02

현재완료시제, 과거완료시제

1교시 Grammar Point

1 현재완료시제

- 형태: 〈have/has + 과거분사〉
- 용법: 과거부터 현재까지 일어난 동작이나 상태를 나타낼 때 사용
- 부정문: 〈have/has + not/never + 과거분사 ~〉
- 의문문: 〈(의문사) + Have/Has + 주어 + 과거분사 ~?〉

용법	의미	함께 쓰이는 부사
경험	~해본 적이 있다	ever, never, once, twice, many times 등
계속	지금까지 ~해왔다	for, since 등
완료	이미(막/아직) ~했다	already(이미), just(이제 막), yet(아직) 등
결과	~해서 …하다	–

Humans **have** never **traveled** to Mars. 경험

Cathy **has lived** in Seoul for 30 years. 계속

My new laptop **hasn't arrived** yet. 완료

Yuna **has gone** to Toronto. 결과 [So, she isn't here.]

A: Have you already **read** this novel?
B: Yes, I **have**. / No, I **haven't**.

A: How long **have** you **known** your friends?
B: I **have known** them for 10 years.

2 과거완료시제

- 형태: 〈had + 과거분사〉
- 용법: 대과거부터 과거까지 일어난 동작이나 상태를 나타낼 때 사용

용법	의미	함께 쓰이는 부사
경험	~한 적이 있었다	ever, never, once, twice, many times 등
계속	~해 왔었다	for, since 등
완료	~했었다	already(이미), just(이제 막), yet(아직) 등
결과	~해버렸다	–

Had you **gone** to the jazz festival before then? 경험

When I met her, she **had talked** with him for 2 hours. 계속

When he arrived at the restaurant, she **had** already **left**. 완료

He simply walked in. He **had forgotten** to lock the door. 결과

cf. before, after와 같은 사건의 전후관계가 분명한 접속사가 쓰인 경우 과거시제로 씀
After we **(had) discussed** it, we went to bed.

3 과거시제 vs. 현재완료시제

과거	과거에 발생된 동작이나 상태 [현재의 상태는 알 수 없음]	Wonseok **lost** his pen. [과거에 펜을 잃어버림. 현재는 찾았는지 못 찾았는지는 모름]
현재완료	과거부터 현재까지의 동작이나 상태 [현재의 상태를 알 수 있음]	Wonseok **has lost** his pen. [과거부터 지금까지 펜을 잃어버림. 현재도 못 찾음]

Grammar Tips

for vs. since

〈for + 숫자 기간〉 '~동안'
〈since + 특정 시점〉 '~이후로'

for thirty minutes, **for** 3 days ...
since last year, **since** I was young ...

have been to vs. have been in vs. have gone to

have been to '~에 가본 적이 있다' [경험]
have been in '~에 쭉 있다' [계속]
have gone to '~에 가버렸다' [결과]

I **have been to** England.
I **have been in** England.
The man **has gone to** England.
(have/has gone to는 1, 2인칭 주어는 불가능)

현재완료시제를 쓸 수 없는 경우

과거를 나타내는 부사어(when, yesterday, last ~, ago, just now 등)는 현재완료와 함께 쓸 수 없다.

Marie **has gone** to the station **last night**. (×)
Marie **went** to the station **last night**. (o)

2교시 In - Class Questions

STEP A

괄호 안에서 알맞은 말을 고르시오.

1 Some of my friends have **(yet / never / for)** been abroad.

2 Linda has known her music teacher **(since / for / twice)** last year.

3 The new computers haven't arrived **(already / yet / just)**.

4 We **(have / had / will have)** never seen the woman before then.

STEP B

주어진 말을 문장의 빈칸에 알맞은 형태로 바꿔 쓰시오.

1 Her grandparents ________________ ill for years when they died. (be)

2 I ________________ whether I will buy a car or not. (not, decide)

3 Hojun ________________ to take some rest a few days ago. (want)

4 Jessica ________________ solve the math question because she had seen it before. (be able to)

어법상 어색한 부분을 찾아 바르게 고치시오.

1 My cousin has been feeding her cat when I saw her. __________ → __________

2 He has gone to his friend's house many times. __________ → __________

3 What Henry has been writing since he became 30 years old? __________ → __________

4 I have never seen such beautiful scenery until I went to Ireland. __________ → __________

우리말과 같은 뜻이 되도록 주어진 말을 사용하여 문장을 완성하시오.

1 Sophia는 전에 어떤 시험에도 실패를 한 적이 없다. (fail)
→ Sophia ________________________ any exams before.

2 내가 그에게 전화했을 때 그는 이미 그녀에게 편지를 보냈었다. (send)
→ When I called him, he ________________________ her a letter.

3 종민이는 파리에서 5년 동안 프랑스어를 공부했다. (study)
→ Jongmin ________________________ French in France for five years.

3교시 After-Class Questions

[01-03] 문장의 빈칸에 알맞은 동사의 형태를 고르시오.

01 The airplane _________ the airport when I got there.

① left ② leaves ③ will leave
④ has already left ⑤ had already left

02 Both Sam and Nancy _________ together since last May.

① work ② will work ③ has worked
④ had worked ⑤ have worked

03 My brother lost the train ticket I _________ for him yesterday.

① bought ② was bought ③ has bought
④ had bought ⑤ had been bought

04 다음 질문에 대한 응답으로 알맞은 것은?

How long have you been a dentist?

① For last year. ② Since 2012.
③ Before 10 o'clock. ④ After I arrived in Korea.
⑤ Until I became a teacher.

05 두 문장이 같은 뜻이 되도록 빈칸에 알맞은 말을 쓰시오.

Keilen went to Russia and she is not here.
→ Keilen _________ _________ to Russia.

06 다음 중 어법상 어색한 문장은?

① My relatives have always lived on Jeju Island.
② Cathy has been to the national library many times.
③ They had lost their jobs, so they could not earn any money.
④ He has never seen an elephant until he visited the zoo.
⑤ He had practiced as a lawyer for 10 years before he died.

07 우리말과 같은 뜻이 되도록 문장의 빈칸에 알맞은 말을 쓰시오.

엄마는 직장에 다시 나가시기 전에 며칠간 아프셨다.
→ Mom _________ _________ sick for days before she went to work again.

Vocabulary Tips

- airport 공항
- relative 친척
- earn (돈을) 벌다
- practice (의사, 변호사 등 전문직에) 종사하다

08 문장의 빈칸에 had가 들어갈 수 없는 것은?

① We ______ expected to finish the work by 8 p.m., but we didn't.
② The ground was moist because it ______ rained the night before.
③ Mom found a laptop that someone ______ left in the waiting room.
④ I ______ not seen Daniel for a long time. I don't remember his face.
⑤ Greg ______ finished his project when his teammates came to the office.

[09-10] 주어진 말을 사용하여 문장의 빈칸에 알맞은 말을 쓰시오.

09

One of my best friends passed me the fashion magazine, but I didn't want to have it because I ________________(finish) reading it during my break. So I gave it back to him.

10

I was born in New York and moved to Seattle in 2011. Since then, I ________________(stay) there with my parents and elder sisters.

11 우리말과 같은 뜻이 되도록 대화의 빈칸에 알맞은 말을 쓰시오.

A: ________ ________ ________ what the announcement said just now? (방금 전에 안내방송에서 뭐라고 했는지 들었니?)
B: No, I ________. I ________ ________ to music since one o'clock. (아니. 나는 1시부터 계속 음악을 듣고 있었어.)

12 대화의 빈칸에 알맞은 동사의 형태는?

A: Where is Jenny?
B: She is not here. She ________ the drugstore.

① has been to ② had been to ③ have been to
④ has gone to ⑤ had gone to

13 다음 중 어법상 올바른 문장은?

① When has Jimin been in Busan?
② They have come up with a new theory in 2001.
③ My daughter has just won the special award.
④ We had met novice teachers since last year.
⑤ Have they gotten their admission letters last week?

Vocabulary Tips

- moist 촉촉한
- announcement 안내방송
- just now 방금 전에
- drugstore 약국
- theory 이론
- special award 특별상
- novice 초보
- admission letter 입학 허가서

14 밑줄 친 부분 중 어법상 어색한 것은?

① Linda has dated him since last month.
② Someone broke the vase I had put on the table.
③ My uncle has just painted the fence, and it looks great.
④ My family had to delay the trip we had planned before.
⑤ The groups have attended the conference before I came.

15 주어진 말을 사용하여 글의 빈칸을 완성하시오.

This morning, I was going to travel to Korea. However, the airplane for Korea (1)________________(take off, already) when I got to the airport. Now, it's 1:00 p.m. I (2)________________(wait) for the next airplane for over two hours.

16 문장의 빈칸에 알맞은 말끼리 짝지은 것은?

(a) I found that nobody ________ an emergency call.
(b) Since I was young, I ________ to financial lectures.

① had received – have listened
② had received – had listened
③ have received – have loved
④ have received – listened
⑤ has received – listened

17 어법상 어색한 부분을 찾아 바르게 고치시오.

Jay prepared for the audition since last year.

____________________ → ____________________

18 문장의 빈칸에 알맞은 동사의 형태는?

How long ________ Tim ________ at this company?

① does – work
② did – worked
③ have – work
④ have – worked
⑤ has – worked

19 밑줄 친 부분의 쓰임이 같은 것을 모두 고르시오.

① Ralph has broken the window.
② Have you ever eaten raw fish?
③ He has lived in America since 1995.
④ I have lost my passport at the airport.
⑤ My baseball team has won the Korean series this year.

Vocabulary Tips

- delay 연기하다, 미루다
- attend 참석하다
- conference 회의
- take off 이륙하다
- emergency call 비상호출
- financial 재무의
- prepare 준비하다
- audition 오디션
- raw fish 생선회

20 〈보기〉의 밑줄 친 부분과 쓰임이 같은 것은?

보기 I've never seen such a great player in my whole life.

① Abigail has gone to Tibet.
② I have just arrived home.
③ Amber has visited Australia before.
④ I have been in the classroom since this morning.
⑤ Olivia has just completed her homework assignment.

21 주어진 말을 문장의 빈칸에 알맞은 형태로 바꿔 쓰시오.

Isabella ________________(leave) Cambridge, England, in 2012 and ________________(teach) English in Seoul since then.

서술형 대비

22 두 문장을 한 문장으로 바꿔 쓰시오.

I bought a laptop computer in 2009. I still have the laptop computer.
→ ____

23 다음 중 어법상 어색한 문장은?

① Victor has just arrived at the classroom.
② My cell phone has been broken since last week.
③ Stanley and I have known each other for last year.
④ Tommy has gone to England, so he is not in Seoul.
⑤ Sue has lost her hat, so she doesn't have it anymore.

24 두 문장을 한 문장으로 나타낼 때 빈칸에 알맞은 말을 쓰시오.

Audrey began to learn the piano ten years ago. She is still learning it.
→ Audrey __________ __________ the piano __________ ten years.

25 문장의 빈칸에 알맞은 말을 쓰시오.

(1) I have played this computer game __________ I was a middle school student.
(2) My best friend has __________ to Hawaii, so I miss him.
(3) My daughter has been sick __________ two days.

Vocabulary Tips

- arrive 도착하다
- anymore 더 이상
- miss 그리워하다

미래완료시제, 완료진행시제

1교시 Grammar Point

1 미래완료시제

- 형태: ⟨will + have + 과거분사⟩
- 의미: '~일 것이다' (현재부터 시작하여 미래의 어느 시점까지 계속되거나 완료되는 동작이나 상태를 나타냄)

We **will have known** each other for 5 years next month. 계속
(다음 달이면 우리가 서로 알고 지낸 지 5년이 된다.)

He **will have finished** the work by this time tomorrow. 완료
(그는 내일 이맘때까지 그 일을 끝냈을 것이다.)

2 현재완료 진행시제

- 형태: ⟨have/has + been + -ing⟩
- 의미: '~하는 중이다' (과거에 시작되어 현재까지 계속 진행되는 일을 나타낼 때 쓰임)

Many employees **have been hoping** for receiving a bonus.
(많은 직원들은 성과급을 받기를 바라고 있다.)
⇒ 과거부터 현재까지 '성과급을 받기를 바라는' 동작이 현재까지 계속적으로 이어져왔음을 나타냄

3 과거완료 진행시제

- 형태: ⟨had + been + -ing⟩
- 의미: '~하던 중이었다' (과거의 특정 시점을 기준으로 하여 그 이전에 시작되어 기준 시점까지 동작이 계속 진행되었던 일을 나타낼 때 쓰임)

When I got up in the morning, there was a flood in my hometown. It **had been raining** all night long. (아침에 일어났을 때, 우리 동네는 홍수가 났다. 밤새도록 비가 내렸었다.)
⇒ 아침에 홍수가 난 모습을 본 시점을 기준으로, 기준 시점 이전부터 비가 내리고 있었음을 의미함

4 미래완료 진행시제

- 형태: ⟨will + have + been + -ing⟩
- 의미: '~하고 있을 것이다' (현재나 미래의 언젠가에 시작하여 미래의 특정 시점에 그 동작이 계속 진행되는 일을 나타낼 때 쓰임)

I **will have been learning** English for ten years **by next year**.
(내년이면 영어를 배운 지 10년이 될 것이다.)
⇒ 내년을 기준 시점으로, 그 시점이 되면 10년 동안 계속적으로 영어를 배우고 있을 것이라는 의미이며, 미래에도 계속 그 동작이 진행 중임을 강조

5 현재완료시제 vs. 현재완료 진행시제

현재완료 시제	과거에 시작된 동작이 현재까지 계속되거나 완료되어 경험, 결과, 완료됨	I **have made** a dish for Mom. (나는 엄마를 위해 요리를 만들었다.) [현재 요리가 완료됨]
현재완료 진행시제	과거에 시작된 동작이 현재까지 계속 진행되고 있음	I **have been making** a dish for Mom. (나는 엄마를 위해 요리를 만드는 중이다.) [현재까지 요리를 만들고 있음]

Grammar Tips

- **현재완료 진행시제와 함께 쓰이는 시간 표시 어구들**

⟨since + 과거 시점⟩ (~이래로)
⟨for + 기간⟩ (~ 동안)
over the years (수년 간)

- **미래완료시제나 미래완료 진행시제와 함께 쓰이는 시간 표시 어구들**

⟨by + 미래⟩ (~까지)
⟨as of + 미래⟩ (~이면)
⟨next + 시간⟩ (다음 ~)
tomorrow (내일)

- **진행형을 쓸 수 없는 동사**

have(가지다), believe(믿다), know(알다), want(원하다) 등의 상태를 나타내는 동사

I **have been believing** Santa Claus since I was a little kid. (×)
I **have believed** in Santa Claus since I was a little kid. (o)

2교시 In-Class Questions

괄호 안에서 알맞은 말을 고르시오.

1 I **(has studied / has been studying / had been studying)** for two hours before my tutor came home.

2 This time tomorrow, I **(will have met / have met / had met)** Gina at the shopping mall. I'm really looking forward to it.

3 Yuna Kim **(will have been practicing / has been practicing / had been practicing)** figure skating very hard for the Olympics since last month.

주어진 동사를 알맞은 형태로 바꿔 완료진행시제 문장을 만드시오.

1 I ________________ this novel for an hour. (read)

2 Adrian ________________ when Kate called him. (sleep)

3 How long ________ you ________________ here? (live)

4 My brother and I ________________ the dishes before Mom came back. (wash)

밑줄 친 부분을 어법상 바르게 고치시오.

1 If I go to England again, I <u>will be</u> there three times. ________________

2 Kevin, what <u>had you been</u> doing here? ________________

3 When she came, I <u>has waited</u> for her for two hours. ________________

STEP D

주어진 말을 사용하여 다음 우리말을 영어로 옮기시오.

1 나는 오후 내내 TV에서 방송하는 야구 경기를 시청하고 있었다.
(been, all afternoon, watching, have, on)
→ ____

2 올해 연말이면 그가 학생들을 가르쳐 온 지 20년이 될 것이다.
(teaching, by the end of this year, have, for)
→ ____

3 나는 미국에 가기 전까지 3년 동안 영어를 공부하던 중이었다.
(before, had, went, been, the US, studying)
→ ____

3교시 After-Class Questions

[01-03] 두 문장을 한 문장으로 바꿔 쓸 때 빈칸에 알맞은 말을 쓰시오.

01 My brother started building a school six months ago. He is still building it.
→ My brother ________ ________ ________ a school for six months.

02 Please visit my house today. I'm going on a picnic tomorrow.
→ I ________ ________ ________ on a picnic by this time tomorrow.

03 A lot of girls and boys stood in line. We got to the theater.
→ Before we got to the theater, a lot of girls and boys ________ already ________ ________ in line.

04 밑줄 친 부분 중 어법상 어색한 것은?

① My son has been sick since last week.
② It has been raining for a couple of weeks.
③ I have been waiting for a taxi for ten minutes.
④ My family had already finished dinner when I went home.
⑤ We have been working together for three years next month.

05 우리말과 같은 뜻이 되도록 주어진 말을 알맞은 형태로 바꿔 쓰시오.

나의 아버지는 2년 전에 구입한 SUV를 지금까지 운전하고 계신다. (drive)
→ My father ________________ an SUV that he bought two years ago.

[06-08] 대화의 빈칸에 알맞은 동사의 형태를 고르시오.

06

A: What are you watching?
B: I'm watching a documentary film about Korean history. I ________ it since this morning.

① watched ② has watched ③ had watched
④ had been watching ⑤ have been watching

Vocabulary Tips

- stand in line 줄을 서다
- a couple of 둘의
- together 함께
- SUV 스포츠 실용차 (sports utility vehicle)
- documentary film 다큐멘터리 영화

07
A: Why didn't you come to the concert yesterday?
B: My car suddenly broke down. It ________ well for a long time.

① runs ② has run ③ is running
④ has been running ⑤ had been running

08
A: How long have you been in Paris?
B: Well, I ________ in Paris for 10 months by next month.

① will be ② have been ③ will have been
④ will be staying ⑤ am going to be

[09-10] 우리말과 같은 뜻이 되도록 빈칸에 알맞은 말을 쓰시오.

09 나의 부모님이 나를 방문했을 때 나는 3년간 외국에서 공부하고 있었다.
→ I ________ ________ ________ abroad ________ three years when my parents visited me.

10 우리가 영화관에 도착했을 때, 영화는 10분 넘게 상영하던 중이었다.
→ When we arrived at the theater, the movie ________ ________ ________ for over 10 minutes.

[11-12] 밑줄 친 부분을 어법상 알맞은 형태로 고치시오.

11 When we arrived, Jean <u>has been talking</u> on the phone for more than one and a half hours. → ________________

12 The city council <u>had been supporting</u> taxi companies since 2012.
→ ________________

13 **다음 중 어법상 <u>어색한</u> 문장은?**
① What have you been doing since we met last?
② How long has she been waiting for the subway?
③ The CEO has been making a speech since 10 a.m.
④ Minho hasn't eaten any food for the last few days.
⑤ By the time Mr. Park reaches 50, he will work for the company for 25 years.

Vocabulary Tips
- **talk on the phone** 전화 통화하다
- **council** 의회
- **support** 지원하다
- **make a speech** 연설하다

[14-15] 우리말과 같은 뜻이 되도록 빈칸에 알맞은 말을 고르시오.

14 그녀가 아이를 찾았을 때, 그 아이는 3시간 동안 계속 울고 있었다.

→ When she found the child, she ________ for three hours.

① was crying ② has cried ③ had cried
④ have been crying ⑤ had been crying

15 너는 몇 시간 동안 최 선생님을 기다리는 중이니?

→ How many hours ________ for Mrs. Choi?

① do you wait ② you have waited
③ you have been waiting ④ have you been waiting
⑤ had you been waiting

서술형 대비

16 다음 문장을 의문문으로 바꿔 쓰시오.

He had been sleeping when you arrived.

→ ______________________________

17 주어진 말을 문장의 빈칸에 알맞은 형태로 바꿔 쓰시오.

It's 4 o'clock in the afternoon. Hank starts exercising. By 6 o'clock, he will ______________(finish) exercising.

18 밑줄 친 부분에 유의하여 다음 문장을 우리말로 옮기시오.

Mr. Kim <u>will have worked</u> here for ten years by the end of this year.

→ ______________________________

19 우리말과 같은 뜻이 되도록 주어진 말을 빈칸에 알맞은 형태로 바꿔 쓰시오.

(1) 비가 3일 동안 내린다. (rain)
→ It ______________________ for 3 days.

(2) 비가 3일 동안 내리는 중이다. (rain)
→ It ______________________ for 3 days.

20 어법상 <u>어색한</u> 부분을 찾아 바르게 고치시오.

Kelly has been wanting to buy her own apartment since she got married.

______________________ → ______________________

Vocabulary Tips

- exercise 운동하다
- get married 결혼하다

21 대화에서 어법상 어색한 부분은?

A: Where have your sons been hiding?
B: They have been in the closet.

① Where ② have your sons ③ been hiding
④ have been ⑤ 어색한 부분 없음

[22-24] 대화의 빈칸에 알맞은 동사의 형태를 고르시오.

22

A: What has Sean been doing here?
B: He ________ for his next class.

① waited ② have waited ③ have been waiting
④ has been waiting ⑤ had been waiting

23

A: My sister and I are reading some books.
B: Oh, how many books have you read?
A: If I finish reading this book, I ________ five books.

① have read ② have been reading ③ had read
④ will have read ⑤ will be read

24

A: Austin is working at the cafeteria now.
B: I see, how many hours ________?

① has he be worked ② has he working ③ has he been worked
④ has he been working ⑤ has he being worked

25 두 문장 중 어법상 어색한 문장을 골라 바르게 고치시오.

(a) Rodin looks sleepy today. He hasn't been sleeping enough last night.
(b) Linda had been sleeping soundly before she was surprised at the noise.

________________ → ________________

Vocabulary Tips

- hide 숨다
- closet 옷장, 벽장
- cafeteria 구내식당
- soundly 곤히, 깊이
- be surprised at ~에 놀라다
- noise 소리, 소란

Final Test

01 다음 중 어법상 올바른 문장을 모두 고르시오.

① I will have been fixing this car by 5 p.m.
② He has been studying since he got here.
③ Dad has locked the windows this afternoon.
④ We have been watching a movie before you came.
⑤ My classmates have collected these flags last year.

[02-03] 다음 중 어법상 어색한 문장을 고르시오.

02 ① Sumi has been waiting for me for three hours.
② All of us drank the tea he had made before.
③ It had rained a lot at night, so the bus didn't come.
④ My brother has been in the US since a long time.
⑤ Ryan has been taking Spanish lessons for five months.

03 ① Bill has been lying on the bed since I came.
② I have been knowing him for more than ten years.
③ The stock market has been rising since last week.
④ My mother has been suffering from cold for several days.
⑤ My wife has been watching dramas since this morning.

04 밑줄 친 부분 중 어법상 어색한 것을 골라 바르게 고치시오.

A: ①Have your parents ②ever ③gone to Austria before?
B: No, they ⑤haven't.

__________ → __________

05 괄호 안에서 알맞은 말을 고르시오.

(1) We **(didn't see / haven't seen)** her the day before yesterday.
(2) I want to change the door key that I **(used / have used)** so far.

06 문장의 빈칸에 알맞은 것끼리 짝지은 것은?

(a) Huey ________ to Europe. He is still in Japan.
(b) Maria ________ him for years.

① didn't go – knows
② hasn't gone – has been knowing
③ hasn't gone – has known
④ hasn't been – has been knowing
⑤ hasn't been gone – has known

[07-08] 문장의 빈칸에 알맞은 동사의 형태를 고르시오.

07

For a couple of hours, soccer players from all over the region ________ together.

① play ② plays
③ had been played ④ have been playing
⑤ has played

08

I ________ for my girlfriend for about half an hour when I figured out that I was in the wrong place.

① waited ② had been waited
③ have been waiting ④ had been waiting
⑤ will have been waiting

서술형 대비

09 다음 문장을 현재완료 진행시제로 바꿔 쓰시오.

I read a news article about Steve Jobs.

→ ______________________________

10 밑줄 친 부분 중 어법상 어색한 것은?

① I will have finished my homework by tonight.
② It has been raining when we went out.
③ Bill had been working at his office when the power went out.
④ I had been waiting for her for an hour when Isabella arrived at the bus stop.
⑤ My girlfriend has been watching TV for six hours.

11 밑줄 친 부분을 어법상 바르게 고친 것은?

> Jimmy ①saw a movie with Sally last Saturday. They ②had fun, so they ③made another plan to meet each other. But today they ④can't meet together. Jimmy ⑤has been to his grandparents' house.

① saw → has seen
② had → have been
③ made → had made
④ can't meet → couldn't meet
⑤ has been → has gone

12 두 문장을 한 문장으로 바꿔 쓸 때 빈칸에 알맞은 말을 쓰시오.

> Cathy's mom scolded her. Then, she started to do her homework.
> → Cathy __________ her homework when her mom __________ her.

13 문장의 빈칸에 been과 gone 중에서 알맞은 말을 쓰시오.

(1) David has __________ to the grocery store because he has no food at home.

(2) Rebecca has __________ to the grocery store, so she has lots of food at home.

[14-15] 두 문장이 같은 뜻이 되도록 빈칸에 알맞은 것을 고르시오.

14

> John began to take some pictures an hour ago and is still taking pictures now.
> → John ________ pictures for an hour.

① is taking ② was taking
③ have taken ④ has been taking
⑤ had been taking

15

> Both Minhee and Minji started solving some difficult questions at 7 p.m., and their teacher arrived in the classroom at 8 p.m.
> → When the teacher arrived in the classroom at 8 p.m., both Minhee and Minji ________ some difficult questions for one hour.

① was solving ② has solved
③ had solved ④ has been solving
⑤ had been solving

16 우리말과 같은 뜻이 되도록 할 때 빈칸에 알맞은 것은?

> Andy는 머리가 아팠다. 그는 온종일 컴퓨터게임을 해왔었다.
> → Andy had a headache. He ________________ computer games all day.

① has played　② has been playing
③ had been playing　④ had been played
⑤ have been played

[17-19] 문장의 빈칸에 알맞은 말끼리 짝지은 것을 고르시오.

17

> (a) When I got home, my other family members _________ their lunch. So I had to have lunch alone.
> (b) Jason _________ 15 next year. He expects a wonderful year.

① finished – has been
② have already finished – will be
③ have already finished – will have been
④ had already finished – will be
⑤ had already finished – has been

18

> (a) Jackie _________ how to use this device last week.
> (b) Helen _________ how to use this device since last week.

① learns – learns
② learned – learned
③ learned – has been learning
④ has learned – has been learning
⑤ has learned – had been learning

19

> (a) Sandy _________ in Canada by this time tomorrow.
> (b) I _________ others by donating money in my later years.

① will have been – will have helped
② will have been – will help
③ will be – will have been helping
④ will be – will be helping
⑤ has been – will help

20 문장의 빈칸에 be동사를 알맞은 형태로 바꿔 쓰시오.

(1) My elder brother ______________ married now.

(2) My elder sister ______________ married for 5 years now.

(3) My parents ______________ married over 30 years by the time I graduate from university.

[21-22] 다음 중 어법상 어색한 문장을 고르시오.

21 ① Have you ever seen a real giraffe and lion?
② When have you given up submitting the document?
③ She has been practicing table tennis for four years.
④ Their team has already made their hotel reservations.
⑤ My grandparents have taken vitamins A and C since 2013.

22 ① I have not met your brother yet.
② I have just finished cleaning my room.
③ He has gone to L.A. He is not here now.
④ My friend has lost her pen.
⑤ It has rained yesterday.

23 주어진 단어를 빈칸에 알맞은 형태로 바꿔 쓰시오.

Frank ________(lose) his iPad two days ago. So he cannot listen to music and record his schedule.

24 대화의 밑줄 친 부분 중 어법상 어색한 것은?

A: ①Did you wash your car? Your car ②was very dirty.
B: No. When I ③saw my car, I found that it ④has been washed by someone. So I ⑤had nothing to do.

25 우리말과 같은 뜻이 되도록 빈칸에 알맞은 말을 쓰시오.

나는 그때까지 토끼 고기를 먹어본 적이 없었다.
→ I ______________ rabbit until that time.

서술형 대비

26 주어진 말을 사용하여 다음 우리말을 영어로 옮기시오.

나는 이모를 배웅하기 위해 방금 공항에 갔다 왔다.
(see off, just)
→ ________________________________

27 대화의 빈칸에 알맞은 것은?

A: Have you seen Philip?
B: No, I haven't seen him ________.

① yet ② already
③ still ④ just now
⑤ since

28 다음 질문에 대한 응답으로 어법상 어색한 것은?

How long have you studied abroad?

① I came to New York last month.
② I have studied abroad only one year ago.
③ I have studied abroad since last year.
④ I have studied abroad for almost five years.
⑤ I have just arrived here from Korea.

29 문장의 빈칸에 알맞은 말끼리 짝지은 것은?

(a) Jerry had a bad injury two months ______.
(b) Vivian has studied for her midterm exam ______ last week.

① before – since ② before – for
③ ago – for ④ ago – during
⑤ ago – since

30 대화에서 어법상 어색한 부분이 있는 것은?

① A: Matthew and I have known each other for a long time.
② B: When have you met him?
③ A: I met him when I was 11 years old. We've spent almost all of our weekends together.
④ B: Wow, that's great! By the way, I have not seen him lately.
⑤ A: Oh, he has been sick since last week.

≫ 정답 및 해설 6쪽

Extracurricular Activities

▸ *Sentence Writing*

PART A Complete the sentences describing the pictures.

1

lose weight

2

run

3

drive

1 Suji is going to start exercising because she thinks she is too fat. She ______________ (그녀는 이번 여름이면 살이 빠질 것이다.) by this summer.

2 Tina was out of breath. She ______________ on the track for two hours.
(그녀는 트랙을 두 시간 동안 달리고 있었다.)

3 Man: Why are you so nervous?
Woman: Frankly speaking, this is the first time I ______________ a car.
(솔직히 말하면, 저는 처음으로 차를 운전해 보는 거예요.)

PART B Change the Korean into English by using the given words.

1 나는 지금까지는 한국을 그리워한 적이 없다. (miss, so far)
→ ______________________________

2 그 두 노인은 2003년부터 서울에서 살고 있다. (old man, living, since)
→ ______________________________

3 그것은 그가 그의 인생을 돌아보았던 두 번째 순간이었다. (look back on, second time)
→ ______________________________

4 다음 주면 내가 결혼한 지 10년이 될 것이다. (be married)
→ ______________________________

▸ Further Studies 불규칙동사 변화표 ①

동사	변화형(현재-과거-과거분사)	동사	변화형(현재-과거-과거분사)
arise 생겨나다, 일어나다; (…의 결과로서) 생기다	arise – arose – arisen	fall 떨어지다, ~에 빠지다	fall – fell – fallen
awake 깨어나다, 일어나다, 눈뜨다	awake – awoke [awakened] – awoken	feed 먹이다	feed – fed – fed
be ~이다, 있다	be (is, am, are) – was (were) – been	feel 느끼다	feel – felt – felt
bear 참다, 낳다, 몸에 지니다	bear – bore – born [borne]	fight 싸우다	fight – fought – fought
beat 치다, 때리다	beat – beat – beat [beaten]	find 찾다, 알다	find – found – found
become ~가 되다, 어울리다	become – became – become	fly 날다	fly – flew – flown
begin 시작하다	begin – began – begun	forget 잊다	forget – forgot – forgotten
blow 불다	blow – blew – blown	forgive 용서하다	forgive – forgave – forgiven
break 깨다, 어기다	break – broke – broken	get 갖다, 얻다, 취하다	get – got – got [gotten]
bring 가져오다, 야기하다	bring – brought – brought	give 주다	give – gave – given
build 짓다, 건설하다	build – built – built	go 가다	go – went – gone
burn 태우다	burn – burnt [burned] – burnt [burned]	grow 자라다, 키우다	grow – grew – grown
buy 사다	buy – bought – bought	hang 매달다, 걸다	hang – hung – hung
cast 던지다	cast – cast – cast	cf. hang 교수형에 처하다	hang – hanged – hanged
catch 잡다	catch – caught – caught	have 가지다, 먹다	have – had – had
choose 고르다, 선택하다	choose – chose – chosen	hear 듣다	hear – heard – heard
come 오다	come – came – come	hide 숨기다	hide – hid – hidden
cost 비용이 들게 하다	cost – cost – cost	hit 치다, 때리다, 히트하다	hit – hit – hit
cut 자르다, 삭감하다	cut – cut – cut	hold 잡다, 지탱하다, 개최하다	hold – held – held
deal 다루다, 거래하다	deal – dealt – dealt	hurt 다치게 하다	hurt – hurt – hurt
dig 파다	dig – dug – dug	keep 유지하다, 키우다	keep – kept – kept
do ~을 하다	do – did – done	kneel 무릎 꿇다	kneel – knelt [kneeled] – knelt [kneeled]
draw 당기다, 그리다, 끌다	draw – drew – drawn	know 알다	know – knew – known
dream 꿈꾸다	dream – dreamt [dreamed] – dreamt [dreamed]	lay 놓다, 낳다, 눕히다	lay – laid – laid
drink 마시다	drink – drank – drunk	lead 이끌다, 지도하다	lead – led – led
drive 운전하다, 추진하다	drive – drove – driven	learn 배우다	learn – learned [learnt] – learned [learnt]
eat 먹다	eat – ate – eaten	leave 떠나다, 남겨두다	leave – left – left

조동사 (Modal Verbs)

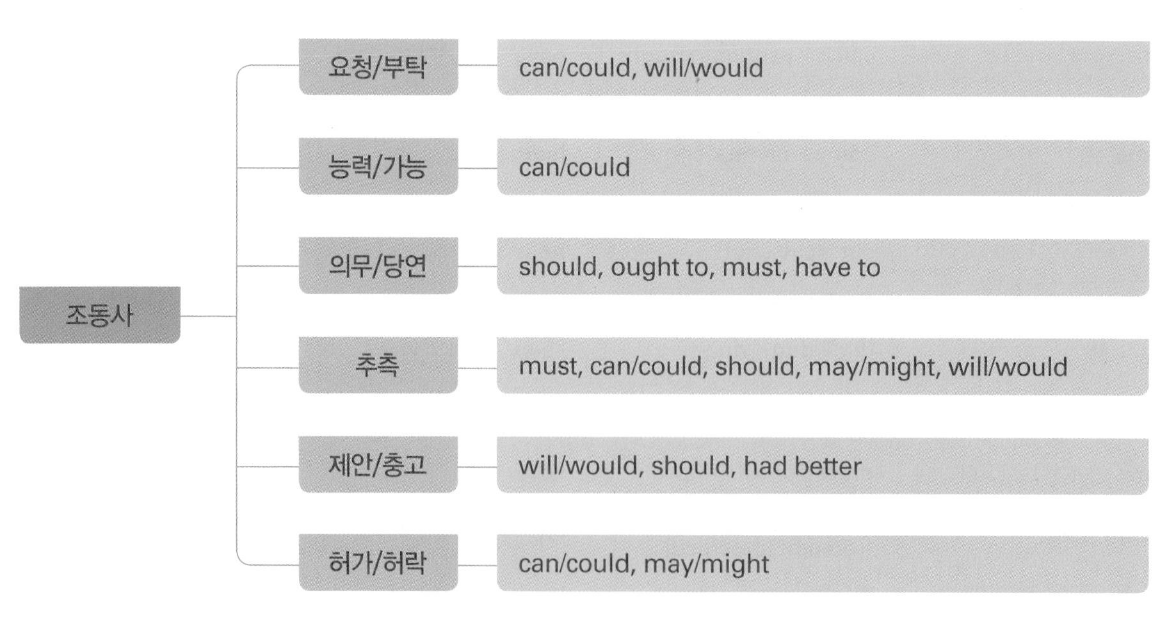

기출 맛보기

대화의 빈칸에 알맞은 것을 고르시오. (송파구 ○○중학교)

A: I think my supervisor is at the office.
B: No, he ________ be at the office, for he called me from his home just half an hour ago.

① can't
② mustn't
③ shouldn't
④ used to not
⑤ had better not

해설
문맥상 '~일 리가 없다'라는 현재의 부정적 추측을 나타내는 can't가 알맞다.
① ~일 리가 없다, ② ~해서는 안 된다, ③ ~안 하는 것이 좋을 것이다, ④ ~안 하곤 했다, ⑤ ~안 하는 게 좋다

해석
A: 나는 공장장님이 사무실에 있다고 생각해.
B: 아니야, 그가 사무실에 있을 리가 없어. 왜냐하면 그가 그의 집에서 30분 전에 나에게 전화했거든.

정답 ①

will/would, can/could

1교시 Grammar Point

1 will/would

(1) **미래/예정** | '~할 것이다'

Girls' Generation **will** probably come to the festival tomorrow.

(2) **부탁, 권유** | '~해주시겠어요?'

Will [Would] you please open the door for me?

(3) **과거의 불규칙적인 습관** | '~하곤 했다' (= used to)

I **would** often go hiking with my father when I was young.

(4) **간절한 희망(would like to)** | '~하고 싶다' (= wish to)

I **would like to** find a different occupation.

(5) **의지, 강한 거절** | '~할 것이다', '~하려고 하지 않다'

I **will** finish my homework before the due date.

Mr. Simpson **wouldn't** listen to my excuse.

2 can/could

(1) **능력/가능** | '~할 수 있다' (= be able to, be capable of -ing)

Sunny **can** speak English a little, but she **can't** write it at all.

I **could** not meet you last week because I was very busy.

(2) **허가/허락** | '~해도 좋다' (= may)

You **can** use my cell phone.

Could I talk to you for just a moment?

(3) **요청/부탁** | '~해주시겠어요?'

Can [Could] I borrow your pen? [could는 can보다 더 정중한 표현]

(4) **추측/가능성** | '~일 리 없다', '~일 수도 있다'

He **cannot** come here. 부정적 추측

It **could** rain tomorrow. 가능성

(5) **완료 조동사** | 과거 사실에 대한 추측이나 후회

〈can't + have + 과거분사〉 '~했을 리가 없다'
〈could + have + 과거분사〉 '~할 수 있었는데 (하지 못했다)'
〈couldn't + have + 과거분사〉 '~하지 않을 수도 있었는데 (했다)'

Bob **can't have bought** the wallet.

I **could have lent** you my iPad. Why didn't you ask me?

Matthew **couldn't have solved** the math problem.

Grammar Tips

- **will vs. be going to**

(1) 미래의 동작, 상태, 예정을 나타낼 때는 will 또는 be going to 둘 다 쓰임

I **will [am going to]** be 16 years old next year.

(2) 말하는 시점에서 미래의 일을 결정할 때는 will, 이미 계획된 일을 말할 때는 be going to

I **will** watch a movie with my friend tonight. (지금 결정한 일)

I **am going to** watch a movie with my friend tonight. (이미 계획된 일)

- **will이 가까운 미래를 나타낼 때 (= be + -ing)**

I **will leave** for L.A. tomorrow.
= I'**m leaving** for L.A. tomorrow.

- **would rather (차라리 ~하겠다)**
would rather A than B (B 하느니 차라리 A 하겠다)

I **would rather** not go out for a walk in this weather. [= I'd rather]

I **would rather** drink water **than** have some food.

- **be able to의 쓰임**

can처럼 단독으로 쓰이기보다는 will be able to(~할 수 있을 것이다)처럼 다른 조동사와 함께 잘 쓰인다.

2교시 In - Class Questions

우리말과 같은 뜻이 되도록 빈칸에 알맞은 말을 쓰시오.

1 Kyle은 영어를 매우 잘할 수 있다.
→ Kyle ______________ speak English very well.

2 Nelson은 공부를 매우 열심히 했을 리가 없다.
→ Nelson ______________ have studied very hard.

3 저와 결혼해 주시겠어요?
→ ______________ you marry me?

4 나는 Cathy와 함께 그 영화를 보러 가고 싶다.
→ I ______________ like to go to the movie with Cathy.

괄호 안에서 알맞은 말을 고르시오.

1 You **(can see / can't see / can't have seen)** Alex at the party. He didn't go there.

2 Scarlet **(cannot solve / cannot have solved / could not solved)** the problem by herself. I'm sure her mom helped her.

3 We **(can / can't / will / won't)** hardly understand it. Please say that again.

4 Margaret didn't finish her homework. So she **(can't / couldn't / wasn't able)** go shopping with her family.

어법상 어색한 부분을 찾아 바르게 고치시오.

1 You will be able meet me at the library. __________ → __________

2 Both Gina and I are capable of play the flute. __________ → __________

3 I would rather clean the house to go shopping with Mom. __________ → __________

우리말과 같은 뜻이 되도록 주어진 말을 사용하여 문장을 완성하시오.

1 그녀는 혼자 힘으로 그것을 할 수 있을 것이다. (do)
→ She ______________________ it for herself.

2 너는 그 순간에 잠자코 있을 수 있었는데. (hold one's tongue)
→ You ______________________ at that moment.

3 그녀가 그렇게 행동했을 리가 없다. (do)
→ She ______________________ that.

3교시 After - Class Questions

01 밑줄 친 부분 중 어법상 어색한 것은?

①When I ②was young, I ③would go to the beach ④near my house with my friends and ⑤had fun in the water.

02 다음 중 어법상 어색한 문장은?

① Would you get me the bill?
② My car wouldn't start this morning.
③ I would rather joined the dance club.
④ Would you please stay with me for a while?
⑤ I would like to get the brand-new cell phone.

[03-04] 문장의 빈칸에 알맞은 조동사를 고르시오.

03 The weather is very nice for a baseball game. It _________ be better.

① can ② can't ③ could
④ couldn't ⑤ could have

04 Don't worry about your mistake. I think the manager _________ the boss about it.

① is not telling ② was not told ③ won't tell
④ could have not told ⑤ should have not told

05 두 문장이 같은 뜻이 되도록 할 때 빈칸에 알맞은 것은?

It is impossible that my mother said that.
→ My mother ______________________________ that.

① would have said ② couldn't have said ③ should have said
④ cannot have said ⑤ must have said

06 밑줄 친 말 대신에 쓸 수 있는 것은?

(a) Kate is going to have a blind date this weekend.
(b) Can you and your sister come to my reception party tonight?

① are [Are] ② were [Were] ③ will [Will]
④ does [Does] ⑤ must [Must]

Vocabulary Tips

- bill 계산서
- weather 날씨
- impossible 불가능한
- blind date 소개팅
- reception party 환영 파티

07 문장의 빈칸에 able to가 들어갈 수 없는 문장은?

① Some people may be ________ help you find out the secret.
② Ted and Laura are ________ speak five different languages.
③ Many employees hope to be ________ travel to Brazil and Peru.
④ You are ________ use my camera this weekend. I won't use it then.
⑤ I won't be ________ buy the bag that I really want to have.

[08-09] 밑줄 친 can의 쓰임이 나머지와 다른 것을 고르시오.

08 ① Can you look for this file for the boss?
② You can say something if you have to.
③ Can I stay longer? I feel lonely.

09 ① James can write poems and novels.
② You can't bring your dog in the store.
③ You can park anywhere in this parking lot.

10 문장의 빈칸에 알맞은 것은?

Many adoptees might ________ see their mothers someday.

① can ② will ③ have to
④ be able to ⑤ are able to

[11-12] 우리말과 같은 뜻이 되도록 주어진 말을 사용하여 빈칸을 완성하시오.

11 Sarah가 그 결혼식을 잊었을 리가 없다. (forget)

→ Sarah ________________ the wedding.

12 그는 매우 어렸을 때 몇 시간씩 농구를 하곤 했다. (play)

→ When he was very young, he ________________ basketball for hours.

13 대화의 빈칸에 알맞은 조동사는?

A: Hey, Ellie. How was the movie?
B: It was really funny. The actor in this movie looks very handsome.
I ________ see it once again.

① shall ② can't ③ wouldn't
④ would like to ⑤ won't able to

Vocabulary Tips

- employee 직장인, 근로자
- lonely 외로운
- poem 시
- parking lot 주차장
- adoptee 입양아
- someday 언젠가
- forget 잊다 (-forgot-forgotten)

[14-16] 두 문장이 같은 뜻이 되도록 빈칸에 알맞은 말을 쓰시오.

14 Cathy is going to have a baby in May.

→ Cathy ________ have a baby in May.

15 Her plane will arrive at Incheon Airport at 12 o'clock.

→ Her plane ________ arriving at Incheon Airport at 12 o'clock.

16 It is possible that Dr. Neilson will forgive my big mistake.

→ Dr. Neilson ________ forgive my big mistake.

17 괄호 안에서 알맞은 말을 모두 고르시오.

(1) It **(can / could / will)** rain tomorrow.
(2) I **(can / could)** read and write when I was 8.

18 우리말과 같은 뜻이 되도록 할 때 빈칸에 알맞은 것은?

그는 수업시간에 늦지 않을 수도 있었는데.
→ He ________ late for the class.

① cannot be ② won't be ③ cannot have been
④ would have been ⑤ could not have been

[19-20] 문장의 빈칸에 알맞은 말끼리 짝지은 것을 고르시오.

19

(a) I ________ be 28 years old next month.
(b) The train for Busan ________ depart soon.
(c) Your books look heavy. I ________ help you.

① will – will – am going to ② will – is going to – will
③ will – is going to – am going to ④ am going to – will – will
⑤ am going to – will – am going to

20

(a) Bill was a hardworking person. So I thought that he ________ succeed to his parents' business.
(b) Sam said we ________ have more free time.

① will – can ② will – could ③ will – were able to
④ would – could ⑤ would – were able to

Vocabulary Tips

- possible 가능한
- forgive 용서하다
- depart 출발하다
- hardworking 부지런한
- succeed 계승하다, 이어받다

21 밑줄 친 would의 의미가 나머지와 다른 것은?

① Mom would learn how to swim.
② My sister would take a walk after dinner.
③ Dad would sometimes tell interesting stories.
④ My brother would play soccer during lunch break.
⑤ The teacher told me not to go there, but I would go there.

서술형 대비
22 주어진 말을 사용하여 다음 우리말을 영어로 옮기시오.

나는 그 소설책을 보느니 재테크에 관한 책을 읽겠다. (would rather)
→ ______________________________

23 밑줄 친 부분에 유의하여 다음 문장을 우리말로 옮기시오.

You couldn't have caught a bad cold.
→ ______________________________

24 문장의 빈칸에 공통으로 알맞은 것은?

(a) He ________ swim a lot faster three years ago.
(b) A man is knocking on the door. Who ________ that be?

① can ② is able to ③ is capable of
④ could ⑤ was able to

서술형 대비
25 조동사 can을 이용하여 다음 우리말을 영어로 옮기시오.

(1) Maria는 그 학교의 교장일 가능성이 있다. (principal)
→ ______________________________

(2) Maria는 그 학교의 교장이 될 수 있다. (principal)
→ ______________________________

Vocabulary Tips
- take a walk 산책하다
- sometimes 가끔
- investment 재테크
- a lot (비교급을 수식하여) 훨씬
- principal 교장

may/might, must/have to

1교시 Grammar Point

1 may/might

(1) **불확실한 추측** | '~일지도 모른다, ~일 수도 있다'

The government **may** not accept your suggestion.

Nancy said that her teacher **might** change her mind.

(2) **허가/허락** | '~해도 좋다' (= can)

You **may** go home if you want.

You **may** not enter this area without permission.

(3) **완료 조동사** | 과거 사실에 대한 불확실한 추측

〈may/might + have + 과거분사〉 '~이었을 지도 모른다'

Cathy **may have been** rich when she was young.

2 must/have to

(1) **의무/당연** | '~해야 한다' (= have to)

People **must** watch this movie.
→ People **have to** watch this movie.

(2) **추측** | '~임에 틀림없다'

She looks sad. She **must** break up with her boyfriend.
→ She **has to** break up with her boyfriend. (×)
[must가 추측으로 쓰일 때는 have to로 바꿔 쓸 수 없다.]

(3) **부정문**

must가 의무의 의미일 때 (~해야 한다)	must not (~해서는 안 된다)
	don't have [need] to (~할 필요가 없다) [= need not + 동사원형]
must가 추측의 의미일 때 (~임에 틀림없다)	cannot (~일 리가 없다)

Pattinson **must not** leave home forever.

Bella **didn't have [need] to** go to London.

Taylor **cannot** get married. He is only 20 years old.

(4) **완료 조동사** | 과거 사실에 대한 강한 추측

〈must + have + 과거분사〉 '~이었음에 틀림없다'

Alice **must have lost** her birthday gift.

Edward **must have forgotten** his key.

Grammar Tips

might의 용법

(1) 현재시제에 쓰이면 may보다 약한 추측을 의미

(2) may의 과거형

may의 관용표현

may well (~하는 것은 당연하다)
may/might as well (~하는 것이 낫다)

Parents **may well** love their children.
We **may as well** memorize words to get better scores.

의무로 쓰일 때 must의 시제

과거: had to
미래: will have to

Ashley **had to** meet the president at the last meeting.
Dakota **will have to** take part in the social group soon.

2교시 In - Class Questions

괄호 안에서 알맞은 말을 고르시오.

1 Andy **(may / will / should)** be allergic to peaches and peanuts.

2 It's only 3 o'clock. You **(must not / cannot / don't have to)** hurry.

3 People **(must not / will not / don't need to)** drive a car without a license.

우리말과 같은 뜻이 되도록 주어진 말을 사용하여 빈칸을 완성하시오.

1 Evan은 얼굴이 좋아 보이지 않는다. 그는 아픈 것이 틀림없다. (be)
→ Evan doesn't look well. He __________ __________ sick.

2 우리에게는 다른 숙제가 있을지도 모른다. (have)
→ We __________ __________ some other homework.

3 그녀가 그의 예전 여자 친구였을지도 모른다. (be)
→ She __________ __________ __________ his ex-girlfriend.

두 문장이 같은 뜻이 되도록 빈칸에 알맞은 말을 쓰시오.

1 Patrick must send this package to the client.
→ Patrick ____________________ this package to the client.

2 May I see your boarding pass?
→ ____________________ I see your boarding pass?

3 You don't have to go to school today because it's Sunday.
→ You ____________________ to school today because it's Sunday.

대화의 빈칸에 알맞은 말을 〈보기〉에서 골라 쓰시오.

보기	
No, you may not.	Yes, you may.
She must have some food.	She might have caught a cold.

1 A: Do you know why Hana kept coughing?
B: I'm not sure. ____________________

2 A: May I have some chocolate cake?
B: ____________________ You are on a diet now.

3교시 After - Class Questions

[01-03] 문장의 빈칸에 알맞은 조동사를 고르시오.

01 Justin has been driving for 10 hours. He ________ be tired.

① can't　　② must　　③ won't
④ didn't　　⑤ has to

02 I thought that what the teachers said about the future ________ be true.

① may　　② will　　③ had to
④ should　　⑤ might

03 I emailed my partner several times. But he did not answer. He ________ his email address.

① must change　　② might change　　③ might have changed
④ might as well　　⑤ should have changed

04 밑줄 친 부분 중 어법상 어색한 부분을 찾아 바르게 고치시오.

People say ①that employees ②may as well ③doing without ④any ⑤samples.

________________ → ________________

05 밑줄 친 must가 추측의 의미로 쓰인 것을 모두 고르시오.

① My family must visit my grandparents' this holiday.
② Either Jane or Frank must be a suspect in the car accident.
③ Parents must take care of their kids as well as feed them.
④ You must not park your car in front of this building.
⑤ Dinosaurs must have been cold-blooded animals.

06 문장의 빈칸에 공통으로 알맞은 조동사는?

(a) ________ I take your coat, sir?
(b) Teachers ________ well love their students a lot.
(c) Cathy ________ not have missed the bus.

① Can[can]　　② Will[will]　　③ May[may]
④ Must[must]　　⑤ Should[should]

Vocabulary Tips

- without ~없이
- sample 샘플, 견본
- either A or B A와 B 둘 중 하나
- suspect 용의자, 혐의자
- A as well as B B뿐만 아니라 A도
- feed 밥을 먹이다
- dinosaur 공룡
- cold-blooded 냉혈의, 냉혹한
- miss 놓치다

[07-09] 주어진 말을 이용하여 다음 우리말을 영어로 옮기시오.

07 Cathy는 아픈 것이 틀림없다. 그녀는 지금 창백해 보인다. (must, sick, pale)

→ Cathy ____________. She ____________ now.

08 살을 빼기 위해서는 조금 덜 먹는 편이 낫다. (may, eat less)

→ ________________________

09 Edward는 그때 그의 차 열쇠를 잃어버렸음이 틀림없다. (must, then)

→ ________________________

[10-11] 두 문장이 같은 뜻이 되도록 빈칸에 알맞은 말을 고르시오.

10 It is certain that his aunt was smart when she was young.
→ His aunt ________ have been smart when she was young.

① would ② should ③ must
④ can ⑤ could

11 It doesn't seem that Kelly learned anything about ethics and physics.
→ Kelly ________ not have learned anything about ethics and physics.

① would ② should ③ must
④ may ⑤ could

12 두 문장이 같은 의미가 되도록 빈칸에 알맞은 말을 쓰시오.

Max must send a text message to his team members.
→ Max ________ ________ send a text message to his team members.

[13-14] 우리말과 같은 뜻이 되도록 주어진 말을 사용하여 빈칸을 완성하시오.

13 지금쯤 내 남자 친구가 여기에 도착했을지도 모른다. (arrive)

→ My boyfriend ________ ________ ________ here by now.

14 민희는 모두 A학점을 받았다. 그녀가 장학금을 받는 것은 당연하다. (receive)

→ Minhee aced all of her subjects. She ________ ________ ________ a scholarship.

Vocabulary Tips

- **pale** 창백한
- **certain** 확실한
- **ethics** 윤리학
- **physics** 물리학
- **ace** A학점을 받다
- **scholarship** 장학금

15 우리말을 영어로 바르게 옮긴 것은?

우리는 어제 그 식당에 들어가기 위해 줄을 서서 기다려야 했다.

① We should wait in line to enter the restaurant yesterday.
② We would wait in line to enter the restaurant yesterday.
③ We might wait in line to enter the restaurant yesterday.
④ We could wait in line to enter the restaurant yesterday.
⑤ We had to wait in line to enter the restaurant yesterday.

16 다음 글에서 밑줄 친 부분을 어법상 바르게 고치시오.

> Mina was elected president of our school. So she has to prepare for all of the upcoming events on behalf of us. First of all, she has to take part in the school campaigns next week.

→ ______________________

17 다음 글의 빈칸에 알맞은 것은?

> Somi is my best friend. She worked really hard in order to have better life in the future. I was pretty sure that she would achieve her goal. Now, she ________, and she can relax.

① must not work hard
② must not have worked hard
③ might not have worked hard
④ might not work hard
⑤ doesn't have to work hard anymore

18 밑줄 친 부분 중 어법상 어색한 것은?

① I would eat pasta very often.
② Would you like some more juice?
③ We had better not go inside. There is a bad smell.
④ I would rather see a movie than listen to music.
⑤ Dana must be angry when we talked about that issue.

19 밑줄 친 must의 의미가 나머지와 다른 것은?

① All staff members must be kind to customers. It's a rule.
② I must get up early in order to go to school.
③ Sam must take a final exam.
④ Owen has a lot of money. He must be rich.
⑤ You must study hard to pass the exam.

Vocabulary Tips

- wait in line 줄을 서서 기다리다
- upcoming 다가오는
- on behalf of ~을 대신하여
- take part in ~에 참석하다
- in oder to ~하기 위해서
- achieve 이루다, 성취하다
- relax 쉬다
- issue 문제
- customer 고객, 손님

20 밑줄 친 may의 의미를 '추측'인지 '허락'인지 판단하여 쓰시오.

(1) My parents <u>may</u> not know the truth. ________

(2) Thomas <u>may</u> be tired from studying and want to go to bed. ________

(3) You <u>may</u> open your present and take a look at it. ________

[21-22] 대화의 빈칸에 알맞은 조동사를 고르시오.

21

A: Did you know that Jessica had a bad car accident?
B: Really? Is she okay now?
A: Yes. She is nearly recovered, but she ________ be in the hospital for four weeks.

① had to ② have to ③ has to
④ should ⑤ doesn't have to

22

A: I have my driver's licence test tomorrow. I am a bit worried.
B: Oh, come on. You've practiced a lot. You ________ worry about it. All you have to do is do your best.

① need to ② must ③ are not able to
④ ought to ⑤ don't have to

23 문장의 빈칸에 공통으로 알맞은 조동사는?

I ________ to stay up late last night. So I ________ better go home early and get some sleep.

① should ② have ③ had
④ may ⑤ need

24 밑줄 친 부분과 바꿔 쓸 수 있는 것은?

You <u>don't have to</u> hand in your report today because the due date has been postponed until next Monday.

① need not ② should not ③ must not
④ ought to ⑤ had better

25 우리말과 같은 뜻이 되도록 빈칸에 알맞은 말을 쓰시오.

John은 내일 버스 터미널로 그를 데리러가야 할 것이다.
→ John ________ ________ ________ pick him up at the bus terminal tomorrow.

Vocabulary Tips

- be tired from ~로 피곤하다
- take a look at ~을 보다
- a bit 약간, 조금
- do one's best 최선을 다하다
- due date 마감일, 제출일
- postpone 연기하다, 미루다
- pick up ~를 차로 데리러가다

1교시 Grammar Point

1 should

(1) 도덕적 의무나 충고 | '~해야 한다' (= ought to)

We **should** bow to our elders. 도덕적 의무

You **should** take a walk at least once a day. 충고

You **should not[ought not to]** take any photos in the bookstore.
부정문: '~하면 안 된다' (금지)

(2) 완료 조동사 | 과거 사실에 대한 후회

〈should + have + 과거분사〉 '~했어야 했는데 (하지 않았다)'
〈shouldn't + have + 과거분사〉 '~하지 말았어야 했는데 (했다)'

You **should have talked** on the phone while you were driving.

I **shouldn't have fallen** asleep. I missed my favorite TV drama.

2 had better

• 강한 충고, '~하는 게 좋다'

You **had better** go back to your accommodations.

You **had better not** try this unless your parents approve it.
부정문: '~하지 않는 게 좋다'

= You**'d better not** try this unless your parents approve it.

3 used to

• 과거의 규칙적인 습관이나 상태, '(과거에) ~하곤 했다 (지금은 아니다)'

I **used to** own three dogs and eleven cats in Canada.

There **used to** be many vendors on this street.

She **didn't use to** swim when she was young. 부정문: '~하지 않곤 했다'
= used not to

Grammar Tips

• **〈should + have + 과거분사〉 vs. had to**

〈should + have + 과거분사〉: '~했어야 했는데 (하지 않았다)'
had to: '~해야 했다 (했다)'

• **used to vs. would**

과거의 습관	used to, would
과거의 상태	used to

I **used to[would]** play golf every weekend. (o)
There **would** be a big tree. (x)
There **used to** be a big tree. (o)

• **〈be[get] used to + -ing〉**
〈be accustomed to + -ing〉
'~에 익숙하다'

Brian **got used to eating** spicy food.

• **used to의 의문문**

〈Did + 주어 + use to + 동사원형 ~?〉

Grammar Plus+

need, dare

(1) need: '~할 필요가 있다'

긍정문에서는 일반동사로, 부정문/의문문에서는 일반동사나 조동사로 쓰임

He **needs** to buy a car. [긍정문: 일반동사]

He **need not** buy a car. [부정문: 조동사]
= He **doesn't need to** buy a car. [부정문: 일반동사]

Need he buy a car? [의문문: 조동사]
= **Does** he **need to** buy a car? [의문문: 일반동사]

(2) dare: '감히 ~하다'

긍정문에서는 일반동사로, 부정문/의문문에서는 일반동사나 조동사로 쓰임

A: **Dare** you ask your teacher? (= **Do** you **dare to** ask your teacher?)
B: Yes, I **dare to** ask her.
No, I **dare not** ask her. (= No, I **don't dare to** ask her.)

2교시 In-Class Questions

STEP A

빈칸에 알맞은 말을 〈보기〉에서 골라 쓰시오.

보기 had better used to should

1 If you feel sick, you ______________ see a doctor. It is necessary.

2 She ______________ order food to be delivered when she was at college.

3 He isn't honest. You ______________ not trust him.

STEP B

괄호 안에서 알맞은 말을 고르시오.

1 Ms. Kim **(used to / is used to)** work as a teacher.

2 There **(used to / would)** be a university here.

3 She **(has better / have better / had better)** say something.

4 They **(not ought to / ought not to / ought to not)** eat anything.

STEP C

우리말과 같은 뜻이 되도록 빈칸에 알맞은 말을 쓰시오.

1 너는 영어회화에 더 많은 시간을 보내야 해.
→ You ______________________ more time studying English conversation.

2 어두워지기 전에 집으로 돌아가는 게 좋겠다.
→ You ______________________ back home before it gets dark.

3 너의 아들은 그 시험에 대비해서 공부를 열심히 했어야 했는데.
→ Your son ______________________ hard for the test.

STEP D

주어진 말을 사용하여 다음 우리말을 영어로 옮기시오.

1 Tim은 예전에 캐나다에서 살았었다. (used to)
→ ____

2 David는 그녀에게 이메일을 보내지 말았어야 했는데. (should)
→ ____

3 Joan은 LA에서 혼자 거리를 걷지 않는 편이 낫다. (had better)
→ ____

3교시 After - Class Questions

01 다음 질문에 대한 응답으로 알맞은 것은?

Can I park here although it says, "No Parking," here?

① No, you didn't use to.
② Yes, you should.
③ No, you'd rather.
④ No, you'd better not.
⑤ Yes, you have to.

02 두 문장이 같은 의미가 되도록 빈칸에 알맞은 말을 쓰시오.

My brother and I feel bad for my grandmother because we didn't follow any of her advice.

→ My brother and I ________ ________ ________ some of her advice.

03 밑줄 친 부분이 나머지와 다른 것은?

① You'd like to go home before it gets dark.
② You'd rather drink this juice than that one.
③ You'd lie down on the bench when you were young.
④ You'd have solved the issues already without my support.
⑤ You'd better study by yourself instead of studying with your friends.

04 밑줄 친 부분 중 어법상 어색한 것은?

① She need not keep the dog.
② You must not take pictures in this gallery.
③ We ought not to use our cell phones in class.
④ We had not better touch these strange flowers.
⑤ Cindy wasn't used to giving speeches in front of the audience.

Grammar Plus+

05 다음 질문에 대한 알맞은 응답을 두 개로 쓰시오.

Dare you ask your mother-in-law?

→ No, I ________ ________ ask my mother-in-law.

→ No, I ________ ________ ________ ask my mother-in-law.

[06-07] 다음 중 어법상 어색한 문장을 고르시오.

06 ① We should have given more money to the poor.
② Ellen had better study in the library this weekend.
③ I'd rather take the subway. Traffic jam is terrible.
④ Soldiers need not go to the site where civilians were killed.
⑤ Paula didn't use to playing computer games when she was a child.

Vocabulary Tips

- follow 따르다
- advice 충고
- lie 눕다
- support 도움, 지지
- gallery 미술관, 갤러리
- give a speech 연설하다
- audience 관중
- civilian 시민

Grammar Plus+

07 ① He needs to sell his car.
② Need he sell his car?
③ He needs not sell his car.
④ Does he need to sell his car?
⑤ He doesn't need to sell his car.

08 어법상 어색한 부분을 찾아 바르게 고치시오.

(1) There would be a tall building around this area.

________________ → ________________

(2) My daughter would be very shy at middle school.

________________ → ________________

09 글의 빈칸에 알맞은 것은?

My friends and I planned to go on a picnic this weekend. I was in charge of bringing the paper cups and plates for lunch. The morning of the picnic, I realized that there were no paper cups and plates available at the store. I ________ them earlier.

① could have bought
② should have bought
③ must have bought
④ had to buy
⑤ might have bought

10 문장의 빈칸에 알맞은 조동사 두 개를 고르시오.

Look at the messy room. You ________ clean your room after finishing your meal.

① will
② may
③ can
④ should
⑤ must

11 문장의 빈칸에 알맞은 조동사는?

Think of your health first. You ________ a balanced diet to stay healthy.

① had better keep
② have better keep
③ should have kept
④ would rather keep
⑤ might have kept

12 우리말과 같은 뜻이 되도록 주어진 말을 사용하여 문장을 완성하시오.

Sally는 레스토랑에서 시간제 근무를 하곤 했다. (have, use, a part-time job)

→ Sally ________________ at a restaurant.

Vocabulary Tips

- sell 팔다
- area 지역
- in charge of ~을 담당한
- available 구입할 수 있는, 사용할 수 있는
- messy 지저분한
- balanced diet 균형 잡힌 식단
- part-time job 시간제 근무

13 **문장의 빈칸에 used to만 들어갈 수 있으면 ①, would만 들어갈 수 있으면 ②, 둘 다 들어갈 수 있으면 ③을 쓰시오.**

(1) My husband and I ________ go bowling for hours on Mondays.

(2) There ________ be a huge monument in front of City Hall.

(3) Hank ________ have a complex about his appearance, but he doesn't have one now.

[14-15] 밑줄 친 부분 중 어법상 어색한 것을 고르시오.

14

Tyler ①must ②have failed the final exam. He ③might not ④have studied harder for the ⑤examination.

Grammar Plus+

15

My dad and I planned ①to go to Europe in order to go sightseeing. So we decided ②to go to a bookstore to buy a few travel guides. I wanted ③to buy only one book, which I thought was ④enough. However, Dad bought five books. He need not ⑤to buy all of those books.

[16-17] 우리말을 영어로 바르게 옮긴 것을 모두 고르시오.

16 당신은 여기에 주차하시면 안 됩니다.

① You will not park here.
② You have to park here.
③ You have not to park here.
④ You should not park here.
⑤ You ought not to park here.

Grammar Plus+

17 너는 영어로 말할 필요가 없다.

① You need not to speak in English.
② You need not speak in English.
③ You needs not speak in English.
④ You don't need to speak in English.
⑤ You do need not to speak in English.

18 **문장의 밑줄 친 부분을 어법상 바르게 고치시오.**

Emily has a horrible stomachache today, so she doesn't have to eat anything. → ________________

Vocabulary Tips

- go bowling 볼링 치러 가다
- monument 기념비(물)
- complex 콤플렉스, 강박관념
- appearance 외모
- sightsee 관광하다, 구경하다
- a few 약간의
- park 주차하다
- stomachache 위통, 복통

[19-20] 밑줄 친 부분 중 어법상 어색한 것을 고르시오.

19 ① The machine used to operate all day long.
② Young musicians don't have to sing songs.
③ Students didn't have better take this examination.
④ I would rather stay home than go out today.
⑤ Government officials ought not to avoid these problems.

20 ① This building used to be a hospital.
② He will have to arrive at class on time.
③ Where should I put these eggs? In the refrigerator?
④ You had better forget the bad experience.
⑤ Our family not used to eat bread for breakfast.

[21-24] 문장의 빈칸에 알맞은 조동사를 고르시오.

21 You ________ ask your teacher first before you leave the classroom.

① might ② could ③ used to
④ had better ⑤ need

22 You ________ skip class. It will affect your grade.

① may ② had better ③ used to
④ should not ⑤ would not

23 I was sure that everything ________ be all right.

① need ② should ③ used to
④ would ⑤ had better

24 I ________ not stand in front of the class. I get really nervous.

① need ② dare ③ used to
④ should ⑤ must

25 대화의 빈칸에 알맞은 조동사는?

A: Excuse me. Does Kevin live in this house?
B: He ________ be here, but he does not anymore. He moved.

① must ② had better ③ shouldn't
④ dare ⑤ used to

Vocabulary Tips

- operate 작동하다
- government official 공무원
- avoid 피하다
- refrigerator 냉장고
- skip 빼먹다, 거르다
- affect 영향을 끼치다
- not anymore 더 이상 아니다

Final Test

[01-02] 두 문장이 같은 뜻이 되도록 빈칸에 알맞은 말을 쓰시오.

01

I cannot stand the noise that many students make in the classroom.
→ I ________ ________ ________ ________ stand the noise that many students make in the classroom.

02

It is impossible that Jessica could be a member of MENSA when she was very young.
→ Jessica ________ ________ ________ a member of MENSA when she was very young.

03 다음 중 어법상 어색한 문장은?

① Evan shouldn't do such a thing.
② You would rather doing it again.
③ Passengers will be able to use this phone.
④ Mr. Kim can't have told you this serious story.
⑤ She could have passed this exam if she had taken it.

04 주어진 조건에 맞게 다음 우리말을 영어로 옮기시오.

나는 5시간 동안 걸어야 했다.

(1) [의무] ________________________________

(2) [후회] ________________________________

[05-07] 문장의 빈칸에 알맞은 말을 <보기>에서 골라 쓰시오.

보기	might	had to	should	would

05 We ________ spend time together in Mok-dong, but now we go to Cheongdam-dong.

06 I can't concentrate on this book. I ________ not have watched so much TV.

07 They ________ have played a lot when their parents were out.

08 다음 문장과 뜻이 같은 문장을 <보기>에서 고르시오.

보기
① He may be an interesting man.
② He must be an interesting man.
③ He must have been an interesting man.
④ He may have been an interesting man.
⑤ He can't be an interesting man.

(1) I am sure that Jaedong is an interesting man. ________

(2) It's possible that Jaedong was an interesting man. ________

09 대화의 빈칸에 알맞은 조동사는?

A: Mom, where's my cell phone? I want to check my Facebook page.
B: I don't know. It ______________ be in your backpack.

① ought to ② has to
③ must ④ shall
⑤ may

10 〈보기〉의 밑줄 친 must와 의미가 다른 것은?

보기 All students must come back to the dormitory before 11 p.m.

① You must not talk loudly in the library.
② Kelly must get a checkup tomorrow.
③ My parents must be upset with me.
④ I must not expect too much on my first attempt.
⑤ My family must get up early to catch the airport shuttle.

11 밑줄 친 may의 의미가 나머지와 다른 것 두 개를 고르시오.

① Kyle may speak English well.
② They may be our classmates.
③ Bob may come to the graduation party.
④ You may use my smartphone to play a game.
⑤ You may not enter this area without permission.

12 밑줄 친 부분과 바꿔 쓸 수 있는 것은?

You don't have to do this assignment anymore.

① may not　② don't need to
③ should not　④ must not
⑤ cannot

13 밑줄 친 부분에 유의하여 다음 문장을 우리말로 옮기시오.

(1) We used to study in the library together.
→ ______________________

(2) We are used to studying in the library together.
→ ______________________

[14-15] 우리말과 같은 뜻이 되도록 빈칸에 알맞은 것을 고르시오.

14
Kate가 벌써 그 과제를 끝냈을 리가 없다.
→ Kate ________ the assignments already.

① ought not to have completed
② don't need to have completed
③ must have not completed
④ may not have completed
⑤ can't have completed

15
나는 그 영화를 보느니 차라리 잠을 자겠다.
→ I ________ than see that movie.

① would sleep　② have to sleep
③ rather sleeping　④ would rather sleep
⑤ would rather sleeping

16 밑줄 친 부분의 의미가 나머지와 다른 것은?

① It could rain later this evening.
② I can get to the museum without any help.
③ It could be true that Steve is an honors student.
④ She can't have gone to school. It was Saturday.
⑤ Jason can't have helped you yesterday. He was very busy.

17 대화의 빈칸에 알맞은 조동사는?

A: Why do you have a long face?
B: I lost a chance.
A: What does it mean?
B: I met a beautiful girl at the monthly meeting. However, I was too busy to share anything with her.
A: Hmm... You ________ for her cell phone number.
B: You can say that again.

① must have asked　② will have asked
③ should have asked　④ can have asked
⑤ may have asked

[18-19] 밑줄 친 부분 중 어법상 어색한 것을 고르시오.

18

I ①used to ②have a good time with Lucy. But these days, I ③wouldn't rather talk to her ④in person because Lucy is very rude to everyone. So I try ⑤not to talk with her.

19

I am ①out of town now. It suddenly starts ②raining. I ③could have ④brought my umbrella. I ⑤have to wait until the rain stops.

20 우리말과 같은 뜻이 되도록 할 때 빈칸에 알맞은 말끼리 짝지은 것은?

너는 그 서류를 갖고 있을 필요가 없다. 그것들을 재활용하는 것이 낫다.
→ You ________________ have the papers.
You ________________ recycle them.

① have not to – hadn't better
② don't need – had better
③ need not – had better not
④ don't have to – had better
⑤ don't have to – had better not

서술형 대비

21 주어진 말을 사용하여 다음 우리말을 영어로 옮기시오.

내가 감히 나의 영어 선생님께 그런 질문을 할 수 있을까? (ask, dare)

→ ________________________ such a question?

22 문장의 빈칸에 들어갈 수 없는 말은?

________ Jane borrow the dress that you bought for the previous party?

① Can ② Could ③ May
④ Might ⑤ Would

23 두 문장이 같은 뜻이 되도록 할 때 빈칸에 알맞은 조동사는?

It is possible that Sarah won first prize at the writing contest.
→ Sarah ________ have won first prize at the writing contest.

① must ② should ③ ought to
④ can't ⑤ may

24 밑줄 친 부분 중 어법상 어색한 것을 찾아 바르게 고치시오.

When my daughter was in middle school, she ①used to be very shy. She ②would not enjoy talking with her friends and ③could not have express her feelings because she was too worried about her friends' negative responses. Now that she is older, she ④can make presentations in front of her classmates. She ⑤may well realize that she is the most important person herself.

________________ → ________________

25 (A), (B)의 각 네모 안에서 어법상 알맞은 말을 고르시오.

> What (A) [could / may] cause a celebrity to commit suicide in Korea? The most serious problem is that the suicide rate is increasing. It seems that there is no specific reason for them to have ended their lives. However, it is assumed that they (B) [must have suffered / had to suffer] from malicious replies.
>
> *malicious reply 악성 댓글

(A) ________________

(B) ________________

26 다음 우리말을 영어로 옮기시오.

(1) 민수는 지난달에 휴대전화를 샀음에 틀림없다.
→ ________________

(2) 민수는 지난달에 휴대전화를 샀어야 했다.
→ ________________

(3) 민수는 지난달에 휴대전화를 샀어야 했는데.
→ ________________

27 문장의 빈칸에 알맞은 말끼리 짝지은 것은?

> (a) She ________ argue about her unfair treatment with her boss.
> (b) My teacher ________ give her students snacks all of the time.

① dares not – doesn't need
② dare not – needs not
③ dare not – need not
④ doesn't dare to – needs not
⑤ doesn't dare – doesn't need

28 문장의 빈칸에 알맞은 조동사는?

> Many members of the young generation ________ well love to have expensive cars and luxury bags.

① will ② may ③ can
④ must ⑤ may as

29 우리말과 같은 뜻이 되도록 할 때 빈칸에 알맞은 조동사는?

> 모든 학생들이 지난 수업에 늦었음에 틀림없다.
> → Every student ________ late for the last class.

① can be ② must be
③ must have been ④ could have been
⑤ may have been

30 밑줄 친 may의 의미가 나머지와 <u>다른</u> 것은?

① Either you or your friend <u>may</u> be right.
② Linda <u>may</u> look happy and excited.
③ <u>May</u> I check your luggage for a minute?
④ My parents and grandparents <u>may</u> be late tonight.
⑤ His grandfather <u>may</u> be old, but he is still strong.

≫ 정답 및 해설 11쪽

Extracurricular Activities

▸ Sentence Writing

PART A Complete the sentences describing the pictures.

1

take

2

not / touch / monument

3

eat

1 ______________________ pets into the Super Store.
(너는 Super Store에 애완동물을 데리고 들어갈 수 없다.)

2 Kids ______________________ in the museum.
(아이들은 박물관에서 그 기념비를 만질 수없다.)

3 The cat taking a nap ______________________ fish.
(낮잠을 자고 있는 고양이가 그 물고기를 먹었음에 틀림없다.)

PART B Change the Korean into English by using the given words.

1 예전에는 여기에 상점이 있었지만 지금은 공원이 있다. (there)
→ ______________________

2 Jimmy는 그것에 대해서 불평하지 않는 게 좋겠어. (complain)
→ ______________________

3 비가 매우 많이 왔다. 나는 밖으로 나가지 말았어야 했는데. (go out, heavily)
→ ______________________

4 그녀는 친절하기 때문에 사랑받는 것은 당연하다. (since)
→ ______________________

▸ *Further Studies* 불규칙동사 변화표 ②

동사	변화형(현재-과거-과거분사)	동사	변화형(현재-과거-과거분사)
lend 빌려주다	lend – lent – lent	send 보내다	send – sent – sent
let 시키다	let – let – let	set 놓다, 정하다	set – set – set
lie 눕다, 놓여 있다	lie – lay – lain	show 보여주다	show – showed – shown [showed]
lose 잃다	lose – lost – lost	shut 닫다	shut – shut – shut
make 만들다	make – made – made	sing 노래하다	sing – sang – sung
mean 의미하다, 의도하다	mean – meant – meant	sit 앉다	sit – sat – sat
meet 만나다	meet – met – met	sleep 자다	sleep – slept – slept
mistake 실수하다, 잘못 알다	mistake – mistook – mistaken	smell 냄새가 나다	smell – smelled [smelt] – smelled [smelt]
misunderstand 오해하다	misunderstand – misunderstood – misunderstood	speak 말하다	speak – spoke – spoken
overcome 극복하다	overcome – overcame – overcome	spend 쓰다, 소비하다	spend - spent - spent
overeat 과식하다	overeat – overate – overeaten	stand 서다, 주장하다, 참다	stand – stood – stood
overhear 우연히 듣다	overhear – overheard – overheard	steal 훔치다	steal – stole – stolen
oversleep 너무 자다	oversleep – overslept – overslept	swim 수영하다	swim – swam – swum
pay 지불하다, 갚다	pay – paid – paid	take 취하다, 갖다, 가져가다	take – took – taken
prove 증명하다, 검증하다	prove – proved – proven [proved]	teach 가르치다	teach – taught – taught
put 놓다	put – put – put	tear 눈물을 흘리다, 찢다	tear – tore – torn
quit 중단하다	quit – quit [quitted] – quit [quitted]	tell 말하다	tell – told – told
read 읽다	read – read [red] – read [red]	think 생각하다	think – thought – thought
rid 제거하다	rid – rid – rid	throw 던지다	throw – threw – thrown
ride 타다, 태워다주다	ride – rode – ridden	understand 이해하다	understand – understood – understood
ring 종을 울리다	ring – rang – rung	upset 뒤엎다, 전복시키다, 어지럽히다	upset – upset – upset
rise 증가하다, 떠오르다	rise – rose – risen	wake 일어나다, 깨어나다	wake – woke [waked] – woken [waked]
run 뛰다, 달리다	run – ran – run	wear 입다	wear – wore – worn
say 말하다	say – said – said	weep 울다	weep – wept – wept
see 보다	see – saw – seen	win 이기다	win – won – won
seek 찾다, 추구하다	seek – sought – sought	write 쓰다	write – wrote – written
sell 팔다	sell – sold – sold		

Unit 04 수동태 (Passives)

동사의 태
- 능동태 〈타동사 + 목적어〉
- 수동태 〈be + 과거분사〉

능동태는 주어가 동작을 하는 것을 말할 때 쓰인다. [일반적 동사의 형태]
수동태는 주어가 동작을 받는 것(당하는 것)을 말할 때 쓰인다. [동사의 형태가 〈be동사 + 과거분사〉로 바뀜]

기출 맛보기

다음 중 어법상 알맞은 것을 고르시오. (영등포구 ○○중학교)

① The bookshelf was filled of a lot of books.

② I am sick and tired by your excuses.

③ Almost all of my friends are made impressed by the film.

④ Someone was seen go off fireworks.

⑤ Several universities has been applied for by me.

해설

③ 5형식 문장 The film makes almost all of my friends impressed.를 수동태로 나타낸 것이다. 5형식의 목적격 보어가 과거분사일 경우는 수동태에서 그대로 동사 뒤에 온다.

① [of → with] be filled with(~으로 가득 차 있다)

② [by → of] be sick and tired of(~에 진력이 나다)

④ [go → to go] 지각동사의 수동태 문장은 목적격 보어인 원형부정사가 to부정사로 바뀐다.

⑤ [has → have] 주어가 복수이므로 동사도 복수형이 와야 한다.

해석

① 그 책장은 많은 책들로 가득 차 있었다.

② 나는 네 변명에 진력이 난다.

③ 내 친구들 중 거의 대부분이 그 영화에 감명 받았다.

④ 누군가가 폭죽을 터뜨리는 것이 보였다.

⑤ 몇 개의 대학교가 나에 의해 지원되었다.

정답 ③

DAY 07

4, 5형식 문장의 수동태

1교시 Grammar Point

1 4형식 문장의 수동태

- 간접목적어와 직접목적어를 주어로 한 두 개의 수동태 가능
- 직접목적어가 주어일 경우 간접목적어 앞에 전치사 to, for, of를 씀

Sam **gave** Kelly (① 간접목적어) a letter (② 직접목적어).

→ ① Kelly **was given** a letter by Sam.
→ ② A letter **was given to** Kelly by Sam.

She **asked** him (① 간접목적어) a question (② 직접목적어).

→ ① He **was asked** a question by her.
→ ② A question **was asked of** him by her.

2 직접목적어를 주어로 한 수동태만 가능한 동사

- buy, make, read, sell, find, write, pass, cook 등

He **bought** me (① 간접목적어) a ring (② 직접목적어).

→ ① I **was bought** a ring by him. (×)
→ ② A ring **was bought for** me by him. (o)

3 5형식 문장의 수동태

- 목적어를 주어로 한 수동태 가능
- 목적격 보어를 주어로 한 수동태는 없음

Jason **named** his son (목적어) Rick (목적격 보어).

→ Jason's son **was named** Rick by Jason.

He **encourages** Mr. Park (목적어) to pass the exam (목적격 보어).

→ Mr. Park **is encouraged** to pass the exam by him.

4 지각동사, 사역동사의 수동태

- 능동태의 목적격 보어인 원형부정사는 수동태에서 to부정사로 바뀜
- 사역동사는 make만 수동태 가능

We **saw** some birds (목적어) **fly(flying)** over the tree (목적격 보어). [지각동사]

→ Some birds **were seen to fly(flying)** over the tree by us.

They **made** him (목적어) **go** away (목적격 보어). [사역동사]

→ He **was made to go** away by them.

Grammar Tips

간접목적어 앞의 전치사

to	give, teach, send, offer, promise, show, tell 등
for	buy, get, make, find, cook, build, order 등
of	ask, beg, inquire 등

사역동사 let의 수동태: be allowed to

Our manager didn't **let** him go.
→ He **was not allowed to** go by our manager.

2교시 In-Class Questions

괄호 안에서 알맞은 말을 고르시오.

1 James **(sends / sent / was sent)** a letter by his girlfriend three days ago.

2 I was told **(turn / to turn / to be turned)** on the radio.

3 Her life was made **(happy / to happy / be happy)** by his love.

문장의 빈칸에 of, to, for 중에서 알맞은 것을 골라 쓰시오.

1 Some drunken people were asked ______________ leave by the manager.

2 The opinions are asked ______________ students by the math teacher.

3 Some gifts were sent ______________ him by someone.

4 This sweet cake was made ______________ kids.

우리말과 같은 뜻이 되도록 주어진 말을 사용하여 문장을 완성하시오.

1 그 여자는 5일 전에 그 서류를 받았다. (give)
→ The woman ____________________________ the document five days ago.

2 그 노트북 컴퓨터는 그 가난한 학생을 위해 교장에 의해 구입되었다. (buy)
→ The laptop ____________________________ the poor student by the principal.

3 그의 강아지는 부모님에 의해 Tony라고 이름 붙여졌다. (name)
→ His puppy ____________________________ by his parents.

4 Jenny는 그녀의 친구에 의해 그 남자와 결혼하게 되었다. (make)
→ Jenny ____________________________ the man by her friend.

능동태 문장을 수동태 문장으로 바꿔 쓰시오.

1 Monica left the door open.
→ ____

2 Mom cooked me some hot potato soup.
→ ____

3 Fred wrote his girlfriend a love letter.
→ ____

3교시 After - Class Questions

[01-02] 우리말과 같은 뜻이 되도록 빈칸에 알맞은 동사의 형태를 고르시오.

01 이 반지는 내가 19살 되던 생일에 나의 엄마가 주셨다.

→ This ring ________ me on my 19th birthday by my mom.

① gave ② given ③ was given
④ was given to ⑤ has given

02 그는 그 남자에 의해 그 숙제를 끝내는 것을 부탁받았다.

→ He ________ finish the homework by the man.

① asks ② is asked ③ was asked
④ was asked to ⑤ was asked of

[03-05] 능동태 문장을 수동태 문장으로 바꿔 쓸 때 빈칸에 알맞은 것을 고르시오.

03 Many people heard the singer sing a famous song.

→ The singer was heard ________ a famous song (by many people).

① sing ② to sing ③ sang
④ for singing ⑤ to be singing

04 My friends made me a big birthday card.

→ A big birthday card ________ by my friends.

① made for me ② was made of me ③ was made for me
④ were made to me ⑤ were made for me

05 Everyone calls her the "Queen of Singers."

→ She ________ the "Queen of Singers" by everyone.

① called ② is called ③ is call to
④ was called ⑤ was called to

06 **다음 중 어법상 어색한 문장은?**

① His mother was helped to do the laundry.
② She was made to feel guilty by the young boy.
③ Some hot chocolate was made for my sister.
④ The girl was seen getting out of a big van.
⑤ Some difficult questions were asked from Daniel.

Vocabulary Tips

- do the laundry 세탁하다
- guilty 죄책감이 드는
- get out of ~에서 나오다

07 밑줄 친 말을 수동태의 주어로 만들 수 없는 것은?

① Her family named their pet Bob.
② Kelly gave some documents to Jane.
③ The teacher thinks Jenny a great student.
④ Will you teach Cathy both English and Spanish?
⑤ People saw a stranger standing there.

서술형 대비

[08-09] 능동태 문장을 수동태로 바꿔 쓸 때 빈칸에 알맞은 말을 쓰시오.

08 The scent in the room made us feel comfortable.

→ We were ________ ________ ________ comfortable by the scent in the room.

09 They won't let their friends leave the country.

→ Their friends ________ ________ ________ ________ leave the country.

10 대화의 빈칸에 알맞은 말끼리 짝지은 것은?

A: Both Yuna and Tim were seen ______ on the bed. What happened to them?
B: They caught a bad cold.
A: Hmm... They ______ eat any ice cream.

① lying – are allowed
② lying – allowed to
③ lying – are not allowed to
④ to lying – are allowed to
⑤ to lying – are not allowed to

11 문장의 빈칸에 공통으로 알맞은 것은?

(a) The masculine man was seen ________ pushups.
(b) The woman was made ________ the dishes by her mother-in-law.

① do
② to do
③ did
④ doing
⑤ were done

12 밑줄 친 부분 중 어법상 어색한 것은?

Amber ①was elected ②as ③president. She ④is thought of ⑤as a brave girl.

Vocabulary Tips

- document 문서
- scent 향기
- masculine 근육질의
- pushup 팔굽혀펴기
- mother-in-law 시어머니, 장모
- elect 선출하다
- president 학급회장, 대통령

13 문장의 빈칸에 알맞은 말끼리 짝지은 것은?

Our science teacher showed us a microscope.
→ We ________ a microscope by our science teacher.
→ A microscope ________ by our science teacher.

① was shown – were shown to us
② was shown – was shown to me
③ was shown – was shown for us
④ were shown – was shown to us
⑤ were shown – was shown for us

서술형 대비

14 능동태 문장을 수동태 문장으로 바꿔 쓰시오.

(1) People didn't see Audrey enter the house yesterday.
→ Audrey ______________________________ yesterday.

(2) People didn't see Audrey entering the house yesterday.
→ Audrey ______________________________ yesterday.

15 능동태 문장을 수동태 문장으로 바르게 고친 것은?

① Anne made me wash her car by today.
→ I made to wash Anne's car by her by today.
② Carol lets Donna go outside.
→ Donna is let to go outside by Carol.
③ Olivia let Lora get in her class.
→ Lora is allowed to get in Olivia's class by her.
④ Jennifer sometimes asked the teachers silly questions.
→ Silly questions were sometimes asked of the teachers by Jennifer.
⑤ Emily bought me some interesting toys.
→ I was bought some interesting toys by Emily.

16 문장의 빈칸에 알맞은 말끼리 짝지은 것은?

(a) Jasmine was made ________ walk to the office.
(b) The soup was made ________ Jasmine in the office.

① to – to　② to – for　③ to – of
④ for – to　⑤ for – for

17 괄호 안에서 알맞은 말을 고르시오.

(1) We were **(told / heard)** to do our homework.

(2) I was **(given / bought)** a new car as a prize from the contest.

Vocabulary Tips

- microscope 현미경
- enter 들어가다
- silly 어리석은

[18-19] 문장의 빈칸에 알맞은 것을 고르시오.

18 Something was heard ________ on the window down the hall.

① fall ② fell ③ falls
④ to fall ⑤ be fallen

19 The news about the dictator's death in the North Korea ________ by the announcer.

① reported ② were reporting ③ was reported
④ were reported ⑤ is reporting

서술형 대비

20 능동태 문장을 수동태 문장으로 바꿔 쓰시오.

We saw our homeroom teacher walking with her boyfriend along the river.

→ ____

21 문장의 빈칸에 알맞은 말을 쓰시오.

This computer game was given ________ me by my uncle.

22 다음 중 어법상 어색한 문장은?

① A question was asked of me by him.
② The information was given to the applicants.
③ They were heard to come up the stairs by us.
④ A long text message was sent to me by my boyfriend.
⑤ He was bought a pair of mittens by his girlfriend.

[23-24] 어법상 어색한 부분을 찾아 바르게 고치시오.

23 I was made clean my room by my mother. __________ → __________

24 She is called to sweetheart by him. __________ → __________

25 능동태 문장을 수동태 문장으로 바꿔 쓸 때 빈칸에 알맞은 말을 쓰시오.

My professor gave me one more chance to do the presentation.

→ (1) ________ was given one more chance to do the presentation by my professor.

→ (2) ______________________________ was given to me by my professor.

Vocabulary Tips

- dictator 독재자
- announcer 아나운서
- homeroom teacher 담임선생님
- applicant 지원자
- text message 문자메시지
- mittens 벙어리장갑
- presentation 발표

주의해야 할 수동태

1교시 Grammar Point

1 수동태의 시제

(1) **현재/과거, 미래시제 수동태** | 〈be동사 + 과거분사〉, 〈will be + 과거분사〉

The classroom **is [was] cleaned** by all of my classmates. 현재/과거

The Eiffel Tower **will be repaired** next year. 미래

(2) **조동사가 있는 수동태** | 〈조동사 + be + 과거분사〉

My car **can be fixed** (by the mechanic) tomorrow.

← The mechanic can fix my car tomorrow.

(3) **진행형의 수동태** | 〈be동사 + being + 과거분사〉

The criminals **are being arrested** by the police officer.

← The police officer is arresting the criminals.

(4) **완료시제의 수동태** | 〈have/has/had + been + 과거분사〉

The light in my room **has been turned off** since last night.

← Someone has turned off the light in my room since last night.

2 주의해야 할 수동태

(1) **구동사의 수동태: 항상 하나의 단어로 취급**

I **was looked at** by her. ← She **looked at** me.

My grade **was laughed at** by them. ← They **laughed at** my grade.

(2) **that절을 목적어로 하는 문장의 수동태**

- 동사 say, think, believe, consider, hope 등의 목적어가 that절인 경우
- 〈It + be동사 + 과거분사 + that ~〉 혹은
  〈that절의 주어 + be동사 + 과거분사 + to부정사 (to have + 과거분사) ~〉의 형태

People **say that** exercising regularly is a very good habit.

→ **It is said that** exercising regularly is a very good habit.

→ Exercising regularly **is said to be** a very good habit.

People **think that** Sumi went to the hospital.

→ **It is thought that** Sumi went to the hospital.

→ Sumi is thought **to have gone** to the hospital.

cf. that절이 주절보다 앞선 시제일 때는 완료부정사(to have + 과거분사) 사용

3 의문문의 수동태

- 〈(의문사) + be동사/조동사 + 주어 + 과거분사 ~?〉

Was your room **locked**?

Has your work **been done** already?

Who **was** the dish **cooked by**? (= **By whom was** the dish **cooked**?)

Grammar Tips

수동태로 쓰지 않는 타동사

have, lack, fit, become, cost, resemble, meet, remember 등

Jane **is resembled** by her mom. (x)

Jane **resembles** her mom. (o)

수동태로 쓸 수 없는 자동사

appear, disappear, take place, consist of, occur 등

All of a sudden, my brother **was disappeared**. (x)

All of a sudden, my brother **disappeared**. (o)

by 이외의 전치사를 쓰는 수동태

be known to (~에게 알려지다)
be known as (~로서 유명하다)
be known for (~로 알려지다)
be satisfied with (~에 만족하다)
be pleased with (~에 기뻐하다)
be surprised at (~에 놀라다)
be tired of (~에 싫증나다)
be tired from (~로 피곤하다)
be filled with (~로 가득 차다)
be made of (~로 만들어지다_물리적 변화)
be made from (~로 만들어지다_화학적 변화)
be based on (~을 근거로 하다)

자주 쓰이는 구동사

put off (연기하다)
depend on (~에 의지하다)
run over (~을 (차로) 치다)
think of (~에 대해 생각하다)
take care of (~을 돌보다) [= look after]
think of A as B (A를 B로 간주하다)
pay attention to (~에 주의를 기울이다)

> 정답 및 해설 12쪽

2교시 In-Class Questions

STEP A

문장의 빈칸에 알맞은 말을 〈보기〉에서 골라 알맞은 형태로 바꿔 쓰시오.

보기 send publish prepare build

1 Dinner ____________ for you by the time you arrive home.

2 That email ____________ to me by my sister tomorrow.

3 The auditorium for the students ____________ by a charity.

4 A series of English grammar books ____________ by the end of this month.

STEP B

문장이 어법상 올바르면 O, 올바르지 않으면 X표 하고 바르게 고치시오.

1 The movie was based by a true story. ____________

2 By whom was this gift sent? ____________

3 It is said that Hawaii is famous for its beaches. ____________

STEP C

문장의 빈칸에 알맞은 말을 〈보기〉에서 골라 쓰시오.

보기 for by with at to as

1 The restaurant is known ____________ its delicious cuisine.

2 Dr. Lee is known ____________ the Hippocrates of Korea.

3 His name is known ____________ all of us at the company.

4 My parents were surprised ____________ my report card.

STEP D

능동태 문장을 수동태 문장으로 바꿔 쓰시오.

1 You should not forget the due date for the homework assignment.

→ ____________

2 My brother is making a model of the Gundam.

→ ____________

3 The university has held a concert in November.

→ ____________

4 The volunteer workers looked after the orphans in the village.

→ ____________

3교시 After-Class Questions

[01-03] 문장의 빈칸에 알맞은 것을 고르시오.

01 It ________ that many students don't like to take midterm exams.

① says ② said ③ is said
④ is saying ⑤ was said

02 The criminals were taken care ________ us.

① by ② of ③ with
④ by of ⑤ of by

03 A new tower bridge is ________ built across the Thames River.

① be ② being ③ been
④ having ⑤ has been

[04-05] 다음 중 어법상 어색한 문장을 고르시오.

04 ① The killer has been arrested by the police.
② My sister is resembled by my mom and dad.
③ The little kid was run over by a big truck.
④ She is believed to be clever by her uncle.
⑤ The seniors had their hair cut by the hair designer.

05 ① Independence could be gained by the people.
② Those actors are be cast by the famous director.
③ The rumor and the truth have been spread by girls.
④ The trip had to be put off because of the heavy rain.
⑤ Her stupid joke was laughed at by most of the students.

[06-07] 〈보기〉와 의미가 같은 문장을 고르시오.

06 보기 The mayor believes that the policy can solve this problem.

① The policy believed to solve this problem by the mayor.
② The policy believed to be solved this problem by the mayor.
③ The policy is believed to solve this problem by the mayor.
④ The policy was believed to be solved this problem by the mayor.
⑤ The policy can be believed to solve this problem by the mayor.

Vocabulary Tips

- midterm exam 중간고사
- criminal 범죄자
- take care of ~을 돌보다 (= look after)
- arrest 체포하다
- run over ~을 (차로) 치다
- clever 영리한
- independence 독립
- cast 배역을 정하다
- rumor 소문
- spread 퍼지다
- mayor 시장
- policy 정책

07 보기 My mother kept our house clean every day.

① My mother was kept our house clean every day.
② My mother is kept our house clean every day.
③ Our house is kept clean by my mother every day.
④ Our house was kept clean by my mother every day.
⑤ Our house kept my mother clean every day.

08 밑줄 친 부분 중 어법상 어색한 것은?

Calcium ①is said ②to playing an important role ③in our bodies, and it ④is believed that it ⑤affects the metabolism.

서술형 대비

[09-11] 능동태 문장을 수동태 문장으로 바꿔 쓸 때 빈칸에 알맞은 말을 쓰시오.

09 Workers have made a lot of cars in Korea.

→ A lot of cars ______________ in Korea by workers.

10 They will finish this construction project soon.

→ This construction project ______________ soon.

11 She must take care of her family.

→ Her family ______________ by her.

12 우리말과 같은 뜻이 되도록 주어진 말을 빈칸에 알맞은 형태로 바꿔 쓰시오.

북한에 가난한 아이들을 위한 학교들이 세워지고 있다. (build)
→ Schools for poor children ______________ in North Korea.

13 문장의 빈칸에 공통으로 알맞은 것은?

(a) The backyard is covered ________ a lot of leaves.
(b) Are you satisfied ________ your job?

① for ② by ③ to
④ with ⑤ in

14 다음 중 어법상 올바른 문장은?

① I am worried by my health.
② The new laptop was bought for me.
③ My boyfriend was made dinner by me.
④ My father is tired by his tedious work.
⑤ The classroom is filled to many students.

Vocabulary Tips

- calcium 칼슘
- affect the metabolism 신진대사에 영향을 주다
- construction 공사
- tedious 지루한

15 문장의 빈칸에 by가 들어갈 수 없는 것은?

① The space shuttle was made ______ the engineers.
② Kelly loves getting invited ______ people's houses.
③ Jupiter has been visited ______ a space probe.
④ Was that crystal vase knocked onto the floor ______ my son?
⑤ The new baseball stadium will have been built ______ next year.

16 어법상 어색한 부분을 찾아 바르게 고치시오.

Thanks to modern technology, carts have been disappeared from the street.

______________________ → ______________________

17 문장의 빈칸에 알맞은 동사의 형태는?

We learned that the final test had __________.

① postpones ② postponed ③ be postponed
④ being postponed ⑤ been postponed

18 문장의 빈칸에 알맞은 말끼리 짝지은 것을 고르시오.

It __________ that Taemin is going to receive the award. __________ is thought to be a great artist.

① is said – He ② is said – It ③ told – He
④ is told – It ⑤ is told – He

19 빈칸에 들어갈 말이 나머지와 다른 것은?

① The bottle is filled __________ soy sauce.
② Nahyun was surprised __________ her test score.
③ Junmo is satisfied __________ the news.
④ The road is covered __________ lots of snow.
⑤ The mother is pleased __________ her son's performance.

20 밑줄 친 부분 중 어법상 어색한 문장을 모두 고르시오.

① French is spoken in Quebec, Canada.
② Brenda has elected president of her class.
③ The new house is heat by gas.
④ This novel was written by Emily.
⑤ The bike is washed quickly by my brother.

Vocabulary Tips

- space shuttle 우주왕복선
- Jupiter 목성
- space probe 우주 탐사용 로켓
- crystal 수정
- baseball stadium 야구장
- modern technology 현대기술
- cart 마차
- postpone 연기하다
- receive 받다
- award 상
- soy sauce 간장
- performance 공연, 수행

21 우리말을 영어로 바르게 옮긴 것은?

그녀의 블로그는 2010년부터 많은 사람들에 의해 방문되고 있다.

① Her blog has visited by lots of people since 2010.
② Her blog has been visited by lots of people since 2010.
③ Her blog visited by lots of people since 2010.
④ Her blog is visited by lots of people since 2010.
⑤ Her blog has been visiting lots of people since 2010.

22 능동태 문장을 주어진 말로 시작하는 수동태 문장으로 바꿔 쓰시오.

People think that the new movie is really interesting.

→ (1) It ______________________________.

→ (2) The new movie ______________________________.

[23-24] 문장의 빈칸에 알맞은 말끼리 짝지은 것을 고르시오.

23

(a) Woojin is tired ________ eating pizza.
(b) Bella is tired ________ studying all day.

① of – in ② of – from ③ of – at
④ from – of ⑤ from – at

24

(a) The utility bill has to ________ until the end of this week.
(b) How much money is going to ________ during this winter vacation?

① be paid – be spent ② be pay – be spend ③ pay – spend
④ pay – be spent ⑤ be pay – spend

25 우리말을 영어로 잘못 옮긴 것은?

① 많은 학생들이 녹색 옷을 입고 있다.
→ Many students are dressed in green.
② 치즈는 우유로 만들어진다.
→ Cheese is made from milk.
③ 그 차는 먼지로 덮여 있다.
→ The car is covered with dust.
④ 우리는 그 점수에 만족하지 않았다.
→ We weren't satisfied with the score.
⑤ 그 집은 가구로 가득 차 있다.
→ Furniture is filled with the house.

Vocabulary Tips

- **blog** 블로그(글, 사진을 시간 순서대로 업데이트 할 수 있는 공간)
- **utility bill** 관리비
- **furniture** 가구

Final Test

01 능동태 문장을 수동태 문장으로 바르게 바꿔 쓴 것은?

Janet painted her garden fence yellow.

① Janet's garden fence yellow is painted by her.
② Janet's garden fence was painted yellow by her.
③ Janet's garden fence was painting yellow by her.
④ Janet's garden fence yellow was painted by her.
⑤ Janet's garden fence is painted yellow by her.

02 다음 중 어법상 <u>어색한</u> 문장은?

① Were they raised in a countryside?
② This work must be done by this weekend.
③ That factory has been in this city since 2010.
④ The professor considered one of the greatest scholars.
⑤ Many cars were towed away from in front of this building.

03 우리말을 영어로 바르게 옮긴 것을 <u>모두</u> 고르시오.

이 전구는 누구에 의해서 발명되었니?

① Who did this light bulb invent?
② Who was this light bulb invented by?
③ By who was this light bulb invented?
④ Who was this light bulb invent by?
⑤ By whom was this light bulb invented?

04 주어진 말을 문장의 빈칸에 알맞은 형태로 바꿔 쓰시오.

(1) The truck can ________ twenty boxes of Coke. (hold)

(2) The picture frame can ________ by the wire. (hold)

05 문장의 빈칸에 들어갈 수 <u>없는</u> 것을 <u>두 개</u> 고르시오.

Kate was ________ nothing for her birthday.

① bought ② cooked
③ given ④ told
⑤ offered

06 대화의 빈칸에 알맞은 것은?

A: How may I help you?
B: I am looking for a pair of sneakers.
A: We have a collection of items. How about these?
B: Are they ________ genuine leather?
A: Actually, no. They are imitation leather.

① made by ② made in
③ made at ④ made of
⑤ made from

07 능동태 문장을 수동태 문장으로 바르게 바꿔 쓴 것은?

① I can't depend on you.
→ You can't be depended by me.
② People believe that she is honest.
→ She is believed being honest.
③ I gave Sean the computer.
→ The computer was given for Sean by me.
④ We heard them come up the stairs.
→ They were heard came up the stairs by us.
⑤ My professor put off the final project.
→ The final project was put off by my professor.

08 문장의 빈칸에 알맞은 말끼리 짝지은 것은?

(a) New York is well known ________ shopping and its remarkable landmarks.
(b) This table is made ________ willow wood.
(c) Something was heard ________ fall outside the door.

① to – from – of ② to – of – by
③ for – from - about ④ for – of – to
⑤ as – from – to

09 주어진 동사를 문장의 빈칸에 알맞은 형태로 바꿔 쓰시오.

If you ___________(interest) watching a movie, you may want to go to a CGV at the AK Department Store. The theater is showing a variety of new movies now.

10 다음 중 어법상 어색한 문장은?

① English is taught to us by Kyle.
② I am remembered by my teacher.
③ This historic event must not be forgotten.
④ A question was asked of me by him.
⑤ Her husband was made to clean the room by her.

11 문장의 빈칸에 들어갈 수 없는 것을 모두 고르시오.

Mr. Simpson was ________ with the trip to Mexico.

① delighted ② surprised
③ satisfied ④ pleased
⑤ tired

12 우리말과 같은 뜻이 되도록 주어진 말을 빈칸에 알맞은 형태로 바꿔 쓰시오.

(1) 우리는 최근에 몇 가지 놀라운 소식을 들었다.
→ We have ________ ________ some amazing news recently. (tell)

(2) 이 물건은 영어로 뭐라고 불리나요?
→ What ________ this object ________ in English? (call)

[13-14] 능동태 문장을 수동태 문장으로 바꿔 쓸 때 빈칸에 알맞은 말을 쓰시오.

13

The mechanic couldn't fix my car in three days.
→ My car ________ ________ ________ by the mechanic in three days.

14

Who sings these songs?
→ ________ ________ ________ these songs ________?

서술형 대비

15 능동태 문장을 수동태 문장으로 바꿔 쓰시오.

Where did the students take the test?

→ ______________________________

[16-17] 문장의 빈칸에 공통으로 알맞은 것을 고르시오.

16

(a) The national museum was very crowded ________ elementary school students.
(b) She wasn't satisfied ________ her singing at the audition.

① within ② by
③ of ④ with
⑤ about

17

(a) Karl was made ________ drink some milk by Mom.
(b) The girl was seen ________ dance on stage.

① by ② with
③ for ④ about
⑤ to

18 다음 중 어법상 어색한 문장을 모두 고르시오.

① Was the report write by Kyle?
② Her room is kept tidy by her.
③ My pretty cats were taken care of by him.
④ Her pillow made comfortable by her mom.
⑤ The surprising news considered a new chance.

[19-20] 〈보기〉의 능동태 문장을 수동태 문장으로 바르게 바꿔 쓴 것을 고르시오.

19

보기 Steve taught me how to play dominoes yesterday.

① I taught me how to play dominoes yesterday.
② I was taught how to play dominoes to Steve yesterday.
③ How to play dominoes was taught to me by Steve yesterday.
④ How to play dominoes taught me by Steve yesterday.
⑤ How to play dominoes was taught by Steve yesterday.

20

보기 Patrick's classmates called him a coward.

① Patrick called a coward by his classmates.
② Patrick was called a coward by his classmates.
③ Patrick was called to a coward by his classmates.
④ A coward called Patrick by his classmates.
⑤ A coward was called Patrick by his classmates.

21 다음 중 어법상 올바른 문장은?

① Some fried chicken was ordered to me by my father.
② A campaign pledge promised to the local people by the politician.
③ I was bought a toy doll as a Christmas present by my daddy.
④ I was made wake up at 8 a.m. by my pet.
⑤ Lullabies were sung to Serena by her mother.

22 주어진 말을 빈칸에 알맞은 형태로 바꾼 것끼리 짝지은 것은?

(a) This bell ______ ringing when Vicky entered the room. (hear)
(b) Some dogs are trained ______ the blind. (help)
(c) The brain ______ more active by hormones. (make)

① hears – help – made
② heard – to help – made
③ is heard – to help – are made
④ was heard – helping – is made
⑤ was heard – to help – is made

서술형 대비

23 우리말과 같은 뜻이 되도록 빈칸에 알맞은 말을 쓰시오.

실종된 아이들을 보았을 가능성이 있는 사람은 모두 경찰에 연락하도록 요청받고 있다. (ask)
→ Anyone who might have seen the missing children ______________ to call the police.

24 문장의 빈칸에 알맞은 말끼리 짝지은 것은?

(a) A set of story books was found ________ little children at school.
(b) Jessica was being laughed ________ by her friends.

① for – at
② for – over
③ of – on
④ to – at
⑤ to – on

25 우리말을 영어로 바르게 옮긴 것을 두 개 고르시오.

그녀가 곧 돌아올 것이라고 생각된다.

① She thinks that she will come back soon.
② She is thought to come back soon.
③ It is thought for her will come back soon.
④ It is thought that she will come back soon.
⑤ It was thought that she would come back soon.

26 문장의 빈칸에 알맞은 말을 〈보기〉에서 골라 쓰시오.

보기 of　with　about　at　from

(1) This chair and drawer are made ________ iron.
(2) My classmates were surprised ________ the test score.
(3) Everybody is worried ________ her health.
(4) Those cups are filled ________ grapefruit juice.

[27-28] 다음 글을 읽고, 물음에 답하시오.

Most Koreans like bibimbap, and people from other countries also enjoy eating it these days. It is especially popular in America. Different kinds of bibimbap (a)**(served / is served / are served)** at many restaurants in America. In addition, many housewives (b)**(is learning / are learning / are learned)** how to make bibimbap. Because of its popularity, (c)한국 비빔밥은 수출되고 있다.

27 위 글 (a), (b)의 괄호 안에서 어법에 맞는 말끼리 짝지은 것은?

① served – is learning
② is served – is learning
③ is served – are learning
④ are served – are learning
⑤ are served – are learned

28 위 글의 밑줄 친 우리말 (c)를 다음 조건에 맞게 영어로 옮기시오.

한국 비빔밥은 수출되고 있다. (현재완료, export) → Korean bibimbap ________________.

[29-30] 다음 글을 읽고, 물음에 답하시오.

Constructing a pyramid was the main part of the king's work. It (a)believe that after the king died, he would live forever and would want to watch over the country. Besides, it was a symbol by which the King would lead the country successfully. The location of the pyramids as well as internal decoration (b)design to match the location of the stars in the heavens. Materials of the Pyramids were various. For instance, Khufu's Pyramid (1)was build mainly of limestone and (2)considered an architectural masterpiece.

*limestone 석회암

29 위 글의 밑줄 친 (a), (b)의 말을 올바른 형태로 바꾼 것끼리 짝지은 것은?

① believed – was designed
② is believed – was designed
③ was believed – was designed
④ was believed – were designed
⑤ were believed – were designed

30 위 글의 밑줄 친 (1), (2)를 어법상 올바른 형태로 고치시오.

(1) ________________
(2) ________________

≫ 정답 및 해설 15쪽

Extracurricular Activities

▸ *Sentence Writing*

PART A Complete the sentences describing the pictures.

1
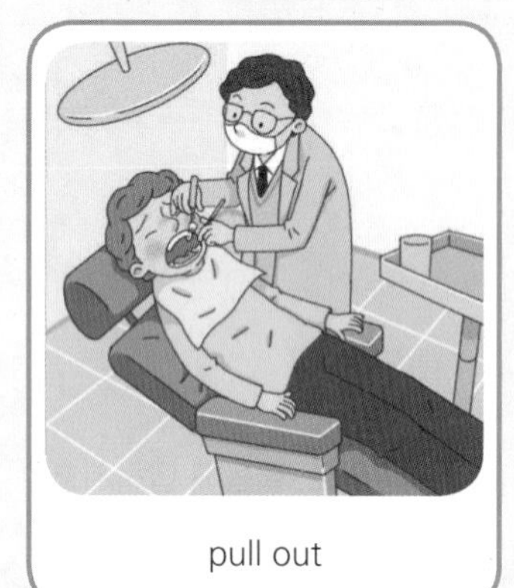
pull out

2

see

3

give

1 A tooth ______________ (진행형 수동태) by the dentist. The patient feels sick.

2 Gary ______________ (5형식 수동태) in his room. His family is surprised.

3 Kelly and Kay ______________ (4형식 수동태) by their mother. They are very happy to get it.

PART B Change the Korean into English by using the given words.

1 이 케이크는 그에 의해 그녀에게 오늘 아침 배달되었다. (deliver)
→ ______________

2 이 컴퓨터는 나의 엄마에 의해서 오랫동안 사용되지 않았다. (use, for a long time)
→ ______________

3 Kevin은 우진이에 의해서 비웃음을 당했다. (laugh at)
→ ______________

4 Keilen은 그녀의 미래 계획에 대해서 걱정한다. (worry)
→ ______________

▸ Further Studies 학교 시험에 자주 나오는 Idioms ①

- once in a blue moon 드물게 일어나는, 아주 가끔
- a man of one's word 자신이 한 말을 잘 지키는 사람
- a mixed blessing 잘된 일인지 잘못된 일인지 분간하기 힘든
- a piece of cake 너무 쉬운, 누워서 식은 죽 먹기인
- a steal 너무 싸서 훔친 것 같은 (↔ rip off 바가지 쓰다)
- a sweet tooth 단 음식을 좋아하는
- a tall order 많은 양의 주문
- a wet blanket 흥을 깨는 사람, 분위기 파악 못하는 사람
- a white lie 선의의 거짓말
- all ears 주의를 기울이고 있는, 바싹 긴장을 하고 있는
- all thumbs 손재주가 없는
- around the corner 가까이에
- as is often the case 자주 그렇듯이, 흔히 그렇듯이
- at gunpoint 즉석에서 바로 요구하는, 다급하게 요구하는
- stop beating around the bush 빙빙 돌리지 않고 요점을 말하다
- bark up the wrong tree 대상을 잘못 선택하다
- be broke 무일푼이다, 한 푼도 없다
- be my guest 마음대로 하세요, 편안하게 하세요
- beat around the bush 초점을 피해 말을 빙빙 돌리다
- beat it 꺼져버려
- Beats me. (= I don't know.) 모르겠다.
- to jump on the bandwagon 시류에 편승하다, 유리한 편에 붙다
- better left unsaid 말을 하지 않은 채로 남겨두는 것이 좋겠다
- black sheep of the family 집안의 골칫거리, 문제아
- break the ice 어색한 분위기를 깨다
- bring home the bacon 가족의 생계를 책임지다, 집에 돈을 벌어오다
- burn the midnight oil 밤새 공부하다
- butter up 아부하다, 아첨하다 (= brown-nose)
- butterflies in one's stomach 신경이 곤두선, 심경이 불편한, 긴장이 되는
- by the skin of one's teeth 간발의 차이로, 간신히

부정사 (Infinitives)

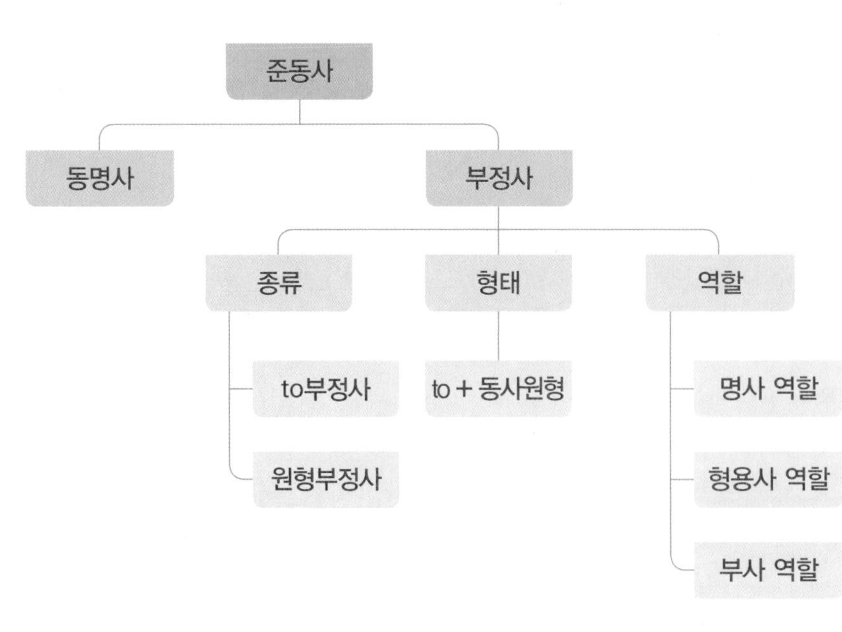

기출 맛보기

〈보기〉의 밑줄 친 to부정사의 쓰임과 같은 것을 고르시오. (서초구 ○○중학교)

> 보기 I have lots of things to do this weekend.

① Tom is not old enough to go to school.

② I stayed up late last night in order to finish my homework.

③ To know oneself is difficult.

④ There are many famous sights to see here.

⑤ One fine morning, she awoke to find herself beautiful.

해설

〈보기〉와 ④는 to부정사가 형용사적 용법으로 쓰여 앞의 명사를 수식한다.

① to부정사의 부사적 용법 중 앞의 부사 enough를 수식한다.

② to부정사의 부사적 용법 중 목적의 의미를 나타낸다.

③ to부정사의 명사적 용법 중 주어 역할을 한다.

⑤ to부정사의 부사적 용법 중 결과의 의미를 나타낸다.

해석

〈보기〉 나는 이번 주말에 할 일이 많다.

① Tom은 학교에 갈 나이가 되지 않았다.

② 나는 나의 과제를 끝내기 위해 지난밤에 늦게까지 깨어있었다.

③ 자기 자신을 안다는 것은 어렵다.

④ 여기에는 볼만한 많은 명소가 있다.

⑤ 그녀는 어느 좋은 아침에 깨어보니 그녀 자신이 아름답다는 것을 깨달았다.

정답 ④

to부정사의 명사적 용법

1교시 Grammar Point

1 주어, 목적어, 보어 역할

To meet a famous singer in person is very special for us. 주어 역할
→ It(가주어) is very special for us **to meet**(진주어) a famous singer in person.

My dream is **to be** a well-known writer. 보어 역할

I hope **to finish** my final project soon. 목적어 역할

2 〈의문사 + to부정사〉

- 명사 역할
- 〈의문사 + 주어 + should + 동사원형〉으로 바꿔 쓸 수 있음

We don't know **where to go**.

I can't decide **what to wear** to her birthday party.
→ I can't decide **what I should wear** to her birthday party.

3 to부정사를 목적격 보어로 쓰는 동사

ask(묻다), want(원하다), advise(조언하다), tell(말하다), order(명령하다), wish(바라다), recommend(권하다), allow(허락하다), enable(~을 할 수 있게 하다) 등	+	목적어	+	to부정사

My brother **wants** me **to help** him with his homework.

Mom **allowed** us **to play** computer games.

4 to부정사의 의미상 주어

(1) **문장의 주어와 to부정사의 주어가 다를 때** | 〈for + 목적격〉

This box is heavy **for you** to carry.

It is dangerous **for you** to swim here.

(2) **사람의 성격을 나타내는 형용사가 앞에 올 때** | 〈of + 목적격〉

It is very kind **of you** to help me.

(3) **to부정사가 목적격 보어로 쓰일 때** | 〈목적격 + to부정사〉

Mom allowed **me to go** to the concert. [목적어 = to부정사의 의미상 주어]

5 가목적어 it

- feel, find, think, make, believe, consider 등과 같은 5형식 동사의 목적어로 to부정사가 올 때 가목적어 it을 사용함
- 〈동사 + it + 목적격 보어(형용사, 명사) + to부정사〉

I make it a rule **to get up early**. (o)

I make **to get up early** a rule. (×)

Grammar Tips

- **〈의문사 + to부정사〉의 뜻**

how to-v (어떻게 ~해야 할지)
what to-v (무엇을 ~해야 할지)
when to-v (언제 ~해야 할지)
where to-v (어디에서 ~해야 할지)
which to-v (어느 것을 ~해야 할지)

- **5형식 동사 help는 목적격 보어로 원형부정사와 to부정사를 모두 취한다.**

Gina **helped** me **do[to do]** my homework.

- **〈사역동사 + 목적어 + ①원형부정사/②과거분사〉 (~가 ①…하도록/②…되도록 시키다)**

① Dan **made** me **clean** his car. 차를 세차하도록 (능동 관계)

② Dan **made** his car **cleaned**. 차가 세차되도록 (수동 관계)

cf. Mom **got** me **to clean** the car. (엄마는 나에게 세차하도록 시켰다.)
Mom **got** the car **cleaned**. (엄마는 세차되도록 했다.)

- **〈지각동사 + 목적어 + ①원형부정사/②-ing/③과거분사〉 (~가 ①…하는 것을/②…하고 있는 것을/③…되는 것을 ...하다)**

① I **saw** my mom **cook** dinner. 엄마가 요리를 하는 것을 (능동 관계)

② I **felt** my dog **licking** my toe. 개가 핥고 있는 (진행의 의미 강조)

③ We **saw** my lunch **packed**. 도시락이 포장되는 것을 (수동 관계)

2교시 In - Class Questions

괄호 안에서 알맞은 말을 모두 고르시오.

1 David wants me **(help / to help / helping / helped)** him with his math project.

2 I heard Peter **(play / to play / playing / played)** the cello in his room.

3 My English teacher made us **(finish / to finish / finishing / finished)** our project.

밑줄 친 to부정사를 주어, 목적어, 보어로 구분하여 쓰시오.

1 To keep a promise is important for close friends. ______________

2 Sally told me to learn how to improve my English skills. ______________

3 A few famous actresses tried to help the poor in Africa. ______________

우리말과 같은 뜻이 되도록 주어진 말을 빈칸에 알맞은 형태로 바꿔 쓰시오.

1 나의 할머니는 나에게 온종일 벽을 페인트칠하도록 시키셨다. (paint)
→ My grandmother made me ______________ the wall all day long.

2 나는 Cathy가 한국어 배우는 것을 도와주었다. (learn)
→ I helped Cathy ______________ Korean.

3 나의 아버지는 어제 자동차를 세차하셨다. (wash)
→ My father had his car ______________ yesterday.

STEP D

어법상 어색한 부분을 찾아 바르게 고치시오.

1 It is very generous for you to bring this heavy box. __________ → __________

2 Anderson doesn't realize how solve this matter with colleagues.
__________ → __________

3 My friends advised me buy a used car as soon as possible.
__________ → __________

4 The application makes it possible provide very useful information to people.
__________ → __________

3교시 After-Class Questions

01 우리말과 같은 뜻이 되도록 할 때 빈칸에 알맞은 것은?

LA에서 맛있는 한국식당을 찾는 것은 어렵지 않다.
→ It is not difficult ________ delicious restaurants in L.A.

① find ② found ③ to find
④ to finding ⑤ for finding

02 밑줄 친 부분의 의미가 같은 문장을 두 개 고르시오.

① I had a great dinner.
② I had a little money left.
③ I had a great dinner cooked.
④ I had my mom pay my tuition.
⑤ I had a good time with my friends.

[03-05] 문장의 빈칸에 들어갈 수 없는 것을 고르시오.

03 It is ________ of the students to help their community.

① thoughtful ② nice ③ kind
④ necessary ⑤ wise

04 My siblings ________ me find a construction job.

① had ② made ③ let
④ helped ⑤ got

05 Sally ________ Austin to get married to Leslie.

① asked ② wanted ③ allowed
④ helped ⑤ made

[06-07] 문장의 빈칸에 알맞은 것을 고르시오.

06 Some people don't know how ________ the new tablet PC.

① use ② using ③ to use
④ me use ⑤ me to use

07 Frank found ________ very easy to solve those questions.

① her ② his ③ one
④ it ⑤ that

Vocabulary Tips

- tuition 수업료, 학원비
- community 지역사회
- sibling 형제자매
- construction 건축, 건설

[08-10] 다음 중 어법상 <u>어색한</u> 문장을 고르시오.

08 ① We need to have our hair cut.
② Mary loves to make speeches in public.
③ My sister helped me to clean my room.
④ Both Jade and Jack made me wash their trucks and bikes.
⑤ It is important of you not to miss any phone calls from your boss.

09 ① Sarah told me to carry her heavy boxes.
② Dad wouldn't let me to go to the concert.
③ The teacher got me to join the guitar club.
④ Mom heard me turn on the radio on the desk.
⑤ The doctor advised me not to drink coffee for a while.

10 ① Parents make their children do their best at school.
② The Korean government helps adopted people to find their real parents.
③ They saw some young people practicing songs on stage yesterday.
④ Suddenly, Whitney felt her backpack touched by a stranger.
⑤ My mom used to have me washing the dishes when she felt very tired.

서술형 대비

11 주어진 말을 사용하여 다음 우리말을 영어로 옮기시오.

Matthew가 내 영어 실력을 이기는 것은 불가능하다. (beat, skills, impossible)
→ It ______________________________.

12 〈보기〉의 밑줄 친 부분과 쓰임이 같은 것은?

보기 All Koreans decided <u>to wear</u> red devil T-shirts for the Korean World Cup in 2002.

① He grew up <u>to be</u> a dentist.
② Don't rely on anybody for you not <u>to know</u>.
③ We are <u>to make</u> some food for the food festival.
④ Roland didn't want <u>to major</u> in psychology in America.
⑤ What are the new school assignments <u>to finish</u>?

13 밑줄 친 부분 중 어법상 <u>어색한</u> 것은?

① Paul heard her <u>singing</u> beautifully.
② Evan watched the bugs <u>move</u> slowly.
③ It takes me 4 hours <u>to get</u> to the airport.
④ We made it a rule <u>to be</u> quiet in the library.
⑤ Hank asked his friend <u>do</u> some very difficult work for him

Vocabulary Tips

- make a speech 연설하다
- in public 공개적으로
- for a while 잠시 동안
- government 정부
- adopted 입양된
- rely on 의지하다, 믿다
- psychology 심리학
- bug 벌레
- make a rule 규칙을 정하다

서술형 대비

14 두 문장이 같은 뜻이 되도록 빈칸에 알맞은 말을 쓰시오.

My brother will teach me how to ride a skateboard.
→ My brother will teach me how _________ _________ _________ a skateboard.

15 다음 중 어법상 올바른 문장을 모두 고르시오.

① It was wise of Jerry to save money last year.
② The police officer helped an old woman to open the door.
③ Mom asked me to bring some food like kimchi.
④ Harry made it a rule to go jogging every morning.
⑤ Please tell me which way choose if you know.

16 다음 중 어법상 올바른 문장을 두 개 고르시오.

① Let me carry those books for you.
② Mr. Park suddenly heard his name call.
③ Laurie allowed us taking her classes at her university.
④ Both Mom and Dad expected us do something special.
⑤ He will get me to determine what he should do in the future.

[17-18] 어법상 어색한 부분을 찾아 바르게 고치시오.

17 Her dog never lets her to sleep well.

_________________ → _________________

18 I got a bad grade in English. I don't know why to improve my English skills.

_________________ → _________________

19 우리말과 같은 뜻이 되도록 빈칸에 알맞은 말을 쓰시오.

선생님은 우리에게 쉬는 시간 동안 조용히 하라고 말씀하셨다.
→ The teacher ordered us _________ _________ _________ during the break.

20 문장의 빈칸에 알맞은 것을 두 개 고르시오.

All of the students watched the Korean soccer team _________ the game.

① played ② plays ③ play
④ playing ⑤ to play

Vocabulary Tips

- skateboard 스케이트보드
- determine 결정하다
- improve 향상시키다

21 문장의 빈칸에 들어갈 말이 나머지와 다른 것은?

① It is nice _________ Austin to help me with my work.
② It is dangerous _________ us not to lock the door.
③ It is necessary _________ Teddy to buy a large house.
④ It is so exciting _________ me to listen to K-pop.
⑤ It was not difficult _________ you to find a new job.

[22-23] 문장의 빈칸에 알맞은 말끼리 짝지은 것을 고르시오.

22

(a) The teacher had our science assignment _________.
(b) All of the people felt the building _________.

① finish – shake
② finished – shaking
③ finished – to shake
④ to finish – shaking
⑤ to finish – shake

23 다음 중 어법상 어색한 문장은?

① The dictionary enables for you to understand English words.
② The snow forced us to take the bus back to the camp.
③ It was important for me to meet the deadline.
④ They encourage him to keep reading books as many as possible.
⑤ It is kind of her to delay her plans for my convenience.

[24-25] 다음 대화를 읽고, 물음에 답하시오.

A: What happened to you? I heard you ①missed your plane.
B: Yes. I had a hard time ②coming back from New York trip. Do you know what? Right before I got to the airport, I realized that I had forgotten ③to bring my passport with me. I ④had left my passport at the hotel. So I hurried back there. When I asked a hotel employee _________(search) my room, the manager helped me ⑤finding my passport. Finally, I managed to come back home.

24 위 대화의 ①~⑤ 중 어법상 어색한 것은?

① missed
② coming
③ to bring
④ had left
⑤ finding

25 위 대화의 빈칸에 주어진 search를 알맞은 형태로 바꿔 쓰시오.

____

Vocabulary Tips

- meet the deadline 기한을 맞추다
- as ~ as possible 가능한 한 ~한(하게)
- delay 연기하다, 미루다
- convenience 편의
- manage to ~ 가까스로 ~하다

DAY 10

to부정사의 형용사적, 부사적 용법

1교시 Grammar Point

1 형용사적 용법

(1) **한정적 용법** | 명사 수식, '~하는, ~할'

He wants *some water* **to drink.** (마실 물)

I have *only a few friends* **to talk to.** ← talk to friends [to부정사 + 전치사]

(2) **서술적 용법** | 〈be + to부정사〉

예정	~할 예정이다 (= be going to, be scheduled to, be due to, will)
의무	~해야 한다 (= should, ought to, must)
운명	~할 운명이다 (= be doomed to, be destined to)
가능	~할 수 있다 (= be able to, can)
의도	~하려고 하다 (= intend to, wish to, mean to)

I **am to go** to Japan next week. 예정

You **are to follow** the school rules. 의무

He **was** never **to meet** Kelly again. 운명

No one **was to be seen** in the dark. 가능

If you **are to succeed**, you must study hard. 의도

2 부사적 용법

(1) **의미** | 목적, 감정의 원인, 결과, 판단의 근거, 조건, 형용사 수식

목적	~하기 위해서, ~하려고 (= in order to, so as to)	판단의 근거	~하다니
감정의 원인	~해서 …하다	조건	~한다면
결과	~해서 (그 결과) …되었다	형용사 수식	~하기에

Some students went to the Internet cafe **to play** computer games. 목적

She was so happy **to pass** the exam. 감정의 원인

She grew up **to be** a famous singer. 결과 (자라서 ~이 되었다)

They must be crazy **to go** out in this cold weather. 판단의 근거

You will take him for a singer **to hear** his song. 조건

The river isn't *safe* **to swim** in. 형용사 수식

(2) **관용표현**

- **〈too + 형용사/부사 + to부정사〉 '매우 ~해서 …할 수 없다'**
  = 〈so + 형용사/부사 + that + 주어 + cannot/could not ...〉
- **〈형용사/부사 + enough + to부정사〉 '…할 만큼 충분히 ~하다'**
  = 〈so ~ that + 주어 + can ...〉

Jina got up **too late to catch** the school bus.
= Jina got up **so late that she could not catch** the school bus.

Tiffany is **rich enough to buy** a smartphone.
= Tiffany is **so rich that she can buy** a smartphone.

Grammar Tips

- **to부정사가 -thing으로 끝나는 말을 수식할 때의 어순**
  〈-thing + 형용사 + to부정사〉
  nothing to have
  something new to have
  anything comfortable to wear
- **only to**
  '(결국) ~하고 말았다'의 뜻으로 '결과'의 관용표현이다.
  I studied so hard **only to fail** the exam.

2교시 In-Class Questions

STEP A

밑줄 친 to부정사의 의미를 〈보기〉에서 골라 쓰시오.

보기 목적 감정의 원인 결과 판단의 근거 조건 형용사 수식

1 She was very sad to hear the news about your grandmother. ______________

2 He went to Korea to look for freedom and peace. ______________

3 My grandmother lived to be 96. ______________

4 To hear him talk, you would take him for a foreigner. ______________

STEP B

밑줄 친 〈be + to부정사〉의 의미를 〈보기〉에서 골라 쓰시오.

보기 예정 의무 운명 가능 의도

1 They are to arrive at the subway station at 10 a.m. ______________

2 If they are to eat ice cream, they must finish their homework first. ______________

3 Dr. Lee went to France in 2012 and was never to come back. ______________

4 You are to do the dishes after you have a meal. ______________

STEP C

두 문장이 같은 뜻이 되도록 to부정사를 사용하여 빈칸을 완성하시오.

1 Cathy couldn't find her dog.
→ Cathy ______________________ her dog.

2 The Simpsons are going to see the art exhibition.
→ The Simpsons ______________________ the art exhibition.

우리말과 같은 뜻이 되도록 to부정사와 주어진 단어를 사용하여 문장을 완성하시오.

1 여러분은 학교에 공부하러 오는 거지, 놀기 위해 오는 것이 아닙니다. (study, play)
→ You come to school ______________________, ______________________.

2 우리 집은 역에서 볼 수 없다. (see)
→ Our house is never ______________________ from the station.

3교시 After - Class Questions

01 〈보기〉와 의미가 같은 문장은?

보기 Kids should go to the library to study quietly.

① Kids wish to go to the library to study quietly.
② Kids are to go to the library to study quietly.
③ Kids are going to the library to study quietly.
④ Kids may go to the library so as to study quietly.
⑤ Kids go to the library in order to study quietly.

02 문장의 빈칸에 알맞은 것은?

He has no friends to ________.

① talk ② talk with ③ talking
④ talked ⑤ be talked

[03-06] 두 문장이 같은 뜻이 되도록 빈칸에 알맞은 말을 고르시오.

03 If you listen to his voice, you will take him for a singer.

→ ________ his voice, you will take him for a singer.

① Listen to ② Listened to ③ To listen to
④ Being listened to ⑤ Having been listened to

04 Kelly is to hand in her homework by tomorrow.

→ Kelly ________ hand in her homework by tomorrow.

① ought to ② is able to ③ is doomed to
④ intend to ⑤ is due to

05 Jason is to play golf with me this weekend.

→ Jason ________ play golf with me this weekend.

① is able to ② ought to ③ means to
④ is going to ⑤ is destined to

06 Kelly opened the door, but she found the classroom empty.

→ Kelly opened the door ________ the classroom empty.

① find to ② never to find ③ only to find
④ to find ⑤ so as to find

Vocabulary Tips

- take A for B A를 B로 생각하다, 여기다
- hand in 제출하다
- empty 비어 있는, 텅빈

07 두 문장이 같은 의미가 되도록 주어진 단어를 바르게 배열하시오.

You should not make any noise in this room.

→ ______________________________

(in / noise / not / are / this / make / to / you / room / any)

08 우리말과 같은 뜻이 되도록 주어진 말을 빈칸에 알맞은 형태로 바꿔 쓰시오.

당신은 들어오기 전에 노크를 해야 합니다. (knock)

→ You ______________________ before you come in.

[09-10] 밑줄 친 to부정사의 쓰임이 나머지와 다른 것을 고르시오.

09 ① He woke up to find himself famous.
② We are sad not to watch the soap opera.
③ To lose weight is not easy for me.
④ To turn left, you can see the beautiful building.
⑤ Travelers are standing in line to buy souvenirs.

10 ① They failed to pass the midterm exam.
② His next plan is to return to his home.
③ She wants to make money to buy a lot of clothes.
④ It is impossible for me to finish my homework.
⑤ We decided to choose some books for our classroom.

[11-12] 우리말을 영어로 바르게 옮긴 것을 고르시오.

11 내 친구들은 살 집을 구했다.

① My friends have bought to live in.
② My friends have bought to live.
③ My friends have bought living in a house.
④ My friends have bought a house to live in
⑤ My friends have bought a house living.

12 우리는 선생님이 하시는 말씀을 따라야 한다.

① We obeyed what our teacher says.
② We will obey what our teacher says.
③ We are to obey what our teacher says.
④ We are obeying what our teacher says.
⑤ We will have to obey what our teacher says.

13 문장의 빈칸에 주어진 단어를 바르게 배열하시오.

I was pleased that Hank gave me ______________________.

(to drink / cold / something)

Vocabulary Tips

- make a noise 소란을 피우다
- soap opera 드라마, 연속극
- souvenir 기념품
- obey 따르다

서술형 대비

14 **to부정사를 사용하여 다음 우리말을 영어로 옮기시오.**

그는 내일 런던에 갈 것이다.

→ ______________________________

15 **다음 중 어법상 올바른 문장을 모두 고르시오.**

① Actually, they need a friend to play.
② We are looking for to read something about this topic.
③ That's enough money to buy a laptop computer.
④ What is the most expensive bag buying in Rome?
⑤ Teachers give students many opportunities to practice this action.

16 **우리말과 같은 뜻이 되도록 to부정사를 사용하여 빈칸을 완성하시오.**

너는 훌륭한 연설가가 되려면 실수를 두려워해서는 안 된다.

→ You shouldn't be afraid of making mistakes if you ______________ a good speaker.

17 **밑줄 친 to부정사의 의미가 나머지와 다른 것을 두 개 고르시오.**

① She woke up to find herself in a strange place.
② They made it to the finals, only to lose there.
③ The honest boy grew up to be a lawyer.
④ To hear him talk, you would take him for an expert.
⑤ We turned down the volume not to disturb my roommate.

18 **〈보기〉의 밑줄 친 to부정사와 쓰임이 같은 것은?**

보기 I am sorry to interrupt you.

① Cathy wears a hat to look cute.
② The wine is good enough to drink.
③ She was surprised to find him gone.
④ They are to arrive here tomorrow morning.
⑤ He taught me how to solve that question.

19 **밑줄 친 to부정사의 쓰임이 같은 것을 두 개 고르시오.**

① They are to listen to the lecture soon.
② This is the best thing to do in this situation.
③ His girlfriend wanted a letter to read.
④ He asked his sister to move the chair.
⑤ My mother went to the hospital to have a checkup.

Vocabulary Tips

- actually 사실, 실제로
- opportunity 기회
- be afraid of ~을 두려워하다
- make it to the finals 결승전에 진출하다
- expert 전문가
- disturb 방해하다
- interrupt 방해하다
- checkup 건강검진

[20-21] 다음 글을 읽고, 주어진 단어를 바르게 배열하시오.

Are you having a hard time losing weight recently? Here are some good tips for you. These are **20. (too / follow / to / difficult / not)**. First, try to eat vegetables instead of eating junk food. Secondly, drink enough water. Finally, **21. (are / upstairs / to / go / you / if)**, take the stairs instead of an elevator. Not using your legs keeps you from losing weight.

20 → These are ______________________________.

21 → Finally, ______________________________,
take the stairs instead of an elevator.

[22-23] 두 문장이 같은 뜻이 되도록 빈칸에 알맞은 말을 쓰시오.

22 I'm too sleepy to watch the rest of the documentary film.

→ I'm ________ ________ ________ I ________ watch the rest of the documentary film.

23 They were so old that they could travel by themselves.

→ They were old ________ ________ ________ by themselves.

[24-25] 밑줄 친 부분에 유의하여 다음 문장을 우리말로 옮기시오.

24 Their classmates <u>are to see</u> a movie next Monday.

→ ______________________________

25 <u>To hear</u> him speak Korean, you will take him for a Korean.

→ ______________________________

Vocabulary Tips

- **recently** 최근
- **instead of** ~대신에
- **upstairs** 위층으로
- **stairs** 계단, 층계
- **keep ~ from -ing** ~가 …하지 못하게 하다

DAY 11

to부정사의 기타 용법

1교시 Grammar Point

1 to부정사의 시제

	단순부정사	완료부정사
용법	to부정사의 시제가 문장의 동사와 같은 시제일 때	to부정사의 시제가 문장의 동사보다 앞선 시제일 때
형태	〈to + 동사원형〉	〈to + have + 과거분사〉

My friend **seems to like** my boyfriend. 단순부정사
→ It **seems** that my friend **likes** my boyfriend.
She **seems to have been** sick. 완료부정사
→ It **seems** that she **was** sick.

2 to부정사의 부정과 수동형

(1) **to부정사의 부정** | 〈not/never + to부정사〉

Many women try **not to eat** chocolate.

It is easy for me **not to do** my homework.

(2) **to부정사의 수동형**

	능동형 부정사	수동형 부정사
용법	to부정사와 의미상 주어의 관계가 능동일 때	to부정사와 의미상 주어의 관계가 수동일 때
형태	〈to + 동사원형〉	〈to be + 과거분사〉

I want **to invite** Keilen to the wedding. [의미상 주어 I가 초대하는 것]

I'm so sorry not **to be invited** to the wedding. [의미상 주어 I가 초대받은 것]

3 독립부정사, 대부정사

(1) **독립부정사** | to부정사가 독립적으로 쓰여 문장 전체를 수식할 때 쓰임

strange to say (이상한 말이지만)	to be brief (간단히 말하면)
to be frank with you (솔직히 말하면)	to say nothing of (~은 말할 것도 없이)
to make matters worse (설상가상으로)	to tell the truth (사실을 말하자면)
to be sure (확실히)	so to speak (소위, 이른바)
to begin with (우선, 먼저)	needless to say (말할 필요도 없이)

To be frank with you, I don't like the clothes you are wearing.

Mason can speak Spanish, **to say nothing of** English.

(2) **대부정사** | 문장 내에서 반복될 경우, 문맥상으로 유추가 가능할 때 to 다음의 내용을 생략함

You may go out if you want **to**. [to = to go out]

Grammar Tips

- **seem 뒤에 나오는 to be는 생략 가능하다.**

Mina **seems to be** sick.
→ Mina **seems** sick.

2교시 In – Class Questions

STEP A

문장의 빈칸에 알맞은 것을 고르시오.

1 I've never played golf, but ____________________.

① I'd like to ② I'd like it ③ I'd like to do

2 Kevin is so sorry ____________________ you waiting for so long.

① to keep ② to have keep ③ to have kept

STEP B

두 문장이 같은 뜻이 되도록 빈칸에 알맞은 말을 쓰시오.

1 It seems that Hank is ill.
→ Hank ____________________ ill.

2 It seemed that she was satisfied with the present.
→ She ____________________ satisfied with the present.

3 It seems that the reporter enjoyed writing on his blog.
→ The reporter ____________________ writing on his blog.

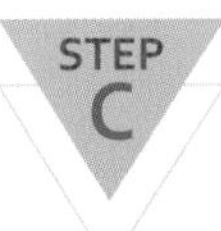

STEP C

괄호 안에서 알맞은 말을 고르시오.

1 My mother always tries (**to not eat** / **not to eat**) chocolate.

2 You may take the book if you (**want** / **want to**).

3 I don't know him, and I don't (**wanted** / **want** / **want to**).

STEP D

우리말과 같은 뜻이 되도록 빈칸에 알맞은 말을 쓰시오.

1 솔직히 말하면, 누리는 정말 예뻐.
→ ____________________, Nuri is so pretty.

2 말할 필요도 없이, 나의 영어 선생님은 잘 가르치신다.
→ ____________________, my English teacher teaches well.

3교시 After-Class Questions

[01-02] 문장의 빈칸에 알맞은 것을 고르시오.

01 It ________ that my boyfriend has another girlfriend.

① seem ② seems ③ seems to
④ is seem ⑤ seem to

02 Cathy seems ________ hard in her school days.

① to study ② to studying ③ to have studied
④ to be studying ⑤ to be studied

03 다음 중 어법상 어색한 문장을 모두 고르시오.

① The movie seems to be boring.
② It seems that like you so much.
③ We haven't eaten the cake, but we'd like.
④ I love to go to the theater with my friends.
⑤ They seem to have had a similar problem before.

04 대화의 빈칸에 알맞은 것은?

A: What do you think of him? Is he handsome? B: Yeah, I think so. But, ________, he is not smart.

① to be sure ② so to speak ③ needless to say
④ to be brief ⑤ to be frank with you

05 문장의 빈칸에 주어진 단어를 바르게 배열하시오.

Mom told us ____________________ the room.
(to / enter / not)

06 우리말과 같은 뜻이 되도록 주어진 말을 사용하여 빈칸을 완성하시오.

친구가 내게 그 책을 사라고 충고했지만 나는 거절했다. (refuse)
→ My friend advised me to buy the book, but I ________ ________.

Vocabulary Tips

- boring 지루한
- similar 비슷한
- refuse 거절하다

07 밑줄 친 부분 중 어법상 어색한 것은?

① To meet many friends is not good.
② We advised tourists to take the subway.
③ I still have not decided where to go.
④ To make matters worse, it was getting cold.
⑤ They seem to be famous K-pop stars when they were young.

08 어법상 올바른 문장끼리 짝지은 것은?

(a) They seem to have worked together in the past.
(b) Many supermodels are pretty enough to wearing any kinds of clothes.
(c) It seemed that she likes the boy who was wearing the cap.

① (a) ② (a), (b) ③ (a), (c)
④ (b), (c) ⑤ (c)

09 우리말과 같은 뜻이 되도록 할 때 문장의 빈칸에 알맞은 것은?

나는 지난밤에 그녀에게 전화를 했던 것 같다.
→ I ________________ her last night.

① seems to call ② seems to be called ③ seem to have called
④ seemed to call ⑤ seemed to be called

서술형 대비

[10-12] 두 문장이 같은 뜻이 되도록 빈칸에 알맞은 말을 쓰시오.

10 It seemed that she was satisfied with the present.
→ She seemed ________________________ with the present.

11 It seemed that the students stayed up late last night.
→ The students seemed ________________________.

12 It seemed that he had been a policeman.
→ He seemed ________________________.

Vocabulary Tips

- **stay up late** 늦게까지 깨어있다

13 우리말과 같은 뜻이 되도록 주어진 말을 사용하여 빈칸을 완성하시오.

우선, 그 대통령은 그 편지를 읽기 시작했다. (begin)

→ ______________________, the president started reading the letter.

14 다음 중 어법상 올바른 문장은?

① They told him not tell a lie.
② To so speak, he is a famous pianist.
③ They tried to not gain weight every day.
④ We saw them to play soccer on the playground.
⑤ We can speak English, to say nothing of Korean.

15 대화의 빈칸에 알맞은 말끼리 짝지은 것은?

> A: You may go home if you want ________.
> B: No, I don't want ________. ________, I hate going home. I don't know why.
> A: ________, neither do I.

① for – to – To begin with – Strange to say
② to – for – Needless to say – Needless to say
③ to – to – Strange to say – To be frank with you
④ of – to – Strange to say – To be frank with you
⑤ too – too – Not to mention – To tell the truth

16 어법상 어색한 부분을 찾아 바르게 고치시오.

Professor Kim advised us to not plagiarize our essays.

______________________ → ______________________

17 〈보기〉의 밑줄 친 부분을 to부정사로 바꿀 때 형태가 같은 것을 모두 고르시오.

> 보기 Jason thought that he had done his best.

① Hank hoped that he had a girlfriend.
② I'm sorry that I misunderstood him.
③ The accident seems that it happened when I was young.
④ They thought that they had passed the exam.
⑤ Kelly thinks that she is very smart.

Vocabulary Tips

- president 대통령
- tell a lie 거짓말을 하다
- plagiarize 표절하다
- misunderstand 오해하다

[18-19] 대화의 밑줄 친 to 다음에 생략된 말을 찾아 쓰시오.

18

A: When will you be back home?
B: I'll try to as soon as possible.

____

19

A: Did he come here?
B: No, I asked him to, but he didn't want to.

____

20 대화의 빈칸에 알맞은 것은?

A: Would you like something to drink?
B: Yes, I would ________.

① love ② to love ③ loving
④ love to ⑤ to loving

[21-25] 주어진 말을 이용하여 각 빈칸에 문맥상 알맞은 독립부정사를 쓰시오.

A: You know Keilen, don't you? She is, **21.** ________(speak), a walking dictionary.
B: Really? I didn't know that. Anyway, the meeting will be held next Friday, **22.** ________(brief), July 4th.
A: Oh, I forgot! Thank you for reminding me. **23.** ________(honest), I am a little worried about the meeting.
B: How come?
A: **24.** ________(begin), it needs a lot of money. **25.** ________(worse), one of the members is sick.
B: That's terrible.

21 ________________

22 ________________

23 ________________

24 ________________

25 ________________

Vocabulary Tips

- anyway 어쨌든
- remind 상기시키다, 다시 일깨우다

Final Test

01 우리말과 같은 뜻이 되도록 할 때 빈칸에 알맞은 것은?

> 한국 학생이 영어로 글을 쓰는 것은 어렵다.
> → It is difficult ________ essays in English.

① for Korean students write
② for Korean students for write
③ for Korean students to write
④ of Korean students write
⑤ of Korean students to write

[02-04] 문장의 빈칸에 들어갈 수 없는 것을 고르시오.

02

> It was ________ of the children to raise money for the sick.

① thoughtful ② nice
③ kind ④ necessary
⑤ wise

03

> Most parents don't ________ their young children watch TV at late night.

① have ② make
③ let ④ help
⑤ get

04

> Mike ________ his daughter to go to Africa.

① asked ② wanted
③ allowed ④ helped
⑤ made

05 다음 중 어법상 어색한 문장은?

① Jin heard us talking about the problems.
② Sue didn't want us to help the poor and the sick.
③ The teacher got us to make a study group with our classmates.
④ My sister never had her room clean by anyone.
⑤ The doctor told me to exercise every morning to stay healthy.

06 두 문장이 같은 뜻이 되도록 빈칸에 알맞은 말을 쓰시오.

> Cookbooks let us know how to cook various foods.
> → Cookbooks let us know ________ ________ ________ ________ various foods.

[07-09] 어법상 어색한 부분을 찾아 바르게 고치시오.

07

> Only a few writers make the readers interesting.

________ → ________

08

> Mr. Park cannot be gentle to be behave like that.

________ → ________

09

> The professor came here so as he will get some more information.

________ → ________

10 문장의 빈칸에 알맞은 것을 두 개 고르시오.

> People of different ages saw the dolphins ________ in the show at the zoo.

① performed ② performs
③ perform ④ to perform
⑤ performing

11 문장의 빈칸에 알맞은 말끼리 짝지은 것은?

> (a) My parents sometimes made their cousin ________ me money.
> (b) My math teacher had my homework ________.

① lend – check ② lend – to check
③ lend – checked ④ to lend – checked
⑤ to lending – checked

12 주어진 조건에 맞게 다음 우리말을 영어로 옮기시오.

> 바다에서 어떻게 수영하는지 나에게 가르쳐줄 수 있니?

(1) [의문사 + to부정사]
→ ____________________
(2) [should를 사용하여]
→ ____________________

[13-14] 두 문장이 같은 뜻이 되도록 빈칸에 알맞은 것을 고르시오.

13

> The room was so dark that I couldn't find her ring.
> → The room was ________ her ring.

① as dark as possible
② too dark for finding
③ so dark for me to find
④ too dark for me to find
⑤ enough dark for me to find

14

> It seems that my friends got good grades.
> → My friends seem ________ good grades.

① got ② get
③ to get ④ to have gotten
⑤ to be gotten

15 밑줄 친 to부정사의 쓰임이 나머지와 다른 것은?

① The American travelers are <u>to arrive</u> Korea at noon.
② No one is <u>to be seen</u> in the street.
③ Some senators are never <u>to meet</u> the president these days.
④ The new student's dream is <u>to get</u> a high GPA at school.
⑤ Students are <u>to follow</u> what the teacher says in the classroom.

[16-17] 주어진 말의 위치로 알맞은 곳을 고르시오.

16 (passionate)

> They (①) were (②) enough (③) to teach (④) students, (⑤) even teachers.

17 (not)

> The girls who are (①) more than 100kg (②) decided (③) to (④) eat (⑤) chocolate cakes and hamburgers.

[18-19] 〈보기〉와 의미가 같은 문장을 고르시오.

18

> 보기 Terry was so clever that he could solve the important matters.

① Terry was enough clever solve the important matters.
② Terry was clever enough solve the important matters.
③ Terry was clever enough solving the important matters.
④ Terry was clever enough to solve the important matters.
⑤ Terry was enough clever to solve the important matters.

19

> 보기 He seems to have heard the last call in the airport.

① It seems that he hears the last call in the airport.
② It seems that he heard the last call in the airport.
③ It seems that he is hearing the last call in the airport.
④ It seems that he is heard the last call in the airport.
⑤ It seems that he has been heard the last call in the airport.

20 문장의 빈칸에 알맞은 것은?

> Hundreds of wildlife refuges have been established to provide animals with safe places _________.

① which to live ② to live
③ to live in ④ to living
⑤ on to live

21 우리말을 영어로 바르게 옮긴 것은?

> 당신은 부모님을 잘 따라야 한다.

① You are to obey your parents.
② You obeyed your parents.
③ You are obeyed your parents.
④ You are obeying your parents.
⑤ You will have to obey your parents.

22 밑줄 친 말의 의미와 가장 가까운 것은?

> A lot of celebrities <u>are to</u> arrive Incheon Airport this evening.

① will ② can
③ may ④ should
④ must

23 대화의 빈칸에 알맞은 것은?

> A: Hey, what is that on your pants? There is something on them.
> B: Oh, no. I think it is ketchup.
> A: Your pants ought _________.
> B: Okay, I will put them in the laundry basket.

① wash ② to wash
③ to be washed ④ to washing
⑤ to be washing

24 다음 중 어법상 <u>어색한</u> 문장은?

① Ellen heard her father snoring in the bedroom.
② John was smart enough to escape from the problem.
③ Jordan decided not to go to the Internet cafe with his friends.
④ Catherine seems being sad about the results of the final exam.
⑤ Needless to say, everyone gave up everything they didn't want.

≫ 정답 및 해설 18쪽

25 우리말과 같은 의미가 되도록 할 때 빈칸에 알맞은 것은?

그 학생들은 지각하지 않기 위해 빨리 달렸다.
→ The students ran fast ________ for school.

① to late
② not to be late
③ to not be late
④ to have been late
⑤ not to have been late

26 우리말과 같은 뜻이 되도록 주어진 말을 빈칸에 알맞은 형태로 바꿔 쓰시오.

그 섬은 화산 분출에 의해 파괴되었다고 여겨진다. (destroy)
→ The island is believed ______________ by volcanic eruption.

[27-29] 두 문장이 같은 뜻이 되도록 빈칸에 알맞은 말을 쓰시오.

27
They seem to be happy with their lives.
→ It seems that they ________ happy with their lives.

28
They seemed to be happy with their lives.
→ It seemed that they ________ happy with their lives.

29
They seemed to have been happy with their lives.
→ It seemed that they ________ happy with their lives.

30 밑줄 친 부분에 유의하여 다음 문장을 우리말로 옮기시오.

(1) We decided not to go there.
→ ______________________________

(2) We didn't decide to go there.
→ ______________________________

≫ 정답 및 해설 19쪽

Extracurricular Activities

▸ Sentence Writing

 Complete the sentences describing the pictures.

1

explain / careful

2

cooperate

3

get hurt

1 In science class, the teacher ______________________ when students do experiments in the laboratory.
(얼마나 조심해야 할지를 설명하고 계신다)

2 Certain liquid can be very dangerous because they can damage the skin. So students should remember ______________________.
(서로 어떻게 협력해야 하는지)

3 Students should also wear goggles and special gloves ______________________ during the experiments.
(상처입지 않기 위해서)

PART B Change the Korean into English by using the given words.

1 Kelly는 상금을 어떻게 쓸지 이미 결정했다. (prize money, already)
→ ______________________

2 유명한 사람들은 평범한 인생을 갖는 것이 어렵다는 것을 알게 된다. (find, normal life)
→ ______________________

3 그녀는 매우 슬프게 보인다. (seem, that)
→ ______________________

4 한국인들은 북한에 방문하기 위해서 비자가 있어야 한다. (visa, North Korea)
→ ______________________

▸ *Further Studies* 학교 시험에 자주 나오는 Idioms ②

▶ Let's call it a day. 오늘은 이만하도록 합시다.

▶ call somebody names 욕을 하다

▶ make heads and tails of something 전체를 이해(파악)하다

▶ come in handy (도구 등이) 유용한, 도움이 되는, 편리한

▶ rip off 바가지 쓰다

▶ cost an arm and a leg 값비싼 대가를 치루다

▶ crocodile tears 위선적인 눈물, 양면성이 있는

▶ cut corners 지름길을 택하다

▶ Don't be such a stranger. 자주 방문해라.

▶ a Cock and bull story 믿기 어려운 이야기, 말도 안 되는 소리

▶ cook the books 사람을 속이기 위해 숫자 또는 기록을 조작하다

▶ come of age 나이가 차다, 성년이 되다

▶ call the tune 영향력 있는 위치 또는 지위

▶ under the microscope (= scrutinize) 면밀하게 조사하다

▶ cross the Rubicon 돌이키지 못할 상황에 처하다

▶ call the shots (= call the tune) 지시하다, 명령하다, 제 뜻대로 하다

▶ blow the whistle on 비밀을 폭로하다

▶ hit the road 여행을 떠나다

▶ hit the roof [ceiling] 몹시 화가 나다

▶ raise the roof 소란을 피우다, 함성을 지르다

▶ couch potato TV앞에 앉아 감자칩 먹으면서 할 일 없이 빈둥거리는 사람

▶ under the weather (= feel blue, have a long face) 몸 상태가 안 좋은, 아픈

▶ spill the beans 비밀을 폭로하다

▶ up close and personal 밀착취재

▶ rule of thumb 주먹구구식, 눈대중, 경험법칙

▶ around the clock 주야로, 쉬지 않고(24시간 내내)

▶ on cloud nine (= in seventh heaven) 매우 기분이 좋은

▶ cloud somebody's judgment [memory] 판단(기억)을 흐리게 하다

▶ on the rocks 파산(파멸) 상태인, 위기에 처한

▶ pay through the nose 엄청난 대가를 치르다

동명사
(Gerund)

Day 12 | 동명사의 용법, 시제, 능동과 수
Day 13 | 동사에 따른 목적어의 형태, 관용표현

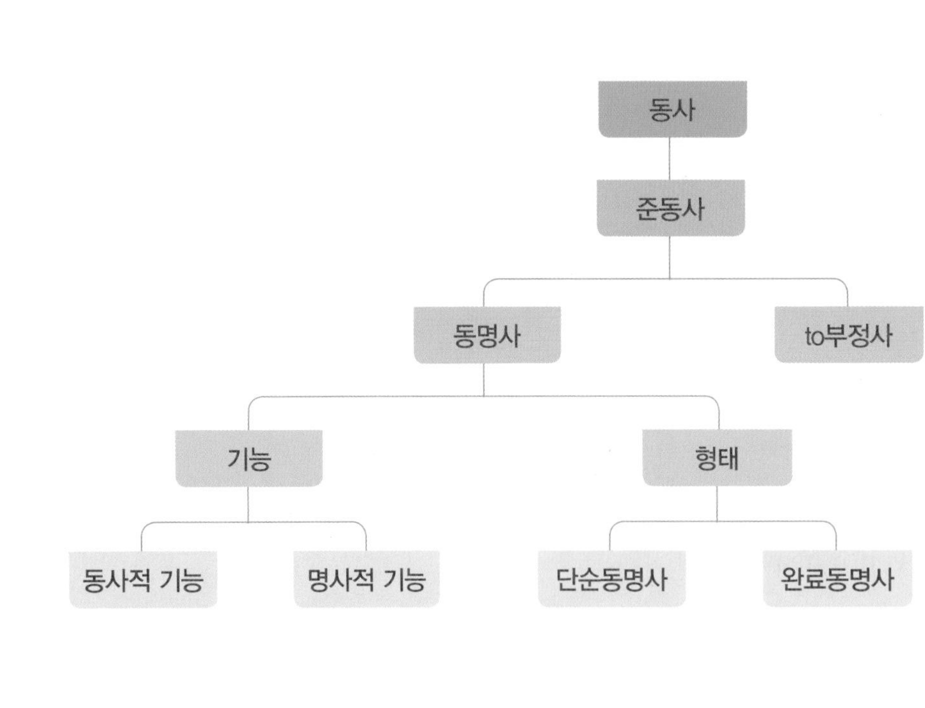

기출 맛보기

우리말과 같은 뜻이 되도록 빈칸에 알맞은 것을 고르시오. (경기도 부천시 ○○중학교)

Joshua는 어제 기말고사에서 실수한 것을 후회했다.
→ Joshua regretted ________ a mistake on the final exam yesterday.

① make
② made
③ making
④ to make
⑤ had making

해설
〈regret + to부정사〉는 '유감스럽게도 (미래에) ~하다'라는 뜻이고, 〈regret + 동명사〉는 '(과거에) ~했던 것을 후회하다'라는 뜻이다. 내용상 과거의 일을 후회하는 것이므로 동명사가 와야 한다.

정답 ③

DAY 12

동명사의 용법, 시제, 능동과 수동

1교시 Grammar Point

1 동명사의 용법

- 형태: 〈동사원형 + –ing〉
- 쓰임: 문장에서 주어, 보어, 목적어 역할

Learning from friends is a part of life. 주어 역할
[*동명사 주어는 단수 취급]

My job is **consulting** teenager's worries. 보어 역할

The group members began **having** regular meetings. 동사의 목적어 역할

The best aim of **studying** English is to use it properly. 전치사의 목적어 역할

2 동명사의 의미상 주어

- 용법: 문장의 주어와 동명사의 주어가 일치하지 않을 때
- 형태: 소유격이나 목적격 형태로 동명사 앞에 위치

I like **reading** English books. (내가 영어책을 읽음)

I like **his[him] reading** English books. (그가 영어책을 읽음)

I like **my son** reading English books. (나의 아들이 영어책을 읽음)
[= my son's]

3 동명사의 시제

	단순동명사	완료동명사
용법	동명사의 시제가 문장의 동사와 같은 시제	동명사의 시제가 문장의 동사보다 앞선 시제
형태	〈동사원형 + -ing〉	〈having + 과거분사〉

The parents **are** proud of **having** a well-known daughter. 단순동명사
→ The parents **are** proud that they **have** a well-known daughter.

I **am** sorry for **having lost** my loved dog. 완료동명사
→ I **am** sorry that I **lost[have lost]** my loved dog.

4 동명사의 능동과 수동

	능동형 동명사	수동형 동명사
용법	동명사와 의미상 주어의 관계가 능동일 때	동명사와 의미상 주어의 관계가 수동일 때
형태	〈동사원형 + -ing〉	〈being + 과거분사〉

Charlie is upset about **being treated** like a young kid. 단순수동 동명사

Linda forgot **having been given** a big birthday gift. 완료수동 동명사

Grammar Tips

- **동명사가 목적어로 올 때 수동의 뜻으로 쓰이는 동사: need, want 등**

All dishes **need washing**.
→ All dishes **need to be washed**.
(모든 접시들은 설거지 될 필요가 있다.)

2교시 In - Class Questions

STEP A

밑줄 친 동명사가 문장에서 어떤 역할을 하는지 쓰시오.

1 In cities, driving a car is an unevitable tool to commute. ____________

2 The next step to completing this project is to set a goal. ____________

3 Do you remember going to the museum last year? ____________

4 One small way to help the environment is recycling all cans and bottles. ____________

STEP B

괄호 안에서 알맞은 말을 고르시오.

1 Tom enjoys **(being played / playing)** an important role in the school play.

2 Jack knows of my **(learning / having learned)** Chinese when I was young.

3 Austin was proud of **(selecting / being selected)** as class president.

STEP C

우리말과 같은 뜻이 되도록 주어진 단어를 바르게 배열하시오.

1 엄마는 내가 학창시절에 공부를 잘했던 것을 매우 좋아하신다.
(well / loves / studied / my / having / in my school days)
→ Mom ____.

2 Chuck은 그 학회에서 많이 배웠던 것에 신이 난다.
(taught / been / having / is excited about / at the conference / a lot)
→ Chuck ____.

3 그녀는 그녀의 아들이 길을 잃을까봐 걱정한다.
(her son / losing / is worried about / his way)
→ She ____.

STEP D

우리말과 같은 뜻이 되도록 주어진 말을 사용하여 빈칸을 완성하시오.

1 내 아이들은 강아지와 노는 것을 좋아한다. (like)
→ My kids ____________ ____________ with dogs.

2 그 노부부는 새로운 차를 샀던 것을 부인했다. (deny)
→ The old couple ____________ ____________ a new car.

3교시 After - Class Questions

01 문장의 빈칸에 들어갈 수 없는 것은?

Eating a variety of food ______________________.

① makes you healthy
② will help you stay in good shape
③ gives you lots of energy
④ is better than eating instant food
⑤ becoming my good habit

[02-03] 두 문장이 같은 뜻이 되도록 할 때 빈칸에 알맞은 것을 고르시오.

02 The audience is aware that they made a lot of effort on this play.

→ The audience is aware of ________ a lot of effort on this play.

① they made ② they making ③ their making
④ their having making ⑤ their having made

03 William doesn't regret that he attended vocational high school.

→ William doesn't regret ________ vocational high school.

① attend ② attending ③ being attended
④ having attended ⑤ having been attended

04 다음 중 어법상 어색한 문장은?

① It will stop raining in a few minutes.
② People are used to using credit cards.
③ The musician gave up releasing for the new album.
④ Everyone left without say goodbye to us.
⑤ What about going to his birthday party with me?

05 우리말을 영어로 바르게 옮긴 것은?

나의 아버지는 3년 전에 대표이사로 승진되신 것을 자랑스러워하신다.

① My father is proud of being promoted to CEO 3 years ago.
② My father is proud of having promoted to CEO 3 years ago.
③ My father is proud of having been promoted to CEO 3 years ago.
④ My father was proud of being promoted to CEO 3 years ago.
⑤ My father was proud of having been promoted to CEO 3 years ago.

Vocabulary Tips

- audience 관객
- make an effort 노력하다
- regret 후회하다
- vocational high school 직업 고등학교
- release 발표하다, 출시하다
- be proud of ~을 자랑스러워하다
- promote 승진시키다
- CEO 대표이사

서술형 대비

[06-09] 주어진 말을 사용하여 다음 우리말을 영어로 옮기시오.

06 내 바지는 기장 수선이 필요하다. (need, hem)

→ ______________________________

07 아이들은 바보처럼 취급받는 것을 싫어한다. (hate, treat, fool)

→ ______________________________

08 인터넷에서 영화를 다운받는 것은 네가 생각하는 것만큼 어렵지 않다. (download, as difficult as)

→ ______________________________

09 나의 어머니는 내가 그 창문을 깨뜨렸다고 확신하신다. (sure of, break)

→ ______________________________

10 대화의 빈칸에 알맞은 것은?

A: I am so sorry for ________ the living room last night.
B: That's okay. But never do that again.

① to mess up ② to be messed up ③ messing up
④ having messed up ⑤ having messing up

[11-12] 문장의 빈칸에 알맞은 것을 고르시오.

11 Young, famous actors get tired of ________ everywhere they go these days.

① recognize ② recognizing ③ be recognized
④ being recognized ⑤ being to recognize

12 Danny couldn't fall asleep all night because of ________.

① the baby cry ② the baby to crying ③ the crying baby's
④ the baby's crying ⑤ the baby's to cry

Vocabulary Tips

- hem 단을 만들다, 기장을 수선하다
- treat 취급하다, 다루다
- fool 바보
- mess up 어지럽히다, 엉망으로 만들다
- recognize 알아보다

After - Class Questions

13 괄호 안에서 알맞은 말을 고르시오.

(a)(Give / Giving) your kids a lot of chances to speak with American students is the best way for them (b)(to improve / improving) their language skills.

14 두 문장이 같은 뜻이 되도록 빈칸에 알맞은 말을 쓰시오.

His bicycle needed to be fixed.
→ His bicycle needed ________.

15 밑줄 친 부분을 바르게 고치시오.

Andy was sure of his roommate being gotten good grades on the previous exam. → ____________

16 우리말을 영어로 바르게 옮긴 것은?

나의 아버지는 젊었을 때 열심히 공부하지 않았던 것을 부끄럽게 여기신다.

① My father is ashamed of not studying hard when he was young.
② My father is ashamed of studying not hard when he was young.
③ My father is not ashamed of having studied hard when he was young.
④ My father is ashamed of not having studied hard when he was young.
⑤ My father was ashamed of not having studied hard when he was young.

[17-18] 밑줄 친 동명사의 쓰임이 어법상 어색한 것을 고르시오.

17 ① Lucy was ashamed of scolding by her parents due to her mistake.
② The writer admitted being rejected by many publishing company.
③ Amy hopes you enjoy listening to her music and lyrics forever.
④ Her paintings are one way of expressing her personality.
⑤ Most singers in Korea spend a lot of time training themselves.

18 ① Please forgive me for interrupting you.
② Talking with you at the seminar was nice.
③ Why didn't you suggest installing this program?
④ Aaron's happiness depends on having lots of trustworthy friends.
⑤ Attend the music festival will be an unforgettable experience.

Vocabulary Tips

- language skill 언어능력
- fix 수리하다
- be ashamed of ~ ~을 부끄럽게 여기다
- scold 꾸짖다
- admit 인정하다
- reject 거절하다
- publishing company 출판사
- lyrics (노래) 가사
- personality 성격
- interrupt 방해하다
- suggest 제안하다
- install (프로그램 등을) 설치하다
- depend on ~에 달려있다
- trustworthy 믿을 수 있는
- attend 참석하다

[19-20] 대화의 밑줄 친 부분 중 어법상 어색한 것을 고르시오.

19

A: I am having difficulty ①sharing this music file.
B: Hey, sharing music is not a good way ②to listen to music.
A: Really? But it is the easiest and fastest way.
B: I want you ③to stop sharing, and I suggest that you ④buy the file or album.
A: All right. Don't blame me for ⑤share it.

20

A: Why ①did the cashier at the convenience store ②insist on ③paying only in cash?
B: I ④think that the credit card checker ⑤was broken at that moment.

[21-23] 밑줄 친 동명사의 시제를 〈보기〉에서 골라 쓰시오.

보기	현재 또는 미래	과거	대과거

21 Ethan was afraid of having made some mistakes while speaking English.

→ ____________________

22 Don't be ashamed of making any mistakes while speaking English.

→ ____________________

23 Alexander is proud of having been your student.

→ ____________________

24 다음 문장을 동명사가 주어인 문장으로 바꿔 쓰시오.

It is hard to take advanced English grammar courses.

→ ____

25 주어진 말을 문장의 빈칸에 알맞은 형태로 바꿔 쓰시오.

There is a possibility of her ____________________ several days ago. (arrive)

Vocabulary Tips

- insist 주장하다, 요구하다
- blame 비난하다
- cashier 계산원
- convenience store 편의점
- credit card checker 신용카드 단말기
- be afraid of ~하는 것을 두려워하다
- advanced 상급인
- possibility 가능성

DAY 13

동사에 따른 목적어의 형태, 관용표현

1교시 Grammar Point

1 동사에 따른 목적어의 형태

(1) to부정사와 동명사를 목적어로 취하는 동사

to부정사만을 취하는 동사	want, wish, hope, decide, promise, expect, learn, fail, choose, refuse 등
동명사만을 취하는 동사	mind, miss, enjoy, finish, give up, quit, avoid, postpone, put off, appreciate, stop, suggest, imagine, consider, deny 등
둘 다 취하는 동사	begin, start, continue, like, love, hate, intend, prefer 등

Evan **decided to learn** English and Chinese when he was 10 years old.

Many senators are **considering writing** a letter to their citizens.

Don was worried that his friends **preferred to take [taking]** another course.

(2) to부정사, 동명사를 둘 다 목적어로 취하면서 의미가 다른 동사

forget remember	to부정사	'(미래에) ~할 것을 잊다/기억하다'
	동명사	'(과거에) ~했던 것을 잊다/기억하다'
stop	to부정사	'~하기 위해서 멈추다'(to부정사의 부사적 용법)
	동명사	'~하는 것을 멈추다'
try	to부정사	'~하려고 노력하다'
	동명사	'시험 삼아 ~하다'

The students **remember to find** what they have to do in class.

The students **remember finding** what they have to do in class.

Lucas **stopped to talk with** his staff.

Lucas **stops talking with** his staff.

Many fat people **try to eat** small portions of food.

Many fat people **try eating** small portions of food.

2 동명사의 관용표현

go -ing (~하러 가다)	it is no use -ing (~해도 소용없다)
cannot help -ing (~하지 않을 수 없다)	when it comes to -ing (~에 관해서는)
have difficulty [trouble] -ing (~하는 데 어려움을 겪다)	How [What] about -ing? (~하는 게 어때?)

Do you want to **go shopping**?

Suji **cannot help eating** pizzas and hamburgers.

Mike **has difficulty studying** math for the final exam.

It is no use crying all day long.

When it comes to going to Hawaii, Edward thinks that it is a good idea.

How about dancing with me?

Grammar Tips

- **to부정사, 동명사를 둘 다 취하면서 의미가 다른 동사 regret**

regret + to부정사 (유감스럽게도 ~하다)
regret + 동명사 (~한 것을 후회하다)

- **기타 관용표현**

look forward to -ing (~하기를 고대하다)
feel like -ing (~하고 싶다)
be busy -ing (~하느라 바쁘다)
be used to -ing (~하는 데 익숙하다)
on [upon] -ing (~하자마자)
object to -ing (~하는 것에 반대하다)
be devoted to -ing (~에 헌신하다)
stop A from -ing (A가 ~을 못하게 하다)
spend 시간/돈 -ing (~하는 데 시간/돈을 쓰다)
be worth -ing (~할 만한 가치가 있다)

- **How [What] about + -ing? (~하는 게 어때?)**

= Why don't you + 동사원형?
= What do you say to + -ing?
= Let's + 동사원형.

- **cannot help -ing (~하지 않을 수 없다)**

= cannot but + 동사원형
= have no choice but + to부정사

- **동명사 vs. 현재분사**

	동명사	현재분사
역할	명사 역할 (주어, 목적어 보어로 쓰임)	형용사 역할 (명사 수식)
의미	목적, 용도 (~하기 위한)	상태, 동작 (~하고 있는)
예	a sleeping bag (= a bag for sleeping)	a sleeping baby (= a baby who is sleeping)

2교시 In-Class Questions

괄호 안에서 알맞은 말을 모두 고르시오.

1 Some employees chose **(stay / to stay / staying)** at this company until next year.

2 The doctors need to postpone **(check / to check / checking)** those documents.

3 Her boyfriend begins **(learn / to learn / learning)** jazz dance at his university.

밑줄 친 부분을 어법상 바르게 고치시오.

1 For an appetizer, I highly suggest to have the fried chicken wings. ________

2 We also offer ice cream for $4. You cannot help to eat it. ________

3 These cups are worth to buy and keep in the living room. ________

4 Due to the foggy weather, the truck driver cannot continue deliver your products. ________

밑줄 친 부분이 동명사이면 '동', 현재분사이면 '현'이라고 쓰시오.

1 Young kids are really likely to buy magnifying glasses. ________

2 Speeding cars on highways are very dangerous. ________

3 Does Mom know that our washing machine broke yesterday? ________

4 A few reporters would like to meet the woman making a speech in the square. ________

우리말과 같은 뜻이 되도록 주어진 말을 이용하여 문장을 완성하시오.

1 그들은 커피 마시는 것을 끝낸 후에 백화점에 갈 것이다. (finish)
→ After they ________________, they will go to the department store.

2 십대들은 자신들에게 관심이 집중되는 것을 원하지 않는다. (want, attract)
→ Teenagers ________________ attention to themselves.

3 한국 정부는 시민들에게 집을 찾는 것을 도와주기로 약속했다. (promise)
→ The Korean government ________________ the citizens find houses.

3교시 After-Class Questions

01 **문장의 빈칸에 알맞은 말끼리 짝지은 것은?**

(a) I can't imagine ________ the national entrance exam.
(b) My family considered ________ to New York next month.
(c) Mom wished ________ one day off to do nothing.

① to fail – to go – to have
② to fail – going – to have
③ failing – going – having
④ failing – to go – to have
⑤ failing – going – to have

서술형 대비

[02-03] 주어진 말을 이용하여 다음 우리말을 영어로 옮기시오.

02 우리는 시장에서 그 맛있는 음식을 사지 않을 수 없었다. (help)

→ ______________________________

03 Bella는 Edward와 함께 노는 데 4시간을 보냈다. (spend)

→ ______________________________

04 **문장의 빈칸에 들어갈 수 없는 것은?**

Harry and his girlfriend ________ collecting unique antique teapot sets.

① considered
② suggested
③ put off
④ stopped
⑤ refused

[05-07] 주어진 말을 빈칸에 알맞은 형태로 바꿔 쓰시오.

05 Most women like to go ____________. (shop)

06 What do you say ____________ a movie? (see)

07 Fathers often have difficulty ____________ money. (earn)

08 **우리말과 같은 뜻이 되도록 주어진 말을 사용하여 문장을 완성하시오.**

선배 학생들은 신입생들을 위한 환영파티를 준비하느라 분주하다. (busy)

→ The senior students ________ ________ ________ for the welcoming party for the freshmen.

Vocabulary Tips

- national entrance exam 수능시험
- unique 독특한, 특이한
- antique 고풍의
- freshman 신입생

[09-10] 밑줄 친 부분을 어법상 바르게 고친 것을 고르시오.

09 Help me, please! I forgot ①reading *Hamlet*, ②and I ③must hand ④in the paper ⑤by Tuesday!

① reading → to read ② and → but ③ must → should
④ in → on ⑤ by → until

10 Most employees prefer ①to work at ②widely ③known companies ④while most women don't mind ⑤to have part-time jobs in various fields.

① to work → work ② widely → wide ③ known → knowing
④ while → on the other hand ⑤ to have → having

[11-12] 밑줄 친 부분의 성격이 나머지와 다른 것을 고르시오.

11 ① Willy saw some boys dancing in the shopping mall.
② Making a proper decision for young children is really crucial.
③ Go home, or you might wake up the sleeping baby in the room.
④ When you drive on the highway, you should watch out speeding cars.
⑤ The president would like to meet the lady talking about the big issue.

12 ① Not having sweets is a key habit for children to have.
② One of my hobbies is collecting magnetic stickers.
③ Nancy feels like watching an exciting soccer game.
④ We are sorry for not having you around us anymore.
⑤ He won't postpone attending the meeting.

13 밑줄 친 부분이 옳지 않는 것은?

① Because Rose got lots of stress, she continued to overeat.
② Local artists are considering to give a workshop on Saturday.
③ Attention, visitors. The museum will begin to close in 20 minutes.
④ Young children like to experience some turbulence on airplanes.
⑤ Mac started to understand the difference between illusion and reality.

Vocabulary Tips

- paper 과제
- prefer 선호하다
- various 다양한
- field 분야
- crucial 중요한
- highway 고속도로
- issue 주제, 안건, 사안
- magnetic 자석의
- postpone 연기하다
- overeat 과식하다
- workshop 워크샵
- attention 주목하다, 주의하다
- turbulence 난기류
- illusion 환상
- reality 현실

14 어법상 올바른 문장끼리 짝지은 것은?

(a) Try to put the vase and the lamp between the windows if you want.
(b) Kyle and Sunny couldn't help to drink an Americano after having a heavy dinner.
(c) Lucas stopped looking for the lost money at home and sat down for a while.
(d) Many teachers hope to teach as much as possible.

① (a)(b) ② (b)(c)(d) ③ (c)(d)
④ (a)(b)(c) ⑤ (a)(b)(c)(d)

[15-16] 우리말과 같은 뜻이 되도록 빈칸에 알맞은 말을 쓰시오.

15 이 영화는 몇 번 볼만한 가치가 있다.

→ This movie is ________ ________ several times.

16 우리 부모님을 설득하려 노력해도 소용없다.

→ It is ________ ________ ________ to persuade our parents.

17 두 문장이 같은 의미가 되도록 빈칸에 알맞은 말을 쓰시오.

Terry forgot that he brought his ball to the game, so he was disqualified from the game.

→ Terry forgot ________ his ball to the game, so he was disqualified from the game.

[18-22] 문장의 빈칸에 알맞은 것을 고르시오.

18 Serena appreciates ________ her friends last weekend.

① you help ② you to help ③ your to help
④ your helping ⑤ your help

19 I still remember ________ my first cell phone.

① buy ② bought ③ to buying
④ buying ⑤ to buy

20 Let's stop ________ a break for a while. I'm really exhausted.

① take ② to take ③ taking
④ being taken ⑤ taken

Vocabulary Tips

- vase 꽃병
- persuade 설득하다
- bring 가져오다(-brought-brought)
- disqualify 자격을 박탈하다
- appreciate 고맙게 생각하다
- for a while 잠시 동안
- exhausted 피곤한, 기진맥진한

21 When it comes _________ English, we have the best teaching skills in Seoul.

① teach ② teaching ③ to teach
④ to teaching ⑤ to having taught

22 At last, the Pope in the Vatican stopped _________, and every citizen was in great sorrow.

① breathe ② to breathe ③ breathing
④ being breathed ⑤ to be breathed

23 두 문장을 한 문장으로 만들 때 빈칸에 알맞은 말을 쓰시오.

It is rainy outside now. I can't go on the field trip to the amusement park.
→ The rain stopped _________ _________ _________ on the field trip to the amusement park.

24 밑줄 친 부분 중 어법상 어색한 것은?

① Helen avoids walking alone on the streets at night.
② Diana kept her son from falling into the deep lake.
③ Mary had great trouble understand her violent husband.
④ Joshua is used to taking some medicine after eating each meal.
⑤ The students in the classroom stopped talking when their teacher entered the room.

25 세 문장이 같은 의미가 되도록 빈칸에 알맞은 말을 쓰시오.

Whitney couldn't help laughing at the funny scene.
→ Whitney _________ _________ laugh at the funny scene.
→ Whitney had _________ _________ _________ to laugh at the funny scene.

Vocabulary Tips

- Pope (가톨릭교의) 교황
- citizen 시민
- be in sorrow 슬픔에 빠지다
- breathe 숨을 쉬다
- field trip 현장학습
- amusement park 놀이공원
- violent 폭력적인
- medicine 약
- funny scene 재미있는 광경

Final Test

01 대화의 빈칸에 알맞은 것은?

A: Jack, I need your help.
B: What is it, Mom?
A: I am baking some cookies, but I have run out of eggs and sugar. Can you buy some for me?
B: Sure, I will leave now.
A: Jack, don't forget ________ the prices.
B: I won't.

① check ② checking
③ to check ④ to checking
⑤ to be checked

서술형 대비

[02-03] 주어진 말을 사용하여 다음 우리말을 영어로 옮기시오.

02 네 돈을 훔쳐간 것에 대해 그들을 비난해도 소용이 없다.
(blame ~ for, use)

→ ________________________________

03 나의 부모님은 내가 집에 늦게 돌아오는 것을 싫어하신다.
(hate, my)

→ ________________________________

[04-05] 밑줄 친 부분 중 어법상 어색한 것을 고르시오.

04 ① Sandy feels like listening to classical music.
② It is so hard for my dad to stop smoking.
③ We will definitely remember to see you there soon.
④ How can we forget to meet them in Paris last year?
⑤ My son is trying to write some thank-you cards to his teachers.

05 ① Many visitors object to paying the entrance fee.
② She enjoyed her making pizza and pasta for her friends.
③ The writer postponed sending the scenario because of the contract.
④ Tim is aware of his girlfriend's having problems with her finances.
⑤ Despite the proof, the witness denied having seen the accident that had happened.

06 두 문장이 같은 뜻이 되도록 빈칸에 알맞은 말을 쓰시오.

We are sure that she told us a lie.
→ We are sure of ________________________.

07 우리말과 같은 뜻이 되도록 할 때 빈칸에 알맞은 것은?

나는 그녀가 장학금을 받을 학생으로 선택될 것을 학수고대하고 있다.
→ I'm looking forward to ________ for a scholarship.

① her choosing ② her to choose
③ choose for her ④ her being chosen
⑤ her having chosen

[08-10] 문장의 빈칸에 알맞은 것을 고르시오.

08 I can't remember ________ to my house after I got drunk last night.

① to take ② to be taken
③ taking ④ being taken
⑤ for taking

09

The smartphone is portable enough ________ around in your pocket.

① carry ② to carry
③ carrying ④ carried
⑤ carries

10

There were few chances of their ________.

① hurt ② hurting
③ being hurt ④ to be hurt
⑤ having hurt

11 문장의 빈칸에 알맞은 말끼리 짝지은 것은?

(a) The theme of these buildings is ________ in nature.
(b) The architects have decided ________ eco-friendly buildings in this area.

① living – to build ② living – building
③ to live – building ④ to live – to building
⑤ to living – to build

12 밑줄 친 부분 중 어법상 어색한 것을 골라 바르게 고치시오.

Nowadays, all citizens ①are used to ②select their own president ③every five ④years, which was not ⑤allowed even until 1987.

________ → ________

[13-14] 〈보기〉의 밑줄 친 부분과 성격이 같은 것을 고르시오.

13

보기 Stewart likes assembling model cars.

① Nobody heard her speaking English.
② Who was the lady sitting over there?
③ Look! The sleeping cat is mine.
④ We started going on the field trip.
⑤ Some people were asking about the event.

14

보기 My son is looking for magnifying glasses.

① Don't wake up the sleeping baby.
② Speeding cars and motorcycles are very dangerous.
③ We need to meet the girl making the cake in the kitchen.
④ Please give me this swimming suit for my birthday.
⑤ Have you ever talked to the man wearing that weird T-shirt?

15 우리말과 같은 뜻이 되도록 빈칸에 알맞은 말을 쓰시오.

우리는 며칠 전에 다투었기 때문에 그녀가 여기에 오는 것이 불편하다.
→ ________ ________ here is uncomfortable because we argued a few days ago.

16 대화의 밑줄 친 부분 중 어법상 어색한 것은?

A: What is your dream?
B: I am dreaming of ①becoming a successful songwriter.
A: Wow, have you started ②attending any auditions?
B: Not yet. I'm afraid of ③being scolding by my parents.
A: Oh, I know. My parents also object to ④my becoming a dancer.
B: No way. Why don't you try ⑤persuading them? You can do it.

[17-19] 다음 중 어법상 어색한 문장을 고르시오.

17 ① Before you start learning how to swim, you should buy a swimming suit.
② Do you love to do what your parents want to do?
③ Many employees prefer staying the same position as far as they can do.
④ Let's continue working on this project instead of doing something else.
⑤ Only a few children finished to write their essays about the future.

18 ① Ellie was used to working even on Sundays.
② The protestors objected to import American beef.
③ The clerks feel like having some snacks around 5 p.m.
④ My parents spent most of their time playing golf last weekend.
⑤ Some students are busy making portfolios for their final projects.

19 ① Please forgive me for interrupting you.
② Everybody dreams of having his or her own car.
③ I spent three days preparing for the English exam.
④ My father woke me up by turn on the MP3 player.
⑤ My wife worries about spending too much money.

20 우리말과 같은 뜻이 되도록 주어진 단어를 배열할 때 네 번째 오는 단어는?

> 영어 공부를 하는 것에 관해서는 최 선생님의 의견을 듣는 것이 가장 좋은 생각이다.
> (Ms. Choi's opinion / it / listening to / comes to / is / studying English / the best idea)
> → When ______________________.

① Ms. Choi's opinion ② it
③ listening to ④ comes to
⑤ studying English

21 네 문장이 같은 뜻이 되도록 빈칸에 알맞은 말을 쓰시오.

> How about starting learning yoga for your health?
> → Why don't you ________ learning yoga for your health?
> → What do you say ________ ________ learning yoga for your health?
> → Let's ________ learning yoga for your health.

22 대화의 밑줄 친 부분 중 어법상 어색한 것을 두 개 고르시오.

> A: Is it true that William wishes ①to write a biography?
> B: Yes, I heard about it. I keep ②to persuade him not to do it.
> A: You don't need to do that. I think he will quit ③writing it soon.
> B: How come?
> A: Don't you remember? Last year, he started ④to write one, but he finally gave up ⑤to do it.

[23-25] 주어진 말을 사용하여 다음 우리말을 영어로 옮기시오.

23

너는 내일의 영화표 예매하는 것을 기억하고 있지? (book, remember)

→ ____________________

24

저희는 당신에게 이 슬픈 소식을 알리게 되어 유감입니다. (regret, inform~of)

→ ____________________

25

Helen은 사실을 말하지 않음으로써 그녀의 친구들을 속였다. (deceive, by)

→ ____________________

[26-27] 두 문장이 같은 뜻이 되도록 할 때 빈칸에 알맞은 것을 고르시오.

26

Sam regrets that he didn't study hard. → Sam regrets _________ hard.

① not to study ② not studying
③ not to have studied ④ not having studied
⑤ not having been studied

27

Joe denied having ordered several books from eBay. → Joe denied that he _________ several books from eBay.

① has ordered ② not ordering
③ my ordering ④ was ordering
⑤ had ordered

28 문장의 빈칸에 알맞은 말끼리 짝지은 것은?

(a) Somi appreciated _________ helping her parents. (b) Even at night, we can't fall asleep because of _________.

① he – the baby cry
② to him – the crying baby
③ his – the baby to cry
④ his – the baby's crying
⑤ himself – the baby's to cry

29 짝지은 두 문장의 의미가 다른 것은?

① The women started to chat while sitting on a bench.
→ The women started chatting while sitting on a bench.
② Sora remembered looking for the lost purse.
→ Sora remembered to look for the lost purse.
③ I had difficulty finding a place to live in.
→ It was difficult for me to find a place to live in.
④ I woke up early so that I could catch the first train.
→ I woke up early to catch the first train.
⑤ I like to go to see PSY's concert with Mina.
→ I like going to see PSY's concert with Mina.

30 대화의 빈칸에 알맞은 것은?

A: Why did Juniper miss her bus stop? B: The bus was so crowded that she had a hard time _________.

① got off ② to get off
③ getting off ④ get off
⑤ gets off

> 정답 및 해설 23쪽

Extracurricular Activities

▸ Sentence Writing

PART A Complete the sentences describing the memo. 

How to Prepare for the Final Exam

1. Write down your name first.
2. Check the instructions.
3. Don't spend too much time on one question.
4. Never watch what your friends are doing on the exam.
5. Double-check all of your answers.
6. Never cheat during the exam.

When you prepare for the final exam, please notice the following.

1 Don't put off ________________.

2 Don't solve any questions before ________________.

3 It is no use ________________.

4 Don't waste time ________________.

5 Avoid careless mistakes by ________________.

6 It's never worth ________________.

PART B Change the Korean into English by using the given words.

1 그 컴퓨터는 수리를 해도 소용없다. 새 컴퓨터를 구입하는 것이 더 낫겠다. (it, use, fix, had better)
→ ________________

2 그 록 콘서트에 참석한 것은 잊지 못할 경험이다. (attend, unforgettable)
→ ________________

3 우리는 그가 회사로부터 해고당했던 것을 이해할 수 없다. (be fired, his)
→ ________________

4 네가 슬프다면 긍정적인 생각을 하도록 노력해라. (if, try, positive, develop)
→ ________________

▸ Further Studies 학교 시험에 자주 나오는 Idioms ③

▶ make a beeline 직선코스, 최단거리 코스
▶ kick oneself 후회하다
▶ hot under the collar 화를 내어, 흥분하여
▶ get hot 인기가 있다, 한창 뜨고 있다
▶ for love or money 모든 수단과 방법을 다 써도
▶ set the world on fire 세상을 떠들썩하게 만들다
▶ rob the cradle 훨씬 나이 어린 상대와 결혼(연애, 데이트)하다
▶ bone up on (= cram) 벼락치기 공부를 하다
▶ taper off (음주 습관 등을) 차차 버리다
▶ rock the boat 평지풍파를 일으키다
▶ eat crow 잘못을 인정하다, 실언을 취소하다
▶ scratch the surface 수박 겉핥기식으로 하다
▶ skate on thin ice 살얼음판을 걷다
▶ win hands down 낙승하다, 쉽게 이기다
▶ nose out 신승하다 (어렵게 또는 근소한 차이로 이기다)
▶ sink in 완전히 이해되다
▶ have/get a frog in one's throat 목이 잠기다, 목이 쉬다
▶ crop up 갑자기 발생하다
▶ play cat and mouse with (= tease) 놀리다
▶ come out of nowhere 갑자기 나타나다
▶ jump the gun 신호 전에 출발하다
▶ egg on 사주하다, 선동하다
▶ spell out 정확하게 설명하다
▶ black out (= faint, pass out) 기절하다
▶ keep a straight face 엄숙한 표정을 짓다
▶ under the counter 부정한 뒷거래
▶ off the top of my head 얼른 생각하건대
▶ have it in (= be capable of) 능력이 있는
▶ pain in the neck 불쾌하게 하는 사람/것
▶ lemon 불량품, 결함상품, 매력이 없는 여성, 한물간 여성

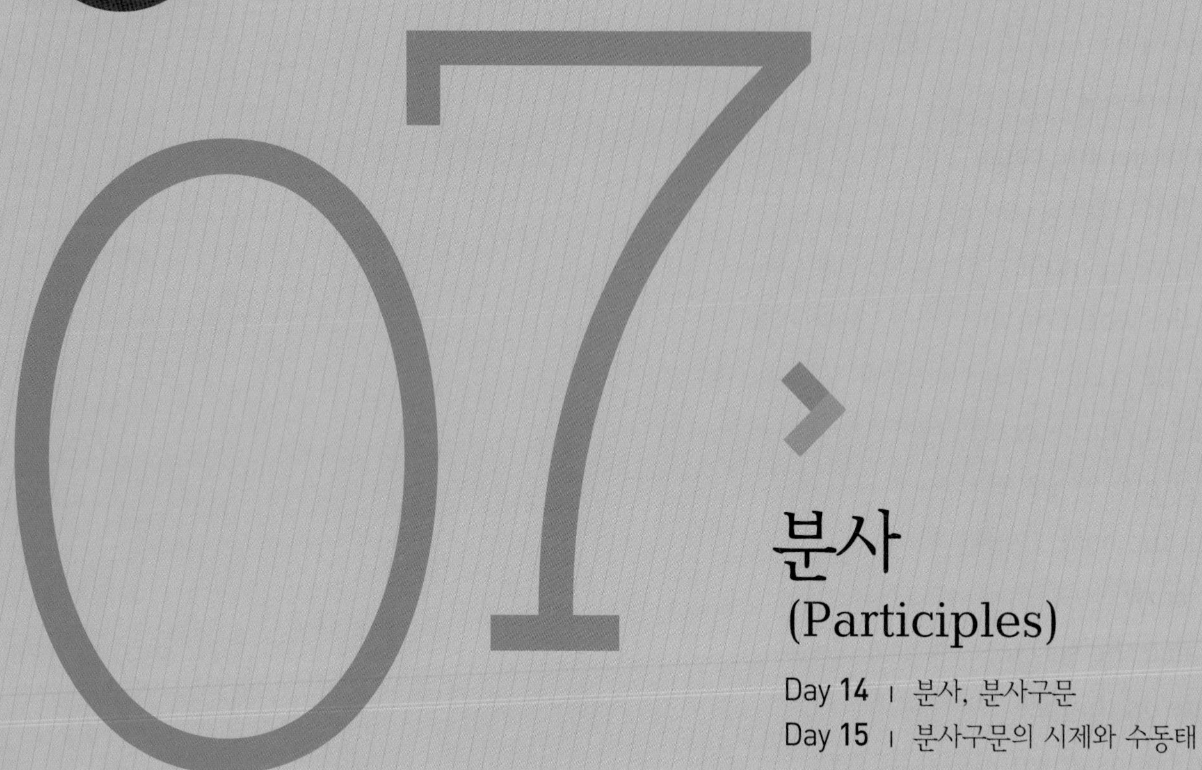

분사 (Participles)

Day 14 | 분사, 분사구문
Day 15 | 분사구문의 시제와 수동태

기출 맛보기

대화의 빈칸에 알맞은 것을 고르시오. (경기도 광명시 ○○중학교)

A: What did the audience think about this performance?
B: Everyone was so happy and ________ about it.

① excite
② exciting
③ excited
④ excites
⑤ to excite

해설
관중들이 '신이 나게 된' 것이므로 수동을 의미하는 과거분사가 와야 한다.

해석
A: 청중들은 그 공연에 대해 어떻게 생각하니?
B: 모든 사람들이 그 공연에 대해 아주 기뻐했고 신이 났어.

정답 ③

DAY 14

분사, 분사구문

1교시 Grammar Point

1 분사의 종류와 역할

현재분사	과거분사
〈동사원형 + -ing〉 능동, 진행을 의미(~하는, ~하고 있는) 명사 수식, 진행시제	〈동사원형 + -ed〉 수동, 완료를 의미(~받은, ~된, ~당한) 명사 수식, 수동태, 완료시제
an **interesting** subject (재미있는 과목)	a **given** task (주어진 과업)

Have you heard the **surprising** news? 명사 수식 (놀라운 소식)

The window was **broken** yesterday. 수동태 (창문이 깨진)

2 분사구문

- 분사구문: 문장의 종속절을 분사를 이용하여 간단하게 만든 구문
- 의미: 접속사에 따라 시간, 이유, 양보, 조건, 연속동작/동시동작을 의미

(1) **분사구문을 만드는 법**

As Ellen is surprised by some questions, she looks embarrassed.
└ ①~~As~~ ②~~Ellen~~ ③~~is~~ surprised by some questions, (주어가 같을 때)
→ **Being surprised by some questions**, she looks embarrassed.

While I was reading a book, Mom was preparing dinner.
└ ①~~While~~ I ②~~was~~ reading a book, (주어가 다를 때: 독립분사구문)
→ **I reading a book**, Mom was preparing dinner.

(2) **의미**

시간 (when, while, after, before, as 등)	When Yuri heard the news, she started to cry. → **Hearing** the news, she started to cry.
이유 (as, because, since 등)	Since Cathy had lots of work to do, she couldn't surf the Internet. → **Having** lots of work to do, she couldn't surf the Internet.
양보 (although, though, even though, even if 등)	Even though it was written in German, this book is easy to understand. → **Being written** in German, this book is easy to understand.
조건 (if, unless 등)	If you don't trust people, you cannot make friends. → **Not trusting** people, you cannot make friends.
연속동작/동시동작	I was thinking about her, and I looked at her photos. → I was thinking about her, **looking at** her photos.

Grammar Tips

분사의 서술적 역할

5형식 문장에서 분사가 목적격 보어 역할을 한다.

Tony sees him **crossing** the road. 보어 역할 (건너고 있는 것)

I heard my name **called**. 보어 역할 (불리는 것)

감정을 나타내는 분사

현재분사: 명사가 감정을 줄 경우
과거분사: 명사가 감정을 받을 경우

현재분사	과거분사
tiring (지치게 하는)	tired (지친)
exciting (흥미진진한)	excited (흥분한, 신 난)
boring (지루한)	bored (지루해진)
disappointing (실망스러운)	disappointed (실망한)
shocking (충격을 주는)	shocked (충격을 받은)

분사구문의 부정

분사 앞에 부정어(not, never)를 둔다.

Not meeting his girlfriend, he was very depressed.

〈with + 명사 + 분사〉 '~한 채로'

Ron left his house **with the phone ringing**. [현재분사: 능동 관계]

David sat in the chair **with his arms crossed**. [과거분사: 수동 관계]

2교시 In - Class Questions

괄호 안에서 알맞은 말을 고르시오.

1 Chanel felt her legs (**touch** / **touched** / **touching**) by a stranger.

2 Did you hear their names (**call** / **calling** / **called**)?

3 Everybody was able to see the man (**sings** / **sung** / **singing**) a song on stage.

우리말과 같은 뜻이 되도록 주어진 말을 빈칸에 알맞은 형태로 바꿔 쓰시오.

1 Jessy는 잠긴 문을 열 수가 없었다. (lock)
→ Jessy couldn't open the ______________ door.

2 Linda는 중고차를 사서 거기에서 몇 년 동안 살았다. (use)
→ Linda bought a ______________ car and lived in it for years.

3 그 선생님은 그 학생이 시험에서 부정행위 하는 것을 적발했다. (cheat)
→ The teacher caught the student ______________ on the test.

4 우리는 타고 있는 초들을 껐다. (burn)
→ We blew out the ______________ candles.

STEP C

두 문장이 같은 뜻이 되도록 빈칸에 알맞은 말을 〈보기〉에서 골라 쓰시오.

보기 if and because though

1 Turning to the left, you can see your close friend.
→ ______________ you turn to the left, you can see your close friend.

2 Not having a good grade, Victor couldn't get a decent job.
→ ______________ he didn't have a good grade, Victor couldn't get a decent job.

3 James started at noon, arriving in Sweden around 6 p.m.
→ James started at noon, ______________ he arrived in Sweden around 6 p.m.

4 Seeing the car accident, he didn't help the wounded people on the road.
→ ______________ he saw the car accident, he didn't help the wounded people on the road.

STEP D

어법상 어색한 부분을 찾아 바르게 고치시오.

1 Knowing never what to say to the poor, I just kept silent.
______________ → ______________

2 Be young, Frank and Sophia are so considerate that they can help anybody.
______________ → ______________

3교시 After-Class Questions

[01-03] 주어진 동사를 빈칸에 알맞은 분사로 바꿔 쓰시오.

01 boil (1) I don't like ________ sweet potatoes.
(2) ________ water is dangerous.

02 fall (1) He is sweeping the ________ leaves in the garden.
(2) I am ready to catch the ball ________ from the sky.

03 close (1) He gave a ________ address at the meeting.
(2) They made a decision in the ________ session.

[04-05] 문장의 빈칸에 알맞은 것을 고르시오.

04 Who is the woman ________ at us?

① wave ② waves ③ waving
④ to wave ⑤ to have waved

05 Tony and Andy took a walk for a while with their dogs ________ them.

① follow ② follows ③ followed
④ following ⑤ having followed

[06-08] 밑줄 친 분사의 쓰임이 어법상 어색한 것을 고르시오.

06 ① Emily has seen the man riding the bike.
② We were scared when we met the barking dog.
③ The man wearing the red shirt is my friend.
④ These buildings have remained deserting.
⑤ The students heard their teacher singing a song.

07 ① George Bush had a dream shared by lots of Americans.
② My father had his shoes polished by us.
③ Magma moved inside a volcano causes a lot of small earthquakes.
④ Terry may feel frustrated and confused due to his poor scores.
⑤ Teachers feel so surprised at the behavior of teenagers.

Vocabulary Tips

- sweep 쓸다
- address 연설
- make a decision 결심하다
- session 회의
- wave 손을 흔들다
- take a walk 산책하다
- follow 따라가다(오다)
- bark 짖다
- remain 남아 있다, 계속 ~이다
- desert 버리다
- polish 닦다, 광을 내다
- volcano 화산
- earthquake 지진
- frustrated 좌절감을 느끼는
- confused 혼란스러운
- behavior 행동

08 ① I know the boy <u>called</u> Tommy.
② Look at the <u>broken</u> windows in your room.
③ I like the fantasy novels <u>written</u> by Tolkien.
④ She went up the mountain <u>covered</u> with snow.
⑤ James saw the baby <u>cried</u> in that restroom.

서술형 대비

[09-10] 우리말과 같은 뜻이 되도록 주어진 말을 사용하여 문장을 완성하시오.

09 나의 선생님은 내 발표에 만족하신 것 같다. (my presentation, seem, satisfy)
→ My teacher ______________________________.

10 Mack은 온종일 아무것도 먹지 못해서 피곤하고 배가 고팠다. (eat, not, all day)
→ ____________________, Mack was very tired and hungry.

[11-13] 두 문장이 같은 뜻이 되도록 빈칸에 알맞은 접속사를 고르시오.

11 Being late for school, I was scolded by my homeroom teacher.
→ ________ I was late for school, I was scolded by my homeroom teacher.

① Since ② For ③ Even if
④ Even though ⑤ In case of

12 Smiling brightly, Lisa still looked very sad and gloomy.
→ ________ she smiled brightly, Lisa still looked very sad and gloomy.

① When ② As ③ After
④ Though ⑤ Since

13 Walking down the street, I saw your family talking to my parents.
→ ________ I was walking down the street, I saw your family talking to my parents.

① Even though ② Since ③ If
④ Because ⑤ When

Vocabulary Tips

- **satisfy** 만족시키다
- **scold** 꾸짖다(–scolded–scolded)
- **homeroom teacher** 담임선생님
- **gloomy** 우울한, 어둑어둑한

14 밑줄 친 분사구문 중 어법상 어색한 것은?

① Watching a movie, they had popcorn and Coke.
② Attending this party, Rocky and Jack became close friends.
③ Looking for his lost cats, Rick was crying again and again.
④ Traveled by car, Lucas may suffer from headaches.
⑤ Being busy, Elisa couldn't keep in touch with you for a long time.

[15-16] 주어진 말을 빈칸에 알맞은 형태로 바꿔 쓰시오.

15 Ms. Hathaway had a valuable diamond ring ________. (steal)

16 The main character in this essay is very ________ because spring has gone and her favorite season, summer, has come back again. (excite)

[17-19] 문장의 빈칸에 알맞은 말끼리 짝지은 것을 고르시오.

17

(a) The group of girls ________ on stage is my favorite idol group. (b) The building ________ blue on the hill is Julie's house.

① sung – painted ② sung – painting ③ sing – painted
④ singing – painting ⑤ singing – painted

18

The Gift for Room 7 was a very ________ movie. It made everyone ________.

① touch – touch ② touching – touching ③ touched – touching
④ touching – touched ⑤ touched – touched

19

There were some serious car accidents last night. Lots of ________ people were taken to the hospital downtown, and many cars were also ________.

① injure – damage ② injured – damaging ③ injured – damaged
④ injuring – damage ⑤ injuring – damaging

Vocabulary Tips

- suffer from ~로 고통을 겪다
- headache 두통
- keep in touch with ~와 연락하다
- valuable 값비싼, 귀중한
- main character 주인공
- The Gift for Room 7 (영화) 7번방의 선물
- damage 손상시키다
- be taken to ~로 이송되다

[20-21] 주어진 말을 빈칸에 알맞은 형태로 바꿔 쓰시오.

20 ________________ hard for the midterm exam, I could not pass the English presentation. (study)

21 ________________ too quickly due to the lack of time, your food didn't taste good. (cook)

22 두 문장을 한 문장으로 바꿔 쓸 때 빈칸에 알맞은 말을 쓰시오.

A crying kid was left alone on the playground. He was wearing a black shirt.
→ A crying kid ________ a black shirt was left alone on the playground.

23 주어진 의미를 추가하여 다음 문장의 빈칸을 완성하시오.

(1) My lovely kids fell asleep ____________________________. (TV를 보면서)

(2) My lovely kids fell asleep ____________________________. (팔짱을 낀 채로)

24 밑줄 친 부분을 분사구문으로 바꿔 쓰시오.

The summer festival finally got started <u>and made people excited</u>.
→ The summer festival finally got started, ____________________________.

서술형 대비

25 주어진 말과 분사구문을 이용하여 다음 우리말을 영어로 옮기시오.

너는 열심히 일하지 않아서 해고당했다. (fire)

→

Vocabulary Tips

- presentation 발표
- lack 부족, 결핍
- playground 운동장
- fire 해고하다

분사구문의 시제와 수동태

1교시 Grammar Point

1 분사구문의 시제

	단순분사구문	완료분사구문
용법	부사절과 주절의 시제가 같을 때	부사절이 주절의 시제보다 앞설 때
형태	〈동사원형 + -ing〉	〈having + 과거분사〉

Because I run too much, I am exhausted. 부사절 시제 = 주절 시제
→ **Running** too much, I am exhausted.

Unless I get a student loan, I can't go to college. 부사절 시제 = 주절 시제
→ **Getting** a student loan, I can't go to college.

Since I stayed up last night, I am exhausted. 부사절 시제 ≠ 주절 시제
→ **Having stayed** up last night, I am exhausted.

Though I just had dinner, I am hungry. 부사절 시제 ≠ 주절 시제
→ **Having** just **had** dinner, I am hungry.

2 분사구문의 수동태

	단순수동태 분사구문	완료수동태 분사구문
용법	부사절과 주절의 시제가 같을 때	부사절이 주절의 시제보다 앞설 때
형태	〈being + 과거분사〉	〈having been + 과거분사〉

*수동태 분사구문에 쓰인 being이나 having been은 생략할 수 있다.

When we were asked to leave here, we felt humiliated.
→ **(Being) Asked** to leave here, we felt humiliated.

Although I was invited to the party, I am still at home.
→ **(Having been) Invited** to the party, I am still at home.

Because she was disappointed with me, she doesn't talk to me.
→ **(Having been) Disappointed** with me, she doesn't talk to me.

Grammar Tips

- **독립분사구문**

부사절의 주어와 주절의 주어가 달라서 부사절의 주어를 남겨둔 분사구문

It snowing a lot, we can ski.
← As **it** snows a lot, we can ski.

- **분사의 생략**

수동태를 분사구문으로 바꿀 때 being, having been은 생략 가능하지만 수동이 아닌 경우는 생략할 수 없다.

(Being) Written in easy words, this book can be read by kids.
Being young, he is wise.

- **분사구문의 의미 혼동을 피하기 위해 접속사를 남겨두기도 한다.**

When turning around, Ron saw a beautiful girl.

Grammar Plus+ 비인칭 독립분사구문

관용적으로 쓰이는 분사구문을 말하며, 다음과 같은 것들이 있다.

generally speaking (일반적으로 말해서)	frankly speaking (솔직히 말해서)
strictly speaking (엄격히 말해서)	judging from (~으로 판단하건데)
compared with (~과 비교하자면)	speaking of (~에 대해 말하자면)
considering (~을 고려하면)	supposing (만약 ~라면)

> 정답 및 해설 24쪽

2교시 In - Class Questions

빈칸에 알맞은 말을 〈보기〉에서 골라 완료분사구문으로 쓰시오.

보기 finish watch join bear

1 ______________ the choir last year, she didn't practice.

2 ______________ in Canada, I can speak English well.

3 ______________ his work, he is going shopping.

4 ______________ TV until late at night, the boy went to school without his homework.

괄호 안에서 알맞은 말을 고르시오.

1 **(Not having / Not having had)** the toy, the boy wants to buy it.

2 **(Working / Having worked)** outside all day, he has quite dark skin.

3 **(Being told / Having been told)** the news, we were very surprised.

4 **(Meeting / Having met)** them before, I got along with them easily.

우리말과 같은 뜻이 되도록 주어진 말을 사용하여 문장을 완성하시오.

1 우리는 목동에 도착한 후에 식당으로 들어갔다. (arrive)
→ ________ ________ in Mok-dong, we went to the restaurant.

2 그 책은 아랍어로 쓰여서 읽을 수가 없다. (written)
→ ________ ________ ________ in Arabic, the book could not be read.

3 그 컵은 아주 오래 전에 만들어졌지만 나는 매일 사용한다. (make)
→ ________ ________ ________ ________ ________ long time ago, I use it every day.

우리말과 같은 뜻이 되도록 빈칸에 알맞은 말을 쓰시오.

1 날씨가 더워져서 엄마는 창문을 여셨다.
→ ________ ________ warmer, Mom opened the window.

2 그녀의 외모에 대해 말하자면, 그녀는 모델같이 보인다.
→ ________ ________ her appearance, she seems to be a model.

3 모든 새들이 총소리에 놀라서 날아가 버렸다.
→ ________ by the shot, all of the birds flew away.

3교시 After-Class Questions

[01-03] 문장의 빈칸에 알맞은 것을 고르시오.

01 ________________ his homework, he went to bed to get up early tomorrow.

① Finish ② Finished ③ Having finished
④ Having been finished ⑤ To be been finished

Grammar Plus+

02 ________________, my sister and I are not good at helping my mom at home.

① Compared with ② Frankly speaking ③ Judging from
④ Supposing ⑤ Considering

03 ________________ notified, the policemen and CSI arrived too late to arrest the criminals and to secure witnesses.

① Have been ② Having been ③ Not having been
④ Having not been ⑤ No having been

04 밑줄 친 부분 중 생략할 수 있는 것은?

①Being left alone ②at home, ③Terry ④could watch the interesting TV program ⑤and play the computer game.

05 〈보기〉와 같은 의미로 쓰인 문장을 두 개 고르시오.

보기 As they had been injured in the car accident, Ellen and his parents couldn't take the airplane.

① Injured in the car accident, Ellen and his parents couldn't take the airplane.
② Ellen and his parents had been injured in the car accident, they couldn't take the airplane.
③ Had been injured in the car accident, Ellen and his parents couldn't take the airplane.
④ Have been injured in the car accident, Ellen and his parents couldn't take the airplane.
⑤ Having been injured in the car accident, Ellen and his parents couldn't take the airplane.

서술형 대비

06 주어진 말을 사용하여 다음 우리말을 영어로 옮기시오.

그 어린 남자아이는 그 영화를 보고 난 후에 마치 영웅인 것처럼 행동했다. (see)
→ ______________________________, the young boy acted as if he were a hero.

Vocabulary Tips

- notify 알리다, 통보하다
- arrest 체포하다
- criminal 범죄자
- secure 확보하다
- witness 목격자
- injure 부상을 입다, 부상을 입히다
- car accident 자동차 사고
- hero 영웅

Grammar Plus+

07 우리말과 같은 뜻이 되도록 할 때 빈칸에 알맞은 것은?

네가 원어민이 아닌 것을 고려한다면, 너의 일본어 실력은 훌륭하다.

→ ________ you are not a native speaker, your Japanese is excellent.

① Speaking of ② Considering that ③ Talking of
④ Supposing that ⑤ Granting that

08 문장의 빈칸에 알맞은 말끼리 짝지은 것은?

(a) ________ in English, those magazines are easy to read.
(b) ________ in Korea, Minji is good at speaking Korean.

① Write – Born ② Having written – Being born
③ Wrote – Having been born ④ Being written – Being born
⑤ Written – Born

09 밑줄 친 부분 중 어법상 어색한 것은?

You have had some experiences ①that you are very ②disappointed when you watch some musicals with high expectations. Here is an example. ③Having been watched a new musical, your acquaintances tell you that it is not only very ④interesting but is also a must-see musical. However, in reality, it ⑤depends on your personal preference.

[10-13] 주어진 말을 빈칸에 알맞은 형태로 바꿔 쓰시오.

10 ________________ the newly issued journals all night, Jonathan feels extremely tired during the lecture. (research)

11 ________________ long ago, the Bible is considered quite believable. (write)

12 ________________ very much money for my parents, they told me that the food was really bad at the restaurant at that time. (pay)

13 ________________ a lot last night, the roads are slippery. So the city has decided to scatter calcium chloride on it. (snow)

Vocabulary Tips

- expectation 기대
- example 예
- acquaintance 지인, 아는 사람
- must-see 반드시 봐야 할
- in reality 사실은
- depend on ~에 달려있다
- personal preference 개인적인 선호
- issue 출판하다
- extremely 매우
- slippery 미끄러운
- scatter 뿌리다
- calcium chloride 염화칼슘(얼음, 눈을 녹여주는 물질)

[14-15] 밑줄 친 부사절을 분사구문으로 바르게 바꾼 것을 고르시오.

14 When you signed a contract for your new apartment, you should have reviewed all of the provisions carefully, which was your big mistake.

① You signing a contract for your new apartment,
② You having signed a contract for your new apartment,
③ Signing a contract for your new apartment,
④ Signed a contract for your new apartment,
⑤ You signed a contract for your new apartment,

15 Though Grandma had been hit by a car last night, no one dared to tell the news to my mom until now because her farther just died in a car accident last month.

① Being hit by a car last night,
② Hit by a car last night,
③ Grandma having been hit by a car last night,
④ Grandma was hit by a car last night,
⑤ Grandma being hit by a car last night,

16 밑줄 친 부분을 생략할 수 없는 것은?

① Being interested in dancing, I will attend an audition.
② Having learned many Chinese characters, I can study Chinese easily.
③ Having been cooked by me, the food tastes good.
④ Although being young, she can manage this project.
⑤ While I was watching TV, I fell asleep.

서술형 대비

[17-19] 다음 문장을 분사구문으로 바꿔 쓰시오.

17 Since Minju hadn't worked very hard, she missed a chance to be promoted.

→ ______________________________

18 When the little girl was left alone, she began to get scared.

→ ______________________________

19 Because the due date for the books had passed, I paid the late fee.

→ ______________________________

Vocabulary Tips

- contract 계약서
- provision 조항
- Chinese character 한문
- promote 승진시키다
- due date 만기일
- late fee 연체료

[20-21] 주어진 문장을 분사구문으로 바꿔 쓸 때 빈칸에 알맞은 것을 고르시오.

20 After Jack had completed his homework assignment, he went to an Internet cafe to play computer games.

→ ________________ his homework assignment, Jack went to an Internet cafe to play computer games.

① Complete ② To complete ③ Having completed
④ Being completed ⑤ It being completed

21 When her class was finished, Sunny went to her part-time job.

→ ________________, Sunny went to her part-time job.

① Finishing ② Being finished ③ It being finished
④ Having finished ⑤ Her class being finished

[22-23] 어법상 어색한 부분을 찾아 바르게 고르시오.

22 Not having published, his novel is getting popular through the Internet.

________________ → ________________

23 Having not understand English, Hannah tried to communicate with her foreign friends.

________________ → ________________

Grammar Plus+

[24-25] 밑줄 친 부분의 쓰임이 올바른 것을 고르시오.

24 ① Strictly spoken, the answer is not correct.
② Walked down the street, I met my ex-girlfriend.
③ I bought a brand-new camera making in Japan.
④ Speaking of her journey, have you ever been to Hawaii?
⑤ Having not a ticket, Adam is not able to enter the concert hall.

25 ① Alice was lying on the couch with her eyes closing.
② Inviting to her birthday party, I was so happy.
③ Supposing you are wrong, what will you do then?
④ After finished my daily chores, I sat down for a cup of coffee.
⑤ The car accident, happened half an hour ago, is still hindering the flow of traffic.

Vocabulary Tips

- part-time job 아르바이트, 시간제 일
- publish 출판하다
- communicate 의사소통을 하다
- hinder 방해하다
- flow 흐름

Final Test

01 주어진 말을 빈칸에 알맞은 형태로 바꿔 쓰시오.

(1) Lily and her sister were praying with their hands ________. (hold)

(2) Bruce sat down on the armchair with his legs ________. (shake)

02 문장의 빈칸에 들어갈 수 없는 것은?

> ________ at the accident, Paul called one of his friends.

① Surprised ② Being surprised
③ As surprised ④ Having been surprised
⑤ As he is surprised

[03-04] 두 문장이 같은 뜻이 되도록 할 때 빈칸에 알맞은 것을 고르시오.

03

> Preparing lunch, my mother thought that why she had to prepare it for her children.
> → ________ my mother prepared lunch, she thought that why she had to prepare it for her children.

① If ② Since
③ When ④ Even if
⑤ Because

04

> Because Emily has never ridden an elephant before, she can't teach her friend how to ride one.
> → ________ an elephant before, she can't teach her friend how to ride one.

① Not riding ② Never riding
③ Never have ridden ④ Never having ridden
⑤ Never having been ridden

[05-06] 다음 중 어법상 어색한 문장을 고르시오.

05 ① Being no empty rooms, we can't sleep here.
② Being only fifteen, Jonathan couldn't watch this movie.
③ Judging from my experience, she will be very late.
④ Wasting lots of time, you were not able to pass the entrance exam.
⑤ It being a beautiful sunny day, Sam didn't go out and stayed at home.

06 ① Having been deceived by my students, I cannot trust them anymore these days.
② Having failed ten times, I passed the national exam at last.
③ Having been seen Vanessa before, I recognized her at once.
④ Not having been read very often, these books are covered with dust.
⑤ Having checked this information in advance, Maria knows how to handle some problems.

[07-08] 우리말을 영어로 바르게 옮긴 것을 고르시오.

07

> 너는 더 많은 노력을 한다면 더 좋은 고등학교에 진학할 수 있다.

① You make more of an effort, you can enter a better high school.
② Make more of an effort, you can enter a better high school.
③ If making more of an effort, you can enter a better high school.
④ Having making more of an effort, you can enter a better high school.
⑤ It making more of an effort, you can enter a better high school.

08

오늘은 월요일이어서 직원 중 한 명이 그 안건에 대해 논쟁하지 말자고 제안했다.

① Today, Monday, one of the employees suggests not arguing about the agenda.
② Today is Monday, one of the employees suggests not arguing about the agenda.
③ Today having Monday, one of the employees suggests not arguing about the agenda.
④ It is Monday, one of the employees suggests not arguing about the agenda.
⑤ It being Monday, one of the employees suggests not arguing about the agenda.

09 **〈보기〉와 의미가 같은 문장은?**

보기 Since my car had broken down, I had to commute by bus.

① Had broken down, I had to commute by bus.
② Having broken down, I had to commute by bus.
③ My car had broken down, I had to commute by bus.
④ My car having broken down, I had to commute by bus.
⑤ My car having been broken down, I had to commute by bus.

서술형 대비

10 **우리말과 같은 뜻이 되도록 주어진 말을 사용하여 문장의 빈칸을 완성시오.**

일반적으로 말하면, 어린아이들은 어떤 것이든 더 쉽고 더 빠르게 습득한다. (speak)

→ ______________________, young children can acquire anything more easily and quickly.

11 **주어진 말을 빈칸에 알맞은 형태로 바꿔 쓰시오.**

When we take this medicine, it can kill viruses, change __________ cells, and even destroy cancer cells. (age)

12 **다음 중 어법상 어색한 문장을 모두 고르시오.**

① There are two glasses filled with water.
② They're looking at a menu wrote in English.
③ He was very embarrassing to look at her face.
④ The woman wearing the red dress is Kevin's mom.
⑤ *The Gift for Room 7* is a very interesting and touching movie.

13 **밑줄 친 분사의 쓰임이 어법상 어색한 것은?**

① I saw a girl singing on the street.
② I met my friend sitting in the park.
③ There is an old tree standing in the garden.
④ There are many nice cars making in Korea.
⑤ The girl holding the dog in front of the vending machine is Jane.

14 **다음 중 어법상 올바른 문장은?**

① I know the man walk with his dog.
② Qualifying for the job, he should be hired.
③ There is a destroying building next to the bank.
④ Not having enough time, I have to take a taxi instead of a bus.
⑤ Admitted what you did to him, I still cannot forgive you.

15 밑줄 친 부분을 동명사와 현재분사로 구분하시오.

① He likes playing soccer.
② Look at the rising sun.
③ He got in the waiting taxi.
④ We bought a new washing machine.
⑤ There's a man sleeping on the bench.
⑥ You can meet him in the waiting room.
⑦ I need a sleeping bag to go camping.
⑧ I was cooking in the kitchen when you called me.
⑨ We don't use this outdoor swimming pool in the winter.
⑩ You cannot smoke here. Please use the smoking room over there.

(1) 동명사(6개): ____________________

(2) 현재분사(4개): ____________________

16 밑줄 친 부분 중 어법상 어색한 것은?

①Having not ②finished the courses, he ③could not get his ④master's degree ⑤from his university.

17 밑줄 친 부분 중 어법상 올바른 것은?

① My sister had her purse stole.
② We saw people danced on stage.
③ Sandy had his hair cutting.
④ From judging his behavior, he is not nice.
⑤ A broken arm should be in cast.

18 밑줄 친 분사구문을 부사절로 바꿔 쓰시오.

Many teens look in the mirror, wearing clothes.
→ Many teens look in the mirror, ____________ ____________________.

19 밑줄 친 분사구문을 부사절로 바르게 바꿔 쓴 것은?

Not sleeping much, I looked very energetic while attending the meeting.

① If I didn't sleep much,
② When I don't sleep much,
③ Even though I didn't sleep much,
④ As I didn't sleep much,
⑤ Though I don't sleep much,

서술형 대비

[20-21] 밑줄 친 부사절을 분사구문으로 바꿔 쓰시오.

20

If your book is written in a hurry, it will have lots of errors.
→ ____________________, your book will have lots of errors.

21

While I was putting up green wallpaper, my wife cleaned the attic.
→ ____________________, my wife cleaned the attic.

[22-23] 문장의 빈칸에 알맞은 말끼리 짝지은 것을 고르시오.

22

(a) ________ to many foreign countries, Keilen has many exotic souvenirs at home.
(b) People often feel their lives ________.

① Travel – boring
② Traveled – bored
③ Traveling – boring
④ Having traveled – boring
⑤ Having been traveled – bored

23

(a) ________, you are not supportive enough to do this group work.
(b) Mina sat in the classroom with her legs ________.

① Frankly speaking – crossed
② Generally speaking – crossing
③ Frankly speaking – having crossed
④ Judging from – crossing
⑤ Speaking of – having crossed

24 주어진 말과 지시에 맞게 다음 우리말을 영어로 옮기시오.

너는 엄마를 놀라게 하고 싶지 않다면 그 사실을 말하지 않는 것이 좋다. (surprise, had better)

(1) [부사절로] ____________________

____

(2) [분사구문으로] ____________________

____

25 주어진 말과 분사구문을 이용하여 다음 우리말을 영어로 옮기고, 생략 가능한 부분에 괄호를 치시오.

아기가 매운 음식을 먹게 되어서 배가 아픈 것이다. (feed, stomachache)

→ ____________________

____

26 주어진 말을 빈칸에 알맞은 형태로 바꿔 쓰시오.

(1) ____________ in paintings, we plan to visit some museums. (interest)

(2) At the museums, we looked at many ____________ paintings. (interest)

27 두 문장이 같은 뜻이 되도록 할 때 빈칸에 알맞은 것은?

Being injured, Alice was not able to go to the wedding ceremony.
→ ________ Alice was injured, she was not able to go to the wedding ceremony.

① Though ② If ③ So
④ Because ⑤ With

[28-29] 문장의 빈칸에 들어갈 수 없는 것을 고르시오.

28

The subway ________, I was late for an important meeting with a client.

① having delayed ② arriving late
③ breaking down ④ delayed
⑤ crowded

29

So many trees and flowers ________ it, the garden looks beautiful.

① filling ② covered
③ brightening ④ being around
⑤ surrounding

30 문장의 빈칸에 알맞은 것은?

________, glasses can correct most sight defects.

① When well fitted ② Well fitting
③ Well fitted when ④ Well fitting when
⑤ When having well fitted

≫ 정답 및 해설 27쪽

Extracurricular Activities

▸ *Sentence Writing*

PART A Complete the sentences describing the picture.

According to the Billboard chart, *Hey, Jude* was the most popular song in the 1960s.

1 ________________ in 1968, it topped the Billboard chart for almost 9 weeks.
(발표가 되었을 때, release)

2 *Hey, Jude* ________________ as one of the bestselling songs in the 1960s,
(기록된 후에, record)
composer Paul McCartney became famous.

3 ________________ so much money, he felt very depressed and lonely due to his
(매우 많은 돈을 벌었지만, earn)
parents' divorce.

4 ________________ the song, people can feel how much he wanted to send us a hopeful
(그 노래를 들어보면, listen to)
message.

PART B Change the Korean into English by using the given words.

1 몇몇 아이들은 그들의 친구들로부터 고립된 느낌을 받을 수 있다. (can, from their friends, isolate)
→ ________________

2 Lucy는 피곤했기 때문에 평소보다 일찍 잠잤다. (than usual, being)
→ ________________

3 그의 억양으로 판단하건데, 그는 영국사람임에 틀림없다. (accent, Englishman)
→ ________________

▸ Further Studies 학교 시험에 자주 나오는 Idioms ④

- have ants in one's pants 부산스럽다, 안절부절 못하다
- give someone the creeps 섬뜩하게 하다, 소름끼치게 하다
- drive a hard bargain 흥정을 잘하다
- peter out (= fizzle out) 용두사미가 되다
- pick up the bill (= pick up the tab = foot the bill) 계산을 치르다, 돈을 내다
- get cold feet 자신(용기)을 잃다, 겁먹다
- on the house (= free of charge, complimentary) 공짜로, 무료로
- the real go of it (= the hang of it = the knack of it) 요령, 감각, 감
- feel the pinch 압박/위기감을 느끼다
- fringe benefits 급료 이외의 혜택, 부가 급여
- be sent packing (= be kicked out) 쫓겨나다
- keep a straight face 엄숙한/웃지 않는 표정을 짓다
- bite the bullet 힘든 상황을 잘 견뎌내다
- back out of ~을 취소하다
- ace in the hole 비장품, 비장의 무기
- rain check 뒤로 미루다, 연기하다
- put something on the back burner 문제를 보류하다, 뒤로 미루다
- a slight edge on ~보다 약간 우세한
- in seventh heaven 매우 기분이 좋은
- the cream of the crop 최상의 것, 최상의 사람
- high as a kite 기분이 매우 좋은
- have an eye for ~에 대한 심미안이 있다
- a makeshift 미봉책, 임시변통
- corny (= old-fashioned) 너무 구식인
- come to terms with 타협할 수 있는
- clamp down on 억압/탄압하다
- pink slip 해고 통지서
- gym rat 운동광, 운동에 미친 사람
- game geek 게임광
- alcoholic/fitaholic/workaholic 알코올 중독/운동 중독/일 중독

비교
(Comparisons)

Day 16 | 비교급, 최상급

비교
- 원급 〈as + 형용사/부사의 원급 + as〉
- 비교급 〈형용사/부사의 비교급 + than〉
- 최상급 〈형용사/부사의 최상급 + in/of + 장소 명사/집합 명사〉

기출 맛보기

다음 중 어법상 어색한 문장을 고르시오. (강동구 ○○중학교)

① My class played soccer better than the other classes.

② This restaurant's service is as worse as Pizza World's.

③ It is still one of the most remarkable landmarks in Seoul.

④ No other student at school is as tall as me.

⑤ Gangwon-do is not as hot as Jeju Island.

해설

② [worse → bad] 동등비교는 〈as + 형용사의 원급 + as ...〉로 표현해야 한다.

① 〈비교급 + than〉: '~보다 더 …한'

③ 〈one of the + 형용사의 최상급 + 복수명사〉: '가장 ~한 것들 중의 하나'

④ 〈no other + 단수명사 ~ as + 형용사 + as ...〉는 최상급 표현이다.

⑤ 〈not as + 형용사 원급 + as ...〉: '…만큼 ~하지 않다'

해석

① 우리 반은 다른 반들보다 축구를 더 잘한다.

② 이 식당의 서비스는 Pizza World 만큼이나 나쁘다.

③ 그곳은 여전히 서울에서 가장 주목할 만한 랜드마크 중 하나이다.

④ 학교에서 다른 어떤 학생도 나만큼 키가 크지 않다. (내가 가장 크다.)

⑤ 강원도는 제주도만큼 덥지 않다.

정답 ②

DAY 16

비교급, 최상급

1교시 Grammar Point

1 원급 표현

〈as + 원급 + as ~〉 '~만큼 …한'
〈not + as[so] + 원급 + as ~〉 '~만큼 …하지 않은'
〈배수사 + as + 원급 + as ~〉 '~보다 몇 배 더 …한'
〈as + 원급 + as possible〉 '가능한 한 …하게'
(= as + 원급 + as + 주어 + can)

Cathy can run **as** fast **as** Kelly.
Jay has **not as[so]** many books **as** I do.
Gina studies **twice as** hard **as** Jay does.
She will bake **as** many pies **as possible**. [= as many as she can]

2 비교급 표현

〈the + 비교급 ~, the + 비교급 ...〉 '~할수록 더 …한'
〈비교급 + and + 비교급〉 '점점 더 ~한'
비교급 강조 〈much, far, even, still, a lot + 비교급〉 '훨씬 더 ~한'

The more I eat, **the fatter** I get. (나는 더 많이 먹으면 먹을수록 더 뚱뚱해진다.)
It is getting **darker and darker**. (날이 점점 더 어두워진다.)
The population of China is **much larger** than that of Korea. [that = the population]

3 최상급 표현

〈the + 최상급 + in 단수명사(장소, 집단)/of 복수명사〉 '~ 중에서 가장 …한'
〈one of the + 최상급 + 복수명사〉 '가장 ~한 것 중에 하나'
〈최상급 + 주어 + have + ever + 과거분사〉 '~가 (경험)한 것 중에 가장 …한'
최상급의 여러 가지 표현: 〈the + 최상급 + in 장소 / of 복수명사〉
= 〈No (other) + 단수명사 + 동사 + 비교급 + than〉
= 〈No (other) + 단수명사 + 동사 + as + 원급 + as〉
= 〈비교급 + than any other + 단수명사〉

Brian is **the tallest** in our class/of six boys.
This is **one of the best dishes** in Korea.
My mom is **the most diligent woman I have ever seen**.
Hangeul is **the best** writing system in the world.
= **No other** writing system in the world is **better than** *Hangeul*.
= **No other** writing system in the world is **as good as** *Hangeul*.
= *Hangeul* is **better than any other** writing system in the world.

Grammar Tips

- **than 대신에 to를 쓰는 라틴 비교급**

senior to (~보다 선배인, 손위인)
junior to (~보다 후배인, 손아래인)
superior to (~보다 나은)
inferior to (~보다 못한)
prefer A to B (B보다 A를 더 좋아하다)

Fiona is ten years **senior to** me. [= older than]

- **열등비교**

〈less + 원급 + than〉 '~보다 덜 …한'
(= not + as[so] + 원급 + as ~)

He is **less tall than** I.
= He is **not as[so] tall as** I.

- **비교급 앞에 the를 쓰는 경우**

문장에 of the two가 있을 때

You are **the older** *of the two*.

- **최상급에 the를 쓰지 않는 경우**

(1) 부사의 최상급
He can drink milk **fastest**.

(2) 동일 대상을 비교할 때
I am **prettiest** after the shower.

- **비교 대상의 일치**

비교 구문에서 비교하는 대상은 서로 같은 형태여야 한다.

My sneakers look more comfortable than **yours**. [yours = your sneakers]

The color of my shirt is different from that of your shirt. [that = the color]

The **ears** of a rabbit are longer than those of a monkey. [those = the ears]

2교시 In-Class Questions

STEP A

빈칸에 알맞은 말을 〈보기〉에서 골라 알맞은 형태로 고쳐 쓰시오.

보기 good high expensive

1 Your English is getting ______________ and ______________.

2 Mt. Everest is ______________ ______________ mountain in the world.

3 My jacket is twice as ______________ as yours.

STEP B

괄호 안에서 알맞은 말을 모두 고르시오.

1 Chris is the cleverest (among / between / of) us.

2 Today is the happiest day (as / in / for) my life.

3 I ran as fast as I (can / could / possible).

4 Sean isn't poor. He has as (much / more / better) money as Tom.

STEP C

우리말과 같은 뜻이 되도록 주어진 말을 사용하여 문장을 완성하시오.

1 나이가 들면 들수록 기억력이 점점 더 나빠진다. (bad)
→ ______________ ______________ we grow, ______________ ______________ our memories become.

2 기린은 가장 키가 큰 동물 중 하나이다. (tall)
→ A giraffe is ______________ of ______________ ______________ ______________.

3 강아지는 고양이보다 덜 똑똑하다. (intelligent)
→ A dog is ______________ ______________ ______________ a cat.

4 인도의 인구는 독일의 인구보다 훨씬 더 많다. (far, large)
→ The population of India is ______________ ______________ ______________ ______________ of Germany.

STEP D

주어진 말을 사용하여 다음 우리말을 영어로 옮기시오.

1 다이아몬드는 다른 어떤 물질보다 단단하다. (material, than, any)
→ ____

2 이 식탁의 다리가 저 식탁의 다리보다 더 길다. (long, leg)
→ ____

3 날씨가 점점 따뜻해지고 있다. (get, and)
→ ____

Final Test

[01-02] 문장의 빈칸에 알맞은 말을 고르시오.

01

> His first movie was not as ________ as the second one.

① successful ② successfully
③ more successful ④ more successfully
⑤ the most successful

02

> This device is technically inferior ________ its competitors.

① in ② as
③ to ④ than
⑤ then

03 다음 문장에서 twice의 위치로 알맞은 곳은?

> The population of South Korea (①) is (②) as (③) large (④) as (⑤) that of your country.

04 두 문장이 같은 의미가 되도록 할 때 빈칸에 알맞은 것은?

> Please let those students know the results as soon as possible.
> → Please let those students know the results ________.

① as possible ② as soonly as
③ as soon as you ④ as possible as you
⑤ as soon as you can

[05-06] 다음 중 어법상 어색한 문장을 고르시오.

05 ① Monica is more overweight than fat.
② Mr. Hong is superior to the other members.
③ Her disease is not as serious as I thought.
④ The size of your house is very bigger than that of mine.
⑤ Gina is less wise and intelligent than Suyeong.

06 ① My condition was more worse than his.
② Mina is even taller than her father.
③ The horse is the fastest one of all.
④ This bag is even heavier than that one.
⑤ Her dancing is far more popular than her singing.

07 문장의 의미가 나머지와 다른 것은?

① Vatican City is the smallest country in the world.
② No country in the world is smaller than Vatican City.
③ No country in the world is as small as Vatican City.
④ Vatican City is not as small as any other country in the world.
⑤ Vatican City is smaller than any other country in the world.

08 주어진 말을 문장의 빈칸에 알맞은 형태로 바꿔 쓰시오.

(1) Hyunmin is the third ________ student in his class. (nice)

(2) Their friend Luna is even ________ than Jen. (honest)

09 우리말을 영어로 바르게 옮긴 것은?

> 당신은 그 일을 더 빨리 시작하면 할수록 더 빨리 끝낼 것이다.

① The soon you start the work, you will finish it.
② Sooner you start the work, sooner you will finish it.
③ The sooner you start the work, the sooner you will finish it.
④ You start the work the sooner, you will finish it the sooner.
⑤ The more you start the work, the more you will finish it.

10 대화의 빈칸에 들어갈 수 없는 것은?

> A: Who is the ________ player on your team?
> B: I think Blair is the ________.

① smartest　　② best
③ fastest　　④ difficulties
⑤ greatest

서술형 대비

[11-12] 우리말과 같은 뜻이 되도록 빈칸에 알맞은 말을 쓰시오.

11

> 민재는 기말고사에서 네 번째로 높은 점수를 받은 학생이다.
> → Minjae is the student who got ________ ________ ________ ________ on the final exam.

12

> 너는 더 일찍 일어날수록 더 긴 하루를 보낼 수 있다.
> → ________ ________ you get up, ________ ________ a day you can spend.

[13-14] 두 문장이 같은 뜻이 되도록 빈칸에 알맞은 말을 쓰시오.

13

> Brian shouted at me as loudly as possible.
> → Brian shouted at me as loudly as ________ ________.

14

> Studying math is not as difficult as I expected.
> → Studying math is ________ difficult ________ I expected.

15 어법상 어색한 부분을 찾아 바르게 고치시오.

> The size of my cell phone is bigger than yours.

________ → ________

16 다음 중 어법상 어색한 문장을 두 개 고르시오.

① The more, the better.
② I don't have as much money as you.
③ No other city in Korea is bigger than Seoul.
④ Health is more important than any other things.
⑤ The weather here is getting more and more warmer.

17 문장의 빈칸에 알맞은 말끼리 짝지은 것은?

Insu ________ playing dodge ball ________ playing tennis.

① would rather – than ② would rather – to
③ prefer – to ④ prefers – than
⑤ prefers – to

18 괄호 안에서 알맞은 말을 고르시오.

(1) Mr. Kim speaks Arabic more (**better / fluently**) than me.

(2) Juhee is (**tall / the taller**) of the two.

(3) We want to move to a (**little / less**) crowded place.

19 밑줄 친 부분 중 어법상 어색한 것은?

①During the field trip, our group members will study ②twice as ③many stars ④as we ⑤possible.

20 대화에서 어법상 어색한 곳을 모두 고르시오.

① A: Seoul has the most crowded population in the world.
② B: No, I guess it isn't as worse as New York.
③ A: Really? What about the traffic?
④ B: The traffic is also a lot worse there.
⑤ A: Wow, it seems to be one of the busiest city that I have ever heard of.

21 문장의 의미가 나머지와 다른 것은?

① Tom is the strongest boy in his class.
② Tom is stronger than any other boy in his class.
③ No other boy in his class is stronger than Tom.
④ No other boy in his class is as strong as Tom.
⑤ Tom is not as strong as the other boys in his class.

22 두 문장이 같은 뜻이 되도록 빈칸에 알맞은 말을 쓰시오.

As you study harder, your score will be better.
→ ________ ________ you study, ________ ________ your score will be.

23 다음 중 어법상 올바른 문장은?

① She is one of the best actress in Korea.
② He is the most nice guy in the world.
③ No other students at our school aren't kinder than you.
④ His father was on the most famous soccer team.
⑤ The further you leave your family, the more you miss them.

24 밑줄 친 말을 어법상 알맞은 형태로 바꾸시오.

This smartphone is probably the good cell phone in the world.

① better ② well
③ nice ④ best
⑤ great

25 짝지은 두 문장의 의미가 같지 않은 것은?

① This car is more expensive than that one.
→ That car is cheaper than this one.
② Bob is smarter than James.
→ James isn't as smart as Bob.
③ My sister's room is not as large as my room.
→ My room is larger than my sister's room.
④ Bill eats two times as much food as I eat.
→ Bill eats two times more food than I eat.
⑤ Wayne plays the piano better than Raymond.
→ Wayne plays the piano as well as Raymond.

서술형 대비

26 우리말과 같은 뜻이 되도록 주어진 단어를 바르게 배열하시오.

Jason은 나보다 세 살이 많다.
(Jason / I / to / years / is / senior / three)

→ ____________________

27 우리말과 같은 뜻이 되도록 빈칸에 알맞은 말을 쓰시오.

Brian은 우리 반의 모든 학생들 중에서 가장 열심히 공부한다.
→ Brian studies ________ of all of the students in the class.

28 표의 내용과 일치하지 않는 문장은?

이 름	Cathy	Sean	Kyle	Keilen
점 수	80	40	95	75

① Cathy got twice as many points as Sean.
② Cathy did not get as many points as Kyle.
③ Kyle got more points than any other student.
④ Cathy got as good points as Keilen.
⑤ Sean got the fewest points of all.

[29-30] 〈보기〉의 두 문장을 한 문장으로 바르게 바꾼 것을 고르시오.

29

보기 This movie is very good. I have never seen a movie like that.

① This is the best movie I have ever seen.
② This movie is as good as that one.
③ The more movies I see, the better I feel.
④ I feel better and better when I see the movie.
⑤ Whenever I see this movie, I feel very good.

30

보기 The weather was warm last week. This week, the weather is getting warmer.

① I like the warmer weather here.
② The warmer the weather is, the better I feel.
③ The weather is warm as it becomes summer.
④ The weather here is the warmest in the world.
⑤ The weather is getting warmer and warmer.

≫ 정답 및 해설 29쪽

Extracurricular Activities

▸ *Sentence Writing*

 Complete the sentences describing the picture.

1 The Golden Gate Bridge is ______________ in the United States.
(가장 유명한 다리 중 하나, famous)

2 When it was proposed to be built, the estimated cost was over 100 million dollars. Joseph Strauss, a young engineer, came up with a new idea. It was ______________ the original one.
(처음 것만큼 비싸지는 않았다, expensive)

3 First, he had thought it would cost 17 million dollars. However, it cost ______________ he expected. Anyway, the bridge has become a symbol of the city of San Francisco.
(그가 예상했던 것보다 두 배의 비용이 들었다, much)

PART B Change the Korean into English by using the given words.

1 이 책은 내가 기대했던 것보다 훨씬 더 재미있다. (even, expect, interesting)
→ ______________

2 이 상점은 저 상점만큼 붐빈다. (store, crowded)
→ ______________

3 서울은 한국에서 가장 큰 도시 중 하나다. (one, big)
→ ______________

4 우리의 세계는 점점 더 좁아지고 있다. (get, small)
→ ______________

▸ Further Studies 학교 시험에 자주 나오는 Idioms ⑤

- ▶ jump on the bandwagon 시류에 편승하다(유리한 쪽으로 붙다)
- ▶ hit the books 열심히 공부하다
- ▶ sharp dresser 옷을 환상적으로 잘 입는 사람
- ▶ I am in my birthday suit 난 알몸이야
- ▶ for the birds (= silly) 어리석은 (*cf.* for birds 새를 위하여)
- ▶ bring down the house 사람들을 포복절도하게 만들다
- ▶ to die for 너무나 매력적인
- ▶ pros and cons 찬반, 장점과 단점
- ▶ just the ticket 꼭 필요한 그 무엇
- ▶ clockwatcher 퇴근시간만 목이 빠지게 기다리는 사람
- ▶ a homeless romantic 백마 탄 왕자님을 만날 거라는 가망 없는 꿈을 쫓는 사람
- ▶ jump out of the frying pan and into the fire 설상가상, 갈수록 태산, 산 너머 산
- ▶ make a drama out of everything 작은 문제를 심각한 문제로 만들다
- ▶ two-timer 양다리 걸치는 사람
- ▶ word of mouth 입소문
- ▶ bigmouth 입이 가벼운 사람, 비밀을 잘 지키지 않는 사람
- ▶ potty mouth 말씨가 거친 사람
- ▶ lip service (= sweet talk) 사탕발림
- ▶ backstabber 중상 모략하는 사람
- ▶ kiss somebody's ass (= brown-nose) 아첨하다, 아부하다
- ▶ sleep like a log 업어 가도 모를 정도로 깊이 잠든
- ▶ hit the bottle 밥 먹듯 술을 마시다
- ▶ hit the headlines 신문이나 TV 등의 언론에 대서특필 되다
- ▶ turncoat 변절자
- ▶ fussy eater 편식하는 사람
- ▶ Beggars can't be chooser. 얻어먹는 처지에 찬밥 더운밥 가리게 생겼냐.
- ▶ a come-from-behind victory 역전우승
- ▶ be on everyone's lips 인구에 회자되다(세상 사람들 입에 자주 오르내리다)
- ▶ shoot a hole in (= damage) ~에 흠집을 내다
- ▶ pickup line 여자의 환심을 사기 위해 하는 말

Unit 09 관계사 (Relatives)

관계사
- 관계대명사: who (사람), which (사물, 동물), that (사람, 사물, 동물), what
- 관계부사: where (장소), when (때), how (방법), why (이유)
- 복합관계사: 복합관계대명사, 복합관계부사

기출 맛보기

밑줄 친 부분의 쓰임이 나머지와 다른 것은? (영등포구 ○○중학교)

① We heard the rumor that he passed away.

② Did you purchase any merchandise that celebrities advertise?

③ They make us feel that we need the products.

④ I didn't know that they attend the same high school.

⑤ I believed that she could solve the problem.

해설

②는 목적격 관계대명사 that으로, 선행사 merchandise를 수식한다. 나머지는 모두 명사절을 이끄는 접속사 that이다. 접속사 that 뒤에는 완전한 문장이 오고, 관계대명사 that 뒤에는 불완전한 문장이 온다.

해석

① 우리는 그가 사망했다는 소문을 들었다.
② 너는 유명인들이 광고하는 제품을 구입했니?
③ 그들은 우리가 그 물건을 필요로 한다는 것을 느끼게 만들었다.
④ 나는 그들이 같은 고등학교를 다녔다는 것을 알지 못했다.
⑤ 나는 그녀가 그 문제를 해결할 수 있다고 믿었다.

정답 ②

DAY 17

관계대명사

1교시 Grammar Point

1 주격 관계대명사

The woman is Cathy. + **She** respects Dr. Park.
[Cathy: 사람, She: 주어 역할 → who / that]
→ The woman **who [that]** respects Dr. Park is Cathy.

Fred bought me **a ball**. + **The ball** is very expensive.
[a ball: 사물, The ball: 주어 역할 → which / that]
→ Fred bought me a ball **which [that]** is very expensive.

2 목적격 관계대명사

The boy is not a famous actor. + I saw **him** last night.
[The boy: 사람, him: 목적어 역할 → who(m)]
→ The boy **who(m)** I saw last night is not a famous actor.

Those songs were excellent. + Our family listened to **them**.
[Those songs: 사물, them: 전치사의 목적어 역할 → which/that]
→ Those songs **to which** our family listened were excellent.
→ Those songs **which [that]** our family listened **to** were excellent.

cf. 전치사의 목적어로 쓰일 경우 〈전치사 + 관계대명사〉로 쓰일 수 있지만, that, who는 전치사가 앞에 놓이지 않는다.

That's the woman **for who** he is waiting. (x) [→ for whom (o)]

The town **in that** she was born is in the countryside. (x) [→ that ~ born in (o)]
→ The town **in which** she was born is in the countryside. (o)

3 소유격 관계대명사

• 〈소유격 관계대명사 + 명사 + 동사 + 목적어/보어〉

The man died in 2013. + **His** daughter cried a lot.
[The man: 사람, His: 소유격, 명사 수식 → whose]
→ The man **whose** daughter cried a lot died in 2013.

Hank has **a black dog**. + **Its** name is Blackie.
[a black dog: 동물, Its: 소유격, 명사 수식 → whose, of which]
→ Hank has a black dog **whose [of which the]** name is Blackie.

4 관계대명사의 생략

(1) 목적격 관계대명사

The bookstore doesn't have the book **(which [that])** I wanted.

cf. 〈전치사 + 목적격 관계대명사〉는 생략할 수 없다.

The man **to whom** you spoke is my manager.

(2) 〈주격 관계대명사 + be동사〉

Look at the singers **(who are)** singing on stage.

Grammar Tips

• 관계대명사의 역할

두 문장 모두에 관련 있는 (대)명사를 관계대명사로 연결하여 〈접속사 + (대)명사〉 역할을 한다.

• 관계대명사의 종류

선행사	주격	목적격	소유격
사람	who	who whom	whose
사물, 동물	which	which	of which whose
사람, 사물, 동물	that	that	x
선행사 없음	what	what	x

• 관계대명사가 이끄는 절의 구조

(1) 〈주격 관계대명사 + 동사 + 목적어/보어〉

(2) 〈목적격 관계대명사 + 주어 + 동사〉

(3) 〈소유격 관계대명사 + 명사 + 동사 + 목적어/보어〉

• 〈주격 관계대명사 + be동사〉의 생략 = 분사구(명사 수식)

Jane helped an old man **who was** carrying a heavy bag.
[an old man: 선행사]

Jane helped an old man **carrying** a heavy bag.
[an old man: 분사의 수식을 받는 명사]

2교시 In - Class Questions

괄호 안에서 알맞은 말을 고르시오.

1 The bicycle (**who / which / what**) was stolen belonged to Kelly.

2 This is the book in (**which / that**) I'm interested.

3 My sister (**whom / whose / that**) major is mathematics teaches at a middle school.

두 문장을 who, whose, whom, which, of which를 이용하여 한 문장으로 바꿔 쓰시오.

1 They telephoned Mrs. Choi. + She was the family doctor.
→ ________________________________

2 This is Cathy. + I told you about her.
→ ________________________________

3 I saw a car. + Its windows were all broken.
→ ________________________________

4 The book is in the drawer. + He is reading the book these days.
→ ________________________________

다음 문장에서 생략해도 되는 부분에 괄호를 치고, 생략 가능한 부분이 없으면 X표 하시오.

1 The movie which is known to many Koreans is still playing at the theater.

2 Those teenagers who are standing in front of that broadcasting station are waiting for a famous singing groups.

3 I couldn't trust some of my teammates with whom I played.

우리말과 같은 뜻이 되도록 주어진 말과 관계대명사를 사용하여 빈칸을 완성하시오.

1 내게 겉표지가 하얀색인 그 공책을 건네 주세요. (cover)
→ Please pass me the notebook ______________ ______________ is white.

2 그 학생들은 매우 재미있는 수업을 듣고 있다. (be)
→ The students are taking a lesson ______________ ______________ very interesting.

3 내가 만난 그 남자는 유명한 가수였다. (meet)
→ The man ______________ ______________ ______________ was a famous singer.

4 런던을 통과하여 흐르는 강은 템스 강이다. (flow)
→ The river ______________ ______________ through London is the Thames.

3교시 After-Class Questions

[01-02] 문장의 빈칸에 알맞은 관계대명사를 <u>모두</u> 고르시오.

01 This is my lost wallet ________ colors are brown and purple.

① that ② who ③ whom
④ whose ⑤ of which the

02 The professor ________ you must meet right now is Mrs. Choi.

① who ② whom ③ whose
④ which ⑤ that

03 다음 중 어법상 <u>어색한</u> 문장은?

① Hank whom I believed to be intelligent failed the exam.
② Are you sure these are the pants which you want to buy?
③ The man whom she saw was not a famous person at all.
④ Kent gave me a book which was about Thomas Jefferson.
⑤ The text message of which came from her said that she wouldn't finish her homework.

04 밑줄 친 관계대명사를 <u>생략</u>할 수 있는 것은?

① This is the the city in <u>which</u> I was born.
② The music <u>which</u> Bumkie composed for everyone is too noisy.
③ Help is needed for families <u>whose</u> homes were destroyed by the hurricane.
④ She wants to see the movie <u>which</u> is very romantic and sometimes sad.
⑤ Jack gave up interviewing the actor <u>who</u> is very popular.

05 다음 문장에서 관계대명사가 생략된 곳을 찾은 다음, 문장의 동사에 밑줄을 치시오.

Some books (①) I read (②) in the library (③) for 4 hours (④) provide (⑤) a lot of information about alternative energy.

서술형 대비

06 밑줄 친 말을 어법상 올바른 형태로 고치시오.

The guy who often (1)<u>play</u> tennis after school (2)<u>live</u> near my house.

(1) ____________________ (2) ____________________

Vocabulary Tips

- purple 보라색
- intelligent 똑똑한
- text message 문자메시지
- compose 작곡하다
- destroy 파괴하다, 망치다
- interview 인터뷰하다
- alternative energy 대체에너지

07 밑줄 친 부분 중 어법상 어색한 부분을 찾아 바르게 고치시오.

In Africa, there ①are a lot of people ②who doesn't have enough food to eat and clothes to wear. There are over one million children in Africa ③whose families ④don't have both of them. Some children work because their parents have died from diseases. So government and charities ⑤have taken some actions in order to improve children's lives.

__________________ → __________________

08 문장의 빈칸에 알맞은 말끼리 짝지은 것은?

(a) The meaning of the word ________ Harry is looking for is in the dictionary.
(b) The meaning of the word ________ Harry is looking is in the dictionary.

① which – which
② which – of which
③ which – for which
④ of which – for which
⑤ for which – for which

09 우리말을 영어로 바르게 옮긴 것은?

머리카락이 회색인 여자 분은 Murray의 담임선생님이다.

① The woman who hair is gray is Murray's homeroom teacher.
② The woman that hair is gray is Murray's homeroom teacher.
③ The woman which is gray is Murray's homeroom teacher.
④ The woman whose hair is gray is Murray's homeroom teacher.
⑤ The woman of which hair is gray is Murray's homeroom teacher.

10 문장의 빈칸에 공통으로 알맞은 관계대명사는?

(a) Last weekend, my family heard about the terrible news ________ happened in a France prison.
(b) My aunt wears a necklace ________ her mother left her as a legacy.

① who
② whose
③ which
④ of which
⑤ what

11 어법상 어색한 부분을 찾아 바르게 고치시오.

The little girl was talking with you yesterday morning was my younger sister.

__________________ → __________________

Vocabulary Tips

- disease 병, 질병
- charity 자선단체
- take an action ~에 대해 행동(조치)을 취하다
- improve 향상시키다
- prison 감옥
- legacy 유산

3교시 After-Class Questions

[12-13] 밑줄 친 관계대명사를 생략할 수 없는 것을 고르시오.

12 ① English is the subject which I like the most.
② I have a friend who lives in London.
③ They are the students whom he taught last year.
④ She is the woman whom Rick fell in love with.
⑤ This is the computer game which I bought for my son.

13 ① Linda drank the Coke that I gave her.
② I brought the invitation card that she had given me before.
③ Tell your father the story which you heard.
④ That is the building in which I learn foreign languages.
⑤ We tore some pages of the books which we had borrowed from the library.

서술형 대비

[14-15] 주어진 말을 사용하여 다음 우리말을 영어로 옮기시오.

14 나는 아버지가 치과의사인 친구 몇 명이 있다. (dentist)

→ I have ______________________________.

15 토끼는 당근을 먹는 동물이다. (a rabbit)

→ ______________________________

[16-17] 문장에서 생략 가능한 부분에 밑줄을 그으시오.

16 Jenny will help the sick people who are suffering from cancer.

17 I can't forget the photos which you showed me last night.

18 밑줄 친 말과 바꿔 쓸 수 있는 것은?

Would you like to buy that bag whose price is over 2,000 dollars?

① who ② that ③ which
④ of which ⑤ for which

19 우리말과 같은 뜻이 되도록 빈칸에 알맞은 말을 모두 고르시오.

부모님이 칭찬을 많이 했던 아이들은 자신감으로 가득 차있다.

→ The children ________ the parents praised a lot are filled with confidence.

① who ② whom ③ which
④ whose ⑤ that

Vocabulary Tips

- invitation card 초대장
- tear 찢다(-tore-torn)
- suffer from ~으로 고통 받다
- cancer 암
- praise 칭찬하다
- confidence 자신감

20 〈보기〉의 문장을 두 문장으로 바르게 분리한 것은?

보기 The car whose bumper was dented is my mother's.

① The bumper was dented. The car is my mother's.
② The bumper was dented. It is my mother's.
③ The bumper of my mother's car was dented.
④ The car is my mother's. Her bumper was dented.
⑤ The car is my mother's. Its bumper was dented.

21 문장의 빈칸에 알맞은 관계대명사는?

These are the cookies ________ his grandmother made yesterday.

① who ② when ③ what
④ that ⑤ where

22 밑줄 친 who의 쓰임이 나머지와 다른 것은?

① I employed the man who was kind and honest.
② I have a friend who can lead me.
③ I don't remember who you are and where you are from.
④ We need a person who can solve this problem.
⑤ My ideal wife is someone who I think should be honest and have an open mind.

23 대화의 빈칸에 알맞은 것은?

A: Do you know ________ laptop this is?
B: I guess it is Jimmy's laptop. It is the same model ________ I have.
A: No, his laptop is a different model than yours.

① what – who ② which – that ③ that – whose
④ who – whom ⑤ whose – that

24 생략된 말을 넣어 다음 문장을 다시 쓰시오.

The old lady you spoke with is my Chinese teacher.
→ ____________________________

25 밑줄 친 부분 중 어법상 어색한 것은?

① The teacher we met was very kind.
② He is a man who everybody likes very much.
③ Mr. Smith has a camera which I always wanted to get.
④ Look at the K-pop singer singing on stage.
⑤ That is the novel in that I am interested.

Vocabulary Tips

- bumper 자동차 범퍼
- dent (움푹하게) 들어가다
- employ 고용하다
- open mind 열린 마음

DAY 18

주의해야 할 관계대명사

1교시 Grammar Point

1 what의 쓰임

① 선행사를 포함하는 관계대명사이므로 선행사 없음
② 명사절을 이끌어 문장 안에서 주어, 목적어, 보어 역할을 함
③ '~한 것'으로 해석하며, the thing(s) which [that]로 바꿔 쓸 수 있음

What I really want to buy is the new convertible car. [주어 역할]
[= The thing which/that]

Show me what is in your backpack. [목적어 역할]
[= the thing which/that]

This is not **what** I ordered. [보어 역할]

2 that의 쓰임

① 선행사가 사람, 사물, 동물일 때 모두 쓰임
② 주격 또는 목적격 관계대명사 who, whom, which를 대신해서 쓸 수 있음
③ that만 써야 하는 경우: 선행사가 〈사람 + 동물〉 혹은 〈사람 + 사물〉일 때 / 선행사가 서수, 최상급, all, no, every, any, only, very, same, last, -thing일 때 / 의문사가 있는 의문문에서 who, what, which의 중복을 피하기 위해서

Look at the girl and the dog **that** are running in the playground.
The main actor is the only reason **that** I watched this soap opera.
Tell me something **that** you bought last night.
Who is the girl **that** studies in the library every day?

3 관계대명사의 제한적 용법 vs. 계속적 용법

	제한적 용법	계속적 용법
형태	선행사 + 관계대명사	선행사 + 콤마(,) + 관계대명사 [관계대명사 = 접속사 + 대명사]
역할	선행사를 수식(한정)	선행사를 보충하여 설명
해석	선행사 ← 관계대명사절 (뒤에서부터 해석)	선행사 → 관계대명사절 (앞에서부터 해석)
종류	who, which, that, what	who, which

I have a daughter **who** became a teacher. [제한적 용법: 딸이 한 명 이상일 수 있음]
I have a daughter, **who** became a teacher. [계속적 용법: 딸이 한 명임]
→ I have a daughter, **and she** became a teacher.

4 〈전치사 + 관계대명사〉

• 관계대명사가 전치사의 목적어로 쓰이는 경우에 전치사는 관계대명사 앞이나 관계대명사절 끝에 올 수 있음(단, 〈전치사 + that〉으로는 쓰이지 않음)

This is the apartment **in which** my sister lives.
= This is the apartment **(which)** my sister lives **in**.

Grammar Tips

• **관계대명사 that vs. what**

that	what
선행사 o	선행사 ×
뒤에 오는 문장이 불완전함	뒤에 오는 문장이 불완전함
형용사절 (선행사 수식)	명사절 (주어, 목적어, 보어 역할)

• **관계대명사 that을 사용할 수 없는 경우**

(1) 소유격으로 쓸 수 없다.
(2) 전치사와 나란히 쓸 수 없다.
(3) 계속적인 용법으로 쓸 수 없다.

• **관계대명사 vs. 접속사 vs. 동격의 that**

that 뒤에 오는 문장 성분과 생략 가능 여부로 구분할 수 있다.

관계대명사	불완전한 문장이 옴 목적격은 생략 가능 선행사 o
접속사	완전한 문장이 옴 목적어 역할을 할 때 생략 가능 선행사 ×
동격	완전한 문장이 옴 생략 불가능 동격 부분에 명사 (fact, idea, belief, truth…) 등이 옴

The baseball game **(that)** I watched was exciting. [관계대명사]
(내가 본 그 야구 경기는 흥미진진했다.)

I love **(that)** I can play baseball with my friends. [접속사]
(내가 친구들과 야구를 할 수 있다는 것이 정말 좋다.)

I love the fact **that** I can play baseball with my friends. [동격]
(내가 친구들과 야구를 할 수 있다는 사실이 정말 좋다.)

• **계속적 용법으로 쓰인 which**

앞문장의 일부나 문장 전체의 내용을 받을 때는 which만 쓰인다.

• 관계대명사 that, what은 계속적 용법으로 쓰이지 않는다.

2교시 In-Class Questions

STEP A

빈칸에 알맞은 관계대명사를 쓰시오.

1 Do ______________ you think is right.

2 Sunny lost the most valuable ring ______________ she had.

3 Who was the first employee ______________ came to office this morning?

4 My dad bought the sedan ______________ was very luxurious.

STEP B

괄호 안에서 알맞은 말을 모두 고르시오.

1 My uncle took his girlfriend **(who / that)** is beautiful, to our home.

2 The dogs were all obedient and did **(what / that)** the trainer ordered them to do.

3 You are the only person in the world **(that / which / whom)** knows everything about me.

4 There were many students at my university **(what / that)** wanted to listen to my lecture.

STEP C

밑줄 친 That[that]의 역할을 〈보기〉에서 골라 쓰시오.

보기 접속사 관계대명사 지시형용사

1 That smartphone is hers, not mine. ______________

2 Toys that are dangerous should not be given to children. ______________

3 That he doesn't want to see us is quite obvious. ______________

4 Look at the children that are running in the park. ______________

STEP D

어법상 어색한 부분이 있으면 바르게 고치고, 없으면 X표 하시오.

1 It is the planner what my wife made for me. ___________ → ___________

2 He is the very man which I have been looking for. ___________ → ___________

3 This is the very question that has long been in my mind. ___________ → ___________

4 Although I expected something different, I was surprised by that he said.
___________ → ___________

3교시 After - Class Questions

[01-02] 문장의 빈칸에 알맞은 관계대명사를 고르시오.

01 ________ Ben bought for her yesterday will be good for her health.

① That ② What ③ Who
④ Which ⑤ Those

02 Look at the girl and her cats ________ are running in the yard.

① that ② what ③ who
④ which ⑤ whom

03 두 문장을 한 문장으로 바꿔 쓸 때 빈칸에 알맞은 관계대명사를 쓰시오.

She is the only woman. + I want to date her.
→ She is the only woman ________ I want to date.

04 두 문장이 같은 뜻이 되도록 빈칸에 알맞은 말을 쓰시오.

Anne tried to open the door, which she found impossible.
→ Anne tried to open the door, ________ she found ________ impossible.

05 다음 문장의 의미로 알맞은 것을 〈보기〉에서 고르시오.

> 보기 ⓐ 내가 나의 반 친구에게 말했더니 그는 그 상황을 설명해주었다.
> ⓑ 나는 그 상황을 설명해주었던 나의 반 친구에게 말했다.

(1) I spoke to my classmate who explained the situation. ________

(2) I spoke to my classmate, who explained the situation. ________

[06-09] 문장의 빈칸에 알맞은 말끼리 짝지은 것을 고르시오.

06

> (a) There are a lot of chairs in the auditorium ________ we can sit.
> (b) The boys and girls ________ they talked are Gary's sons and daughters.

① of which – to whom ② on which – in whom
③ in which – about who ④ in which – to that
⑤ in which – to whom

Vocabulary Tips

- yard 마당, 뜰
- impossible 불가능한
- explain 설명하다
- situation 상황
- auditorium 강당

07

(a) Megan lets me use her smartphone, _________ has variety functions.
(b) The only thing _________ matters at the moment is your advice.

① that – what ② that – who ③ who – that
④ which – what ⑤ which – that

08

(a) He found the last candy _________ I had hid under the table.
(b) She may not find _________ I put under the table.

① which – which ② which – that ③ that – what
④ that – that ⑤ what – what

09

(a) Money is not everything _________ Kaymi works for.
(b) Who is this man _________ has lots of experience?

① what – who ② which – that ③ that – that
④ that – who ⑤ which – who

10 밑줄 친 that의 쓰임을 관계대명사, 접속사, 동격 중에서 골라 쓰시오.

(1) We didn't know that the only van has fewer than 10 seats. _________
(2) All that children in Africa need is some food. _________
(3) People in the country believe the fact that the economy is getting better. _________

11 다음 중 어법상 어색한 문장은?

① Linda passed the driving test, which made everyone surprised.
② The smallest table that is in the middle is my father's.
③ The large pears which are ripening on the trees look very delicious.
④ The pastime in the United Kingdom on that people spend the most time is gardening.
⑤ His habit of reading the newspaper every morning is what gives him lots of pleasure.

12 우리말과 같은 뜻이 되도록 빈칸에 알맞은 말을 쓰시오.

아이는 아무 말도 하지 않았고, 그것이 어머니를 화나게 했다.
→ The child said nothing, _________ made the mother upset.

Vocabulary Tips

- variety 다양한
- function 기능
- hide 숨기다(–hid–hidden)
- economy 경제
- ripen 익다
- pastime 취미
- gardening 정원 가꾸기
- pleasure 기쁨
- upset 화가 난

3교시 After - Class Questions

13 〈보기〉의 밑줄 친 that과 쓰임이 같은 것은?

> **보기** Facebook is a social network services that was founded by Mark Zuckerberg with his college roommates.

① The rumor that all of the students failed the exam proved to be false.
② Eve said that she would take action to make the store better.
③ The car and the driver that fell down the cliff were not found.
④ What I want is that both my parents and sisters be happy.
⑤ Everyone knew that the ship had changed its course because there was a strong storm.

14 밑줄 친 관계대명사의 쓰임이 어법상 어색한 것은?

① I saw a famous singer, who won an award this year.
② I began to watch the movie, that was very exciting.
③ Charlotte likes her friend, who teaches psychology at a university.
④ My family visited the Louvre Museum, which has the *Mona Lisa*.
⑤ The reporter interviewed Billy, who had traveled around the world.

15 〈보기〉의 밑줄 친 what과 쓰임이 다른 것은?

보기 Owen thinks deeply about what he does.

① This is what we wanted to buy.
② What we have is strong will.
③ I remember what she said.
④ What I want is that blue vehicle.
⑤ Do you know what her phone number is?

16 다음 중 어법상 올바른 문장은?

① Sue was the first person that said the right answer.
② Thomas sold his book, that he no longer needed, to his friend.
③ She sang a song and played the piano, who everyone enjoyed a lot.
④ Marylin Monroe, who real name was Norma Jean, died a long time ago.
⑤ My sister read us many interesting stories, some of them were not true.

17 글의 빈칸에 알맞은 관계대명사를 쓰시오.

> Both of the young men wanted to climb the top of Mt. Everest, __________ is the world's tallest mountain. Independently, both climbers reached the mountain, but they could not arrive at the top of the mountain due to bad weather.

Vocabulary Tips

- social 사회의, 사회적인
- found 설립하다, 창설하다 (–founded–founded)
- cliff 절벽
- deeply 깊이
- vehicle 자동차
- independently 각각
- climber 등산객
- due to 때문에

18 **두 문장을 한 문장으로 바꿔 쓴 문장이 어색한 것은?**

Hank bought a chair. + He could sit in it.

① Hank bought a chair which he could sit in.
② Hank bought a chair in which he could sit.
③ Hank bought a chair he could sit in.
④ Hank bought a chair that he could sit in.
⑤ Hank bought a chair in that he could sit.

[19-20] 밑줄 친 부분의 쓰임이 나머지와 다른 것을 고르시오.

19 ① This was what he really wanted.
② What my son learns is nothing.
③ Do you know what he is doing?
④ Show me what you have in your hand.
⑤ What makes me happy is your true love.

20 ① We believed that she is smart.
② It is sad that your pet passed away.
③ Please recommend a song that is good for us.
④ It is important that you should keep your promise.
⑤ Have you heard that Jason bought a luxury sedan?

[21-22] 밑줄 친 부분을 어법상 바르게 고치시오.

21 Ophelia was very exhausted. That's which made her stay in bed all day long.

→ ________________

22 My father argued with a stranger, who seldom happened.

→ ________________

23 **다음 중 어법상 어색한 문장을 두 개 고르시오.**

① Sandy is the woman whom I don't get along with.
② Rebecca is the very good teacher who I respect.
③ Music is the subject which I am interested in.
④ I will auction her laptop which she has used so far.
⑤ He suddenly canceled the concert which he had planned it before.

24 **우리말과 같은 뜻이 되도록 빈칸에 알맞은 말을 쓰시오.**

내가 정말로 원하는 것은 고양이를 나의 애완동물로 갖는 것이다.
→ ________ I really want is to have a cat as a pet.
→ ________ ________ ________ I really want is to have a cat as a pet.

25 **문장의 빈칸에 알맞은 관계대명사를 쓰시오.**

All ________ people need to survive is water.

Vocabulary Tips

- pass away 죽다
- recommend 추천하다
- keep one's promise 약속을 지키다
- luxury 호화로운
- sedan 세단 자동차
- respect 존경하다
- auction 경매하다
- survive 생존하다

DAY 19

관계부사, 복합관계사

1교시 Grammar Point

1 관계부사

- 역할: 〈접속사 + 부사〉
- 관계부사 = 〈전치사 + 관계대명사〉

	선행사	관계부사	전치사 + 관계사
장소	the place	where	in/at/on which
시간	the time/day/year	when	in/at/on which
이유	the reason	why	for which
방법	the way	how	in which

*the way는 관계부사 how와 함께 쓰일 수 없으며 둘 중 하나만 씀

There is a very famous hotel. I want to stay **at the hotel**. [전치사 + 명사]
→ There is a very famous hotel **where** I want to stay. 장소
→ There is a very famous hotel **at which** I want to stay.
→ There is a very famous hotel **which** I want to stay **at**.

This is the time **when** I have to do my best to pass the test. 시간

I don't know the reason **why** she is disappointed at me. 이유

Can you show me (the way) **how** we get to the airport? 방법

2 복합관계사

- 형태: 〈관계사 + -ever〉, 선행사 포함
- 종류: 복합관계대명사, 복합관계부사

복합관계대명사	명사절	양보의 부사절
whoever	~하는 누구나 (= anyone who)	누가 ~할지라도 (= no matter who)
whomever	~하는 사람은 누구에게나 (= anyone whom)	누구를 ~하더라도 (= no matter whom)
whichever	~하는 어느 것이나 (= anything that)	어느 것이[을] ~할지라도 (= no matter which)
whatever	~하는 무엇이나 (= anything that)	무엇을 ~할지라도 (= no matter what)

Whoever [= Anyone who] comes in first will be the winner. 명사절: 주어 역할
(첫 번째로 오는 사람은 누구나)

Whatever [= No matter what] you said, I didn't care. 양보의 부사절
(당신이 뭐라고 말했던지 간에)

복합관계부사	부사절	양보의 부사절
whenever	~할 때마다 (= at any time when)	언제 ~하더라도 (= no matter when)
wherever	~하는 어디든 (= at any place where)	어디에 ~하더라도 (= no matter where)
however	–	아무리 ~하더라도 (= no matter how)

Wherever [= At any place where] you go, I will follow you. 부사절
(당신이 가는 곳은 어디든지)

However [= No matter how] cold it is, I want to go for a walk. 양보의 부사절
(아무리 춥더라도)

Grammar Tips

관계대명사 vs. 관계부사

관계사절에서 관계사가 어떤 역할을 하는지에 따라 구별할 수 있다.
관계대명사: 주어, 목적어, 보어 역할
관계부사: 부사 역할

관계부사 = 전치사 + which

the hotel **where** [**at which**] I stay
(= the hotel **which** I stay **at**)
the reason **why** [**for which**] I go
(= the reason **which** I go **for**)
* when은 〈전치사 + which〉만 가능함

관계부사와 선행사의 생략

(1) 선행사가 일반적인 장소인 the place, the time, the reason일 때 생략할 수 있다. 이때 관계부사절 → 명사절로 바뀐다.
This is the reason [why I don't go there]. 형용사절
This is [**why** I don't go there]. 명사절(보어 역할)

(2) 계속적 용법으로 쓰인 관계부사는 생략할 수 없다.
I love spring, **when** I can go on a picnic.

(3) that은 모든 관계부사를 대신하여 쓸 수 있다.
Go to the school **where** [**that**] your friends are studying.
Tell me the **way that** you get here. [the way how (x), the way that (o)]

2교시 In - Class Questions

괄호 안에서 알맞은 말을 모두 고르시오.

1 Ames is the city **(which / in which / where)** we studied.

2 What is the reason **(which / for which / why)** you like it?

3 Give this ticket to **(who / whoever / whomever)** wants to go.

4 **(Whatever / Wherever / However)** stupid your sister is, she won't follow you.

우리말과 같은 뜻이 되도록 빈칸에 알맞은 말을 쓰시오.

1 당신이 도착할 시간을 예약해 주세요.
→ Please make a reservation ____________ you arrive.

2 우리는 그가 화가 났던 이유가 궁금했다.
→ We wondered the ____________ ____________ ____________ he had been upset.

3 이곳은 내가 너를 만났던 그 서점이다.
→ This is the bookstore ____________ I met you.

4 Tina가 1등을 했던 방법은 그렇게 효과적이지 않다.
____________ Tina won first place is not that effective.

STEP C

두 문장이 같은 뜻이 되도록 빈칸에 알맞은 말을 쓰시오.

1 Greg will give advice to anyone who needs help.
→ Greg will give advice to ____________ needs help.

2 Don't do whatever you don't want to do.
→ Don't do ____________ ____________ you don't want to do.

3 Whomever he wants to meet, he won't be allowed to do it.
→ ____________ ____________ ____________ he wants to meet, he won't be allowed to do it.

STEP D

주어진 말을 사용하여 다음 우리말을 영어로 옮기시오.

1 나는 민준이가 여기에 도착했던 방법이 궁금하다. (reach, wonder)
→ ____

2 이곳은 내가 이 그림을 매일 봤던 곳이다. (선행사 생략, painting)
→ ____

3 송연이는 아무리 유명해도 매우 외롭다고 느낀다. (feel, lonely)
→ ____

3교시 After - Class Questions

[01-02] 문장의 빈칸에 알맞은 관계사끼리 짝지은 것을 고르시오.

01

(a) The guest house ________ we will stay at during the holiday is very inexpensive.
(b) Has she ever visited a place ________ Spanish is spoken?

① which – where ② which – which ③ that – which
④ where – which ⑤ where – where

02

(a) ________ the doctor suggests, I won't do it.
(b) Mom will pay for the art materials ________ much they cost.

① Wherever – whenever ② Whenever – whichever
③ Whoever – however ④ Whatever – however
⑤ Whatever – whenever

03 우리말을 영어로 옮긴 것이 어법상 어색한 것은?

이곳은 내가 자주 커피를 마시는 카페이다.

① This is the cafe where I often drink coffee.
② This is the cafe that I often drink coffee at.
③ This is the cafe which I often drink coffee at.
④ This is the cafe at which I often drink coffee.
⑤ This is the cafe where I often drink coffee at.

[04-05] 다음 중 어법상 어색한 문장을 고르시오.

04
① That is the right place at which we can rest.
② This was the way they found out the fallacy.
③ This is the shoe store which I work every day.
④ Today is the day when we are going to Tongyeong.
⑤ The game is the main reason why you aren't focusing on your study.

05
① Whoever wants to get an A must study hard.
② The books show how you can make the broth.
③ This is the way how some friends treat me all of the time.
④ No matter what you do at home, don't be late for class.
⑤ Andrew stayed up until midnight, when his mom went into his room.

06 두 문장이 같은 뜻이 되도록 빈칸에 알맞은 말을 쓰시오.

I won't forget you no matter what happens later.

→ I won't forget you, ________ happens later.

Vocabulary Tips

- inexpensive 비싸지 않은
- fallacy 오류
- focus on ~에 집중하다
- broth 국
- treat 대하다
- all of the time 항상

07 밑줄 친 when의 쓰임이 나머지와 다른 것은?

① We are waiting for the week when we will visit Paris.
② Did you remember the day when you first met me?
③ June is the month when Justin and Keilen got married.
④ Alice had lunch when I was sleeping.
⑤ Austin told you the time when he could stop by your home.

08 밑줄 친 부분을 대신하여 쓸 수 있는 말을 모두 고르시오.

Whenever I chatted with my partner during the discussion, my teacher stared at me.

① No matter when ② At any time when ③ Each time
④ Every time ⑤ Most of the time

09 밑줄 친 부분 중 어법상 어색한 부분을 골라 바르게 고치시오.

A: Jack, ①it's time to do what I told you to do.
B: Mom, ②I'm too exhausted. I want to skip it ③only today.
A: Hey! ④However you are tired, you should keep your promise. You got a new game package by saying, "I will exercise ⑤whenever you want me to."

________________ → ________________

[10-13] 문장의 빈칸에 알맞은 관계사를 고르시오.

10 Jessica will introduce you to ________ comes here.

① whoever ② whomever ③ whenever
④ whatever ⑤ however

11 After the Civil War, many soldiers returned to their hometowns ________ they were born.

① when ② where ③ why
④ how ⑤ what

12 Everybody remembered the day ________ the accident occurred.

① when ② why ③ how
④ where ⑤ which

13 Do you fasten your seatbelt ________ you ride in a car?

① whichever ② wherever ③ however
④ whenever ⑤ whatever

Vocabulary Tips

- stop by 들르다
- chat 떠들다, 잡담하다
- stare 응시하다, 노려보다
- soldier 군인, 병사
- return 되돌아가다
- occur 발생하다
- fasten the seatbelt 안전벨트를 매다

14 두 문장이 같은 뜻이 되도록 할 때 빈칸에 알맞은 것은?

No matter which MP3 you choose, I will buy it for your birthday.
→ ________________, I will buy it for your birthday.

① Which you choose MP3
② Which MP3 you choose
③ Whatever you choose MP3
④ Whichever MP3 you choose
⑤ Whichever you choose MP3

15 빈칸에 Whoever[whoever]가 들어갈 수 없는 것은?

① ________ wishes to succeed in the field can succeed.
② Give this poster to ________ brings the movie ticket.
③ People welcome ________ wants to invest in this project.
④ Harry will give this book to ________ comes in the room first.
⑤ ________ rich people are, they always want more and more.

서술형 대비

16 우리말과 같은 뜻이 되도록 빈칸에 알맞은 말을 쓰시오.

당신이 뭐라고 말하든 나는 내 마음을 바꾸지 않을 것이다.
→ I won't change my mind ________________________________.

17 주어진 단어를 바르게 배열할 때 두 번째로 오는 말은?

You should call me, ________________________________.
(you / late / arrive / however / at night)

① you
② late
③ arrive
④ however
⑤ at night

18 글의 빈칸에 공통으로 알맞은 복합관계사를 쓰시오.

> Daniel Henney, a Korean-American movie star, is very popular these days after he starred in a recently released movie. He gathers a crowd ________ he goes. According to an interview last week, he mentioned a unique fan who always follows him ________ he stays.

19 문장의 빈칸에 알맞은 관계사를 〈보기〉에서 골라 쓰시오.

보기	when	whoever	whatever	wherever

(1) ________ comes to the event will get a souvenir.

(2) ________ he went, he made trouble.

(3) I will do ________ you tell me to do.

(4) January is the month ________ I finish a series of grammar books.

Vocabulary Tips

- invest 투자하다
- star 영화에 출연하다
- recently 최근에
- release 개봉하다
- gather a crowd 군중을 끌다
- according to ~에 따르면
- souvenir 기념품
- series 시리즈, 일련

20 밑줄 친 where의 쓰임이 나머지와 다른 것은?

① This is the school where we graduated.
② Bill visited the village where he was born.
③ The parents didn't know where their kids were.
④ Kyle went to Hawaii, where he got his diploma.
⑤ The tour guide led the tourists to the place where most people visit.

21 다음 중 어법상 올바른 문장은?

① There's something what we should know.
② The cities where I visited in Japan were beautiful.
③ What we have to do is very annoying and difficult.
④ They live in a house that garden is full of flowers.
⑤ Are you interested in the girl who she is standing in front of the vending machine?

22 문장의 빈칸에 알맞은 관계부사끼리 짝지은 것은?

(a) This is the reason ________ I am calling you.
(b) I want to visit the place ________ Wolfgang Amadeus Mozart was born.
(c) Kimberly asked the professor ________ she could get a better grade.

① how – where – who
② where – who – the reason
③ where – when – how
④ why – where – who
⑤ why – where – how

[23-24] 밑줄 친 부분 중 어법상 어색한 것을 고르시오.

23 ① I won't forget the day when he won first prize.
② This is the reason why she left me.
③ The place where Harry often met Carol was in the library.
④ Do you remember that spring when we fell in love?
⑤ Tell me the way how I can get along with you.

24 ① The reason why I broke up with her is complicated.
② His house is not far from the house in which Ralph lives.
③ Did you remember the exact date when you moved to Seoul?
④ I will try to find out which this computer broke down today.
⑤ This is the restaurant where you can taste the best Korean food.

25 문장의 빈칸에 알맞은 관계사를 쓰시오.

Most of my friends want to know the way ________ I could get a good grade without difficulty.

Vocabulary Tips

- diploma 졸업장, 수료증
- vending machine 자판기
- first prize 1등
- get along with ~와 잘 지내다
- complicated 복잡한
- far from ~에서 먼
- difficulty 어려움

Final Test

[01-02] 문장의 빈칸에 알맞은 말끼리 짝지은 것을 고르시오.

01

(a) The traffic problems which the city is facing _________ a big issue these days.
(b) We saw the car whose doors _________ all dented. *dent: 찌그러뜨리다

① is – is ② is – were
③ are – was ④ are – were
⑤ were – was

02

(a) Can you recognize the woman _________ Benjamin is talking?
(b) This is the best team _________ I have ever seen.

① to who – which ② whom – that
③ on whom – that ④ to whom – which
⑤ to whom – that

03 문장의 빈칸에 알맞은 관계대명사를 모두 고르시오.

Wendy wore the silk scarf _________ was in style with young girls.

① who ② whose
③ which ④ that
⑤ of which

서술형 대비

04 주어진 말을 사용하여 다음 우리말을 영어로 옮기시오.

너는 CGV에서 지금 상영되고 있는 그 영화를 본 적이 있니? (play, have seen)

→ ______________________________

05 밑줄 친 부분 중 어법상 어색한 것은?

There is always a generation gap between parents and their teenage children. Parents think ①that their children, ②who consider themselves grown-ups, are still kids. It is one of the main reasons ③that prevent them from communicating with each other. Children ④whom are treated as kids also don't want to talk about their problems. So the parents don't understand ⑤what their children are worrying about.

06 두 문장을 한 문장으로 바꿔 쓸 때 빈칸에 알맞은 말을 쓰시오.

Sandra passed the driving test. And it was very difficult.
→ Sandra passed the driving test, _________ was very difficult.

07 대화의 밑줄 친 부분 중 어법상 어색한 것은?

A: ①Should I bring ②anything to the party?
B: ③That you'd like ④to drink. We'll ⑤order some food for dinner.

[08-09] 다음 중 어법상 어색한 문장을 고르시오.

08 ① The people whose dogs were lost tried to find them.
② Who that is normal can believe such a strange story?
③ The news that she got injured proved to be true.
④ There was nothing which interested Jane at the museum.
⑤ This is the same drawing test, which has many levels.

09 ① This is the restaurant where I want to go.
② The reason why he did it is hard to tell.
③ Today is the only day where I can take a rest.
④ There are times when I wonder why I do this job.
⑤ We moved to London, where my family lived for three years.

10 밑줄 친 that의 쓰임이 나머지와 다른 것은?

① It was true that Mike stole the bike.
② He is not the police officer that he used to be.
③ This is the last book of the series that I wrote.
④ I met some sports stars that are very popular in Korea.
⑤ Mr. Edwards is the teacher that I like the most at this school.

11 밑줄 친 부분을 생략할 수 없는 것은?

① Is he your friend whom you helped?
② These are the trousers which I want to buy.
③ She ate the chicken curry and pork cutlet that her boyfriend made.
④ Show me some pictures that you took during your vacation.
⑤ What is the name of the student who won the competition?

12 다음 문장을 두 문장으로 분리하시오.

The men whose legs were injured by the accident are my school teachers.

→ ________________________________
____

13 짝지은 두 문장의 의미가 다른 것은?

① That is the house where Henry grew up.
→ That is the house in which Henry grew up.
② Jack remembers the day when he took his first airplane ride.
→ Jack remembers the day on which he took his first airplane ride.
③ What was the reason why Gary gave up singing at the concert?
→ What was the reason for which Gary gave up singing at the concert?
④ He didn't know how Brian fixed this TV.
→ He didn't know the way in which Brian fixed this TV.
⑤ Cindy was in bed until noon when her mom came to pick her up.
→ Cindy was in bed until noon which her mom came to pick her up.

14 대화의 빈칸에 알맞은 관계사는?

A: What is that? Did you buy a T-shirt for 100 dollars? B: Sorry, Dad. I really want to wear it. A: ________ you say, I won't forgive you this time.

① What ② Which
③ Whoever ④ Whatever
⑤ Whenever

15 문장의 빈칸에 알맞은 복합관계사를 쓰시오.

(1) Helen is busy ________ I call her.
(2) ________ hard you try, you cannot win this game.
(3) I will be with you, ________ you go.
(4) ________ comes in first will be given a great gift.

16 밑줄 친 who와 바꿔 쓸 수 있는 것은?

> Have you ever worked together with someone? Working with a partner can make work easier and more fun. This article is about two friends, Steve and Bill, who worked together to found a great computer game company.

① but they ② but her
③ and he ④ and it
⑤ and they

[17-19] 〈보기〉의 밑줄 친 부분과 쓰임이 같은 것을 고르시오.

17

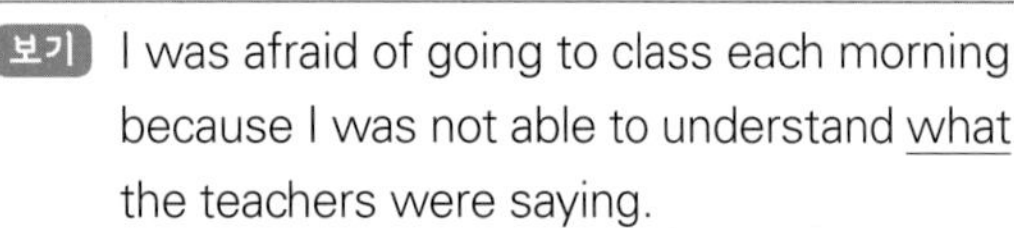

보기 I was afraid of going to class each morning because I was not able to understand what the teachers were saying.

① What food do you like best?
② What is your cell phone number?
③ I don't know what the problem is.
④ You can tell me what you want.
⑤ Do you know what he is doing in his classroom?

18

보기 A service is any kind of work that someone does to satisfy our needs.

① She is not that pretty.
② She said that I was lucky.
③ That he is a doctor is true.
④ It means that there are not enough resources.
⑤ Make a list of the things that you want to buy.

19

> 보기 Think about a moment when you had to speak in front of many people.

① When and where did she go?
② When is your boyfriend's birthday?
③ I know the time when you left home.
④ My mother went out when she received a phone call.
⑤ When my father comes, my family will go out to eat.

20 (a), (b), (c)의 각 네모 안에서 어법에 맞는 표현끼리 짝지은 것은?

> March is the month (a) [when / which] comes after the long cold winter. I like March the best of months because of the warm spring. March is the month (b) [when / which] I can set out on a journey with my family. This year, I'm going to Austria because I really like the scenery in the country and want to visit the mansion (c) [where / which] the movie *The Sound of Music*, was shot.

① which – which – which
② which – when – where
③ when – which – where
④ when – when – where
⑤ when – which – which

21 두 문장을 한 문장으로 바꿔 쓴 문장이 잘못된 것은?

> This is the perfect woman. + I am looking for her.

① This is the perfect woman for whom I am looking.
② This is the perfect woman I am looking for.
③ This is the perfect woman whom I am looking for.
④ This is the perfect woman for which I am looking for.
⑤ This is the perfect woman that I am looking for.

22 문장의 빈칸에 알맞지 않은 것은?

> Good Will is a store ________________.

① sells very inexpensive products
② which sells what people want
③ where you bought the rug in your house
④ where many workers donate their old items
⑤ in which young children like to go

23 문장의 밑줄 친 what이 관계대명사로 쓰인 것은?

① Does she know what my teacher looks like?
② Don't tell him what food you can't eat.
③ I am pretty sure what her favorite music is.
④ Nobody guesses what I am drawing.
⑤ Make a list of what to do for the test.

24 두 문장이 같은 뜻이 되도록 할 때 빈칸에 알맞은 것은?

We met Keilen, whom we had learned English from for more than four years.
→ We met Keilen, ________ for more than four years.

① and we had learned English
② and we had learned English from
③ and we had learned English from her
④ but we had learned English from
⑤ but we had learned English from her

25 밑줄 친 whatever [Whatever]의 쓰임이 같은 것끼리 묶인 것은?

(a) Thomas buys whatever Luz wants.
(b) Don't take anything, whatever he gives you.
(c) Whatever the man tells you is not the right information.
(d) You can present whatever you choose.
(e) Whatever he said, I don't care.

① (a), (b)　② (b), (e)
③ (b), (c)　④ (c), (e)
⑤ (a), (e)

26 두 문장을 한 문장으로 바꿔 쓸 때 어색한 부분을 찾아 바르게 고치시오.

Ryan works at a government office.
I sometimes go there.
→ Ryan works at a government office which I sometimes go.

__________ → __________

27 빈칸에 알맞은 관계사끼리 짝지은 것은?

(a) I hope to buy a TV ________ price is very expensive.
(b) Sunday is the day ________ we go to church.
(c) The high school ________ I attended was a prestigious one.

① whose – on which – where
② whose – when – which
③ whose – which – where
④ which – which – that
⑤ which – when – which

28 문장의 빈칸에 알맞은 관계사를 쓰시오.

(1) Marie will give a boxed lunch to __________ arrives here first.
(2) Marie won't marry __________ she doesn't like.
(3) Invite the people __________ Marie knows.

29 문장의 빈칸에 공통으로 알맞은 관계사를 쓰시오.

(a) He forgot the day ________ he had to submit his final paper.
(b) I don't know the reason ________ I was scolded.

30 빈칸에 알맞은 관계사끼리 짝지은 것은?

I had to study hard for the midterm exam in the library, ________ air conditioner was broken. It was too hot there, ________ annoyed me a lot. So I left and went home.

① which – that　② who – which
③ that – that　④ whom – what
⑤ whose – which

> 정답 및 해설 34쪽

Extracurricular Activities

▸ Sentence Writing

PART A Complete the sentences describing the pictures.

1

look at / whenever

2

win / whoever

3

take place / FIFA World Cup

1 ______________________________, she smiles at me. I think she likes me.
(내가 그녀를 볼 때마다)

2 ______________________________ will go to Paris as the winner of the NFM prize.
(우승하는 사람은 누구든지)

3 Eric wants to know the year ______________________________ in Korea.
(한국에서 FIFA 월드컵이 열렸던 해)

PART B Change the Korean into English by using the given words.

1 우리는 어머님이 배우이신 친구 한 명이 있다. (we, actress)
→ ______________________________

2 이 케이크 한 조각이 오늘 내가 먹은 전부이다. (piece, all)
→ ______________________________

3 민이가 보고 있는 것은 새로 나온 영화이다. (watch, newly released movie)
→ ______________________________

4 Cathy가 누구와 사랑에 빠졌든지 나는 신경 쓰지 않는다. (fall in love with, mind)
→ ______________________________

▸ Further Studies 학교 시험에 자주 나오는 Idioms ⑥

- drop someone a line 메일이나 글로 연락하다
- pull strings (권력이나 돈 따위에) 줄을 대다
- ding-dong (= stupid person) 멍청한 사람들
- seize the day 매순간을 즐겨라
- the life of the party (↔ icebreaker) 분위기 메이커 (↔ 분위기 깨는 사람)
- a people person 사람들과 두루 뭉실하게 잘 어울리는 사람
- two thumbs up 강력추천
- make one's blood run cold 머리카락이 쭈뼛 서게 만들다
- hot stuff 멋진 사람이나 물건
- like a cat on a hot tin roof 안절부절 못하는
- draw up a paper 문서를 작성하다
- cold turkey 금단증상
- drama queen 호들갑을 떠는 여자
- be one's own boss 개인 사업을 하다
- go-getter 도전적인 야심가
- God's gift to men 공주병 환자
- God's gift to women 왕자병 환자
- good from far, far from good 멀리서는 멋진데 가까이서 보면 꽝인
- be packed like sardines 콩나물시루 같이 들어차 있다
- You rule. 네가 짱이야.
- chin up (= cheer up) 기운 내
- pick on (= torment) ~를 따돌리다, 왕따 시키다
- rat race 극심한 경쟁
- All that's fair must fade. 화무십일홍.
- What's with the long face? 왜 그렇게 우울한 표정이니?
- by the book 규칙에 따라, 원리원칙대로
- a flash in the pan 빛깔 좋은 성공이 금방 끝나버리고 다시는 그런 기회가 오지 않는 것
- practice what you preach (남의 일 참견 말고) 너나 잘해
- busy bee 늘 바쁘고 활동적인 사람
- on the tip of one's tongue 혀끝에서 맴도는데 생각이 안나는

Unit 10 관사 (Articles)

Day 20 | 관사의 의미와 용법 (심화)

기출 맛보기

다음 중 어법상 어색한 문장을 고르시오. (양천구 ○○중학교)

① Do you remember the Mexican restaurant we used to go to?
② I can play the drum and the guitar well.
③ I want to look for North Star in the sky at night.
④ Stanley goes to bed early in the evening.
⑤ It may take an hour to complete this task.

해설

③ [North Star → the North Star] 세상에 하나뿐인 것을 나타낼 때는 정관사 the를 사용해야 한다.
① 서로 알고 있는 대상에 관해 이야기할 때 the를 사용해야 한다.
② 악기 앞에는 정관사 the를 사용한다.
④ 사물(bed)이 원래의 목적으로 사용될 때 관사를 사용하지 않는다.
⑤ '하나, 한'의 수를 나타낼 때 부정관사 a(n)을 사용한다.

해석

① 너는 우리가 가곤 했던 그 멕시코 식당을 기억하니?
② 나는 드럼과 기타를 잘 연주할 수 있다.
③ 나는 밤하늘에 있는 북극성을 찾아보고 싶다.
④ Stanley는 저녁 일찍 잠자리에 든다.
⑤ 이 일을 끝내는 데 한 시간이 걸릴지도 모른다.

정답 ③

관사의 의미와 용법 (심화)

1교시 Grammar Point

1 부정관사 a(n)

> 하나(one), 어떤(certain), 마다(per), ~같은 사람, 제품/작품, 종족 대표

Eating an apple keeps you healthy. 하나의 사과

An old man suggested this option. 어떤 노인이

I was asked to take the exam once a month. 한 달마다

The man was a Mozart of the time. 모차르트 같은 사람

The little girl is playing a Chopin. 쇼팽의 곡

Raising a dog is not always easy. 개를 기르는 것

2 정관사 the

the + 특정 대상 (대상을 아는 경우)	The sun rises. (유일한 대상) The food goes bad. (정해진 대상)
the + 익숙한 장소	in the room (우리 집 방) ⇔ in a room (막연한 방) the street (우리 동네 거리) ⇔ a street (모르는 어떤 거리)
the + 한정 명사 (수식어구에 의해 한정을 받는 명사)	The cars on the freeway look dangerous. The roof of my house is similar to that of your house.
the + 방위, 방향	We drive to the north.
the + 신체부위	I punch you in the face.

3 무관사

> 식사, 운동/게임, 호칭/직책, 교통수단, 심각한 병 등의 명사

I haven't eaten **lunch** yet. 식사

We are playing **tennis** and **chess**. 운동/게임

President Park will visit this town. 직책

by **taxi** / by **bus** (*cf.* in **a taxi** / on **the bus**) 교통수단

get **cancer** (*cf.* have **the flu**, get **a cold**) 심각한 병

4 〈the + 고유명사〉

the + 보통명사	the North Pole (북극), the Great Wall (만리장성)
the + 복수 지명	the Philippines (필리핀), the Netherlands (네덜란드), the Himalayas (히말라야 산맥), the West Indies (서인도제도)
the + 관광물 (박물관, 탑, 호텔)	the Louvre (루브르 박물관), the Eiffel Tower (에펠탑)
the + 물 관련 이름 (강, 바다, 다리, 운하)	the Nile (나일강), the Golden Gate Bridge (금문교)

Grammar Tips

- **무관사: 불가산 명사와 복수 명사**

We bought **a gold**. (x) 불가산 명사
We spent **a coins**. (x) 복수 명사

- **혼동하기 쉬운 가산 명사와 불가산 명사**

가산 명사	불가산 명사
a mistake	furniture
an X-ray	machinery
a relationship	homework
a word	toast
an assignment	fruit
	grammar
	vocabulary

- **방향 관련 주의해야 할 표현**

in front of (~의 앞에)
in the front of (~의 앞쪽에)

on top of (~의 위에)
at the top of (~의 윗부분에)

- **〈관사 + 식사명〉**

(1) 특정 식사를 나타낼 때
The lunch was wonderful.

(2) 형용사를 동반하는 경우
I had **a delicious dinner**.

- **기타 무관사를 취하는 경우**

(1) 단수형 나라명
Korea, Japan, China 등

(2) 도로명, 공원명, 광장명, 공항명, 대학명
Broadway, Central Park, Times Square, Yale University

(3) 공휴일
on New Year's Day

2교시 In - Class Questions

STEP A

괄호 안에서 알맞은 말을 고르시오.

1 My family loves to have good (food / meal).

2 (The gold / Gold) is a precious metal.

3 I always go to school by (bus / the bus).

4 We are going to travel in (France / Philippines) next month.

STEP B

빈칸에 알맞은 관사를 쓰시오. (관사가 필요하지 않으면 ×표 할 것)

1 This room needs ______________ furniture.

2 John finally became ______________ astronaut.

3 Kelly is ______________ Canadian singer.

4 Were you going to read ______________ newspaper today?

STEP C

어법상 어색한 부분을 찾아 바르게 고치시오.

1 I sometimes eat a breakfast in the cafeteria. ___________ → ___________

2 On the Christmas, Americans decorate their Christmas trees. ___________ → ___________

3 The club members climbed Himalayas. ___________ → ___________

4 Sally wants to visit the Times Square in New York. ___________ → ___________

STEP D

주어진 말을 사용하여 다음 우리말을 영어로 옮기시오.

1 전화벨이 울리고 있었지만 집에는 아무도 없었다. (nobody, house, although)

→ ____

2 나의 가족은 저녁식사 후에 공원에서 배드민턴을 쳤다. (dinner, badminton)

→ ____

3 나는 책 읽는 것을 좋아해. 그 책의 이름은 뭐니? (book, name)

→ ____

Final Test

01 밑줄 친 부정관사가 per(~마다)의 의미로 쓰인 것은?

① It was a big accident last night.
② You must take the medicine three times a day.
③ A dog has four legs, and a spider has eight legs.
④ A lot of visitors are waiting in line to see the monument.
⑤ My parents always drink a cup of milk in the morning.

02 밑줄 친 부정관사가 the same(같은)의 의미로 쓰인 것은?

① His father is a movie director.
② Mr. Park is playing a Mozart.
③ One of my friends has a new iPad.
④ Birds of a feather flock together.
⑤ Sam goes to the movies once a month.

[03-04] 밑줄 친 부분 중 어법상 어색한 것을 고르시오.

03 ① Why don't you open the window?
② His son is always in the room.
③ People looked me in the eyes.
④ You have to turn left at the second traffic light.
⑤ Kelly sat down on a bench near the newstand.

04 ① Goodbye! Have a nice day.
② Don't touch a child on head.
③ The last meal of the day is called dinner.
④ Please tell me the way to the bus stop.
⑤ Amber usually goes for a walk in the morning.

05 문장의 빈칸에 들어갈 관사가 나머지와 다른 것은?

① Jane wants to learn how to play _________ violin.
② Do you remember _________ man on stage?
③ Have you ever seen _________ Amazon River?
④ A few members want to visit _________ Netherlands.
⑤ _________ rose symbolizes passion and love.

06 주어진 말을 사용하여 다음 우리말을 영어로 옮기시오.

David는 채식주의자이다. 그래서 그는 고기를 먹지 않는다. (vegetarian, meat)

→ _______________________________________

07 문장의 빈칸에 알맞은 말끼리 짝지은 것은?

(a) I'd like to travel to _________ someday. (b) We are staying in the _________.

① United Kingdom – South America
② North Pole – Jeju Island
③ Alaska – Korea
④ Alaska – Netherlands
⑤ China – Hawaii

08 우리말과 같은 뜻이 되도록 할 때 빈칸에 알맞은 말끼리 짝지은 것은?

필요는 발명의 어머니이다. → _________ necessity is _________ mother of _________ invention.

① × – the – the
② × – the – ×
③ A – × – the
④ × – a – the
⑤ The – × – ×

[09-10] 문장의 빈칸에 알맞은 관사끼리 짝지은 것을 고르시오.

09

_________ hippo has _________ big mouth.

① A – a
② A – the
③ A – ×
④ × – the
⑤ × – ×

10

Some of them are staying at _________ home instead of being at _________ school.

① a – a
② a – the
③ a – ×
④ × – ×
⑤ × – the

11 밑줄 친 부분 중 어법상 어색한 것을 찾아 바르게 고치시오.

①Eiffel Tower is one of ②the most famous landmarks in ③Paris. Constructed in 1889, it was ④a symbol of democracy of ⑤France.

_________________ → _________________

12 문장의 빈칸에 알맞은 관사를 쓰고, 그 이유를 간략히 쓰시오.

(1) _________ gold in this bracelet is of high quality.
이유: ______________________________

(2) This is _________ best gold ring that I have.
이유: ______________________________

(3) Mom gave me _________ useful advice to help me make my decision.
이유: ______________________________

(4) We have never been to _________ north.
이유: ______________________________

13 대화의 밑줄 친 부분 중 어법상 어색한 것을 고르시오.

A: Alice is going to have ①a big party tonight. Can you go with me ②in a car?
B: Sorry. I can't. I have other plans.
A: Oh, no. I will do ③a magic show ④at a party. I want you to give me ⑤some flowers.
B: Really? Okay, I will try to cancel my plans.

14 문장의 빈칸에 알맞은 관사를 넣으시오. (관사가 필요 없으면 ×표 할 것)

_________ Columbia University is in _________ state of New York.

15 밑줄 친 부분에 유의하여 다음 문장을 우리말로 옮기시오.

(1) There is an eraser on top of the paper.
→ ______________________________

(2) Read the topic at the top of the page.
→ ______________________________

16 우리말을 영어로 옮길 때 빈칸에 알맞은 관사를 넣으시오. (넣을 필요가 없으면 ×표 할 것)

Cathy는 공항을 가기 위해 택시를 불러 세웠다. 그래서 우리는 택시로 공항에 갔다.
→ Cathy hailed _________ taxi to go to the airport. So we went to the airport by _________ taxi.

17 주어진 문장을 바르게 고치지 않은 것은?

① Gary was a wisest boy in my class.
→ Gary was the wisest boy in my class.
② Steve is the polite person. He's also the good listener.
→ Steve is a polite person. He's also a good listener.
③ A Louvre is bigger than any other museum in the world.
→ Louvre is bigger than any other museum in the world.
④ Let's take the Route 1. We have to go to an east.
→ Let's take the Route 1. We have to go to the east.
⑤ The President Park has decided to pass the bill.
→ President Park has decided to pass the bill.

18 문장의 빈칸에 관사가 필요한 것은?

① Teddy's brother went to ________ prison to meet Teddy.
② The people at this meeting haven't had ________ lunch yet.
③ ________ skin cancer is caused by too much exposure to the sun.
④ We were supposed to send this package to France by ________ airmail.
⑤ ________ Queen Mary was the greatest woman in England's history.

19 대화의 빈칸에 알맞은 것은?

A: How did you pay the part-time workers?
B: As a rule, they were paid ________.

① by an hour ② by a hour
③ by the hour ④ by hours
⑤ by the hours

20 밑줄 친 관사의 쓰임이 올바른 것끼리 묶인 것은?

(a) A day has twenty-four hours.
(b) Could you turn off a light?
(c) Chan and Helen are of an age.
(d) Elizabeth caught me by the hand.
(e) The mathematics is an interesting subject.

① (a)(d) ② (a)(c)(d)
③ (a)(d)(e) ④ (a)(b)(d)
⑤ (b)(c)(d)(e)

21 문장의 빈칸에 부정관사 a(n)을 넣을 수 없는 것은?

① ________ cat is a selfish animal.
② I hung ________ Monet in my living room.
③ It is quite ________ helpful class.
④ ________ knowledge can be gained from the Internet.
⑤ There was ________ fire near my house.

[22-23] 어법상 어색한 부분을 찾아 바르게 고치시오.

22

Would you please bring me a paper from the bookshelf if you're not busy now?

________ → ________

23

It is necessary that a person drinks several glasses of the water daily if he wishes to remain healthy.

________ → ________

24 밑줄 친 부분 중 어법상 어색한 부분을 모두 고르시오.

> Daniel is ①a police. ②One day, he came across ③the vicious criminal at ④the corner of ⑤the busy street and arrested him immediately.

25 글의 빈칸에 a, an, the 중 하나를 쓰시오. (관사가 불필요한 경우는 x를 쓸 것)

> This is (1)________ last call for New York passengers. Now departing from gate 50, flight 075 is bound for New York with stops in Detroit and Philadelphia. This is (2)________ last New York flight from (3)________ Incheon International Airport today. All passengers should be on (4)________ board with their boarding passes and passports. Thank you.

26 〈보기〉의 밑줄 친 부분과 쓰임이 같은 것은?

> 보기 A Mr. Jones called on you while you were out.

① Rome was not built in a day.
② Birds of a feather flock together.
③ How many days are in a common year?
④ I play baseball once or twice a month.
⑤ Once, there lived an old king in a small country.

서술형 대비

27 우리말을 영어로 옮긴 문장에서 어법상 어색한 부분을 고쳐 다시 쓰시오.

> Joshua는 내 형의 친한 친구 중 하나이다.
> → Joshua is a my older brother's close friend.

→ ________________________________

28 밑줄 친 부분에 들어갈 말이 나머지와 다른 것은?

① He was ________ MVP this season.
② It took ________ hour to finish my homework.
③ Both of ________ women are beautiful.
④ ________ backpacks there are all mine.
⑤ All of ________ oranges in the box are very delicious.

[29-30] 다음 글을 읽고, 물음에 답하시오.

> When it comes to English, many Korean students have difficulty studying (a)[a grammar / grammar]. So most English teachers give (b)[an assignment / assignment]. However, students really don't like to do (c)[a homework / homework]. What is more, they don't bother with memorizing (d)________ vocabulary. If they figured out the relationship between words, it would be easier to memorize them. They don't know the truth.

29 위 글의 (a), (b), (c) 네모 안에서 어법상 올바른 표현끼리 짝지은 것은?

	(a)	(b)	(c)
①	a grammar	– assignment	– homework
②	a grammar	– an assignment	– a homework
③	grammar	– an assignment	– a homework
④	grammar	– assignment	– homework
⑤	grammar	– an assignment	– homework

30 위 글의 빈칸 (d)에 알맞은 관사를 넣고, 필요 없다면 X표 하시오.

(d)________

> 정답 및 해설 36쪽

Extracurricular Activities

▸ Sentence Writing

PART A Complete the sentences describing the picture. Use the given words.

Two weeks ago, ________________(elephant) was found in ________________(hallway) of Page Elementary School in L.A. This big animal probably went to ________________ (school) after escaping from ________________(zoo). One of the students believed that ________________(elephant) followed him back to school from ________________(field trip) which his school took to the California Zoo.

PART B Change the Korean into English by using the given words.

1 떠나기 전에 불을 끄고 창문을 닫아라. (shut, turn off, leaving)

→ ____

2 나는 보통 저녁을 먹고 난 후에 바이올린을 연주한다. (violin, dinner)

→ ____

3 하루에 두 번씩 이 약을 복용하세요. (take)

→ ____

4 공항으로 가는 버스가 하나 있다. 너는 저기에서 그 버스를 탈 수 있다. (there, take)

→ ____

▸ Further Studies 학교 시험에 자주 나오는 Idioms ⑦

▶ sharp tongue 가시 담긴 말투

▶ silver tongue 부드러운 말투

▶ tone-deaf 음치

▶ It's all Greek to me. / It sounds all Greek to me. 난 그런 것엔 까막눈이야. 봐도 몰라.

▶ big fat 떠들썩한

▶ no brainer 머리를 굴릴 필요가 없는 매우 쉬운 결정

▶ Don't add insult to injury. 그건 날 두 번 죽이는 거야.

▶ brain box 매우 지적인 사람

▶ pop one's clogs (= pass away, die) 죽다

▶ southpaw 왼손잡이 투수, 왼손잡이 복서

▶ spare tire 두툼한 뱃살

▶ It's what's inside that counts. 중요한 건 외모가 아니라 내면의 모습이다.

▶ crow's feet 눈가의 잔주름

▶ sweetheart deal 짜고 치는 고스톱

▶ hold out for (원하는 것을 얻을 때까지) 기다리다

▶ in a million 가능성이 희박한, 최고의

▶ get all choked up (눈물이 나지 않지만) 목이 미어지다

▶ leave no stone unturned 온갖 수단을 다 써보다

▶ put one's John Hancock 서명하다 (John Hancock은 미국 독립선언서 최초 서명자)

▶ look a gift horse in the mouth 선물 받은 물건에 대해 이러쿵저러쿵 험담하다

Unit 11 가정법 (Conditionals)

Day 21 | 가정법 과거, 과거완료, 혼합가정법
Day 22 | 기타 가정법

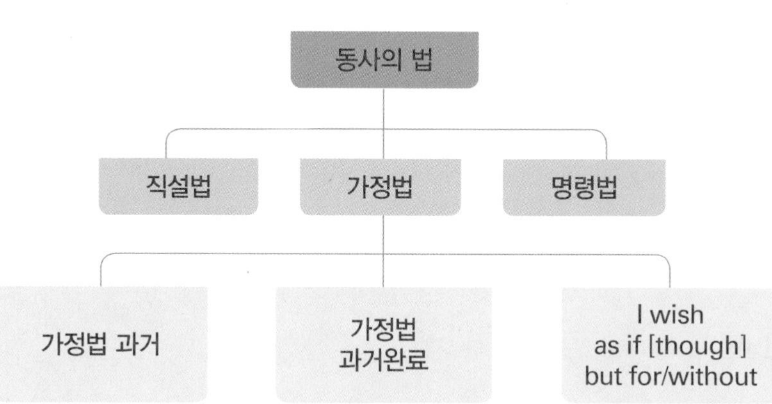

기출 맛보기

다음 중 어법상 어색한 문장을 고르시오. (강동구 ○○중학교)

① If I had known you were coming, I would have stayed at the office.

② If we hadn't started last week, we would not complete our project now.

③ If I earned enough money, I could purchase a new smartphone.

④ Without fresh water, all living things would die.

⑤ I wish I am a famous athlete.

해설

⑤ 〈I wish + 가정법 과거(주어 + 동사의 과거형)〉는 '~하면 좋을 텐데'라는 뜻이다. I wish 가정법에서 동사로 현재시제 am을 쓸 수 없다. 시제에 따라 were 또는 had been을 사용해야 한다.

① 가정법 과거완료는 〈If + 주어 + had + 과거분사 ~, 주어 + 조동사의 과거형 + have + 과거분사 ...〉로 쓰며, '~했다면 …했을 텐데'라는 뜻이다.

② 혼합가정법은 〈If + 주어 + had + 과거분사 ~, 주어 + 조동사의 과거형 + 동사원형 ...〉으로 쓰며, '~였다면 …할 텐데'라는 뜻이다.

③ 가정법 과거는 〈If + 주어 + 동사의 과거형 ~, 주어 + 조동사의 과거형 + 동사원형 ...〉으로 쓰며, '~하다면 …할 텐데'라는 뜻이다.

④ 〈Without + 명사, 주어 + 가정법 과거(조동사의 과거형 + 동사원형)〉는 '~이 없으면 …일 텐데'라는 뜻이다.

해석

① 네가 오는 것을 알았더라면 나는 사무실에 있었을 텐데.

② 우리가 지난주에 시작하지 않았다면 우리 프로젝트를 지금 끝내지 못할 텐데.

③ 내가 충분히 돈을 번다면 새 스마트폰을 구입할 수 있을 텐데.

④ 신선한 물이 없으면 모든 살아 있는 것들은 죽을 것이다.

⑤ 내가 유명한 운동선수면 좋을 텐데.

정답 ⑤

DAY 21

가정법 과거, 과거완료, 혼합가정법

1교시 Grammar Point

1 가정법 과거

- 현재 사실과 반대되는 일을 가정

> 형태: 〈If + 주어 + 과거동사 ~, 주어 + 조동사의 과거형 + 동사원형 ...〉
> (if절의 동사가 be동사일 경우 주어와 상관없이 항상 were를 사용)
> 의미: '만일 ~라면 …할 텐데'

If I **were** you, I **would** buy the car. (내가 너라면 그 차를 살 텐데.)
→ As I **am not** you, I **can't buy** the car. (나는 네가 아니라서 그 차를 살 수 없다.)

If she **were** not sick, she **would come** to the party. (그녀는 아프지 않으면 파티에 갈 텐데.)
→ As she **is** sick, she **will not come** to the party.
(그녀는 아프기 때문에 파티에 가지 않을 것이다.)

2 가정법 과거완료

- 과거 사실과 반대되는 일을 가정

> 형태: 〈If + 주어 + had + 과거분사 ~, 주어 + 조동사의 과거형 + have + 과거분사 ...〉
> 의미: '만일 ~했다면 …했을 텐데'

If he **had been** there, he **would have eaten** it. (그가 거기에 있었다면 그것을 먹었을 텐데.)
→ As he **wasn't** there, he **could not eat** it.
(그는 그곳에 없었기 때문에 그것을 먹을 수가 없었다.)

If she **had studied** hard, she **could have passed** the exam.
(그녀는 열심히 공부했다면 시험에 합격할 수 있었을 텐데.)
→ As she **didn't study** hard, she **could not pass** the exam.
(그녀는 열심히 공부하지 않았기 때문에 시험에 합격할 수 없었다.)

3 혼합가정법

- 가정법 과거완료와 가정법 과거가 혼합된 형태
- 과거에 실현되지 못한 사실이 현재까지 영향을 미칠 때 사용
- 시간의 차이를 알 수 있는 부사어(구)인 now, today, tonight 등이 사용됨

> 형태: 〈If + 주어 + had + 과거분사 ~ (과거 부사어), 주어 + 조동사의 과거형 + 동사원형 + ~ (현재 부사어)〉
> 의미: '만일 ~였다면 …할 텐데'

If I **had not gained** weight then, I **could wear** this swimming suit now.
(나는 체중이 늘지 않았더라면 지금 이 수영복을 입을 수 있을 텐데.)
→ As I **gained** weight then, I **can't wear** this swimming suit now.
(나는 체중이 늘었기 때문에 지금 이 수영복을 입을 수 없다.)

Grammar Tips

가정법 → 직설법으로 바꿀 때

현재/과거 사실에 반대되는 가정법 문장이므로 현재/과거 사실을 나타내는 직설법 문장으로 바꾼다.

(1) if를 없애고 so, as, because 등의 접속사를 쓴다.
(2) 가정법과 반대되는 문맥으로 나타낸다. (긍정 가정법 → 부정 직설법 / 부정 가정법 → 긍정 직설법)
(3) 동사의 시제는 현재/과거로 쓴다.

If I **were** rich, I **could buy** the boat.
→ As I **am not** rich, I **can't buy** the boat.

가정법 현재 vs. 가정법 과거

가정법 현재는 단순 조건문으로 실제로 발생 가능한 일을 가정한다. 반면에 가정법 과거는 실현 가능성이 희박할 경우에 사용한다.

If she **knows** his number, she **will call** him. [가정법 현재: 전화를 할 가능성이 어느 정도 있음]
If she **knew** his number, she **would call** him. [가정법 과거: 실제로 전화번호를 몰라서 전화를 걸 가능성이 거의 없음]

if절의 대동사

문장에서 반복되는 부분(동사구)을 대동사로 나타낼 수 있다.

I don't have any money. If I **did**, I could buy a brand-new car.
[did: had money]

2교시 In - Class Questions

괄호 안에서 알맞은 말을 고르시오.

1 If I **(studied / had studied)** harder while at school, I would be a doctor now.

2 If I **(win / won)** the lottery, I would buy a big mension with swimming pool.

3 If I **(knew / have known)** the truth, I would tell it to you.

4 If we **(taken / had taken)** the airplane, we would be in Busan now.

주어진 말을 빈칸에 알맞은 형태로 바꿔 쓰시오.

1 If I ______________ enough money, I could travel around the world. (have)

2 If you ______________ the parcel before 2 p.m., it will arrive by tomorrow afternoon. (send)

3 If Jim had not ______________ his arm, he could be playing baseball here in the postseason. (break)

두 문장이 같은 뜻이 되도록 빈칸에 알맞은 말을 쓰시오.

1 If I had become a pro-gamer, I'd have been happier.
→ I ____________________ a pro-gamer, so I ____________________ happy.

2 If he had been a man of strong will, he would have succeeded.
→ As he ____________________ a man of strong will, he ____________________.

3 As I like basketball very much, my dream is to be an NBA professional basketball player.
→ If I ____________________ basketball very much, my dream ____________________ to be an NBA professional basketball player.

4 My mother didn't have time, so she didn't watch the soap opera.
→ If my mother ____________________ time, she ____________________ the soap opera.

직설법 문장을 if를 이용한 가정법 문장으로 바꿔 쓰시오.

1 As Mike doesn't take care of his car regularly, his car frequently breaks down.
→ ____

2 As you helped me then, I am here now.
→ ____

3 As he did not have enough time, he could not do it better.
→ ____

3교시 After-Class Questions

[01-02] 빈칸에 알맞은 동사의 형태를 고르시오.

01 If my school ________ closer to my house, I would not be late often.

① is ② were ③ would be
④ has been ⑤ had been

02

A: You played the piano very well.
B: Well, if I had had longer fingers, I ________ the piano better.

① play ② played ③ could play
④ could have played ⑤ could had played

[03-04] 우리말을 영어로 바르게 옮긴 것을 고르시오.

03 내가 너라면 나는 그것에 대해 나중에 이야기할 텐데.

① I'll talk about it later if I am you.
② I'll talk about it later if I was you.
③ I'd talk about it later if I were you.
④ I'd have talked about it later if I were you.
⑤ I'd have talked about it later if I had been you.

04 그녀가 그 파티에 갔다면 범블비를 볼 수 있었을 텐데.

① If she comes to the party, she can see Bumblebee.
② If she came to the party, she could see Bumblebee.
③ If she has come to the party, she could have seen Bumblebee.
④ If she had come to the party, she could have seen Bumblebee.
⑤ If she had come to the party, she could had seen Bumblebee.

[05-06] 다음 중 어법상 어색한 문장을 고르시오.

05 ① Gary could get a job to earn some money if he were not lazy.
② If you had asked me a question, I would have helped you.
③ I would not be in the hospital now if I had driven carefully.
④ I wouldn't have broken my leg if I hadn't slipped on the stairs.
⑤ If I had not joined the club, I would have not been tired now.

06 ① I wish I had studied English hard.
② She looks as if she were an honors student.
③ If I had enough time, I would spend it with my family.
④ If I had enough money, I can buy a brand-new bike.
⑤ If it had not rained this morning, we could have gone on the field trip.

Vocabulary Tips

- earn (돈 등을) 벌다
- slip 미끄러지다
- honors student 우등생
- brand-new 아주 새로운

[07-08] 두 문장이 같은 뜻이 되도록 빈칸에 알맞은 말끼리 짝지은 것을 고르시오.

07 Because Andrew had breakfast in the morning, he isn't hungry right now.

→ If Andrew ________ breakfast in the morning, he ________ hungry right now.

① had – wouldn't be
② hadn't – would be
③ had had – wouldn't be
④ hadn't had – would be
⑤ hadn't had – wouldn't have been

08 Joe didn't follow the rules. So he is in trouble now.

→ If Joe ________ the rules, he ________ in trouble now.

① didn't follow – was
② followed – isn't
③ had followed – wouldn't be
④ followed – would be
⑤ hadn't followed – wouldn't be

[09-11] 어법상 어색한 부분을 찾아 바르게 고치시오.

09 If he told me the truth, I wouldn't have suspected him of stealing my purse.

________________ → ________________

10 If Bill didn't help me yesterday, I might not be alive now.

________________ → ________________

서술형 대비

11 If she is smart, she could solve the problem.

________________ → ________________

12 직설법 문장을 가정법 문장으로 바꿔 쓰시오.

Linda didn't finish her homework yesterday, so she can't watch this show.

→ ________________________________

13 문장의 빈칸에 알맞은 말끼리 짝지은 것은?

If the singer GD ________ my close friend, I ________ more proud to others at that time.

① had been – would feel
② had been – would have felt
③ were – would feel
④ were – would have felt
⑤ was – would feel

Vocabulary Tips

- be in trouble 곤경에 처하다
- suspect A of B A를 B로 의심하다
- proud 자랑스러운

[14-15] 문장의 빈칸에 알맞은 동사의 형태끼리 짝지은 것을 고르시오.

14

(a) If Jack ________ money, he would call you.
(b) If Jack ________ money, he will call you.
(c) If Jack ________ money, he would have called you.

① needed – needs – had needed
② needed – need – had needed
③ needs – needs – needed
④ had needed – needs – needed
⑤ would need – will need – has needed

15

(a) If I ________ just five minutes earlier, I wouldn't have missed the school bus.
(b) If it ________ not raining now, I would be enjoying my trip.

① had gotten up – were
② had gotten up – is
③ had gotten up – had been
④ got up – were
⑤ got up – had been

16 밑줄 친 부분 중 어법상 어색한 것은?

① The boss will not employ you if you are not honest.
② If I were you, I wouldn't take the bus.
③ I could lend you my car if I had one.
④ If my father was the president, he wouldn't let people cry.
⑤ What would your wife do if you got a big bonus?

[17-18] 문장의 빈칸에 알맞은 동사를 한 단어로 쓰시오.

17 Betty is horribly sick. If she ________, she could come to the swimming pool.

18 John doesn't know any English. If he ________, he could enjoy this movie without Korean subtitle.

[19-20] 우리말과 같은 뜻이 되도록 주어진 말을 빈칸에 알맞은 형태로 바꿔 쓰시오.

19 내가 그것을 하는 것을 망설이지 않았다면, 그때 무슨 일이 일어났을까? (happen, hesitate)

→ What ________________ if I ________________ to do it then?

Vocabulary Tips

- horribly 끔찍하게
- Korean subtitle 한국어 자막
- happen 일어나다
- hesitate 망설이다

20 너는 복권에 당첨된다면 직장을 그만둘 텐데. (win, quit)

→ If you ________________ the lottery, you ________________ your job.

[21-22] 가정법 문장을 직설법 문장으로 바꿔 쓸 때 빈칸에 알맞은 말을 쓰시오.

21 If Jinhee hadn't watched the documentary, she wouldn't have applied for this job.

→ As Jinhee __________ the documentary, she __________ for this job.

22 If I were hungry, I would have lunch with them.

→ As I __________ __________ hungry, I __________ __________ lunch with them.

23 **주어진 말을 사용하여 다음 우리말을 영어로 옮기시오.**

어젯밤에 비가 내리지 않았다면 내가 너를 집까지 태워다주었을 텐데.
(rain, drive you home)

→ ____

24 **짝지은 두 문장의 뜻이 다른 것은?**

① If he had stayed longer, he could have met her there.
→ He didn't stay longer, so he couldn't meet her there.
② If I had been 10 years younger, I could have traveled around the world.
→ I wasn't 10 years younger, so I couldn't travel around the world.
③ If I had had a camera, I could have taken pictures of it.
→ As I don't have a camera, I can't take pictures of it.
④ If I had remembered my mom's birthday, I would have bought her a present.
→ I didn't remember my mom's birthday, so I wouldn't buy her a present.
⑤ If he had had the operation, he would not use a wheelchair now.
→ As he didn't have the operation, he uses a wheelchair now.

25 **〈보기〉의 직설법 문장을 가정법 문장으로 바르게 고친 것은?**

보기 As he was not satisfied with his silver medal, he could not stop training.

① If he had been satisfied with his silver medal, he could have stopped training.
② If he had been satisfied with his silver medal, he could stop training.
③ If he was satisfied with his silver medal, he could have stopped training.
④ If he were satisfied with his silver medal, he have stopped training.
⑤ If he had been satisfied with his silver medal, he could had stopped training.

Vocabulary Tips

- lottery 복권
- apply for ~에 지원하다
- operation 수술
- silver medal 은메달

DAY 22

기타 가정법

1교시 Grammar Point

1 I wish + 가정법

I wish + 가정법 과거	I wish + 가정법 과거완료
현재에 이룰 수 없는 소망	과거에 이루지 못한 일에 대한 아쉬움
〈I wish + 주어 + 동사의 과거형 ~〉	〈I wish + 주어 + had + 과거분사 ~〉
'~하면 좋을 텐데'	'~했다면 좋았을 텐데'

I wish I could speak English like my English teacher.
→ I am sorry that I **can't speak** English like my English teacher.

My final grade is not so good. **I wish I had studied** harder for this class.
→ My final grade is not so good. I am sorry that I **didn't study** harder for this class.

2 as if[though] + 가정법

as if + 가정법 과거	as if + 가정법 과거완료
〈주절 + as if + 주어 + 동사의 과거형〉	〈주절 + as if + 주어 + had + 과거분사〉
'마치 ~처럼'	'마치 ~였던 것처럼'

He talks **as if** he **knew** my mind. → In fact, he **doesn't know** my mind.

She looks **as if** she **had been** sick. → In fact, she **wasn't** sick.

3 if의 생략

- 과거완료에서 종종 일어남(과거는 were일 경우만)
- if를 생략하면 주어와 동사의 위치가 바뀜

If I had been at the party, I would have had a lot of fun.
→ **Had I been** at the party, I would have had a lot of fun.

4 without + 가정법

without + 명사, 가정법 과거	without + 명사, 가정법 과거완료
〈without + 명사, 주어 + 조동사의 과거형 + 동사원형 ...〉	〈without + 명사, 주어 + 조동사 과거형 + have + 과거분사 ...〉
'만약 ~이 없다면 …할 텐데'	'만약 ~이 없었다면 …했을 텐데'

Without water, nothing could live.
→ **But for water**, nothing could live.
→ **If it were not for water**, nothing could live.
→ **Were it not for water**, nothing could live.

Without water, nothing could have lived.
→ **But for water**, nothing could have lived.
→ **If it had not been for water**, nothing could have lived.
→ **Had it not been for water**, nothing could have lived.

Grammar Tips

as if의 시제

(1) 주절과 as if의 시제가 일치하면
→ 가정법 과거

(2) 주절보다 as if의 시제가 앞서면
→ 가정법 과거완료

She **acts** as if she **were** young.
→ In fact, she is not young.
[현재 젊은 척 행동함]

She **acts** as if she **had been** young.
→ In fact, she was not young.
[과거에 젊은 척 행동함]

She **acted** as if she **were** young.
→ In fact, she was not young.
[과거에 젊은 척 행동했음]

She **acted** as if she **had been** young.
→ In fact, she had not been young.
[과거보다 더 과거에 젊었던 것처럼 행동했음]

가정법 과거 were의 도치

If it **were** not for dreams, life would be nothing.
= **Were it** not for dreams, life would be nothing.

〈It's time + 가정법〉

〈It's time + 주어 + 동사의 과거형〉의 형태로 쓰며, 할 일을 하지 않은 것에 대한 유감을 표현한다. '~해야 할 때이다'라는 의미이다. 〈It is time + 주어 + should + 동사원형〉으로 바꿔 쓸 수 있다.

It is time we **went** to bed.
→ It is time **we should go** to bed.
→ It is time **for us to go** to bed.

2교시 In - Class Questions

STEP A

직설법 문장은 가정법 문장으로, 가정법 문장은 직설법 문장으로 바꿔 쓰시오.

1 I am sorry I was not in the office when you stopped by.
→ I wish I ______________________________.

2 I am sorry the journey is over.
→ I wish ______________________________.

3 I wish they had come and seen us last class.
→ I am sorry ______________________________.

4 I wish I knew her cell phone number.
→ I am sorry I ______________________________.

STEP B

두 문장이 같은 뜻이 되도록 빈칸에 알맞은 말을 쓰시오.

1 If it had not been for the navigation system, we might have gotten lost.
→ __________ the navigation system, we might have gotten lost.

2 But for the sun, nothing could live.
→ If it __________ __________ __________ the sun, nothing could live.

3 Without your help, I couldn't have finished my assignment on time.
→ If it __________ __________ __________ __________ your help, I couldn't have finished my assignment on time.

STEP C

밑줄 친 부분을 어법상 바르게 고치시오.

1 I had hurried up, I couldn't have missed the train. → __________

2 He talks as if he knew everything. In fact, he didn't know anything. → __________

3 She looked as if she had not been sick. In fact, she is sick. → __________

STEP D

주어진 말을 사용하여 다음 우리말을 영어로 옮기시오.

1 내가 할리우드 영화를 알아들을 수 있으면 좋을 텐데. (Hollywood, understand)
→ ______________________________

2 그는 마치 그 영화를 봤던 것처럼 말한다. (talk, see)
→ ______________________________

3 공기가 없다면 세상의 어떤 생물도 존재할 수 없을 것이다. (without, no creatures, exist)
→ ______________________________

3교시 After-Class Questions

01 문장의 빈칸에 알맞지 않은 것은?

_________ your help, I would have failed the final exam.

① If it were not for ② Had it not been for
③ But for ④ Without
⑤ If it had not been for

02 주어진 말을 빈칸에 알맞은 형태로 바꿔 쓰시오.

Kelly wishes she _____________________ hard when she was a high school student. (study)

[03-04] 〈보기〉와 의미가 같은 문장을 고르시오.

03 보기 Helen sings on stage as if she were a musical actress.

① Helen is a real musical actress.
② Helen will be a musical actress.
③ Helen doesn't like to be a real musical actress.
④ In fact, Helen isn't a musical actress.
⑤ Helen was a musical actress, but she is not one now.

04 보기 It is time that you went to bed.

① It is time that you will go to bed.
② It is time that you can go to bed.
③ It is time that you shall go to bed.
④ It is time that you would go to bed.
⑤ It is time that you should go to bed.

[05-06] 문장의 빈칸에 알맞은 말을 고르시오.

05 I wish I ________ a competent employee when I worked for the company.

① am ② was ③ were
④ have been ⑤ had been

06 Gary wishes his parents ________ him a present last Christmas.

① give ② gave ③ would give
④ has given ⑤ had given

[07-08] 밑줄 친 부분 대신에 쓸 수 있는 것을 고르시오.

07 Without him, our soccer team couldn't win the game.

① If it is not for him ② If it were not for him
③ If it were for him ④ If it has not been for him
⑤ If it had not been for him

Vocabulary Tips

- competent 유능한
- employee 직원, 근로자

08 But for the research, I wouldn't have gotten my master's degree.

① Had it not been for the research
② It had not been for the research
③ If it have not been for the research
④ If it were not for the research
⑤ Were it not for the research

09 밑줄 친 부분의 쓰임이 어법상 어색한 것은?

① My grandmother likes her dog as if it were her daughter.
② I wish I have done my best to study hard when I was young.
③ My father works for us as if there were no tomorrow.
④ They wish they could play baseball very well this season.
⑤ Without my parents' financial support, I couldn't have gotten my degree.

서술형 대비

10 다음 글을 읽고, 빈칸에 알맞은 말을 쓰시오.

This morning, I woke up late because I went to bed too late last night. I had to get to school on time to take an exam. I hurried to the bus stop. But I found that I had no cash or bus card with me. I came across Shawn, a friend of mine. He was my lifesaver. I asked him to lend me some money and took the bus. Luckily, I was not late for the exam. Without his help, I ______________________ the exam.

11 문장의 빈칸에 공통으로 알맞은 것은?

(a) ________ you, I wouldn't have survived in this environment.
(b) Sandra couldn't finish her work ________ your help.
(c) I wouldn't be happy ________ my wife.

① With [with]　② For [for]　③ On [on]
④ Without [without]　⑤ If [if]

서술형 대비

12 어법상 어색한 부분을 찾아 바르게 고치시오.

Had it not been for the tsunami, the buildings would not be damaged.

______________ → ______________

13 두 문장이 같은 뜻이 되도록 빈칸에 알맞은 말을 쓰시오.

Without her sacrifice, we could not have succeeded.

→ ________ ________ ________ ________ ________ her sacrifice, we could not have succeeded.

Vocabulary Tips

- master's degree 석사학위
- financial support 재정 지원
- on time 정시에
- come across 우연히 만나다
- lifesaver 생명의 은인
- luckily 다행히도, 운이 좋은
- survive 살아남다
- environment 환경
- tsunami 쓰나미
- damage 손상시키다
- sacrifice 희생

14 다음 중 어법상 어색한 문장은?

① He talks as if he had seen a ghost.
② It is time that we start to study math.
③ It would be difficult, but for their support.
④ If it had not been for you, I wouldn't have succeeded.
⑤ I wish Mr. Kim had been generous to his students.

[15-16] 대화의 빈칸에 알맞은 것을 고르시오.

15

A: Could you tell me why no one likes Mr. Kim?
B: Hmm... He always talks ________ he knew everything. In fact, he doesn't know anything at all.

① if ② as if ③ even if
④ without ⑤ but for

16

A: What's wrong with you?
B: I failed the test, and I'm disappointed. I wish I ________ for the exam.

① studied ② had studied ③ haven't studied
④ hadn't studied ⑤ didn't study

[17-18] 두 문장이 같은 뜻이 되도록 빈칸에 알맞은 것을 고르시오.

17 We are sorry that Mina isn't our co-worker.

→ We wish Mina ________ our co-worker.

① is ② was ③ would be
④ were ⑤ had been

18 She acts as if she didn't care about the fact.

→ In fact, she ________ about the fact.

① cares ② cared ③ doesn't care
④ didn't care ⑤ had cared

19 어법상 어색한 부분을 바르게 고친 것은?

The instructor says, "Was she 5 centimeters taller, she could be a supermodel."

① says → said ② Was → Were ③ Was she → She was
④ Was she → She were ⑤ Was she → If she was

Vocabulary Tips

- support 지원
- generous 관대한
- co-worker 동료
- instructor 강사

20 괄호 안에서 알맞은 것끼리 짝지은 것은?

I **(was / were)** told some shocking news last night. Someone acted as if he **(was / were)** the owner of a house. A guard mistakenly helped open the door. I wish he **(didn't help / hadn't helped)** him.

① was – was – didn't help
② was – were – didn't help
③ was – were – hadn't helped
④ were – was – didn't help
⑤ were – were – hadn't helped

21 두 문장이 같은 뜻이 되도록 빈칸에 알맞은 말을 쓰시오.

(1) Tim keeps it as if it had been his laptop.
→ In fact, it ________________ Tim's laptop.

(2) My family was hilarious as if we had been in the first position.
→ In fact, we ________________ in the first position.

22 문장의 빈칸에 들어갈 수 없는 것은?

________ with Woojin, you would have recognized that something on his face changed.

① Were you
② If you had been
③ Had you been
④ If you had talked
⑤ Had you talked

23 밑줄 친 부분 중 어법상 어색한 것은?

①When the little boy ②asks for his allowance, he usually ③talks ④as if he ⑤has no money.

24 밑줄 친 부분 대신에 쓸 수 있는 것을 모두 고르시오.

Without enough money, I couldn't have studied in the US.

① Were it not for enough money
② If it were not for enough money
③ If it had not been for enough money
④ Had it not been for enough money
⑤ But for enough money

25 우리말과 같은 뜻이 되도록 주어진 단어 중에서 필요한 것만 골라 바르게 배열하시오.

Leslie가 한국말을 잘할 수 있다면 좋을 텐데.
(can / could / speak / spoke / had spoken)
→ I wish Leslie ________________ Korean well.

Vocabulary Tips

- mistakenly 실수로
- hilarious 기분이 좋은
- recognize 알아차리다
- allowance 용돈

Final Test

01 대화의 빈칸에 알맞은 동사의 형태는?

> A: What does your father do?
> B: He teaches English grammar at a school.
> A: Does he enjoy teaching grammar at school?
> B: Not really. He wishes he ________ a doctor.

① is ② be
③ were ④ will be
⑤ becomes

02 짝지은 두 문장의 뜻이 다른 것은?

① They wish they had known how to make the cheesecake.
→ They are sorry they didn't know how to make the cheesecake.
② If it were not for food, no one could live.
→ Without food, no one could live.
③ James talks about Rome as if he had been there.
→ In fact, he has been to Rome.
④ If I had driven more slowly, I would not be in the hospital now.
→ Because I didn't drive more slowly, I am in the hospital now.
⑤ If she had had tomatoes, she would have made spaghetti for them.
→ Because she didn't have tomatoes, she didn't make spaghetti for them.

03 밑줄 친 부분 중 어법상 어색한 것은?

> If Mary ①practiced singing a lot ②when she ③was in middle school, her skills ④would ⑤be a lot better now.

[04-05] 〈보기〉와 의미가 같은 문장을 고르시오.

04

> 보기 Richard is sorry that he can't go to his hometown.

① Richard wishes he goes to his hometown.
② Richard wishes he can go to his hometown.
③ Richard wishes he can't go to his hometown.
④ Richard wishes he could go to his hometown.
⑤ Richard wishes he couldn't go to his hometown.

05

> 보기 Tyler speaks as if he knew everything.

① In fact, Tyler knows everything.
② In fact, Tyler doesn't know anything.
③ In fact, Tyler knew everything.
④ In fact, Tyler didn't know anything.
⑤ In fact, Tyler hadn't know anything.

06 다음 중 어법상 어색한 문장은?

① We wish we were intelligent students.
② Jay would help the poor if he were not sick.
③ I could visit your home if my mom allows it.
④ Justine wishes she were not in trouble.
⑤ Austin wouldn't waste so much time if he were smart.

서술형 대비

07 밑줄 친 부분을 주어진 말로 시작하는 말로 바꿔 쓰시오.

> But for his bad cold, he could go to school.
> → If ________________________,
> he could go to school.

08 문장의 빈칸에 알맞은 동사의 형태는?

> If I ________ you, I would have stopped to talk to you.

① was ② were
③ had seen ④ have seen
⑤ would have seen

09 〈보기〉의 문장을 통해 알 수 있는 것은?

보기 Victor and Stella act as if they were in love.

① They will love each other.
② They love each other.
③ They don't love each other.
④ They loved each other.
⑤ They didn't love each other.

10 〈보기〉와 같이 대화의 밑줄 친 문장을 I wish ~와 If ~를 사용하여 바꿔 쓰시오.

보기 A: What do you want, Edward?
B: I want to have a cute girlfriend.
→ I wish I had a cute girlfriend.
→ If I had a cute girlfriend, I would be happy.

A: What do you want, Joshua?
B: I want to earn a lot of money.

→ ____________________
→ ____________________

11 〈보기〉의 밑줄 친 if와 쓰임이 같은 것은?

보기 Your kids would be happier if you bought them a CD.

① Don't ask me if I know the truth about it.
② I want to know if he can be a winner.
③ I am wondering if Andrew can come to my party.
④ If Sam didn't like her, she might be disappointed.
⑤ Even if you know everything, you still need to learn more.

12 두 문장이 같은 뜻이 되도록 빈칸에 알맞은 말을 쓰시오.

If it had been very snowy, we would have gone sledding.
→ As it ________ ________ very snowy, we ________ ________ sledding.

13 다음 상황을 읽고, Mike에게 해줄 말이 어법상 알맞은 것은?

Hello, I am Mike. Currently, I work at a bank. Now I am concerned about my job. I failed to get promoted. I was very disappointed. What should I do?

① What will you do if you stopped working?
② What would you want to do if you get a new job?
③ If I were you, I would just keep doing my best.
④ I was you, I would have worked harder.
⑤ Had I been you, I would give a better performance.

14 어법상 어색한 부분을 찾아 바르게 고치시오.

Molly played the most important role in this play. But she says as if she didn't do it.

____________ → ____________

15 밑줄 친 가정법이 어법상 어색한 것은?

① My sister thinks herself ugly. I wish she didn't think like that.
② I live in a foreign country. I wish I didn't live in a foreign country.
③ Jin ate too much instant food. He wishes he didn't eat too much instant food.
④ Yang wasn't friendly to people at all. He wishes he had been friendly to people.
⑤ Joe can't bake a chocolate cake. He wishes he could bake a chocolate cake.

16 빈칸에 알맞은 표현을 〈보기〉에서 골라 문장을 완성하시오.

보기 ⓐ he would not have been scolded
ⓑ you went to bed
ⓒ people could not live on the Earth

(1) Without air, ____________________.
(2) If Jack had not skipped his class, ____________.
(3) It is time ____________________.

Final Test

[17-19] 〈보기〉와 뜻이 같은 문장을 고르시오.

17

> 보기 Our team wishes we had passed the pre-test.

① We are sorry our team passes the pre-test.
② We are sorry our team doesn't pass the pre-test.
③ We are sorry our team passed the pre-test.
④ We are sorry our team didn't pass the pre-test.
⑤ We are sorry our team hadn't passed the pre-test.

18

> 보기 As Keilen didn't bring her own tools, she couldn't fix the computer.

① If Kellen brings her own tools, she can fix the computer.
② If Keilen brought her own tools, she could fix the computer.
③ If Keilen had brought her own tools, she could fix the computer.
④ If Keilen had brought her own tools, she could have fixed the computer.
⑤ If Keilen had brought her own tools, she couldn't fix the computer.

19

> 보기 As I don't know her cell phone number, I can't call her now.

① If I know her cell phone number, I will call her now.
② If I don't know her cell phone number, I would call her now.
③ If I didn't know her cell phone number, I would call her now.
④ If I knew her cell phone number, I would call her now.
⑤ If had known her cell phone number, I would call her now.

20 대화의 빈칸에 알맞은 것은?

> A: What are you going to do this winter vacation?
> B: I don't know what I am going to do.
> A: If I were you, ________ a class during the winter session.

① I'll take ② I'd take
③ I'd taken ④ I'd have taken
⑤ I'd had taken

21 우리말과 같은 뜻이 되도록 빈칸에 알맞은 말을 쓰시오.

> 내가 학창시절에 좀 더 열심히 공부했다면 지금 더 좋은 대학교 학생일 텐데.
> → If I ________ ________ ________ in my school days, I ________ ________ a student at a better college now.

22 문장의 빈칸에 공통으로 알맞은 말을 두 개 고르시오.

> (a) Modern people couldn't stand ________ watching TV.
> (B) I wouldn't have been in that expensive school ________ my parents' support.

① but ② with
③ within ④ without
⑤ but for

23 직설법 문장을 가정법 문장으로 바꿔 쓸 때 빈칸에 알맞은 말끼리 짝지은 것은?

> As I don't have a laptop computer, I can't lend one to you.
> → If I ________ a laptop computer, I ________ one to you.

① had – couldn't lend
② had – could lend
③ didn't have – could lend
④ hadn't have – could have lent
⑤ had had – couldn't have lent

24 짝지은 두 문장의 의미가 서로 <u>다른</u> 것은?

① Victor wishes he could go to school.
→ Victor is sorry he can't go to school.
② He talks as if he were my teacher.
→ In fact, he isn't my teacher.
③ If they raised gasoline prices, it would be a big issue.
→ As they don't raise gasoline prices, it will not be a big issue.
④ If he had had enough experience, they would have hired him.
→ As he had enough experience, they would hire him.
⑤ If Hank had gone by KTX, he could have saved a lot of time.
→ As Hank didn't go by KTX, he couldn't saved a lot of time.

25 밑줄 친 부분 중 어법상 <u>어색한</u> 것을 찾아 바르게 고치시오.

> Thomas Edison ①<u>lit up</u> the world ②<u>with his invention</u> of the electric light. ③<u>With him</u>, the world ④<u>would still be</u> dark. However, surprisingly, the electric light ⑤<u>was</u> not his only invention.

__________ → __________

26 밑줄 친 부분 중 어법상 <u>어색한</u> 것은?

① I wish I <u>met</u> you when I was young.
② Had it not been for her skills, he would <u>have died</u>.
③ He talked as if he <u>had been</u> an expert in that field.
④ Had Jane <u>been born</u> in better times, she would have become famous.
⑤ If he had taken the doctor's advice, he <u>might be</u> healthy now.

서술형 대비

27 직설법 문장을 가정법 문장으로 바꿔 쓰시오.

> As Amy is very busy, she won't come here to talk about the matter.

→ ____________________
____

28 문장의 빈칸에 알맞은 말끼리 짝지은 것은?

> (a) If you don't leave now, you ________ late for work.
> (b) If the weather ________ fine, we could have played baseball.

① were – had been　　② are – was
③ would be – were　　④ will be – had been
⑤ won't be – have been

29 우리말을 영어로 바르게 옮긴 것은?

> 내가 너였다면 그의 충고를 들었을 텐데.

① If I was you, I would take his advice.
② If I am you, I will take his advice.
③ Have I been you, I would take his advice.
④ Were I you, I would have taken his advice.
⑤ Had I been you, I would have taken his advice.

30 대화의 밑줄 친 부분 중 어법상 <u>어색한</u> 것은?

> A: Did you eat out with your family last night?
> B: No, I couldn't go. If I ①<u>had been</u> there with my family, I ②<u>would have had</u> a wonderful time.
> A: Why didn't you have dinner with them?
> B: Because of my work. If it ③<u>had not been</u> for my work, I ④<u>could have eaten</u> a lot of delicious food there.
> A: You know, if your brother had not eaten so much there, he ⑤<u>would not have had</u> a stomachache now.

≫ 정답 및 해설 40쪽

Extracurricular Activities

▸ Sentence Writing

 Complete the sentences describing the picture.

For decades, many colleges have run successful financial aid programs.

1 If there ________(be) no programs, almost a third of the students ____________________ (register) for classes. (프로그램들이 없다면 학생들의 3분의 1은 수업을 위해 등록할 수 없을 것이다.)

2 For example, ________ scholarships, I ____________________(graduate) from my school, either. (예를 들어, 장학금이 없었다면 나도 학교를 졸업할 수 없었을 것이다.)

3 I wish all alumni ________(donate) money for promising students. (촉망되는 학생들을 위해 모든 졸업생들이 돈을 기부하면 좋을 텐데.)

PART B Change the Korean into English by using the given words.

1 Cathy가 그녀의 약속을 지켰으면 좋았을 텐데. (wish, promise, keep)
→ ____________________

2 내가 이탈리아에 산다면 스파게티를 좋아할 텐데. (spaghetti, Italy)
→ ____________________

3 네가 그 문제에 대해 나에게 말했다면 내가 널 도왔을 텐데. (tell, help, problem)
→ ____________________

4 그는 마치 부자인 것처럼 돈을 썼다. (rich, spend)
→ ____________________

▸ Further Studies 내신, 수능에 많이 나오는 속담 ①

▶ No news is good news. 무소식이 희소식이다. (99, 96 수능)

▶ Like father, like son. 부전자전이다. (99 수능)

▶ Many drops make a shower. 티끌 모아 태산이다. (99 수능)
= Water will wear away stone. 낙숫물이 바위 뚫는다. (96 수능)

▶ Strike while the iron is hot. 쇠뿔도 단김에 빼라. (99 수능)

▶ A bad workman blames his tools. 서투른 목수가 연장 탓한다. (99 수능)

▶ A bird in the hand is worth two in the bush. 남의 돈 천 냥이 내 돈 한 푼만 못하다. (99 수능)

▶ There is no place like home. 집 만한 곳은 없다. (99 수능)

▶ Practice makes perfect. 연습이 최고를 만든다. (99 수능)

▶ Easier said than done. 말하기는 쉬워도 실천하기는 어렵다. (99, 96 수능)

▶ Out of sight, out of mind. 눈에서 멀어지면 마음도 멀어진다. (99 수능)

▶ A friend in need is a friend indeed. 어려울 때 친구가 진짜 친구다. (99, 95 수능)

▶ A picture is worth a thousand words. 백문이 불여일견이다. (99 수능)

▶ Look before you leap. 돌다리도 두드려보고 건너라. (99 수능)

▶ Blood is thicker than water. 피는 물보다 진하다. (97 수능)

▶ The pot calls the kettle black. 똥 묻은 개가 겨 묻은 개 나무란다. (97 수능)

▶ Slow and steady wins the race. 느려도 착실하면 이긴다. (97 수능)

▶ Two heads are better than one. 백짓장도 맞들면 낫다. (97 수능)

▶ First come, first served. 선착순이다. (96 수능)

▶ Ignore is bliss. 모르는 게 약이다. (96 수능)

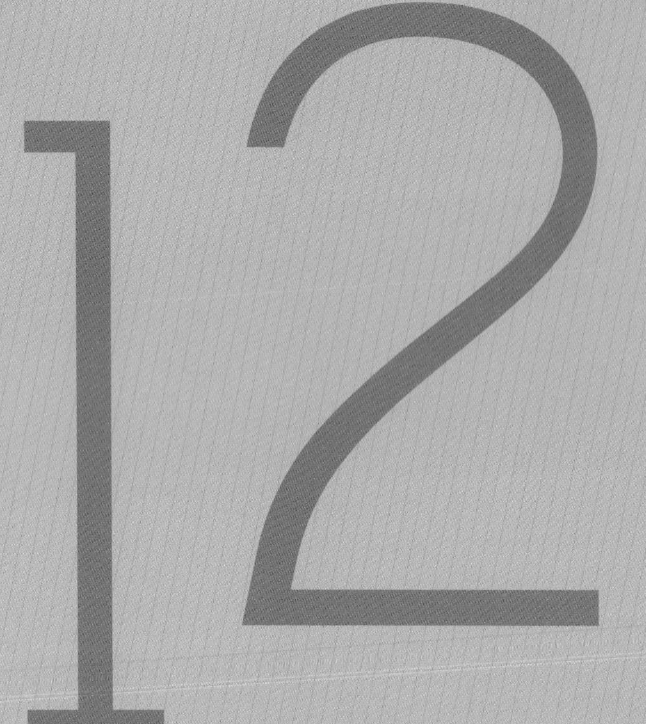

일치, 화법
(Agreement, Narration)

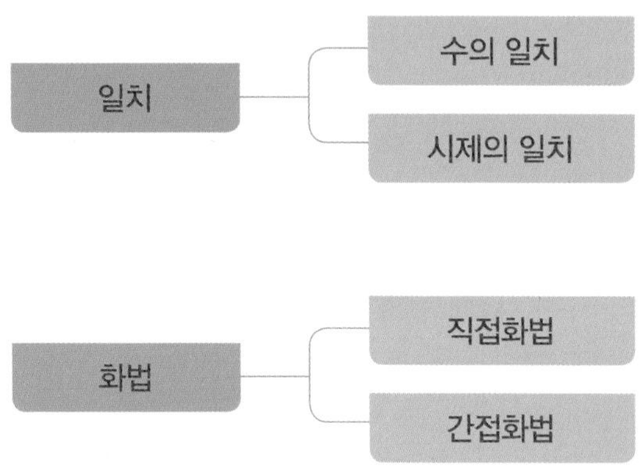

일치: 한 문장 안에서 수, 인칭, 태, 시제 등을 일치시켜 표현한다.

화법: 어떤 사람이 한 말을 다른 사람에게 전달하는 방식을 화법이라고 한다.

기출 맛보기

직접화법을 간접화법으로 바꿀 때 빈칸에 알맞은 말을 고르시오. (강남구 ○○중학교)

He said to me, "I met your girlfriend at Times Square last night."
→ He told me that he ________ at Times Square the night before.

① had meet my girlfriend
② has met my girlfriend
③ had met my girlfriend
④ met my girlfriend
⑤ have meet my girlfriend

해설

평서문의 화법 전환 방법은
(1) 전달동사를 바꾼다. [said to → told]
(2) 쉼표와 큰따옴표(" ")를 없애고 접속사를 that을 넣는다.
(3) 말하는 사람의 입장에 맞게 피전달문(큰 따옴표 안의 말)의 대명사를 바꾼다. [I → he / your → my]
(4) 피전달문 안의 동사의 시제를 전달동사의 시제에 맞추어 바꾼다. 피전달문의 시제가 전달동사의 시제보다 앞선 일이므로 과거완료시제로 바꾼다. [met → had met]
(5) 피전달문 안의 시간이나 장소의 부사(구)를 상황에 맞게 바꾼다. [last night → the night before]

해석

그는 나에게 "나는 지난밤에 타임스퀘어에서 너의 여자 친구를 만났어."라고 말했다.
→ 그는 나에게 전날 밤에 타임스퀘어에서 나의 여자 친구를 만났었다고 말했다.

정답 ③

DAY 23 일치

1교시 Grammar Point

1 수의 일치

단수 취급 (단수 동사 오는 경우)	복수 취급 (복수 동사 오는 경우)
every, each, -thing, -body	항상 짝을 이루는 명사 (jeans, glasses, pants, shoes 등)
시간, 거리, 금액, 학과명 등	both A and B
분수, some, most, half, the rest + (of) + 단수 명사	분수, some, most, half, the rest + (of) + 복수 명사
the number of + 복수 명사(~의 수)	a number of 복수명사(많은 ~)

Every student has a laptop.
Ten dollars is cheap for a meal.
One third of his story is not true.
The number of teams is important.

Jeans are very expensive.
Both you and I are happy.
Some cars are made in Korea.
A number of singers are excited.

2 상관접속사가 포함된 수의 일치

• B에 동사를 일치시킴

not A but B(A가 아니라 B), either A or B(A와 B 둘 중에 하나), not only A but also B(A뿐만 아니라 B도 역시) [= B as well as A], neither A nor B(A도 B도 아닌)

Not Dan but I am going to go to Paris next month.
Either you or Jessy makes a good impression on the boss.
Not only she but also I wasn't good at giving speeches.
Neither the blue jeans nor the T-shirt is dirty.

3 시제의 일치

주절의 시제	종속절의 시제
현재, 현재완료, 미래	내용에 따라 모든 시제 가능
과거	과거 또는 과거 완료

We **think** that he passes/passed/will pass the final exam.
They **believed** that the actor got/had gotten married recently.

4 시제 일치의 예외

• 불변의 진리, 격언, 현재의 습관, 과학적 사실일 경우 항상 현재시제
• 종속절이 역사적 사실일 경우 항상 과거시제

The teacher **told** us that the Earth moves around the sun. [불변의 진리]
They **said** that she takes a walk every day. [습관]
We **learned** that World War I broke out in 1914. [역사적 사실]

Grammar Tips

• **항상 단수 취급하는 경우**

(1) 주어로 쓰인 구나 절
To study English **is** important. (to부정사구)
What she has done **is** helpful. (명사절)

(2) 병명, 복수 형태의 국가명
A heart attack is a serious problem. 병명(심장마비)
The Netherlands is pretty country. 복수형태 국가명

(3) A and B가 하나의 물건/사람을 말할 때
bread and butter (버터 바른 빵)
curry and rice (카레라이스)
a poet and teacher (시인이자 교사)

• **항상 복수 취급하는 경우**

(1) (a) few, many, 〈the + 형용사〉
The rich **are** interested in money.
[the rich = rich people]

(2) the police(경찰), cattle(소)
The police **are** searching for proof.
The cattle **are** under the tree.

• **시제 일치 추가 예문**

I **knew** that my aunt visited/had visited N.Y.

• **시제 일치의 예외 추가 예문**

Mom **told** me that life is short. (격언)

She **knew** that water boils at 100℃. (과학적 사실)

2교시 In-Class Questions

괄호 안에서 알맞은 말을 고르시오.

1 Every **(student / students / a student)** in the classroom will receive this book.

2 Diabetes **(is / are / was)** a serious and dangerous disease these days.

3 The number of babies **(keep / keeps)** increasing.

STEP B

주어진 동사를 문장의 빈칸에 알맞은 형태로 바꿔 쓰시오.

1 Neither Jane nor her friends ______________ students anymore. (be)

2 The police in the building ______________ waiting for backup. (be)

3 Some people said that the sun ______________ round and hot. (be)

4 We learned that the Korean War ______________ in 1953. (end)

어법상 어색한 부분을 찾아 바르게 고치시오.

1 Nancy told me that she went to church every Sunday. ___________ → ___________

2 What Brian had done were not helpful at all. ___________ → ___________

3 Two-thirds of her stories is about Paris fashion. ___________ → ___________

4 The poor has much different points of views than the rich. ___________ → ___________

우리말과 같은 뜻이 되도록 빈칸에 알맞은 말을 쓰시오.

1 Keilen은 그가 그녀에게 서류를 이미 보냈다는 것을 깨달았다.
→ Keilen realized that he ______________ ______________ ______________ the document to her.

2 나의 부모님은 '피는 물보다 진하다'고 내게 말씀하셨다.
→ My parents ______________ me, "Blood ______________ thicker than water."

3 내가 생각하기에 내 코뿐만 아니라 눈도 매우 작다.
→ I think that not only my nose but also my eyes ______________ very small.

4 20마일은 이런 날씨에 걷기에는 먼 거리이다.
→ Twenty miles ______________ a long distance to walk in this weather.

3교시 After-Class Questions

[01-03] 문장의 빈칸에 알맞은 것을 고르시오.

01 What I want to know ________ how long it is going to take.

① is ② are ③ has
④ have ⑤ will have

02 Her professor said that Columbus ________ America in 1492.

① discover ② discovers ③ discovered
④ has discovered ⑤ had discovered

03 Each boy in my class ________ me ________ enthusiasm.

① show – their ② show – his ③ showed – their
④ shows – their ⑤ shows – his

[04-05] 우리말을 영어로 바르게 옮긴 것을 고르시오.

04 Matilda는 지구가 점점 더 따뜻해진다는 것을 알았다.

① Matilda knows that the Earth is getting warmer.
② Matilda knows that the Earth was getting warmer.
③ Matilda knew that the Earth is getting warmer.
④ Matilda knew that the Earth was getting warmer.
⑤ Matilda knew that the Earth had been getting warmer.

05 10년은 내가 기다리기에는 오랜 시간이다.

① Ten year is a long time for me to wait.
② Ten years is a long time for me to wait.
③ Ten years was a long time for me to wait.
④ Ten years are a long time for me to wait.
⑤ Ten years were a long time for me to wait.

[06-09] 밑줄 친 부분 중 어법상 어색한 것을 고르시오.

06 ① Each boy has a different favorite game.
② Most of the students as well as you are ready for the test.
③ The number of babies born in the town isn't on the rise.
④ Mathematics deals with the problems of numbers and formulas.
⑤ Two thirds of this story were about a real accident in Canada.

Vocabulary Tips

- professor 교수
- discover 발견하다
- enthusiasm 열정
- formula (수학) 공식

07 ① Mr. Brown said that he had met Jacky before.
② Jason believed that his sister would study hard.
③ My teacher says that honesty is the best policy.
④ They didn't know that light traveled faster than sound.
⑤ Mom told me that her father gets up early every morning.

08 ① Today's news were shocking to us.
② One and two equals three.
③ Diabetes is a serious disease.
④ A poet and novelist is my neighbor.
⑤ Bread and butter is my lunch.

09 ① There were cattle under the trees.
② The Netherlands is well known for flowers.
③ The rich are not always satisfied with their lives.
④ Studying English and math together are challenging.
⑤ To eat and sleep well is the most important thing to me.

[10-11] 밑줄 친 부분 중 어법상 어색한 부분을 고르시오.

10

Some teachers told Catherine ①that most of the students ②will visit the museum next Friday. The reason ③was that they ④should finish their projects. So she asked her teachers if she ⑤could go with them.

11

There are 10 professors for my final presentation. Among them, I have already taken classes with five of them. Thus, five of them ①are already familiar to me. But the other professors ②are new to me. I am very nervous. I guess that ③either my roommates ④or Thomas ⑤take their classes.

12 문장의 빈칸 어느 곳에도 들어갈 수 없는 것은?

(a) Kelly believes her friend _________ a job. (b) I knew that the actress _________ an award.

① get ② got ③ gets
④ will get ⑤ had gotten

Vocabulary Tips

- policy 정책
- travel (빛 · 소리 등이) 나아가다, 전해지다
- equal 합이 ~이다
- diabetes 당뇨
- challenging 힘든, 도전적인
- final presentation 학기말 발표
- familiar 친근한
- get an award 수상하다

서술형 대비

13 어법상 어색한 부분을 찾아 바르게 고치시오.

Half of the money are not yours but your parents'.

_______________ → _______________

14 대화의 빈칸에 알맞은 말끼리 짝지은 것은?

A: How many of your friends will come to this party on Sunday?
B: ________ my friends will come and play card games. Please come!
A: I'm afraid I can't. It's too far from my home. Fifty minutes ________ a long time for me to travel.

① A number of – are
② A number of – is
③ A number of – was
④ The number of – is
⑤ The number of – are

[15-17] 문장의 빈칸에 알맞은 것끼리 짝지은 것을 고르시오.

15

(a) Five years ________ since my father passed away.
(b) Five years ________ not that long a period.

① has passed – is
② has passed – are
③ has passed – were
④ have passed – is
⑤ have passed – have been

16

(a) The rest of my money ________ given to Mom.
(b) Half of the animals here ________ from China.

① is – are
② is – is
③ are – is
④ are – are
⑤ be – is

17

(a) My teacher said that Canada ________ the second largest country in the world.
(b) My teacher said that World War I ________ in 1918.

① is – had ended
② is – ended
③ was – ended
④ was – had ended
⑤ had been – ended

[18-19] 문장의 빈칸에 be동사를 알맞은 형태로 바꿔 쓰시오.

18 We didn't know that Hong Kong ________ once England's territory.

19 My son learned that bats ________ the only mammal that can fly.

Vocabulary Tips

- pass away 죽다
- World War I 1차 세계대전
- territory 영토
- mammal 포유류

[20-22] 다음 중 어법상 어색한 문장을 고르시오.

20 ① Everyone likes me except him.
② No one likes him because of his behavior.
③ Each girl received some candy from the boy.
④ Every man and woman were surprised at the news.
⑤ Watching movies and listening to music are my two favorite things to do.

21 ① Half of the tangerines are not fresh.
② The Netherlands is known for windmills.
③ Five kilometers are not far away from here.
④ I think economics is a difficult subject to learn.
⑤ Some of the money was sent to the orphanage by him.

22 ① Tom and Jane are good friends.
② The teacher and poet is my cousin.
③ I know that her family is happy and kind.
④ The people sometimes visits famous sites.
⑤ The curry and rice on the table was prepared for my dad.

23 다음 중 어법상 어색한 문장을 모두 고르시오.

① Plenty of furniture were sold yesterday.
② Two-thirds of these strawberries is rotten.
③ A watch and chain was found on the desk.
④ The number of illegal immigrants are increasing rapidly.
⑤ A number of supermarkets are open today even though it is a holiday.

24 밑줄 친 부분 중 어법상 올바른 것을 모두 고르시오.

① Ten years are not a long time.
② One of my friends speak Japanese very well.
③ Early to bed and early to rise makes me healthy.
④ Many a child have been spoiled by smartphones.
⑤ The Philippines is a country which has many islands.

25 두 문장이 같은 뜻이 되도록 빈칸에 알맞은 말을 쓰시오.

Not only he but also they are responsible for the situation that happened last week.
→ ________ as well as ________ ________ responsible for the situation that happened last week.

Vocabulary Tips

- behavior 행동
- tangerine 귤
- windmill 풍차
- economics 경제학
- orphanage 고아원
- rotten 썩은
- illegal 불법의
- immigrant 이민자
- rapidly 급속히
- spoil 망치다
- responsible 책임이 있는

DAY 24

화법 전환

1교시 Grammar Point

화법

직접화법	다른 사람이 한 말을 인용부호(" ")를 이용해서 그대로 전달하는 표현 방법
간접화법	다른 사람이 한 말을 말하는 사람의 입장에서 풀어 전달하는 표현 방법

1 평서문의 화법 전환

① 전달동사를 바꾼다. [say → say, say to → tell]
② 쉼표와 큰따옴표(" ")를 없애고 접속사 **that**을 쓴다.
③ 말하는 사람의 입장에 맞게 피전달문 안의 **대명사**를 바꾼다.
④ 전달동사의 시제에 맞게 피전달문 안의 동사의 **시제**를 바꾼다.
⑤ 피전달문 안의 **시간이나 장소의 부사(구)**를 상황에 맞게 바꾼다.

He **said to** me, "I love you." [직접화법]
→ He **told**① me (that)② he③ **loved**④ me③. [간접화법]

2 명령문의 화법 전환

① 전달동사를 tell(일반적 지시), ask(부탁), order(명령), advise(충고)로 바꾼다.
② 쉼표와 큰따옴표(" ")를 없애고, 긍정명령문은 **〈전달동사 + 목적어 + to부정사〉**로, 부정명령문은 **〈전달동사 + 목적어 + not + to부정사〉**로 바꾼다.

My mother **said to** me, "**Don't eat** too much." [직접화법: 부정명령문]
→ My mother **told/advised**① me **not to eat**② too much. [간접화법]

3 의문문의 화법 전환

① 전달동사를 바꾼다. [say → ask, say to → ask]
② 쉼표와 큰따옴표(" ")를 없애고, 의문사가 있는 경우는 **〈의문사 + 주어 + 동사〉**의 순으로, 의문사가 없는 경우는 **〈If/whether + 주어 + 동사〉**의 순으로 배열한다.
③ 피전달문의 대명사, 인칭, 시제, 부사(구)를 바꾼다. (평서문의 화법 전환과 동일)

She said to me, "**What did you** do yesterday?" [의문사 있는 의문문]
→ She asked① me **what I had done**②③ the day before③.

Sue said to me, "**Will you go** to the library with me?" [의문사 없는 의문문]
→ Sue asked me① **if I would go**②③ to the library with her③.

Grammar Tips

● 화법 전환 시 문장에 따른 전달동사

	전달동사
평서문	say → say say to → tell
명령문	tell, ask, order, advise
의문문	say → ask say to → ask

● 화법 전환 시 주의해야 할 지시대명사와 시간의 부사

직접화법	간접화법
now	then
ago	before
here	there
this	that
these	those
today	that day
tomorrow	the next day the day after the following day
last night	the night before
yesterday	the day before the previous day

● 화법 전환 시 시제의 사용

주절의 시제	피전달문의 시제
현재	현재 → 현재
과거	현재 → 과거
	미래 → 과거
	과거 → 과거완료
	현재완료 → 과거완료

2교시 In-Class Questions

직접화법을 간접화법으로 바꿔 쓸 때 괄호 안에서 알맞은 것을 고르시오.

1 The old lady said to me, "Can you help me?"
→ The old lady **(told / asked)** me **(if / that)** I **(can / could)** help her.

2 He said, "I bought this wristwatch last week."
→ He said that he **(bought / had bought)** that wristwatch the week before.

3 I said to my girlfriend, "What kind of beverage do you want?"
→ I asked my girlfriend **(if / what)** kind of beverage **(wanted she / she wanted)**.

STEP B

직접화법을 간접화법으로 바꿔 쓸 때 나머지 문장을 완성하시오.

1 Wayne promised, "I'll behave myself."
→ Wayne promised ______________________________.

2 June asked him, "When do you want to leave?"
→ June asked him ______________________________.

3 My wife said to me, "Don't drink beer anymore."
→ My wife advised me ______________________________.

4 She said to me, "Will you go or stay here?"
→ She asked me ______________________________.

STEP C

화법을 전환한 문장 중 어법상 어색한 부분을 찾아 바르게 고치시오.

1 Joan said to me, "Did you have any money?"
→ Joan told me if I had had any money. __________ → __________

2 Audrey said, "Have you met Ralph before?"
→ Audrey asked if I met Ralph before. __________ → __________

3 You said to me, "You are my best friend."
→ You told me that you were my best friend. __________ → __________

직접화법을 간접화법으로 바꿔 쓰시오.

1 James said to his wife, "Where did you get this bag?"
→ ______________________________

2 I said to my mother, "I'm totally exhausted and starving."
→ ______________________________

3 My daughter said to me, "Don't use your smartphone while you are driving."
→ ______________________________

3교시 After-Class Questions

01 직접화법을 간접화법으로 바꿔 쓸 때의 부사 변화가 잘못된 것은?

① now → then　　② ago → before
③ here → there　　④ tomorrow → the next day
⑤ yesterday → the day after

[02-04] 직접화법을 간접화법으로 바꿔 쓸 때 빈칸에 알맞은 말끼리 짝지은 것을 고르시오.

02 Her doctor said, "You will get well quickly."

→ Her doctor ________ that she ________ well quickly.

① said – will get　　② said – would get
③ said – would have got　　④ told – would get
⑤ told – would have got

03 Thomas told me, "I want to visit Paris this year."

→ Thomas ________ me that he ________ to visit Paris ________.

① said – wanted – that year　　② said – had wanted – that year
③ told – wanted – this year　　④ told – wanted – that year
⑤ told – had wanted – this year

04 My mom said to me, "I will buy you books tomorrow."

→ My mom ________ me that she ________ books ________.

① said to – would buy me – the following day
② said to – will buy you – the next day
③ told to – will buy you – tomorrow
④ told – would buy me – the following day
⑤ told – would buy you – the next day

05 간접화법을 직접화법으로 바꿔 쓸 때 빈칸에 알맞은 말끼리 짝지은 것은?

Bobby asked her where she was from.
→ Bobby ________ her, "________________________?"

① said – Where are you from?　　② said – Where you are from?
③ told – Where you are from?　　④ said to – Where are you from?
⑤ said to – Where you are from?

06 밑줄 친 if와 바꿔 쓸 수 있는 것은?

Jake asked her if she liked autumn better than summer.

① that　　② how　　③ what
④ which　　⑤ whether

Vocabulary Tips
- get well 좋아지다
- quickly 빠르게

07 주어진 말을 사용하여 문장의 빈칸을 바르게 완성한 것은?

People asked Hojun ______________________________________.

(cost, MP3 player, how, that, much)

① that how much MP3 player cost
② that how much MP3 player costs
③ how much that MP3 player costs
④ how much that MP3 player cost
⑤ how much cost that MP3 player

08 직접화법을 간접화법으로 바꿔 쓴 문장이 잘못된 것은?

① She says to me, "What do you want to do?"
→ She asks me what I want to do.
② Lucy said, "I can repair the bike today."
→ Lucy said that she could repair the bike that day.
③ My friend said to Ken, "Stop talking."
→ My friend said to Ken to stop talking.
④ He said to them, "I'm watching TV now."
→ He told them that he was watching TV then.
⑤ Anne said to him, "Have you ever read these novels?"
→ Anne asked him if he had ever read those novels.

서술형 대비

[09-10] 직접화법을 간접화법으로 바꿔 쓸 때 빈칸에 알맞은 말을 쓰시오.

09 Charlie said to me, "I met Anne here."
→ Charlie told me that he ________ ________ Anne ________.

10 You said to me, "Is everything okay?"
→ You asked me ________ ________ ________ okay.

11 〈보기〉의 직접화법을 간접화법으로 바꿔 쓴 문장이 잘못된 것은?

보기 His brother said to me, "Don't worry about this problem."

① His brother told me not to worry about that problem.
② His brother told me to not worry about that problem.
③ His brother asked me not to worry about that problem.
④ His brother ordered me not to worry about that problem.
⑤ His brother advised me not to worry about that problem.

12 직접화법을 간접화법으로 바꿔 쓸 때 어법상 어색한 부분을 찾아 바르게 고치시오.

A government officer said to me, "Do you need any help?"
→ A government officer asked me if did I need any help.

______________________ → ______________________

Vocabulary Tips

- cost 비용이 들다
- repair 고치다
- government officer 공무원

13 다음 중 어법상 올바른 문장은?

① Nobody says, "What you like the most?"
② He asked me if I know Mr. Lee well.
③ I didn't tell to them, "Where are you?"
④ You told me when they had been happy.
⑤ He asked how can I solve it.

[14-16] 〈보기〉의 직접화법을 간접화법으로 바르게 바꿔 쓴 것을 고르시오.

14 보기 Sean said, "I usually keep my word."

① Sean said that I usually keep my word.
② Sean said that he usually kept my word.
③ Sean said that he usually keeps his word.
④ Sean told that he usually keep his word.
⑤ Sean told that he usually kept his word.

15 보기 My sister said to him, "Did you attend the meeting?"

① My sister asked him if he attended the meeting.
② My sister asked him if he had attended the meeting.
③ My sister asked him whether he attended the meeting.
④ My sister asked him that he had attended the meeting.
⑤ My sister asked him that he had attend the meeting.

16 보기 David said to me, "Can you sing and dance for me?"

① David asked me what could I sing and dance for me.
② David asked me can I sing and dance for him.
③ David asked me if I can sing and dance for me.
④ David asked me if I could sing and dance for me.
⑤ David asked me if I could sing and dance for him.

17 다음 중 어법상 어색한 문장은?

① Miranda said that she works in Chicago.
② My boys said that 4 times 5 is twenty.
③ The teacher told us that Japan colonized Korea in 1909.
④ We knew that our parents could come to the conference.
⑤ He told us we could not live without water.

18 간접화법을 직접화법으로 바꿔 쓸 때의 부사 변화가 잘못된 것은?

① that → this
② this day → today
③ the day before → yesterday
④ the day after → tomorrow
⑤ before → ago

Vocabulary Tips

- keep one's word 약속을 지키다
- attend 참석하다
- times 곱하기
- colonize 식민지화하다
- conference 회의

서술형 대비

[19-20] 직접화법을 간접화법으로 바꿔 쓰시오.

19 James said to me, "Go on a diet."

→ ______________________

20 Ben said to me, "I have been to Australia."

→ ______________________

[21-22] 직접화법을 사용하여 다음 우리말을 영어로 옮긴 다음, 간접화법으로 바꿔 쓰시오.

21 Andrew는 Belle에게 "나는 어제 그녀와 함께 영화관에 갔어."라고 말했다.

(1) ______________________

(2) [간접화법] ______________________

22 내 옆에 앉아있는 신사는 나에게 "너는 몇 살이니?"라고 물었다.

(1) ______________________

(2) [간접화법] ______________________

23 주어진 문장을 간접화법으로 바꿔 쓸 때 일곱 번째로 오는 말은?

My mom asked me, "Where did you have supper?"

① mom ② asked ③ where ④ had ⑤ supper

24 밑줄 친 부분 중 어법상 어색한 것을 골라 바르게 고치시오.

> In the last class, Ms. Edward ①said that the Earth ②is round and ③moved around the sun. So the sun ④rises in the east and ⑤sets in the west.

______________ → ______________

25 대화의 밑줄 친 부분을 간접화법으로 바꿔 쓰시오.

> A: Billy, do you have any plan after work?
> B: Yes. My wife called me and she said to me, "I will make a delicious dinner for you."
> A: You had better go home quickly after work.
> B: I'd like to, but I need more time to finish my work. I will go home as soon as I finish my work.
> A: Don't worry. I can help you.

→ ______________________

Vocabulary Tips

- Australia 호주
- supper 저녁식사
- rise 뜨다
- set 지다

Final Test

01 대화의 빈칸에 알맞은 것끼리 짝지은 것은?

> A: How many people are there in your club?
> B: I guess _________ people in our club _________ over one hundred.

① a number of – is ② a number of – are
③ the number of – be ④ the number of – is
⑤ the number of – are

02 문장의 빈칸에 알맞은 말끼리 짝지은 것은?

> (a) Bella, the poet and singer, _________ going to open a new restaurant.
> (b) The police _________ very popular in many countries.
> (c) When we were young, we _________ that one and one _________ two.

① is – is – learn – equal
② is – is – learned – equals
③ is – are – learned – equals
④ are – are – learned – equal
⑤ are – are – learn – equals

03 밑줄 친 부분 중 어법상 어색한 것은?

① Three fourths of this potato has gone sour.
② Not Gary but Lisa has gone bankrupt this month.
③ Each of them goes on a journey with their parents.
④ Every student goes to the job fair to get some information.
⑤ Neither my hat nor my pants goes with this long jacket.

04 우리말을 영어로 바르게 옮긴 것은?

> 이 동물원의 동물들의 수가 점점 줄어들고 있다.

① The number of animal in the zoo gets smaller and smaller.
② The numbers of animals in the zoo get smaller and smaller.
③ The number of animals in the zoo is getting smaller and smaller.
④ The numbers of animal in the zoo are getting smaller and smaller.
⑤ The number of animals in the zoo are getting smaller and smaller.

서술형 대비

05 어법상 어색한 부분을 찾아 바르게 고치시오.

> Kelly met Henry, and she asked him to decide the day of the meeting. She suggested Sunday. However, he told her that he went to church every Sunday.

_________________ → _________________

06 직접화법을 간접화법으로 바꿔 쓸 때 빈칸에 들어갈 수 없는 것은?

> Walter said to me, "Can you go there with me?"
> → Walter _________ me _________ _________ _________ go there with _________.

① I ② if ③ can
④ asked ⑤ him

07 대화의 밑줄 친 부분 중 어법상 어색한 것은?

> A: What's up, Andy? Cathy ①told me that you looked embarrassed. What ②happened?
> B: Hmm... Something happened concerning my son Eric.
> A: Eric? ③What happened to him?
> B: I stayed at home with him yesterday, and he said to me he ④will watch a movie with his girlfriend.
> A: Really? That's strange. He ⑤said to me, "I have never had a girlfriend."

[08-10] 〈보기〉의 직접화법을 간접화법으로 바르게 바꿔 쓴 문장을 고르시오.

08

보기 The teacher said to us, "Finish this project now."

① The teacher said to us finish that project then.
② The teacher said to us to finish that project now.
③ The teacher told us to finish that project now.
④ The teacher told us to finish that project then.
⑤ The teacher told to us to finish that project then.

09

보기 Yeojun said to himself, "Where am I going?"

① Yeojun said to himself where am I going.
② Yeojun said himself where he was going.
③ Yeojun told himself where am I going.
④ Yeojun asked himself where he was going.
⑤ Yeojun asked himself where was he going.

10

보기 Professor Parker told me, "Who helped you with your presentation?

① Professor Parker asked me who had helped me with my presentation.
② Professor Parker asked me who helped me with my presentation.
③ Professor Parker asked me who had helped you with my presentation.
④ Professor Parker asked me who you had helped with my presentation.
⑤ Professor Parker asked me who I helped with my presentation.

서술형 대비

11 우리말과 같은 뜻이 되도록 빈칸에 알맞은 말을 쓰시오.

그 경찰관은 도둑에게 "지금 뭐하는 중이에요?"라고 물었다.
→ The policeman asked the thief ______________ ______________.

12 두 문장이 같은 뜻이 되도록 빈칸에 알맞은 말을 쓰시오.

(1) Junmo says to me, "Do I know you?"
→ Junmo ________ me ________________.

(2) Myung said to her, "When did I meet her?"
→ Myung ________ her when ____________ ______ her.

[13-14] 〈보기〉의 간접화법을 직접화법으로 바르게 바꿔 쓴 문장을 고르시오.

13

보기 Mike asked me if I had had dinner with her the day before.

① Mike said to me, "Did you have dinner with her yesterday?"
② Mike said to me, "Did you have dinner with her the day before?"
③ Mike told me, "Do you have dinner with her the day before?"
④ Mike asked me, "Do you have dinner with her yesterday?"
⑤ Mike asked me, "Did you have dinner with her the day before?"

14

보기 Mr. Brown told her that he would come back home the next day.

① Mr. Brown told her, "I would come back home tomorrow."
② Mr. Brown asked her, "I will come back home the next day."
③ Mr. Brown said to her, "I would come back home tomorrow."
④ Mr. Brown said to her, "He will come back home the next day."
⑤ Mr. Brown said to her, "I will come back home tomorrow."

15 대화의 내용을 요약한 문장의 빈칸에 알맞은 말을 쓰시오.

Morris: Can I ask a few questions about my assignment?
Cindy: Why not? You can visit my office today.
Morris: Thanks a lot.

⬇

Morris asked Cindy ____________ a few questions about ______ assignment. Cindy agreed, and she told him ____________ her office ____________.

16 문장의 빈칸에 알맞은 말끼리 짝지은 것은?

(a) Mr. Kim told me that he had met her 3 days ________.
(b) We asked her if she was angry ________.

① ago – before
② ago – tonight
③ ago – that night
④ before – that night
⑤ before – tonight

17 밑줄 친 부분 중 어법상 어색한 것은?

① The scissors were sold out.
② Every girl needs her own room.
③ Half of the work was done in 5 hours.
④ A number of people are waiting for the guest.
⑤ 40 dollars are too much money to give to your son.

18 각 문장의 빈칸에 알맞은 말끼리 짝지은 것을 모두 고르시오.

(a) Either speaking ______ writing ______ fun.
(b) Neither listening ______ reading ______ fun.
(c) Money as ______ as people ______ important.

① (a) and – is
② (a) or – is
③ (b) or – are
④ (c) well – are
⑤ (c) well – is

19 주어진 말을 이용하여 다음 우리말을 영어로 옮기시오.

그녀뿐만 아니라 나 역시 영어를 말하는 것에 어려움이 있다. (not only, have difficulty -ing)

→ ________________________________

20 문장의 빈칸에 가장 많이 들어갈 수 있는 말은?

(a) Some of the shirts ______ made in Japan.
(b) One third of my lecture ______ about science.
(c) Studying animals ______ very interesting.
(d) My father told me that life ______ short.
(e) Not Dana but you ______ my classmate then.
(f) Physics ______ one of the hardest subjects for girls.

① is
② are
③ was
④ were
⑤ be

21 밑줄 친 부분 중 어법상 어색한 것은?

To study oceans ①give lots of useful information. For people, seafood ②is a source of protein. Many countries, Thailand and Japan included, depend on ocean tourism activities. In addition, about 50 percent of the world's population ③lives close to the seas. So once oceans ④are contaminated, there ⑤are many negative financial impacts on people.

22 직접화법을 간접화법으로 바꿔 쓸 때 빈칸에 알맞은 말을 쓰시오.

I said to a flight attendant, "Please, bring me a blanket"
→ I asked a flight attendant ________ ________ me a blanket.

23 직접화법을 간접화법으로 바꿔 쓴 문장이 잘못된 것은?

① A waiter said, "Do you need anything else?"
→ A waiter asked if I needed anything else.
② A student said, "May I leave the classroom now?"
→ A student asked if she might leave the classroom then.
③ Owen said to me, "Do you really want my care?"
→ Owen asked me if you really wanted his care.
④ My friend Jack said to me, "Where are you going?"
→ My friend Jack asked me where I was going.
⑤ She said to me, "Can you come to my birthday party?"
→ She asked me if I could come to her birthday party.

24 다음 중 어법상 어색한 문장을 두 개 고르시오.

① My teacher said that water boiled at 100°C.
② She asked me whether I used SNS.
③ Emily said that she had changed her cell phone number.
④ He asked me if I wanted to go to an amusement park.
⑤ She asked me where did I purchase that bag.

[25-28] 다음 중 어법상 어색한 문장을 고르시오.

25 ① Jay told Emma that he loved her very much.
② Mika said that she wanted thin crust pizza and cream spaghetti.
③ Blair said to me she had been to China many times.
④ Tom told Abigail that he could come to the class.
⑤ He told me that he was a class president at school.

26 ① The fact that he loves me is unbelievable.
② Reading books is my favorite hobby.
③ To keep practicing will make you successful.
④ Using credit cards in place of cash are not a good way to save money.
⑤ The stairs which lead to the top are rather dangerous.

27 ① He said that he would buy a brand-new camera.
② Mr. Kim told me that failure is but a stepping stone to success.
③ She said that she gets up at 6 every morning and goes to school at 7:30
④ I know that the Korean War broke out in 1950.
⑤ People of that era didn't believe that the Earth was round.

28 ① These statistics show deaths per 1,000 people in 2013.
② A total of 300 Chinese people lives in Chinatown.
③ The police is looking for the ruthless murderers.
④ There is always a lot of traffic in this area at this time of the day.
⑤ Some firefighters believe that more than one person is to blame for the fire.

29 주어진 문장의 시제를 과거로 바꿔 쓸 때 빈칸에 알맞은 말을 쓰시오.

My father knows that I have been interested in drawing cartoons. → My father ________ that I ________ ________ interested in drawing cartoons.

30 문장의 빈칸에 알맞은 것은?

When I was young, I didn't know that Bern ________ the capital of Switzerland.

① had been ② has been ③ be
④ is ⑤ was

≫ 정답 및 해설 45쪽

Extracurricular Activities

▸ *Sentence Writing*

PART A **Complete the sentences describing the picture.**

1 Amy told me that she ______________________________ Joe.
(그녀의 친구 Joe와 어울리지 않을 것이라고, get along with)

2 Last Friday, they attended a college reunion party.
Joe said Amy, "______________________________ yours,"
(내 딸의 영어가 네 딸보다 훨씬 낫다고, much)
and also ________ that ______________________________ than Amy's.
(그녀의 아들이 더 잘생겼다고 그녀에게 말했다, handsome)

3 Eventually, Amy told me ______________________________ anymore.
(나에게 Joe와 더 이상 이야기하지 않겠다고 말했다, talk)

PART B **Change the Korean into English by using the given words.**

1 그는 나에게 "나는 당신에게 이 집을 사줄게요."라고 말했다. (say to, buy, this house)
→ ______________________________

2 나의 남동생은 나에게 6시에 깨워달라고 요청했다. (wake up, ask)
→ ______________________________

3 아빠는 나에게 외출하지 말라고 말했다. (go out, tell)
→ ______________________________

4 Helen은 Hank에게 저것이 수필인지 시인지 물어보았다. (an essay or a poem, ask)
→ ______________________________

▸ Further Studies 내신, 수능에 많이 나오는 속담 ②

- A drowning man would catch at a straw. 물에 빠진 사람은 지푸라기라도 잡으려고 한다.
- One man's meat is another man's poison. 한 사람의 고기는 다른 사람에게는 독이 될 수 있다.
- The longest way around is the shortest way. 가장 멀리 돌아가는 길이 가장 짧은 길이다. (바쁠수록 돌아가라.)
- There is no accounting for taste. 취미는 설명할 수 없다. (취미도 가지가지다.)
- Too many cooks spoil the broth. 요리사가 많으면 국을 망친다. (사공이 많으면 배가 산으로 간다.)
- Kill two birds with one stone. 일석이조(一石二鳥)
- There is no smoke without fire. 아니 땐 굴뚝에 연기 나랴.
- To say is one thing, and to practice is another. 말하는 것과 행하는 것은 별개이다.
- As you sow, so shall you reap. 뿌린 대로 거둘 것이다.
- Heaven helps those who help themselves. 하늘은 스스로 돕는 자를 돕는다.
- No gain without pain. 고통 없이 얻어지는 것은 없다.
  = No pain, no gain.
- Rome was not built in a day. 로마는 하루아침에 이루어지지 않았다.
- A man is known by the company he keeps. 사람은 친구를 보면 알 수 있다.
- Birds of a feather flock together. 날개가 같은 새들이 함께 모인다. (유유상종)
- Honesty is the best policy. 정직이 최선의 방책이다.
- Every dog has its day. 쥐구멍에도 볕 들 날이 있다.
- Don't judge a book by its cover. 책을 표지로 판단하지 마라.
- Empty vessels make the greatest noise. 빈 수레가 요란하다.
- Cut your coat according to your cloth. 천에 맞게 코트를 잘라라.
- Don't count your chickens before they are hatched. 부화하기 전에 병아리를 세지 마라.
- Every Jack has his Jill. 모든 Jack에게는 Jill이 있다. (짚신도 짝이 있다.)
- It never rains, but it pours. 비가 왔다하면 쏟아 붓는다.

Unit 13 특수구문

Day 25 | 강조, 부정
Day 26 | 도치, 생략

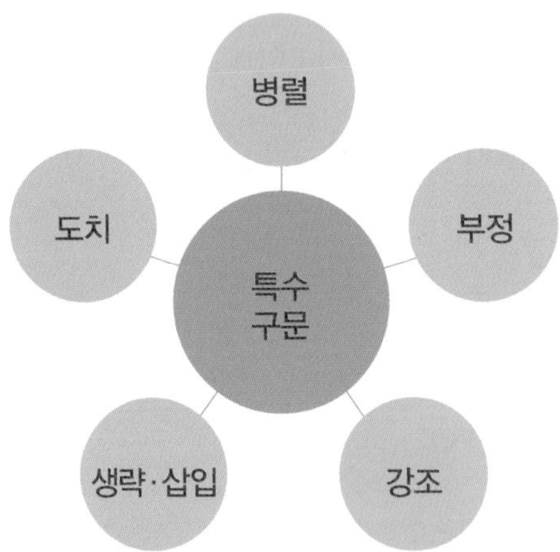

강조: 단어와 구 등의 표현을 이용하여 특정 부분의 의미를 강조한다.

부정: 부정을 나타내는 어휘가 있는 문장으로, 전체부정, 부분부정, 준부정, 이중부정 등이 있다.

도치: 일반적인 어순과는 달리 어순이 바뀐 것을 말한다.

생략: 문장에서 공통되는 부분이나 반복되는 말을 생략한다.

기출 맛보기

다음 중 어법상 <u>어색한</u> 문장을 고르시오. (서초구 ○○중학교)

① Neither of us was ready to be a doctor.

② My daughter hardly ever doesn't wake up by herself in the morning.

③ It was last Sunday that James met a Bond girl at a party.

④ What on earth is the matter with you?

⑤ Not all of the students enjoy watching movies.

해설

② [doesn't wake → wakes] hardly는 '거의 ~없는'이라는 의미를 가진 준부정어이다. 자체에 부정의 의미가 있으므로, not, never 등의 부정어와 함께 사용할 수 없다.

① 전체부정: 부정어구 never, none, no 등이 문장에 사용되어 '아무도(아무 것도) ~않다'의 의미를 나타낸다.

③ 강조: 부사구(last Sunday)를 강조할 때 〈It was ~ that ...〉 강조 구문으로 사용할 수 있다.

④ 강조: 의문문을 강조할 때는 의문사 뒤에 on earth, in the word가 오며, '도대체'라고 해석한다.

⑤ 부분부정: not all은 '모두가 ~인 것은 아니다'라는 부분부정을 만든다.

해석

① 우리 중 누구도 의사가 될 준비가 되어 있지 않았다.

② 내 딸은 아침에 거의 스스로 일어나지 못한다.

③ James가 Bond girl을 파티에서 만난 때는 지난 일요일이었다.

④ 도대체 너에게 무엇이 문제니?

⑤ 모든 학생들이 영화 보는 것을 즐기는 것은 아니다.

정답 ②

DAY 25

강조, 부정

1교시 Grammar Point

1 강조

(1) **동사 강조** | 〈do/does/did + 동사원형〉 '정말 ~하다'

He **does** look excited.

(2) **명사 강조** | 〈the very + 명사〉 '바로 그 ~'

Justin is **the very** man I have dreamed of.

(3) **의문문 강조** | 〈의문사 + on earth/in the world〉 '도대체'

I don't know what **on earth** Mark is thinking. (마크가 도대체 무엇을 생각하는지)

(4) **부정문 강조** | not ~ at all/in the least '전혀, 결코'

I don't want to waste too much money **at all**. (전혀 낭비하기를 원치 않는다)

(5) **〈It + be동사 + 강조 대상 + that ...〉 강조구문** | '…한 것은 바로 ~였다'

원문	Sam picked up the apples in the yard yesterday. ① ② ③ ④
① 주어 강조	**It was** Sam **that[who]** picked up the apples in the yard yesterday. (어제 마당에서 사과를 땄던 사람은 바로 Sam이었다.)
② 목적어 강조	**It was** apples **that[which]** Sam picked up in the yard yesterday. (Sam이 어제 마당에서 땄던 것은 바로 사과였다.)
③ 수식어 강조	**It was** in the yard **that[where]** Sam picked up the apples yesterday. (Sam이 어제 사과를 땄던 곳은 바로 마당이었다.)
④ 수식어 강조	**It was** yesterday **that[when]** Sam picked up the apples in the yard. (Sam이 마당에서 사과를 땄던 것은 바로 어제였다.)

2 부정

(1) **부분부정** | 〈not/never + all/always/both/every/quite/necessarily〉
'모두/항상/둘 다/반드시 ~한 것은 아니다'

Not all animals have four legs. (모든 동물이 4개의 다리를 가진 것은 아니다.)

The rich are **not always** happy. (부자들이 항상 행복한 것은 아니다.)

(2) **전체부정** | no, none, never, neither

None of them is in my family. (그들 중 누구도 우리 가족이 아니다.)

Neither of them is disappointing. (그들 중 아무도 실망스럽지 않다.)

(3) **준부정** | few, little, rarely, hardly, seldom, scarcely '거의 ~않다'

We can get **little** advice from him.

I **hardly** practice the cello.

Grammar Tips

- **〈It be동사 ~ that ...〉 강조구문 vs. 〈It(가주어) ~ that(진주어) ...〉 구문**

〈It is ~ that ...〉 생략 시
강조 구문: 완벽한 문장
~~It is~~ Tom ~~that~~ likes me.
→ Tom likes me. (o)

가주어-진주어 구문: 불완전한 문장
~~It is~~ true ~~that~~ I don't know it.
→ I don't know it true. (×)

- **〈It is ~ that ...〉 강조구문은 동사를 강조할 수 없다.**

동사는 do/does/did로 강조

- **강조구문에서 that 이외에 쓸 수 있는 접속사**

사람 강조: who, whom
사물, 동물 강조: which
시간 강조: when
장소 강조: where

- **기타 부정 표현**

no sooner A than B
(A 하자마자 B하다)
not A until B (B해서야 비로소 A하다)

- **전체부정 표현**

no = not ~ any
neither = not ~ either

I have **no** friends.
= I do**n't** have **any** friends.
I studied **neither** subject.
= I did**n't** study **either** subject.

2교시 In - Class Questions

STEP A

빈칸에 알맞은 말을 〈보기〉에서 골라 쓰시오. (필요하면 어형을 바꿀 것)

보기 do the very on earth at all who

1 Keilen is ___________ woman that everyone wants to meet.

2 The new couple ___________ want to look very happy then.

3 What ___________ is the problem with transfering schools?

4 Now, I don't have to buy an expensive printer ___________.

STEP B

주어진 말을 사용하여 밑줄 친 부분을 강조하는 문장으로 바꿔 쓰시오.

1 John made many grammar mistakes in his writing. (that)
→ ___________________________

2 I used her computer the day before yesterday. (when)
→ ___________________________

3 She worked at a hospital for 20 years. (do)
→ ___________________________

STEP C

우리말과 같은 뜻이 되도록 주어진 말을 사용하여 문장을 완성하시오.

1 나는 수학에서 항상 맞는 답을 구하는 것은 아니다. (always)
→ I ___________ ___________ get the right answer in math.

2 그들 중 누구도 피아노를 연습하지 않는다. (neither)
→ ___________ ___________ ___________ practices the piano.

3 모든 포유류가 육지에서 사는 것은 아니다. (all, live)
→ ___________ ___________ mammals ___________ on land.

STEP D

주어진 말을 사용하여 다음 우리말을 영어로 옮기시오.

1 지수는 그 사고에 대해서 전혀 모른다. (anything, at all)
→ ___________________________

2 나는 교수님이 말씀하시는 것을 도무지 이해할 수 없었다. (least, what)
→ ___________________________

3 윤호가 내 지갑을 주웠던 곳은 바로 우리 집 앞이었다. (it, where)
→ ___________________________

3교시 After-Class Questions

[01-02] 두 문장이 같은 뜻이 되도록 〈보기〉에서 알맞은 표현을 골라 빈칸을 완성하시오.

보기	not always	neither A nor B	none	both A and B

01 People are usually satisfied with their lives, but sometimes they are not satisfactory.

→ Life is ______________________ satisfactory for people.

02 Dad doesn't like to go shopping. My brother also doesn't like to go shopping.

→ ______________________ likes to go shopping.

03 밑줄 친 부정구문의 성격이 나머지와 다른 것은?

① Ken has little doubt about it.
② None of them came to help the poor.
③ My girlfriend hardly ever calls me.
④ Many teenagers seldom read novels and poems.
⑤ Few people understand the difference between the two concepts.

04 밑줄 친 that 대신에 쓸 수 있는 것은?

It was yesterday that the new movie was released.

① who　② where　③ which
④ when　⑤ how

05 밑줄 친 It의 쓰임이 나머지와 다른 것은?

① It was her voice that attracted me all day long.
② It was in the hall that Sally met her teacher.
③ It is true that the store is closed on Sunday.
④ It is Jane that goes to school with Hank and Nick.
⑤ It is an unbelievable story that I read in a magazine.

06 우리말을 영어로 바르게 옮긴 것은?

이곳은 그가 5년 동안 공부한 바로 그 장소이다.

① This is a place he has studied for 5 years.
② It is place in the world he studied for 5 years.
③ It is the same place he has studied for 5 years.
④ This is on earth place he has studied for 5 years.
⑤ This is the very place he has studied for 5 years.

Vocabulary Tips

- satisfactory 만족스러운
- doubt 의심
- teenager 십대
- concept 개념
- release 개봉하다

[07-08] 〈보기〉의 밑줄 친 부분을 강조하는 문장으로 바르게 바꿔 쓴 것을 고르시오.

07 보기 A doctor tries to help the poor children in a small town.

① A doctor do try to help the poor children in a small town.
② A doctor did try to help the poor children in a small town.
③ A doctor do tries to help the poor children in a small town.
④ A doctor does try to help the poor children in a small town.
⑤ A doctor does tries to help the poor children in a small town.

08 보기 Victoria reserved a ticket to Bangkok.

① It is a ticket that Victoria reserved to Bangkok.
② It is a ticket to Bangkok that Victoria reserved.
③ It was a ticket that Victoria reserved to Bangkok.
④ It was a ticket to Bangkok that Victoria reserved.
⑤ It was to Bangkok that Victoria reserved a ticket.

09 부정문을 강조하는 표현이 잘못된 문장을 골라 바르게 고치시오.

(a) Harry was not at the last worried about this matter.
(b) Ron doesn't understand in the least what Brian said.

________________ → ________________

10 밑줄 친 부분 중 강조구문 (a)에 들어갈 수 없는 것은?

Hank(①) bought(②) this notebook(③) at the bookstore(④) yesterday(⑤).

→ It was ____(a)____ that ________________.

11 밑줄 친 부분 중 어법상 어색한 것은?

There ①are few people ②in line at this curry restaurant. ③None of ④the customers arrive here ⑤yet.

12 글의 빈칸에 알맞은 말끼리 짝지은 것은?

My grandmother ________ remember the day I first entered the elementary school ________. I was disappointed but never gave up reminding her about it. At the end, she mentioned ________ school I went to.

① can't – at the least – that
② didn't – at all – the very
③ didn't – not at all – the very
④ did – not at all – very
⑤ can't – at all – that

Vocabulary Tips

- **reserve** 예약하다
- **customer** 고객
- **give up** 포기하다
- **mention** 언급하다

After-Class Questions

[13-14] 다음 중 강조구문이 아닌 문장을 고르시오.

13 ① Sarang does obey her father.
② What on earth did your friend tell you?
③ Jeff won't say anything to your mom.
④ It was milk that she needed for her pasta.
⑤ Mr. Yun is the very teacher I would like to learn from.

14 ① Kelly is not in the least clever.
② It was I who repaired this expensive device.
③ Jack did not give any further information at all.
④ What on earth is the matter with your brother?
⑤ Both Sam and Josh did their homework together.

15 우리말과 같은 뜻이 되도록 빈칸에 알맞은 말을 쓰시오.

(1) 미나가 모든 자료를 다 가지고 있지는 않다.
→ Mina ______________________ of the materials.

(2) 미나는 아무 자료도 가지고 있지 않다.
→ Mina ______________________ of the materials.

16 주어진 말을 사용하여 다음 우리말을 영어로 옮기시오.

네가 그 병원에서 봤던 사람이 바로 Paul과 그녀였다. (it, who)
→ ______________________________________

17 〈보기〉의 밑줄 친 부분을 강조하는 문장으로 바꾼 것이 잘못된 것은?

보기 ①Brian ②packed ③lunch ④for his kids ⑤early in the morning.

① It was Brian who packed lunch for his kids early in the morning.
② It was packed that Brian lunch for his kids early in the morning.
③ It was lunch which Brian packed for his kids early in the morning
④ It was for his kids that Brian packed lunch early in the morning.
⑤ It was early in the morning when Brian packed lunch for his kids.

18 괄호 안에서 알맞은 말을 고르시오.

(1) It was **(Iowa / in Iowa)** that I first met my husband.
(2) It was **(you and me / you and I)** who they invited to their laboratory.

Vocabulary Tips

- material 자료, 재료
- laboratory 연구소

19 부정구문의 성격이 나머지와 다른 것은?

① Both of my parents are not dead.
② Even my mom cannot do everything herself.
③ Not all of the students followed the teacher's instructions.
④ He spent time playing with neither of his brothers.
⑤ People who look nice are not always nice to you.

서술형 대비

[20-21] 밑줄 친 부분을 강조하는 문장으로 바꿔 쓸 때 빈칸에 알맞은 말을 쓰시오.

20 What do you want to do?

→ What ________ ________ ________ do you want to do?

21 Juliet fell in love with Romeo on her cousin's wedding day.

→ ________ ________ Romeo who Juliet fell in love with on her cousin's wedding day.

[22-23] 밑줄 친 부분의 쓰임이 나머지와 다른 것을 고르시오.

22 ① It was last night that I realized my mistake.
② It was not a true that she had married twice.
③ It was I that wrote an email to Sean this morning.
④ It was your girlfriend that I met on the street this afternoon.
⑤ It was on the street that Jim picked up a hundred-dollar bill yesterday.

23 ① I did do everything I could.
② I did inform you in advance.
③ They do meet each other.
④ Your best friends do care about you.
⑤ Do as I tell you.

24 우리말과 같은 뜻이 되도록 할 때 빈칸에 알맞은 것은?

나는 너의 부모님 두 분을 다 만난 것은 아니었다.
→ I didn't meet ________ of your parents.

① some ② none ③ either ④ neither ⑤ both

25 우리말과 같은 뜻이 되도록 빈칸에 알맞은 말을 쓰시오.

나는 엄마가 나를 깨워야만 비로소 일어난다.
→ I don't get up ________ my mom wakes me up.

Vocabulary Tips

- instruction 지도사항, 가르침
- one hundred-dollar bill 100달러짜리 지폐
- in advance 미리

DAY 26

도치, 생략

1교시 Grammar Point

1 도치

(1) 장소부사(구) 도치 | 〈장소부사구 + 자동사 + 주어〉 [*타동사 도치 불가]

In the room slept her sister.
(slept: 자동사, her sister: 주어)

Here he comes. → Here comes he. (x) [주어가 대명사일 경우 도치 불가]
(he: 주어(대명사), comes: 동사)

In the living room finished Trey the project. (×) [타동사 도치 불가]
(finished: 타동사, Trey: 주어)

(2) 부정어 도치 | 〈부정어 + be동사 + 주어〉
〈부정어 + do/does/did/조동사 + 주어 + 동사원형〉

부정어: never, few, little, hardly, scarcely, rarely, seldom, not only, not until, no sooner, nowhere 등

Never was my son tired after he played soccer.
(Never: 부정어, was: 동사, my son: 주어)

Seldom does she go to bed late.
(Seldom: 부정어, does: 동사, she: 주어)

(3) so, neither, nor 도치

〈so + 동사(be/일반/조동사) + 주어〉	〈neither[nor] + 동사(be/일반/조동사) + 주어〉
긍정문에 대한 동의	부정문에 대한 동의
'~또한 그렇다'	'~도 또한 아니다'
= 〈주어 + 동사(be/일반/조동사) too.〉	= 〈주어 + 동사(be/일반/조동사) + not either.〉

Caroline can dance well, and so can her husband.
= her husband can dance well, too.

Henry didn't pass the exam, and neither did Lisa.
= Lisa did not pass the exam either.

2 생략

(1) 접속사로 연결되어 반복되는 부분

Nayoung went home **and (she)** washed the dishes.

(2) 비교구문의 than, as 뒷부분이 반복되는 부분

Irene swims faster **than** Ron **(does)**.

(3) to부정사의 동사 반복되는 부분

You can come if you want **to (come)**.

(4) if, when, while, etc. 부사절에서 주절 주어와 같을 때 〈주어 + be동사〉 생략

While (you are) in Austria, you should visit Vienna.

Grammar Tips

도치 추가 예문

In the classroom studied John.
(In the classroom: 장소부사구, studied: 동사, John: 주어)

Over my house flew airplanes.
(Over my house: 장소부사구, flew: 동사, airplanes: 주어)

Here comes Eric.
(Here: 장소부사, comes: 동사, Eric: 주어)

〈not until A + 조동사 + 주어 + 본동사 + B〉

'A하고 나서야 비로소 B하다'

Not until yesterday did we know the secret.
→ We didn't know the secret until yesterday.

〈only ~ + 조동사 + 주어 + 본동사〉

Only after leaving the house did she discover she had left her purse at home.

so, neither, nor 도치 추가 예문

A: I can't go.
B: Neither can I. [부정에 동의]
(나 또한 못갈 것 같아.)
A: I studied hard.
B: So did I. [긍정에 동의]
(나 또한 그랬어.)

생략 추가 용법

(1) 〈주격 관계대명사 + be동사〉
There is a boy **(who is)** sleeping on the sofa.

(2) 목적격 관계대명사
He lost the pen **(that)** his father had given to him.

(3) think, believe, know 등의 목적어 역할을 하는 명사절의 접속사 that
I think **(that)** Cathy is pretty.

2교시 In - Class Questions

STEP A

괄호 안에서 알맞은 말을 고르시오.

1 Never **(does she go / does go she / did she go)** to the doctor these days.

2 Under the table **(two little girls are / are two little girls)**.

3 Seldom **(Jennifer does meet / does Jennifer meet / does meet Jennifer)** many people.

4 Keilen didn't get the certificate, and neither **(did Lily / Lily did / does Lily)**.

STEP B

다음 문장을 주어진 말로 시작하는 문장으로 바꿔 쓸 때 빈칸에 알맞은 말을 쓰시오.

1 Jeongmin ran into the classroom.
→ Into the classroom ___________ ___________.

2 He drank a cup of milk tea at the cafe.
→ At the cafe ___________ ___________ a cup of milk tea.

3 You don't want it, and he doesn't want it either.
→ You don't want it, and ___________ ___________ ___________.

STEP C

생략할 수 있는 부분에 밑줄을 치시오.

1 Jane missed the subway, so she took the bus.

2 Someone may go out if he wants to go out.

3 Frank hopes that he gets a decent job soon.

4 When I was young, I liked to play with many of my friends.

STEP D

밑줄 친 부분을 강조하는 문장으로 바꿔 쓰시오.

1 This food not only looks good, but it is also delicious.
→ ____

2 We do not realize its importance until we lose our health.
→ ____

3 People with gray hair walk down the street.
→ ____

4 Susan hardly dreamed that she would visit here.
→ ____

3교시 After-Class Questions

[01-03] 밑줄 친 부분 대신에 쓸 수 있는 표현을 고르시오.

01 Brian will do his homework this weekend, and I will, too.

① so he will ② do will he ③ so I will
④ so I do ⑤ so will I

02 I had never seen so many dogs and cats in the street.

① Never I had seen ② Never had I seen ③ Never had seen I
④ I never had seen ⑤ Never did I have seen

03 Your dad won't give you any money. I won't give you any either.

① Neither won't I. ② Neither I won't. ③ Neither will I.
④ Either I won't ⑤ Either will I.

[04-06] 다음 중 어법상 어색한 문장을 고르시오.

04 ① You may go home if you want to.
② They walked as fast as they could.
③ When in danger, just call me.
④ Here five girls and two boys are.
⑤ Minji is going to the concert, and so am I.

05 ① Not until you apologize will I forgive you.
② No sooner had she met him than she ran away.
③ Jiho left right after dinner, and so Minsu did.
④ Not only did he come late, but he also forgot his homework.
⑤ Never do I play computer games at home before finishing my homework.

06 ① Seldom have I been late for school.
② At no time did she open the window.
③ Not until September will I have a holiday.
④ Never I have seen such a beautiful girl.
⑤ Not a word has my mom said since last week.

Vocabulary Tips

- in danger 위험에 처해 있는
- apologize 사과하다
- forgive 용서하다
- run away 도망가다

07 〈보기〉의 밑줄 친 부분을 강조한 문장으로 바르게 바꿔 쓴 것은?

보기 Gary has little dreamed that he will become the best pilot.

① Little Gary has dreamed that he will become the best pilot.
② Little has Gary dream that he will become the best pilot.
③ Little has Gary dreamed that he will become the best pilot.
④ Little have Gary dreamed that he will become the best pilot.
⑤ Little Gary have dreamed that he will become the best pilot.

08 밑줄 친 부분 중 생략할 수 있는 것은?

On ①Saturday morning, when ②I was in the room, I was doing my homework. Suddenly, the doorbell rang. ③As I went to open the door, I was told not ④to open the door by my parents. Even though ⑤the bell kept ringing, I didn't open the door.

09 밑줄 친 부분 중 생략할 수 없는 것은?

① Both Nancy and Rick were interested in art when they were young.
② This is my best friend whom I met in the kindergarten.
③ Some thought that these problems seem hard to solve.
④ Victoria writes essays better than Dan does.
⑤ Though Kevin was very tired, he finished all of the work he had to do.

[10-11] 대화의 빈칸에 알맞은 말을 고르시오.

10

A: Is it okay to save this file in my USB?
B: Yes, if my sister allows you ________.

① are ② will ③ to
④ can ⑤ on

11

A: I didn't finish my history report.
B: ______________________________

① So did I. ② So I did. ③ I did, too.
④ Neither I did. ⑤ Neither did I.

12 우리말을 영어로 바르게 옮긴 것은?

우리는 전에 그런 이상한 이름을 결코 들어본 적이 없다.

① Never did we have heard such a weird name.
② Never have we hear such a weird name before.
③ Never have we heard such a weird name before.
④ Never didn't we hear such a weird name before.
⑤ Never did we hear such a weird name before.

Vocabulary Tips

- pilot 비행기 조종사
- suddenly 갑자기
- kindergarten 유치원
- weird 이상한

서술형 대비

13 우리말과 같은 뜻이 되도록 주어진 단어를 바르게 배열하시오.

서울의 도심을 통해 한강이 흐른다. (the Han River / flows)
→ Through the city of Seoul ______________________________.

14 〈보기〉와 의미가 같은 문장은?

보기 Our airplane flies over a large farm.

① Over a large farm our airplane flies.
② Over a large farm flies our airplane.
③ Our airplane over a large farm flies.
④ Files our airplane over a large farm.
⑤ Over a large farm does our airplane fly.

15 두 문장을 한 문장으로 바꿔 쓸 때 빈칸에 알맞은 말을 쓰시오.

The girls look very similar. They also like the same food.
→ Not only ______________ very similar, but ______________ the same food.

16 두 문장이 같은 뜻이 되도록 할 때 빈칸에 알맞은 말끼리 짝지은 것은?

It was not until yesterday that my mom found my TEPS test score.
→ ________ yesterday ________ my TEPS test score.

① Until – my mom not found
② Until – did my mom find
③ Until – my mom didn't find
④ Not until – my mom found
⑤ Not until – did my mom find

17 우리말과 같은 뜻이 되도록 괄호 안에서 알맞은 말을 고르시오.

토끼는 밖으로 뛰어나오고 독수리는 날아 들어왔다.
→ Out **(jumped a rabbit / did a rabbit jump)**, and in **(flew an eagle / did an eagle fly)**.

18 밑줄 친 부분 중 어법상 어색한 것은?

(a) My family knew the fact only with her help.
→ ①Only with her help ②did my family ③know the fact.
(b) Mary was so exhausted that she fell asleep right away.
→ ④So exhausted ⑤Mary was that she fell asleep right away.

19 어법상 어색한 부분을 찾아 바르게 고치시오.

(1) My Chinese is not good, and either is his. ________ → ________
(2) I am happy to speak Spanish, and nor is she. ________ → ________
(3) Eventually, you got an award, so did I. ________ → ________

Vocabulary Tips

- fly 날다(–flew–flown)
- similar 비슷한
- exhausted 지친
- fall asleep 잠들다
- right away 곧바로
- eventually 결국

20 어법상 올바른 문장끼리 묶은 것은?

(a) There lived a woman in this town.
(b) On the desk by the window her lamp lay.
(c) Not until you were twelve did you eat pizza.
(d) Hardly have he noticed the announcement.
(e) To this classroom she comes.

① (a) ② (a), (e) ③ (c), (d)
④ (b), (c), (d) ⑤ (a), (c), (e)

21 생략할 수 있는 말에 밑줄을 그으시오.

I like basketball more than I like baseball.

서술형 대비

22 두 문장이 같은 뜻이 되도록 빈칸에 알맞은 말을 쓰시오.

I never told him who I met yesterday.
→ Never ________ ________ ________ him who I met yesterday.

[23-24] 다음 중 어법상 어색한 문장을 모두 고르시오.

23 ① Down the street walked he.
② Some dishes broke my mom again.
③ Enclosed in the envelope is my invitation.
④ Not a trace did she leave from the room.
⑤ Happy are people who know the joy of helping others.

24 ① Only in his house does he feel comfortable and happy.
② Only after I came back to the hotel I could take a rest.
③ Only a few of my friends know that I have a new boyfriend.
④ Only my little sister has been to Canada with my parents.
⑤ Only last week my mom met my homeroom teacher for the first time.

25 다음 중 어법상 올바른 문장은?

① Over my head a bird passed.
② On a flower sat some bees.
③ Rarely it snows in Busan.
④ Little she realizes how pretty she is.
⑤ At the top of the mountain many trees stood.

Vocabulary Tips

- lie 놓여있다 (-lay-lain)
- announcement 공고문
- enclose 동봉하다
- envelope 봉투
- trace 자국, 흔적

Final Test

01 밑줄 친 It의 쓰임이 나머지와 다른 것은?

① It was easy for you to stay up late.
② It is today that my parents come back home.
③ It was Mike that loved you so much.
④ It is on the road where the snow piles up.
⑤ It is the famous actor who all of the students wants to see.

02 밑줄 친 부분을 강조한 문장으로 올바른 것은?

Eunice took the picture while Anne was smiling.

① It was took the picture that Anne was smiling.
② Eunice on earth took the picture while Anne was smiling.
③ Eunice does take the picture while Anne was smiling.
④ Eunice in the least took the picture while Anne was smiling.
⑤ Eunice did take the picture while Anne was smiling.

03 문장의 의미가 잘못된 것은?

① The rich are not always happy. (부자들이 항상 행복한 것은 아니다.)
② Not every woman can be a good wife. (모든 여자가 좋은 아내가 될 수 있는 것은 아니다.)
③ None of them knew that they were dolls. (그들 중 아무도 그것들이 인형이라는 것을 알지 못했다.)
④ Neither of us thinks about solving the riddle. (우리 둘 중 하나는 이 수수께끼를 푸는 것에 대해 생각한다.)
⑤ We don't know what on earth Matilda is drawing. (우리는 Matilda가 도대체 무엇을 그리고 있는지 모른다.)

[04-06] 다음 중 어법상 어색한 문장을 고르시오.

04 ① You can buy this car if you want to.
② Eric is very man all women want to go out with.
③ Vicky dances well, and so does Micky.
④ Scarcely did Cathy pass the entrance exam.
⑤ It was Jane that decided to buy a new computer.

05 ① When old, they are bored to do every work.
② On the top of the roof a hen stood.
③ In his house are a number of people.
④ Many members of the jury did believe that he is innocent.
⑤ In the basket were a small pin and a clip.

06 ① All students in Korea are not happy.
② Here was the man, and there she was.
③ It is the detective that helps the victims.
④ She is a nurse, and so do I.
⑤ I'm not in the least concerned about his future.

07 밑줄 친 부분 중 어법상 어색한 것은?

Yesterday, I ①met a man, and he wanted ②to have a dinner with me. We had dinner and a great time. He was a wonderful man. Not only ③he was kind, ④but he also had good manners. I ⑤do want to meet him again.

서술형 대비

08 주어진 말을 이용하여 다음 우리말을 영어로 옮기시오.

그 상자가 도착한 시간은 바로 6시였다. (deliver)
→ It was ______________________________
______________________________.

09 밑줄 친 부분을 강조하는 문장으로 바꿔 쓸 때 빈칸에 알맞은 것은?

My sisters said not a word after fighting with each other last night.
→ Not a word ________ after fighting with each other last night.

① my sisters said ② said my sisters
③ did my sisters said ④ my sisters did
⑤ did my sisters say

10 생략된 부분이 있는 문장을 모두 고르시오.

(a) Frank saw the smart bird which was going back to its cage.
(b) Jinseok went home and played computer games.
(c) While in Italy, we had to stay at that hotel.
(d) Karen believes that man wants to take the course.

____

11 문장의 빈칸에 알맞은 것은?

Jane and Dona were in a traffic jam, and ________ were their husbands.

① so ② only
③ never ④ not until
⑤ scarcely

12 밑줄 친 부분 중 생략할 수 없는 것은?

① Yuki drove more carefully than Hunter did.
② Sunny is a dancer who is majoring in ballet.
③ Minjun was very excited about football when he was young.
④ If it is possible, stop by my house for a while.
⑤ While you were at home, the mailman knocked at the door.

13 대화의 빈칸에 알맞은 말끼리 짝지은 것은?

A: I am so afraid of going to Russia. Because I can't speak ________ Russian ________ English.
B: ________ ________ I. But it doesn't really matter. You can get help from information center.

① either – or – Neither – can
② either – or – Neither – can't
③ both – and – So – can
④ both – and – So – can't
⑤ neither – nor – Neither – can

14 밑줄 친 부분을 강조하여 (1), (2)의 문장을 다시 쓰시오.

Many people suffer sleep disorders. The most common symptom is that (1)they rarely fall asleep at night. So in Korea, people suffering from insomnia start to count sheep. (2)100 sheep are on the green grass. That's the first setting.

(1) ______________________________
(2) ______________________________

15 도치된 문장을 원래 문장으로 복원하여 다시 쓰시오.

Not until the boy left did I know he was my student.

→ ______________________________
____

16 밑줄 친 부분에서 생략된 부분을 복원하여 다시 쓰시오.

(1) Although invited to the party, I won't go.
→ ______________________, I won't go.

(2) If necessary, he will ask a favor of you.
→ ____________, he will ask a favor of you.

17 우리말과 같은 뜻이 되도록 빈칸에 알맞은 말을 〈보기〉의 말을 이용하여 쓰시오.

보기 both either neither nor or and

(1) 우리는 그것 중 어느 것도 좋아하지 않는다.
→ We like ________ of them.

(2) 그는 그것 둘 다 좋아하는 것은 아니다.
→ He doesn't like ________ of them.

(3) 너는 부지런하지도 않고, 열심히 공부도 하지 않는다.
→ ________ ________ ________ diligent,
________ ________ ________ study hard.

[18-19] 다음 중 어법상 올바른 문장을 고르시오.

18 ① It was the library where I met him.
② It was you and her that gave him a gift.
③ It was last night where we had a party.
④ Only this morning did he find the answer.
⑤ Little did he homework, so he was in trouble.

19 ① It was in front of my house which I met her.
② He do want to travel all around the world.
③ What your teacher teaches you is not always right.
④ Little dreamed I that I would meet the idol group EXO.
⑤ It was Jim whom caused a big problem last night.

20 괄호 안에서 알맞은 말을 고르시오.

(1) Across the street (a mall lay / lay a mall).

(2) Here (we are / are we).

(3) Nothing (we said / did we say) was the truth.

(4) It was (Manhattan / in Manhattan) that Gina studied.

21 밑줄 친 부분을 강조한 문장으로 바르게 바꿔 쓴 것은?

(a) The famous bakery was near this town. (b) David lost his bike in the park.

(a) ________ (b) ________

① Near this town the famous bakery was.
② Near this town was the famous bakery.
③ In the park David lost his bike.
④ In the park did David lose his bike.
⑤ In the park lost David his bike.
⑥ In the park lost his bike David.

22 문장의 빈칸에 알맞은 말을 〈보기〉에서 골라 쓰시오.

보기 did on earth that neither

(1) What ________ are you trying to do?

(2) It was the news that he got married to Emma ________ I was shocked by.

(3) I think my wife was upset with me. She ________ talked to me nor looked at me this morning.

(4) The firefighters ________ try hard to save the victim's life.

서술형 대비

23 밑줄 친 부분을 강조하는 문장으로 바꿔 쓰시오.

I played baseball with a famous player in this baseball park last Sunday.

→ ______________________________________
____

24 〈보기〉의 밑줄 친 부분과 쓰임이 같은 것은?

보기 I did meet Kenny at the department store the day before yesterday.

① They did their best to win the game.
② She does look happy recently.
③ Is she doing her homework assignment?
④ What did you do the day before yesterday?
⑤ Didn't she want you to ask for some help?

25 밑줄 친 부분의 쓰임이 나머지와 다른 것은?

① It was this toy that I wanted to get.
② It was Mother Teresa that took care of the poor.
③ It is true that he got a 100 on the midterm exam.
④ It is this Saturday that my family will go fishing.
⑤ It was in front of the post office that the lost child was found.

26 대화의 빈칸에 들어갈 수 없는 문장은?

A: ____________________   B: Neither do I.

① I don't like English.
② I don't eat tomatoes.
③ He doesn't study hard.
④ I have no chance to talk to him.
⑤ My father has written a letter to my mom.

27 밑줄 친 부분 중 어법상 올바른 것은?

① Sumin can drive, and so do I.
② I am very short, and so does my sister.
③ Jane lives in Hawaii, and so do Bob.
④ She will go hiking, and so does he.
⑤ My sister has finished her homework, and so has Hannah.

28 우리말과 같은 뜻이 되도록 주어진 단어를 바르게 배열하시오.

이 마을 어느 곳에서도 일요일에 문을 연 가게를 찾기 힘들 것이다. (stores / will / find / you / any)   → Hardly anywhere in this town ____________ ____________ open on Sundays.

29 대화에서 어법상 어색한 부분을 찾아 바르게 고치시오.

A: It's cold out there. Please give me something hot to drink.   B: Okay. Wait a minute. ... Here are you. Enjoy it.   A: Thanks a lot. What is it?   B: It's ginger tea. It helps your blood circulation.   A: Oh, I have never tasted it before. It's delicious.

____________ → ____________

30 밑줄 친 부분 중 생략할 수 있는 것은?

① Who is your new English teacher?
② She has a son who is 13 years old.
③ People who are very sick need to go to a hospital.
④ Do you know the girl who is talking to John over there?
⑤ Her brother who was very nice and kind often bought us food.

≫ 정답 및 해설 49쪽

Extracurricular Activities

▸ Sentence Writing

PART A Complete the sentences describing the picture.

1 On the playground ______________________________.
(많은 나무들과 꽃들이 있다)

2 Under the big tree ______________________. A boy and a girl are sitting there,
(나무로 만들어진 벤치가 하나 있다)
and they are eating ice cream.

3 Here ______________________ who is wearing a big hat.
(여자 한 분이 오고 있다)

4 It is ______________________ that ______________________.
(그 여자분은 바로 이 학교의 교장선생님이다)

PART B Change the Korean into English by using the given words.

1 Jeff는 그곳에 가지 않을 것이고, 나도 그럴 것이다. (will)
→ ______________________

2 모든 학생들 중 그 선생님이 가장 좋아하는 사람은 바로 너이다. (best of, it)
→ ______________________

3 수두는 Edward가 전에 발견했던 바로 그 병이다. (the chicken pox, had discovered)
→ ______________________

4 저 언덕 너머에서 갑작스런 소나기가 시작되었다. (over, sudden shower)
→ ______________________

▸ Further Studies 내신, 수능에 많이 나오는 속담 ③

▸ A sound mind in a sound body. 건강한 신체에 건전한 정신

▸ Penny-wise and pound-foolish. 작은 돈에는 현명하고 큰 돈에는 어리석다.

▸ No new is good news. 무소식이 희소식이다.

▸ A stitch in time saves nine. 제 때의 한 바늘은 아홉 바늘의 수고를 덜어준다.

▸ Make hay while the sun shines. 볕이 있을 때 건초를 만들어라.

▸ Necessity is the mother of invention. 필요는 발명의 어머니이다.

▸ Time and tide wait for no man. 세월은 사람을 기다리지 않는다.

▸ Walls have ears. 벽에도 귀가 있다.

▸ A rolling stone gathers no moss. 구르는 돌에는 이끼가 끼지 않는다.

▸ A watched pot never boils. 지켜보는 냄비는 끓지 않는다. (일을 서두르지 마라.)

▸ All work and no play make Jack a dull boy. 공부만 하고 놀지 않으면 아이를 바보로 만든다.

▸ Better late than never. 늦는 것이 아예 하지 않는 것보다 낫다.

▸ Easy come, easy go. 쉽게 얻은 것은 쉽게 잃는다.

▸ Haste makes waste. 서두르면 일을 망친다.

▸ Never put off till tomorrow what you can do today. 오늘 할 일을 내일로 미루지 마라.

▸ A leopard cannot change its spots. 표범은 그의 반점을 변화시킬 수 없다. (성격은 좀처럼 고치기 힘들다.)

▸ Beauty is in the eye of the beholder. 제 눈에 안경이다.

▸ Don't put all your eggs in one basket. 한 바구니에 모든 달걀을 담지 마라.

▸ Nothing ventured, nothing gained. 모험하지 않으면 얻는 것도 없다.

▸ One cannot eat one's cake and have it. 케이크를 먹으면서 가지고 있을 수는 없다. (양쪽 다 좋을 수는 없다.)
= You cannot have your cake and eat it, too.

▸ What's done cannot be undone. = Don't cry over spilt milk. 이미 이루어진 일은 되돌릴 수 없다.

▸ The whole is more than the sum of its parts. 전체는 부분의 합 이상이다.

총정리 모의고사

1회 / 2회

총정리 모의고사 1회

01 문장의 형식이 나머지와 다른 것을 고르시오.

① The CEO made him retired.
② The truth made her really disappointed.
③ The teacher made them solve the questions.
④ Jessica made him something delicious.
⑤ Her advice made me regret what I had done.

[02-04] 우리말을 영어로 바르게 옮긴 것을 고르시오.

02

너는 그녀가 도착했을 때 그녀를 계속 기다리고 있었니?

① Are you waiting for her when she arrives?
② Was you waiting for her when she arrived?
③ Have you been waiting for her when she arrived?
④ Have you been waited for her when she arrived?
⑤ Had you been waiting for her when she arrived?

03

이 차 사고에 대해 책임을 져야 할 사람은 바로 너와 나이다.

① It is you and I that am to blame for this car accident.
② It is you and I that are to blame for this car accident.
③ It is you and me that are to blame for this car accident.
④ This is you and I that am to blame for this car accident.
⑤ This is you and me that are to blame for this car accident.

04

Harry는 그의 친구를 만나길 기대하고 있다.

① Harry is looking forward meet his friend.
② Harry is looking forward to met his friend.
③ Harry is looking forward to meet his friend.
④ Harry is looking forward to meeting his friend.
⑤ Harry is looking forward to be meeting his friend.

05 대화에서 어법상 어색한 것을 고르시오.

A: Jason, why didn't you ①clean your room?
B: When I ②entered my room, I found that it ③has been cleaned. I ④thought that you had done it. So I ⑤had nothing to do.

서술형 대비

[06-07] 두 문장이 같은 뜻이 되도록 빈칸에 알맞은 말을 쓰시오.

06

Harry lived in that apartment, but now he doesn't live there.
→ Harry _________ _________ live in that apartment.

07

My husband is so smart that he knows everything.
→ My husband is smart _________ _________ _________ everything.

08 대화의 빈칸에 알맞은 것을 고르시오.

A: I didn't pass the exam this afternoon. It was too difficult.
B: You ________________ harder last night. However, you played computer games.

① had better study ② should have studied
③ would have studied ④ must have studied
⑤ might have studied

09 능동태 문장을 수동태 문장으로 바르게 바꾼 것을 고르시오.

They gave me a good book as a gift.

① A good book is given me as a gift by them.
② A good book was given for me as a gift by them.
③ A good book was given to me as a gift by them.
④ A good book was given of me as a gift by them.
⑤ A gift was given me as a good book by them.

서술형 대비

10 빈칸에 알맞은 말을 넣어 대화를 완성하시오.

A: Who is taking care of the elderly?
B: They ____________________________ by woman named Catherine.

11 문장의 빈칸에 알맞은 것을 고르시오.

Lonely people need some friends ________.

① to live ② to play
③ to play on ④ to play with
⑤ to live in

12 밑줄 친 부분 중 어법상 어색한 것을 고르시오.

When I ①was studying in the cafe, I ②saw Danny ③cross the street and ④to go into a convenience store ⑤with his girlfriend.

13 두 문장을 한 문장으로 바꿔 쓸 때 빈칸에 알맞은 말을 쓰시오.

Yesterday, my father shouted loudly at me. I couldn't understand his action.
→ I couldn't understand ________ ________ ________ loudly at me yesterday.

14 다음 중 어법상 어색한 문장을 고르시오.

① Diana fell asleep with the TV turned on.
② Those girls ran around with their hair untied.
③ All of those people worked with their faces painting.
④ It was a busy day with the phone ringing all day long.
⑤ The couple took a walk with their dogs following them.

15 우리말과 같은 뜻이 되도록 할 때 주어진 단어를 바르게 배열한 것을 고르시오.

> Anna는 먹을 게 없어서 COOL 편의점에 갔다.
> (to / nothing / there / eat / being)
> → ______________, Anna went to the COOL convenience store.

① There being nothing to eat
② There eat nothing to being
③ There being eat nothing to
④ Being nothing to eat there
⑤ To eat nothing there being

16 두 문상이 같은 뜻이 되도록 할 때 빈칸에 알맞은 말끼리 짝지은 것을 고르시오.

> My home is the most comfortable place.
> → ________ place is ________ comfortable than my home.

① No other – more
② No other – most
③ Another – more
④ Any other – more
⑤ The other – most

17 우리말과 같은 뜻이 되도록 빈칸에 알맞은 말을 고르시오.

> 그가 나에게 진실을 말했으면 좋았을 텐데.
> → I wish he ________ me the truth.

① will tell　② would tell
③ has told　④ have told
⑤ had told

18 밑줄 친 if의 쓰임이 나머지와 다른 것을 고르시오.

① Yuna asked if it was right to do.
② He'll stay at home if it rains tomorrow.
③ Nobody knows if our team will win or not.
④ I'm not sure if I can arrive there on time.
⑤ Don't tell me if he has not decided yet.

19 문장의 빈칸에 알맞은 말을 고르시오.

> ________ you need most is your teacher's comments on this essay.

① Who　② How
③ That　④ What
⑤ Which

20 어법상 어색한 문장끼리 묶은 것을 고르시오.

> (a) I met a man with who I used to work.
> (b) Andrew saw a car whose windows were all broken.
> (c) This is the house in that Jack lived when he was young.
> (d) This is the house in which Jack lived when he was young.

① (a), (c)　② (b), (d)
③ (b), (c), (d)　④ (a), (c), (d)
⑤ (a), (b), (c), (d)

21 밑줄 친 부분 중 어법상 어색한 것을 고르시오.

① A doctor must love sick people.
② Rome was not built in the day.
③ Frank and Sue go to the same school.
④ You should visit this room twice a week.
⑤ The book on the table isn't very interesting.

22 **가정법 문장을 직설법 문장으로 바꿔 쓴 문장이 잘못된 것을 고르시오.**

① If Lucy had longer legs, she could run faster.
→ As Lucy does not have longer legs, she cannot run faster.

② If you had taken my advice, you would have had a better life.
→ As you didn't take my advice, you didn't have a better life.

③ She looks as if she had had a severe backache.
→ In fact, she didn't have a severe backache.

④ I wish I had studied all of the subjects last semester.
→ I'm sorry I didn't study all of the subjects last semester.

⑤ If I had had lunch a few minutes ago, I would not be hungry now.
→ As I didn't have lunch a few minutes ago, I was hungry now.

[23-24] 대화의 밑줄 친 부분 중 어법상 어색한 것을 고르시오.

23

A: Jack ①has not arrived here yet. I wonder if he ②will be here soon. I have something to ask him.
B: He caught a severe cold; if he had been healthy, he ③would come already.
A: Really? I ④didn't know that. I ⑤should call him and ask whether he is all right.

24

A: Have you ①checked the newspaper? I read an interesting article.
B: About what? The missing children?
A: Yeah. The number of missing children ②are not known.
B: No way. Either the police or government ③knows the number.
A: Unfortunately, both ④don't know. That's ⑤shocking news.

25 **밑줄 친 부분을 직접화법으로 바르게 바꿔 쓴 것을 고르시오.**

One rainy day, Kevin took a puppy home and asked his father if he could keep it as a pet. His father said, "As long as you promise two things, you can keep it. The first is that it does not cause any trouble. The second is you must take care of it by yourself."

① told his father, "Can he keep it as a pet?"
② told his father, "Can I keep it as a pet?"
③ told his father, "Could I keep it as a pet?"
④ said to his father, "Can you keep it as a pet?"
⑤ asked his father, "Could I keep it as a pet?"

총정리 모의고사 2회

[01-02] 문장의 빈칸에 알맞은 말을 고르시오.

01

Our plane ________ at Incheon International Airport in 30 minutes.

① arrive ② arrives
③ has arrived ④ will arrive
⑤ arrived

02

The value of Korean movies is considered ________ American movies.

① as higher as
② as high as those of
③ as high as that of
④ as higher as that of
⑤ as high as

03 우리말과 같은 뜻이 되도록 〈보기〉의 단어를 사용하여 빈칸을 완성하시오.

보기 must take care of tired

(1) 그 의사는 밤새 환자를 돌봐야 했었다.
→ The doctor ________________ his patients all night.

(2) 그 의사는 밤새 피곤했었음에 틀림없다.
→ The doctor ________________ all night.

[04-05] 밑줄 친 부분 중 어법상 어색한 문장을 고르시오.

04 ① Tom is thought to have been sick.
② The rumor could not have been true.
③ I learned that water freezes at 0 degrees.
④ If I were you, I wouldn't let her feel lonely.
⑤ Having written in hurry, the book didn't get recognized.

05 ① Everyone thinks him an honest guy.
② I have not watched his new movie so far.
③ His brother didn't meet any of us until then.
④ The team tried to rehearse for its first performance.
⑤ Semi visited Lina's apartment in order to cheer her up.

[06-09] 문장의 빈칸에 알맞은 말끼리 짝지은 것을 고르시오.

06

(a) My car is ________ by a mechanic now. (b) His laptop ________ yet.

① repaired – is not repaired
② being repaired – has not been repaired
③ being repaired – has been repaired
④ being repairing – has not been repaired
⑤ being repairing – has been repairing

07

(a) James had his car ________ by a stranger. (b) Chun got me ________ breakfast.

① stolen – cooked
② stolen – to cook
③ steal – cook
④ to steal – to cook
⑤ to steal – cooked

08

(a) The lady talks as if she ________ the best teacher.
(b) The boy wishes he ________ a foreign language at that time.

① is – speaks ② is – could speak
③ were – had spoken ④ were – spoken
⑤ was – had spoke

09

(a) Please tell me if he ________ back home tomorrow.
(b) Sungwoo will go to Hawaii for his honeymoon if he ________ his fiance next year.

① comes – marries
② comes – will marry with
③ will come – marries
④ will come – will marry
⑤ will come – marry with

10 문장의 빈칸에 알맞은 말끼리 짝지은 것을 모두 고르시오.

(a) Mr. Song allowed me ________ at his bangalow.
(b) We saw the student ________ off the tree.

① staying – fall ② staying – to fall
③ to stay – falling ④ to stay – to fall
⑤ to stay – fall

[11-13] 문장의 빈칸에 알맞은 말을 고르시오.

11

I am a shy girl. I didn't use to talk with people a lot when I was young. Now, I am in a public speech class, so I ________ with people.

① did used to talk ② used to talk
③ used to talking ④ get used to talk
⑤ am getting used to talking

12

I heard a popular speaker was coming to my town. I singed up to attend his speech. Unfortunately, I was very disappointed because his speech ________.

① too bored ② too boring
③ was too bored ④ was too boring
⑤ to be boring

13

My son is in trouble. He bullied his classmate. The victim's parents will not forgive him. You can't imagine ________.

① how disappointing he is
② how disappointed he is
③ how disappointing is he
④ how is he disappointing
⑤ how he is disappointed

14 주어진 말을 문장의 빈칸에 알맞은 형태로 바꿔 쓰시오.

Mr. Smith forgot ________ my mom at the Nordstrom Mall before. (meet)

15 우리말과 같은 뜻이 되도록 빈칸에 알맞은 말을 고르시오.

두 언니 모두가 나와 친한 것은 아니다.
→ ________ of my sisters are not close to me.

① Both
② Any
③ Either
④ One
⑤ All

16 문장의 빈칸에 알맞은 말끼리 짝지은 것을 고르시오.

________ Jihee ________ her mom, her mom could have finished her degree.

① If – could support
② If – has supported
③ If – supported
④ Had – supported
⑤ Had – been supported

17 밑줄 친 부분 중 어법상 어색한 것을 골라 바르게 고치시오.

(a) The residents ①prefer building a gym ②than building a factory.
(b) The young ③would rather hang out with their friends ④than ⑤stay at their houses.

________________ → ________________

18 대화의 빈칸에 알맞은 말끼리 짝지은 것을 고르시오.

A: ________ makes you come here?
B: The first man ________ I talked to there recommended your store.

① That – that
② Who – whom
③ Who – who
④ What – whom
⑤ What – that

19 우리말과 같은 뜻이 되도록 주어진 말을 사용하여 빈칸을 완성하시오.

(1) 말할 필요도 없이, 그는 내 입장에서 생각해준다.
(need, say)
→ ________________, he always puts himself in my shoes.

(2) 이 강의는 두 번 들을 만한 가치가 있다.
(attend, lecture)
→ It is worthy ________________ twice.

20 밑줄 친 부분과 같은 뜻의 말로 바꿔 쓰시오.

> But for the money, my family could not have gone abroad for summer vacation.
> → (1) ________ the money,
> → (2) ________ ________ ________ ________ ________ ________ the money,
> → (3) ________ ________ ________ ________ ________ the money,

21 대화에서 어법상 어색한 부분을 찾아 바르게 고치시오.

> A: When have Sera and you reach this hotel?
> B: We have just arrived here.

____________________ → ____________________

22 문장의 빈칸에 알맞은 동사의 형태를 〈보기〉에서 골라 쓰시오.

> 보기 attend attends attending to attend to attending

(1) A large number of people ________ his class.
(2) Most of them ________ the project meeting.

23 문장의 빈칸에 알맞은 관계사를 쓰시오.

(1) ________ hot it is outside, we will go swimming.
(2) ________ finishes first will be the winner.

24 밑줄 to부정사의 용법이 나머지와 다른 것을 고르시오.

① My plan was to get a better score.
② It is nice of you to bring my chair.
③ To look up new words is my study habit.
④ I have a goal to get to the top of the mountain.
⑤ I won't forget to stop by your office at 4 o'clock.

25 두 문장이 같은 뜻이 되도록 바꿔 쓴 문장에서 어법상 어색한 부분을 찾아 바르게 고치시오.

> This box is so heavy that I can't carry it.
> → This box is too heavy for me to carry it.

____________________ → ____________________

방과 후

Review Test

Day 01 ▸ Day 26

Class ____________ Name ______________________ Score ____________

A

Choose the correct answers.

1 A hard workout helps your muscles (**works / to work / working**) better.

2 Sam heard some kids (**sing / to sing / sung**) in the bathroom.

3 My parents make me (**wash / to wash / washing**) their car every weekend.

4 You might be attracted to someone who always allows you (**speak / to speak / speaking**).

B

Correct any errors. Write OK if there are not any.

1 Melanie watched them played tennis on the court. ____________ → ____________

2 The movie director helps us making a good presentation. ____________ → ____________

3 My friends eventually made me to buy a new smartphone. ____________ → ____________

4 Too many patients are here. They have to have their temperatures taken soon.
____________ → ____________

C

Change the Korean into English by using the given words.

1 나는 좋은 선생님이 되는 것이 어렵다는 것을 알았다. (**good, difficult, teacher, found, it**)
→ ____

2 Thomas는 자신을 매우 똑똑하다고 생각한다. (**smart boy, himself, think of, pretty**)
→ ____

Review Test

Class ____________ Name ____________________ Score ____________

A Choose the correct answers.

1 Eric and Harry try to remember that they have met her **(ago / before / since)**.

2 **(How long / When / Did)** has he worked for the government?

3 Kevin lost the contact lenses I **(buy / have bought / had bought)** the day before.

4 My father had gone to Germany when I **(was / have been / had been)** born.

B Correct any errors.

1 When have you become a poet? ____________ → ____________

2 We don't find any survivors for a week. ____________ → ____________

3 It has snowed heavily on Sunday. ____________ → ____________

4 Sam is a farmer. He raises 50 pigs since he bought the farm. ____________ → ____________

C Put the words in the correct order.

1 내 컴퓨터는 어젯밤 이후로 고장이 나 있다. **(has / last night / my computer / been / broken / since)**
→ ____

2 나는 일생 동안 외국에 가본 적이 없었다. **(have / abroad / in / never / I / life / my / been)**
→ ____

Review Test

Class ____________ Name ______________________ Score ____________

A Choose the correct answers.

1 By the time I turned on a movie channel, *Harry Potter* **(had been going / has been going / had been gone)** for the climax.

2 Jake will **(have drunk / have drinking / had drunk)** a cup of coffee when his parents arrive at the airport.

3 I **(had been playing / had been played / have been playing)** soccer until my mom came to pick me up.

B Correct any errors. Write OK if there are not any.

1 Tina is my mentor. She has been helping me since last year. ____________ → ____________

2 My sister has been skating for three hours when I called her. ____________ → ____________

3 We will know each other for 10 years next year. ____________ → ____________

C Change the Korean into English by using the given words.

1 Ethan은 30분 동안 그의 여자 친구와 전화 통화를 하는 중이다. **(talk, half an hour)**
→ ____

2 내 동생은 몇 년 동안 중국어를 배우고 있다. **(learn, several)**
→ ____

3 내가 친구에게 전화했을 때, 그녀는 노래를 부르고 있었다. **(phone, songs)**
→ ____

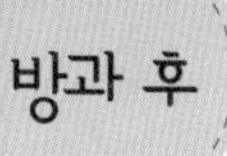

Review Test

Class ____________ Name ____________________ Score ____________

A Choose the correct answers.

1 **(Will / Can / May)** you be able to suggest a new plan instead of Paul?

2 Susan **(can't finish / couldn't finished / cannot have finished)** the project yesterday. She didn't work on it at all.

3 Susan **(will / is going to / can / is able to)** be thirty years old next year.

4 **(May / Shall / Could)** you tell me what is going on these days?

5 Jen **(would like / should like / would rather)** start for Paris now than stay Rome.

B Correct any errors.

1 Hillary always tells lies. She may not be honest. ____________ → ____________

2 I would rather to go home earlier. ____________ → ____________

3 It was sunny yesterday. Your bike must have been wet. ____________ → ____________

4 If you answer this question, you can be going to get more points.
____________ → ____________

C Put the words in the correct order.

1 Abigail는 그렇게 큰 실수를 했을 리가 없다. **(Abigail / big / such / made / cannot / have / a / mistake)**
→ ____

2 나는 더 좋은 컴퓨터를 살 수도 있었지만, 돈이 충분하지 않았다.
(money / could / enough / have / have / bought / didn't / a better / I / but / computer / I)
→ ____

Class ____________ Name ____________________ Score ____________

Choose the correct answers.

1 He **(must have been / should have been)** sick since he failed the examination.

2 Kate **(should have been / might have been)** pretty when she was young.

3 A few people **(must / have to / had to)** perform this dangerous work yesterday.

4 All of the students don't look well. I think they **(need / will / must)** have food poisoning.

5 You **(may well / may as well)** get some rest. You look tired. You have had a hard time finishing this project.

Correct any errors.

1 We might went to the same church last Sunday. ____________ → ____________

2 John must have buy a new car. Its color is changed. ____________ → ____________

3 James must win the game since he practiced a lot. ____________ → ____________

C Put the words in the correct order.

1 그의 의견은 사실이 아닐지도 모른다.
(be / not / true / his / opinion / may)
→ ______________________________

2 나는 다음 월요일까지 나의 보고서를 제출해야 할 것이다.
(next / I / Monday / will / by / have to / report / submit / my)
→ ______________________________

Review Test

Class ____________ Name ____________________ Score ____________

A Choose the correct answers.

1 Stella **(need / needs / should)** not play the violin since the contest was called off.

2 She **(uses to buy / used to buy / is used to buy)** a loaf of bread at the store on her way home.

3 William **(has better / had better / had better not)** get his visa before he departs.

4 Kate **(dare not / need not)** go on a trip alone. She wants someone to travel with.

B Correct any errors.

1 I failed the test. I shouldn't have studied harder. ____________ → ____________

2 She has better not go to such a dangerous place. ____________ → ____________

3 Sam would have short hair when he was young. ____________ → ____________

C Change the Korean into English by using the given words.

1 너는 그 컴퓨터게임을 하곤 했니? (used to)

→ ____

2 그는 젊었을 때 자주 인터넷 카페에 가곤 했었다. (would)

→ ____

3 대학에 입학하기 위해 더 열심히 공부하는 게 좋겠다. (should, enter)

→ ____

Review Test

Class ________ Name ______________ Score ________

A Choose the correct answers.

1 Linda was seen **(cross / to cross / to be crossed)** the street.

2 We are made **(feel / to feel / to be felt)** comfortable like we are at home.

3 A new car was bought **(to / for / of)** me by my grandfather.

4 The students was **(made / seen / given)** the books by their homeroom teacher.

B Correct any errors. Write OK if there are not any.

1 Sumi's bike was lent for him by her. ________ → ________

2 His car was stealed last night. ________ → ________

3 Justin was proved guilty by the judge. ________ → ________

4 They were seen drive too fast on the highway. ________ → ________

C Change the Korean into English by using the given words.

1 나는 9시까지 집에 돌아와야 한다고 들었다. (tell, come back)
→ ____

2 나는 남편으로부터 우리의 결혼기념일을 위한 꽃다발을 받았다. (give, a bouquet of, wedding anniversary)
→ ____

Class ____________ Name ____________________ Score ____________

A Choose the correct answers.

1 One of our club members **(was run by / was run over by / ran over)** a car.

2 It **(is believe / is believed / being believed)** that the new research is unexpected.

3 I couldn't buy the apartment. It **(costs / is cost / will cost)** too much.

4 This street has already **(closed / be closed / been closed)** because of the typhoon.

B Correct any errors.

1 The coffee should be serve to everyone here. ____________ → ____________

2 The disabled have taught Korean by her. ____________ → ____________

3 Lots of plants and flowers are taken care by me. ____________ → ____________

4 Some of the candles are being preparing by the staff. ____________ → ____________

C Change the Korean into English by using the given words.

1 이 문제는 즉시 처리되어야 한다. **(matter, handle, as soon as possible)**

→ ____

2 우리는 다음 금요일까지 학기말 과제를 제출하도록 요청받았다. **(term paper, ask, submit, by)**

→ ____

Review Test

Class ____________ Name ____________ Score ____________

A Choose the correct answers.

1 Kelly must have heard her sister **(to cry / cried / crying)** yesterday.

2 My father made me **(throw / to throw / thrown)** my game CDs away.

3 Joe will ask you **(do / to do / doing)** all of the work alone.

4 It is necessary **(for / of / x)** you to come home earlier.

B Correct any errors.

1 Dora didn't tell me when to comes back her house. ____________ → ____________

2 Many people didn't know who should we vote for in the election. ____________ → ____________

3 The old wanted for the young to get along with their friends. ____________ → ____________

4 Jill had her husband to repair the window yesterday. ____________ → ____________

C Change the Korean into English by using the given words.

1 엄마는 내가 친구들과 컴퓨터게임 하는 것을 허락하실 것이다. (allow)

→ ____________

2 나는 L.A.에 있었을 때 아파트가 흔들리는 것을 느꼈다. (feel)

→ ____________

Review Test

Class ____________ Name ____________________ Score ____________

A Choose the correct answers.

1 My pocket money was **(big enough / enough big / big to enough)** for me to buy this MP3.

2 The cheetah ran so fast that I **(can / cannot / couldn't)** catch it.

3 She worked hard **(only to / only / to only)** fail the exam.

4 Riding a bike is a good way **(increase / to increase / to increasing)** your chances of meeting people.

B Correct any errors.

1 The new pool is too small for your family to swim. ____________ → ____________

2 My son is sorry for breaking your glass cup. ____________ → ____________

3 Dona exercised in order not become sick. ____________ → ____________

4 The Japanese book is so difficult for your kid to read. ____________ → ____________

C Change the Korean into English by using the given words.

1 나의 어머니는 백화점에서 할인을 받기 위해 쿠폰을 사용하셨다. **(use, coupon, discount, get)**
→ ____

2 너는 네 발표를 도와줄 누군가가 필요하니? **(need, presentation, someone, help, with)**
→ ____

방과 후

Review Test

Class ____________ Name ______________________ Score ____________

A Choose the correct answers.

1 The boy seems **(to have / have / having)** some complaints.

2 You can go there if you want **(to / to going / to be gone)**.

3 I don't want Kara **(to invite / to be invited)** to my wedding.

4 They are said **(to stay / to have stayed)** in England for the last two years.

B Make the two sentences have the same meaning.

1 It seems that he forgot what to do.
→ He seems ________________________ what to do.

2 My computer seems to be out of order.
→ It ____________ that ________________________ out of order.

3 It seemed that he was famous.
→ He ________________________ famous.

4 He seems to have been famous.
→ It ____________ that ________________________ famous.

Change the Korean into English by using the given words.

1 나는 축구는 말할 것도 없고 야구도 좋아한다. **(mention)**
→ ____

2 나는 길을 잃었다. 설상가상으로 비가 내리기 시작했다. **(lost, matters)**
→ ____

Review Test

Class ____________ Name ____________________ Score ____________

A Choose the correct answers.

1 Frank is seriously thinking of **(change / changing / to change)** his career.

2 He was sorry for **(make / to make / having made)** a big mistake.

3 Erica rejected **(promote / promoting / being promoted)** to a new position in the company.

4 A few teachers don't like **(students / students's / students')** studying Chinese characters.

5 **(Help / Helping / Being helped)** children in Africa is a necessary activity for young students to let them know what volunteers do.

B Correct any errors.

1 Following not the class rules might cause a big problem. ____________ → ____________

2 Everyone in the pool must wear a swim suit. ____________ → ____________

3 Tina is worried about telling some bad comments about her novel by her classmates.
____________ → ____________

C Change the Korean into English by using the given words.

1 엎질러진 물을 놓고 우는 것은 소용없는 일이다. (use)
→ ____

2 Ben은 걸어서 출근하는 데 익숙해졌다. (used to)
→ ____

Review Test

Class ____________ Name ____________________ Score ____________

A Choose the correct answers.

1 His doctor suggested **(eat / to eat / eating)** several meals on high-stress days.

2 Would you mind **(pass / to pass / passing)** the bread next to you?

3 It is no use **(worry / to worry / worrying)** about what happened recently.

4 Do you remember **(give / to give / giving)** me a ride in that big truck last Monday?

5 Catherine felt so thirsty that she stopped **(work / to work / working)** and got some water.

B Correct any errors.

1 My family is looking forward to go to Europe next month. ____________ → ____________

2 These interesting books are worth to share with your friends. ____________ → ____________

3 My mom never wants me to forget to have plans last week. ____________ → ____________

4 Tim felt like to drive out of town this weekend. ____________ → ____________

C Change the Korean into English by using the given words.

1 어떤 학생들은 고등학교에서 일본어를 공부하기 시작한다. (start, learn)

→ ____

2 나는 네가 내 블로그에 방문하기를 기대하고 있다. (look forward to, visit)

→ ____

Review Test

Class ____________ Name ____________________ Score ____________

Choose the correct answers.

1 Earthquakes **(occur / occurred / occurring)** in every country are predictable these days.

2 **(Locate / Being located / Being locating)** at a high level, the city is a little bit cold, and the average temperature is pretty low.

3 My boyfriend didn't say anything; he just stood next to the window with his face **(turn / turning / turned)** away from me.

4 **(Having not / Not having / Having never)** any reference books, Linda had difficulty solving those problems.

5 Since Rick, her son, doesn't like to go to the hair salon, she has his hair **(cut / cuts / cutting)** at home.

Correct any errors.

1 The boy played the computer game is my brother. __________ → __________

2 Everyone is tiring because of the hiking trip. __________ → __________

3 A teacher found the door broke. __________ → __________

Change the Korean into English by using the given words.

1 몸무게를 줄이는 데 관심이 있는 많은 사람들은 그 뉴스에 신이 났다. **(interest, lost, excite)**
→ ____

2 그녀는 눈을 감은 채 음악을 듣는 데 집중했다. **(concentrate, close, with)**
→ ____

Review Test

Class ___________ Name ___________________ Score ___________

A Choose the correct answers.

1 (Be / Being / Been) thirsty, he had some water.

2 (Spend / Spent / Spending / Having spent) all of her money, Lucia didn't have enough money to buy a new bag.

3 (Being / Having been / There being) no bus service, many people had to take the subway.

4 (Frankly speaking / Generally speaking / Considering), I have never been to Spain with my family.

5 (Impressing / Impressed / Having impressed) by her performance, William was determined to learn about her.

B Correct any errors.

1 Be angry at me a few days ago, she won't talk to me. __________ → __________

2 Don't finished her homework, she can't take a rest. __________ → __________

3 Injuring last night, I am in the hospital now. __________ → __________

C Change the Korean into English by using the given words.

1 솔직히 말하자면, Emma는 그렇게 아름다운 건 아니야. **(frankly, that)**
→ ____

2 그는 어떻게 해결해야 할지 몰라서 그 문제를 포기하기로 결정했다. **(분사구문, solve, give up on)**
→ ____

Review Test

Class ____________ Name ____________ Score ____________

A Choose the correct answers.

1 *Before Sunset* is **(romantic / more romantic / the most romantic)** movie I have ever seen.

2 Diamonds are more precious than **(other / another / any other)** gem in the world.

3 Their team project is not so good **(as / so / than)** the other teams' projects.

4 The legs of the small table are **(far / more / most)** weaker than those of the big one.

B Correct any errors.

1 I prefer taking a bus better to taking a taxi. ____________ → ____________

2 No other doctors is nicer than him. ____________ → ____________

3 We are trying to catch as many insects as we could. ____________ → ____________

4 Gold is twice as more expensive as it was last year. ____________ → ____________

C Change the Korean into English by using the given words.

1 Ellen은 Jonathan보다 한국말을 훨씬 더 유창하게 말한다. (much, fluently)

→ ____

2 너는 기말고사를 위해 더 많이 공부할수록 더 좋은 성적을 받을 수 있다. (final exam, the)

→ ____

Review Test

Class ____________ Name ____________________ Score ____________

A Choose the correct answers.

1 Sam glanced at the strange man **(who / which / whom)** was wearing sunglasses and was standing in the corner.

2 These are the essays **(that / who / whose)** authors are all my students.

3 Both Angela and Tiffany are women **(whom / on whom / with whom)** everybody wants to work.

4 He can't find his cell phone **(which / whom / what)** I put in his briefcase.

B Correct any errors.

1 The woman whom respected Dr. Jeff was Keilen. __________ → __________

2 The old couple that daughter learned the clarinet felt happy. __________ → __________

3 That person to who Fiona is speaking will be my teacher. __________ → __________

4 I have a dog of which is very friendly and cute. __________ → __________

C Put the Korean into English by using the given words.

1 이것은 내가 어릴 때부터 써왔던 나의 일기이다. **(this, diary, since)**
→ ______________________________

2 나는 신용카드를 분실한 사람을 찾았다. **(the man, look for, lose)**
→ ______________________________

Review Test

Class ____________ Name ____________________ Score ____________

A Choose the correct answers.

1 Stop bothering me about everything **(which / that / what)** goes wrong!

2 Nobody can believe **(which / that / what)** you've just said.

3 He will show me China's 10 richest people, many of **(who / whom / what)** are under 30 years old.

4 Would you lend me a pen **(on which / with which / of which)** I can write now?

B Correct any errors.

1 Tell me something which I have to buy by tonight. ____________ → ____________

2 Please let me know that you want to buy for your party. ____________ → ____________

3 Athena has three uncles, that became popular composers. ____________ → ____________

4 My parents are the only people who I can rely on. ____________ → ____________

C Change the Korean into English by using the given words.

1 Bossman 선생님이 나에게 이 영문법 책을 주셨는데, 그것은 매우 도움이 되었다.
(English grammar book, helpful)
→ ____

2 Dora는 그녀가 가진 가장 예쁜 인형을 잃어버렸다. **(the prettiest, lose)**
→ ____

방과 후

Class ____________ Name ____________________ Score ____________

A Choose the correct answers.

1 We will discuss (**what** / **why** / **how**) we can run the new business better.

2 Cathy looks gorgeous, (**whatever** / **whoever** / **however**) she wears.

3 Jack made the door open, (**whichever** / **whenever** / **however**) cold it is outside.

4 Pick up (**no matter which** / **anything that** / **at any time when**) you like.

B Correct any errors. Write OK if there are not any.

1 Whatever cold it is outside, I want to go hiking. ____________ → ____________

2 Whoever gets the highest score will be the winner. ____________ → ____________

3 I don't have any reason I like going to the zoo. ____________ → ____________

4 Let's go the Lorenz School where we visited before. ____________ → ____________

C Change the Korean into English by using the given words.

1 너는 너의 어머니가 그 종이학들을 어떻게 접었는지 아니? (**paper cranes, fold**)
→ ______________________________

2 그 수업을 수강하고 싶어 하는 학생들은 누구든지 환영받을 것이다. (**be welcomed, lesson**)
→ ______________________________

Review Test

Class ____________ Name ____________________ Score ____________

A Choose the correct answers.

1 Let's play (a / the / x) basketball this weekend.

2 Have you ever met (a / the / x) man in the car?

3 Our family visited (a / the / x) Netherlands last year.

B Correct any errors. Write OK if there are not any.

1 There was a store in the front of the hotel. ____________ → ____________

2 My brothers are in a backyard and are playing soccer. ____________ → ____________

3 What are names of the cities? ____________ → ____________

4 Mr. Smith punched me in the face. ____________ → ____________

C Put the words in the correct order.

1 Mary의 아버지는 대한민국 공군 장교이다.
(the / an / is / in / officer / ROK Air force)
→ Mary's father ______________________________.

2 나는 길에서 휴대폰을 주웠다. 그런데 그 전화가 갑자기 울렸다.
(rang / the / cell phone / on / suddenly / a / phone / and / street / the)
→ I picked up ______________________________.

Class ____________ Name ______________________ Score ____________

A Choose the correct answers.

1 If he **(knows / knew / had known)** my address, he would have sent a package to me.

2 If Anne had taken his advice then, she would **(be / been / have been)** successful now.

3 Cathy would **(walk / be walking / have walked)** with her dog if she had one.

4 We could **(do / done / have done)** much better if we had practiced more.

B Correct any errors.

1 If she had read many books, she wouldn't feel difficult at the test. ____________ → ____________

2 If there was a room available, we could go camping today. ____________ → ____________

3 What could he do if he had left alone now? ____________ → ____________

4 If we didn't study yesterday, we would be embarrassed today. ____________ → ____________

C Change the Korean into English by using the given words.

1 내가 대학교에 다시 갔다면 외과의사가 되었을 텐데. **(go back, might, surgeon)**
→ ____

2 내가 바쁘지 않으면 지금 너를 만날 수 있을 텐데. **(busy, could, meet)**
→ ____

Review Test

Class ____________ Name ____________________ Score ____________

A Choose the correct answers.

1 The king acts as if he **(is / were / has been)** a beggar.

2 I wish I **(have / had / had had)** a beautiful girlfriend now.

3 If it **(will not be / were not / had not been)** for her leadership, we wouldn't have been successful.

4 He talks as if he **(were / has been / had been)** in New York when he was younger.

B Correct any errors.

1 I wish she was my sister. ____________ → ____________

2 I had been at the party, I could have met her. ____________ → ____________

3 The guy acts as if he saw the event. In fact, he wasn't there. ____________ → ____________

C Change the Korean into English by using the given words.

1 인터넷이 없다면 우리는 이 귀중한 정보를 찾을 수 없을 것이다.
(but for, information, valuable, find, could)
→ ____

2 Isabella는 마치 혼자서 그 일을 끝냈던 것처럼 행동한다.
(as if, complete, presentation, acts)
→ ____

Class ____________ Name ____________________ Score ____________

A Choose the correct answers.

1 I learned that the French Revolution **(breaks / broke / had broken)** out in 1789.

2 Statistics **(is / are / have been)** a boring subject to some students.

3 I wish I **(study / would study / had studied)** hard when I was in middle school.

4 Not only the poor but also the rich **(was / were / has been)** disappointed with the news.

B Correct any errors. Write OK if there are not any.

1 Each of the boys have great potential. ____________ → ____________

2 Nobody want to talk about that issue. ____________ → ____________

3 Neither you nor he is very tired. ____________ → ____________

4 The police is very supportive of the citizens. ____________ → ____________

C Change the Korean into English by using the given words.

1 나의 어머니는 결코 그녀의 커피에 설탕과 크림을 넣지 않는다고 말씀하셨다.
(that, cream, never, sugar, put, said)
→ ____

2 모든 학생들이 기말고사를 위해서 열심히 공부한다. **(final exam, every, hard, on, study)**
→ ____

Review Test

Class ____________ Name ____________________ Score ____________

A Choose the correct answers.

1 My best friend asked me what (**was my favorite food / my favorite food was / my favorite food is**).

2 Jane (**say to / said / said to**) the kids, "Don't run in the hall."

3 William told them that he had met an old friend (**yesterday / the day after / the previous day**).

4 Some clerks told the customers (**to not touch / not to touch / not touch**) the products.

B Correct any errors.

1 I told her if she would help me with my project. ____________ → ____________

2 Mom asked me to not go to the museum late. ____________ → ____________

3 He asked us when did he leave for Busan. ____________ → ____________

C Change the Korean into English by using the given words.

1 나의 어머니는 나에게 영화 보러 가지 말라고 말씀하셨다. (not, tell, go)
→ ____

2 그 비서는 나에게 전에 커피를 좋아했었는지 물었다. (secretary, if, ask)
→ ____

Class ____________ Name ____________________ Score ____________

A Choose the correct answers.

1 These are (very / only / the very) books that some students need.

2 Everybody (do / did / does) hope he will try harder and harder this year.

3 (None / No / Not) of them has ever been to Europe with his family.

4 What (in earth / on earth / at earth) are some solutions for this matter?

B Correct any errors.

1 What on the world would you talk to him about? ____________ → ____________

2 It was him that encouraged you to study so much. ____________ → ____________

3 They both got A's. Neither of them wasn't disappointed. ____________ → ____________

 Change the Korean into English by using the given words.

1 나는 기타를 연주하는 방법을 전혀 모른다. (at all, how to, the guitar)
→ ______________________________

2 내가 Jim을 만났던 곳은 바로 공원에서였다. (at the park, come across, where)
→ ______________________________

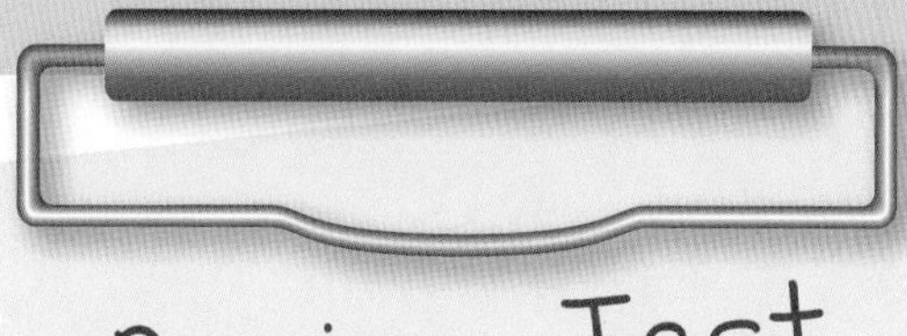

Class ____________ Name ____________________ Score ____________

A Choose the correct answers.

1 Right over his head (it pass / passed it / it passed).

2 Never (her son was tired / was her son tired / her son tired was), she kept playing with him.

3 A: I have been to England recently.
B: Really? (So have / Neither have / So do) I. It was so great.

4 A: Martin and Brian didn't show up at the party.
B: (Neither do / Neither did / Nor do) Susan.

B Correct any errors.

1 Not only she gave us money, but she also prayed for us. ____________ → ____________

2 If you are possible, you can work at this store. ____________ → ____________

3 So crowded the bus is that I can seldom move. ____________ → ____________

4 Henry couldn't pass the exam, neither could Laurie. ____________ → ____________

C Change the Korean into English by using the given words.

1 어떤 학생들은 수학을 좋아하고, 다른 학생들은 영어를 좋아한다. [반복되는 부분은 생략할 것]
(some, others, like)
→ ____

2 내가 그녀를 다시 만날 거라고는 거의 꿈도 꾸지 못했다. [부정어를 강조할 것]
(dream, would, again, little, that)
→ ____

memo

memo

memo

memo

중학 영문법

저자 Kyle Cho · Keilen Yun · Cathy Choi
감수 Michael A. Putlack

초판 11쇄 발행 2024년 12월 5일

편집장 조미자
책임편집 류은정 · 김미경 · 정진희 · 권민정 · 최수경
디자인 김교빈 · 임미영
인쇄 북토리

펴낸이 정규도
펴낸곳 Happy House
주소 경기도 파주시 문발로 211 다락원 빌딩
전화 02-736-2031 (내선 250)
팩스 02-732-2037
출판등록 1977년 9월 16일 제406-2008-000007호

ISBN 978-89-6653-098-4 53740

진단평가, Study Plan, 정답 및 해설 무료 다운로드 **www.ihappyhouse.co.kr**
*Happy House는 다락원의 임프린트입니다.

COOL grammar

중학 영문법

자율학습

정답 및 해설

Book 3

Unit 01 문장의 형식

DAY 01 5형식 문장

2교시 In - Class Questions ▶ 본문 9쪽

STEP A 1 to borrow 2 apologize 3 take 4 to keep
STEP B 1 disappear, disappearing 2 wake 3 done
STEP C 1 Jessica will help him assemble the bookshelves.
2 The cell phone ringing caused me not to focus on driving.
3 Jason got me to stay with them for several days.
STEP D 1 I saw the clerk mop[mopping] the floor.
2 Keilen felt her bag touched by a stranger.
3 We always leave the door open.

STEP A
1 그 새로운 정책은 학생들이 한 달에 세 권의 책을 빌릴 수 있게 한다.
2 민이는 내가 엄마를 화나게 한 것에 대해 엄마에게 사과하도록 시켰다.
3 그 가수는 그 파파라치가 그녀의 사진을 찍게 하지 않았다.
4 그 의사는 그의 환자들에게 담배를 피우지 못하게 했다.

STEP B
1 그들은 그 배들이 사라지는(사라지고 있는) 것을 볼 것이다.
2 Victoria는 그녀의 남동생에게 그녀를 아침 6시에 깨우도록 시켰다.
3 나의 아빠는 저녁식사 전에 나의 숙제가 완료되기를 원하신다.

STEP C
1 Jessica는 그가 책장을 조립하는 것을 도와줄 것이다.
2 휴대전화벨이 울리는 소리는 나를 운전에 집중하지 못하게 했다.
3 Jason은 나를 며칠 동안 그들과 함께 머물도록 했다.

Final Test ▶ 본문 10 - 13쪽

01 ③ 02 ② 03 ⑤ 04 ⑤ 05 ③ 06 ③, ⑤ 07 ② 08 published 09 ⑤ 10 ① 11 check → checked 12 as → 삭제 13 ⑤ 14 ③ 15 ② 16 ② 17 ③ 18 (1) Jay는 길에서 잃어버렸던 그의 강아지를 찾았다 (2) 그의 태도가 매우 무례하다는 것을 알게 되었다 19 wash, to wash 20 ⑤ 21 ①, ④, ⑤ 22 calls the rival team Monster 23 me an honest person, me as an honest person 24 ④ 25 ② 26 ③ 27 ①, ⑤ 28 me, not, to, listen, to 29 ① 30 to stop

01 그 레스토랑 매니저는 나에게 탁자를 정리하라고 시켰다.
* get이 이끄는 5형식 문장에서 목적격 보어와 목적어의 관계가 능동일 때는 〈get + 목적어 + to부정사〉 형태로 쓴다.

02 ① 그 소식은 그녀를 매우 우울하게 만들었다.
② Jane은 그녀의 옷을 직접 만든다.
③ 그 사장은 지난밤에 그 프로그램이 설치되도록 시켰다.
④ 내 친구들 중 한 명이 나를 몇 시간 동안 기다리게 했다.
⑤ 나는 내일 아침까지 이 일이 완료되도록 시킬 것이다.
* ②는 3형식 문장(주어 + 동사 + 목적어)이고, 나머지는 5형식 문장(주어 + 동사 + 목적어 + 목적격 보어)이다.

03 ① 무엇이 그를 열심히 공부하게 만들었을까?
② Max는 나에게 그의 컴퓨터를 사용하도록 했다.
③ 우리는 어린 남자아이가 그 강을 수영해서 건너는 것을 보았다.
④ 우리는 네가 파티에서 좋은 시간을 보내기를 원해.
⑤ 나의 어머니는 우리에게 점심으로 호박파이를 만들어주셨다.
* ⑤는 4형식 문장(주어 + 동사 + 간접목적어 + 직접목적어)이고, 나머지는 5형식 문장(주어 + 동사 + 목적어 + 목적격 보어)이다.

04 ① 나의 아내는 나에게 집을 청소하라고 시켰다.
② 나는 호텔 메이드에게 나를 방해하지 말라고 요청했다.
③ 나의 부모님은 나에게 새 컴퓨터를 사라고 시키셨다.
④ 그 의사는 나에게 내일 다시 오라고 말했다.
⑤ 그녀의 노래는 멋지게 들리고, 그녀의 외모는 아름답다.
* ⑤는 2형식 문장(주어 + 동사 + 주격 보어)이고, 나머지는 모두 5형식 문장(주어 + 동사 + 목적어 + 목적격 보어)이다.

05 ① 엄마는 모든 창문을 닫아 두었다.
② 임금 상승에 대한 압박은 회사로 하여금 임금을 올리게 할 수 있다.
③ 과학자들은 껌을 씹는 것이 뇌를 활동하게 한다는 것을 발견했다.
④ 가능한 어디든지, 당신이 읽게 할 수 있는 책을 선택해라.
⑤ 나는 매일 비행기가 하늘로 이륙하는 것을 본다.
* [to working → work] makes는 사역동사로 쓰였으므로 목적격 보어 자리에 동사원형이 와야 한다.

06 * 지각동사 watch는 목적어와 목적격 보어의 관계가 능동일 때 목적격 보어로 동사원형이나 현재분사가 온다.

07 (a) 학구열이 높은 학생들은 항상 그들의 선생님을 기쁘게 한다.
(b) 그 상담자는 Hank에게 운동하라고 충고했다.
* (a) 동사 make는 5형식 동사로 목적격 보어 자리에 형용사(happy)를 취한다. 5형식의 목적격 보어 자리에 부사는 올 수 없다.
(b) 동사 advise는 목적격 보어로 to부정사를 취한다.

08 William은 그의 소설이 출판되도록 노력했지만, 그의 노력은 헛된 일이었다.
* 동사 get은 목적어와 목적격 보어의 관계가 수동일 경우(소설이 출판되는 것) 〈get + 목적어 + 과거분사〉 형태로 쓴다.

09 ① 나의 시어머니는 나에게 설거지를 하라고 시키셨다.
② 그 질문들은 사람들을 당황하게 했다.
③ 우리는 서로 도와 에너지를 아껴야 한다.
④ 지나는 나에게 책상 위의 책들을 가져 오라고 시켰다.
⑤ 모든 사람들은 그 남자가 정원에서 노래 부르는 것을 보았다.
* [to sing → sing 혹은 singing] 지각동사 see는 목적격 보어로 동사원형이나 현재분사를 취한다.

10 ① 지난밤에 우리가 본 그 영화는 나를 지루하게 만들었다.
② 나는 화가 났을 때 주로 1에서 10까지 센다.
③ 영어를 배우는 것은 매우 어렵지만 나는 계속할 것이다.
④ 나는 Paul Gauguin과 같은 유명한 화가가 되고 싶다.
⑤ 나는 어머니를 도와서 저녁과 설거지, 그리고 빨래를 했다.
* [boring → bored] 지각동사 watch가 이끄는 5형식 문장에서 목적어와 목적격 보어의 관계가 수동(내가 지루하게 된)이면 목적격 보어로 과거분사가 와야 한다.

11 김 선생님은 혈압이 측정되도록 하기 위해 병원에 갔다.
* 사역동사 have의 목적어인 혈압(blood pressure)이 '측정되는' 수동의 의미이므로 목적격 보어로 과거분사가 와야 한다.

12 우리 모두는 올해 우진이를 우리의 새 회장으로 선출했다.
* 동사 elect는 5형식 문장을 만들 때 목적격 보어 앞에 as를 쓰지 않는다.

13 학교에서 몇몇 선생님들은 특정한 학생들을 좋아하는데, 때때로 그것은 학생들을 화나게 한다. 예를 들면, 내가 초등학교에 다녔을 때 나의 음악 선생님은 한 학생을 정말 좋아하셨다. 나는 어른들이 어떻게 하는 것이 공평한 것인지 이미 알고 있다고 생각했기 때문에 매우 화가 났다. 그들은 왜 특정한 학생들을 좋아하는지에 대해 설명함으로써 학생들을 이해시켜야 했다.
* [to understand → understood] 사역동사 make의 목적어(their students)가 '이해되는' 수동의 의미이므로 목적격 보어는 과거분사가 와야 한다.

14 * 지각동사 see의 목적어인 그 여자(the woman)가 '들어가는' 능동의 의미이므로 목적격 보어로 동사원형이나 현재분사가 와야 한다.

15 이 선생님은 학생들이 쉬는 시간에 휴대전화를 사용하도록(사용하는 것을) ______. ①④⑤ 시켰다 ② 허락했다 ③ 보았다
* 목적격 보어로 동사원형을 취하지 않는 동사는 allow이다. allow는 목적격 보어로 to부정사를 취한다.

16 우리는 우리 교관이 ______는 것을 알게 되었다.
① 친절하다 ② 행복하게 ③ 귀엽다 ④ 조용하다 ⑤ 잘생겼다
* 5형식 문장에서 목적격 보어로는 형용사나 명사가 쓰이므로 부사 happily는 들어

갈 수 없다.

17 김 선생님은 나를 이 팀의 리더로 ___________.
① 생각했다 ② 이름 지었다 ③ 선택했다 ④ 불렀다 ⑤ 이루어졌다
* 〈as + 목적격 보어〉 형태로 쓰이는 동사는 chose이다.

18 * 동사 find는 3형식으로 쓰일 때는 '찾다', 5형식으로 쓰일 때는 '알게 되다, 깨닫다'의 뜻이다.

19 Tim은 나에게 저녁식사 전에 손을 닦으라고 했다.
* 사역동사 have의 목적어인 me가 '손을 닦는' 능동의 의미이므로 목적격 보어로 동사원형이 와야 하고, 동사 get의 목적어인 me가 '손을 닦는' 능동의 의미이므로 목적격 보어로 to부정사가 와야 한다.

20 ① 엄마는 나의 낡은 정장이 수선되도록 했다.
② Danny는 우리에게 그 의자들을 정돈하라고 시켰다.
③ Mason은 우리에게 땅을 파도록 시켰다.
④ Sera는 그녀의 학생들이 시간을 낭비하게 했다.
⑤ 그는 그녀의 아기를 한 시간 동안 혼자 두지 않을 것이다.
* leave는 목적격 보어로 형용사(alone)를 취하는 동사이다.
① [alter → altered] '정장이 수선되는' 수동의 의미.
② [arranged → arrange] '우리가 정돈하는' 능동의 의미.
③ [to dig → dig] '우리가 땅을 파는' 능동의 의미(made는 사역동사).
④ [wasting → waste] '학생들이 낭비하는' 능동의 의미(made는 사역동사)

21 ① 그들은 우리가 그들에게 외치는 소리를 들었다.
② 진이는 그의 가방에 있던 공책을 도둑맞았다.
③ 그녀는 네가 그 영화를 보게 하지 않을 것이다.
④ 나의 엄마는 그 아이들을 즐겁게 했다.
⑤ 진희는 그 남자가 바이올린 켜고 있는 것을 듣는다.
* ① '우리가 소리치는' 능동의 의미이므로 동사원형이 왔다.
④ '아이들이 즐겁게 되는' 수동의 의미이므로 과거분사가 왔다.
⑤ '그 남자가 바이올린을 켜고 있는' 능동의 의미이므로 현재분사가 왔다.
② [to steal → stolen] '그의 공책이 도둑을 맞은' 수동의 의미
③ [watch → to watch] '네가 보는' 능동의 의미(get + 목적어 + to부정사)

22 나의 팀은 그 라이벌 팀을 괴물이라고 부른다.
* 〈call + 목적어 + 목적격 보어〉의 5형식 문장으로 배열한다.

23 *5형식 동사 think는 〈think + 목적어 + 목적격 보어〉의 형태로 쓰이며, think of는 〈think of + 목적어 + as + 목적격 보어〉의 형태로 쓰인다.

24 A: 야, 네가 이 창문을 닫았니? 여기는 정말 더워.
B: 아니, 엄마한테 문을 열어놔 달라고 부탁했는데.
* leave는 5형식 문장을 만들 때 목적격 보어로 형용사를 취하는 동사이다.

25 2060년에 사람들은 친구를 방문할 새로운 수단을 갖게 될 것이다. 그들은 그들의 날개를 살 수 있을 것이다. 날개는 사람들을 자유롭게 움직이도록 해줄 것이다. 그래서 그 날개들은 사람들이 시간을 절약하도록 할 것이다. 그들의 비행이 안전하도록 하기 위해 새로운 교통 규칙이 필요할지도 모른다.
* 사역동사 let은 목적격 보어로 동사원형을 취하며, help는 목적격 보어로 to부정사 혹은 동사원형을 취한다. keep은 목적격 보어로 형용사를 취한다.

26 ① Nicole은 뭔가 맛있는 것을 원한다.
② Billy는 Noah와 함께 포켓볼 치기를 원하지 않는다.
③ Brian은 그의 아버지가 자신과 함께 놀기를 원한다.
④ 그 사장님은 모든 직원이 그 회의에 참석하기를 원했다.
⑤ 모든 학생들은 그 수학 문제를 풀 시간을 원했다.
* ③은 〈want + 목적어 + 목적격 보어(to부정사)〉의 5형식 문장이다. 나머지는 〈want + 목적어〉의 3형식 문장이다.

27 대부분의 한국사람들은 국가대표 야구팀이 최초로 금메달을 따는 것을 보았다.
* 5형식 문장을 이끄는 지각동사 see는 목적어와 목적격 보어의 관계가 능동(국가대표 야구팀이 금메달을 따는)의 의미일 때 목적격 보어로 동사원형이나 현재분사가 온다.

28 *동사 tell이 이끄는 5형식 문장이므로 〈주어(My mother) + 동사(tells) + 목적어(me) + 목적격 보어(not to listen to music)〉로 나타낸다. 동사 tell의 목적격 보어는 to부정사가 오는데, 이때 to부정사의 부정은 〈not + to부정사〉로 쓴다.

29 내 꿈이 실현되도록 하기 위해 나는 돈을 저축하기로 결심했다.
* 사역동사 make는 목적어와 목적격 보어의 관계가 능동(내 꿈이 이루어지는)의 관계일 때 목적격 보어로 동사원형이 온다.

30 (a) 내 여자 친구는 내가 담배 끊는 것을 도와주었다.
(b) 그 경찰관은 나의 아빠에게 차를 멈추라고 명령했다.
* (a) 〈help + 목적어 + 목적격 보어(동사원형/to부정사)〉, (b) 〈order + 목적어 + 목적격 보어(to부정사)〉이므로 공통으로 알맞은 것은 to부정사이다.

Sentence Writing

▶ 본문 14쪽

Part A
1 made us finish
2 heard their names called
3 allow me to enter

Part B
1 We think of him as the best teacher at this school.
2 Mr. Jackson expected his employees to work this weekend.
3 The woman on the bus felt her shoulder touched by someone.
4 My parents made me earn my tuition.

Unit 02  시제

DAY 02 현재완료시제, 과거완료시제

2교시 In - Class Questions

▶ 본문 19쪽

STEP A 1 never 2 since 3 yet 4 had
STEP B 1 had been 2 have not decided 3 wanted 4 was able to
STEP C 1 has been → was or had been 2 gone → been 3 Henry has → has Henry 4 have → had
STEP D 1 has never failed 2 had already sent 3 has studied

STEP A
1 나의 친구들 중 몇 명은 해외에 다녀온 적이 한 번도 없다.
2 Linda는 지난해 이래로 그녀의 음악 선생님을 안다.
3 그 새로운 컴퓨터들은 아직 도착하지 않았다.
4 우리는 그때 이전에 그 여자를 본 적이 없었다.

STEP B
1 그녀의 조부모님들은 돌아가셨을 때, 몇 년 동안 아프셨다.
2 나는 차를 살지 안 살지를 결정하지 않았다.
3 호준이는 며칠 전에 쉬고 싶었다.
4 Jessica는 전에 그 수학문제를 본 적이 있기 때문에 그 문제를 풀 수 있었다.

STEP C
1 내가 사촌을 보았을 때 그녀는 자신의 고양이에게 먹이를 주고 있었다.
2 그는 그의 친구의 집에 여러 번 간 적이 있다.
3 Henry는 30세가 된 이래로 무엇을 써 오고 있니?
4 나는 아일랜드에 갈 때까지 그와 같이 아름다운 풍경을 본 적이 없었다.

3교시 After - Class Questions

▶ 본문 20 - 23쪽

01 ⑤ **02** ⑤ **03** ④ **04** ② **05** has, gone **06** ④ **07** had, been **08** ④ **09** had finished **10** have stayed **11** Did, you, hear, didn't, have, listened **12** ④ **13** ③ **14** ⑤ **15** (1) had already taken off (2) have waited **16** ① **17** prepared → has prepared **18** ⑤ **19** ①, ④, ⑤ **20** ③ **21** left, has taught **22** I have had the laptop computer since 2009. **23** ③ **24** has, learned, for **25** (1) since (2) gone (3) for

01 내가 공항에 도착했을 때 그 비행기는 이미 떠났다.
* 내가 도착한 과거시점보다 이전에 비행기가 떠난 것이므로 과거완료시제가 알맞다.

02 Sam과 Nancy 둘 다 지난 5월 이래로 함께 일하고 있다.
* 5월 이래로 함께 계속 일하고 있으므로 현재완료시제가 알맞다.

03 내 남동생은 내가 어제 그에게 사주었던 기차표를 잃어버렸다.
* 기차표를 잃어버린 과거시점보다 이전에 표를 산 것이므로 대과거시제가 알맞다.

04 너는 얼마나 오랫동안 치과의사로 있었니?
① 작년 동안. ② 2012년 이래로. ③ 10시 전에.
④ 내가 한국에 도착한 후에. ⑤ 내가 선생님이 되었을 때까지.
* 〈의문사(How long) + have + 주어+ 과거분사 ~?〉로 묻는 말에 대한 응답은 '~이래로(since)'의 표현이 알맞다.

05 Keilen은 러시아에 가서 여기에 없다. → Keilen은 러시아에 갔다.
* 러시아에 가서 '현재 여기 없다'라는 의미는 현재완료시제의 결과를 의미하는 has gone to가 알맞다.

06 ① 나의 친척들은 언제나 제주도에서 살고 있다.
② Cathy는 국립 도서관에 많이 가봤다.
③ 그들은 직업을 잃어서 돈을 벌 수 없었다.
④ 그는 동물원을 방문하기 전까지 코끼리를 본 적이 없었다.
⑤ 그는 죽기 전에 10년 동안 변호사로서 일을 했었다.
* [has → had] 동물원에 방문했던 과거시점보다 그 이전에 가본 적이 없으므로 과거완료시제로 표현해야 한다. ③은 돈을 벌 수 없는 과거시점보다 이전에 직업을 잃어버린 결과가 과거까지 영향을 미친 것이므로 과거완료시제(결과)가 알맞다.

07 * 엄마가 직장에 다시 나간 과거시점보다 먼저 아팠던 것이므로 과거완료시제로 써야 한다.

08 ① 우리는 8시까지 그 일을 끝내기로 기대했었지만 그렇게 하지 못했다.
② 땅은 젖어있었는데, 그것은 전날 밤에 비가 내렸기 때문이다.
③ 엄마는 누군가 대기실에 놓고 갔던 노트북 컴퓨터를 발견했다.
④ 나는 오랫동안 Daniel을 보지 못했다. 나는 그의 얼굴을 기억하지 못한다.
⑤ Greg는 그의 팀원들이 사무실에 왔을 때 그의 프로젝트를 끝냈다.
* 현재 그의 얼굴을 기억하지 못한다고 했으므로 과거부터 현재까지의 상태를 나타내는 현재완료시제가 알맞다. 따라서 빈칸에는 have가 와야 한다.

09 나의 친한 친구들 중 한 명이 나에게 그 패션잡지를 건넸지만 나는 그것을 갖고 싶지 않았다. 왜냐하면 나는 쉬는 시간 동안에 그것을 읽었기 때문이다. 그래서 나는 그것을 다시 그에게 주었다.
* 친구가 건네준 과거시점보다 더 먼저 내가 읽었으므로 과거완료시제로 표현해야 한다.

10 나는 뉴욕에서 태어났고, 2011년에 시애틀로 이사 갔다. 그때 이후로 나는 부모님과 언니들과 함께 시애틀에서 살고 있다.
* 과거부터(since 2011) 지금까지 시애틀에 살고 있으므로 현재완료시제로 표현한다.

11 * just now(방금 전에)는 과거시제와 함께 쓰이는 부사구이다. 1시부터 계속 음악을 듣고 있다고 했으므로 현재완료시제로 표현한다.

12 A: Jenny는 어디에 있니?
B: 그녀는 여기에 없어. 그녀는 약국에 갔어.
* '약국에 가고 없다'는 표현은 현재완료시제의 결과적 용법으로 표현한다.

13 ① 지민이는 언제 부산에 갔니?
② 그들은 2001년에 새로운 이론을 발견했다.
③ 나의 딸은 특별상을 받았다.
④ 우리는 작년부터 초보 선생님들을 만나고 있다.
⑤ 그들은 지난주에 그들의 입학 허가서를 받았니?
* just는 현재완료시제와 함께 쓰이는 부사이다.
① [has Jimin been → was Jimin] When은 현재완료시제와 함께 쓸 수 없다.
② [have come → came] in 2001은 과거를 나타내는 부사구이므로 현재완료시제와 함께 쓸 수 없다.
④ [had → have] 문맥상 현재완료시제가 알맞다.
⑤ [Have they gotten → Did they get] last week는 과거를 나타내는 부사구이므로 현재완료시제와 함께 쓸 수 없다.

14 ① Linda는 지난달부터 그와 데이트를 하고 있다.
② 내가 탁자 위에 올려놓았던 꽃병을 누군가가 깨뜨렸다.
③ 나의 삼촌은 울타리를 방금 칠하셨는데, 그것은 멋져 보인다.
④ 나의 가족은 우리가 전에 계획했던 여행을 연기해야 했다.
⑤ 그 그룹들은 내가 도착하기 전에 회의에 참석했다.
* [have → had 혹은 삭제] 내가 도착했던 과거시점 이전에 그 그룹이 참석했으므로 과거완료시제나 과거시제로 써야 한다.

15 오늘 아침, 나는 한국으로 여행을 갈 예정이었다. 그러나 내가 공항에 도착했을 때 한국으로 가는 비행기는 이미 이륙했다. 지금은 1시이다. 나는 두 시간이 넘게 다음 비행기를 기다리고 있다.
* (1) 내가 도착했던 과거시점 이전에 비행기가 출발한 것이므로 과거완료시제가 알맞다. (2) 지금이 1시이고 두 시간 넘게 기다리고 있는 것이므로 현재완료시제(계속)가 알맞다.

16 (a) 나는 비상호출을 받은 사람이 아무도 없었다는 것을 알았다.
(b) 나는 젊었을 때부터 재무 강의를 듣고 있다.
* (a) 주절이 과거시제이므로 종속절은 과거완료시제가 와야 한다. (b) 〈Since + 주어 + 과거동사〉 다음에 나오는 주절에는 현재완료시제가 와야 한다.

17 Jay는 작년부터 그 오디션을 준비해왔다.
* '작년부터(since last year)'라는 말이 있으므로 현재완료시제로 써야 한다.

18 Tim은 이 회사에 얼마나 오랫동안 일했니?
* How long ~?은 현재완료시제(계속)와 함께 쓰이는 의문문이다. 주어가 3인칭 단수이므로 has를 써야 한다.

19 ① Ralph는 그 유리창을 깨뜨렸다.
② 너는 생선회를 먹어본 적이 있니?
③ 그는 1995년 이후로 미국에서 살고 있다.
④ 나는 공항에서 내 여권을 잃어버렸다.
⑤ 나의 야구팀이 올해 코리안 시리즈에서 우승을 했다.
* ①④⑤는 현재완료시제의 결과를 나타낸다. ② 경험, ③ 계속

20 **보기** 나는 내 인생을 통틀어 이렇게 훌륭한 선수를 본 적이 없다.
① Abigail는 티베트에 가고 없다.
② 나는 지금 막 집에 도착했다.
③ Amber는 전에 호주에 방문한 적이 있다.
④ 나는 오늘 아침부터 교실에 있었다.
⑤ Olivia는 그녀의 과제를 막 끝냈다.
* 〈보기〉와 ③은 현재완료시제의 경험을 나타낸다. ① 결과, ②⑤ 완료, ④ 계속

21 Isabella는 2012년에 영국 캠브리지를 떠났고, 그 이후로는 서울에서 영어를 가르치고 있다.
* 과거를 나타내는 부사구 in 2012가 있으므로 첫 번째 빈칸에는 과거시제가 알맞고, since then이 있으므로 두 번째 빈칸에는 현재완료시제가 알맞다.

22 나는 2009년에 노트북 컴퓨터를 하나 샀다. 나는 그 노트북 컴퓨터를 여전히 갖고 있다.
→ 나는 2009년 이후로 그 노트북 컴퓨터를 가지고 있다.
* 과거에 구입한 노트북을 현재까지 가지고 있음을 나타내는 것이므로 현재완료시제로 표현한다.

23 ① Victor은 방금 교실에 도착했다.
② 내 휴대전화는 지난 주 이래로 고장이 난 상태이다.
③ Stanley와 나는 작년부터 알고 지낸다.
④ Tommy은 영국으로 갔다, 그래서 그는 서울에 없다.
⑤ Sue는 그녀의 모자를 잃어버렸다. 그래서 그녀는 모자가 더 이상 없다.
* [for → since] 〈since + 특정 시점〉, 〈for + 숫자 기간〉으로 쓰인다.
① 완료, ②③ 계속, ④⑤ 결과

24 Audrey는 10년 전에 피아노를 배우기 시작했다. 그녀는 여전히 피아노를 배우고 있다.
→ Audrey는 10동안 피아노를 배우고 있다.
* 과거에 시작해서 현재까지 계속하고 있는 일이므로 현재완료시제로 표현한다. 문맥상 '10년 동안'이므로 for가 알맞다.

25 (1) 나는 중학생 때부터 이 컴퓨터게임을 해오고 있다.
(2) 나의 가장 친한 친구는 하와이에 가고 없다. 그래서 나는 그가 그립다.
(3) 내 딸은 이틀 동안 아팠다.
* (1)(3) 〈for + 숫자 기간〉, 〈since + 특정 시점〉으로 표현한다.
(2) '하와이로 떠나고 없다'는 has gone to로 표현한다.

03 미래완료시제, 완료진행시제

2교시 In - Class Questions ▶ 본문 25쪽

STEP **A** **1** had been studying **2** will have met **3** has been practicing

STEP **B** **1** have been reading **2** had been sleeping **3** have, been living **4** had been washing

STEP **C** **1** will have been **2** have you been **3** had waited 혹은 had been waiting

STEP **D** **1** I have been watching baseball games on TV all afternoon. **2** By the end of this year, he will have been teaching students for twenty years. **3** I had been studying English for 3 years before I went to the US.

STEP **A** **1** 나는 나의 과외 선생님이 집에 오시기 전에 두 시간 동안 공부를 하고 있었다. **2** 내일 이맘때면 나는 쇼핑몰에서 지나를 만날 것이다. 나는 그것이 몹시 기다려진다. **3** 김연아는 올림픽을 위해 지난달부터 피겨 스케이팅 연습을 매우 열심히 해오고 있다.

STEP **B** **1** 나는 한 시간 동안 이 소설을 읽고 있다. **2** Adrian은 Kate가 그에게 전화를 했을 때 잠을 자고 있었다. **3** 너는 얼마나 오랫동안 여기에 살고 있니? **4** 나의 남동생과 나는 엄마가 돌아오시기 전에 설거지를 하고 있었다.

STEP **C** **1** 내가 영국에 다시 간다면 세 번 가는 것이다. **2** Kevin, 너는 여기서 뭐하고 있었니? **3** 그녀가 왔을 때 나는 그녀를 두 시간 동안 기다리고 있었다.

3교시 After - Class Questions ▶ 본문 26 - 29쪽

01 has, been, building **02** will, have, gone **03** had, been, standing **04** ⑤ **05** has been driving 혹은 has driven **06** ⑤ **07** ⑤ **08** ③ **09** had, been, studying, for **10** had, been, playing **11** had been talking **12** has been supporting **13** ⑤ **14** ⑤ **15** ④ **16** Had he been sleeping when you arrived? **17** have finished **18** 김 선생님은 올 연말이면 이곳에서 일한 지 10년째가 될 것이다. **19** (1) has rained (2) has been raining **20** been wanting → wanted **21** ⑤ **22** ④ **23** ④ **24** ④ **25** (a) hasn't been sleeping → didn't sleep

01 나의 형은 6개월 전에 학교를 짓기 시작했다. 그는 여전히 그 학교를 짓고 있다.
→ 나의 형은 6개월 동안 학교를 짓고 있다.
* 과거에 시작한 동작이 현재까지 계속되고 있으므로 현재완료 진행시제가 알맞다.

02 나의 집에 오늘 방문해 주세요. 나는 내일 소풍을 갈 예정이에요.
→ 내일 이맘때면 나는 소풍을 갔을 거예요.
* 미래의 한 시점까지 완료되는 상태를 나타내므로 미래완료시제가 알맞다.

03 많은 여자아이와 남자아이들이 줄을 서고 있었다. 우리는 극장에 도착했다.
→ 우리가 극장에 도착하기 전에 많은 여자아이들과 남자아이들이 이미 줄을 서고 있었다.
* 극장에 도착한 시점이 과거이며 그 시점에 많은 소녀와 소년들이 이미 줄을 서고 있었으므로 과거완료 진행시제가 알맞다.

04 ① 나의 아들은 지난주부터 계속 아프다.
② 2주 동안 비가 내리고 있다.
③ 나는 버스를 10분 째 기다리고 있다.
④ 내가 집에 갔을 때 나의 가족은 이미 저녁식사를 끝냈다.
⑤ 다음 달이면 우리가 함께 일한 지 3년이 될 것이다.
* [have been working → will have worked] 미래를 나타내는 next month가 있으므로 미래완료시제로 써야 한다.

05 * 과거에 시작하여 현재까지 계속되는 동작(drive)을 나타내므로 현재완료 진행시제가 알맞다.

06 A: 너는 무엇을 보고 있니?
B: 한국 역사에 관한 다큐멘터리 영화를 보고 있어. 나는 오늘 아침부터 그것들을 보고 있어.
* 과거에 시작한 동작이 현재까지 진행되고 있으므로 현재완료 진행시제가 알맞다.

07 A: 너는 왜 어제 콘서트에 안 왔어?
B: 갑자기 내 차가 고장이 났어. 그 차는 오랫동안 잘 달렸었거든.
* 차가 고장 난 것은 과거이며 과거 이전부터 오랫동안 잘 달렸다는 표현은 과거완료 진행시제가 알맞다.

08 A: 너는 파리에서 얼마동안 있었니?
B: 음, 다음 달이면 10개월 동안 파리에 있는 거야.
* 미래시점인 '다음 달이면 10개월 동안 파리에 머물게 된다'는 표현이므로 미래완료시제가 알맞다.

09 * 나를 방문한 시점이 과거이고, 그 이전에 시작된 동작(study)이 과거시점까지 계속 진행되는 일을 나타내므로 과거완료 진행시제로 표현한다.

10 * 도착한 시점이 과거이고, 그 이전부터 영화가 상영 중이었으므로 과거완료 진행시제로 표현한다.

11 우리가 도착했을 때 Jean은 한 시간 반 넘게 전화 통화를 하고 있었다.
* 과거의 동작 이전에 이미 진행 중이던 동작을 나타낼 때는 과거완료 진행시제가 알맞다.

12 시의회는 2012년 이래로 택시 회사들을 지원하고 있다.
* '2012년 이래로 지원한다'는 내용이 되어야 하므로 현재완료 진행시제로 고쳐야 한다.

13 ① 우리가 마지막으로 만난 이후로 너는 무엇을 하고 있었니?
② 그녀는 얼마나 오랫동안 지하철을 기다리고 있었니?
③ 그 CEO는 아침 10시 이래로 연설을 하고 있다.
④ 민호는 지난 며칠 동안 어떤 음식도 먹지 못했다.
⑤ 박 선생님이 50이 되면, 그는 그 회사에서 25년 동안 근무하게 될 것이다.
* [will work → will have worked] 미래시점인 '50이 되면 회사에서 일한 지 25년이 된다'는 의미이므로 미래완료시제로 표현해야 한다.

14 * 아이를 찾은 것이 과거(found)이고 그 이전부터 찾은 시점까지 계속되었던 동작을 나타내는 것이므로 과거완료 진행시제로 표현한다.

15 * 과거부터 현재까지 기다리고 있는 상태이므로 현재완료 진행시제로 표현한다. 현재완료 진행시제의 의문문은 〈의문사 + have + 주어 + been + -ing ~?〉로 쓴다.

16 네가 도착했을 때 그는 잠을 자고 있었다.
* 과거완료 진행시제의 의문문은 〈Had + 주어 + been -ing ~?〉의 형태로 쓴다.

17 오후 4시다. Hank는 운동을 시작한다. 6시까지면 그는 운동을 끝낼 것이다.
* 4시에 시작된 운동이 6시까지 끝날 것이라는 표현은 미래완료시제로 표현한다.

18 * 미래완료시제는 '(미래에) ~일 것이다'라는 의미이다.

19 * (1) 과거에 시작해서 현재까지 계속되는 동작이나 상태는 현재완료시제로 나타낸다.
(2) 과거에 시작해서 현재까지 계속 진행되는 의미를 강조할 경우 현재완료 진행시제로 나타낸다.

20 Kelly는 그녀가 결혼한 이래로 그녀 소유의 아파트를 사기를 원하고 있다.
* want는 진행형으로 쓸 수 없는 동사이다.

21 A: 너의 아들들은 어디에 숨어 있었니?
B: 그들은 옷장 안에 있었어.
* Where는 현재완료 진행시제와 함께 사용할 수 있다. 어디에 숨어 있었는지를 묻는 말에 현재 벽장 안에 있다고 응답해야 하므로 현재완료시제로 나타냈다.

22 A: Sean은 여기에서 무엇을 하고 있었니?
B: 그는 다음 수업을 기다리고 있었어.
* 현재완료 진행시제로 물었으므로 현재완료 진행시제로 답해야 한다.

23 A: 내 여동생과 나는 책을 몇 권 읽고 있어.
B: 오, 몇 권이나 읽었니?
A: 내가 이 책을 읽는 것을 끝내면 다섯 권을 읽는 거야.
* 문맥상 '다섯 권을 읽는 거야'라는 뜻이므로 미래완료시제가 알맞다.

24 A: Austin은 지금 구내식당에서 일하고 있어.
B: 그렇구나. 그는 몇 시간 동안 일하고 있는 거니?
* 문맥상 '몇 시간 동안 일하고 있니?'라는 질문이 되어야 하므로 현재완료 진행시제로 표현해야 한다.

25 (a) Rodin은 오늘 졸려 보인다. 그는 지난밤에 잠을 충분히 자지 못했다.
(b) Linda는 그 소리에 의해 놀라기 전에는 곤히 잠을 자고 있었다.
* 과거를 나타내는 last night이 있으므로 과거시제가 와야 한다.

Final Test

▶ 본문 30 - 33쪽

01 ①, ② **02** ④ **03** ② **04** ③, gone to → been to **05** (1) didn't see (2) have used **06** ③ **07** ④ **08** ④ **09** I have been reading a news article about Steve Jobs. **10** ② **11** ⑤ **12** did, had scolded **13** (1) gone (2) been **14** ④ **15** ⑤ **16** ③ **17** ④ **18** ③ **19** ② **20** (1) is (2) has been (3) will have been **21** ② **22** ⑤ **23** lost **24** ④ **25** had never eaten **26** I have just been to the airport to see off my aunt. **27** ① **28** ② **29** ⑤ **30** ②

01 ① 나는 5시까지 이 차를 고치고 있을 것이다.
② 그는 여기에 도착한 이후로 공부를 하고 있다.
③ 아빠는 오늘 오후 그 창문들을 잠그셨다.
④ 우리는 네가 오기 전에 영화를 보고 있었다.
⑤ 나의 같은 반 친구들은 작년에 이 깃발들을 모았다.
* ① 미래의 시점을 나타내는 by 5 p.m.이 있으므로 미래완료 진행시제가 왔다.
② 과거의 한 시점 이래로(since) 현재까지의 진행을 나타내므로 현재완료 진행시제가 왔다.
③ [has locked → locked] 과거를 나타내는 this afternoon과 현재완료는 함께 쓸 수 없다.
④ [have → had] 오기 전부터 영화를 보고 있다는 내용이므로 과거완료 진행시제가 와야 한다.
⑤ [have collected → collected] 과거를 나타내는 last year와 현재완료는 함께 쓸 수 없다.

02 ① 수미는 나를 세 시간 동안 기다리고 있다.
② 우리 모두는 그가 전에 만들어 놓은 차를 마셨다.
③ 밤에 비가 많이 왔었다. 그래서 버스가 오지 않았다.
④ 내 남동생은 오랫동안 미국에 있다.
⑤ Ryan은 다섯 달 동안 스페인어 수업을 듣고 있다.
* [since → for] 문맥상 '오랫동안'이라는 뜻이므로 for가 와야 한다. 〈since + 특정 시점〉, 〈for + 기간〉으로 쓰인다.

03 ① Bill은 내가 온 이후로 계속 침대에 누워 있다.
② 나는 그를 알고 지낸 지 10년이 넘었다.
③ 주식시장은 지난주 이후로 오르고 있다.
④ 나의 어머니는 며칠 동안 감기 때문에 고생하고 계신다.
⑤ 나의 아내는 오늘 아침부터 드라마를 보고 있다.
* [been knowing → known] know와 같이 상태를 나타내는 동사는 현재완료 진행시제를 쓸 수 없다.

04 A: 너의 부모님은 전에 오스트리아에 다녀오신 적이 있니?
B: 아니, 없으셔.
* 전에 다녀온 적이 있는지 경험을 묻는 질문이 되어야 한다. have gone to는 '가고 없다'는 결과를 의미한다.

05 (1) 우리는 엊그제 그녀를 보지 못했다.
(2) 나는 지금까지 써오던 문 열쇠를 바꾸고 싶다.
* (1) 과거를 나타내는 부사구 the day before yesterday가 있으므로 과거시제가 와야 한다.
(2) 문맥상 '지금까지 써오던 문 열쇠'를 뜻하는 것이므로 현재완료시제가 와야 한다.

06 (a) Huey는 유럽에 가지 않았다. 그는 여전히 일본에 있다.
(b) Maria는 몇 년 동안 그를 알고 지낸다.
* (a) 아직 유럽에 가지 않았으므로 hasn't gone으로 나타내야 한다.
(b) 상태동사 know는 진행형으로 쓸 수 없다.

07 몇 시간 동안 전 지역에서 온 축구선수들이 함께 축구를 하고 있다.
* '몇 시간 동안'이라는 부사구가 있고, 주어가 soccer players이므로 have played 또는 have been playing이 와야 한다.

08 내가 잘못된 장소에 있다는 것을 깨달았을 때 나는 내 여자 친구를 30분 동안 기다리고 있었다.
* 내가 깨달았던 과거의 시점보다 이전부터 계속 기다리고 있었다는 표현이므로 과거완료 진행시제가 알맞다.

09 나는 Steve Jobs에 관한 뉴스 기사를 읽었다.
* 현재완료 진행시제는 〈have been + -ing〉로 쓴다.

10 ① 나는 오늘 밤까지 내 숙제를 끝낼 것이다.
② 내가 밖에 나갔을 때 비가 내리고 있었다.
③ Bill은 전기가 나갔을 때 사무실에서 일을 하고 있었다.
④ 나는 Isabella가 버스 정류장에 도착했을 때 그녀를 한 시간 동안 기다리고 있었다.
⑤ 나의 여자 친구는 여섯 시간 동안 TV를 보고 있다.
* [has been raining → had been raining] 과거의 어느 시점을 기준으로 그 이전에 발생한 일이 기준 시점까지 계속되었음을 나타낼 때는 과거완료 진행시제를 쓴다.

11 Jimmy는 지난 토요일에 Sally 함께 영화를 보았다. 그들은 즐거웠고, 그래서 서로 다시 만날 계획을 세웠다. 그러나 오늘 그들은 만날 수 없다. Jimmy가 그의 조부모님 댁에 가고 없다.
* ⑤의 has been은 갔다 온 것을 의미하므로, 만날 수 없다는 문장과 어울리지 않는다. 문맥상 '가고 없다'는 의미가 되려면 has gone으로 고쳐야 한다. 나머지는 모두 맞는 표현이다.

12 Cathy의 엄마는 그녀를 혼냈다. 그 후 그녀는 숙제를 시작했다.
→ Cathy는 그녀의 엄마가 그녀를 혼낸 후에 숙제를 했다.
* 엄마가 혼을 낸 것이 먼저 일어난 일이므로 과거완료시제로, 숙제를 한 것이 그 다음의 일이므로 과거시제로 쓴다.

13 (1) David는 집에 음식이 없어서 식료품점에 가고 없다.
(2) Rebecca는 식료품점에 다녀왔다. 그래서 집에 음식이 많다.
* (1) 문맥상 '음식이 없어서 식료품점에 가고 없다(gone)'라고 하는 것이 알맞다.
(2) 문맥상 '갔다 왔기(been) 때문에 음식이 많다'라고 하는 것이 알맞다.

14 John은 한 시간 전에 사진을 찍기 시작했고 지금도 여전히 사진을 찍는 중이다.
→ John은 한 시간 동안 사진을 찍고 있다.
* 한 시간 전부터 지금까지 계속 사진을 찍고 있으므로 현재완료 진행시제로 표현한다.

15 민희와 민지 둘 다 7시에 어려운 문제들을 풀기 시작했고, 그들의 선생님은 8시에 교실에 도착했다.
→ 선생님이 8시에 교실에 도착했을 때 민희와 민지 둘 다 한 시간 동안 문제를 풀고 있었다.
* 도착하기 한 시간 전부터 문제를 풀고 있다고 했으므로 과거완료 진행시제로 표현한다.

16 * 머리가 아팠던 과거시점보다 이전부터 컴퓨터게임을 하고 있었으므로 과거완료 진행시제가 와야 한다.

17 (a) 내가 집에 갔을 때 나의 다른 가족들은 이미 점심을 끝냈다. 그래서 나는 혼자 점심을 먹어야 했다.
(b) Jason은 내년이면 15살이 된다. 그는 멋진 한해를 기대한다.
* (a) 집에 갔던 과거시점보다 이전에 가족들이 식사를 끝낸 것이므로 과거완료시제가 알맞다. (b) 내년이면 15살이 된다는 표현은 미래시제로 표현한다.

18 (a) Jackie는 지난주에 이 장치를 사용하는 법을 배웠다.
(b) Helen은 지난 주 이래로 이 장치를 사용하는 법을 배우는 중이다.
* (a) last week는 과거를 나타내는 부사구이므로 과거시제가 와야 한다.
(b) 지난 주 이래로 계속 배우고 있다는 내용이므로 현재완료 진행시제가 와야 한다.

19 (a) Sandy는 내일 이맘때면 캐나다에 있을 것이다.
(b) 나는 내 인생의 후반에 돈을 기부함으로써 남을 도울 것이다.
* (a) by this time tomorrow는 미래의 한 시점까지 완료하는 의미의 부사구이므로 미래완료시제가 와야 한다. (b) in one's later years는 '인생 후반에'라는 뜻이므로 미래시제가 알맞다.

20 (1) 나의 형은 지금 결혼했다.
(2) 나의 누나는 결혼한 지 5년이 되었다.
(3) 나의 부모님은 내가 대학을 졸업할 때면 결혼한 지 30년이 될 것이다.
* (1) 현재를 나타내는 부사 now가 있으므로 현재시제로 써야 한다.
(2) 지금까지의 결혼한 기간을 나타내므로 현재완료시제로 써야 한다.
(3) 미래의 한 시점을 나타내므로 미래완료시제로 써야 한다.

21 ① 너는 기린과 사자를 실제로 본 적이 있니?
② 너는 언제 그 서류 제출하는 것을 포기했니?
③ 그녀는 4년 동안 탁구를 연습하고 있다.
④ 그들의 팀은 이미 호텔 예약을 했다.
⑤ 나의 조부모님은 2013년 이래로 비타민 A와 C를 드신다.
* [have you given up → did you give up] When은 현재완료시제와 함께 쓰일 수 없다.

22 ① 나는 아직 너의 남동생을 만나지 못했다.
② 나는 내 방의 청소를 방금 끝냈다.
③ 그는 LA로 떠났다. 그는 지금 여기에 없다.
④ 내 친구는 그녀의 펜을 잃어버렸다.
⑤ 어제 비가 왔다.
* [has rained → rained] 과거를 나타내는 부사 yesterday가 있으므로 과거시제가 와야 한다.

23 Frank는 이틀 전에 그의 iPad를 잃어버렸다. 그래서 그는 음악을 들을 수 없고 스케줄을 기록할 수 없다.
* 과거를 나타내는 부사구 two days ago가 있으므로 과거시제로 써야 한다.

24 A: 너는 세차를 했니? 차가 매우 지저분하던데.
B: 아니. 내 차를 봤을 때 누군가에 의해 세차가 되었다고 생각했어. 그래서 난 아무것도 하지 않았어.
* [has been → had been] 내가 봤던 과거시점보다 이전에 이미 세차가 된 것을 나타내야 하므로 과거완료시제로 써야 한다.

25 * until that time은 과거를 나타내는 부사구이므로 그 이전의 일은 과거완료시제로 표현해야 한다.

26 * '~에 갔다 왔다'는 have been to로 표현한다.

27 A: 너는 Philip을 본 적이 있니?
B: 아니, 나는 아직 그를 본 적이 없어.
* 문맥상 '아직'이라는 말이 알맞다.
② 이미, 벌써, ③ 여전히, ④ 이제 막, 방금 전, ⑤ ~이래로

28 너는 외국에서 공부한 지 얼마나 되었니?
① 나는 지난달에 뉴욕에 왔어.
② 나는 단지 일 년 전에 여기에 왔어.
③ 나는 작년부터 외국에서 공부해왔어.
④ 나는 거의 5년 동안 외국에서 공부해왔어.
⑤ 나는 한국에서 여기에 방금 도착했어.
* ago는 '~전에'라는 뜻으로 과거를 나타내는 부사이므로 현재완료시제와 함께 쓰일 수 없다.

29 (a) Jerry는 두 달 전에 심한 부상을 입었다.
(b) Vivian은 지난주부터 중간고사를 위해 공부해왔다.
* (a) 과거시제가 쓰였으므로 과거를 나타내는 부사 ago가 알맞다.
(b) 현재완료시제가 쓰였으므로 since나 for가 알맞다. 〈since + 특정 시점〉, 〈for + 숫자 기간〉이므로 since가 알맞다.

30 A: Matthew와 나는 서로 알고 지낸 지 오래 되었어.
B: 언제 그를 만났니?
A: 내가 11살 때 그를 만났어. 우리는 거의 모든 주말을 함께 보내왔지.
B: 와, 멋지다! 그런데, 나는 최근에 그를 만난 적이 없어.
A: 오, 그는 지난주 이래로 아파.
* [→ When did you meet him?] When은 현재완료시제와 함께 쓸 수 없다.

Sentence Writing

▶ 본문 34쪽

Part A
1 will have lost weight
2 had been running
3 have driven

Part B
1 I have not missed Korea so far.
2 The two old man have been living in Seoul since 2003.
3 It was the second time he had looked back on his life.
4 I will have been married for 10 years by next week.

Part A
1 수지는 자신이 매우 살이 쪘다고 생각하기 때문에 운동을 시작할 것이다. 그녀는 이번 여름이면 살이 빠질 것이다.
2 Tina는 숨이 찼다. 그녀는 트랙을 두 시간 동안 달리고 있었다.
3 남: 당신은 왜 그렇게 긴장해 있어요?
여: 솔직히 말하면, 저는 처음으로 차를 운전해 보는 거예요.

Unit 03  조동사

DAY 04 will/would, can/could

2교시 In - Class Questions

▶ 본문 39쪽

STEP A 1 can 2 cannot 3 Will 4 would
STEP B 1 can't have seen 2 cannot have solved 3 can 4 couldn't
STEP C 1 meet → to meet 2 play → playing 3 to → than
STEP D 1 will be able to do 2 could have held your tongue 3 can't have done

STEP B
1 너는 그 파티에서 Alex를 봤을 리가 없다. 그는 거기에 가지 않았다.
2 Scarlet 혼자 그 문제를 풀었을 리가 없다. 그녀의 엄마가 틀림없이 그녀를 도와주었다.
3 우리는 그것을 거의 이해할 수가 없어요. 다시 한 번 말해주세요.
4 Margaret은 그녀의 숙제를 끝내지 못했다. 그래서 그녀는 그녀의 가족과 함께 쇼핑을 갈 수 없었다.

STEP C
1 너는 나를 도서관에서 만날 수 있을 것이다.
2 지나와 나는 둘 다 플루트를 연주할 수 있다.
3 나는 엄마와 함께 쇼핑을 가느니 차라리 집을 청소하겠다.

3교시 After - Class Questions

▶ 본문 40 - 43쪽

01 ⑤ 02 ③ 03 ④ 04 ③ 05 ④ 06 ③ 07 ④ 08 ① 09 ① 10 ④ 11 cannot have forgotten 12 would play 13 ④ 14 will 15 is 16 can 17 (1) could, will (2) could 18 ⑤ 19 ② 20 ④ 21 ⑤ 22 I would rather read a book about investments than read the novel. 23 너는 독감에 걸리지 않을 수도 있었을 텐데. 24 ④ 25 (1) Maria could be the principal at the school. (2) Maria can be the principal at the school.

01 나는 어렸을 때 집 근처의 해변에 친구들과 함께 가서 물속에서 즐거운 시간을 보내곤 했다.
* [had → have] '~하곤 했다'라는 과거의 습관을 나타내는 조동사 would는 go와 have를 병렬구조로 연결하고 있다. 따라서 and 다음에는 동사원형이 와야 한다.

02 ① 계산서 좀 가져다주시겠어요?
② 오늘 아침에 내 차가 시동이 걸리지 않았다.
③ 나는 차라리 댄스 동아리에 가입하는 게 좋겠다.
④ 잠시 동안 저와 함께 있어주실래요?
⑤ 나는 최신 휴대전화를 사고 싶다.
* [joined → join] would rather 다음에는 동사원형이 와야 한다.

03 날씨가 야구 경기를 하기에 매우 좋다. 이보다 더 좋을 수 없다.
* It couldn't be better.는 '이보다 더 좋을 수 없다.'는 표현으로, 여기에 쓰인 could는 가능성을 의미한다.

04 네 실수에 대해서는 걱정하지 마. 내 생각에는 과장님이 사장님께 그것에 대해 이야기하지 않을 거야.
* 문맥상 '이야기하지 않을 것이다(won't tell)'라는 의미가 알맞다.

05 나의 어머니가 그렇게 말했던 것은 불가능하다.
→ 나의 어머니가 그렇게 말했을 리가 없다.
* 과거 사실에 대한 강한 부정을 나타내는 '~했을 리가 없다'는 〈cannot + have + 과거분사〉로 나타낸다.

06 (a) Kate는 이번 주에 소개팅을 할 것이다.
(b) 당신과 당신의 여동생은 오늘밤 내 환영 파티에 와줄래요?
* will은 미래를 나타내거나 부탁의 말에 사용한다.

07 ① 몇몇 사람들은 비밀을 찾아내기 위해 당신을 도와줄 수 있을지도 모른다.
② Ted와 Laura는 5개의 다른 언어를 말할 수 있다.
③ 많은 직장인들은 브라질과 페루로 여행할 수 있기를 희망한다.
④ 이번 주말에 내 카메라를 써도 돼. 나는 그때 그것을 쓰지 않을 거야.
⑤ 나는 내가 정말로 갖고 싶어 하는 가방을 살 수 없을 것이다.
* be able to는 능력/가능의 의미로 쓰일 수 있지만, ④와 같이 허가/허락의 의미로 쓰이지 않는다.

08 ① 사장님을 위해 이 파일을 찾아줄래요?
② 해야 할 말이 있으면 어떤 것도 말해도 된다.
③ 제가 좀 더 있어도 될까요? 외로워요.
* ①은 요청을 의미하고, ②③은 허가/허락을 의미한다.

09 ① James는 시와 소설을 쓸 수 있다.
② 이 가게에 개를 데리고 올 수 없습니다.
③ 이 주차장 어디에든 주차할 수 있습니다.
* ①은 능력을 의미하고, ②③은 허가/허락을 나타낸다.

10 많은 입양아들은 언젠가 그들의 어머니를 볼 수 있을지도 모른다.
* 조동사 다음에 조동사가 올 수 없으므로 조동사를 대체할 수 있는 동의어가 필요하다. have to는 의미상 맞지 않고, 가능을 나타낼 수 있는 be able to가 알맞다.

11 * 과거 사실의 부정적인 추측은 〈cannot + have + 과거분사〉로 표현한다.

12 * 과거의 습관을 표현할 때 would를 사용한다.

13 A: 저기, Ellie야. 영화는 어땠어?
B: 정말 재미있었어. 이 영화의 배우가 정말 멋져 보여. 나는 다시 한 번 보고 싶어.
* 문맥상 '다시 한 번 보고 싶다'는 표현인 would like to가 알맞다.

14 Cathy는 5월에 아이를 낳을 예정이다.
* be going to는 미래를 나타내는 조동사 will과 바꿔 쓸 수 있다.

15 그녀의 비행기는 12시에 인천공항에 도착할 것이다.
* will이 가까운 미래를 나타낼 때 현재진행시제(be동사 + 현재분사)로 바꿔 쓸 수 있다.

16 Neilson 박사님은 나의 큰 실수를 용서해 줄 수 있다.
* 가능의 의미를 나타낼 때 조동사 can이 알맞다.

17 (1) 내일 비가 올 수도 있다[올 것이다].
(2) 나는 8살 때 읽고 쓸 수 있었다.
* (1) 미래의 불확실한 가능성을 표현할 때는 could가 와야 한다.
(2) 문장이 과거시제이므로 could가 알맞다.

18 * '~하지 않을 수도 있었는데'라는 표현은 〈couldn't + have + 과거분사〉로 나타낸다.

19 (a) 나는 다음달에 28살이 될 것이다.
(b) 부산행 기차가 곧 출발할 예정이다.
(c) 너의 책들이 무거워 보여. 내가 도와줄게.
* (a) 나이를 먹는 것은 will로 표현한다.
(b) 기차가 출발하는 시간은 예정된 것이므로 is going to로 표현한다.
(c) 즉석에서 결정한 사항은 will로 쓴다.

20 (a) Bill은 부지런한 사람이었다. 그래서 나는 그가 부모님의 가업을 이어 받을 것이라고 생각했다.
(b) Sam은 우리가 자유 시간을 좀 더 가질 수 있다고 말했다.
* (a) 주절이 과거시제이므로 종속절에도 과거시제를 나타내는 would가 와야 한다.
(b) 주절의 시제(과거)에 맞게 종속절에도 과거시제가 와야 한다. be able to는 능력의 의미일 때만 바꿔 쓸 수 있으므로 가능성의 의미로 쓰이는 could가 와야 한다.

21 ① 엄마는 수영하는 법을 배우곤 하셨다.
② 나의 여동생은 저녁식사 후에 산책을 하곤 했었다.
③ 아빠는 가끔 재미있는 이야기를 해주곤 하셨다.
④ 나의 남동생은 점심시간에 축구를 하곤 했었다.
⑤ 그 선생님은 거기에 가자 말라고 하셨지만 나는 거기에 갈 것이다.
* ⑤는 주어의 의지를 나타내고, 나머지는 과거의 습관을 나타낸다.

22 * 'B 하느니 차라리 A 하겠다'는 〈would rather A than B〉로 나타낸다.

23 * 〈couldn't + have + 과거분사〉는 '~하지 않을 수도 있었을 텐데'라는 의미이다.

24 (a) 그는 3년 전에 훨씬 더 빨리 수영할 수 있었다.
(b) 어떤 사람이 문을 두드리고 있다. 그가 누구일까?
* (a) 과거를 나타내는 three years ago가 있으므로 could가 와야 한다.
(b) 가능성을 나타낼 때는 could만 가능하다.

25 * (1) 현재의 가능성에는 can이 아니라 could가 쓰인다.
(2) 현재의 능력/가능은 can이 쓰인다.

DAY 05 may/might, must/have to

2교시 In - Class Questions ▶ 본문 45쪽

STEP A **1** may **2** don't have to **3** must not
STEP B **1** must, be **2** may, have
3 may[might], have, been
STEP C **1** has to send **2** Can
3 don't need to go 혹은 need not go
STEP D **1** She might have caught a cold.
2 No, you may not.

STEP A **1** Andy는 복숭아와 땅콩에 알레르기가 있을지도 모른다.
2 3시밖에 안 됐어. 서두를 필요 없어.
3 사람들은 면허증 없이 차를 운전하면 안 된다.

STEP C **1** Patrick은 이 소포를 그 고객에게 보내야 한다.
2 제가 당신의 비행기 표를 봐도 될까요?
3 오늘이 일요일이므로 너는 학교에 갈 필요가 없다.

STEP D **1** A: 너는 하나가 왜 계속 기침하는지 아니?
B: 잘 모르겠어. 그녀는 감기에 걸렸을지도 몰라.
2 A: 초콜릿 케이크를 먹어도 돼요?
B: 아니, 안 돼. 너는 지금 다이어트 중이잖아.

3교시 After - Class Questions ▶ 본문 46 - 49쪽

01 ② **02** ⑤ **03** ③ **04** ③ doing → do **05** ②, ⑤ **06** ③ **07** must be sick, looks pale **08** You may as well eat less to lose weight. **09** Edward must have lost his car key then. **10** ③ **11** ④ **12** has, to **13** may[might], have, arrived **14** may, well, receive **15** ⑤ **16** will have to **17** ⑤ **18** ⑤ **19** ④ **20** (1) 추측 (2) 추측 (3) 허락 **21** ① **22** ⑤ **23** ③ **24** ① **25** will, have, to

01 Justin은 10시간 동안 운전을 하고 있다. 그는 피곤함에 틀림없다.
* 문맥상 '~임에 틀림없다'라는 추측의 must가 와야 한다.

02 나는 선생님들께서 미래에 대해 말씀하셨던 것이 진짜일지도 모른다고 생각했다.
* 문맥상 '~일지도 모른다'는 추측의 may나 might가 와야 하는데, 주절의 시제가 과거이므로 might가 알맞다.

03 나는 내 동료에게 여러 번 이메일을 보냈다. 하지만 그는 아무 답변이 없었다. 그는 이메일 주소를 바꿨을지도 모른다.
* 문맥상 '이메일 주소를 바꿨을지도 모른다'는 표현인 ⟨might + have + 과거분사⟩로 나타내야 한다.

04 사람들은 직장인들이 어떠한 샘플도 없이 일을 하는 것이 더 낫다고 이야기한다.
* ⟨may as well + 동사원형⟩의 형태로 쓰이며 '~하는 것이 낫다'라는 의미이다.

05 ① 나의 가족은 이번 휴일에 조부모님을 방문해야 한다.
② Jane과 Frank 둘 중 하나는 그 자동차 사고의 용의자임에 틀림없다.
③ 부모는 그들의 아이들을 먹여야 할 뿐만 아니라 돌봐주어야 한다.
④ 이 빌딩 앞에 차를 주차하면 안 됩니다.
⑤ 공룡은 냉혈동물이었음에 틀림없다.
* ②는 '~임에 틀림없다', ⑤는 '~이었음에 틀림없다'라는 추측의 의미이고, 나머지는 '~해야 한다'라는 의무의 의미이다.

06 (a) 제가 당신의 코트를 받아드릴까요?
(b) 교사들이 학생들을 많이 사랑하는 것은 당연하다.
(c) Cathy는 버스를 놓치지 않았을지도 모른다.
* (a) May[Can] I ~?는 허가를 묻는 표현이다. (b) ⟨may well + 동사원형⟩은 '~하는 것이 당연하다'라는 뜻으로 may의 관용표현이다. (c) ⟨may not have + 과거분사⟩는 '~이 아니었을지도 모른다'라는 뜻으로 과거 사실에 대한 불확실한 추측을 나타낸다.

07 * 현재의 일에 대한 강한 추측인 '~임에 틀림없다'는 ⟨must + 동사원형⟩으로, '~처럼 보이다'는 ⟨look + 형용사⟩로 표현한다.

08 * '~하는 것이 낫다'는 may as well로 나타낸다.

09 * 과거의 일에 대한 강한 추측인 '~였음에 틀림없다'는 ⟨must + have + 과거분사⟩로 나타낸다.

10 그의 이모는 어렸을 때 영리했다는 것이 확실하다.
→ 그의 이모는 어렸을 때 영리했음에 틀림없다.
* 과거의 확실한 추측(~했음에 틀림없다)은 ⟨must + have + 과거분사⟩로 나타낸다.

11 Kelly는 윤리학과 물리학에 대해 어떤 것도 배우지 않았던 것처럼 보인다.
→ Kelly는 윤리학과 물리학에 대해 어떤 것도 배우지 않았을지도 모른다.
* 주절의 동사 seem으로 보아 과거의 일에 대한 불확실한 추측(~했을지도 모른다)을 나타내는 ⟨may + have + 과거분사⟩가 알맞다.

12 Max는 그의 팀원들에게 문자메시지를 보내야 한다.
* must가 의무를 나타낼 때는 have to로 바꿔 쓸 수 있으며, 주어가 3인칭 단수이므로 has to가 와야 한다.

13 * 과거의 일에 대한 불확실한 추측은 ⟨may[might] + have + 과거분사⟩로 표현한다.

14 * '~하는 것은 당연하다'는 ⟨may well + 동사원형⟩으로 표현한다.

15 * '~해야 했다'는 의무의 과거형은 had to로 나타낸다.

16 미나는 우리 학교의 학생회장으로 선출되었다. 그래서 그녀는 우리를 대신해서 다가오는 모든 행사를 준비해야 한다. 첫 번째로, 그녀는 다음 주에 있는 학교 홍보에 참석해야 할 것이다.
* 문맥상 '~해야 할 것이다'라는 미래시제로 나타내야 한다. will과 must는 함께 쓰일 수 없으므로 will have to로 쓴다.

17 소미는 내 친한 친구이다. 그녀는 미래에 더 나은 삶을 살기 위해서 정말로 열심히 일을 했다. 나는 그녀가 목표를 이룰 것이라고 확신했다. 지금 그녀는 더 이상 열심히 일할 필요가 없고 쉴 수 있다.
* 그녀의 목표를 이룬 것이 확실하다고 했으므로, '더 이상 열심히 일할 필요가 없다'는 의미의 doesn't have to work hard anymore가 와야 한다.

18 ① 나는 매우 자주 파스타를 먹곤 했었다.
② 주스를 더 마시겠습니까?
③ 우리는 안에 들어가지 않는 게 좋겠다. 나쁜 냄새가 난다.
④ 나는 음악을 듣느니 영화를 보겠다.
⑤ 다나는 우리가 그 문제에 대해 이야기했을 때 화가 났음이 분명하다.
* [must be → must have been] 과거에 일어난 일이므로 ⟨must + have + 과거분사⟩가 되어야 한다.

19 ① 모든 직원들은 고객들에게 친절해야 한다. 그것이 규칙이다.
② 나는 학교에 가기 위해서 일찍 일어나야 한다.
③ Sam은 기말고사를 봐야 한다.
④ Owen은 돈이 많다. 그는 부자임에 틀림없다.
⑤ 너는 그 시험에 통과하기 위해서 열심히 공부해야 한다.
* ④는 추측을 의미하고, 나머지는 의무를 의미한다.

20 (1) 나의 부모님은 그 사실을 모를지도 모른다.
(2) Thomas는 공부로 인해 피곤해서 잠자러 가기를 원할지도 모른다.
(3) 너는 선물을 열어서 봐도 돼.
* (1)(2) 문맥상 '~일지도 모른다'는 불확실한 추측의 의미이다.
(3) '~해도 좋다'는 허가의 의미이다.

21 A: 너는 Jessica가 심한 자동차 사고가 난 것을 알고 있니?
B: 정말! 그녀는 지금 괜찮니?
A: 응, 그녀는 거의 다 회복되었지만 병원에 4주 동안 입원해 있어야 했어.
* must의 과거형인 had to(~해야만 했다)가 시제에 맞는 표현이다.

22 A: 나는 내일 운전면허 시험을 봐. 나는 약간 걱정돼.
B: 오, 힘 내. 너는 그동안 연습을 많이 했잖아. 너는 시험에 대해서 걱정할 필요 없어. 네가 해야 할 것은 최선을 다하는 거야.
* 문맥상 '걱정할 필요 없다'라는 의미인 don't have to가 와야 한다.

23 나는 지난밤에 늦게까지 깨어 있어야만 했어. 그래서 나는 집에 일찍 가서 잠을 자는 게 낫겠어.
* '지난밤에 늦게까지 깨어 있어야만 했다'는 의미가 되어야 하므로 첫 번째 빈칸에는 had to가 와야 하고, '잠을 자는 게 좋겠다'라는 의미가 되어야 하므로 두 번째 빈칸에는 had better가 와야 한다.

24 너는 오늘 네 보고서를 제출할 필요가 없어. 왜냐하면 마감일이 다음 주 월요일로 연기되었거든.
* don't have to는 don't need to 또는 need not으로 바꿔 쓸 수 있다.

25 * must의 미래형은 will have to로 나타낸다.

DAY 06 should, had better, used to

2교시 In - Class Questions ▶ 본문 51쪽

STEP A 1 should 2 used to 3 had better
STEP B 1 used to 2 used to
3 had better 4 ought not to
STEP C 1 should spend 2 had better go
3 should have studied
STEP D 1 Tim used to live in Canada.
2 David shouldn't have sent her an email.
3 Joan had better not walk on the street alone in L.A.

STEP A 1 너는 아프면 병원에 가야 한다. 그것이 필요하다.
2 그녀는 대학교에 있을 때 배달되는 음식을 주문하곤 했다.
3 그는 정직하지 않다. 너는 그를 신뢰하지 않는 게 좋다.

STEP B 1 김 선생님은 교사로서 일했었다.
2 여기에 대학교가 하나 있었다.
3 그녀는 뭔가를 얘기하는 편이 좋다.
4 그들은 어떤 것도 먹어서는 안 된다.

3교시 After - Class Questions ▶ 본문 52 - 55쪽

01 ④ 02 should, have, followed 03 ⑤ 04 ④ 05 dare, not, don't, dare, to 06 ⑤ 07 ③ 08 (1) would → used to (2) would → used to 09 ② 10 ④, ⑤ 11 ① 12 used to have a part-time job 13 (1) ③ (2) ① (3) ① 14 ③ 15 ⑤ 16 ④, ⑤ 17 ②, ④ 18 should not 혹은 had better not 19 ③ 20 ⑤ 21 ④ 22 ④ 23 ④ 24 ② 25 ⑤

01 여기에 '주차 금지'라고 쓰여 있기는 하지만 여기에 주차해도 될까요?
* '~하지 않는 편이 좋다'라는 강한 충고는 had better not으로 나타낸다.

02 내 남동생과 나는 우리가 할머니의 충고를 따르지 않았던 것 때문에 매우 기분이 좋지 않다.
→ 내 남동생과 나는 할머니의 충고를 따랐어야 했는데.
* 과거에 할머니의 충고를 따르지 않았던 것에 대한 후회는 〈should have + 과거분사〉로 나타낸다.

03 ① 너는 어두워지기 전에 집에 돌아가고 싶어 한다.
② 너는 저 주스보다 차라리 이 주스를 마시겠다.
③ 너는 어렸을 때 벤치에 누워 있곤 했다.
④ 너는 나의 도움 없이 그 문제들을 이미 해결했을 것이다.
⑤ 너는 친구들과 공부하는 대신에 너 혼자서 공부하는 것이 낫다.
* ⑤의 You'd better는 You had better의 줄임말이고, 나머지는 You would가 축약된 것이다.

04 ① 그녀는 그 개를 기를 필요가 없다.
② 이 미술관에서 사진을 찍어서는 안 됩니다.
③ 우리는 수업 시간에 휴대전화를 사용하지 말아야 한다.
④ 우리는 이 이상한 꽃들을 만지지 않는 것이 좋다.
⑤ Cindy는 관중들 앞에서 연설하는 것에 익숙하지 않았다.
* [had not better → had better not] had better의 부정은 had better not 이다.

05 너는 너의 장모님께 여쭤볼 수 있니?
→ 아니, 나는 장모님께 여쭤볼 수 없어.
* dare는 의문문과 부정문에서 조동사로 쓰인다. dare로 물었을 때의 대답은 dare not이나 don't dare to로 할 수 있다.

06 ① 우리는 가난한 사람들에게 더 많은 돈을 줬어야 했다.
② Ellen은 이번 주말에 도서관에서 공부하는 것이 좋다.
③ 나는 지하철을 타는 게 낫겠다. 교통체증이 너무 심하다.
④ 군인들은 민간인들이 살해되었던 그 장소를 갈 필요가 없다.
⑤ Paula는 어렸을 때 컴퓨터게임을 하지 않았었다.
* [playing → play] 문맥상 '~하지 않았었다'는 과거의 습관을 나타내므로 use to 다음에 동사원형이 와야 한다. 〈be used to -ing〉는 '~하는 데 익숙해지다'라는 뜻이다.

07 ① 그는 그의 차를 팔 필요가 있다.
②④ 그가 그의 차를 팔 필요가 있니?
③⑤ 그는 그의 차를 팔 필요가 없다.
* [needs → need] 부정문에서 need가 조동사로 쓰일 경우 인칭과 수에 상관없이 항상 need로 써야 한다.

08 (1) 이 지역 주변에 높은 빌딩이 하나 있었다.
(2) 내 딸은 중학교 때 매우 소심했었다.
* '과거에 ~였다'는 과거의 상태를 나타낼 때는 would로 쓸 수 없다.

09 내 친구들과 나는 이번 주말에 소풍을 가기로 계획했다. 나는 점심 때 사용할 종이컵과 접시를 가져오는 것을 담당했다. 소풍가는 날 아침에 나는 가게에 살 수 있는 종이컵과 종이접시가 없다는 것을 알았다. 나는 좀 더 일찍 그것들을 사놨어야 했다.
* '미리 사놨어야 했는데 사지 않았다'는 과거 사실에 대한 후회는 〈should have + 과거분사〉로 표현한다.

10 그 지저분한 방을 봐라. 너는 식사를 끝낸 후에 방을 치워야 한다.
* 문맥상 '방을 치워야 한다'는 의무를 나타내야 하므로 조동사 should와 must가 알맞다.

11 당신의 건강을 먼저 생각하세요. 당신은 건강을 위해 균형 잡인 식단을 유지하는 것이 좋습니다.
* 문맥상 '~하는 것이 좋다'는 강한 충고를 나타내야 하므로 조동사 had better가 알맞다.

12 * '~하곤 했다'는 과거의 습관은 〈used to + 동사원형〉으로 나타낸다.

13 (1) 나의 남편과 나는 월요일마다 몇 시간씩 볼링을 치곤 했다.
(2) 시청 앞에 큰 기념물이 하나 있었다.
(3) Hank는 그의 외모에 콤플렉스가 있었지만 지금은 없다.
* (1) 과거의 습관을 나타낼 때 used to와 would 둘 다 쓰인다. (2)(3) 과거의 상태에는 would를 사용할 수 없고 used to만 가능하다.

14 Tyler는 기말고사에서 낙제했음에 틀림없다. 그는 시험공부를 좀 더 열심히 했어야 했는데.
* [might not → should] 문맥상 '공부를 좀 더 열심히 해야 했는데'라는 유감을 나타내야 하므로 〈should + have + 과거분사〉가 와야 한다.

15 나의 아빠와 나는 관광하기 위해 유럽에 가기로 계획했다. 그래서 우리는 여행책자 몇 권을 사기 위해 서점에 가기로 결심했다. 나는 책 한 권만 사길 원했는데, 한 권이면 충분하다고 생각했기 때문이다. 하지만 아빠는 다섯 권을 사셨다. 그는 그 모든 책을 살 필요는 없다.
* [to buy → buy] need가 조동사로 쓰였기 때문에 to가 삭제되어야 한다.

16 * 금지의 '~해서는 안 된다'는 should not이나 ought not to로 표현한다.

17 * '~할 필요가 없다'는 〈need not + 동사원형〉, 〈do(es)n't need to + 동사원형〉, 〈do(es)n't have to + 동사원형〉으로 표현한다.

18 Emily는 오늘 심한 위통이 있다. 그래서 그녀는 아무것도 먹지 말아야 한다[먹지 않는 것이 좋다].
* 문맥상 '~하지 말아야 한다'라는 충고를 의미하기 위해서는 should not이나 좀 더 강한 충고인 had better not이 알맞다.

19 ① 그 기계는 하루 종일 작동되곤 했다.
② 젊은 음악가들은 노래를 부를 필요가 없다.
③ 학생들은 이 시험을 보지 않는 게 낫다.
④ 나는 오늘 외출하느니 집에 있는 게 낫겠다.
⑤ 공무원들은 이 문제들을 피해서는 안 된다.
* [didn't have better take → had better not take] had better의 부정은 had better not이다.

20 ① 이 건물은 (예전에) 병원이었다.
② 그는 그 수업에 정시에 도착해야 할 것이다.
③ 이 달걀을 어디에 두어야 할까? 냉장고에?
④ 너는 나쁜 경험을 잊는 것이 좋을 거야.
⑤ 우리 가족은 아침에 빵을 먹지 않았었다.
* ⑤ [not used to → didn't use to 혹은 used not to] used to의 부정문은 didn't use to나 used not to로 쓴다.

21 너는 교실을 떠나기 전에 먼저 너의 선생님께 여쭤보는 게 좋을 것이다.
* 문맥상 '~하는 것이 좋다'는 강한 충고를 나타내야 하므로 had better가 알맞다.

22 너는 수업을 빠져서는 안 된다. 그것은 너의 성적에 영향을 줄 것이다.
* 문맥상 '~해서는 안 된다'는 금지를 나타내야 하므로 should not이 알맞다.

23 나는 모든 것이 잘 될 것이라고 확신했다.
* 문맥상 '~일 것이다'라는 미래 조동사 will이 와야 하는데, 주절에 이어지는 종속절에서 시제 일치를 해야 하므로 would가 알맞다.

24 나는 감히 교실 앞에 서 있을 수가 없다. 나는 정말 긴장된다.
* 문맥상 '감히 ~할 수 없다'는 의미가 되어야 하므로 dare not이 알맞다.

25 A: 실례합니다만, Kevin이 이 집에서 살고 있나요?
B: 그는 전에 이곳에 살았습니만, 더 이상은 아니에요 .그는 이사 갔어요.
* 현재는 아닌 과거의 상태는 〈used to + 동사원형〉으로 나타낸다.

Final Test

▶ 본문 56 - 59쪽

01 am, not, able, to **02** cannot, have, been **03** ② **04** (1) I had to walk for five hours. (2) I should have walked for five hours. **05** would **06** should **07** might **08** (1) ② (2) ④ **09** ⑤ **10** ③ **11** ④, ⑤ **12** ② **13** (1) 우리는 도서관에서 함께 공부하곤 했다. (2) 우리는 도서관에서 함께 공부하는 것에 익숙하다. **14** ⑤ **15** ④ **16** ② **17** ③ **18** ③ **19** ③ **20** ④ **21** Dare I ask my English teacher **22** ④ **23** ⑤ **24** ③ could not have → could not **25** (A) could (B) must have suffered **26** (1) Minsu must have bought a cell phone last month. (2) Minsu had to buy a cell phone last month. (3) Minsu should have bought a cell phone last month. **27** ③ **28** ② **29** ③ **30** ③

01 나는 교실에서 학생들이 만드는 소음을 참을 수가 없다.
* can이 능력을 나타낼 때는 be able to로 바꿔 쓸 수 있다.

02 Jessica가 어렸을 때 MENSA 회원이었던 것은 불가능하다.
→ Jessica가 어렸을 때 MENSA 회원이었을 리가 없다.
* 과거의 강한 부정적 추측을 나타낼 때는 '~했을 리가 없다'는 뜻의 〈cannot + have + 과거분사〉가 알맞다.

03 ① Evan은 그러한 일을 해서는 안 된다.
② 너는 차라리 그것을 다시 하는 것이 낫다.
③ 승객들은 이 전화를 사용할 수 있을 것이다.
④ 김 선생님이 너에게 이 심각한 이야기를 했을 리가 없다.
⑤ 그녀가 이 시험을 봤다면 통과할 수 있었을 텐데.
* [doing → do] would rather 다음에는 동사원형이 와야 한다.

04 * (1) 의무의 과거형은 had to로 나타낸다.
(2) 과거의 일에 대한 후회는 〈should + have + 과거분사〉로 나타낸다.

05 우리는 목동에서 함께 시간을 보냈었지만, 지금은 청담동으로 간다.
* 더 이상 하지 않는 과거의 습관은 would로 나타낸다.

06 나는 이 책에 집중을 할 수 없다. 나는 TV를 너무 많이 보지 말았어야 했다.
* 과거의 일에 대한 후회는 〈should + have + 과거분사〉로 나타낸다.

07 그들은 부모님이 외출하신 동안 많이 놀았을지도 모른다.
* '~였을지도 모른다'는 약한 추측은 〈might + have + 과거분사〉로 나타낸다.

08 (1) 나는 제동이가 재미있는 사람이라는 것을 확신한다.
② 그는 재미있는 사람임에 틀림없다.
(2) 제동이가 재미있는 사람이었을 가능성이 있다.
④ 그는 재미있는 사람이었을지도 모른다.
① 그는 재미있는 사람일지도 모른다.
③ 그는 재미있는 사람이었음에 틀림없다.
⑤ 그는 재미있는 사람일 리가 없다.
* (1) 현재의 확실한 추측은 must로 나타낸다.
(2) 과거의 불확실한 추측은 〈may have + 과거분사〉로 쓴다

09 A: 엄마, 내 휴대전화가 어디 있어요? 내 페이스북을 확인하고 싶어요.
B: 모르겠는데. 그건 아마 네 배낭에 있을지도 몰라.
* 문맥상 '배낭 안에 있을지도 몰라'라는 불확실한 추측을 나타내야 하므로 may가 알맞다.

10 보기 모든 학생들은 저녁 11시 전에 기숙사에 돌아와야 한다.
① 너는 도서관에서 크게 이야기하지 말아야 한다.
② Kelly는 내일 건강검진을 받아야 한다.
③ 나의 부모님은 나에게 화가 났음에 틀림없다.
④ 나는 첫 번째 시도에서 너무 많은 것을 기대하지 말아야 한다.
⑤ 나의 가족은 공항버스를 타기 위해 일찍 일어나야만 한다.
* ③은 '~임에 틀림없다'는 강한 추측을 나타내고, 〈보기〉와 나머지는 '~해야 한다'는 의무를 나타낸다.

11 ① Kyle은 영어를 잘할지도 모른다.
② 그들은 우리의 반 친구일지도 모른다.
③ Bob은 졸업 파티에 올지도 모른다.
④ 너는 게임을 하기 위해 내 스마트폰을 사용해도 된다.
⑤ 너는 허락 없이 이 지역에 들어오면 안 된다.
* ④⑤는 허락을 나타내고, 나머지는 불확실한 추측을 나타낸다.

12 너는 이 과제를 더 이상 할 필요가 없다.
* don't have to = don't need to (~할 필요가 없다)

13 * (1) 〈used to + 동사원형〉 '~하곤 했다'
(2) 〈be used to + 명사/동명사〉 '~에 익숙하다'

14 * 과거 사실에 대한 강한 부정적 추측을 나타내는 '~이었을 리가 없다'는 〈can't + have + 과거분사〉로 나타낸다.

15 * '~하느니 차라리 …하겠다'는 〈would rather + 동사원형 + than + 동사원형〉으로 나타낸다.

16 ① 오늘 저녁 늦게 비가 올 수도 있다.
② 나는 어떤 도움도 없이 박물관에 갈 수 있다.
③ Steve가 우수학생이라는 것은 사실일 수도 있다.
④ 그녀가 학교에 갔을 리가 없어. 토요일이었거든.
⑤ Jason은 어제 너를 도와주었을 리가 없다. 그는 매우 바빴다.
* ②는 '~할 수 있다'는 가능의 의미이고, 나머지는 추측/가능성을 의미한다.

17 A: 너는 왜 우울해 보이니?
B: 난 기회를 놓쳤어.
A: 무슨 말이야?
B: 난 월례 모임에서 한 아름다운 여자를 만났어. 그런데 내가 너무 바빠서 어떤 것도 공유할 수 없었어.
A: 흠... 너는 그녀의 전화번호라도 물어봤어야 했는데.
B: 그러게 말이다.
* '~했었어야 했다'라는 과거 사실에 대한 후회를 나타낼 때는 〈should + have + 과거분사〉가 알맞다.

18 나는 Lucy와 즐거운 시간을 보내곤 했다. 하지만 요즘, Lucy는 모든 사람들에게 무례하기 때문에 나는 그녀와 직접 이야기하지 않는 것이 낫다. 그래서 나는 그녀와 이야기하지 않으려고 노력한다.
* [wouldn't rather → would rather not] would rather의 부정은 would rather not이다.

19 나는 지금 교외에 나와 있다. 갑자기 비가 내리기 시작한다. 나는 우산을 가지고 왔어야 했다. 나는 비가 그칠 때까지 기다려야 한다.
* [could → should] 과거에 하지 않은 일에 대한 후회를 나타내는 표현은 〈should + have + 과거분사〉로 나타낸다.

20 * '~할 필요가 없다'는 don't have to, don't need to, need not으로 표현하며, '~하는 것이 낫다'는 had better로 표현한다.

21 * dare는 의문문에서 조동사로 쓰일 수 있다.

22 Jane이 네가 이전 파티를 위해서 샀던 드레스를 빌릴 수 있니?
* 상대방의 허가를 구하는 표현에는 can, could, may, would로 나타낸다.

23 Sarah가 글쓰기 대회에서 1등을 했을 것이다.
* It is possible that ~은 불확실한 추측을 나타내므로 may가 와야 한다.

24 나의 딸은 중학교 때 매우 소심했었다. 그녀는 친구들과 이야기를 하는 것을 즐겨하지 않았고, 그녀의 감정을 표현할 수 없었다. 왜냐하면 다른 친구들의 부정적인 반응에 대해 매우 걱정되었기 때문이었다. 이제 그녀는 나이가 들었기 때문에, 반 친구들 앞에서 발표도 할 수 있다. 그녀가 자신이 가장 중요한 사람이라는 것을 깨닫는 것은 당연하다.
* 능력을 나타내는 can의 과거는 could로 나타내야 한다. 〈could have + 과거분사〉는 과거의 추측을 나타낸다.

25 무엇이 한국의 유명인을 자살하도록 했을까요? 가장 큰 문제는 자살의 비율이 점점 증가하고 있다는 것입니다. 그들이 생을 마감하는 구체적인 이유는 없는 것 같습니다. 하지만 그들이 많은 악성 댓글에 고통을 받았던 것이 틀림없다고 추정됩니다.
* (A) 추측의 의문문에서는 may를 쓸 수 없다.
(B) 문맥상 '~였음에 틀림없다'라는 뜻의 〈must + have + 과거분사〉가 알맞다.

26 * (1) '~였음에 틀림없다'는 〈must + have + 과거분사〉로 나타낸다.
(2) '~해야 했다'는 의무의 과거는 had to로 나타낸다.
(3) 과거의 일에 대한 후회는 〈should + have + 과거분사〉로 나타낸다.

27 (a) 그녀는 그녀의 부당한 대우에 대해서 그녀의 상사와 말싸움을 할 용기가 없다.
(b) 나의 선생님은 학생들에게 항상 간식을 줄 필요는 없다.
* dare와 need의 부정은 〈dare/need not + 동사원형〉 혹은 〈doesn't dare/need to + 동사원형〉으로 표현한다.

28 젊은 세대의 많은 사람들이 비싼 차들과 고급 가방들을 갖고 싶어 하는 것은 당연하다.
* 문맥상 '~하는 것이 당연하다'라는 의미를 나타내는 may well이 알맞다. may as well은 '~하는 것이 낫다'라는 의미이다.

29 * '~였음에 틀림없다'는 과거 사실에 대한 강한 추측은 〈must + have + 과거분사〉가 알맞다.

30 ① 너와 너의 친구 둘 중에 한 사람은 옳을지도 모른다.
② Linda는 행복하고 신 나 보일지도 모른다.
③ 제가 잠시 당신의 가방을 점검해 봐도 될까요?
④ 나의 부모님과 조부모님은 오늘 밤에 늦으실지도 모른다.
⑤ 그의 할아버지는 나이가 드셨을지 모르지만 여전히 강하다.
* ③은 '~해도 좋다'라는 허락을 나타내며, 나머지는 '~일지도 모른다'라는 추측을 나타낸다.

Sentence Writing ▶ 본문 60쪽

Part A
1 You cannot take
2 cannot touch the monument
3 must have eaten

Part B
1 There used to be a store, but there is a park here now.
2 Jimmy had better not complain about it.
3 It rained too heavily. I should not have gone out.
4 Since she is nice, she may well be loved.

Unit 04 › 수동태

DAY 07 4, 5형식 문장의 수동태

2교시 In - Class Questions ▶ 본문 65쪽

STEP A 1 was sent 2 to turn 3 happy
STEP B 1 to 2 of 3 to 4 for
STEP C 1 was given 2 was bought for
3 was named Tony 4 was made to marry
STEP D 1 The door was left open by Monica.
2 Some hot potato soup was cooked for me by Mom.
3 A love letter was written to Fred's girlfriend by him.

STEP A
1 James는 3일 전에 그의 여자 친구에게서 편지를 받았다.
2 나는 라디오를 켜달라는 말을 들었다.
3 그녀의 인생은 그의 사랑으로 인해 행복해졌다.

STEP B
1 몇몇 술 취한 사람들이 그 매니저에 의해 떠나라는 요청을 받았다.
2 그 의견들은 그 수학 선생님에 의해 학생들에게 질문되었다.
3 몇 개의 선물들이 누군가에 의해 그에게 보내졌다.
4 이 달콤한 케이크는 아이들을 위해 만들어졌다.

STEP D
1 Monica는 문을 열어 두었다.
2 엄마는 나에게 뜨거운 감자수프를 만들어주셨다.
3 Fred는 그의 여자 친구에게 연애편지 한 통을 썼다.

3교시 After - Class Questions ▶ 본문 66 - 69쪽

01 ④ **02** ④ **03** ② **04** ③ **05** ② **06** ⑤ **07** ① **08** made, to, feel **09** won't, be, allowed, to **10** ③ **11** ② **12** ② **13** ④ **14** (1) was not seen to enter the house (2) was not seen entering the house **15** ④ **16** ② **17** (1) told (2) given **18** ④ **19** ③ **20** Our homeroom teacher was seen walking with her boyfriend along the river. **21** to **22** ⑤ **23** clean → to clean **24** to sweetheart → sweetheart **25** (1) I (2) One more chance to do the presentation

01 * 4형식 동사 give를 수동태로 바꿀 때는 〈be given to + 간접목적어〉의 형태로 쓴다.

02 * 5형식 동사 ask를 수동태로 바꿀 때는 〈be + 과거분사 + 목적격 보어(to finish)〉의 형태로 쓴다.

03 많은 사람들은 그 가수가 유명한 노래를 하는 것을 들었다.
→ 그 가수가 유명한 노래를 하는 것이 (많은 사람들에 의해) 들렸다.
* 지각동사의 목적격 보어가 원형부정사(sing)일 경우 수동태로 바꿀 때 to부정사로 바꿔야 한다.

04 내 친구들은 나에게 큰 생일 축하 카드 한 장을 만들어주었다.
→ 큰 생일 축하 카드 한 장이 내 친구들에 의해 만들어졌다.
* 4형식 동사 make를 수동태로 바꿀 때는 〈be made for + 간접목적어〉의 형태로 쓴다.

05 모두가 그녀를 '가요의 여왕'이라고 부른다.
→ 그녀는 모두에 의해 '가요의 여왕'이라고 불린다.
* 5형식 동사 call을 수동태로 바꿀 때는 〈be called + 목적격 보어〉의 형태로 쓴다.

06 ① 그의 어머니는 빨래하는 데 도움을 받았다.
② 그녀는 그 어린 남자아이에 의해 죄책감을 느끼게 되었다.
③ 약간의 뜨거운 코코아가 나의 언니를 위해 만들어졌다.
④ 그 여자아이가 큰 차에서 나오는 것이 보였다.
⑤ 어려운 질문들 몇 개가 Daniel에게 질문되었다.
* [from→ of] 4형식 동사 ask를 수동태로 바꿀 경우 간접목적어 앞에 전치사 of가 와야 한다.

07 ① 그녀의 가족은 그들의 애완동물을 Bob이라고 이름 지었다.
② Kelly는 몇 개의 서류를 Jane에게 주었다.
③ 그 선생님은 Jenny가 훌륭한 학생이라고 생각한다.
④ 당신은 Cathy에게 영어와 스페인어 모두를 가르칠 건가요?
⑤ 사람들은 낯선 사람 한 명이 거기에 서있는 것을 보았다.
* 5형식 문장에서 목적격 보어는 수동태의 주어로 만들 수 없다.

08 방안의 향기가 우리를 편안하게 만들었다.
→ 우리는 방 안의 향기에 의해 편안해졌다.
* 사역동사 make가 있는 5형식 문장을 수동태로 바꿀 경우 목적격 보어인 원형부정사(feel)는 to부정사로 바꿔야 한다.

09 그들은 그들의 친구들이 그 나라를 떠나게 하지 않을 것이다.
→ 그들의 친구들은 그 나라를 떠나도록 허락되지 않을 것이다.
* let의 수동태는 없으므로 〈be allowed to + 동사원형〉의 형태로 쓴다.

10 A: 유나와 Tim 둘 다 침대에 누워있는 것이 보여. 그들에게 무슨 일이 있었니?
B: 그들은 심한 감기에 걸렸어.
A: 흠... 그들은 아이스크림을 먹는 것이 허락되지 않겠구나.
* 지각동사 see의 목적격 보어가 현재분사(lying)일 때는 수동태에서 그대로 쓴다. 두 번째 빈칸에는 문맥상 '~이 허락되지 않다'는 의미의 are not allowed to가 알맞다.

11 (a) 그 근육질의 남자가 팔굽혀펴기 하는 것이 보였다.
(b) 그 여자는 그녀의 시어머니에 의해 설거지를 하게 되었다.
* 지각동사와 사역동사는 수동태로 바꿀 때 목적격 보어인 원형부정사가 to부정사로 바뀐다.

12 Amber는 학급회장으로 선출되었다. 그녀는 용감한 여자아이로 생각된다.
* [as → 삭제] 5형식 동사 elect는 〈elect + 목적어+ 목적격 보어〉의 형태이므로 수동태로 바꿀 때 as가 필요 없다.

13 우리의 과학 선생님은 우리에게 현미경을 보여주셨다.
→ 우리는 우리의 과학 선생님에 의해 현미경이 보였다.
→ 현미경이 우리의 과학 선생님에 의해 우리에게 보였다.
* show가 이끄는 4형식 문장은 간접목적어와 직접목적어를 주어로 한, 두 개의 수동태로 바꿀 수 있다. 간접목적어를 주어로 할 때 We가 복수이므로 be동사는 were가 와야 한다. 직접목적어를 주어로 할 때 간접목적어 앞에 전치사 to가 와야 한다.

14 (1)(2) 사람들은 어제 Audrey가 집에 들어가는 것을 보지 못했다.
→ Audrey가 어제 집에 들어가는 것이 목격되지 않았다.
* 〈지각동사 + 목적어 + 목적격 보어〉의 5형식 문장을 수동태로 바꿀 경우 목적격 보어가 원형부정사이면 to부정사로 바뀌고, 현재분사이면 그대로 쓴다.

15 ① Anne은 나에게 그녀의 차를 오늘까지 세차하라고 시켰다.
→ 나는 Anne에 의해 그녀의 차를 오늘까지 세차하게 되었다.
② Carol은 Donna가 밖으로 나가도록 허락한다.
→ Donna는 Carol에 의해 밖으로 나가도록 허락받았다.
③ Olivia는 Lora가 그녀의 수업에 들어오도록 허락했다.
→ Lora는 Olivia에 의해 그녀의 수업에 들어오도록 허락받았다.
④ Jennifer는 때때로 선생님들께 어리석은 질문을 했다.
→ 어리석은 질문이 Jennifer에 의해 선생님들께 질문되었다.
⑤ Emily는 나에게 재미있는 장난감들을 사주었다.
→ 나는 Emily에 의해 재미있는 장난감들이 구입되었다.
(재미있는 장난감들이 나를 위해 Emily에 의해 구입되었다.)
* ask가 이끄는 4형식 문장은 수동태로 바꿀 때 간접목적어 앞에 전치사 of가 온다.
① [made → was made], ② [let → allowed], ③ [is → was],
⑤ [→ Some interesting toys were bought for me by Emily.]

16 (a) Jasmine은 사무실까지 걸어가게 되었다.
(b) 그 수프는 회사에서 Jasmine을 위해 만들어졌다.
* (a) 5형식 문장을 이끄는 사역동사 make는 수동태로 바꿀 때 원형부정사로 쓰인 목적격 보어가 to부정사(to walk)로 바뀐다.
(b) 4형식 문장을 이끄는 동사 make는 수동태로 바꿀 때 간접목적어 앞에 전치사 for가 온다.

17 (1) 우리는 숙제를 하라는 말을 들었다.
(2) 나는 그 대회에서 상으로 새로운 차를 받았다.
* (1) '우리가 들은' 것이므로, 능동태에서는 hear를 써야 하지만, 수동태에서는 be told로 써야 한다.
(2) 4형식 동사 buy는 간접목적어를 주어로 한 I was bought ~라는 수동태로 바꿀 수 없다.

18 복도 쪽에 있는 창문에 무언가가 떨어지는 소리가 들렸다.
* 지각동사 hear가 사용된 문장의 수동태이므로 목적격 보어는 to부정사나 현재분사가 와야 한다.

19 북한 독재자의 사망에 관한 뉴스가 그 아나운서에 의해 보도되었다.
* 주어가 단수(News)인 수동태이므로 was reported가 알맞다.

20 우리는 우리의 담임선생님이 강을 따라 그녀의 남자 친구와 함께 걷고 있는 것을 보았다.
* 지각동사 see가 쓰인 5형식 문장을 수동태로 바꿀 때 목적격 보어가 현재분사이면 그대로 쓴다.

21 이 컴퓨터게임은 삼촌에 의해 나에게 주어졌다.
* 4형식 문장을 이끄는 동사 give의 수동태 문장에서는 간접목적어(me) 앞에 전치사 to가 온다.

22 ① 질문 하나가 그에 의해 나에게 주어졌다.
② 그 정보는 그 지원자들에게 주어졌다.
③ 그들은 우리에 의해 계단을 올라오는 소리가 들렸다.
④ 긴 문자메세지 하나가 내 남자 친구에 의해서 나에게 보내졌다.
⑤ 그는 그의 여자 친구에 의해 벙어리장갑 한 쌍이 구입되었다.
(→ 한 쌍의 벙어리장갑이 그에 의해 그의 여자 친구를 위해 구입되었다.)
* [→ A pair of mittens was bought for him by his girlfriend.] 4형식 동사 buy는 간접목적어를 주어로 한 수동태로 쓸 수 없다.

23 나는 나의 어머니에 의해 내 방 청소를 하게 되었다.
* 사역동사 make의 목적격 보어로 쓰인 원형부정사(clean)는 수동태가 되면 to부정사로 바뀐다.

24 그녀는 그에 의해서 sweetheart라고 불린다.
* 5형식 동사 call의 목적격 보어 sweetheart는 수동태에서 전치사 to가 필요 없다.

25 나의 교수님은 나에게 발표를 할 기회를 한 번 더 주셨다.
→ (1) 나는 나의 교수님에 의해 발표를 한 번 더 할 기회가 주어졌다.
→ (2) 발표를 한 번 더 할 기회가 나의 교수님에 의해 나에게 주어졌다.
* give가 이끄는 4형식 문장은 간접목적어와 직접목적어를 주어로 하여 두 가지의 수동태를 만들 수 있다.

DAY 08 주의해야 할 수동태

2교시 In - Class Questions ▶ 본문 71쪽

STEP A **1** will have been prepared **2** will be sent **3** was built **4** will have been published

STEP B **1** X, by → on **2** O **3** O

STEP C **1** for **2** as **3** to **4** at

STEP D **1** The due date for the homework assignment should not be forgotten.
2 A model of the Gundam is being made by my brother.
3 A concert has been held in November by the university.
4 The orphans in the village were looked after by the volunteer workers.

STEP A **1** 네가 집에 도착할 때 저녁이 준비되어 있을 것이다.
2 그 이메일은 내 여동생에 의해 내일 나에게 보내질 것이다.
3 학생들을 위한 그 강당은 기부에 의해서 지어졌다.
4 영어 문법책 시리즈가 이번 달 말까지 출판될 것이다.

STEP B **1** 이 영화는 실화를 바탕으로 만들어졌다.
2 누구에 의해 이 선물이 보내졌니?
3 하와이는 해변으로 유명하다고들 한다.

STEP C **1** 그 식당은 맛있는 요리로 유명하다.
2 이 박사님은 한국의 히포크라테스로 유명하다.
3 그의 이름은 그 회사의 모든 사람들에게 알려져 있다.
4 나의 부모님은 내 성적표에 놀라셨다.

STEP D **1** 너는 그 숙제의 마감일을 잊지 말아야 한다.
2 나의 형은 건담 모형을 만들고 있다.
3 그 대학은 11월에 콘서트를 열어 왔다.
4 그 자원봉사자들은 그 마을의 고아들을 돌보았다.

3교시 After - Class Questions ▶ 본문 72-75쪽

01 ③ **02** ⑤ **03** ② **04** ② **05** ② **06** ③ **07** ④ **08** ② **09** have been made **10** will be finished **11** must be taken care of **12** are being built **13** ④ **14** ② **15** ② **16** been disappeared → disappeared **17** ⑤ **18** ① **19** ② **20** ②, ③ **21** ② **22** (1) is thought that the new movie is really interesting (2) is thought to be really interesting **23** ② **24** ① **25** ⑤

01 많은 학생들이 중간고사를 보기 싫어한다고 한다.
* that절이 목적어인 문장의 수동태이므로 〈It is said that ~〉으로 나타내며, '~라고 한다'로 해석한다.

02 그 범죄자들은 우리에 의해 돌보아졌다.
* 구동사 take care of는 한 단어로 취급하므로 수동태에서도 〈be taken care of + by + 행위자〉의 형태가 되어야 한다.

03 새로운 타워브리지가 템스 강을 가로질러 건설되고 있다.
* 진행형의 수동태는 〈be동사 + being + 과거분사〉로 쓴다.

04 ① 그 살인자는 경찰에 의해 체포되었다.
② 나의 언니는 엄마와 아빠를 닮았다.
③ 그 어린아이는 대형 트럭에 치었다.
④ 그녀는 삼촌에 의해 영리하다고 믿어진다.
⑤ 어르신들은 그 헤어디자이너에게 머리를 자르도록 했다.
* [is resembled by → resembles] resemble은 수동태가 불가능한 타동사이다.

05 ① 독립은 국민들에 의해 얻어질 수 있었다.
② 저 연기자들은 그 유명한 감독에 의해 배역을 받고 있다.
③ 그 소문과 진실은 여자아이들에 의해 퍼져왔다.
④ 그 여행은 폭우 때문에 연기되어야 했다.

⑤ 그녀의 바보 같은 농담은 대부분의 학생들에 의해 비웃음 당했다.

* [be → being] 현재진행형의 수동태는 〈be being + 과거분사〉의 형태가 와야 한다.

06 그 시장은 그 정책이 이 문제를 해결할 수 있다고 믿는다.
→ 그 정책이 이 문제를 해결할 수 있다고 그 시장에 의해 믿어진다.

* believe의 목적어가 that절이므로 〈It is believed that ~〉이나 〈that절의 주어 + is believed to부정사 ~〉의 형태로 수동태를 만든다.

07 나의 어머니는 우리 집을 매일 깨끗이 유지했다.
→ 우리 집은 나의 어머니에 의해 매일 깨끗이 유지되었다.

* keep이 이끄는 5형식 문장을 수동태로 바꿀 때 동사의 시제가 과거이므로 was kept가 와야 한다.

08 칼슘은 우리의 몸에서 중요한 역할을 한다고 하며, 그것은 신진대사에 영향을 준다고 믿어진다.

* [to playing → to play] is said to 다음에는 동사원형이 와야 한다.

09 근로자들이 한국에서 많은 자동차를 만들어왔다.
→ 많은 자동차들이 한국에서 근로자들에 의해 만들어져 왔다.

* 현재완료시제의 수동태는 〈have been + 과거분사〉의 형태로 쓴다.

10 그들은 이 공사 프로젝트를 곧 끝낼 것이다.
→ 이 공사 프로젝트는 곧 끝날 것이다.

* 미래시제 수동태는 〈will be + 과거분사〉의 형태로 쓴다.

11 그녀는 그녀의 가족을 보살펴야 한다.
→ 그녀의 가족은 그녀에 의해서 보살핌을 받아야 한다.

* 조동사와 구동사가 있는 문장의 수동태이므로 〈조동사 + be + 과거완료(taken care of)〉의 형태로 쓴다.

12 * '현재 세워지고 있는'이라는 현재진행 수동태이므로 〈be동사 + being + 과거분사〉의 형태로 쓴다.

13 (a) 뒷마당은 많은 나뭇잎들로 덮여 있다.
(b) 너는 네 직업에 만족하니?

* by 이외의 전치사를 쓰는 수동태로 (a) be covered with는 '~로 덮여 있다', (b) be satisfied with는 '~에 만족하다'는 뜻이다.

14 ① 나는 나의 건강에 대해 걱정한다.
② 새로운 노트북 컴퓨터가 나를 위해 구입되었다.
③ 나의 남자 친구는 나에 의해 저녁식사가 만들어졌다. (→ 저녁식사가 나의 남자 친구를 위해 나에 의해 만들어졌다.)
④ 나의 아버지는 지루한 일에 싫증이 나 있다.
⑤ 그 교실은 많은 학생들로 가득 차 있다.

* buy가 이끄는 4형식 문장은 직접목적어를 주어로 하는 수동태로만 쓸 수 있으며, 간접목적어 앞에는 전치사 for를 사용한다.
① [by → about] be worried about(~에 대해 걱정하다)
③ [→ Dinner was made for my boyfriend by me.] make는 간접목적어를 주어로 하는 수동태로 쓸 수 없다.
④ [by → of] be tired of(~에 싫증나다)
⑤ [to → with] be filled with(~으로 가득 차다)

15 ① 그 우주왕복선은 그 엔지니어들에 의해서 만들어졌다.
② Kelly는 사람들의 집에 초대되는 것을 좋아한다.
③ 목성은 우주탐사용 로켓에 의해 방문되고 있다.
④ 저 크리스털 꽃병은 내 아들에 의해서 바닥에 떨어졌니?
⑤ 새로운 야구장이 내년까지 건설될 것이다.

* '집에 초대되다'의 뜻이므로 get(be) invited to가 알맞다. '~에 의해 초대되다'일 경우에는 get invited by가 온다.

16 현대 기술 덕분에 마차들이 도로 위에서 사라졌다.

* disappear는 수동태로 쓰이지 않는 동사이다.

17 우리는 기말고사가 연기되었다는 것을 알게 되었다.

* 주절이 과거시제이고 그보다 먼저 일어난 일을 나타내야 하므로 과거완료시제의 수동태인 〈had + been + 과거분사〉로 쓴다.

18 태민이가 그 상을 받을 예정이라고들 한다. 그는 훌륭한 예술가라고 여겨졌다.

* that절이 목적어인 문장의 수동태는 〈It + be동사 + 과거분사 + that ~〉 혹은 〈that절의 주어 + be동사 + 과거분사 + to부정사 ~〉의 형태로 쓴다.

19 ① 그 병은 간장으로 가득 차 있다.
② 나현이는 그녀의 시험 결과에 놀랐다.
③ 준모는 그 소식에 만족한다.
④ 그 도로는 많은 눈으로 덮여 있다.
⑤ 그 어머니는 자신의 아들의 공연에 기뻐한다.

* ②는 be surprised at(~에 놀라다)을 뜻하므로 at이 들어가고, 나머지는 모두 전치사 with가 들어간다.
① be filled with(~로 가득 차다), ③ be satisfied with(~에 만족하다), ④ be covered with(~로 덮여 있다), ⑤ be pleased with(~에 기뻐하다)

20 ① 프랑스어는 캐나다 퀘벡 주에서 통용된다.
② Brenda는 학급 반장으로 선출되었다.
③ 그 새로운 집은 가스에 의해 데워진다.
④ 이 소설은 Emily에 의해 쓰였다.
⑤ 그 자전거는 내 남동생에 의해 재빨리 씻겨졌다.

* ② [has elected → has been elected] 문맥상 '선출되었다'는 완료 수동태가 와야 한다. has elected는 '선출했다'라는 의미이다.
③ [is heat → is heated] 문맥상 '데워진다'는 수동태가 와야 하며, heat의 과거분사는 heated이다.

21 * since가 있고 '방문되는' 수동의 의미이므로 현재완료 수동태인 〈has + been + 과거분사〉의 형태로 쓰는 것이 알맞다.

22 사람들은 그 새 영화가 진짜로 재미있다고 생각한다.
→ 그 새 영화는 진짜로 재미있다고 생각된다.

* that절이 목적어인 문장의 수동태는 〈It + be동사 + 과거분사 + that ~〉 혹은 〈that절의 주어 + be동사 + 과거분사 + to부정사 ~〉의 형태로 쓴다.

23 (a) 우진이는 피자를 먹는 것에 싫증이 난다.
(b) Bella는 온종일 공부했기 때문에 피곤하다.

* (a) be tired of는 '~에 싫증이 나다', (b) be tired from은 '~로 피곤하다'의 뜻이다.

24 (a) 관리비는 이번 주말까지 납부되어야 한다.
(b) 이번 겨울 방학 동안 얼마의 돈이 쓰일 예정이니?

* 조동사 has to와 be going to가 있는 문장의 수동태는 〈조동사 + be + 과거분사〉의 형태로 쓴다.

25 * [→ The house is filled with furniture.] furniture와 the house의 위치가 바뀌어야 한다.

Final Test

▶ 본문 76-79쪽

01 ② **02** ④ **03** ②, ⑤ **04** (1) hold (2) be held **05** ①, ② **06** ④ **07** ⑤ **08** ④ **09** are interested in **10** ② **11** ②, ⑤ **12** (1) been, told (2) is, called **13** couldn't, be, fixed **14** By, whom, are, sung **15** Where was the test taken (by the students)? **16** ④ **17** ⑤ **18** ①, ④, ⑤ **19** ③ **20** ② **21** ⑤ **22** ⑤ **23** is asked **24** ① **25** ②, ④ **26** (1) of (2) at (3) about (4) with **27** ④ **28** has been exported **29** ③ **30** (1) was built (2) is[was] considered

01 Janet은 그녀의 정원 울타리를 노란색으로 칠했다.
→ Janet의 정원 울타리는 그녀에 의해 노란색으로 칠해졌다.

* 목적어 her garden fence를 주어로, 동사 painted를 was painted로 바꾼 다음, 목적격 보어 yellow는 그대로 쓴다.

02 ① 그들은 시골에서 자랐니?
② 이 일은 이번 주말까지 완료되어야 한다.
③ 그 공장은 2010년 이래로 이 도시에 있었다.
④ 그 교수는 가장 위대한 학자 중 한 사람으로 여겨졌다.
⑤ 많은 차들이 이 건물 앞에서 견인되었다.

* [considered → was considered] 문맥상 '~로 여겨지다'는 수동태 문장이 되어야 한다.

03 * by는 전치사이므로 〈by + 목적격〉 형태가 와야 하며, 동사 뒤로 이동할 수 있다. 이 때 의문사는 who로 바뀐다. by who로는 쓰이지 않는다.

04 (1) 그 트럭은 콜라 20박스를 실을 수 있다.
(2) 그 사진 액자는 줄에 의해 지지될 수 있다.

* (1) 트럭이 20박스의 콜라를 실을 수 있는 것이므로 능동태로 써야 한다.
(2) 사진 액자가 줄에 의해 지지되는 것이므로 수동태로 써야 한다.

05 Kate는 그녀의 생일을 위해서 아무것도 ___________ 않았다.

③ 받지 ④ 듣지 ⑤ 제공받지

* buy와 cook은 간접목적어를 주어로 한 수동태를 만들 수 없다.

06 A: 무엇을 도와 드릴까요?

B: 저는 운동화 한 켤레를 찾고 있습니다.

A: 저희는 다양한 종류의 물건을 가지고 있습니다. 이것들은 어떤가요?

B: 이것들은 진짜 가죽으로 만들어진 건가요?

A: 사실은 아닙니다. 이것들은 인조 가죽입니다.

* '~로 만들어지다'는 by 이외의 전치사를 사용하여 수동태로 나타낸다. be made of는 물리적 변화, be made from은 화학적 변화를 나타낼 때 쓰인다.

07 ① 나는 너를 믿을 수 없다.
→ 너는 나에 의해 믿어질 수 없다.

② 사람들은 그녀가 정직하다고 믿는다.
→ 그녀는 정직하다고 믿어진다.

③ 나는 Sean에게 그 컴퓨터를 주었다.
→ 그 컴퓨터는 나에 의해서 Sean에게 주어졌다.

④ 우리는 그들이 계단을 올라오는 소리를 들었다.
→ 그들이 계단을 올라오는 소리가 들렸다.

⑤ 나의 교수님은 그 기말 프로젝트를 연기했다.
→ 그 기말 프로젝트는 나의 교수님에 의해 연기되었다.

* 능동태의 시제가 과거이므로 수동태도 과거시제가 왔다.
① [depended → depended on] depend on은 구동사로 하나의 단어로 취급하므로 수동태에서도 on이 함께 쓰여야 한다.
② [being → to be] that절이 목적어인 문장의 수동태는 that절의 주어(she)를 문장의 주어로 하여 수동태를 만들 수 있는데, 이 때 that절의 동사는 to부정사로 써야 한다.
③ [for → to] give가 이끄는 4형식에서 직접목적어를 주어로 한 수동태로 바꿀 때 간접목적어 앞에 전치사 to를 사용한다.
④ [came → to come] 지각동사가 있는 5형식 문장을 수동태로 바꿀 때 목적격 보어로 쓰인 원형부정사는 to부정사로 바뀐다.

08 (a) 뉴욕은 쇼핑과 그곳의 주목할 만한 명소들로 유명하다.

(b) 이 탁자는 버드나무로 만들어졌다.

(c) 무언가 떨어지는 소리가 문밖에서 들렸다

* (a) '~로 유명하다'는 be well known for로 나타낸다.
(b) '~로 만들어지다(물리적 변화)'는 be made of로 나타낸다.
(c) 지각동사 hear가 사용된 문장의 수동태이므로 원형부정사로 쓰인 목적격 보어가 to부정사로 바뀐다.

09 당신이 영화 보는 것에 관심이 있다면, AK백화점에 있는 CGV에 가기를 원할지도 모른다. 그 영화관은 지금 다양한 종류의 새로 나온 영화를 상영하고 있다.

* '~에 관심이 있다'는 be interested in으로 나타낸다.

10 ① 영어는 Kyle에 의해서 가르쳐진다.

② 나는 나의 선생님에 의해 기억된다. (→ 나의 선생님은 나를 기억하신다.)

③ 이 역사적인 사건은 잊혀지면 안 된다.

④ 질문 하나가 그에 의해서 나에게 주어졌다.

⑤ 그녀의 남편은 그녀에 의해 그 방을 청소하게 되었다.

* remember는 타동사이지만 상태동사이므로 수동태로 쓸 수 없다.

11 Simpson씨는 다가오는 멕시코 여행에 ____________.

① 기뻤다 ③ 만족했다 ④ 기뻤다 ⑤지쳤다

* be surprised at, be tired from의 형태로 쓴다.

12 * (1) tell은 '말해주다'라는 뜻이므로 '들었다'라는 표현이 되려면 수동태로 써야 한다. 빈칸 앞에 have가 있으므로 완료 수동태(have been + 과거분사)로 쓴다.
(2) call은 '부르다'라는 뜻이므로 '불리다'라는 표현이 되려면 수동태로 써야 한다.

13 그 정비기사는 내 자동차를 3일 만에 수리할 수 없었다.
→ 내 자동차는 그 정비기사에 의해서 3일 만에 수리될 수 없었다.

* 부정의 조동사를 포함한 문장의 수동태는 〈조동사 + not + be + 과거분사〉의 형태로 쓴다.

14 누가 이 노래들을 부르니?
→ 이 노래들은 누구에 의해 불려지니?

* 의문사가 주어로 쓰인 의문문의 수동태는 〈By + 목적격 의문사 + be동사 + 주어 + 과거분사 ~?〉의 형태로 쓴다. 수동태의 주어가 복수(songs)이므로 be동사는 are가 와야 한다.

15 그 학생들은 어디에서 그 시험을 봤니?
→ (그 학생들에 의해서) 그 시험은 어디에서 치러졌니?

* 의문문의 수동태는 〈의문사 + be동사 + 주어 + 과거분사 ~?〉의 형태로 쓴다.

16 (a) 국립 박물관은 초등학생들로 매우 붐볐다.

(b) 그녀는 그 오디션에서 그녀의 노래에 만족하지 못했다.

* (a) '~로 붐비다'는 be crowed with, (b) '~에 만족하다'는 be satisfied with이므로, 빈칸에 공통으로 들어갈 말은 with이다.

17 (a) Karl은 엄마에 의해 우유를 마시게 되었다.

(b) 그 여자아이가 무대 위에서 춤추는 것이 보였다.

* 사역동사나 지각동사의 목적격 보어로 쓰인 원형부정사는 수동태가 되면 to부정사로 바뀐다.

18 ① 그 보고서는 Kyle에 의해서 쓰였니?

② 그녀의 방은 그녀에 의해 깔끔하게 유지된다.

③ 내 예쁜 고양이들은 그에 의해 돌보아지고 있다.

④ 그녀의 베개는 그녀의 엄마에 의해서 편안하게 만들어졌다.

⑤ 그 놀라운 소식은 새로운 기회로 여겨진다.

* ② 5형식 문장의 목적격 보어가 형용사(tidy)이면 수동태에서 그대로 쓴다.
③ take care of는 하나의 동사로 취급하여 수동태에서도 그대로 쓴다.
① [write → written], ④ [made → was made], ⑤ [considered → is considered]

19 Steve는 어제 나에게 도미노 하는 방법을 가르쳐 주었다.
→ 어제 도미노 하는 방법이 Steve에 의해 나에게 가르쳐졌다.

* 〈보기〉의 4형식 문장은 간접목적어(me)와 직접목적어(how to play dominoes) 두 가지를 주어로 한 수동태 문장을 만들 수 있다. 간접목적어를 주어로 한 수동태는 I was taught how to play dominoes by Steve yesterday.이다. 직접목적어를 주어로 한 수동태는 간접목적어 앞에 전치사 to가 와야 한다.

20 Patrick의 학급 친구들은 그를 겁쟁이라고 불렀다.
→ Patrick은 그의 학급 친구들에 의해 겁쟁이라고 불렸다.

* 5형식 문장을 수동태로 바꿀 때 목적격 보어가 명사일 경우 변화 없이 그대로 쓴다.

21 ① 프라이드 치킨이 나의 아버지에 의해 내게 수문되었다.

② 선거공약은 그 정치가에 의해 그 지역 사람들에게 공약되었다.

③ 나에게 장난감 인형이 크리스마스 선물로 나의 아빠에 의해 구입되었다.
(→ 장난감 인형이 크리스마스 선물로 나의 아빠에 의해 나를 위해 구입되었다.)

④ 나는 나의 애완동물에 의해 아침 8시에 일어나게 되었다.

⑤ 자장가가 그녀의 어머니에 의해 Serena에게 불려졌다.

* ① [to → for] order는 간접목적어 앞에 to가 아닌 for를 쓴다.
② [promised → was promised] 수동태 문장이므로 〈be동사 + 과거분사〉가 알맞다.
③ [→ A toy doll was bought for me as a Christmas present by my daddy.] 수여동사 buy는 간접목적어를 주어로 하는 수동태로 바꿀 수 없다.
④ [wake → to wake] 사역동사 make가 쓰인 5형식 문장을 수동태로 바꿀 때 원형부정사로 쓰인 목적격 보어는 to부정사로 바꿔야 한다.

22 (a) Vicky는 그 방에 들어갔을 때 이 벨이 울리는 소리가 들렸다.

(b) 어떤 개들은 시각장애인들을 도와주기 위해 훈련받는다.

(c) 뇌는 호르몬에 의해서 더 활동적이게 된다.

* (a) '벨이 울리는 소리가 들리는' 것이므로 수동태로 표현해야 하고, 뒤의 부사절의 시제가 과거이므로 시제 일치로 과거 수동태(was heard)가 와야 한다.
(b) train은 to부정사를 목적격 보어로 취하는 동사이므로 수동태에서도 to help가 와야 한다.
(c) 뇌가 활동적이게 '되는' 것이므로 수동태가 와야 한다.

23 * 주어가 Anyone이므로 단수형 is가 와야 하며, '요청받고 있는' 것이므로 수동태(is asked)가 와야 한다.

24 (a) 스토리북 한 세트가 학교에서 어린아이들을 위해 발견되었다.

(b) Jessica는 그녀의 친구들에게 웃음거리가 되었다.

* (a) 동사 find가 이끄는 4형식 문장을 수동태로 만들 때 간접목적어 앞에 전치사 for를 쓴다.
(b) laugh at은 하나의 동사로 간주하여 수동태로 만들 때 함께 쓰인다.

25 * 목적어로 쓰인 that절의 수동태는 〈It + be동사 + 과거분사 + that ~〉 혹은 〈that절의 주어 + be동사 + 과거분사 + to부정사 ~〉 형태로 쓴다.

26 (1) 이 의자와 서랍은 철로 만들어진다.

(2) 나의 학급 친구들은 그 시험 점수에 놀랐다.

(3) 모든 사람들은 그녀의 건강에 대해 걱정한다.

(4) 저 컵들은 자몽주스로 가득 차있다.

* (1) be made of: '~으로 만들어지다'(물리적 변화)

(2) be surprised at: '~에 놀라다'
(3) be worried about: '~에 대해 걱정하다'
(4) be filled with: '~로 가득 차다'

[27-28] 대부분의 한국인들은 비빔밥을 좋아하며 다른 나라 사람들 또한 요즘 비빔밥 먹는 것을 즐긴다. 그것은 특히 미국에서 인기가 있다. 다양한 종류의 비빔밥들은 미국의 많은 식당에서 제공된다. 게다가, 많은 주부들은 비빔밥 만드는 방법을 배우고 있다. 그것의 인기 때문에 한국 비빔밥은 수출되고 있다.

27 * (a) '비빔밥이 제공되는' 것이므로 수동태가 알맞으며, 주어가 different kinds of bibimbap으로 복수이므로 are served가 와야 한다.
(b) '주부들이 배우는' 것이므로 능동태가 어울리며, 주어가 many housewives로 복수 명사이므로 are learning이 와야 한다.

28 * 현재완료 수동태는 〈has been + 과거분사〉의 형태로 쓴다.

[29-30] 피라미드를 건설하는 것은 왕의 업무의 주요한 부분이었다. 왕은 죽은 후에 영원히 살아서 그 나라를 지켜보길 원한다고 믿어지고 있었다. 그 외에도, 왕이 그 나라를 성공적으로 이끌었는지의 상징이기도 했다. 안의 내부 장식뿐만 아니라 피라미드의 위치도 하늘의 별의 위치와 맞추어서 디자인되었다. 피라미드의 재료들은 다양했다. 예를 들어 쿠푸왕의 피라미드는 석회암을 주로 이용하여 지어졌으며 건축적으로 걸작이라고 간주된다.

29 * (a) that절이 목적어인 경우의 수동태이고 시제가 과거이므로 과거 수동태인 was believed가 알맞다.
(b) '위치가 디자인되는' 것이므로 수동태이며 〈B as well as A〉의 경우 B에 동사의 수를 맞추어야 하므로 was designed가 알맞다.

30 * (1) '쿠푸 왕 피라미드가 지어지는' 것이므로 수동태(be동사 + 과거분사)가 와야 한다.
(2) '쿠푸 왕 피라미드가 간주되는' 것이므로 수동태가 와야 한다.

Sentence Writing

▶ 본문 80쪽

Part A
1 is being pulled out
2 is seen to read the novel
3 are given a computer

Part B
1 This cake was delivered to her by him this morning.
2 This computer has not been used by my mom for a long time.
3 Kevin was laughed at by Woojin.
4 Keilen is worried about her future plans.

Part A
1 치아 하나가 그 치과의사에 의해 뽑혔다. 그 환자는 아프다.
2 Gary가 그의 방에서 소설책을 읽는 것이 보인다. 그의 식구들은 놀란다.
3 Kelly와 Kay는 그들의 어머니에 의해 컴퓨터 한 대를 받았다. 그들은 그것을 받게 되어 매우 행복하다.

Unit 05 부정사

DAY 09 to부정사의 명사적 용법

2교시 In - Class Questions

▶ 본문 85쪽

STEP A 1 to help 2 play, playing 3 finish
STEP B 1 주어 2 보어 3 목적어
STEP C 1 paint 2 learn [to learn] 3 washed
STEP D 1 for → of 2 solve → to solve 3 buy → to buy 4 provide → to provide

STEP A
1 David는 내가 그의 수학 프로젝트를 도와주기를 원한다.
2 나는 Peter가 그의 방에서 첼로를 연주하는(연주하고 있는) 것을 들었다.
3 나의 영어 선생님은 우리에게 우리의 프로젝트를 끝내도록 시키셨다.

STEP B
1 약속을 지키는 것은 친한 친구에게 중요하다.
2 Sally는 나에게 영어 능력을 향상시키는 방법을 배우라고 말했다.
3 유명한 여배우 몇 명이 아프리카의 가난한 사람들을 도와주려고 노력했다.

STEP D
1 이 무거운 상자를 들어주다니 당신은 참 너그럽군요.
2 Anderson은 이 문제를 동료들과 어떻게 해결해야 할지 깨닫지 못한다.
3 나의 친구들은 나에게 가능한 한 빨리 중고차를 사라고 충고했다.
4 그 애플리케이션은 매우 유용한 정보를 사람들에게 제공하는 것을 가능하게 한다.

3교시 After - Class Questions

▶ 본문 86 - 89쪽

01 ③ **02** ③, ④ **03** ④ **04** ⑤ **05** ⑤ **06** ③ **07** ④ **08** ⑤ **09** ② **10** ⑤ **11** is impossible for Matthew to beat my English skills **12** ④ **13** ⑤ **14** I, should, ride **15** ①, ②, ③, ④ **16** ①, ⑤ **17** to sleep → sleep **18** why → how **19** to, be, quiet **20** ③, ④ **21** ① **22** ② **23** ① **24** ⑤ **25** to search

01 * 가주어 It이 쓰인 문장이므로 빈칸에는 진주어인 to부정사가 와야 한다.

02 ① 나는 멋진 저녁을 먹었다.
② 나는 남은 돈이 약간 있었다.
③ 나는 훌륭한 음식이 요리되도록 시켰다.
④ 나는 나의 엄마가 내 학원비를 내도록 했다.
⑤ 나는 내 친구들과 함께 좋은 시간을 보냈다.
* ③④는 사역동사로 '~가 …하도록 시키다'라는 뜻이다.
① 먹다, ② 가지다, ⑤ 보내다

03 그 학생들이 그들의 지역사회를 위해 돕다니 ___________.
① 사려 깊다 ② 멋지다 ③ 친절하다 ④ 필요하다 ⑤ 현명하다
* 의미상 주어가 〈of + 목적격〉이므로 빈칸에는 사람의 감정을 나타내는 형용사가 와야 한다. necessary는 뒤에 〈for + 목적격〉이 와야 한다.

04 나의 형제자매들은 나에게 건설직을 찾도록 ___________.
①②③⑤ 시켰다 ④ 도와주었다.
* 목적격 보어로 원형부정사(동사원형)를 취하지 않는 동사는 get이다. get은 목적격 보어로 to부정사를 취한다.

05 Sally는 Austin에게 Leslie와 결혼할 것을 ___________.
① 요청했다 ② 원했다 ③ 허락했다 ④ 도왔다 ⑤ 시켰다
* 목적격 보어로 to부정사를 취하지 않는 동사는 사역동사 make이다.

06 몇몇 사람들은 그 새로운 태블릿 PC를 어떻게 사용하는지 모른다.
* know의 목적어 역할을 해야 하므로 〈의문사 + to부정사〉가 와야 한다.

07 Frank는 저 문제들을 푸는 것이 매우 쉽다는 것을 깨달았다.
* 동사 find가 이끄는 5형식 문장에서 to부정사가 목적어로 쓰이면 가목적어 it을 사용한다.

08 ① 우리는 머리를 자를 필요가 있다.
② Mary는 공개적으로 연설하는 것을 좋아한다.
③ 나의 여동생은 내가 방 청소하는 것을 도와주었다.
④ Jade와 Jack 둘 다 나에게 그들의 트럭과 자전거를 닦으라고 시켰다.
⑤ 너는 사장으로부터 오는 어떤 전화도 놓치지 않는 것이 중요하다.
* [of you → for you] important는 사람의 성격을 나타내는 형용사가 아니므로 의미상의 주어는 for you로 써야 한다.

09 ① Sarah는 나에게 그녀의 무거운 상자들을 나르라고 말했다.
② 아빠는 내가 그 콘서트에 가는 것을 허락하지 않을 것이다.
③ 그 선생님은 나에게 기타 동아리에 들라고 시켰다.
④ 엄마는 내가 책상 위의 라디오를 켜는 소리를 들었다

⑤ 그 의사는 나에게 잠시 동안 커피를 마시지 말라고 충고했다.
* [to go → go] 사역동사 let은 목적격 보어로 원형부정사(동사원형)를 취한다.

10 ① 부모들은 그들의 아이들이 학교에서 최선을 다하도록 시킨다.
② 한국 정부는 입양된 사람들이 그들의 친부모를 찾도록 도와준다.
③ 그들은 어제 젊은 사람들이 무대에서 노래를 연습하고 있는 것을 보았다.
④ 갑자기 Whitney는 낯선 사람에 의해 그녀의 가방이 만져지는 것을 느꼈다.
⑤ 나의 엄마는 매우 피곤할 때면 나에게 설거지를 하라고 시키시곤 하셨다.
* [washing → wash] 사역동사로 쓰인 have는 목적격 보어로 원형부정사(동사원형)를 취한다.

11 * 가주어 It이 문두에 있고 impossible이 있으므로, 진주어로 쓰인 to부정사의 의미상의 주어는 for Matthew로 쓴다.

12 보기 모든 한국 사람들은 2002년 한국 월드컵을 위해 붉은 악마 티셔츠를 입기로 결심했다.
① 그는 자라서 치과의사가 되었다.
② 너는 알지 못하는 누군가에게 의지하지 마라.
③ 우리는 음식축제에서 음식을 만들 예정이다.
④ Roland는 미국에서 심리학을 전공하는 것을 원하지 않았다.
⑤ 끝낼 새로운 학교 숙제가 뭐니?
* 〈보기〉는 decide의 목적어 역할을 하는 to부정사로 명사적 용법으로 쓰였다. ④는 want의 목적어 역할을 하므로 명사적 용법이다.
① 부사적 용법(결과), ②⑤ 형용사적 용법(명사 수식), ③ 〈be + to부정사〉 용법(예정)

13 ① Paul은 그녀가 아름답게 노래 부르고 있는 것을 들었다.
② Evan은 그 벌레들이 느리게 움직이는 것을 보았다.
③ 내가 공항에 가는 데 4시간이 걸린다.
④ 우리는 도서관에서 조용히 하는 것을 규칙으로 했다.
⑤ Hank는 그의 친구들에게 그를 위해 매우 어려운 일을 해달라고 부탁했다.
* [do → to do] ask는 목적격 보어로 to부정사를 취한다.

14 나의 형은 나에게 스케이트보드 타는 법을 가르쳐줄 것이다.
* 〈의문사 + to부정사〉 = 〈의문사 + 주어 + should + 동사원형〉

15 ① 지난해에 Jerry가 돈을 모은 것은 현명했다.
② 그 경찰관은 늙은 여인이 문을 여는 것을 도와주었다.
③ 엄마는 나에게 김치 같은 음식을 갖고 오라고 요청했다.
④ Harry는 매일 아침 조깅하는 것을 규칙으로 삼았다.
⑤ 네가 안다면 나에게 제발 어느 방법을 선택해야 할지를 알려줘.
* ⑤ [which way choose → which way to choose] 〈의문사 + to부정사〉로 써야 한다.

16 ① 너를 위해 내가 저 책들을 나르도록 해 줘.
② 박 선생님은 갑자기 그의 이름이 불리는 것을 들었다.
③ Laurie는 우리가 그녀의 대학에서 그녀의 수업을 듣는 것을 허락했다.
④ 엄마와 아빠 두 분 다 우리가 특별한 어떤 것을 하는 것을 기대했다.
⑤ 그는 나에게 미래에 무엇을 해야 할지 결정하라고 시킬 것이다.
* ① 사역동사 let은 목적격 보어로 원형부정사(동사원형), ⑤ get은 목적격 보어로 to부정사를 취한다.
② [call → called] '그의 이름이 불리는' 것이므로 목적격 보어로 과거분사가 와야 한다.
③ [taking → to take], ④ [do → to do]

17 그녀의 개는 결코 그녀가 잘 자도록 놔두지 않는다.
* 사역동사 let은 목적격 보어로 원형부정사(sleep)를 취한다.

18 나는 영어에서 나쁜 점수를 받았다. 나는 내 영어 능력을 향상시키는 이유(→ 방법)를 모르겠다.
* 문맥상 '영어 능력을 향상시키는 방법'이 알맞다.

19 * order는 목적격 보어로 to부정사를 취한다.

20 모든 학생들은 한국 축구팀이 그 경기를 하는(하고 있는) 것을 보았다.
* 지각동사 watch는 목적격 보어로 원형부정사와 현재분사 둘 다 취한다.

21 ① Austin이 나의 일을 도와주다니 친절하구나.
② 우리가 그 문을 잠그지 않는 것은 위험하다.
③ Teddy가 큰 집을 구입하는 것이 필요하다.
④ 내가 K-pop을 듣는 것은 매우 신이 난다.
⑤ 네가 새로운 직업을 찾는 것은 어렵지 않았다.
* 사람의 성격을 나타내는 형용사 다음에는 〈of + 의미상의 주어〉가 오고, 그 외의 형용사 다음에는 〈for + 의미상의 주어〉가 온다.

22 (a) 그 선생님은 우리의 과학 숙제가 완료되도록 시키셨다.
(b) 모든 사람들은 그 건물이 흔들리고 있는 것을 느꼈다.
* (a) 사역동사 had 다음에 오는 목적어와 목적격 보어의 관계가 수동(숙제가 완료됨)이므로 목적격 보어는 과거분사가 와야 한다.
(b) 지각동사 felt 다음에 오는 목적어와 목적격 보어의 관계가 능동(건물이 흔들림)이므로 동사원형이나 현재분사가 와야 한다.

23 ① 그 사전은 네가 영어 단어들을 이해할 수 있게 한다.
② 눈 때문에 우리는 캠프장으로 다시 돌아가는 버스를 타게 되었다.
③ 나에게 기한을 맞추는 것은 중요했다.
④ 그들은 그에게 가능한 한 많은 책을 계속 읽도록 장려한다.
⑤ 나의 편의를 위해 우리의 스케줄을 연기해 주다니 그녀는 착하다.
* [for you → you] enable은 5형식 문장을 만들 때 목적격 보어로 to부정사가 오며, 이 때 목적어가 to부정사의 의미상 주어이다.

[24-25]
A: 무슨 일이 있었어요? 당신이 비행기를 놓쳤다는 말을 들었어요.
B: 네. 전 뉴욕 여행에서 돌아오는 데 힘든 시간을 보냈어요. 왜 그런지 알아요? 제가 공항에 도착하기 바로 전에 제 여권을 갖고 올 것을 잊었다는 것을 알게 되었어요. 호텔에 제 여권을 두었어요. 그래서 전 호텔로 급하게 돌아갔죠. 호텔 직원에게 제가 썼던 방에서 찾게 해달라고 요청했을 때, 그 매니저가 제 여권을 찾는 것을 도와주었어요. 마침내 전 가까스로 돌아왔어요.

24 * [finding → find 혹은 to find] help는 목적격 보어로 원형부정사와 to부정사 둘 다 취한다.

25 * 동사 ask는 목적격 보어로 to부정사를 취한다.

DAY 10 to부정사의 형용사적, 부사적 용법

2교시 In - Class Questions ▶ 본문 91쪽

STEP A	**1** 감정의 원인 **2** 목적 **3** 결과 **4** 조건
STEP B	**1** 예정 **2** 의도 **3** 운명 **4** 의무
STEP C	**1** wasn't to find **2** are to see
STEP D	**1** to study, not to play **2** to be seen

STEP A
1 그녀는 너의 할머니에 관한 소식을 듣고 매우 슬펐다.
2 그는 자유와 평화를 찾기 위해 한국에 왔다.
3 나의 할머니는 96세까지 사셨다.
4 그가 말하는 것을 들으면 너는 그를 외국인이라고 여길 것이다.

STEP B
1 그들은 오전 10시에 지하철역에 도착할 예정이다.
2 그들은 아이스크림을 먹고 싶으면 먼저 숙제를 끝내야 한다.
3 이 박사님은 2012년에 프랑스로 가서 결코 돌아오지 못했다.
4 너는 식사를 한 후에는 설거지를 해야 한다.

STEP C
1 Cathy는 그녀의 개를 찾을 수 없었다.
2 Simpson 가족은 그 미술 전시회를 보러 갈 예정이다.

3교시 After - Class Questions ▶ 본문 92 - 95쪽

01 ② **02** ② **03** ③ **04** ① **05** ④ **06** ③ **07** You are not to make any noise in this room. **08** are to knock **09** ③ **10** ③ **11** ④ **12** ③ **13** something cold to drink **14** He is to go to London tomorrow. **15** ③, ⑤ **16** are to be[become] **17** ④, ⑤ **18** ③ **19** ②, ③ **20** not too difficult to follow **21** if you are to go upstairs **22** so, sleepy, that, can't **23** enough, to, travel **24** 그들의 학급 친구들은 다음 주 월요일에 영화를 보러 갈 예정이다. **25** 그가 한국말 하는 것을 들으면 너는 그를 한국인이라고 여길 것이다.

01 보기 아이들은 조용히 공부하기 위해서 도서관에 가야 한다.
① 아이들은 조용히 공부하기 위해서 도서관에 가기를 원한다.
② 아이들은 조용히 공부하기 위해서 도서관에 가야 한다.
③ 아이들은 조용히 공부하기 위해서 도서관에 갈 것이다.
④ 아이들은 조용히 공부하기 위해서 도서관에 갈지도 모른다.
⑤ 아이들은 조용히 공부하기 위해서 도서관에 간다.
* '의무'(~해야 한다)를 의미하는 〈be + to부정사〉로 바꿔 쓸 수 있다.

02 그는 함께 이야기할 친구가 없다.
* 문맥상 '함께 이야기할 친구'라는 의미가 되어야 하므로 talk with가 알맞다.

03 네가 그의 목소리를 듣는다면 그를 가수로 생각하게 될 것이다.
* to부정사의 부사적 용법 중 조건을 나타내는 표현이다.

04 Kelly는 그녀의 숙제를 내일까지 제출해야 한다.
* 〈be + to부정사〉가 의무를 나타내면 ought to, should, must 등으로 바꿔 쓸 수 있다.

05 Jason은 이번 주말에 나와 함께 골프를 칠 예정이다.
* this weekend라는 미래 표시 부사구가 있으므로 〈be + to부정사〉가 예정을 나타내며, be going to, be due to, be scheduled to, will 등으로 바꿔 쓸 수 있다.

06 Kelly는 그 문을 열었지만 그 교실이 비어 있다는 것을 알았다.
* only to는 '결국 ~하고 말았다'는 부정적인 결과를 의미할 때 쓰인다.

07 당신은 이 방에서 어떤 소음도 내서는 안 됩니다.
* should는 의무를 나타내는 〈be + to부정사〉로 바꿔 쓸 수 있다.

08 * 의무를 나타내는 〈be + to부정사〉로 나타낸다.

09 ① 그는 잠에서 깨보니 자신이 유명해졌다는 것을 알았다.
② 우리는 그 드라마를 보지 못해서 슬프다.
③ 살을 빼는 것은 나에게 쉽지 않다.
④ 너는 왼쪽으로 돌면 그 아름다운 건물을 볼 수 있다.
⑤ 관광객들은 기념품을 사기 위해서 줄을 서고 있다.
* ③은 명사적 용법으로 주어 역할을 하는 to부정사이고, 나머지는 부사적 용법으로 쓰였다. ① 결과, ② 감정의 원인, ④ 조건, ⑤ 목적

10 ① 그들은 중간고사를 통과하지 못했다.
② 그의 다음 계획은 그의 집으로 돌아가는 것이다.
③ 그녀는 많은 옷을 살 돈을 벌고 싶어 한다.
④ 내가 숙제를 끝내는 것은 불가능하다.
⑤ 우리는 수업을 위한 책을 선택하기로 했다.
* ③은 money를 수식하는 형용사적 용법이고, 나머지는 명사적 용법으로 쓰였다. ①⑤ 목적어 역할, ② 보어 역할, ④ 주어 역할(진주어)

11 * '(안에서) 살 집'이라는 의미이므로 house to live in으로 나타낸다.

12 * '~해야 한다(의무)'는 〈be + to부정사〉로 나타낼 수 있다.

13 나는 Hank가 나에게 차가운 마실 것을 줘서 기뻤다.
* 〈-thing + 형용사 + to부정사〉의 어순으로 쓴다.

14 * '~할 것이다'(예정)는 〈be + to부정사〉로 나타낸다.

15 ① 사실 그들은 함께 놀 친구가 필요하다.
② 우리는 이 주제에 대해 읽을 무언가를 찾고 있다.
③ 저것은 노트북 컴퓨터를 사기에 충분한 돈이다.
④ 로마에서 살 수 있는 가장 비싼 가방이 뭔가요?
⑤ 선생님들은 학생들에게 이 행동을 연습할 수 있는 많은 기회를 준다.
* ③ 〈enough + 명사 + to부정사〉로 '~할 정도로 충분한 …'라는 의미이다.
⑤ to practice가 many opportunities를 수식하는 형용사적 용법이다.
① [play → play with], ② [to read something → something to read], ④ [buying → to buy]

16 * 의도를 나타내는 〈be + to부정사〉로 표현한다.

17 ① 그녀는 깨어보니 자신이 이상한 장소에 있다는 걸 알았다.
② 그들은 결승까지 갔지만, 결국 그곳에서 실패했다.
③ 그 정직한 소년은 자라서 변호사가 되었다.
④ 그가 이야기하는 것을 듣는다면 너는 그를 전문가로 생각할 것이다.
⑤ 우리는 한 방 친구를 방해하지 않기 위해서 소리를 줄였다.
* ④는 조건, ⑤는 목적의 의미이고, 나머지는 결과의 의미로 쓰였다.

18 보기 당신을 방해해서 죄송합니다.
① Cathy는 귀여워 보이기 위해서 모자를 썼다.
② 그 와인은 마시기 좋다.
③ 그녀는 그가 가버린 것을 알고는 놀랐다.
④ 그들은 내일 아침 여기에 도착할 예정이다.
⑤ 그는 나에게 그 문제를 푸는 방법을 가르쳐주었다.
* 〈보기〉와 ③은 〈감정 형용사 + to부정사〉로 부사적 용법 중 감정의 원인을 나타낸다.
① 부사적 용법 중 목적, ② 부사 enough 수식, ④ 〈be + to부정사〉의 예정, ⑤ 〈의문사 + to부정사〉의 명사적 용법(목적어 역할)

19 ① 그들은 곧 강의를 들을 예정이다.
② 이것이 이 상황에서 할 수 있는 가장 좋은 일이다.
③ 그의 여자 친구는 읽을 편지를 원했다.
④ 그는 그의 여동생에게 그 의자를 옮겨달라고 요청했었다.
⑤ 나의 어머니는 건강검진을 받기 위해 병원에 가셨다.
* ②③은 to부정사의 형용사적 용법으로 쓰여 앞의 명사를 수식한다.
① 〈be + to부정사〉의 예정, ④ 명사적 용법 (목적격 보어 역할), ⑤ 부사적 용법 중 목적

[20-21] 당신은 최근에 살을 빼는 데 어려움을 겪고 있나요? 여기에 당신을 위한 몇 가지 좋은 조언들이 있습니다. 이것들은 따르기에 너무 어려운 것들은 아닙니다. 첫째로, 정크 푸드 대신에 야채를 많이 먹으려고 노력하세요. 둘째로, 충분한 물을 마셔요. 마지막으로, 당신이 위층으로 올라가야 할 때는 엘리베이터 대신에 계단을 이용하세요. 당신의 다리를 사용하지 않는 것은 당신이 살을 빼는 것을 방해합니다.

20 * 〈too + 형용사 + to부정사〉의 어순으로 쓰며, 부정어 not은 too 앞에 쓴다.

21 * 〈be + to부정사〉의 의무를 나타내는 표현이며, '위로 올라가다'는 go upstairs로 나타낸다.

22 나는 매우 졸려서 다큐멘터리 영화의 나머지 부분을 볼 수 없다.
* 〈too ~ to부정사〉 = 〈so ~ that + 주어 + can't ...〉 (매우 ~해서 …할 수 없다)

23 그들은 스스로 여행을 할 수 있을 만큼 나이가 들었다.
* 〈so ~ that + 주어 + can ...〉 = 〈enough + to부정사〉 (…할 정도로 충분히 ~한)

24 * 〈be + to부정사〉와 next라는 미래 표시 부사가 있으므로 예정을 의미한다.

25 * to부정사의 부사적 용법 중 조건(~라면)을 의미한다.

DAY 11 to부정사의 기타 용법

2교시 In - Class Questions

▶ 본문 97쪽

STEP A	1 ① 2 ③
STEP B	1 seems to be 2 seemed to be 3 seems to have enjoyed
STEP C	1 not to eat 2 want to 3 want to
STEP D	1 To be frank with you 2 Needless to say

STEP A
1 나는 골프를 쳐본 적이 없지만 쳐보고 싶다.
2 Kevin은 너를 매우 오래 기다리게 해서 미안하다.

STEP B
1 Hank는 아픈 것처럼 보인다.
2 그녀는 그 선물에 만족한 것처럼 보였다.
3 그 기자는 그의 블로그에 글 쓰는 것을 즐겼던 것처럼 보인다.

STEP C
1 나의 어머니는 항상 초콜릿을 먹지 않으려고 노력하신다.
2 너는 원한다면 그 책을 가져도 좋다.
3 나는 그를 모른다, 그리고 알고 싶지도 않다.

3교시 After - Class Questions

▶ 본문 98 - 101쪽

01 ② 02 ③ 03 ②, ③ 04 ⑤ 05 not to enter 06 refused, to
07 ⑤ 08 ① 09 ③ 10 to be satisfied 11 to stay up late last

night **12** to have been a policeman **13** To begin with **14** ⑤ **15** ③ **16** to not plagiarize → not to plagiarize **17** ②, ③, ④ **18** be back home **19** come **20** ④ **21** so to speak **22** to be brief **23** To be honest **24** To begin with **25** To make matters worse

01 내 남자 친구는 또 다른 여자 친구가 있는 것 같다.
* It이 3인칭 단수이고 현재시제를 나타내야 하므로 seems가 알맞다.

02 Cathy는 학창시절에 열심히 공부했던 것 같다.
* in her school days는 과거시점을 나타내므로 완료부정사 to have studied가 알맞다.

03 ① 그 영화는 지루한 것 같다.
② 나는 너를 아주 많이 좋아하는 것 같다.
③ 우리는 그 케이크를 먹어보지 못했지만 먹어보고 싶다.
④ 나는 친구들과 영화관에 가는 것을 정말 좋아한다.
⑤ 그들은 전에 비슷한 문제를 가졌던 것 같다.
* ② [that like → that I like] that 뒤에는 주어와 동사를 포함하는 절이 와야 한다.
③ [like → like to] to eat the cake에서 반복되는 eat the cake는 생략할 수 있지만 to는 생략할 수 없다.

04 A: 그에 대해서 어떻게 생각하니? 그는 잘생겼니?
B: 응 그런 것 같아, 하지만 솔직히 말해서 그는 똑똑하지 않아.
* 문맥상 '솔직히 말해서'가 알맞다.
① 확실히, ② 소위, 말하자면, ③ 말할 필요도 없이, ④ 간단히 말하면

05 엄마는 우리에게 그 방에 들어가지 말라고 말씀하셨다.
* to부정사의 부정은 not/never를 to 앞에 둔다.

06 * refused to buy the book에서 반복되는 말인 buy the book을 생략할 수 있다.

07 ① 많은 친구를 만나는 것은 좋지 않니.
② 우리는 관광객들에게 지하철을 타라고 조언했다.
③ 나는 어디로 갈지 여전히 결정하지 못했다.
④ 설상가상으로 날이 점점 더 추워지고 있었다.
⑤ 그들은 젊었을 때 유명한 K-pop 스타였던 것 같다.
* [to be → to have been] when they were young이 과거시점을 나타내므로 완료부정사가 와야 한다.

08 (a) 그들은 과거에 함께 일을 했던 것 같다.
(b) 많은 슈퍼모델들은 어떤 종류의 옷도 입을 수 있을 만큼 예쁘다.
(c) 그녀는 모자를 쓰고 있는 그 남자아이를 좋아하는 것 같았다.
* (a) in the past가 과거시점을 나타내므로 완료부정사 to have worked가 왔다.
(b) [to wearing → to wear] 〈형용사 + enough + to부정사〉의 형태가 와야 한다.
(c) [likes → liked] seemed가 과거시제이므로 that절에도 과거시제가 와야 한다.

09 * '~인 것 같다'는 현재시제(seem)이고, 어제 그녀에게 전화를 한 것이므로 to부정사의 시제는 과거시제이다. 따라서 완료부정사가 와야 한다.

10 그녀는 그 선물에 대해서 만족한 것처럼 보였다.
* 주절과 that절의 시제가 같으므로 단순부정사, that절의 동사가 수동태이므로 수동형 부정사인 to be satisfied로 써야 한다.

11 그 학생들은 지난밤에 늦게까지 깨어있던 것 같았다.
* 주절과 that절의 시제가 동일한 과거시제이므로 단순부정사로 쓴다.

12 그는 경찰관이었던 것처럼 보였다.
* 주절이 과거시제(seemed), that절이 대과거(had been)이므로 완료부정사로 쓴다.

13 * '우선'은 독립부정사 To begin with로 표현한다.

14 ① 그들은 그에게 거짓말을 하지 말라고 말했다.
② 그는 소위 유명한 피아니스트다.
③ 그들은 매일 살이 찌지 않으려고 노력했다.
④ 우리는 그들이 운동장에서 축구하는 것을 봤다.
⑤ 우리는 한국어는 말할 것도 없이 영어도 말할 수 있다.
* to say nothing of는 '~은 말할 것도 없이'의 뜻이다.
① [not tell → not to tell], ② [To so speak → So to speak], ③ [to not gain → not to gain], ④ [to play → play 혹은 playing]

15 A: 네가 원한다면 너는 집에 가도 돼.
B: 아니, 가고 싶지 않아. 이상한 말이지만, 나는 집에 가는 게 싫어. 왜 그런지 나도 모르겠어.
A: 솔직히 말하면, 나도 그래.
* 첫 번째와 두 번째 빈칸에 쓰인 대부정사는 앞에 나온 말의 반복을 피하기 위해서 to 다음의 내용을 생략하여 쓰는 부정사이다. 대화의 문맥상 알맞은 의미를 가진 독립부정사를 쓸 수 있다.

16 김 교수님은 우리에게 에세이를 베끼지 말라고 충고하셨다.
* to부정사의 부정은 not/never를 to 앞에 두어야 한다.

17 **보기** Jason은 그가 최선을 다했다고 생각했다.
① Hank는 여자 친구가 있으면 하고 바랬다.
② 내가 그를 오해했던 것이 유감이다.
③ 그 사고는 내가 어렸을 때 일어났던 것 같다.
④ 그들은 시험을 통과했다고 생각했다.
⑤ Kelly는 자신이 매우 똑똑하다고 생각한다.
* 주절의 시제보다 that절의 시제가 앞설 때는 완료부정사(to have + 과거분사)로 나타낸다. 〈보기〉②③④는 완료부정사, 나머지는 단순부정사로 나타낸다.

18 A: 너는 언제 집에 올 거니?
B: 가능한 한 빨리 집에 돌아오도록 노력할게요.
* 반복되는 어구인 be back home이 생략된 대부정사이다.

19 A: 그가 여기 왔니?
B: 아니, 내가 그에게 오라고 요청했지만 그는 오고 싶어 하지 않았어.
* 반복되는 어구인 come이 생략된 대부정사이다.

20 A: 당신은 마실 것을 원하시나요?
B: 네, 마시고 싶어요.
* would love to는 '~하는 것을 좋아하다'의 뜻이며, to 다음에 반복되는 표현인 drink를 생략할 수 있다.

[21-25]
A: 너 Keilen 알지, 그렇지 않니? 그녀는 소위 걸어 다니는 사전이잖아.
B: 진짜? 나는 몰랐어. 어쨌든 회의가 다음 주 금요일, 간단히 말하자면 7월 4일이야.
A: 오, 잊고 있었네! 알려줘서 고마워. 솔직히 말하면 나는 그 회의가 약간 걱정이 돼.
B: 어째서?
A: 우선, 회의에는 돈이 많이 필요해. 설상가상으로 우리 회원 중에 한 명이 아프거든.
B: 그것 참 안 됐다.

Final Test

▶ 본문 102 - 105쪽

01 ③ **02** ④ **03** ⑤ **04** ⑤ **05** ④ **06** how, we, should, cook **07** interesting → interested **08** to be behave → to behave **09** he will get → to get **10** ③, ⑤ **11** ③ **12** (1) Can you teach me how to swim in the sea? (2) Can you teach me how I should swim in the sea? **13** ④ **14** ④ **15** ④ **16** ② **17** ③ **18** ④ **19** ② **20** ③ **21** ① **22** ① **23** ③ **24** ④ **25** ② **26** to have been destroyed **27** are **28** were **29** had been **30** (1) 우리는 거기에 가지 않기로 결정했다. (2) 우리는 거기에 가는 것을 결정하지 못했다.

01 * 가주어 It이 쓰였으므로 진주어 to부정사가 필요하며, to부정사의 의미상 주어는 〈for + 목적격〉의 형태로 쓰인다. 〈of + 목적격〉은 앞에 나온 형용사가 사람의 성격을 나타낼 때 쓰인다.

02 그 아이들이 아픈 사람들을 위해 돈을 모으는 것은 ________.
① 사려 깊었다 ② 좋았다 ③ 친절했다 ④ 필요했다 ⑤ 현명했다
* to부정사의 의미상 주어가 〈of + 목적격〉이므로 빈칸에는 사람의 성격을 나타내는 형용사가 와야 한다. ④의 necessary는 성격을 나타내는 형용사가 아니므로 의미상 주어로 〈for +목적격〉 형태가 와야 한다.

03 대부분의 부모들은 어린아이들이 저녁 늦게 TV를 보도록 하지 않는다.
* 목적격 보어로 원형부정사가 왔으므로 빈칸에 get은 들어갈 수 없다. get은 목적격 보어로 to부정사를 취한다.

04 Mike는 그녀의 딸이 아프리카에 가기를 ________ 않았다.
① 요청하지 ② 원하지 ③ 허락하지 ④ 도와주지 ⑤ 시키지

* 목적격 보어로 to부정사가 왔으므로 사역동사 make는 빈칸에 들어갈 수 없다. make는 원형부정사를 목적격 보어로 취한다.

05 ① 진이는 우리가 그 문제에 대해 이야기하고 있는 것을 들었다.
② Sue는 우리가 가난하고 아픈 사람들을 도와주는 것을 원하지 않았다.
③ 그 선생님은 우리에게 반 친구들과 스터디 그룹을 만들도록 시켰다.
④ 나의 언니는 자신의 방이 누군가에 의해 치워지게 하지 않았다.
⑤ 그 의사는 나에게 건강을 유지하기 위해 매일 아침 운동하라고 말했다.
* [clean → cleaned] 사역동사 have가 이끄는 절에서 목적어와 목적격 보어의 관계가 수동(방이 치워지는 것)이므로 목적격 보어는 과거분사가 와야 한다.

06 요리책은 우리에게 다양한 음식을 요리하는 방법을 알게 해준다.
* 〈의문사 + to부정사〉 = 〈의문사 + 주어 + should + 동사원형〉

07 오직 몇몇의 작가들만이 독자들을 흥미롭게 만든다.
* 목적어와 목적격 보어의 관계가 수동(독자들이 흥미롭게 되는 것)이므로 목적격 보어는 과거분사가 와야 한다.

08 박 선생님이 그와 같이 행동하는 것을 보니 그는 신사적일 리가 없다.
* to부정사의 의미상의 주어인 Mr. Park이 '행동하는' 능동 관계이므로 능동형 부정사가 와야 한다.

09 그 교수는 더 많은 정보를 얻기 위해 여기에 왔다.
* '~하기 위해서'라는 뜻이 되려면 〈so as to + 동사원형〉으로 써야 한다.

10 다른 연령대의 사람들은 동물원에서 돌고래들이 공연하는(공연하고 있는) 것을 보았다.
* 지각동사 see는 목적격 보어로 동사원형과 현재분사 둘 다 취한다.

11 (a) 나의 부모님은 가끔 사촌이 나에게 돈을 빌려주도록 시켰다.
(b) 나의 수학선생님은 내 숙제가 검사되도록 시켰다.
* (a) 사역동사 make가 이끄는 문장에서 목적어와 목적격 보어의 관계가 능동(사촌이 돈을 빌려주는 것)이므로 동사원형이 온다.
(b) 사역동사 have가 이끄는 문장에서 목적어와 목적격 보어의 관계가 수동(내 숙제가 검사되는 것)이므로 과거분사가 온다.

12 * (1) 〈의문사 + to부정사〉 = (2) 〈의문사 + 주어 + should + 동사원형〉

13 방이 너무 어두워서 나는 그녀의 반지를 찾을 수 없었다.
* 〈so + 형용사 + that + 주어 + couldn't + 동사원형〉 = 〈too + 형용사 + for + 목적격 + to부정사〉

14 내 친구들은 좋은 점수를 받았던 것처럼 보인다.
* 주절의 시제가 현재이고 that절의 시제가 과거이므로 완료부정사가 와야 한다.

15 ① 미국인 여행객들은 정오에 한국에 도착할 예정이다.
② 길에는 아무도 보이지 않는다.
③ 몇몇 의원들은 요즘 대통령을 만나려고 하지 않는다.
④ 그 새로운 학생들의 꿈은 학교에서 좋은 성적을 받는 것이다.
⑤ 학생들은 교실에서 선생님이 말씀하시는 것에 따라야 한다.
* ④는 주격 보어 역할을 하는 명사적 용법이고, 나머지는 〈be + to부정사〉 용법으로 쓰였다. ① 예정, ② 가능, ③ 의도, ⑤ 의무

16 그들은 학생들, 심지어 선생님들도 가르칠 정도로 열정적이다.
* 〈형용사(passionate) + enough + to부정사〉의 어순이 알맞다.

17 100kg 이상의 여자아이들은 초콜릿 케이크와 햄버거를 먹지 않기로 결심했다.
* 문맥상 '먹지 않기로 결심했다'라는 의미가 알맞다. 따라서 to eat 앞에 부정어가 와야 한다.

18 Terry는 매우 영리해서 중요한 문제들을 해결할 수 있었다.
* 〈so + 형용사 + that + 주어 + could + 동사원형〉 = 〈형용사 + enough + to부정사〉

19 그는 공항에서 마지막 탑승안내를 들었던 것 같다.
* 완료부정사가 쓰였으므로 that절로 바꿀 때 주절의 시제인 현재보다 한 시제 앞선 과거시제로 써야 한다.

20 수백 개의 야생동물 보호지역들이 동물들에게 거주하기 안전한 장소를 제공하기 위해 설치되어 왔다.
* '~에 거주할 안전한 장소'(to live in a safe place)이므로 to live in이 알맞다.

21 * '~해야 한다'는 의무를 나타내는 표현은 〈be + to부정사〉가 알맞다.

22 많은 유명인들이 오늘 밤 인천공항에 도착할 예정이다.
* 문맥상 〈be + to부정사〉가 예정을 의미하므로 will이나 be going to로 바꿔 쓸 수 있다.

23 A: 이봐, 네 바지에 뭐야? 뭔가 묻은 것 같은데.
B: 오! 안 돼. 케첩인 것 같다.
A: 네 바지는 세탁되어야 해.
B: 알았어, 세탁 바구니에 넣을게.
* '바지가 세탁되는 것'이므로 수동형 부정사(to have + 과거분사)가 와야 한다.

24 ① Ellen은 그녀의 아버지가 침실에서 코고는 소리를 들었다.
② John은 그 문제를 피할 정도로 똑똑했다.
③ Jordan은 그의 친구들과 함께 인터넷 카페에 가지 않기로 결심했다.
④ Catherine은 기말시험 결과에 대해서 슬픈 것처럼 보인다.
⑤ 말할 필요도 없이, 모든 사람들은 그들이 원하지 않는 모든 것을 포기했다.
* [being → to be] seem은 to부정사를 목적어로 취하는 동사이다.

25 * '지각하다'는 to be late이고, 부정어는 to 앞에 온다.

26 * 여겨지는 시점보다 파괴된 시점이 더 이전에 일어난 일이고, '파괴된' 것이므로 완료수동형 부정사(to have been + 과거분사)가 와야 한다.

27 그들은 그들의 삶에서 행복한 것처럼 보인다.
* 단순부정사가 쓰였으므로 that절에서도 주절과 같은 현재시제로 쓴다.

28 그들은 그들의 삶에서 행복한 것처럼 보였다.
* 단순부정사가 쓰였으므로 that절에서도 주절과 같은 과거시제로 쓴다.

29 그들은 그들의 삶에서 행복했었던 것처럼 보였다.
* 완료부정사가 쓰였으므로 that절에서 주절보다 한 시제 앞선 과거완료시제로 쓴다.

30 * (1)은 to부정사를 부정하는 의미이고, (2)는 decide를 부정하는 의미이다.

Sentence Writing

▶ 본문 106쪽

Part A
1 is explaining how to be careful
2 how to cooperate with one another
3 not to get hurt

Part B
1 Kelly has already decided how to spend the prize money.
2 Famous people find it difficult to have normal lives.
3 It seems that she is very sad.
4 Koreans must have a visa to visit North Korea.

Part **A**

1 과학 수업에서 선생님은 학생들이 과학실에서 실험을 할 때 얼마나 조심해야 할지를 설명하고 계신다.

2 어떤 약품은 피부를 다치게 할 수 있기 때문에 매우 위험할 수 있다. 그래서 학생들은 서로 어떻게 협력해야 하는지를 기억해야 한다.

3 학생들은 실험을 하는 동안 상처입지 않기 위해서 고글과 특수 장갑을 껴야 한다.

Unit 06 동명사

DAY 12 동명사의 용법, 시제, 능동과 수동

2교시 In - Class Questions ▶ 본문 111쪽

STEP A 1 주어 2 (전치사의) 목적어 3 (동사의) 목적어 4 보어
STEP B 1 playing 2 having learned 3 being selected
STEP C 1 loves my having studied well in my school days
2 is excited about having been taught a lot at the conference
3 is worried about her son losing his way
STEP D 1 like, playing 2 denied, having, bought

STEP A
1 도시에서는 차를 운전하는 것이 출퇴근을 위한 피할 수 없는 수단이다.
2 이 프로젝트를 끝내기 위한 다음 단계는 목표를 정하는 것이다.
3 너는 작년에 그 박물관에 갔다 온 것을 기억하니?
4 환경을 돕기 위한 한가지 작은 방법은 모든 캔과 병들을 재활용하는 것이다.

STEP B
1 Tom은 학교 연극에서 중요한 역할을 하는 것을 즐긴다.
2 Jack은 내가 어렸을 때 중국어를 배웠던 것을 알고 있다.
3 Austin은 반장으로 선출된 것을 자랑스러워했다.

3교시 After - Class Questions ▶ 본문 112 - 115쪽

01 ⑤ **02** ⑤ **03** ④ **04** ④ **05** ③ **06** My pants need hemming [to be hemmed]. **07** Children hate being treated like fools. **08** Downloading movies on the Internet is not as difficult as you think. **09** My mother is sure of my having broken the window. **10** ④ **11** ④ **12** ④ **13** (a) Giving (b) to improve **14** fixing **15** having gotten **16** ④ **17** ① **18** ⑤ **19** ⑤ **20** ③ **21** 대과거 **22** 현재 또는 미래 **23** 과거 **24** Taking advanced English grammar courses is hard. **25** having arrived

01 다양한 음식을 먹는 것은 ____________.
① 너를 건강하게 만든다 ② 좋은 몸매를 유지하게 도와줄 것이다
③ 너에게 많은 에너지를 준다 ④ 즉석 음식을 먹는 것보다 좋다
⑤ 나의 좋은 습관이 되는 것
* 동명사가 주어 역할을 하기 때문에 빈칸에는 동사구가 와야 한다.

02 관객들은 그들이 이 연극에 엄청난 노력을 쏟았다는 것을 안다.
* 전치사 of 뒤에는 동명사 목적어가 와야 하고, 주절의 시제가 현재(is)이고 that절의 시제가 과거(made)이므로 완료동명사(having + 과거분사)가 와야 한다.

03 William은 직업 고등학교에 다녔던 것에 대해 후회하지 않는다.
* 후회하지 않는 것이 현재이고 다녔던 것은 과거이므로 완료동명사가 와야 한다.

04 ① 몇 분 후면 비가 멈출 것 같아.
② 사람들은 신용카드를 사용하는 것에 익숙해졌다.
③ 그 음악가는 새로운 앨범을 발표하는 것을 포기했다.
④ 모든 사람들이 우리에게 작별인사도 없이 떠났다.
⑤ 나와 함께 그의 생일파티에 가는 게 어떠니?
* [say → saying] 전치사 without 뒤에는 동명사 목적어가 와야 한다.

05 * '자랑스러워하신다'는 현재이고, '3년 전에 승진되신 것'은 과거 수동태이므로 수동형 완료동명사로 표현한다.

06 * need는 동명사와 to부정사 모두를 목적어로 취하며, 수동의 의미를 나타낼 때는 능동형 동명사나 수동형 to부정사로 써야 한다.

07 * 아이들이 '취급받는' 것이므로 수동형 동명사로 나타낸다.

08 * 동명사 downloading이 주어 역할을 하는 문장으로 쓴다.

09 * 전치사 of의 목적어로 동명사가 와야 하며, 과거에 깨뜨린 것이므로 완료동명사를 써야 한다. 동명사의 의미상 주어는 소유격으로 쓴다.

10 A: 지난밤에 거실을 어지럽혀서 죄송해요.
B: 괜찮아. 하지만 다시는 그러지 말아라.
* 전치사 for의 목적어로 동명사가 와야 하고, '지난밤에 어질러 놓았던' 것이므로 완료동명사(having + 과거분사)가 와야 한다.

11 젊고 유명한 배우들은 그들이 요즘 가는 곳은 어디서든 그들을 알아보게 되는 것에 지쳐 있다.
* 전치사의 목적어로 동명사가 와야 하고, 동명사의 의미상 주어인 배우들이 '알아보게 되는' 것이므로 수동형 동명사가 와야 한다.

12 Danny는 아기의 울음 때문에 밤새 잠을 잘 수 없었다.
* 전치사의 목적어는 동명사가 와야 하고, 동명사의 의미상 주어는 소유격이 온다.

13 당신의 아이들에게 미국 학생들과 이야기할 많은 기회를 주는 것은 그들의 언어 능력을 향상시킬 수 있는 최고의 방법이다.
* (a) 문장의 주어 역할을 하는 동명사가 필요하다.
(b) '향상시키기 위한 방법'의 뜻이 되려면 형용사적 용법의 to부정사가 와야 한다.

14 그의 자전거는 수리될 필요가 있다.
* need, want 등의 동사 뒤에는 능동형 동명사가 와서 수동 의미를 나타낸다.

15 Andy는 그의 방 친구가 이전 시험에서 좋은 점수를 받았다는 것을 확신했다.
* 전치사 of의 목적어인 동명사는 의미상 주어인 his roommate가 '좋은 성적을 얻은' 것이므로 능동형 동명사가 와야 한다.

16 * 나의 아버지가 부끄럽게 여기는 것보다 공부를 하지 않은 것이 더 앞선 시제이므로 완료동명사(having + 과거분사)로 나타내며, 동명사의 부정은 not을 동명사 앞에 둔다.

17 ① Lucy는 그녀의 실수 때문에 부모님께 꾸중을 들은 것을 부끄러워했다.
② 그 작가는 많은 출판사에서 거절되었던 것을 인정했다.
③ Amy는 당신이 그녀의 음악과 가사를 듣는 것을 영원히 즐기기를 희망한다.
④ 그녀의 그림은 그녀의 성격을 나타내는 한가지 방법이다.
⑤ 한국의 대부분의 가수들은 그들 자신을 훈련하는 데 많은 시간을 보낸다.
* [scolding → being scolded] 부모님으로부터 Lucy가 '꾸중을 듣는' 수동 관계이므로 수동형 동명사가 와야 한다.

18 ① 당신을 방해한 것을 용서하세요. (당신을 방해해서 정말 죄송합니다.)
② 세미나에서 당신과 이야기한 것이 참 좋았습니다.
③ 너는 왜 이 프로그램을 설치하는 것을 제안하지 않았니?
④ Aaron의 행복은 믿을 만한 많은 친구를 갖는 것에 달려있다.
⑤ 음악축제에 참가하는 것은 잊지 못할 경험일 것이다.
* [Attend → Attending] 뒤에 동사 will be가 있으므로 밑줄 친 부분은 주어 역할을 하는 동명사가 와야 한다.

19 A: 이 음악 파일을 받는 게 어렵네.
B: 이봐, 음악을 공유하는 것은 음악을 듣는 좋은 방법이 아니야.
A: 진짜? 그런데 그게 가장 쉽고 빠른 방법이잖아.
B: 나는 네가 공유하는 것을 그만두고 파일이나 앨범을 살 것을 제안할게.
A: 알았어. 내가 그것을 공유했던 것에 대해 비난하지 마.
* [share → having shared] 전치사 on 다음에는 목적어로 동명사가 와야 하며, 문맥상 과거의 일을 말하므로 완료동명사가 와야 한다.

20 A: 왜 편의점의 계산원이 오직 현금으로만 지불되어야 한다고 주장하니?
B: 내 생각에는 신용카드 단말기가 그 당시에 고장 났던 것 같아.
* [paying → being paid] '계산원이 돈을 지불받는' 것이므로 수동형 동명사가 되어야 한다.

21 Ethan은 영어로 말을 하는 동안에 실수했던 것을 두려워했다.
* 완료동명사이므로 주절의 시제(과거)보다 앞선 시제이다.

22 영어로 말을 하는 동안에 실수하는 것에 대해서 부끄러워하지 마.
* 단순동명사이므로 주절의 시제와 같은 현재시제이거나 미래시제이다.

23 Alexander는 당신의 학생이었던 것을 자랑스럽게 여긴다.
* 완료동명사이므로 주절의 시제(현재)보다 앞선 시제이다.

24 상급 영어 문법 과정을 수강하는 것은 어렵다.

* 주어로 쓰인 to부정사는 동명사로 바꿔 쓸 수 있으며, 동명사는 가주어 구문으로 쓰지 않는다.

25 그녀가 며칠 전에 도착했을 가능성이 있다.
* several days ago는 과거를 나타내는 부사구이므로 완료동명사가 와야 한다.

DAY 13 동사에 따른 목적어의 형태, 관용표현

2교시 In - Class Questions ▶ 본문 117쪽

STEP A 1 to stay 2 checking 3 to learn, learning
STEP B 1 having 2 eating 3 buying and keeping
4 to deliver 혹은 delivering
STEP C 1 동 2 현 3 동 4 현
STEP D 1 finish drinking coffee
2 do not want to attract
3 promised to help

STEP A
1 몇몇 근로자들은 내년까지 이 회사에 머물러 있기를 택했다.
2 그 의사들은 저 서류들을 검토하는 것을 연기할 필요가 있다.
3 그녀의 남자 친구는 그의 대학에서 재즈댄스를 배우기 시작한다.

STEP B
1 전채 요리로 저는 닭 날개 튀김을 강력히 추천합니다.
2 우리는 또한 아이스크림을 4달러에 제공합니다. 당신은 그것을 먹지 않을 수 없을 거예요.
3 이 컵들은 사서 거실에 진열해 둘 가치가 있다.
4 안개 낀 날씨 때문에 그 트럭 운전사는 당신의 물건 배달을 계속할 수 없다.

STEP C
1 어린아이들은 정말로 망원경을 살 것 같다.
2 고속도로에서 과속하는 차들은 매우 위험하다.
3 엄마는 우리 세탁기가 어제 고장 난 것을 알고 계시니?
4 기자 몇 명이 광장에서 연설을 하는 여자를 만나고 싶어 한다.

3교시 After - Class Questions ▶ 본문 118 - 121쪽

01 ⑤ **02** We could not help buying the delicious food at the market. **03** Bella spent 4 hours playing with Edward. **04** ⑤ **05** shopping **06** to seeing **07** earning **08** are, busy, preparing **09** ① **10** ⑤ **11** ② **12** ③ **13** ② **14** ③ **15** worth, watching **16** no, use, trying **17** to bring **18** ④ **19** ④ **20** ② **21** ④ **22** ③ **23** me, from, going **24** ③ **25** couldn't, but, no, choice, but

01 (a) 나는 수능시험을 망치는 것을 상상할 수 없다.
(b) 나의 가족은 다음 달 뉴욕에 가는 것을 고려했다.
(c) 엄마는 아무것도 안 하시고 하루 쉬는 것을 바라셨다.
* (a) imagine, (b) consider는 동명사, (c) wish는 to부정사를 목적어로 취한다.

02 * '~하지 않을 수 없다'는 〈cannot help -ing〉로 표현한다.

03 * '~하는 데 …시간을 보내다'는 〈spend + 시간 + -ing〉로 표현한다.

04 Harry와 그의 여자 친구는 독특한 골동품 찻주전자 세트들을 모으는 것을 __________.
① 고려했다 ② 제안했다 ③ 연기했다 ④ 그만두었다 ⑤ 거절했다
* 목적어로 동명사(collecting)가 왔으므로 refuse가 들어갈 수 없다. refuse는 to부정사를 목적어로 취하는 동사이다.

05 대부분의 여자들은 쇼핑하러 가는 것을 좋아한다.
* 〈go -ing〉는 '~하러 가다'라는 뜻이다.

06 영화를 보는 게 어떠니?
* 〈What do you say to -ing?〉는 '~하는 게 어때?'라는 뜻이다.

07 아버지들은 종종 돈을 버는 것에 어려움을 겪는다.
* 〈have difficulty -ing〉는 '~하는 데 어려움을 겪다'라는 뜻이다.

08 * '~하느라 분주하다'는 〈be busy -ing〉로 나타낸다.

09 저 좀 도와주세요! 전 'Hamlet' 읽는 것을 잊었는데, 화요일까지 과제를 제출해야 해요.
* 〈forget + to부정사〉는 '~할 것을 잊다'라는 뜻이다.

10 대부분의 직장인들은 널리 알려진 회사에서 일하는 것을 선호하는 반면에, 대부분의 여성들은 다양한 분야에서 시간제로 일하는 것을 꺼리지 않는다.
* mind는 동명사를 목적어로 취하는 동사이다.

11 ① Willy는 쇼핑몰에서 춤추는 남자아이들을 보았다.
② 어린아이들이 적절한 결정을 하는 것은 정말로 중요하다.
③ 집에 가라, 그렇지 않으면 너는 방에서 자고 있는 아기를 깨울지도 모른다.
④ 당신은 고속도로를 달릴 때 과속하는 차를 조심해야 한다.
⑤ 대통령은 그 중요한 문제에 대해서 말하고 있는 여자를 만나고 싶어 한다.
* ②의 Making은 주어로 쓰인 동명사이고, 나머지는 현재분사이다.

12 ① 단 것을 먹지 않는 것은 아이들이 가져야 하는 중요한 습관이다.
② 내 취미 중 하나는 자석 스티커를 모으는 것이다.
③ Nancy는 재미있는 축구 경기를 보고 싶어 한다.
④ 우리는 너를 더 이상 못 보는 것에 대해서 유감이다.
⑤ 그는 회의에 참석하는 것을 미루지 않을 것이다.
* ③의 exciting은 뒤의 명사(soccer games)를 꾸며주는 현재분사이고, 나머지는 동명사로 쓰였다.

13 ① Rose는 스트레스를 너무 많이 받아서 계속해서 과식을 했다.
② 지역의 예술가들은 토요일에 워크숍을 개최하는 것을 고려하고 있다.
③ 방문객들에게 알려드립니다. 박물관은 20분 후에 문을 닫기 시작할 것입니다.
④ 어린아이들은 비행기에서 난기류를 경험하는 것을 좋아한다.
⑤ Mac은 환상과 현실의 차이를 이해하기 시작했다.
* consider는 동명사를 목적어로 취하는 동사이며, 나머지는 동명사와 to부정사 둘 다 목적어로 취하는 동사이다.

14 (a) 네가 원하면 두 창문 사이에 램프와 꽃병을 놓아 보세요.
(b) Kyle과 Sunny는 저녁을 많이 먹은 후에 아메리카노를 마시지 않을 수 없었다.
(c) Lucas는 집에서 잃어버린 돈을 찾는 것을 멈추고 잠시 앉았다.
(d) 많은 교사들은 가능한 한 많은 것을 가르치기를 희망한다.
* (c) 문맥상 '~하는 것을 멈추다'라는 의미이므로 stop 다음에 동명사가 왔다.
(d) hope는 to부정사를 목적어로 취한다.
(a) [to put → putting] 〈try + 동명사〉는 '시험 삼아 ~해보다', 〈try + to부정사〉는 '~하려고 노력하다'
(b) [to drink → drinking] 〈cannot help -ing〉는 '~하지 않을 수 없다'

15 * '~할 만한 가치가 있다'는 〈be worth -ing〉로 나타낸다.

16 * '~해도 소용없다'는 〈it is no use -ing〉로 나타낸다.

17 Terry는 그 경기에 자신의 공을 가져가는 것을 잊었다. 그래서 그는 그 경기에 참가할 자격을 박탈당했다.
* 〈forget + to부정사〉는 '~할 것을 잊다'라는 뜻이다.

18 Serena는 지난 주말에 네가 그녀의 친구들을 도와준 것을 고맙게 생각한다.
* 동사 appreciate는 동명사를 목적어로 취하며, 동명사의 의미상 주어는 소유격이 온다.

19 나는 내 첫 번째 휴대전화를 샀던 것을 여전히 기억한다.
* 문맥상 '(과거에) 샀던 것을 기억하다'는 의미이므로 〈remember + 동명사〉가 와야 한다. 〈remember + to부정사〉는 '(미래에) ~할 것을 기억하다'라는 의미이다.

20 잠깐 동안 쉬기 위하여 멈추자. 나는 정말로 피곤해.
* 내용상 '쉬기 위하여'라는 의미가 되어야 하므로 〈stop + to부정사〉가 와야 한다. 〈stop + 동명사〉는 '~하는 것을 멈추다'라는 의미이다.

21 영어를 가르치는 것에 관해서는 우리가 서울에서 최고의 교수 실력을 가지고 있다.
* 〈when it comes to -ing〉(~에 관해서는)로 나타낸다.

22 마침내 바티칸의 교황이 숨을 멈췄고, 모든 시민들은 큰 슬픔에 빠졌다.
* 문맥상 '~하는 것을 멈추다'라는 의미가 되어야 하므로 ⟨stop + 동명사⟩가 알맞다.

23 지금 밖에 비가 오고 있어. 나는 놀이공원으로 현장학습을 갈 수가 없어.
→ 비는 내가 놀이공원으로 현장학습을 가지 못하게 했다. (비 때문에 나는 놀이공원으로 현장학습을 가지 못했다.)
* ⟨stop + A + from -ing⟩는 '~가 …을 못하게 하다'라는 의미이다.

24 ① Helen은 밤에 혼자서 길을 걷는 것을 피한다.
② Diana는 그의 아들이 깊은 호수에 빠지는 것을 막았다.
③ Mary는 그녀의 폭력적인 남편을 이해하는 데 큰 문제가 있다.
④ Joshua는 식사가 끝날 때마다 약을 복용하는 것에 익숙하다.
⑤ 교실에 있는 학생들은 그들의 선생님이 교실에 들어왔을 때 말을 멈췄다.
* [understand → understanding] ⟨have trouble -ing⟩(~하는 데 어려움을 겪다)로 나타낸다.

25 Whitney는 그 재미있는 광경을 보고 웃지 않을 수 없었다.
* ⟨cannot help -ing⟩(~하지 않을 수 없다) = ⟨cannot but + 동사원형⟩ = ⟨have no choice but to + 동사원형⟩

Final Test

▶ 본문 122 - 125쪽

01 ③ **02** It is no use blaming them for stealing your money. **03** My parents hate my coming back home late. **04** ④ **05** ② **06** her having told us a lie **07** ④ **08** ④ **09** ② **10** ③ **11** ① **12** ② select → selecting **13** ④ **14** ④ **15** Her, coming **16** ③ **17** ⑤ **18** ② **19** ④ **20** ③ **21** start, to, starting, start **22** ②, ⑤ **23** Do you remember to book movie tickets for tomorrow? **24** We regret to inform you of this sad news. **25** Helen deceived her friends by not telling the truth. **26** ④ **27** ⑤ **28** ④ **29** ② **30** ③

01 A: Jack, 너의 도움이 필요해.
B: 뭔데요, 엄마?
A: 내가 쿠키를 굽고 있는데 계란이랑 설탕이 떨어졌어. 좀 사다줄 수 있니?
B: 물론이죠, 지금 갈게요.
A: Jack, 가격 체크하는 거 잊지 말고.
B: 네, 잊지 않을게요.
* 문맥상 '가격을 체크하는 것을 잊지 말라'는 의미이므로 ⟨forget + to부정사⟩의 형태가 되어야 한다.

02 * '~해도 소용이 없다'는 ⟨it is no use -ing⟩로 표현한다.

03 * hate는 동명사나 to부정사를 목적어로 취하지만 my는 동명사의 의미상 주어로 쓰이므로, hate 다음에 동명사를 목적어로 쓴다.

04 ① Sandy는 클래식 음악을 듣고 싶어 한다.
② 나의 아빠가 담배를 끊는 것은 매우 어렵다.
③ 우리는 너를 그곳에서 곧 볼 것을 당연히 기억할 것이다.
④ 어떻게 우리가 작년에 그들을 파리에서 만났던 것을 잊을 수 있겠니?
⑤ 내 아들은 그의 선생님들께 감사카드를 쓰려고 노력하는 중이다.
* [to meet → meeting] ⟨forget + to부정사⟩는 '(미래에) ~할 것을 잊다', ⟨forget + 동명사⟩는 '(과거에) ~했던 것을 잊다'는 표현이다. 과거를 나타내는 부사구 last year가 있으므로 동명사가 와야 한다.

05 ① 많은 관광객들은 입장료 내는 것을 반대한다.
② 그녀는 친구들을 위해 피자와 파스타를 만드는 것을 즐겼다.
③ 그 작가는 계약 때문에 시나리오 보내는 것을 연기했다.
④ Tim은 그의 여자 친구가 재정 문제를 갖고 있다는 것을 안다.
⑤ 증거가 있음에도 불구하고, 그 목격자는 발생했던 사건을 본 것을 부인했다.
* [her → 삭제] 동명사의 의미상 주어가 문장의 주어와 일치할 경우 생략한다.

06 우리는 그녀가 우리에게 거짓말을 했다고 확신한다.
* 주절의 시제가 현재이고 that절의 시제가 과거이므로 완료동명사(having + 과거분사)로 나타내야 한다. 주절과 that절의 주어가 다르므로 동명사 앞에 의미상 주어(her)를 써주어야 한다.

07 * ⟨look forward to -ing⟩(~을 학수고대하다)로 쓰이므로 빈칸에는 동명사가 와야 하며, 그녀가 '선택되는' 것이므로 수동형 동명사가 와야 한다.

08 나는 지난밤에 술 취한 후 나의 집으로 오게 된 사실을 기억할 수 없다.
* last night이라는 과거를 나타내는 말이 있으므로 동명사가 와야 하며, 문맥상 내가 '데려오게 된' 수동 관계이므로 수동형 동명사(being + 과거분사)가 와야 한다.

09 그 스마트폰은 당신의 주머니에 넣고 다닐 정도로 휴대가 간편하다.
* ⟨enough + to부정사⟩는 '~할 만큼 충분히 …한'이라는 의미이다.

10 그들이 다칠 기회는 거의 없었다.
* 전치사 of의 목적어로 동명사가 와야 하며, 의미상 그들이 '다치게 되는' 수동의 관계이므로 수동형 동명사가 와야 한다.

11 (a) 이 건물들의 주제는 자연 속에서 사는 것이다.
(b) 그 건축가들은 이 지역에 친환경 빌딩을 짓기로 결정했다.
* (a) be동사의 보어 자리에는 동명사와 to부정사 모두 올 수 있다. (b) decide는 to부정사를 목적어로 취한다.

12 요즘 모든 시민들은 5년마다 그들의 대통령을 뽑는 것에 익숙하다. 이것은 1987년까지는 허락되지 않았던 것이다.
* ⟨be used to -ing⟩는 '~하는 것에 익숙하다'라는 뜻이다.

13 **보기** Stewart는 모형 자동차를 조립하는 것을 좋아한다.
① 아무도 그녀가 영어를 말하는 것을 듣지 못했다.
② 저기 앉아 있는 여자는 누구니?
③ 봐! 저 잠자는 고양이가 내 고양이야.
④ 우리는 현장학습을 가기 시작했다.
⑤ 몇몇 사람들은 그 사건에 대하여 물어보고 있었다.
* ⟨보기⟩의 assembling은 동사 like의 목적어 역할을 하는 동명사이고, ④의 going도 동사 start의 목적어 역할을 하는 동명사이다. 나머지는 모두 현재분사이다.

14 **보기** 내 아들은 망원경을 찾는 중이다.
① 자고 있는 아기를 깨우지 마세요.
② 과속하는 차와 오토바이들은 매우 위험하다.
③ 우리는 부엌에서 케이크를 만들고 있는 그 여자아이를 만날 필요가 있다.
④ 내 생일 선물로 이 수영복을 주세요.
⑤ 너는 저 이상한 티셔츠를 입고 있는 남자와 이야기해본 적이 있니?
* ⟨보기⟩의 magnifying glasses는 동명사(glasses for magnifying)이고, ④의 this swimming suit도 동명사(this suit for swimming)이다. 나머지는 모두 현재분사이다.

15 * 주어 자리는 동명사가 와야 하며, 동명사의 의미상의 주어는 소유격으로 쓴다.

16 A: 너는 꿈이 뭐야?
B: 난 성공한 작곡가 겸 가수가 되는 것을 꿈꾸고 있어.
A: 와, 그럼 오디션에 참가하는 것을 시작했어?
B: 아직 하지 않았어. 난 나의 부모님께 혼날까봐 두려워.
A: 오, 알겠다. 나의 부모님도 내가 댄서가 되는 것을 반대하시거든.
B: 말도 안 돼. 그분들을 설득해 보는 건 어때? 넌 할 수 있어.
* [being scolding → being scolded] 내가 '야단을 맞는' 수동의 관계이므로 수동형 동명사가 와야 한다.

17 ① 너는 수영하는 법을 배우는 것을 시작하기 전에 수영복을 사야 한다.
② 너는 너의 부모가 원하는 것을 하는 것을 좋아하니?
③ 많은 직장인들은 그들이 할 수 있는 한 같은 자리에서 일하는 것을 선호한다.
④ 다른 무언가를 하는 대신에 이 프로젝트를 계속 진행합시다.
⑤ 오직 몇몇 아이들만이 미래에 대한 에세이를 쓰는 것을 끝냈다.
* [to write → writing] finish는 동명사를 목적어로 취한다.

18 ① Ellie는 일요일에도 일하는 것이 익숙했다.
② 항의하는 사람들은 미국산 쇠고기의 수입을 반대했다.
③ 그 점원들은 5시쯤이면 간식을 먹고 싶어 한다.
④ 나의 부모님은 지난 주말에 대부분의 시간을 골프를 치는 데 보내셨다.
⑤ 몇몇 학생들은 기말 프로젝트를 위한 포트폴리오를 만드느라 바쁘다.
* [import → importing] ⟨object to -ing⟩(~하는 것을 반대하다)로 나타낸다.

19 ① 제가 당신을 방해한 것을 용서하세요.
② 모두가 자신의 자동차를 갖는 꿈을 꾼다.
③ 나는 영어시험을 준비하는 데 3일을 보냈다.
④ 나의 아버지는 MP3 플레이어를 켬으로써 나를 깨웠다.
⑤ 나의 아내는 돈을 너무 많이 쓰는 것에 대해서 걱정한다.

* [turn → turning] 전치사 뒤에는 동명사가 와야 한다.

20 * 〈when it comes to -ing〉는 '~에 관해서는'이라는 뜻이다. 주어진 말을 바르게 배열하면 When it comes to studying English, listening to Ms. Choi's opinion is the best idea.이다.

21 당신의 건강을 위해 요가를 배우는 게 어때요?

* How about -ing? = Why don't you + 동사원형? = What do you say to -ing ? = Let's + 동사원형.

22 A: William이 자서전을 쓰고 싶어 하는 게 사실이야?
B: 응, 그것에 관해 들었어. 나는 그에게 하지 말라고 계속 설득하고 있어.
A: 넌 그럴 필요 없어. 내 생각에 그는 곧 글 쓰는 것을 포기할거야.
B: 왜?
A: 기억하지 못하니? 작년에 그는 그것에 관해 쓰기 시작했지만 결국 쓰는 것을 포기했어.

* ② [to persuade → persuading], ⑤ [to do → doing] keep과 give up은 동명사를 목적어로 취하는 동사이다.

23 * 동사 remember는 미래의 일을 나타낼 때 to부정사를 목적어로 취한다. 동명사가 오면 '(과거에) ~했던 것을 기억하다'라는 뜻이다.

24 * 동사 regret은 목적어로 to부정사와 동명사 모두 취하지만 뜻이 달라진다. 〈regret + to부정사〉는 '~하게 되어 유감이다', 〈regret + 동명사〉는 '~한 것을 후회하다'라는 뜻이다.

25 * 동사 deceive는 동명사를 목적어로 취하며, 동명사의 부정은 부정어를 동명사 앞에 둔다.

26 Sam은 공부를 열심히 하지 않았던 것을 후회한다.

* 문맥상 '~하지 않던 것을 후회하다'라는 의미가 되어야 하므로 〈regret + 동명사〉가 알맞으며, 주절과 종속절의 시제가 다르므로 완료동명사(having + 과거분사)가 와야 한다. 〈regret + to부정사〉는 '~하게 되어 유감이다'라는 의미이다.

27 Joe는 eBay에서 몇 권의 책을 주문했던 것을 부인했다.

* 완료동명사가 왔으므로 주절 동사의 시제(과거)보다 앞선 대과거(had + 과거분사)가 와야 한다.

28 (a) 소미는 그가 그녀의 부모님을 도와준 것을 고마워했다.
(b) 심지어 밤에도 아이의 울음소리 때문에 우리는 잠들 수 없다.

* (a) 동명사의 의미상 주어는 소유격이나 목적격으로 쓴다. (b) 문맥상 '아기의 울음소리'라는 의미가 알맞다.

29 ① 그 여자들은 벤치에 앉아서 떠들기 시작했다.
② 소라는 잃어버린 지갑을 찾았던 것을 기억했다.
→ 소라는 잃어버린 지갑을 찾을 것을 기억했다.
③ 나는 살 곳을 찾는 데 어려움을 겪었다.
④ 나는 첫 기차를 타기 위해서 일찍 일어났다.
⑤ 나는 미나와 같이 싸이의 콘서트에 가는 것을 좋아한다.

* remember는 목적어로 to부정사나 동명사가 올 때 의미가 달라진다. 〈remember + to부정사〉는 '(미래에) ~할 것을 기억하다', 〈remember + 동명사〉는 '(과거에) ~했던 것을 기억하다'라는 의미이다.

30 A: Juniper가 왜 버스 정거장을 지나쳤니?
B: 버스가 너무 붐벼서 내리기 힘들었어.

* 〈have a hard time -ing〉는 '~하는 데 어려움을 겪다'라는 의미이다.

Sentence Writing ▶ 본문 126쪽

Part A
1 writing down your name
2 checking the instructions
3 spending too much time on one question
4 trying to see what your friends are doing
5 double-checking all of your answers
6 cheating during the exam

Part B
1 It is no use fixing the computer. You'd better buy a new one.
2 Attending the rock concert is an unforgettable experience.
3 We can't understand his having been fired by the company.
4 If you feel sad, try to develop positive thoughts.

Part **A**

기말시험을 준비하는 방법

1. 먼저 이름을 쓰시오.
2. 주의사항을 검토하시오.
3. 한 문제에 너무 많은 시간을 보내지 마시오.
4. 친구들이 시험에서 하고 있는 것을 절대로 보지 마시오.
5. 정답을 두 번 검토하시오.
6. 시험 중 부정행위를 절대 하지 마시오.

기말시험을 준비할 때 다음 사항을 주의하시오.
1 당신의 이름을 쓰는 것을 미루지 마시오.
2 주의사항을 검토하기 전에 어떤 문제도 풀지 마시오.
3 한 문제에 너무 많은 시간을 보내는 것은 소용이 없습니다.
4 당신의 친구들이 하고 있는 것을 보려고 시간을 낭비하지 마시오.
5 당신의 답을 두 번 검토함으로써 부주의한 실수를 피하시오.
6 시험을 보는 동안에 부정행위를 하는 것은 쓸모없는 일입니다.

Unit 07  분사

DAY 14 분사, 분사구문

2교시 In - Class Questions ▶ 본문 131쪽

STEP **A** 1 touched 2 called 3 singing
STEP **B** 1 locked 2 used 3 cheating 4 burning
STEP **C** 1 If 2 Because 3 and 4 Though
STEP **D** 1 Knowing never → Never knowing
2 Be → Being

STEP **A**
1 Chanel은 그녀의 다리가 낯선 사람에 의해 만져지는 것을 느꼈다.
2 너는 그들의 이름이 불리는 것을 들었니?
3 모든 사람들은 무대에서 노래 부르는 남자를 볼 수 있었다.

STEP **C**
1 너는 왼쪽으로 돌면 친한 친구를 볼 수 있다.
2 Victor는 성적이 좋지 않았기 때문에 좋은 직업을 얻을 수 없었다.
3 James는 정오에 출발해서 저녁 6시쯤에 스웨덴에 도착했다.
4 그는 그 차 사고를 목격했음에도 불구하고 길에 다친 사람들을 도와주지 않았다.

STEP **D**
1 나는 가난한 사람들에게 무슨 말을 해야 할지 몰라서 침묵하고 있었다.
2 Frank와 Sophia는 젊지만 매우 사려 깊어서 어느 누구라도 도와줄 수 있다.

3교시 After - Class Questions ▶ 본문 132 - 135쪽

01 (1) boiled (2) Boiling **02** (1) fallen (2) falling **03** (1) closing (2) closed **04** ③ **05** ④ **06** ④ **07** ③ **08** ⑤ **09** seems satisfied with my presentation **10** Not eating all day **11** ① **12** ④ **13** ⑤ **14** ④ **15** stolen **16** excited **17** ⑤ **18** ④ **19** ③ **20** Studying **21** Being cooked **22** wearing **23** (1) watching TV (2) with the arms crossed **24** making people excited **25** Not working hard, you were fired.

01 (1) 나는 삶은 고구마를 좋아하지 않는다.
(2) 끓는 물은 위험하다.
* (1) '삶아진' 고구마이므로 과거분사, (2) '끓는' 물이므로 현재분사가 와야 한다.

02 (1) 그는 정원에서 낙엽을 쓸고 있다.
(2) 나는 공중에서 떨어지는 공을 잡을 준비를 하고 있다.
* (1) '떨어진' 잎(낙엽)이므로 과거분사, (2) '떨어지고 있는' 공이므로 현재분사가 와야 한다.

03 (1) 그는 회의에서 폐회사를 했다.
(2) 그들은 비밀회의에서 결정을 내렸다.
* (1) '끝내는' 말(폐회사)이므로 현재분사, (2) '제한된' 회의(비밀회의)이므로 과거분사가 와야 한다.

04 우리를 향해 손을 흔들고 있는 여자는 누구니?
* '손을 흔들고 있는'이라는 능동, 진행의 의미인 현재분사가 알맞다.

05 Tony와 Andy는 개들이 그들을 따라오도록 한 채로 한동안 산책을 했다.
* 〈with + (대)명사 + 분사〉에서 개들이 '따라가는' 능동의 관계이므로 현재분사가 와야 한다.

06 ① Emily는 자전거를 타고 있는 남자를 봤다.
② 우리는 그 짖고 있는 개를 만났을 때 무서웠다.
③ 빨간 셔츠를 입고 있는 남자는 나의 친구다.
④ 이 건물들은 버려진 채로 남아 있다.
⑤ 그 학생들은 그들의 선생님이 노래 부르는 것을 들었다.
* [deserting → deserted] '건물이 버려진' 수동의 관계이므로 과거분사가 와야 한다.

07 ① George Bush는 많은 미국인에게 공유되는 꿈을 갖고 있었다.
② 나의 아버지는 우리에게 그의 신발이 닦이도록 시켰다.
③ 화산 안의 움직이는 마그마는 많은 작은 지진을 야기한다.
④ Terry는 나쁜 성적 때문에 좌절하고 혼란스러울지도 모른다.
⑤ 선생님들은 십대들의 행동에 대해 매우 놀란다.
* [moved → moving] 문맥상 '움직이는 마그마'라는 능동을 의미하므로 현재분사가 와야 한다.

08 ① 나는 Tommy라고 불리는 소년을 알고 있다.
② 네 방의 깨진 창문을 봐.
③ 나는 Tolkin에 의해 쓰인 공상소설을 좋아한다.
④ 그녀는 눈으로 뒤덮인 산에 올랐다.
⑤ James는 그 화장실에서 울고 있는 아기를 보았다.
* [cried → crying] '아이가 울고 있는' 것이므로 진행과 능동의 뜻을 가진 현재분사가 와야 한다.

09 * '만족하게 되는' 감정을 받는 것이므로 과거분사로 표현한다.

10 * 분사구문의 부정은 분사 앞에 not을 둔다.

11 나는 학교에 늦었기 때문에 담임선생님께 꾸중을 들었다.
* 문맥상 '늦었기 때문에' 꾸중을 들은 것이므로 이유의 접속사 Since가 알맞다.

12 Lisa는 밝게 웃고 있지만 여전히 매우 슬프고 우울해 보였다.
* 문맥상 '밝게 웃고 있지만' 슬프고 우울해 보인 것이므로 양보의 접속사 Though가 알맞다.

13 나는 길을 걷고 있었을 때 너의 가족이 나의 부모님과 이야기하는 것을 보았다.
* 문맥상 '길을 걷고 있었을 때' 본 것이므로 시간의 접속사 When이 알맞다.

14 ① 그들은 영화를 보면서 팝콘과 콜라를 먹었다.
② Rocky 와 Jack은 이 파티에 참석한 후에 친한 친구가 되었다.
③ Rick은 잃어버린 고양이를 찾으면서 계속 울었다.
④ Lucas는 차로 여행을 할 때 두통으로 고생할지도 모른다.
⑤ Elisa는 바빴기 때문에 오랫동안 너와 연락할 수 없었다.
* [Traveled → Traveling] Lucas가 '여행을 하는' 것이므로 능동을 의미하는 현재분사가 되어야 한다.

15 Hathaway 부인은 값비싼 다이아몬드 반지를 도난당했다.
* 사역동사 have의 목적격 보어는 목적어와의 관계가 수동이면(반지가 도난당한 것) 과거분사를 쓴다.

16 이 에세이의 주인공은 봄이 가고 그녀가 좋아하는 계절인 여름이 다시 돌아오기 때문에 매우 신이 난다.
* 주인공이 '신이 난' 감정을 받았으므로 과거분사인 excited가 알맞다.

17 (a) 무대 위에서 노래를 하고 있는 소녀그룹은 내가 좋아하는 아이돌 그룹이다.
(b) 언덕 위의 파란색으로 칠해진 건물은 Julie의 집이다.
* (a) 소녀들이 '노래를 하는' 능동의 의미이므로 현재분사가 와야 한다.
(b) 건물이 파란색으로 '칠해진' 수동의 의미이므로 과거분사가 와야 한다.

18 '7번 방의 선물'은 매우 감동적인 영화이다. 그 영화는 모든 사람들을 감동받게 했다.
* 영화가 '감동을 주는' 것이므로 현재분사, 사람들이 '감동을 받은' 것이므로 과거분사가 와야 한다.

19 지난밤에 심각한 자동차 사고가 있었다. 다친 많은 사람들은 도심의 병원으로 이송되었고, 많은 차들도 또한 손상되었다.
* '다치게 된' 사람들이므로 과거분사, 차가 '손상된' 것이므로 과거분사가 와야 한다.

20 나는 이번 중간고사를 위해 열심히 공부했지만 영어 발표를 통과할 수 없었다.
* 분사구문의 주어와 시제가 주절과 같으므로 Studying이 알맞다.

21 너의 음식은 시간 부족으로 너무 빨리 요리되어서 맛이 없었다.
* 음식이 '요리되는' 것이므로 Being cooked가 알맞다.

22 울고 있는 한 아이가 운동장에 혼자 남겨졌다. 그는 검정색 셔츠를 입고 있었다.
→ 검정색 셔츠를 입고 있는 한 울고 있는 아이는 운동장에 혼자 남겨졌다.
* '검은 색 셔츠를 입고 있는 아이'이므로 wearing이 와야 한다.

23 (1) 나의 사랑스러운 아이들은 TV를 보면서 잠이 들었다.
(2) 나의 사랑스러운 아이들은 팔짱을 낀 채로 잠이 들었다.
* (1) 아이들이 'TV를 보면서'라는 의미이므로 현재분사가 있는 분사구문으로 쓴다.
(2) with를 사용하여 분사구문으로 나타낸다. 팔이 '껴지는' 것이므로 과거분사로 쓴다.

24 그 여름 축제가 마침내 시작되어 사람들을 신이 나게 했다.
* 접속사 and를 생략하고 동사 made는 현재분사로 바꾼다. 주어는 이미 생략되어 있다.

25 * 분사구문의 부정은 분사 앞에 not이 온다.

DAY 15 분사구문의 시제와 수동태

2교시 In - Class Questions

▶ 본문 137쪽

STEP A	1 Having joined 2 Having been born 3 Having finished 4 Having watched
STEP B	1 Not having 2 Having worked 3 Being told 4 Having met
STEP C	1 Having, arrived 2 Having, been, written 3 The, cup, having, been, made
STEP D	1 It, being 2 Speaking, of 3 Surprised

STEP A
1 그녀는 작년에 합창단에 가입했지만 연습을 하지 않았다.
2 나는 캐나다에서 태어났기 때문에 영어를 잘한다.
3 그는 일을 다 마쳤기 때문에 쇼핑을 가고 있다.
4 그 소년은 밤늦게까지 TV를 봤기 때문에 숙제를 하지 않고 학교에 갔다.

STEP B
1 그 남자아이는 그 장난감을 가지고 있지 않으므로 그것을 사고 싶어 한다.
2 그는 밖에서 온종일 일했기 때문에 피부색이 매우 어둡다.
3 우리는 그 뉴스를 들었을 때 매우 놀랐다.
4 나는 전에 그들을 만난 적이 있기 때문에 그들과 쉽게 어울릴 수 있었다.

3교시 After - Class Questions ▶ 본문 138 - 141쪽

01 ③ **02** ② **03** ③ **04** ① **05** ①, ⑤ **06** Having seen the movie **07** ② **08** ⑤ **09** ③ **10** Having researched **11** Having been written **12** I having paid **13** It having snowed **14** ③ **15** ③ **16** ② **17** Not having worked very hard, Minju missed a chance to be promoted. **18** (Being) Left alone, the little girl began to get scared. **19** The due date for the books having passed, I paid the late fee. **20** ③ **21** ⑤ **22** having published → having been published **23** Having not understand → Not understanding **24** ④ **25** ③

01 그는 숙제를 끝낸 후에 내일 일찍 일어나기 위해 일찍 잠자리에 들었다.

* 주절의 시제보다 종속절의 시제가 앞서 있으므로 완료분사구문(having + 과거분사)이 와야 한다.

02 솔직히 말하면, 나의 언니와 나는 집에서 엄마를 도와드리는 것을 잘하지 못한다.

① ~와 비교하면, ③ ~로 판단하건데, ④ 만약 ~라면, ⑤ ~을 고려하면

* 독립분사구문 frankly speaking은 '솔직히 말하면'이라는 의미이다.

03 경찰관과 CSI는 연락을 받지 못했기 때문에 너무 늦게 도착해서 범인을 잡고 목격자를 확보할 수 없었다.

* 주절의 시제보다 종속절의 시제가 앞서 있고 주어와의 관계가 수동이므로 완료수동태 분사구문(having been + 과거분사)이 알맞다. 의미가 부정이므로 분사 앞에 not이 와야 한다.

04 Terry는 집에 혼자 있어서 재미있는 TV 프로그램을 보고 컴퓨터게임을 할 수 있었다.

* 수동태 분사구문 ⟨being + 과거분사⟩에서 being은 생략할 수 있다.

05 Ellen과 그의 부모님은 그 자동차 사고에서 부상을 당했기 때문에, 그 비행기를 탈 수 없었다.

* 종속절의 시제가 주절의 시제보다 앞서 있으므로 완료분사구문(having + 과거분사)으로 써야 한다. 완료수동태 분사구문에서 having been은 생략할 수 있다.

06 * 종속절의 시제가 주절의 시제보다 앞서 있으므로 완료분사구문으로 표현한다.

07 ① ~에 대해 말하자면, ③ ~에 대해 말하자면, ④ 만약 ~하면, ⑤ 가령 ~라고 하더라도

* 비인칭 독립분사구문에서 '~을 고려하면'은 considering that이다.

08 (a) 저 잡지들은 영어로 쓰였지만 읽기 쉽다.

(b) 민지는 한국에서 태어났기 때문에 한국말을 잘한다.

* (a) 주절과 종속절의 시제가 같고 수동태이므로 단순수동태 분사구문이 와야 한다. 이때 being은 생략 가능하다.
(b) 종속절의 시제가 주절의 시제보다 앞서 있고 수동태이므로 완료수동태 분사구문이 와야 한다. 이때 having been은 생략 가능하다.

09 당신은 기대를 많이 하고 뮤지컬을 볼 때 매우 실망한 경험이 있을 것이다. 그 예가 하나 있다. 당신의 지인들이 새 뮤지컬을 본 후에 당신에게 그것은 재미있을 뿐만 아니라 꼭 봐야 할 공연이라고 당신에게 말한다. 하지만 사실 그것은 개인의 선호에 달려있다.

* [Having been watched → Having watched] 종속절의 시제가 주절보다 한 시제 앞서고 능동의 의미이므로 완료분사구문이 와야 한다.

10 Jonathan은 밤새도록 새로 출판된 잡지들을 연구했기 때문에 강의 내내 엄청나게 피곤하다.

* all night는 과거시점을 나타내는 말이므로 완료분사구문으로 나타내야 한다.

11 성경은 아주 오래전에 쓰였음에도 불구하고 꽤 믿을 수 있는 것으로 여겨진다.

* ago는 과거시점을 나타내는 말이므로 완료분사구문으로 나타내며, 주절의 주어가 성경책이므로 '쓰여야' 하는 수동태이므로 수동완료 분사구문으로 나타내야 한다.

12 나는 부모님을 위해 매우 많은 돈을 냈지만 부모님은 그때 그 식당의 음식이 정말로 별로였다고 말씀하셨다.

* 부모님을 위해 돈을 낸 것이 '나'이고, 주절의 주어는 they이므로 분사구문의 주어를 써주어야 한다. 주절의 at that time으로 보아 돈을 냈던 것이 과거시점의 행위이므로 완료분사구문으로 나타내야 한다.

13 지난밤에 눈이 많이 내렸기 때문에 도로가 많이 미끄럽다. 그래서 그 도시는 염화칼슘을 도로에 뿌리기로 결정했다.

* '눈이 온다'의 주어는 비인칭주어 it을 사용해야 하는데 주절의 주어(the roads)와 주어가 다르므로, 분사구문의 주어 it을 생략해서는 안 된다. last night는 과거시점을 나타내는 말이므로 완료분사구문으로 나타내야 한다.

14 너는 새로운 아파트 계약서에 사인을 할 때 모든 조항들을 꼼꼼하게 살펴보았어야 했는데, 그것이 너의 큰 실수였다.

* 주절과 종속절의 주어와 시제가 같으므로 단순분사구문으로 나타내야 한다.

15 할머니가 지난밤에 차 사고를 당하셨지만, 지난달에 할아버지가 차사고로 돌아가셨기 때문에 지금까지 아무도 엄마에게 이 소식을 말할 엄두를 내지 못하고 있다.

* 부사절의 주어(Grandma)와 주절의 주어(no one)가 다르므로 부사절의 주어를 생략할 수 없다. 부사절이 주절보다 앞선 시제이고 사고를 '당한' 수동태이므로 완료수동태 분사구문으로 나타내야 한다.

16 ① 나는 춤추는 것에 관심이 있기 때문에 오디션에 참가할 것이다.

② 나는 한문을 많이 배웠기 때문에 중국어 공부를 쉽게 할 수 있다.

③ 그 음식은 내가 요리를 했지만 맛있다.

④ 그녀는 어리지만 이 프로젝트를 감당할 수 있다.

⑤ 나는 TV를 보는 동안 잠이 들었다.

* 수동태에 쓰인 being, having been은 생략이 가능하지만 완료분사구문의 having은 생략할 수 없다. ④는 분사구문의 뜻을 명확하게 하기 위해 접속사를 쓴 것이므로 생략할 수 있고, ⑤는 생략을 해도 분사구문 형태로 남아있다.

17 민주는 매우 열심히 일하지 않았으므로 승진될 수 있는 기회를 놓쳤다.

* 종속절과 주절의 시제가 다르므로 완료분사구문으로 나타낸다.

18 한 어린 소녀는 혼자 남겨졌을 때 두려워하기 시작했다.

* 종속절과 주절의 주어와 시제가 일치하므로 접속사를 없애고 ⟨Being + 과거분사⟩로 나타낸다. 이때 Being은 생략 가능하다.

19 나는 책 반납 기한을 넘겨버렸기 때문에 연체료를 냈다.

* 종속절과 주절의 주어가 다르므로 종속절의 주어를 생략할 수 없고, 종속절의 시제가 주절의 시제보다 앞서 있으므로 완료분사구문으로 나타낸다.

20 Jack은 그의 과제를 끝낸 후에 컴퓨터게임을 하기 위해 인터넷 카페에 갔다.

* 종속절과 주절의 주어는 같으나 주절의 시제보다 종속절의 시제가 앞서 있으므로 완료분사구문이 와야 한다.

21 Sunny는 그녀의 수업이 끝났을 때 아르바이트를 하러 갔다.

* 주절과 종속절의 시제는 같지만 주어가 다르므로 종속절의 주어를 생략할 수 없다.

22 그의 소설은 출판되지 않았지만 인터넷을 통해 점점 더 유명해지고 있다.

* 분사구문의 주어인 his novel이 '출판되는' 것이므로 완료수동태 분사구문이 되어야 한다.

23 Hannah는 영어를 이해하지 못했지만 외국인 친구들과 의사소통을 하기 위해 노력했다.

* 종속절의 시제와 주절의 시제가 같으므로 단순분사구문이 되어야 하며, 부정어는 분사 앞에 와야 한다.

24 ① 엄밀하게 말하자면 그 답은 옳지 않다.

② 나는 길을 내려올 때 나의 전 여자 친구를 보았다.

③ 나는 일본에서 만든 최신 카메라를 샀다.

④ 그녀의 여행 이야기가 나와서 말인데 너는 하와이에 가본 적이 있니?

⑤ Adam은 티켓이 없어서 콘서트 장에 들어갈 수 없었다.

* ① [spoken → speaking] 비인칭 독립분사구문으로 strictly speaking은 관용적으로 쓰이는 표현이다.
② [Walked → Walking] 주어인 내가 '걷는' 것이므로 단순분사구문이 와야 한다. ③ [making → made] 카메라가 '만들어지는' 것이므로 과거분사가 와야 한다. ⑤ [Having not → Not having] 부정어는 분사 앞에 위치한다.

25 ① Alice는 눈을 감은 채 소파에 누워있었다.

② 나는 그녀의 생일파티에 초대되어서 매우 기뻤다.

③ 네가 틀렸다면 넌 어떻게 하겠니?

④ 나는 하루 일과를 끝낸 후 커피 한 잔을 마시기 위해 자리에 앉았다.

⑤ 30분 전에 일어난 자동차 사고는 아직도 교통 흐름을 방해하고 있다.

* ① [closing → closed] ⟨with + 목적어 + 분사⟩에서 '눈이 감긴' 것이므로 과거분사가 와야 한다. ② [Inviting → Invited] 분사구문의 주어인 내가 '초대된' 것이므로 단순수동태 분사구문이 와야 한다. ④ [finished → finishing] 분사구문의 주어인 내가 '끝내는' 것이므로 단순분사구문이 와야 한다. ⑤ [happened → having happened] 주절의 시제보다 종속절의 시제가 앞서 있으므로 완료분사구문이 와야 한다.

Final Test ▶ 본문 142 - 145쪽

01 (1) held (2) shaking **02** ⑤ **03** ③ **04** ④ **05** ① **06** ③ **07** ③ **08** ⑤ **09** ④ **10** Generally speaking **11** aging **12** ②, ③ **13** ④ **14** ④ **15** (1) ①, ④, ⑥, ⑦, ⑨, ⑩ (2) ②, ③, ⑤, ⑧ **16** ① **17** ⑤ **18** as they are wearing clothes **19** ③ **20** (Being) Written in a hurry **21** I putting up green wallpaper **22** ④ **23** ① **24** (1) If you don't want to surprise your mom, you had better not tell the truth. (2) Not wanting to surprise your mom, you had better not tell the truth. **25** (Having been) fed spicy food, a baby gets a stomachache. **26** (1) (Being) interested (2) interesting **27** ④ **28** ① **29** ② **30** ①

01 (1) Lily와 그녀의 여동생은 손을 꼭 쥔 채로 기도를 하는 중이었다.
(2) Bruce는 다리를 떨면서 의자에 앉아 있었다.
* '~을 …한 채'를 뜻하는 〈with + 명사 + 분사〉 구문에서, (1) 그들의 손이 '쥐어진' 수동 관계이므로 과거분사가 와야 한다. (2) 그의 다리가 '떠는' 능동 관계이므로 현재분사가 와야 한다.

02 Paul은 그 사고에 놀라서 그의 친구 중 한 명에게 전화를 걸었다.
* [is → was 혹은 had been] 주절의 시제가 과거이므로 종속절의 시제도 과거나 과거완료가 와야 한다. ③⑤의 As는 접속사의 의미를 명확하게 하기 위해 분사구문에 남길 수 있다.

03 어머니는 점심을 준비하실 때 왜 자신이 아이들을 위해 점심을 준비해야 하는지 생각했다.
* 문맥상 시간을 나타내는 접속사가 알맞다.

04 Emliy는 전에 코끼리를 타본 적이 없어서 그녀의 친구에게 어떻게 타는지 가르쳐줄 수 없다.
* 분사의 부정은 부정어를 분사 앞에 둔다. 종속절의 시제가 주절의 시제보다 앞서 있으므로 완료분사구문으로 나타내야 한다.

05 ① 빈방이 없어서 우리는 여기서 잘 수 없다.
② Jonathan은 15살밖에 안 되었기 때문에 이 영화를 볼 수 없다.
③ 내 경험으로 판단하건데, 그녀는 매우 늦을 것이다.
④ 너는 많은 시간을 낭비했기 때문에 이 입학시험에 통과할 수 없었다.
⑤ 아름다운 햇살이 비치는 날임에도 불구하고 Sam은 나가지 않고 집에 머물러 있었다.
* [Being → There being] 주절의 주어(we)와 종속절의 주어(there)가 다르므로 분사 앞에 주어가 있어야 한다.

06 ① 나는 요즘 학생들에게 많이 속아서 더 이상 그들을 믿을 수 없다.
② 나는 국가시험에 열 번 떨어졌지만 마침내 붙었다.
③ 나는 Vanessa를 전에 본 적이 있어서 즉시 그녀를 알아보았다.
④ 이 책들은 매우 자주 읽히지 않아서 먼지로 덮여있다.
⑤ Maria는 이 정보를 미리 검토했기 때문에 몇몇 문제들을 다루는 방법을 알고 있다.
* [Having been seen → Having seen] 내가 '그녀를 본' 능동 관계이고, 종속절의 시제가 주절의 시제보다 앞선 일이므로 완료분사구문이 와야 한다.

07 * 분사구문에 접속사는 의미를 명확히 하기 위해 생략하지 않고 쓸 수 있다. 주절과 종속절의 시제가 같으므로 단순분사구문으로 나타낸다.

08 * 주절의 주어와 종속절의 주어가 다르므로 종속절의 주어인 비인칭주어 It을 생략하지 말아야 한다. 주절과 종속절의 시제가 같으므로 단순분사구문으로 나타낸다.

09 내 차가 고장 났기 때문에 나는 버스로 출퇴근해야 했다.
* 주절과 종속절의 주어가 다르므로 종속절의 주어인 my car는 생략할 수 없다. 종속절의 시제가 주절의 시제보다 앞서 있으므로 완료분사구문으로 나타내야 한다.

10 * '일반적으로 말하면'은 비인칭 독립분사구문인 generally speaking으로 나타낸다.

11 우리가 이 약을 복용할 때, 그것은 바이러스를 죽이고 노화 세포를 변화시키며 암세포들까지도 파괴할 수 있다.
* 세포가 '노화하는' 것이므로 현재분사로 나타내야 한다.

12 ① 물이 가득 찬 잔이 두 개 있다.
② 그들은 영어로 쓰인 메뉴를 보고 있다.
③ 그는 그녀의 얼굴을 보게 되어 매우 당황스러웠다.
④ 빨간색 드레스를 입고 있는 여자는 Kevin의 엄마이다.
⑤ '7번방의 선물'은 매우 흥미롭고 감동적인 영화이다.
* ② [wrote → written] 메뉴가 '쓰인' 수동의 의미이므로 과거분사가 와야 한다.
③ [embarrassing → embarrassed] 사람이 주어로 올 때는 '감정을 받는' 수동의 의미이므로 과거분사가 와야 한다.

13 ① 나는 길에서 노래하는 여자아이 한 명을 보았다.
② 나는 공원에 앉아 있는 내 친구를 만났다.
③ 정원에 서 있는 오래된 나무 한 그루가 있다.
④ 한국에서 만들어진 좋은 차들이 많다.
⑤ 자판기 앞에 개 한 마리를 안고 있는 그 여자아이는 Jane이다.
* [making → made] 차가 '만들어진' 수동의 의미이므로 과거분사로 써야 한다.

14 ① 나는 그의 개와 같이 걷고 있는 남자를 알고 있다.
② 그가 그 일을 하기에 적합하다면 그는 고용되어야 한다.
③ 은행 옆에는 부서진 건물이 있다.
④ 나는 충분한 시간이 없었기 때문에 버스 대신에 택시를 타야 했다.
⑤ 네가 그에게 한 일을 인정하더라도 나는 아직 너를 용서할 수가 없다.
* ① [walk → walking] '걷고 있는 남자'로 walk가 man을 수식해야 하므로 현재분사가 와야 한다.
② [Qualifying → (Being) Qualified] 분사구문의 주어가 he이므로 '~에 적합하게 된'이라는 뜻의 수동태 분사구문이 와야 한다.
③ [destroying → destroyed] '무너진' 건물이라는 수동의 의미이므로 과거분사가 와야 한다.
⑤ [Admitted → Admitting] 분사구문의 주어가 I이므로 '~를 인정하는' 의미의 단순분사구문이 와야 한다.

15 ① 그는 축구하는 걸 좋아한다.
② 저 떠오르는 태양을 봐.
③ 그는 기다리고 있던 택시를 탔다.
④ 우리는 새 세탁기를 한 대 샀다.
⑤ 벤치에서 자고 있는 남자 한 명이 있다.
⑥ 너는 대기실에서 그를 만날 수 있다.
⑦ 나는 야영을 하러 가기 위해서 침낭이 필요하다.
⑧ 네가 나에게 전화했을 때 나는 부엌에서 요리를 하고 있었다.
⑨ 우리는 겨울에 이 야외 수영장을 쓰지 않아요.
⑩ 여기서 담배 피우시면 안 됩니다. 저쪽의 흡연실을 이용해 주세요.
* 진행시제로 쓰이거나 진행 · 능동의 의미를 나타낼 때는 현재분사이고, 문장에서 명사 역할을 하거나 목적 · 용도의 의미를 나타낼 때는 동명사이다.

16 그는 그 과정들을 끝내지 못했기 때문에 그의 대학교로부터 석사학위를 받지 못했다.
* [Having not → Not having] 부정어는 분사 앞에 위치해야 한다.

17 ① 내 여동생의 가방은 도난당했다.
② 우리는 사람들이 무대에서 춤추는 것을 봤다.
③ Sandy는 머리를 자르도록 했다.
④ 그의 행동으로 판단컨대, 그는 좋은 사람이 아니다.
⑤ 부러진 팔은 깁스를 해야 한다.
* ① [stole → stolen], ② [danced → dance 혹은 dancing], ③ [cutting → cut], ④ [From judging → Judging from]

18 많은 십대들은 거울을 보면서 옷을 입는다.
* 동시동작을 나타내므로 접속사는 as로 쓰며, 단순분사구문이므로 주절과 같은 시제로 바꾼다. 문맥상 현재진행시제가 알맞다.

19 나는 비록 잠을 많이 자지는 않았지만 회의에 참석하는 동안 매우 생기 있어 보였다.
* 문맥상 '비록 잠을 많이 자지 못했지만'이 알맞다. 양보를 나타내는 접속사에는 even though, though, even if 등이 있으며, 단순분사구문이므로 주절과 같은 과거시제가 와야 한다.

20 너의 책은 급하게 쓰인다면 많은 오류들이 있을 것이다.
* 부사절과 주절의 주어와 시제가 같으므로 주어를 생략한 단순수동태 분사구문으로 나타낸다. 이때 Being은 생략할 수 있다.

21 내가 벽을 녹색으로 도배하는 동안 나의 아내는 다락방을 청소했다.
* 주절과 부사절의 시제가 같으므로 단순분사구문으로 나타낸다. 주절과 부사절의 주어가 다르므로 종속절의 주어는 생략할 수 없다.

22 (a) Keilen은 많은 나라를 여행했기 때문에 집에 많은 이국적인 기념품을 가지고 있다.
(b) 사람들은 자주 그들의 삶이 지겹다고 느낀다.
* (a) 여행을 한 것은 과거이므로 완료분사구문이 와야 한다.
(b) 삶이 '지루한' 능동 관계이므로 현재분사가 와야 한다.

23 (a) 솔직히 말하자면, 너는 이 그룹 일을 할 정도로 도움이 되지 않는다.
(b) 미나는 그녀의 다리를 꼰 채로 교실에 앉아있었다.
* (a) 문맥상 '솔직히 말하자면, 도움이 안 된다'라는 의미가 알맞다.
(b) 〈with + 명사 +분사〉에서 다리가 '교차되는' 것이므로 과거분사가 와야 한다.

24 * (1) 부사절은 조건을 나타내는 접속사 if를 이용하고, 주절과 시제가 같은 현재시제로 나타낸다.
(2) 부사절과 주절의 주어와 시제가 같으므로 단순분사구문으로 나타낸다. 부정어는 분사 앞에 위치한다.

25 * 분사구문의 주어 a baby가 '먹게 된' 수동태이며, 주절의 시제보다 앞서 있으므로 완료수동태 분사구문(having been + 과거분사)으로 나타내야 한다. 이 때 having been은 생략할 수 있다.

26 (1) 우리는 그림에 관심이 있기 때문에 박물관을 방문할 계획을 한다.
(2) 박물관에서 우리는 많은 흥미로운 그림들을 봤다.
* (1) 분사구문의 주어인 우리가 '관심을 갖게 된' 것이므로 단순수동태 분사구문이 와야 한다.
(2) 그림이 '흥미로운' 것이므로 현재분사가 와야 한다.

27 Alice는 부상을 당했기 때문에 결혼식에 갈 수 없었다.
* 문맥상 이유를 의미하는 Because절로 바꿀 수 있다.

28 내 차가 ____________ 나는 고객과의 중요한 약속에 늦었다.
① 연착해서 ② 늦게 도착해서 ③ 고장 나서 ④ 연착해서 ⑤ 복잡해서
* [having delayed → having been delayed] 주절보다 앞선 시제로 완료형이 올 수 있지만 the subway와 수동 관계이므로 완료수동태 분사구문이 되어야 한다.

29 매우 많은 나무와 꽃이 정원을 ____________ 그곳은 아름다워 보인다.
① 채우고 있어서 ② 뒤덮고 있어서 ③ 밝히고 있어서
④ 주변에 있어서 ⑤ 둘러싸고 있어서
* [covered → covering] 주어 trees and flowers가 '덮고 있는' 능동 관계이므로 현재분사가 와야 한다.

30 안경은 잘 맞춰졌을 때 대부분의 시력 결함을 교정할 수 있다.
* 주절과 종속절의 주어와 시제가 같고 안경이 '맞춰지는' 수동의 의미이므로 단순수동태 분사구문이 와야 한다. 분사구문의 접속사는 의미를 명확하게 하기 위해 생략하지 않고 맨 앞에 쓸 수 있다.

Sentence Writing

▶ 본문 146쪽

Part A
1 Released 2 having been recorded
3 Earning 4 Listening to

Part B
1 Some children can feel isolated from their friends.
2 Being tired, Lucy went to bed earlier than usual.
3 Judging from his accent, he must be an Englishman.

Part A

빌보드 차트를 보면, 'Hey, Jude'는 1960년대에 가장 인기 있는 음악이었다.

1 1968년에 발표되었을 때, 그것은 거의 9주 동안 빌보드 차트에서 정상의 자리를 차지했다.

2 'Hey, Jude'는 1960년대에 가장 인기 있는 노래 중 하나로서 기록된 후 작곡가인 Paul McCartney는 유명해졌다.

3 그는 매우 많은 돈을 벌었지만 부모님의 이혼 때문에 매우 우울하고 외로웠다.

4 그 노래를 들어보면, 사람들은 그가 얼마만큼 우리에게 희망의 메시지를 전달하고 싶었는지 느낄 수 있다.

Unit 08 비교

DAY 16 비교급, 최상급

2교시 In - Class Questions

▶ 본문 151쪽

STEP A 1 better, better 2 the, highest 3 expensive

STEP B 1 among, of 2 in 3 could 4 much

STEP C
1 The, older, the, worse
2 one, the, tallest, animals
3 less, intelligent, than
4 far, larger, than, that

STEP D
1 Diamond is harder than any other material.
2 The legs of this table are longer than those of that table.
3 The weather is getting warmer and warmer.

STEP A
1 너의 영어는 점점 더 좋아지고 있다.
2 에베레스트 산은 세계에서 가장 높은 산이다.
3 나의 재킷은 너의 것보다 두 배 더 비싸다.

STEP B
1 Chris는 우리 중에서 가장 똑똑하다.
2 오늘은 내 인생에서 가장 행복한 날이다.
3 나는 가능한 한 빨리 달렸다.
4 Sean은 가난하지 않다. 그는 Tom만큼의 돈을 가지고 있다.

Final Test

▶ 본문 152 - 155쪽

01 ① **02** ③ **03** ② **04** ⑤ **05** ④ **06** ① **07** ④ **08** (1) nicest (2) more honest **09** ③ **10** ④ **11** the, fourth, highest, score **12** The, earlier, the, longer **13** he, could **14** less, than **15** yours → that of yours **16** ④, ⑤ **17** ⑤ **18** (1) fluently (2) the taller (3) less **19** ⑤ **20** ②, ⑤ **21** ⑤ **22** The, harder, the, better **23** ④ **24** ④ **25** ⑤ **26** Jason is three years senior to I. **27** hardest **28** ④ **29** ① **30** ⑤

01 그의 첫 번째 영화는 두 번째 영화만큼 성공적이지는 않았다.
* 〈not as + 원급 + as〉의 원급비교 표현이므로 successful이 와야 한다. 문장 구조상 보어가 필요한 자리이므로 형용사가 와야 한다.

02 이 제품은 경쟁사의 것보다 기술상 열등하다.
* 라틴 비교급은 than 대신에 to를 쓴다.

03 대한민국의 인구는 너의 나라의 인구보다 두 배 많다.
* 원급비교에서 배수사의 위치는 첫 번째 as 앞이다. 즉, 〈배수사 + as + 원급 + as〉의 어순이다.

04 저 학생들이 가능한 빨리 그 결과를 알게 해주세요.
* 〈as soon as possible〉 = 〈as soon as + 주어 + can〉 '가능한 한 ~하게'

05 ① Monica는 뚱뚱하기보다는 과체중이다.
② 홍 선생님은 다른 멤버들보다 더 월등하다.
③ 그녀의 병은 내가 생각했던 것만큼 심각하지는 않다.
④ 너의 집 크기는 나의 집 크기보다 훨씬 더 크다.
⑤ 지나는 수영이보다 덜 현명하고 덜 똑똑하다.
* [very → much] very는 비교급 강조할 수 없다. much 이외에 even, far, still, a lot 등을 쓸 수 있다.

06 ① 나의 조건은 그의 조건보다 더 나쁘다.
② 미나는 그녀의 아버지보다 훨씬 더 키가 크다.
③ 그 말은 모든 말 중에서 가장 빠른 말이다.
④ 이 가방은 저 가방보다 훨씬 더 무겁다.

⑤ 그녀의 춤은 그녀의 노래보다 훨씬 더 인기가 있다.
* [more → 삭제] worse는 bad의 비교급이므로 more를 삭제해야 한다.

07 ① 바티칸 시국은 세계에서 가장 작은 나라이다.
② 세계의 어떤 나라도 바티칸 시국보다 작지 않다.
③ 세계의 어떤 나라도 바티칸 시국만큼 작지 않다.
④ 바티칸 시국은 세계의 다른 어떤 나라만큼 작지 않다.
⑤ 바티칸 시국은 세계의 다른 어떤 나라보다 더 작다.
* ④를 제외한 문장은 최상급의 의미이다.

08 (1) 현민이는 그의 반에서 세 번째로 좋은 학생이다.
(2) 그들의 친구 Luna는 Jen보다 훨씬 더 정직하다.
* (1) 앞에 third가 있으므로 '세 번째로 좋은'이라는 의미가 되어야 하고, 뒤에 장소를 나타내는 in his class가 있으므로 최상급이 와야 한다.
(2) 비교급을 강조하는 부사인 still이 있고 뒤에 than이 있으므로 비교급이 와야 한다.

09 * '~할수록 더 …한'은 〈the + 비교급 ~, the + 비교급 ...〉 구문으로 나타낸다.

10 A: 누가 네 팀에서 ____________ 선수이니?
① 가장 똑똑한 ② 최고의 ③ 가장 빠른 ⑤ 가장 멋진
B: 내 생각에 Blair가 ____________.
① 가장 똑똑하다 ② 최고다 ③ 가장 빠르다 ⑤ 가장 멋지다
* difficult의 최상급은 most difficult이고, 이 문장에서는 문맥상 알맞지 않다.

11 * '~번째로 가장 …한'은 〈the + 배수사(서수) + 최상급〉으로 나타낸다.

12 * 〈the + 비교급 ~, the + 비교급 ...〉 구문이다. early의 비교급은 earlier, long의 비교급은 longer이다.

13 Brian은 가능한 한 크게 나에게 소리쳤다.
* 〈as + 원급 + as possible〉 = 〈as +원급 + as + 주어 + can[could]〉

14 수학을 공부하는 것은 내가 예상했던 것보다 어렵지 않다.
* 〈not as[so] + 원급 + as〉 = 〈less + 원급 + than〉

15 내 휴대전화의 크기는 네 휴대전화의 크기보다 크다.
* 비교의 대상이 휴대전화가 아닌 휴대전화의 크기이므로 that of yours가 되어야 한다.

16 ① 많으면 많을수록 더 좋다.
② 나는 너만큼 돈을 가지고 있지 않다.
③ 한국의 다른 어느 도시도 서울보다 더 크지는 않다.
④ 건강은 다른 어떤 것보다 더 중요하다.
⑤ 여기의 날씨는 점점 더 따뜻해지고 있다.
* ④ [things → thing] 〈any other + 단수 명사〉로 표현한다.
⑤ [more and more warmer → warmer and warmer] '점점 더 ~한'은 〈비교급 and 비교급〉으로 표현한다.

17 인수는 테니스를 치는 것보다 피구 하는 것을 더 좋아한다.
* 라틴 비교급 표현인 〈prefer A to B〉는 'B보다 A를 더 좋아하다'라는 의미이다. 주어가 3인칭 단수이므로 prefers가 와야 한다. would rather는 뒤에 동사원형이 와야 하므로 빈칸에 올 수 없다.

18 (1) 김 선생님은 나보다 아랍어를 더 유창하게 말한다.
(2) 주희는 둘 중에서 키가 더 크다.
(3) 우리는 덜 붐비는 장소로 옮기기를 원한다.
* (1) 문장 구조상 부사가 와야 하는 자리이며, more 뒤에 또 비교급을 써서는 안 된다.
(2) 비교급 앞에는 the를 쓰지 않으나 두 사람 사이의 비교(of the two)일 경우에는 the를 쓴다.
(3) 문맥상 '덜 붐비는'을 의미하는 less가 알맞다.

19 현장학습을 하는 동안 우리 모둠원들은 가능한 한 두 배로 많은 별들을 연구할 것이다.
* [possible → can] 〈as soon as possible〉 = 〈as soon as + 주어 + can〉이므로 as we 다음에는 can이 와야 한다.

20 A: 서울은 세계에서 가장 붐비는 인구를 가지고 있어.
B: 아니, 내 생각에 뉴욕만큼 나쁘지는 않아.
A: 정말? 교통체증은 어떤데?
B: 교통체증도 거기가 훨씬 더 안 좋아.
A: 와, 내가 지금까지 들었던 가장 분주한 도시 중 하나인 것 같다.
* ② [worse → bad] 〈as + 원급 + as〉로 나타내야 한다.
⑤ [city → cities] 〈one of the + 복수 명사〉로 나타내야 한다.

21 ① Tom은 그의 반에서 가장 힘이 센 남자아이이다.
② Tom은 그의 반에 있는 다른 어떤 남자아이보다 힘이 더 세다.
③ 그의 반에 있는 다른 어떤 남자아이도 Tom보다 힘이 세지 않다.
④ 그의 반에 있는 다른 어떤 남자아이도 Tom만큼 힘이 세지는 않다.
⑤ Tom은 그의 반에 있는 다른 남자아이들만큼 힘이 세지 않다.
* ⑤를 제외한 나머지 문장은 최상급의 의미이다.

22 네가 열심히 공부할수록 너의 점수는 더 좋아질 것이다.
* 접속사 as는 '~함에 따라'라는 의미이므로 〈the + 비교급 ~, the + 비교급 ...〉(~할수록 더 …한)으로 바꿔 쓸 수 있다.

23 ① 그녀는 한국에서 최고의 여배우 중 한 명이다.
② 그는 세계에서 가장 멋진 남자이다.
③ 우리 학교의 다른 어떤 학생들도 너보다 친절하지 못하다.
④ 그의 아버지는 가장 유명한 축구팀에 있다.
⑤ 너는 너의 가족과 멀리 떨어져서 살수록 네 가족을 더 그리워한다.
* 〈the + 최상급 + in + 단수 명사(장소/집단)〉로 나타내므로 맞는 문장이다.
① [actress → actresses] 〈one of the + 최상급 + 복수 명사〉, ② most nice → nicest], ③ [students → student] 〈no other + 단수 명사 + 비교급〉, ⑤ [further → farther] 거리를 나타낼 때의 비교 변화는 far–farther–farthest이다. far–further–furthest는 정도를 나타낼 때의 비교 변화이다.

24 이 스마트폰은 아마도 세계 최고의 휴대전화일 것이다.
* 〈the + 최상급 + in + 단수 명사(장소,집단)〉로 표현한다.

25 ① 이 자동차는 저 자동차보다 더 비싸다.
→ 저 자동차는 이 자동차보다 더 싸다.
② Bob은 James보다 똑똑하다.
→ James는 Bob만큼 똑똑하지 않다.
③ 내 여동생의 방은 내 방만큼 크지 않다.
→ 내 방은 내 여동생의 방보다 크다.
④ Bill은 내가 먹는 음식에 두 배 만큼 먹는다.
→ Bill은 내가 먹는 음식보다 두 배 더 먹는다.
⑤ Wayne은 Raymond보다 피아노를 잘 친다.
→ Wayne은 Raymond만큼 피아노를 잘 친다.
* better than은 '~보다 더 잘하는'(비교급 표현)이라는 뜻이고 as well as는 '~만큼 잘하는'(원급 표현)이라는 뜻이다.

26 * '세 살 많은'은 라틴 비교급(senior to)으로 나타낸다.

27 * hard가 부사로 쓰일 경우, 앞에 the를 생략할 수 있다.

28 ① Cathy는 Sean보다 두 배 많은 점수를 받았다.
② Cathy는 Kyle만큼 점수를 받지 못했다.
③ Kyle은 다른 어떤 학생들보다 더 많은 점수를 받았다.
④ Cathy는 Keilen만큼 좋은 점수를 받았다.
⑤ Sean은 모든 사람 중에서 가장 적은 점수를 받았다.
* [→ Cathy got more points than Keilen.] Cathy가 Keilen보다 점수가 더 높다.

29 보기 이 영화는 매우 좋다. 나는 그와 같은 영화를 본 적이 없다.
→ ① 이것은 내가 지금까지 본 영화 중에서 가장 좋다.
② 이 영화는 저 영화만큼 좋다.
③ 나는 영화를 많이 볼수록 기분이 더 좋다.
④ 나는 그 영화를 볼 때 기분이 점점 좋아진다.
⑤ 나는 이 영화를 볼 때마다 기분이 매우 좋다.
* '내가 지금까지 본 영화 중에서 가장 좋은'이라는 의미인 〈최상급 + 주어 + have + ever + 과거분사〉로 표현한다.

30 보기 지난주에 날씨는 따뜻했다. 이번 주에는 좀 더 따뜻해지고 있다.
→ ⑤ 날씨가 점점 더 따뜻해지고 있다.
① 나는 여기의 좀 더 따뜻한 날씨를 좋아한다.
② 날씨가 따뜻할수록 나는 기분이 좋다.
③ 여름이 됨에 따라 날씨가 따뜻하다.
④ 여기의 날씨는 세계에서 가장 따뜻하다.
* 문맥상 '점점 더 ~한'을 의미하는 〈비교급 and 비교급〉으로 표현한다.

Sentence Writing

▶ 본문 156쪽

Part **A**
1 one of the most famous bridges
2 not as expensive as
3 twice as much as

Part **B**
1 This book is even more interesting than I expected.
2 This store is as crowded as that one.
3 Seoul is one of the biggest cities in Korea.
4 Our world is getting smaller and smaller.

Part **A**

1 금문교는 미국에서 가장 유명한 다리 중 하나이다.

2 그것이 건설되기로 제안되었을 때 견적 비용은 1억 달러가 넘었다. 젊은 건축기사인 Joseph Strauss가 새로운 아이디어를 생각해냈다. 그것은 처음의 비용만큼 비싸지는 않았다.

3 처음에 그는 1,700만 달러가 들 것이라고 생각했다. 하지만 그가 예상했던 것보다 두 배의 비용이 들었다. 어쨌든 그 다리는 샌프란시스코 시의 상징이 되었다.

Unit 09 관계사

17 관계대명사

2교시 In - Class Questions

▶ 본문 161쪽

STEP **A** **1** which **2** which **3** whose

STEP **B**
1 They telephoned Mrs. Choi who was the family doctor.
2 This is Cathy who(m) I told you about. 혹은 This is Cathy about whom I told you.
3 I saw a car whose [of which] windows were all broken.
4 The book which he is reading these days is in the drawer.

STEP **C** **1** which is **2** who are **3** X

STEP **D**
1 whose, cover **2** which [that], is
3 who(m), I, met **4** which, flows

STEP **A**
1 도난당한 그 자전거는 Kelly의 것이었다.
2 이것은 내가 관심이 있는 책이다.
3 전공이 수학인 나의 언니는 중학교에서 가르친다.

STEP **B**
1 그들은 최 선생님에게 전화를 걸었다. + 그녀는 가족 주치의였다.
→ 그들은 가족 주치의인 최 선생님에게 전화를 걸었다.
2 이 사람이 Cathy이다. + 내가 너에게 그녀에 대해 이야기했다.
→ 이 사람이 내가 너에게 이야기했던 Cathy이다.
3 나는 차를 한 대 봤다. + 그 차의 유리창들이 모두 깨졌다.
→ 나는 유리창들이 다 깨진 차를 한 대 봤다.
4 그 책은 서랍에 있다. + 그는 요즘 그 책을 읽고 있다.
→ 그가 요즘 읽고 있는 그 책은 서랍에 있다.

STEP **C**
1 많은 한국 사람들에게 알려져 있는 그 영화는 여전히 극장에서 상영되고 있다.
2 저 방송국 앞에 서 있는 십대들은 유명한 가수 그룹들을 기다리고 있다.
3 나는 내가 같이 경기했던 팀원들 중 몇 명은 믿을 수 없었다.

3교시 After - Class Questions

▶ 본문 162 - 165쪽

01 ④, ⑤ **02** ①, ②, ⑤ **03** ⑤ **04** ② **05** ①, provide **06** (1) plays (2) lives **07** ② doesn't → don't **08** ③ **09** ④ **10** ③ **11** was talking → who [that] was talking **12** ② **13** ④ **14** some friends whose fathers are dentists **15** A rabbit is an animal which [that] eats carrots. **16** who are **17** which **18** ④ **19** ①, ②, ⑤ **20** ⑤ **21** ④ **22** ③ **23** ⑤ **24** The old lady who(m) you spoke with is my Chinese teacher. **25** ⑤

01 이것은 색깔이 갈색과 보라색인 나의 잃어버린 지갑이다.
* 관계대명사 뒤에 〈명사(colors) + 동사(are) + 주격 보어(brown and purple)〉의 완벽한 문장이 왔으므로 소유격 관계대명사 whose나 of which가 와야 한다.

02 당신이 지금 바로 만나야 할 교수님은 최 교수님이다.
* 목적격 관계대명사 whom이 필요하며, who나 that도 목적격 관계대명사로 쓰일 수 있다.

03 ① 내가 똑똑하다고 믿었던 Hank는 그 시험에 떨어졌다.
② 네가 사고 싶었던 바지가 이것이 확실하니?
③ 그녀가 봤던 그 남자는 유명한 사람이 전혀 아니었다.
④ Kent는 나에게 Thomas Jefferson에 관한 책을 한 권 주었다.
⑤ 그녀로부터 온 그 문자메시지는 그녀가 숙제를 끝내지 못할 것이라는 내용이었다.
* [of which → which] came에 대한 주어 역할을 하는 주격 관계대명사가 와야 한다.

04 ① 여기는 내가 태어난 도시이다.
② Bumkie가 모두를 위해 작곡했던 그 음악은 너무 시끄럽다.
③ 허리케인으로 집이 부서진 가족들을 위해 도움이 필요하다.
④ 그녀는 매우 로맨틱하고 슬픈 부분도 있는 영화를 보고 싶어 한다.
⑤ Jack은 매우 인기있는 그 배우를 인터뷰하는 것을 포기했다.
* 목적격 관계대명사는 생략할 수 있다. ① 〈전치사 + 목적격 관계대명사〉일 경우 목적격 관계대명사를 생략할 수 없다. ③ 소유격 관계대명사, ④ 주격 관계대명사, ⑤ 〈주격 관계대명사 + be동사〉는 생략할 수 있지만 주격 관계대명사만 생략할 수 없다.

05 내가 도서관에서 4시간 동안 읽은 몇 권의 책들은 대체에너지에 대한 많은 정보를 준다.
* 문맥상 '내가 읽은 몇 권의 책들'이라는 의미가 되어야 하므로 books와 I 사이에 목적격 관계대명사가 생략 되었다. 관계대명사가 이끄는 절(I read in the library for 4 hours)이 주어인 Some books를 수식하는 구조이므로 동사는 provide이다.

06 방과 후에 자주 테니스를 치는 그 남자는 나의 집 근처에 산다.
* 문장의 주어 The guy를 수식하는 관계대명사절의 동사이므로 plays가 와야 하고, 문장의 동사는 3인칭 단수 현재시제인 lives가 와야 한다.

07 아프리카에서는 먹을 음식과 입을 옷이 충분하지 않은 많은 사람들이 있다. 아프리카에는 가족이 음식과 옷 둘 다 없는 아이들이 백만 명이 넘게 있다. 몇몇 아이들은 그들의 부모가 병으로 죽었기 때문에 일을 한다. 그래서 정부와 자선단체들은 아이들의 삶을 개선하기 위해 조치를 취해 왔다.
* 선행사가 a lot of people로 복수이므로 관계대명사절의 동사는 don't가 와야 한다.

08 (a) (b) Harry가 찾고 있는 단어의 의미는 사전에 있다.
* (a) 목적격 관계대명사이며 선행사가 the meaning of the word이므로 which가 알맞다.
(b) 전치사 for는 관계대명사 앞으로 이동할 수 있으므로 for which로 쓸 수 있다.

09 * 그녀의 머리카락이 회색이라는 부분을 관계대명사절로 하면 된다. 선행사가 사람(the woman)이고 소유격 역할을 해야 하므로 관계대명사 whose가 알맞다. of which는 선행사가 사물일 경우에 쓰인다.

10 (a) 지난 주말에 나의 가족은 프랑스 감옥에서 발생한 끔찍한 뉴스에 대해 들었다.
(b) 나의 이모는 그녀의 어머니가 그녀에게 유산으로 남겨준 목걸이를 한다.
* (a) 선행사가 사물(news)이며 주어 자리가 비었으므로 주격 관계대명사 which가 와야 한다.
(b) 선행사가 사물(a necklace)이며 목적어 자리가 비었으므로 목적격 관계대명사 which가 와야 한다.

11 어제 아침에 너와 함께 이야기하고 있던 그 작은 여자아이는 내 여동생이었다.

* 한 문장에 동사(was talking, was)가 두 번 나올 수 없고, 문맥상 was talking with you yesterday morning이 The little girl을 수식하는 관계대명사절이 되는 것이 알맞다.

12 ① 영어는 내가 가장 좋아하는 과목이다.
② 나는 런던에 살고 있는 친구가 한 명 있다.
③ 그들은 그가 작년에 가르쳤던 학생들이다.
④ 그녀는 Rick이 사랑에 빠졌던 여자이다.
⑤ 이것은 내가 내 아들을 위해 사준 컴퓨터게임이다.
* 목적격 관계대명사는 생략할 수 있지만 주격 관계대명사는 생략할 수 없다. 단, 〈주격 관계대명사 + be동사〉는 생략할 수 있다.

13 ① Linda는 내가 그녀에게 준 콜라를 마셨다.
② 나는 그녀가 전에 나에게 주었던 초대장을 가져왔다.
③ 너의 아버지께 네가 들은 이야기를 해라.
④ 저것은 내가 외국어들을 배우는 건물이다.
⑤ 우리는 도서관에서 빌린 책의 몇 페이지를 찢었다.
* 〈전치사 + 목적격 관계대명사〉는 생략할 수 없다.

14 * '친구의 아버지'이므로 소유격 관계대명사로 나타내야 한다. 친구들이 선행사이므로 관계대명사절의 동사도 복수 동사가 와야 한다.

15 * an animal을 선행사로 한 관계대명사 which[that]가 이끄는 절로 나타낸다.

16 Jenny는 암으로 고통 받는 환자들을 도울 것이다.
* 〈주격 관계대명사 + be동사〉는 생략할 수 있다.

17 나는 네가 지난밤에 나에게 보여줬던 그 사진들을 잊을 수 없다.
* 목적격 관계대명사는 생략할 수 있다.

18 너는 가격이 2,000달러가 넘는 저 가방을 사고 싶니?
* 소유격 관계대명사 whose는 of which로 바꿔 쓸 수 있다.

19 * 사람이 선행사이면서 주격으로 쓰이는 관계대명사는 who, whom, that으로 쓴다.

20 차 범퍼가 움푹 들어간 그 차는 나의 어머니의 것이다.
⑤ 그 차는 나의 어머니의 것이다. 그것의 범퍼는 움푹 들어갔다.
* whose의 선행사가 차(car)이므로 its가 올바른 표현이다.

21 이것들은 어제 그의 할머니가 만드신 쿠키이다.
* 선행사 the cookies가 사물이고 주어 역할을 하는 관계대명사가 들어가야 하므로 that이 알맞다.

22 ① 나는 친절하고 정직한 사람을 고용했다.
② 나는 나를 이끌어줄 수 있는 친구가 한 명 있다.
③ 나는 네가 누구인지 그리고 어디서 왔는지 기억하지 못한다.
④ 우리는 이 문제를 해결할 수 있는 사람이 필요하다.
⑤ 내가 생각하는 아내의 이상형은 정직하고 열린 마음을 가져야 하는 사람이다.
* ③은 의문사로 쓰인 who이고, 나머지는 관계대명사로 쓰인 who이다.

23 A: 이게 누구의 휴대용 컴퓨터인지 너는 아니?
B: 내가 추측하기에 그것은 Jimmy의 휴대용 컴퓨터야. 그것은 내가 가지고 있는 것과 같은 모델이야.
A: 아니야, 그의 휴대용 컴퓨터는 네 것과는 다른 모델이야.
* 문맥상 '누구의 휴대용 컴퓨터인지'라는 의미의 whose가 알맞다. the same model이 사물이므로 빈칸에는 주격 관계대명사 that이 알맞다.

24 네가 말했던 그 나이 든 여자분이 내 중국어 선생님이시다.
* 목적격 관계대명사 who(m)이 생략되었다. 문장의 주어인 The old lady가 선행사이고 관계대명사가 이끄는 절은 you spoke with이다.

25 ① 우리가 만난 그 선생님은 매우 친절했다.
② 그는 모든 사람이 매우 좋아하는 남자이다.
③ Smith 선생님은 내가 항상 사고 싶어 했던 카메라를 갖고 있다.
④ 무대에서 노래를 부르고 있는 한국 가수를 봐.
⑤ 저것은 내가 관심이 있는 소설이다.
* [in that → in which] 관계대명사 that은 앞에 전치사를 둘 수 없다.
① The teacher가 주어이므로 동사는 was가 맞다.
② 사람을 선행사로 하는 목적격 관계대명사는 whom과 who 모두 쓸 수 있다.
③ 선행사가 사물(a camera)이므로 관계대명사 which가 왔다.
④ 〈주격 관계대명사 + be동사〉는 생략할 수 있다. 여기서는 who is가 생략되었다.

DAY 18 주의해야 할 관계대명사

2교시 In - Class Questions ▶ 본문 167쪽

STEP A	1 what 2 that 3 that 4 that[which]
STEP B	1 who, that 2 what 3 that 4 that
STEP C	1 지시형용사 2 관계대명사 3 접속사 4 관계대명사
STEP D	1 what → that[which] 2 which → that 3 X 4 that → what

STEP A
1 네가 옳다고 생각하는 것을 해라.
2 Sunny는 그녀가 가지고 있던 가장 귀중한 반지를 잃어버렸다.
3 오늘 아침에 출근한 첫 번째 직원은 누구인가요?
4 나의 아빠는 매우 호화로운 세단 자동차를 구입하셨다.

STEP B
1 내 삼촌은 그의 여자 친구를 우리 집에 데려 왔는데, 그녀는 아름답다.
2 그 개들은 모두 온순했으며 조련사가 하라고 지시했던 것을 했다.
3 너는 나에 대해서 모든 것을 알고 있는, 세상의 오직 한 사람이다.
4 내가 가르치는 대학에는 내 강의를 듣고 싶어 하는 학생들이 많았다.

STEP C
1 저 스마트폰은 내 것이 아니라 그녀의 것이다.
2 위험한 장난감들은 아이들에게 주어져서는 안 된다.
3 그가 우리를 보기를 원하지 않는다는 것이 매우 확실하다.
4 공원에서 뛰고 있는 아이들을 좀 봐.

STEP D
1 이 다이어리는 나의 아내가 나를 위해 만들어준 것이다.
2 그는 내가 찾고 있던 바로 그 남자이다.
3 이것이야말로 내 마음 속에 오랫동안 갖고 있던 바로 그 의문이다.
4 나는 무엇인가 다른 것을 기대하기는 했지만 그가 한 말에 놀랐다.

3교시 After - Class Questions ▶ 본문 168 - 171쪽

01 ② **02** ① **03** that **04** but, it **05** (1) ⓑ (2) ⓐ **06** ⑤ **07** ⑤ **08** ③ **09** ③ **10** (1) 접속사 (2) 관계대명사 (3) 동격 **11** ④ **12** which **13** ③ **14** ② **15** ⑤ **16** ① **17** which **18** ⑤ **19** ③ **20** ③ **21** what **22** which **23** ②, ⑤ **24** What, The, thing, that[which] **25** that

01 Ben이 어제 그녀를 위해 샀던 것은 그녀의 건강에 좋을 것이다.
* 문맥상 주어 역할을 하는 명사절을 이끌고 앞에 선행사가 없으므로 관계대명사 What이 알맞다.

02 정원에서 뛰고 있는 여자아이와 그녀의 고양이들을 봐라.
* 선행사가 〈사람 + 동물〉일 경우 관계대명사 that을 써야 한다.

03 그녀는 유일한 여자이다. + 나는 그녀와 데이트를 하고 싶다.
→ 그녀는 내가 데이트를 하고 싶은 유일한 여자이다.
* 선행사에 the only가 있을 경우 관계사 that만 쓸 수 있다.

04 Anne은 문을 열려고 노력했지만 그녀는 그것이 불가능하다는 것을 알았다.
* 관계대명사의 계속적 용법은 〈접속사 + 대명사〉로 바꿔 쓸 수 있다. 대명사는 앞 문장의 일부인 open the door를 가리키는 it이 와야 한다.

05 * (1) 선행사를 수식하는 관계대명사의 제한적 용법이므로 〈관계대명사절 → 선행사〉의 순서로 해석한다. (2) 선행사를 보충 설명하는 관계대명사의 계속적 용법이므로 〈선행사 → 관계대명사절〉의 순서로 해석한다.

06 (a) 강당에 우리가 앉을 수 있는 많은 의자들이 있다.
(b) 그들이 이야기했던 남자아이와 여자아이들은 Gary의 아들과 딸들이다.
* 관계대명사가 전치사의 목적어로 사용될 때 〈전치사 + 관계대명사〉로 쓸 수 있다. (a)는 sit in a lot of chairs의 in, (b)는 talked to the boys and girls의 to가 와야 한다. that, who 앞에는 전치사를 쓸 수 없다.

07 (a) Megan은 나에게 그녀의 스마트폰을 쓰도록 했는데, 그것은 다양한 기능이 있다.
(b) 지금 이 순간 중요한 유일한 것은 너의 충고이다.
* (a) 선행사가 사물이고 계속적 용법이므로 which가 와야 한다. that은 계속적 용법으로 쓰이지 않는다.
(b) 선행사에 only가 있으므로 that이 와야 한다.

08 (a) 그는 내가 탁자 아래 숨겨두었던 마지막 캔디를 찾아냈다.
(b) 그녀는 내가 탁자 아래 놓아둔 것을 발견하지 못할지도 모른다.
* (a) 선행사에 the last가 있으므로 that만 올 수 있다.
(b) 선행사가 없으므로 선행사를 포함한 관계대명사 what이 와야 한다.

09 (a) 돈이 Kaymi가 일을 하는 모든 것(목적)은 아니다.
(b) 많은 경험을 가진 이 남자는 누구니?
* (a) 선행사가 everything이므로 that만 올 수 있다.
(b) 의문사 Who가 있는 의문문에서는 관계대명사 who 대신에 that을 쓴다.

10 (1) 우리는 오직 하나뿐인 밴이 10좌석 이하라는 것을 몰랐다.
(2) 아프리카의 아이들이 필요한 모든 것은 약간의 음식이다.
(3) 그 나라의 사람들은 경제가 나아지고 있다는 사실을 믿는다.
* (1) that절이 동사 know의 목적어 역할을 하는 명사절이므로 접속사로 쓰였다.
(2) 주어인 All을 선행사로 하여 that절이 수식하고 있으므로 관계대명사로 쓰였다.
(3) 〈the fact = that절〉이므로 that이 동격절을 이끌고 있다.

11 ① Linda는 운전시험을 통과했는데, 그것은 모두를 놀라게 했다.
② 중간에 있는 가장 작은 탁자는 나의 아버지의 것이다.
③ 나무에서 익어가는 큰 배들은 매우 맛있어 보인다.
④ 영국에서 사람들이 대부분의 시간을 보내는 취미는 정원을 가꾸는 것이다.
⑤ 매일 아침 신문을 읽는 그의 습관은 그에게 많은 기쁨을 주는 것이다.
* [on that → on which] 〈전치사 + that〉의 형태로는 쓰이지 않는다.

12 * 앞 문장 전체를 받는 관계대명사는 which이다.

13 **보기** 페이스북은 Mark Zuckerberg가 그의 대학교 방 친구들과 함께 설립한 소셜 네트워크 서비스 중에 하나이다.
① 모든 학생들이 시험에 떨어졌다는 그 소문은 거짓이라고 증명되었다.
② Eve는 그 가게를 더 좋게 하기 위해 조치를 취할 것이라고 말했다.
③ 절벽에서 떨어졌던 그 차와 운전자는 발견되지 않았다.
④ 내가 원하는 것은 나의 부모님과 여동생이 행복한 것이다.
⑤ 모든 사람은 강력한 폭풍 때문에 그 배가 항로를 바꿨다는 것을 알았다.
* 〈보기〉와 ③의 that은 선행사를 수식하는 주격 관계대명사로 쓰였다.
① 동격, ②④⑤ 명사절을 이끄는 접속사

14 ① 나는 유명한 가수를 보았는데, 그녀는 올해 상을 받았다.
② 나는 영화를 보기 시작했는데, 그 영화는 매우 흥미로웠다.
③ Charlotte는 그녀의 친구를 좋아하는데, 그녀의 친구는 대학에서 심리학을 가르친다.
④ 나의 가족은 루브르 박물관을 방문했는데, 거기에는 '모나리자'가 있다.
⑤ 그 기자는 Billy를 인터뷰했는데, 그는 세계 여행을 했다.
* [that → which] 관계대명사 that은 계속적 용법으로 쓰이지 않는다.

15 **보기** Owen은 그가 하는 것(일)에 대해 매우 깊게 생각한다.
① 이것은 우리가 사고 싶어 했던 것이다.
② 우리가 가지고 있는 것은 강한 의지이다.
③ 나는 그녀가 말한 것을 기억하고 있다.
④ 내가 원하는 것은 저 파란색 자동차이다.
⑤ 너는 그녀의 전화번호가 무엇인지 아니?
* ⑤는 의문사로 '무엇'이라는 의미이고, 〈보기〉와 나머지는 관계대명사로 '~하는 것'이라는 의미이다.

16 ① Sue는 정답을 말한 첫 번째 사람이다.
② Thomas는 더 이상 필요 없는 자신의 책을 친구에게 팔았다.
③ 그녀는 노래를 부르고 피아노를 쳤는데, 모두가 이를 아주 즐겼다.
④ Marylin Monroe는, 본명이 Norma Jean인데, 오래 전에 사망했다.
⑤ 나의 누나는 우리들에게 많은 흥미로운 이야기를 읽어주었는데, 그 중 몇몇은 사실이 아니다.
* 선행사가 the first person으로 서수가 쓰였으므로 관계대명사 that이 왔다.
② [that → which] that은 계속적 용법으로 쓰이지 않는다.
③ [who → which] 선행사가 문장 전체의 내용일 경우 which가 온다.
④ [who → whose] 뒤에 명사가 나왔고, 선행사인 'Marylin Monroe의 본명'이라는 의미가 되려면 소유격 관계대명사가 와야 한다.
⑤ [them → which] 어법상 아무런 접속사 없이 두 개의 문장이 동시에 올 수 없다.

17 두 명의 젊은이들은 둘 다 세계에서 가장 높은 산인 에베레스트 산 정상에 오르기를 원했다. 각각 두 명의 등산객들 모두 그 산에 도착했지만 그들은 나쁜 날씨 때문에 산 정상에는 오를 수 없었다.
* 선행사가 사물이고 주격 관계대명사의 자리이므로 which가 알맞다.

18 Hank는 의자를 하나 샀다. + 그는 거기에 앉을 수 있었다.
→ Hank는 그가 앉을 수 있는 의자 하나를 샀다.
* 관계대명사 that은 〈전치사 + that〉의 형태로 쓰이지 않는다.

19 ① 이것은 그가 진짜로 원했던 것이었다.
② 내 아들이 배우는 것은 아무것도 없다.
③ 너는 그가 무엇을 하고 있는지 아니?
④ 너의 손에 있는 것을 나에게 보여줘.
⑤ 나를 행복하게 만드는 것은 너의 진실한 사랑이다.
* ③은 '무엇'이라는 의미의 의문사이고, 나머지는 '~것'이라는 의미의 관계대명사이다.

20 ① 우리는 그녀가 똑똑하다고 믿는다.
② 너의 애완견이 죽었다니 슬프다.
③ 우리에게 알맞은 노래를 한 곡 추천해주세요.
④ 네가 한 약속을 지키는 것은 중요하다.
⑤ 너는 Jason이 호화로운 세단을 산 것에 대해 들은 적이 있니?
* ③은 주격 관계대명사로 쓰였고, 나머지는 명사절을 이끄는 접속사로 쓰였다.

21 Ophelia는 매우 지쳤다. 그것이 그녀를 온종일 침대에 머물게 했던 것이다.
* which 앞에 선행사가 없으므로 문맥상 '~한 것'이라는 의미의 선행사를 포함한 관계대명사 what이 와야 한다.

22 나의 아버지는 어떤 낯선 사람과 말다툼을 했었는데, 이것은 좀처럼 일어나지 않는 일이었다.
* 문맥상 앞 문장 전체(낯선 사람과 말다툼을 한 일)를 가리키는 관계대명사가 와야 하므로 which가 알맞다.

23 ① Sandy는 내가 함께 어울려 놀지 않는 여자이다.
② Rebecca는 내가 존경하는 매우 훌륭한 선생님이다.
③ 음악은 내가 관심 있어 하는 과목이다.
④ 나는 그녀가 지금까지 사용해왔던 노트북 컴퓨터를 경매할 것이다.
⑤ 그는 전에 계획했던 콘서트를 갑자기 취소했다.
* ② [who → that] 선행사에 very가 있으므로 관계대명사 that만 쓸 수 있다.
⑤ [it → 삭제] 목적격 관계대명사 which가 있으므로 목적어 it을 삭제해야 한다.

24 * 선행사가 없으므로 선행사를 포함한 관계대명사 what이 알맞다. what은 the thing that [which]으로 바꿔 쓸 수 있다.

25 사람들이 생존하기 위해 필요한 모든 것은 물이다.
* 선행사가 All이므로 관계대명사는 that만 올 수 있다.

DAY 19 관계부사, 복합관계사

2교시 In - Class Questions

▶ 본문 173쪽

STEP A 1 in which, where 2 for which, why
3 whoever 4 However

STEP B 1 when 2 reason, for, which 3 where 4 How

STEP C 1 whoever 2 anything, that
3 No, matter, whom

STEP D 1 I wonder how [the way] Minjun reached here.
2 This is where I saw this painting every day.
3 However famous Songyeon is, she feels very lonely.

STEP A 1 에임즈는 우리가 공부했던 도시이다.
2 네가 그것을 좋아하는 이유는 무엇이니?
3 가고 싶어 하는 사람은 누구에게나 이 티켓을 주시오.
4 너의 여동생이 아무리 멍청해도 너를 따라가지는 않을 것이다.

STEP C
1 Greg는 도움이 필요한 누구에게든지 조언을 줄 것이다.
2 당신이 하고 싶지 않은 것은 무엇이든지 하지 마라.
3 그가 누구를 만나고 싶어 하던 간에 그는 그렇게 하는 것이 허락되지 않을 것이다.

3교시 After - Class Questions

▶ 본문 174 - 177쪽

01 ① 02 ④ 03 ⑤ 04 ③ 05 ③ 06 whatever 07 ④ 08 ②, ③, ④ 09 ④ However you are tired → However tired you are 10 ① 11 ② 12 ① 13 ④ 14 ④ 15 ⑤ 16 whatever[no matter what] you say 17 ② 18 wherever 19 (1) Whoever (2) Wherever (3) whatever (4) when 20 ③ 21 ③ 22 ⑤ 23 ⑤ 24 ④ 25 that

01 (a) 우리가 휴가 동안 머물 이 게스트하우스는 매우 비싸지 않다.
(b) 그녀는 스페인어를 사용하는 나라에 가본 적이 있니?
* (a) 관계사가 이끄는 절에 목적어가 필요하므로 목적격 관계대명사가 와야 한다. we will stay at (the guest house)
(b) 관계사가 이끄는 절에서 부사구가 필요하므로 관계부사가 와야 한다. Spanish is spoken (in the place)

02 (a) 그 의사가 무엇을 제안하더라도 나는 그것을 하지 않겠다.
(b) 엄마는 비용이 아무리 많이 들더라도 그 미술 재료를 위해 돈을 지불하실 것이다.
* (a) 문맥상 '무엇을 제안하더라도'의 의미가 알맞다.
(b) 문맥상 '아무리 비용이 많이 들더라도'의 의미가 알맞다.

03 * [at → 삭제] 관계부사 where = at the cage이므로 at을 중복해서 쓰지 말아야 한다.

04 ① 저곳이 우리가 쉴 수 있는 적당한 장소이다.
② 이것이 그들이 그 오류를 발견했던 방법이었다.
③ 이곳은 내가 매일 일하는 신발 가게이다.
④ 오늘은 우리가 통영으로 가는 날이다.
⑤ 그 게임이 네가 공부에 집중을 못하고 있는 주된 이유이다.
* [which → at which 혹은 where] 선행사 the shoe store를 일하는 것이 아니라 at the shoe store에서 일한 것이므로 관계대명사 앞에 at을 쓰거나 관계부사로 써야 한다.

05 ① A를 받고 싶은 사람은 누구든지 열심히 공부해야 한다.
② 그 책들은 너에게 그 국을 만드는 방법을 보여준다.
③ 이것은 몇몇 친구들이 항상 나를 대하는 방식이다.
④ 네가 집에서 무엇을 하더라도 수업에 늦지 마라.
⑤ Andrew는 한밤중까지 깨어 있었는데, 그때 그의 엄마가 그의 방에 들어오셨다.
* 관계부사 how는 선행사 the way와 함께 쓸 수 없다.

06 나중에 무슨 일이 일어나더라도 나는 너를 잊지 못할 것이다.
* no matter what = whatever이며, '무엇을 ~하더라도'라는 의미이다.

07 ① 우리는 파리에 갈 그 주를 기다리고 있다.
② 너는 나를 처음 만났을 때를 기억했니?
③ 6월은 Justin과 Keilen이 결혼을 했던 달이다.
④ Alice는 내가 자고 있었을 때 점심을 먹었다.
⑤ Austin은 그가 너의 집에 들를 수 있는 시간을 너에게 말했다.
* ④는 시간의 접속사로 쓰였고, 나머지는 관계부사로 쓰였다.

08 내가 토론시간에 내 짝과 잡담을 할 때마다, 선생님은 나를 노려보셨다.
* '~할 때마다'의 뜻이 있는 말이 와야 한다. whenever = at any time when, each time, every time

09 A: Jack, 내가 너에게 말했던 것을 할 시간이야.
B: 엄마, 저는 매우 지쳤어요. 오늘만 건너뛰고 싶어요.
A: 얘야! 너는 아무리 피곤하더라도 너의 약속을 지켜야만 해. 너는 "엄마가 원할 때면 언제든지 운동을 할게요."라고 말하면서 새 게임 세트를 샀잖니.
* ⟨however + 형용사 + 주어 + 동사⟩의 어순으로 써야 한다.

10 Jessica는 여기에 오는 누구에게라도 너를 소개할 예정이다.
* 문맥상 '여기에 오는 누구든지'를 의미하고 관계사절에서 주어 역할을 하는 복합관계사가 와야 한다. to가 전치사이기 때문에 whomever를 쓰지 않도록 주의한다.

11 시민전쟁 후에 많은 군인들은 그들이 태어난 고향으로 되돌아갔다.
* 장소를 나타내는 hometown이 선행사이고 빈칸 뒷문장이 완벽하므로 관계부사 where가 와야 한다.

12 모든 사람이 그 사고가 발생했던 그날을 기억했다.
* 선행사가 the day이고 빈칸 뒷문장이 완벽하므로 관계부사 when이 와야 한다.

13 너는 차를 탈 때마다 안전벨트를 매니?
* 문맥상 '~하면 언제든지(= at any time when)'가 알맞다.

14 네가 어느 MP3를 선택하던간에 나는 그것을 너의 생일 선물로 사줄 것이다.
* ⟨no matter which + 명사(MP3) + 주어 + 동사⟩ = ⟨whichever + 명사(MP3) + 주어 + 동사⟩

15 ① 그 분야에서 성공하길 희망하는 사람은 누구든지 성공할 수 있다.
② 그 영화표를 가져오는 사람은 누구나 이 포스터를 주세요.
③ 사람들은 이 프로젝트에 투자하려는 사람은 누구나 환영한다.
④ Harry는 그 방에 처음 오는 사람은 누구에게나 이 책을 줄 것이다.
⑤ 사람들은 아무리 부자여도 항상 더욱 더 많이 원한다.
* ⑤는 문맥상 '아무리 부자라도'라는 의미의 However가 들어가야 한다.

16 * '무엇을 ~하든지'는 ⟨no matter what + 주어 + 동사⟩나 ⟨whatever + 주어 + 동사⟩로 나타낸다.

17 너는 아무리 밤늦게 도착하더라도 나에게 전화해야 한다.
* 양보의 부사절이므로 ⟨however + 형용사/부사 + 주어 + 동사⟩의 어순, 즉 however late at night you arrive로 배열한다.

18 한국계 미국인 영화배우인 다니엘 헤니는 최근에 개봉된 영화에 출연한 후에 요즘 매우 인기가 많다. 그가 가는 곳은 어디든지 많은 인파를 몰고 다닌다. 지난주 인터뷰에 따르면, 그는 그가 머무는 곳은 어디든지 그를 항상 따라다니는 특이한 팬을 언급했다.
* 문맥상 '그가 가는 곳은 어디든지'와 '그가 머무는 곳은 어디든지'를 의미하는 wherever가 알맞다.

19 (1) 이 행사에 오는 사람은 누구든지 기념품을 받을 것이다.
(2) 그는 어디를 가든지 문제를 일으킨다.
(3) 나는 당신이 나에게 하라고 말하는 것은 무엇이든지 할게요.
(4) 1월은 내가 문법책 시리즈를 끝내는 달이다.
* (1) 문맥상 '~에 오는 사람은 누구든지'라는 의미의 복합관계대명사 Whoever가 알맞다.
(2) 문맥상 '~가 어디를 가든지'라는 의미의 복합관계대명사 Wherever가 알맞다.
(3) 문맥상 '~라고 말하는 것은 무엇이든지'라는 의미의 복합관계대명사 wherever가 알맞다.
(4) 선행사가 때를 나타내는 the month이므로 관계부사 when이 와야 한다.

20 ① 여기는 우리가 졸업한 학교이다.
② Bill은 그가 태어난 마을을 방문했다.
③ 그 부모들은 그들의 아이들이 어디에 있는지 알지 못했다.
④ Kyle은 하와이에 갔는데, 거기서 그는 졸업장을 받았다.
⑤ 그 여행가이드는 대부분의 사람들이 방문하는 장소로 그 관광객들을 이끌었다.
* ③은 의문사이고, 나머지는 모두 관계부사이다.

21 ① 우리가 알아야 할 무언가가 있다.
② 내가 일본에서 방문했던 도시들은 아름다웠다.
③ 우리가 해야 할 것은 매우 짜증나고 어렵다.
④ 그들은 정원이 꽃으로 가득찬 집에서 살고 있다.
⑤ 너는 자판기 앞에 서 있는 여자아이에게 관심이 있니?
* ① [what → that] something을 선행사로 하는 관계대명사 that이 와야 한다.
② [where → which] 관계사절 I visit in Japan에서 목적어 자리가 비어 있으므로 목적격 관계대명사가 와야 한다.
④ [that → whose] garden은 선행사 the house와 소유 관계이므로 소유격 관계대명사 whose가 와야 한다.
⑤ [who she is → who is] 주격 관계대명사 who 뒤에 나온 she는 선행사 the girl에 해당하므로 삭제해야 한다.

22 (a) 이것이 내가 너에게 전화한 이유이다.
(b) 나는 Wolfgang Amadeus Mozart가 태어난 곳을 방문하고 싶다.
(c) Kimberly는 교수님에게 그녀가 어떻게 하면 더 좋은 학점을 받을 수 있는지 여쭤보았다.
* (a) 선행사가 이유를 나타내는 the reason이므로 관계부사 why가 와야 한다.
(b) 선행사가 장소를 나타내는 the place이므로 관계부사 where가 와야 한다.
(c) 문맥상 '그녀가 ~할 수 있는 방법'을 나타내는 관계부사 how가 와야 한다.

23 ① 나는 그가 1등을 했던 그날을 잊지 않을 것이다.
② 이것이 그녀가 나를 떠난 이유이다.
③ Harry가 자주 Carol을 만났던 장소는 도서관에서였다.
④ 너는 우리가 사랑에 빠졌던 그 봄을 기억하니?
⑤ 내가 너와 잘 지낼 수 있는 방법을 내게 말해줘.
* [how → 삭제] the way와 관계부사 how는 함께 쓸 수 없다.

24 ① 내가 그녀와 헤어진 이유는 복잡하다.
② 그의 집은 Ralph가 살고 있는 집에서 멀지 않다.
③ 너는 네가 서울로 이사 온 날짜를 정확하게 기억했니?
④ 나는 왜 이 컴퓨터가 고장이 났는지 오늘 알아내려고 할 것이다.
⑤ 여기가 최고의 한국 음식을 맛볼 수 있는 식당이다.
* [which → why] which 이하의 문장이 완전하므로 관계대명사가 아닌 관계부사가 들어가야 한다. 문맥상 '컴퓨터가 고장 난 이유를 찾으려고 하다'라고 해야 한다.

25 대부분의 내 친구들은 내가 어려움 없이 좋은 성적을 받을 수 있었던 방법을 알기를 원한다.
* 선행사가 the way이므로 how는 올 수 없고 모든 관계부사를 대신할 수 있는 that이 알맞다.

Final Test

▶ 본문 178 - 181쪽

01 ④ **02** ⑤ **03** ③, ④ **04** Have you seen the movie which is playing now at CGV? **05** ④ **06** which **07** ③ **08** ④ **09** ③ **10** ① **11** ⑤ **12** The men are my school teachers. Their legs were injured by the accident. **13** ⑤ **14** ④ **15** (1) whenever (2) However (3) wherever (4) Whoever **16** ⑤ **17** ④ **18** ⑤ **19** ③ **20** ② **21** ④ **22** ① **23** ④ **24** ③ **25** ② **26** which → where **27** ② **28** (1) whoever (2) whomever (3) who **29** that **30** ⑤

01 (a) 도시가 직면하고 있는 교통문제들은 요즘 큰 이슈이다.
(b) 우리는 문들이 모두 찌그러진 차를 보았다.
* (a) 관계대명사절이 which the city is facing이고 문장의 주어가 The traffic problems이므로 복수 동사가 와야 한다.
(b) 관계대명사절의 주어가 doors이고 과거시제이므로 과거시제 복수 동사가 와야 한다.

02 (a) 너는 Benjamin과 이야기하고 있는 그 여자를 알아볼 수 있니?
(b) 이 팀은 내가 본 최고의 팀이다.
* (a) 문맥상 '~와 이야기하다'라는 의미의 talk to the woman에서 the woman이 선행사이므로 to가 있어야 한다.
(b) 선행사에 최상급 the best team이 있으므로 관계대명사 that이 와야 한다.

03 Wendy는 젊은 여자아이들 사이에서 유행인 그 실크 스카프를 했다.
* 선행사가 사물(the silk scarf)인 주격 관계대명사는 which, that 둘 다 올 수 있다.

04 * 영화(the movie)를 선행사로 하고 주어 역할을 하는 주격 관계대명사를 이용하여 나타낸다.

05 부모와 십대 아이들 사이에 세대 차이는 항상 있다. 부모들은 다 컸다고 생각하는 아이들을 여전히 아이라고 생각한다. 그것은 서로 대화를 단절시키는 이유들 중에 하나다. 아이로 취급받는 아이들 또한 그들의 문제에 대해서 말하고 싶어 하지 않는다. 그래서 부모들은 그들의 아이들이 걱정하고 있는 것을 이해하지 못한다.
* [whom → who] 선행사가 사람(Children)이고 관계대명사절에 주어가 빠져있으므로 주격 관계대명사 who가 와야 한다.

06 Sandra는 운전면허시험을 통과했다. 그리고 그것은 매우 어려웠다.
→ Sandra는 운전면허시험을 통과했는데, 그것은 매우 어려웠다.
* 〈접속사 + 대명사〉는 계속적 용법의 관계대명사로 바꿔 쓸 수 있으며, 이때 선행사가 사물(the driving test)이므로 which가 와야 한다.

07 A: 파티에 내가 가져가야 할 게 있니?
B: 네가 마시고 싶은 것은 무엇이든지 가지고 와. 우리는 저녁식사로 약간의 음식을 주문할 거야.
* [That → Whatever] That 앞에 You may bring이 생략되었으므로 anything that의 의미인 Whatever가 와야 한다.

08 ① 개를 잃어버린 사람들은 그들을 찾으려고 노력했다.
② 정상적인 사람이 그런 이상한 이야기를 믿을 수 있을까요?
③ 그녀가 다쳤다는 소식은 진짜임이 밝혀졌다.
④ 박물관에서 Jane의 관심을 끈 것은 아무것도 없었다.
⑤ 이것은 똑같은 그림그리기 테스트인데 많은 단계가 있다.
* [which → that] -thing으로 끝나는 명사가 선행사이므로 관계대명사는 that이 와야 한다.

09 ① 이곳은 내가 가고 싶어 하는 식당이다.
② 그가 그 일을 했던 이유는 말하기 어렵다.
③ 오늘은 내가 휴식을 취할 수 있는 유일한 날이다.
④ 내가 이 일을 왜 하는지 궁금할 때가 있다.
⑤ 우리는 런던으로 이사 갔는데, 거기에서 나의 가족은 3년 동안 살았다.
* [where → when] the only day는 때를 나타내는 말이므로 관계부사 when을 써야 한다.

10 ① Mike가 그 자전거를 훔쳤다는 것은 사실이었다.
② 그는 과거의 경찰관이 아니다.
③ 이 책은 내가 썼던 시리즈 중에서 마지막 책이다.
④ 나는 한국에서 매우 인기 있는 운동 스타 몇 명을 만났다.
⑤ Edwards 선생님은 내가 이 학교에서 가장 좋아하는 선생님이다.
* ①은 명사절을 이끄는 접속사로 쓰였고, 나머지는 관계사로 쓰였다.

11 ① 그는 네가 도와준 친구이니?
② 이것이 내가 사고 싶어 하는 그 바지이다.
③ 그녀는 그녀의 남자 친구가 만들어준 치킨 카레와 돈가스를 먹었다.
④ 네가 휴가 동안 찍은 사진을 내게 보여줘.
⑤ 그 시합에서 우승한 학생의 이름이 뭐니?
* 목적격 관계대명사는 생략할 수 있지만 주격 관계대명사는 생략할 수 없다.

12 그 사고로 다리를 부상당한 남자들은 우리 학교 선생님들이시다.
* 주어가 The men, 동사가 are이고, 관계대명사 whose가 이끄는 절은 주어를 수식하는 문장구조이다.

13 ① 저기가 Henry가 자란 집이다.
② Jack은 그가 처음으로 비행기를 탔던 그 날을 기억한다.
③ Gary가 콘서트에서 노래를 부르는 것을 포기한 이유가 무엇이었니?
④ 그는 Brian이 이 TV를 어떻게 고쳤는지 몰랐다.
⑤ Cindy는 그녀의 엄마가 그녀를 데리러 온 오후까지 침대에 누워 있었다.
* [which → at which] 관계부사 = 〈전치사 + 관계대명사〉

14 A: 이게 뭐니? 너는 티셔츠를 100달러를 주고 샀어?
B: 죄송해요, 아빠. 저는 그걸 정말 입고 싶어요.
A: 네가 뭐라고 말해도 이번에는 널 용서하지 않을 거야.
* 부사절을 이끄는 복합관계대명사가 와야 하며, 문맥상 '뭐라고 말해도'라는 의미이므로 Whatever 혹은 No matter what이 알맞다.

15 (1) Helen은 내가 전화할 때마다 바쁘다.
(2) 너는 아무리 노력해도 이 게임에서 이길 수 없다.
(3) 나는 네가 어디를 가든 너와 함께 할 것이다.
(4) 첫 번째로 오는 사람은 누구든지 멋진 선물을 받을 것이다.
* (1) 문맥상 '~할 때면 언제나'를 의미하는 whenever(= at any time when)가 알맞다.
(2) 문맥상 '아무리 ~할지라도'를 의미하는 However(= No matter how)가 알맞다.
(3) 문맥상 '어디에 ~하더라도'를 의미하는 wherever(= at any place where)가 알맞다.
(4) 문맥상 '~하는 누구든지'를 의미하는 Whoever(= Anyone who)가 알맞다.

16 당신은 누군가와 같이 일해본 적이 있는가? 다른 동료와 일을 같이 하는 것은 일을 좀 더 쉽고 재미있게 할 수 있다. 이 기사는 두 명의 친구인 Steve와 Bill에 관한 이야기인데, 두 사람은 함께 일해서 거대한 컴퓨터 게임 회사를 창립했다.
* 계속적 용법으로 쓰인 관계대명사는 〈접속사 + 대명사〉로 바꿔 쓸 수 있다. 이 때 접속사는 문맥에 따라 and, but, for 등으로 쓴다.

17 **보기** 나는 아침마다 수업에 가는 것이 두려웠다. 왜냐하면 나는 선생님들이 하시는 말들을 이해할 수 없었다.
① 너는 무슨 음식을 가장 좋아하니?
② 너의 휴대전화 번호가 어떻게 되니?
③ 나는 무엇이 문제인지 잘 모르겠다.
④ 네가 원하는 것을 내게 말해줘

⑤ 너는 그가 교실에서 무엇을 하고 있는지 알고 있니?

* 〈보기〉와 ④의 what은 선행사를 포함한 관계대명사로 쓰였고, 나머지는 의문사로 쓰였다.

18 **보기** 서비스는 우리가 필요로 하는 것들을 만족시키기 위해 누군가가 하는 어떤 종류의 일이다.

① 그녀는 그렇게 예쁘지 않다.
② 그녀는 내가 운이 좋았다고 말했다.
③ 그가 의사라는 것은 사실이다.
④ 그것은 자원이 충분하지 않다는 것을 뜻한다.
⑤ 네가 사고 싶은 것들의 목록을 만들어라.

* 〈보기〉와 ⑤의 that은 목적격 관계대명사로 쓰였다.
① 부사, ②③④ 명사절을 이끄는 접속사

19 **보기** 네가 많은 사람들 앞에서 이야기해야 했을 때를 생각해봐.

① 그녀는 언제 그리고 어디로 갔니?
② 네 남자 친구의 생일은 언제니?
③ 나는 네가 집을 떠난 시간을 알고 있다.
④ 나의 어머니는 전화 한 통화를 받았을 때 외출하셨다.
⑤ 나의 아버지가 오시면, 나의 가족은 외식을 하러 나갈 것이다.

* 〈보기〉와 ③의 when은 장소를 나타내는 선행사가 왔으므로 관계부사로 쓰였다.
①② 의문사, ④⑤ 시간을 나타내는 접속사

20 3월은 길고 추운 겨울이 지나고 오는 달이다. 나는 따뜻한 봄 때문에 3월을 가장 좋아한다. 3월은 나의 가족과 함께 여행을 갈 수 있는 달이다. 올해, 나는 오스트리아에 갈 것이다. 왜냐하면 나는 그 나라의 풍경을 좋아하고 영화 '사운드 오브 뮤직'을 찍었던 대저택을 방문하고 싶기 때문이다.

* (a) 관계사절의 동사 comes의 주어가 되어야 하므로 주격 관계대명사가 와야 한다.
(b) 선행사가 the month이고 관계사절이 완벽한 문장이므로 관계부사가 와야 한다.
(c) the mansion이 장소를 나타내는 선행사이고 관계사절이 완벽한 문장이므로 where가 와야 한다.

21 이 사람은 완벽한 여성이다. + 나는 그녀를 찾고 있다.
→ 이 사람은 내가 찾고 있는 완벽한 여성이다.

* [for which → who(m)] 문장의 끝에 전치사 for가 있고 선행사가 사람이므로 관계대명사는 who(m)이 와야 한다.
① 전치사의 목적어로 쓰인 관계대명사는 〈전치사 + 목적격 관계대명사〉의 형태로 쓸 수 있다. ② 목적격 관계대명사는 생략할 수 있으며, ⑤ 목적격 관계대명사 who(m)은 that으로 바꿔 쓸 수 있다.

22 Good Will은 ____________ 가게이다.

① 저렴한 물건을 파는
② 사람들이 원하는 것을 파는
③ 너의 집에 있는 양탄자를 샀던
④ 많은 근로자들이 그들의 낡은 물건을 기부하는
⑤ 어린아이들이 가고 싶어 하는

* [sells → which sells] 주절에 이미 주어(Good Will) 동사(is)가 있으므로 the store를 수식하는 주격 관계대명사사절이 와야 한다. 한 문장에 동사가 두 번 올 수 없다.

23 ① 그녀는 나의 선생님이 어떻게 생겼는지 아니?
② 네가 무슨 음식을 먹을 수 없는지 그에게 말하지 마.
③ 나는 그녀가 가장 좋아하는 음악이 뭔지 잘 알고 있어.
④ 누구도 내가 그리고 있는 것을 추측하지 못한다.
⑤ 시험을 대비해서 무엇을 해야 할지 목록을 적어봐.

* 관계사 what은 '무엇'이라는 의미로 해석되지 않는다.

24 우리는 Keilen을 만났는데, 우리는 4년 넘게 그녀로부터 영어를 배웠다.

* 관계대명사절을 문장으로 쓸 때는 의미상 누락되는 부분이 없도록 주의한다. 계속적 용법의 관계대명사 who는 〈접속사 + 대명사〉로 바꿔 쓸 수 있으며, 이때 접속사는 문맥에 맞게 and로 바꾸고, 목적격 관계대명사이므로 문장의 마지막에 from her를 놓치지 않도록 주의한다.

25 (a) Thomas는 Luz가 원하는 것은 무엇이든지 사준다.
(b) 그가 너에게 무엇을 준다 할지라도, 어느 것도 받지 마라.
(c) 그 남자가 너에게 말하는 것은 무엇이든지 올바른 정보가 아니다.
(d) 너는 네가 선택한 것은 무엇이든지 발표할 수 있다.
(e) 그가 뭐라고 말했든지 나는 신경 쓰지 않는다.

* (b)(e)는 양보의 부사절로 쓰여 no matter what의 의미이다. (a)(c)(d)는 명사절로 쓰여 anything that의 의미이다.

26 Ryan은 관공서에서 일한다. 나는 가끔씩 거기에 간다.
→ Ryan은 내가 가끔씩 가는 관공서에서 일한다.

* 부사 there는 관계부사 where로 써야 한다.

27 (a) 나는 가격이 매우 비싼 TV를 사기를 희망한다.
(b) 일요일은 우리가 교회에 가는 날이다.
(c) 내가 다녔던 고등학교는 명문 학교였다.

* (a) 선행사가 a TV이고 빈칸 뒤에 명사가 왔으므로 소유격 관계대명사 whose가 와야 한다.
(b) 선행사가 the day이고 빈칸 다음의 문장이 완전하므로 관계부사 when 혹은 on which가 와야 한다.
(c) 빈칸 다음에 목적어가 없는 불완전한 문장이므로 목적격 관계대명사 which가 와야 한다.

28 (1) Marie는 여기에 먼저 도착하는 사람은 누구든지 점심 도시락을 줄 것이다.
(2) Marie는 그녀가 좋아하지 않는 누구와도 결혼하지 않을 것이다.
(3) Marie가 아는 사람들을 초대해라.

* (1) 선행사를 포함하고 관계절에서 주어 역할을 하며, '~하는 사람은 누구든지'라는 의미를 가진 whoever가 알맞다.
(2) 선행사를 포함하고 관계절에서 목적어 역할을 하며, '~가 좋아하지 않는 누구와도'라는 의미를 가진 whomever가 알맞다.
(3) 선행사가 the people이고 관계절에서 목적어 역할을 하는 who가 알맞다.

29 (a) 그는 그가 기말 과제를 제출해야 하는 날을 잊었다.
(b) 나는 내가 혼났던 이유를 모르겠다.

* 시간(the day)과 이유(the reason)를 선행사로 모두 취할 수 있는 관계사는 that이다.

30 나는 중간고사를 위해 도서관에서 공부를 해야 했는데, 그곳의 에어컨이 고장 났다. 그곳은 너무 더웠는데, 그것이 나를 짜증나게 했다. 그래서 나는 도서관을 나와 집에 갔다.

* 첫 번째 빈칸에는 다음에 명사가 왔으므로 소유격 관계대명사 whose가 와야 한다. 두 번째 빈칸에는 내용상 앞 문장 전체를 받는 계속적 용법의 관계대명사 which가 와야 한다.

Sentence Writing

▶ 본문 182쪽

Part A
1 Whenever I look at her
2 Whoever wins
3 when the FIFA World Cup took place

Part B
1 We have a friend whose mother is an actress.
2 A piece of this cake is all that I ate today.
3 What Min is watching is a newly released movie.
4 Whomever Cathy fell in love with, I don't mind.

Part A

1 내가 그녀를 볼 때마다 그녀는 나를 보고 미소 짓는다. 그녀는 나를 좋아하는 것 같다.
2 우승하는 사람은 누구든지 NFM 상의 우승자로 파리에 갈 것이다.
3 Eric은 한국에서 FIFA 월드컵이 열렸던 해를 알고 싶어 한다.

Unit 10 > 관사

DAY 20 관사의 의미와 용법 (심화)

2교시 In - Class Questions

▶ 본문 187쪽

STEP A 1 food 2 Gold 3 bus 4 France
STEP B 1 × 2 an 3 a 4 the

STEP C　1 a → 삭제　2 On the → At
3 Himalayas → the Himalayas　4 the → 삭제

STEP D　1 Although the phone was ringing, nobody was in the house.
2 My family played badminton in the park after dinner.
3 I like reading books. What is the name of the book?

STEP A　1 나의 가족은 좋은 음식을 먹는 것을 정말 좋아한다.
2 금은 귀중한 금속이다.
3 나는 항상 버스를 타고 학교에 간다.
4 우리는 다음 달에 프랑스를 여행할 예정이다.

STEP B　1 이 방은 가구가 필요하다.
2 John은 결국 우주비행사가 되었다.
3 Kelly는 캐나다 가수이다.
4 너는 오늘 신문을 읽을 예정이었니?

STEP C　1 나는 가끔 구내식당에서 아침을 먹는다.
2 크리스마스에 미국인들은 크리스마스트리를 장식한다.
3 그 동아리 회원들은 히말라야 산맥을 등반했다.
4 Sally는 뉴욕의 타임스퀘어 광장을 방문하고 싶어 한다.

Final Test

▶ 본문 188 - 191쪽

01 ② **02** ④ **03** ⑤ **04** ② **05** ⑤ **06** David is a vegetarian. So he doesn't eat meat. **07** ④ **08** ② **09** ① **10** ④ **11** ① Eiffel Tower → The Eiffel Tower **12** (1) The, 수식어로 한정된 특정한 대상 (2) the, 최상급 앞 (3) ×, advice는 셀 수 없는 명사 (4) the, 방위를 나타내는 명사 **13** ④ **14** ×, the **15** (1) 종이 위에 지우개가 하나 있다. (2) 페이지의 윗부분에 있는 주제를 소리 내어 읽어라. **16** a, × **17** ③ **18** ① **19** ③ **20** ② **21** ④ **22** a paper → a sheet[piece] of paper **23** the water → water **24** ①, ③, ⑤ **25** (1) the (2) the (3) × (4) × **26** ⑤ **27** Joshua is a close friend of my older brother's. **28** ② **29** ⑤ **30** ×

01 ① 지난밤에 큰 사고가 하나 있었다.
② 너는 하루에 세 번 그 약을 먹어야 한다.
③ 개는 네 개의 다리를 갖고 있고 거미는 여덟 개의 다리를 갖고 있다.
④ 많은 방문객들은 그 기념물을 보기 위해 줄을 서서 기다리고 있다.
⑤ 나의 부모님은 항상 아침에 우유 한 잔을 마신다.
* '하루에 세 번씩'이라는 뜻이므로 a가 '~마다(per)'의 의미로 쓰였다.
①⑤ 하나(one), ③ 종족 대표, ④ a lot of는 '많은'(관용어구)

02 ① 그의 아버지는 영화감독이다.
② 박 선생님은 모차르트의 곡을 연주하는 중이다.
③ 내 친구들 중에 한 명은 새로운 아이패드 제품을 갖고 있다.
④ 같은 깃털의 새가 함께 모인다.
⑤ Sam은 한 달에 한 번 영화를 본다.
* '같은 깃털의 새'라는 뜻이므로 a가 '~같은(the same)'의 의미로 쓰였다.
① 하나(one), ② 작품, ③ 제품, ⑤ ~마다(per)

03 ① 창문을 여는 것이 어떨까요?
② 그의 아들은 항상 방에 있다.
③ 사람들은 내 눈을 빤히 보았다.
④ 너는 두 번째 신호등에서 좌회전해야 한다.
⑤ Kelly는 신문 가판대 근처의 벤치에 앉았다.
* [a → the] bench가 수식어구 near the newstand의 수식을 받고 있으므로 앞에 정관사가 와야 한다. ①②④ 〈the + 익숙한 장소〉, ③ 〈the + 신체부위〉

04 ① 잘 가! 좋은 하루 보내.
② 아이의 머리를 만지지 마세요.
③ 하루의 마지막 식사는 저녁이라고 불린다.
④ 버스 정류장으로 가는 길을 가르쳐 주세요.
⑤ Amber는 주로 아침에 산책을 간다.
* [head → the head] 〈the + 신체부위〉이므로 head 앞에 정관사가 와야 한다.
① '하나의(one)' 혹은 하나의 개념, ③ 식사 앞에는 무관사, ④ 〈the + 익숙한 장소〉, ⑤ 관용표현

05 ① Jane은 바이올린을 켜는 방법을 배우고 싶어 한다.
② 너는 무대의 그 남자를 기억하니?
③ 너는 아마존 강을 본 적이 있니?
④ 몇 명의 회원들은 네덜란드를 방문하고 싶어 한다.
⑤ 장미는 정열과 사랑을 상징한다.
* ⑤는 종족대표를 나타내는 부정관사 a가 들어가야 하고, 나머지는 정관사 the가 들어가야 한다.
① 〈the + 악기〉, ② 〈the + 한정 명사〉, ③ 〈the + 강 이름〉, ④ 〈the + 복수 지명〉

06 * vegetarian은 셀 수 있는 명사이므로 앞에 부정관사, meat는 셀 수 없는 명사이므로 무관사로 쓴다.

07 (a) 나는 언젠가 알래스카를 여행하고 싶다.
(b) 우리는 네덜란드에 머무는 중이다.
* 정관사를 쓰는 고유명사는 the United Kingdom, the North Pole, the Netherlands이다. 무관사로 쓰는 고유명사는 South America, Jeju Island, Alaska, Korea, Hawaii이다.

08 * '필요', '발명'과 같은 추상명사는 무관사, mother는 of invention의 수식을 받으므로 the가 필요하다.

09 하마는 큰 입을 가지고 있다.
* 종족 대표를 나타낼 때 부정관사 a를 쓰며, 입은 하나이므로 one을 의미하는 부정관사 a를 써야 한다.

10 그들 중 몇몇은 학교에 있는 대신에 집에서 머물고 있다.
* home, school은 건물이라는 뜻이 아닌 본래의 목적으로 쓰였으므로 무관사이다.

11 에펠탑은 파리의 가장 유명한 명소 중 하나이다. 1889년에 세워진 그 탑은 프랑스 민주주의를 상징하는 것이었다.
* Eiffel Tower는 관광물이므로 정관사를 써야 한다.
② 〈the + 최상급〉, ③⑤ Paris, France는 단수 지명이므로 무관사, ④ a symbol은 '프랑스 민주주의를 상징하는 하나의 물건'이라는 뜻이므로 부정관사

12 (1) 이 팔찌의 금은 좋은 품질이다.
(2) 이것은 내가 가지고 있는 가장 좋은 금반지이다.
(3) 엄마는 내가 결정을 하는 데 도움이 되는 유용한 조언을 주셨다.
(4) 우리는 북쪽에 갔다 온 적이 없다.

13 A: Alice가 오늘밤 큰 파티를 열 예정이래. 나랑 차로 거기에 갈 수 있어?
B: 미안해. 갈 수 없어. 나는 다른 계획이 있어.
A: 오, 이런. 나는 그 파티에서 마술 쇼를 할 거야. 네가 나에게 꽃을 주었으면 좋겠어.
B: 정말로? 알았어, 계획을 취소해 볼게.
* [at a party → at the party] 앞에서 언급된 파티이므로 the로 표현해야 한다.
② by car = in a car

14 컬럼비아 대학교는 뉴욕 주에 있다.
* 대학이름은 무관사이고, state가 of New York의 수식을 받기 때문에 the가 필요하다.

15 * (1) on top of는 '~의 위에', (2) at the top of는 '~의 위쪽에, 윗부분에'라는 의미이다.

16 * 특정하지 않은 택시이므로 부정관사 a가 와야 하며, 〈by + 교통수단〉으로 쓰이므로 무관사이다.

17 ① Gary는 우리 반에서 가장 현명한 남자아이이다.
② Steve는 예절바른 사람이다. 그는 또한 (다른 사람의 이야기를) 잘 들어주는 사람이다.
③ 루브르 박물관은 세계의 다른 어떤 박물관보다 크다.
④ 1번 도로를 타자. 우리는 동쪽으로 가야 해.
⑤ 박 대통령은 그 법안을 통과할 것을 결심했다.
* [A Louvre → The Louvre] 관광물 앞에는 정관사가 와야 한다.
① 〈the + 최상급〉, ② '한 명(one)', ④ 〈the + 방향〉, ⑤ 호칭, 직위는 무관사

18 ① Teddy의 형은 Teddy를 보기 위해 감옥에 갔다.
② 이 회의에 있는 사람들은 아직 점심을 먹지 않았다.
③ 피부암은 태양에 너무 많이 노출됨으로써 발생된다.
④ 우리는 항공우편으로 프랑스에 이 소포를 보내려고 했었다.
⑤ Mary 여왕은 영국 역사에서 가장 위대한 여성이었다.
* prison에 본래의 목적(수감되다)이 아닌 방문하기 위해 간 것이므로 관사 the가 필요하다.

② 식사 앞에는 무관사, ③ 심각한 병명이나 질병 앞에 무관사, ④ 〈by + 교통, 통신수단〉 무관사, ⑤ 관직, 칭호가 고유명사 앞에 쓰일 경우 무관사

19 A: 시간제로 일하는 근로자들에게 어떤 방법으로 임금을 지불했습니까?
B: 규칙상 근로자들은 시간당으로 임금을 지급받았습니다.
* 단위를 나타내는 명사의 경우 by 뒤에 정관사를 써서 나타낸다.

20 (a) 하루는 24시간이다.
(b) 불 좀 꺼주실래요?
(c) Chan과 Helen은 같은 나이이다.
(d) Elizabeth는 나의 손을 잡았다.
(e) 수학은 재미있는 과목이다.
* (a) '하나(one)'를 나타내는 부정관사, (c) '같은(the same)'을 나타내는 부정관사, (d) 〈the + 신체부위〉
(b) [a → the] 〈the + 특정 명사(누구나 아는 것)〉, (e) [the → 삭제] 학과 앞에는 무관사

21 ① 고양이는 이기적인 동물이다.
② 나는 모네의 작품을 거실에 걸어 놓았다.
③ 그것은 꽤 도움이 되는 수업이다.
④ 지식은 인터넷을 통해 얻어질 수 있다.
⑤ 우리 집 근처에서 화재가 한 건 있었다.
* 지식(knowledge)은 추상명사이므로 부정관사를 쓰지 않는다.
① 종족 대표, ② 작품, ③ 〈quite a(n) + 형용사 + 명사〉, ⑤ 하나(one)

22 지금 바쁘지 않으면 책장에서 종이 한 장만 갖다 줄래요?
* paper(종이)는 셀 수 없는 물질명사이므로 개수를 셀 때는 단위명사 a sheet of 나 a piece of를 사용해야 한다.

23 건강을 유지하고자 한다면 매일 물을 몇 잔씩 마시는 것이 필요하다.
* water는 물질명사이므로 앞에 관사를 사용할 수 없다.

24 Daniel은 경찰관이다. 어느 날, 그는 사람이 많은 어느 거리에서 흉악범 한 명을 우연히 마주쳤고, 그를 즉시 검거했다.
* ① [a police → a police officer] 집합명사 police는 셀 수 없는 명사로 복수 취급하므로 관사를 사용하지 못한다. 경찰관 한 명을 나타낼 때는 a police officer로 나타낸다.
③ [the vicious criminal → a vicious criminal] '흉악범 한 명(one)'을 의미이므로 부정관사 a를 사용해야 한다.
⑤ [the busy street → a busy street] '어느(certain) 바쁜 거리'라는 의미이므로 부정관사 a를 사용해야 한다.

25 이것은 뉴욕 행 승객들을 위한 마지막 탑승 안내 방송입니다. 지금 게이트 50에서 출발하는 075항공편은 디트로이트와 필라델피아를 경유하는 뉴욕 행 비행기입니다. 이것은 오늘 인천 국제공항에서의 뉴욕 행 마지막 항공편입니다. 모든 승객은 탑승권과 여권을 가지고 탑승하시기 바랍니다. 감사합니다.
* (1)(2) 최상급 앞에는 정관사가 온다. (3) 공항명 앞에는 무관사이다. (4) on board 와 같은 관용구에는 무관사이다.

26 보기 외출하신 동안 Jones씨라는 어떤 분이 찾아왔어요.
① 로마는 하루아침에 이루어진 것이 아니다.
② 깃털이 같은 새끼리 모인다. (유유상종 類類相從)
③ 보통 한 해에는 며칠이 있니?
④ 나는 한 달에 한두 번 야구 경기를 한다.
⑤ 한때 어떤 늙은 왕이 작은 마을에 살았다.
* 〈보기〉와 ⑤는 '어떤(certain)'이라는 의미로 사용되었다.
①③ 하나(one), ② 같은(the same), ④ ~당, 마다(per)

27 * 부정관사(a)와 소유격(my older brother's)은 나란히 쓰지 않으므로 〈a + 명사 + of + 소유대명사〉로 나타낸다.

28 ① 그는 이번 시즌의 MVP였다.
② 내 과제를 끝내는 데 한 시간이 걸렸다.
③ 그 여자들 둘 다 아름답다.
④ 저기의 배낭들은 모두 내 것이다.
⑤ 그 상자 안에 있는 모든 오렌지는 매우 맛이 있다.
* ②에는 '한 시간'이라는 의미의 부정관사 an이 와야 하고, 나머지는 정관사 the가 와야 한다.

[29–30] 영어에 관해서라면 많은 한국 학생들이 문법을 공부하는 데 어려움이 있다. 그래서 대부분의 영어 교사들은 숙제를 내준다. 하지만 학생들은 숙제하기를 정말로 싫어한다. 더욱이 학생들은 단어를 외우는 것을 귀찮아한다. 단어 간의 관계를 파악하면 외우기 쉬울 텐데, 학생들은 그 사실을 모른다.

29 * (a) grammar는 셀 수 없는 명사이므로 무관사이다.
(b) assignment는 셀 수 있는 명사이므로 부정관사가 와야 한다.
(c) homework는 셀 수 없는 명사이므로 무관사이다.

30 * vocabulary는 셀 수 없는 명사이므로 무관사이다.

Sentence Writing

▶ 본문 192쪽

Part A an elephant, the hallway, the school, the zoo, the elephant, a field trip

Part B
1 Turn off the light and shut the window before leaving.
2 I usually play the violin after dinner.
3 Take this medicine twice a day.
4 There is a bus to the airport. You can take the bus there.

Part A
2주 전에 코끼리 한 마리가 LA의 Page 초등학교 복도에서 발견되었다. 이 큰 동물은 아마도 그 동물원에서 탈출 한 후에 그 학교에 갔을 것이다. 학생들 중 한 명은 캘리포니아 동물원으로 갔던 현장 학습에서 학교로 돌아갈 때 그 코끼리가 그를 따라온 것이라고 믿었다.

Unit 11  가정법

DAY 21 가정법 과거, 과거완료, 혼합가정법

2교시 In - Class Questions

▶ 본문 197쪽

STEP A 1 had studied 2 won 3 knew 4 had taken

STEP B 1 had 2 send 3 broken

STEP C
1 didn't become, was not
2 was not, didn't succeed
3 didn't like, wouldn't[couldn't] be
4 had had, would have watched

STEP D
1 If Mike took care of his car regularly, his car wouldn't frequently break down.
2 If you had not helped me then, I would not be here now.
3 If he had had enough time, he could have done it better.

STEP A
1 내가 학교에 다니는 동안 열심히 공부했다면 지금 의사가 되었을 텐데.
2 내가 복권에 당첨된다면 수영장이 딸린 커다란 저택을 살 텐데.
3 내가 그 사실을 안다면 너에게 그것을 이야기할 텐데.
4 우리가 그 비행기를 탔다면 지금 부산에 있을 텐데.

STEP B
1 내가 충분한 돈이 있다면 세계여행을 할 수 있을 텐데.
2 네가 오후 2시 전에 그 소포를 보내면 그것은 내일 오후까지 도착할 것이다.
3 Jim은 팔이 부러지지 않았다면 포스트 시즌에서 야구 경기를 하고 있었을 텐데.

STEP C
1 내가 프로게이머가 되었다면 행복했을 텐데.
→ 나는 프로게이머가 되지 않았다. 그래서 나는 행복하지 않았다.
2 그가 의지가 강한 사람이었다면 성공했을 텐데.
→ 그는 의지가 강한 사람이 아니었기 때문에 성공하지 않았다.

3 나는 농구를 매우 많이 좋아하기 때문에 내 꿈은 NBA 프로 농구 선수가 되는 것이다.
→ 내가 농구를 매우 많이 좋아하지 않는다면 내 꿈이 NBA 프로 농구 선수가 되는 것이 아닐 텐데.
4 나의 엄마는 시간이 없었다. 그래서 그 드라마를 볼 수 없었다.
→ 나의 엄마가 시간이 있었다면 그 드라마를 보았을 텐데.

STEP **D**

1 Mike는 자동차를 정기적으로 관리하지 않아서 그의 자동차가 자주 고장 난다.
→ Mike가 그의 자동차를 정기적으로 관리한다면 그의 자동차는 자주 고장 나지 않을 텐데.
2 그때 네가 나를 도와주었기 때문에 내가 지금 여기에 있다.
→ 네가 그때 나를 도와주지 않았다면 나는 지금 여기에 있지 않을 것이다.
3 그는 충분한 시간이 없었기 때문에 그것을 더 잘할 수 없었다.
→ 그에게 충분한 시간이 있었다면 그는 그 일을 더 잘할 수 있었을 텐데.

3교시 After - Class Questions

▶ 본문 198 - 201쪽

01 ② **02** ④ **03** ③ **04** ④ **05** ⑤ **06** ④ **07** ④ **08** ③ **09** told → had told **10** didn't help → hadn't helped **11** is → were **12** If Linda had finished her homework yesterday, she could be watching this show. **13** ② **14** ① **15** ① **16** ④ **17** weren't **18** did **19** would have happened, hadn't hesitated **20** won, would quit **21** watched, applied **22** am, not, won't, have **23** If it had not rained last night, I would have driven you home. **24** ③ **25** ①

01 나의 학교가 집과 좀 더 가까이 있다면 나는 자주 지각하지 않을 텐데.
* 주절이 〈주어 + 조동사의 과거형 + 동사원형 ...〉이 왔으므로 가정법 과거의 조건절인 〈If + 주어 + 동사의 과거형 ~〉이 와야 한다.

02 A: 너의 피아노 연주가 정말 좋았어.
B: 음, 내 손가락이 좀 더 길었다면 피아노를 더 잘 연주할 수 있었을 텐데.
* 과거의 사실을 이야기하는 것이므로 가정법 과거완료의 주절인 〈주어 + 조동사의 과거형 + have + 과거분사 ...〉가 와야 한다.

03 * 현재 사실에 반대되는 일을 가정하는 것이므로 가정법 과거인 〈주어 + 조동사의 과거형 + 동사원형 ...., if + 주어 + 동사의 과거형 ~〉으로 나타낸다.

04 * 과거 사실에 반대되는 일을 가정하므로 가정법 과거완료인 〈If + 주어 + had + 과거분사 ~, 주어 + 조동사의 과거형 + have + 과거분사 ...〉의 형태로 나타낸다.

05 ① Gary가 게으르지 않다면 돈을 벌기 위해 일을 구할 수 있을 텐데.
② 네가 나에게 질문했다면 나는 너를 도와줄 수 있었을 텐데.
③ 내가 주의 깊게 운전을 했다면 지금 병원에 있지 않을 텐데.
④ 내가 계단에서 미끄러지지 않았다면 내 다리가 부러지지 않았을 텐데.
⑤ 내가 그 동아리에 가입하지 않았다면 지금 피곤하지 않을 텐데.
* [have not been → not be] 조건절에 가정법 과거완료(had + 과거분사)가 왔고 주절에 now가 있으므로 혼합가정법이다. 혼합가정법의 주절은 〈주어 + 조동사의 과거형 + 동사원형〉으로 나타낸다.

06 ① 영어 공부를 열심히 했더라면 좋을 텐데.
② 그녀는 마치 우등생처럼 보인다.
③ 내가 충분한 시간이 있다면 나의 가족과 함께 보낼 텐데.
④ 나에게 충분한 돈이 있다면 새로 나온 자전거를 살 텐데.
⑤ 오늘 아침에 비가 오지 않았다면 우리는 현장 학습을 갈 수 있었을 텐데.
* [can buy → could buy] 가정법 과거의 주절은 〈조동사의 과거형 + 동사원형〉으로 쓴다.

07 Andrew는 아침을 먹었기 때문에 지금 배고프지 않다.
→ Andrew가 아침을 먹지 않았다면 지금 배고플 텐데.
* 밥을 먹은 것은 과거의 일이고 배가 고프지 않은 것은 현재의 일이므로 혼합가정법 (If + 주어 + had + 과거분사 ~, 주어 + 조동사의 과거형 + 동사원형 ...)으로 나타낸다. 직설법이 부정이므로 가정법은 긍정으로 나타낸다.

08 Joe는 그 규칙을 따르지 않았다. 그래서 그는 지금 곤경에 처해 있다.
→ Joe가 규칙을 따랐다면 지금 곤경에 처해 있지 않을 텐데.
* 규칙을 따르지 않은 것은 과거의 일이고 곤경에 처한 것은 현재의 일이므로 혼합가정법으로 나타낸다. 직설법이 부정이므로 가정법은 긍정으로 나타낸다.

09 그가 나에게 진실을 말했다면 나는 그가 내 지갑을 훔쳤다고 의심하지 않았을 텐데.
* 문맥상 '사실을 말했다면'이라는 과거의 일을 나타내야 하므로 가정법 과거완료가 알맞다. 따라서 조건절은 〈If + 주어 + had + 과거완료〉가 와야 한다.

10 Bill이 나를 어제 도와주지 않았다면 나는 지금 살아있지 않을지도 모른다.
* 조건절에 과거를 나타내는 yesterday가 있고 주절에 현재를 나타내는 now가 있으므로 혼합가정법이다. 따라서 조건절에는 〈had + 과거분사〉가 와야 한다.

11 그녀가 똑똑하다면 그 문제를 풀 수 있을 텐데.
* 가정법 과거의 조건절에 쓰인 be동사는 항상 were로 쓴다.

12 Linda는 어제 숙제를 끝내지 못해서 이 쇼를 볼 수 없다. → Linda가 어제 숙제를 끝냈더라면 이 쇼를 볼 수 있을 텐데.
* 숙제를 끝낸 것은 과거의 일이고 쇼를 보는 것은 현재의 일이므로 혼합가정법(If + 주어 + had + 과거분사 ~, 주어 + 조동사의 과거형 + 동사원형 ...)으로 나타낸다.

13 만약 가수 GD가 내 친한 친구였다면 나는 그때 다른 사람들에게 좀 더 자랑스러워했을 텐데.
* at that time이라는 과거를 나타내는 부사구가 있으므로 가정법 과거완료로 써야 한다.

14 (a) Jack은 돈이 필요하면 너에게 전화할 텐데.
(b) Jack은 돈이 필요하면 너에게 전화할 것이다.
(c) Jack은 돈이 필요했다면 너에게 전화했을 텐데.
* (a) 가정법 과거이므로 동사의 과거형이 와야 한다.
(b) 단순 조건문(가정법 현재)이므로 동사의 현재형이 와야 한다.
(c) 가정법 과거완료이므로 〈had + 과거분사〉가 와야 한다.

15 (a) 내가 5분만 더 일찍 일어났더라면 학교 버스를 놓치지 않았을 텐데.
(b) 지금 비가 내리지 않으면 나는 여행을 즐길 텐데.
* (a) 주절에 〈조동사의 과거형 + have + 과거분사 ...〉가 왔으므로 조건절에는 가정법 과거완료인 〈If + 주어 + had + 과거분사 ~〉가 와야 한다.
(b) 주절에 〈조동사의 과거형 + 동사원형〉이 왔으므로 조건절에는 가정법 과거인 〈If + 주어 + 동사의 과거형 ~〉이 와야 한다.

16 ① 그 사장은 네가 정직하지 않으면 고용하지 않을 것이다.
② 내가 너라면 버스를 타지 않을 텐데.
③ 내가 차를 갖고 있다면 너에게 빌려줄 수 있을 텐데.
④ 나의 아버지가 대통령이라면 사람들을 울게 하지 않을 텐데.
⑤ 네가 많은 보너스를 받는다면 너의 아내는 그것으로 무엇을 할까?
* [was → were] 가정법 과거의 조건절에 쓰인 be동사는 주어의 인칭과 수에 상관없이 항상 were로 쓴다.
① 가정법 현재, ②③⑤ 가정법 과거

17 Betty는 심하게 아프다. 그녀가 아프지 않으면 그 수영장에 올 텐데.
* 앞 문장에서 반복되는 어구(is horribly sick)를 쓸 때는 대동사로 나타낸다. be동사가 쓰였으므로 대동사도 be동사로 쓴다.

18 John은 영어를 전혀 모른다. 그가 안다면 한국어 자막 없이 이 영화를 즐길 수 있을 텐데.
* 앞 문장에서 반복되는 어구(know any English)를 쓸 때는 대동사로 나타낸다. 일반동사가 쓰였으므로 대동사는 do동사로 쓴다.

19 * 과거 사실에 대한 가정이므로 가정법 과거완료로 나타낸다.

20 * 현재 사실에 반대되는 일을 가정할 때는 가정법 과거로 나타낸다.

21 진희가 그 다큐멘터리를 보지 않았다면 이 직업에 지원하지 않았을 텐데.
→ 진희는 그 다큐멘터리를 봤기 때문에 이 직업에 지원했다.
* 가정법 과거완료는 직설법 과거로 바꿔 쓸 수 있다.

22 나는 배가 고프면 그들과 같이 식사를 할 텐데.
→ 나는 배가 고프지 않기 때문에 그들과 같이 식사를 하지 않을 것이다.
* 가정법 과거는 직설법 현재로 바꿔 쓸 수 있다.

23 * 과거 사실에 반대되는 일을 가정할 때는 가정법 과거완료(if + 주어 + had + 과거분사 ~, 주어 + 조동사의 과거형 + have + 과거분사 ...)로 나타낸다.

24 ① 그가 좀 더 오래 머물렀다면 그녀를 그곳에서 만날 수 있었을 텐데.
→ 그는 오래 머무르지 않았기 때문에 그녀를 그곳에서 만날 수 없었다.
② 내가 10살만 더 젊었다면 전 세계를 여행할 수 있었을 텐데.
→ 나는 10살 더 젊지 않았기 때문에 전 세계를 여행할 수 없었다.
③ 내가 카메라가 있었다면 그 사진을 찍을 수 있었을 텐데.

→ 나는 카메라가 없어서 그 사진을 찍을 수가 없다.
④ 내가 엄마의 생신을 기억했다면 엄마에게 선물을 사드렸을 텐데.
→ 나는 엄마의 생신을 기억하지 못해서 엄마에게 선물을 사드리지 못했다.
⑤ 그가 그 수술을 받았다면 지금 휠체어를 사용하지 않을 텐데.
→ 그는 그 수술을 받지 않았기 때문에 지금 휠체어를 사용한다.
* [→ As I didn't have a camera, I couldn't take pictures of it.] 가정법 과거완료이므로 직설법 과거로 나타내야 한다.

25 그는 은메달에 만족하지 못했기 때문에 훈련을 멈출 수가 없었다.
→ 그가 은메달에 만족했다면 훈련을 멈출 수 있었을 텐데.
* 직설법 과거는 가정법 과거완료로 바꿔 쓸 수 있다.

DAY 22 기타 가정법

2교시 In - Class Questions ▶ 본문 203쪽

STEP A 1 had been in the office when you stopped by
2 the journey were not over
3 they didn't come and see us last class
4 don't know her cell phone number

STEP B 1 Without 2 were, not, for
3 had, not, been, for

STEP C 1 Had I hurried 2 doesn't know 3 had been

STEP D 1 I wish I could understand Hollywood movies.
2 He talks as if he had seen the movie.
3 Without air, no creatures in the world could exist.

STEP A
1 네가 사무실에 잠깐 들렀을 때 내가 없어서 유감이다.
→ 네가 사무실에 잠깐 들렀을 때 내가 있었으면 좋았을 텐데.
2 나는 그 여행이 끝나서 유감이다.
→ 그 여행이 끝나지 않으면 좋을 텐데.
3 그들이 지난 수업에 와서 우리를 보았으면 좋았을 텐데.
→ 나는 그들이 지난 수업에 와서 우리를 보지 않아서 유감이다.
4 그녀의 휴대전화 번호를 안다면 좋을 텐데.
→ 나는 그녀의 휴대전화 번호를 알지 못해서 유감이다.

STEP B
1 내비게이션 시스템이 없었다면 우리는 길을 잃었을 텐데.
2 태양이 없다면 아무 것도 살 수 없을 텐데.
3 너의 도움이 없었다면 나는 내 과제를 제시간에 할 수 없었을 텐데.

STEP C
1 내가 서둘렀다면 그 기차를 놓치지 않았을 텐데.
2 그는 마치 모든 것을 아는 것처럼 말한다. 사실, 그는 아무것도 모른다.
3 그녀는 아프지 않았던 것처럼 보였다. 사실, 그녀는 아팠다.

3교시 After - Class Questions ▶ 본문 204 - 207쪽

01 ① **02** had studied **03** ④ **04** ⑤ **05** ⑤ **06** ⑤ **07** ② **08** ① **09** ② **10** wouldn't have taken **11** ④ **12** be → have been **13** Had, it, not, been, for **14** ② **15** ② **16** ② **17** ④ **18** ① **19** ② **20** ③ **21** (1) wasn't (2) hadn't been **22** ① **23** ⑤ **24** ③, ④, ⑤ **25** could speak

01 너의 도움이 없었다면 나는 그 기말고사를 망쳤을 것이다.
* 가정법 과거완료이므로 가정법 과거인 If it were not for는 알맞지 않다. Without과 But for는 가정법 과거와 과거완료에 모두 사용할 수 있다.

02 Kelly는 고등학생일 때 공부를 열심히 했다면 좋았을 것이라고 생각한다.
* when이 이끄는 절이 과거를 나타내므로 과거에 이루지 못한 아쉬움을 표현한 ⟨I wish + 가정법 과거완료⟩로 나타낸다.

03 보기 Helen은 마치 그녀가 뮤지컬 배우인 것처럼 무대에서 노래 부른다.
① Helen은 진짜 뮤지컬 배우이다.
② Helen은 뮤지컬 배우가 될 것이다.
③ Helen은 진짜 뮤지컬 배우가 되는 것을 좋아하지 않는다.
④ 사실 Helen은 뮤지컬 배우가 아니다.
⑤ Helen은 뮤지컬 배우였지만, 지금은 아니다.
* ⟨as if + 가정법 과거⟩ 문장으로 현재 사실에 반대되는 내용이다.

04 네가 잠자리에 들어야 할 때이다.
* ⟨it is time that + 주어 + 과거동사⟩ = ⟨it is time that + 주어 + should + 동사원형⟩

05 내가 그 회사에서 일했을 때 유능한 직원이었으면 좋았을 텐데.
* when이 이끄는 절이 과거를 나타내므로 과거에 이루지 못한 아쉬움을 표현하는 ⟨I wish + 가정법 과거완료⟩로 나타낸다.

06 Gary는 지난 크리스마스에 그의 부모가 그에게 선물을 줬으면 좋았을 것이라고 생각한다.
* 과거를 나타내는 last Christmas가 있으므로 과거에 이루지 못한 아쉬움을 표현하는 ⟨I wish + 가정법 과거완료⟩로 나타낸다.

07 그가 없다면 우리 축구팀은 그 경기에서 이길 수 없을 텐데.
* 주절이 가정법 과거이므로 조건절도 가정법 과거가 와야 한다. without은 if it were not for로 바꿔 쓸 수 있다.

08 그 연구가 없었다면 나는 석사학위를 따지 못했을 텐데.
* 주절이 가정법 과거완료이므로 조건절도 가정법 과거완료가 와야 한다. but for는 if it had not been for로 바꿔 쓸 수 있다. 이때 if를 삭제하면 주어와 동사가 도치된다.

09 ① 나의 할머니는 그녀의 개를 마치 딸인 것처럼 좋아하신다.
② 내가 젊었을 때 최선을 다해 공부를 했다면 좋았을 텐데.
③ 나의 아버지는 마치 내일이 없는 것처럼 우리를 위해 일을 하신다.
④ 그들은 이번 시즌에 야구를 매우 잘할 수 있다면 좋겠다고 생각한다.
⑤ 부모님의 재정 지원이 없었다면 나는 내 학위를 받지 못했을 것이다.
* [have done → had done] 과거를 나타내는 when young이 있으므로 가정법 과거완료(had + 과거분사)가 되어야 한다.

10 나는 오늘 아침에 늦게 일어났다. 왜냐하면 지난밤 늦게 잠자리에 들었기 때문이다. 시험을 보러 나는 학교에 정시에 가야만 했다. 나는 버스 정류장으로 서둘러 갔다. 그러나 나는 현금이나 버스카드가 없다는 것을 알았다. 나는 내 친구 Shawn을 우연히 만났다. 그는 나의 생명의 은인이었다. 나는 그에게 약간의 돈을 빌려달라고 요청했고 버스를 탔다. 다행히 나는 시험에 늦지 않았다. 그의 도움이 없었다면 나는 시험을 못 봤을 텐데.
* 과거에 발생한 일에 대한 내용이므로 ⟨Without + 명사, 가정법 과거완료⟩로 나타낸다.

11 (a) 네가 없었다면 나는 이 환경에서 살아남을 수 없었을 텐데.
(b) Sandra는 너의 도움이 없다면 그녀의 일을 끝낼 수 없을 텐데.
(c) 아내가 없다면 나는 행복하지 않을 텐데.
* 문맥상 '~이 없(었)다면'이라는 뜻의 without으로 나타낸다.

12 쓰나미가 없었다면 그 건물들은 손상되지 않았을 텐데.
* if절이 가정법 과거완료이므로 주절도 가정법 과거완료 형태가 와야 한다. If가 생략되어 주어와 동사가 도치되었다.

13 그녀의 희생이 없었다면 우리는 성공하지 못했을 텐데.
* 주절이 가정법 과거완료인 ⟨could + have + 과거분사⟩이므로 조건절에는 ⟨If it had not been for + 명사⟩가 와야 한다. 이때 If가 생략되면 주어와 동사의 위치가 바뀐다.

14 ① 그는 귀신을 봤던 것처럼 말한다.
② 우리가 수학을 공부할 시간이다.
③ 그들의 지원이 없다면 그것은 어려울 텐데.
④ 네가 없었다면 나는 성공할 수 없었을 거야.
⑤ 김 선생님이 그의 학생들에게 관대했으면 좋았을 텐데.
* [start → started] ⟨It's time + 가정법 (과거)⟩이므로 that절의 동사는 과거형이 와야 한다.

15 A: 왜 아무도 김 선생님을 좋아하지 않는지 말해줄 수 있니?
B: 흠... 그분은 항상 모든 것을 알고 있는 것처럼 얘기하셔. 사실, 그분은 아무것도 모르시거든.
* 내용상 '마치 ~인 것처럼'이라는 의미를 나타내는 as if가 알맞다.

16 A: 무슨 일이니?
B: 나는 그 시험에서 떨어져서 낙담하고 있어. 내가 시험공부를 했으면 좋았을 텐데.
* 과거 일에 대한 후회를 나타내므로 〈I wish + 가정법 과거완료〉로 나타내야 한다.

17 우리는 미나가 우리의 직장 동료가 아니어서 유감이다.
→ 우리는 미나가 우리의 직장 동료이면 좋을 것이라고 생각한다.
* 현재 사실에 대한 소망은 〈we wish + 가정법 과거〉로 나타낸다. 이때 be동사는 항상 were로 쓴다.

18 그녀는 마치 그 사실에 신경 쓰지 않는 것처럼 행동한다.
→ 사실, 그녀는 그 사실에 신경을 쓴다.
* 〈주절 + as if + 가정법 과거〉는 '마치 ~인 것처럼 …하다'라는 뜻이므로 직설법으로 바꿀 때 현재형이 되어야 한다. 직설법에서는 '사실은 그렇지 않다'는 뜻이므로 가정법의 의미와 반대이다.

19 그 강사는 "그녀가 5 센티미터 더 크다면 슈퍼모델이 될 수 있을 텐데."라고 말한다.
* 가정법 과거의 조건절에 be동사가 쓰이면 주어의 인칭에 관계없이 were를 써야 한다. If she were ~에서 If가 생략되면서 주어와 동사가 도치된다.

20 나는 지난밤 충격적인 소식을 들었다. 누군가가 어떤 집의 주인인 것처럼 행동했다. 한 경비원이 실수로 그 문을 여는 것을 도왔다. 그가 그를 돕지 않았으면 좋았을 텐데.
* 첫 번째 괄호에는 last night라는 과거를 나타내는 말이 있으므로 과거형이 와야 한다. 두 번째 괄호에는 〈as if + 가정법〉이므로 was는 사용할 수 없고 were가 와야 한다. 세 번째 괄호에는 과거에 일어난 일에 대한 소망이므로 〈I wish + 가정법 과거완료〉가 와야 한다.

21 (1) Tim은 그것이 자신의 노트북 컴퓨터였던 것처럼 가지고 있다.
→ 사실, 그것은 Tim의 노트북 컴퓨터가 아니었다.
(2) 나의 가족은 우리가 1위 자리에 있었던 것처럼 가뻐했다.
→ 사실, 우리는 1위 자리에 있지 않았다.
* (1) 〈as if + 가정법 과거완료〉이므로 주절보다 앞선 시제인 과거형이 와야 한다.
(2) 〈as if + 가정법 과거완료〉이므로 주절보다 앞선 시제인 과거완료형이 와야 한다.

22 네가 우진이와 함께 ____________ 너는 그의 얼굴에서의 어떤 변화를 알아차렸을 텐데.
②③ 있었다면 ④⑤ 이야기했다면
* 주절에 가정법 과거완료인 〈would + have + 과거분사〉가 있으므로 가정법 과거에 쓰이는 were는 올 수 없다.

23 그 어린 남자아이는 용돈을 요구할 때 보통 돈이 없는 것처럼 말한다.
* [has → had] as if ~ 문장이 현재 사실에 대한 가정이므로 가정법 과거가 와야 한다.

24 충분한 돈이 없었다면 나는 미국에서 공부를 할 수 없었을 텐데.
* 주절에 가정법 과거완료인 〈could + have + 과거분사〉가 왔으므로 조건절에도 가정법 과거완료 형태가 와야 한다. without은 but for나 if it had not been for로 바꿔 쓸 수 있으며, if가 생략되면 주어와 동사가 도치된다.

25 * 현재 사실에 대한 가정이므로 가정법 과거로 나타내야 한다.

Final Test

▶ 본문 208 - 211쪽

01 ③ **02** ③ **03** ① **04** ④ **05** ② **06** ③ **07** it were not for his bad cold **08** ③ **09** ③ **10** I wish I could earn a lot of money. / If I earned a lot of money, I would be happy. **11** ④ **12** was, not, didn't, go **13** ③ **14** didn't do → hadn't done **15** ③ **16** (1) ⓒ (2) ⓐ (3) ⓑ **17** ④ **18** ④ **19** ④ **20** ② **21** had, studied, harder, would, be **22** ④, ⑤ **23** ② **24** ④ **25** ③ With → Without **26** ① **27** If Amy were not very busy, she would come here to talk about the matter. **28** ④ **29** ⑤ **30** ⑤

01 A: 너의 아버지는 뭐하시니?
B: 학교에서 영어 문법을 가르치셔.
A: 너의 아버지는 학교에서 문법 가르치는 것을 좋아하시니?
B: 아니, 그는 의사이면 좋겠다고 생각하셔.
* 현재 사실에 대한 반대를 나타내므로 가정법 과거(were)가 와야 한다.

02 ① 그들은 치즈케이크를 어떻게 만드는지 알았다면 좋을 것이라고 생각한다.
→ 그들은 치즈케이크를 어떻게 만드는지 몰라서 유감이다.
② 음식이 없으면 아무도 살 수 없다.
③ James는 로마에 대해 거기에 갔다 왔던 것처럼 말한다.
→ 사실, 그는 로마에 가본 적이 있다(→ 없다).
④ 내가 좀 더 느리게 운전했다면 지금 병원에 있지 않을 텐데.
→ 내가 좀 더 느리게 운전하지 않았기 때문에 나는 지금 병원에 있다.
⑤ 그녀는 토마토가 있었다면 그들을 위해 스파게티를 만들 수 있었을 텐데.
→ 그녀는 토마토가 없었기 때문에 그들을 위해 스파게티를 만들 수 없었다.
* [has been → hasn't been] 〈as if + 가정법 과거완료〉이므로 과거 사실의 반대를 가정한 것이다. 가정법이 긍정이므로 직설법에서 부정이 되어야 한다.

03 Mary가 중학교 때 노래 연습을 많이 했다면 그녀의 실력은 지금 더 많이 나아졌을 텐데.
* [practiced → had practiced] 조건절에 과거를 나타내는 when절이 있고 주절에 현재를 나타내는 now가 있으므로 혼합가정법 문장이다. 따라서 조건절에는 〈If + 주어 + had + 과거분사〉가 와야 한다.

04 Richard는 고향에 갈 수 없어 유감이다.
④ Richard는 고향에 가면 좋겠다고 생각한다.
* 직설법 현재는 가정법 과거로 바꿔 쓸 수 있다. 직설법이 긍정이면 가정법은 부정으로 나타낸다.

05 Tyler는 모든 것을 아는 것처럼 말한다.
① 사실, Tyler는 아무 것도 모른다.
* 가정법 과거는 직설법 현재로 바꿔 쓸 수 있다. 가정법이 긍정이면 직설법은 부정으로 나타낸다.

06 ① 우리는 명석한 학생이면 좋겠다고 생각한다.
② Jay는 아프지 않으면 가난한 사람들을 도울 텐데.
③ 나는 엄마가 허락하시면 너의 집에 갈 수 있을 텐데.
④ Justine은 곤경에 처해 있지 않으면 좋겠다고 생각한다.
⑤ Austin이 똑똑하다면 많은 시간을 낭비하지 않을 텐데.
* [allows → allowed] 가정법 과거이므로 조건절의 동사는 과거형이 와야 한다.

07 그는 심한 감기가 없다면 학교에 갈 수 있을 텐데.
* 주절이 〈could + 동사원형〉이므로 조건절에 동사의 과거형이 와야 한다.
without은 if it were not for나 but for로 바꿔 쓸 수 있다.

08 내가 너를 보았다면 너와 이야기하기 위해 멈추었을 것이다.
* 주절이 would have stopped로 가정법 과거완료를 나타내므로 조건절에는 〈If + 주어 + had + 과거분사〉가 와야 한다.

09 보기 Victor와 Stella는 사랑하는 것처럼 행동한다.
③ 그들은 서로 사랑하지 않는다.
* as if 다음에 가정법 과거가 왔으므로 현재 사실과 반대되는 일을 가정한 것이다.

10 보기 A: 너는 원하는 게 뭐니, Edward?
B: 나는 예쁜 여자 친구가 생기기를 원해.
→ 내가 예쁜 여자 친구가 있으면 좋을 텐데.
→ 내가 예쁜 여자 친구가 있다면 행복할 텐데.
A: 너는 원하는 게 뭐니, Joshua?
B: 나는 돈을 많이 벌고 싶어.
→ 나는 돈을 많이 벌 수 있으면 좋을 텐데.
→ 내가 돈을 많이 벌 수 있다면 행복할 텐데.
* 현재 상황과 반대되는 일을 가정하는 것이므로 〈I wish + 주어 + 동사의 과거형〉 또는 〈If + 주어 + 동사의 과거형 ~, I would be happy.〉로 바꿔 쓸 수 있다.

11 보기 네가 CD를 사준다면 너의 아이들은 좀 더 기뻐할 텐데.
① 내가 그것에 대한 진실을 알고 있는지에 대해 물어보지 마라.
② 나는 그가 우승자가 될 수 있는지 알고 싶다.
③ 나는 Andrew가 내 파티에 올 수 있는지 궁금하다.
④ Sam이 그녀를 좋아하지 않으면 그녀는 실망할지도 모를 텐데.
⑤ 너는 모든 것을 알고 있다 할지라도 여전히 더 배울 필요가 있다.
* 〈보기〉와 ④는 가정법에 쓰인 if이다.
①②③ 명사절을 이끄는 접속사, ⑤ 양보의 부사절을 이끄는 접속사

12 눈이 매우 많이 왔다면 우리는 썰매를 탔을 텐데.
→ 눈이 매우 많이 오지 않았기 때문에 우리는 썰매를 타지 않았다.
* 가정법 과거완료는 직설법 과거형으로 바꿔 쓸 수 있다.

13 안녕하세요, 저는 Mike입니다. 저는 현재 은행에서 일합니다. 지금 저는 제 직업에 대해 고민하고 있어요. 저는 승진하지 못했어요. 저는 매우 실망했어요. 제가 어떻게 해야 할까요?

① 너는 일을 그만두면 무엇을 할 거니?
② 새로운 직업을 얻는다면, 무슨 일을 하고 싶니?
③ 내가 너라면 나는 그저 계속해서 최선을 다할 텐데.
④ 내가 너라면 나는 정말로 더 열심히 일했을 텐데.
⑤ 내가 너였다면 더 나은 성과를 줄 텐데.

* 현재 사실에 대한 조언이므로 가정법 과거로 써야 한다.
① [will → would], ② [get → got], ④ [→ If I were you, I would work harder.], ⑤ [Had I been → Were I]

14 Molly는 이 연극에서 가장 중요한 역할을 연기했다. 하지만 그녀는 그 역할을 하지 않았던 것처럼 말한다.

* 과거에 했던 일에 대한 가정이므로 가정법 과거완료로 써야 한다.

15 ① 나의 여동생은 자신이 못생겼다고 생각한다. 그녀가 그렇게 생각하지 않으면 좋을 텐데.
② 나는 외국에서 산다. 외국에서 살지 않으면 좋을 텐데.
③ 진이는 너무 많은 인스턴트 음식을 먹었다. 그는 많은 인스턴트 음식을 먹지 않았으면 좋겠다고 생각한다.
④ 양이는 사람들에게 전혀 친절하지 않았다. 그는 사람들에게 친절했으면 좋았을 것이라고 생각한다.
⑤ Joe는 초콜릿케이크를 구울 수 없다. 그는 초콜릿케이크를 구울 수 있으면 좋겠다고 생각한다.

* [didn't eat → hadn't eaten] 앞 문장이 과거시제이므로 가정법 과거완료가 되어야 한다.

16 (1) 공기가 없으면 사람들은 지구에서 살 수 없을 텐데.
(2) Jack이 수업을 빼먹지 않았다면 꾸중을 듣지 않았을 텐데.
(3) 네가 잠자리에 들 시간이다.

* (1) 의미상 ⓒ가 알맞다.
(2) 조건절이 가정법 과거완료이므로 주절에는 〈조동사 과거형 + have + been + 과거분사〉가 와야 한다.
(3) 〈It is time + 가정법 과거〉로 쓰인다.

17 보기 우리 팀은 사전 심사에서 통과했으면 좋았을 것이라고 생각한다.
④ 우리는 우리 팀이 사전 심사에서 통과하지 못했던 것에 대해 유감이다.

* 〈wish + 가정법 과거완료〉이므로 직설법에서는 과거 시제가 와야 한다.

18 Keilen은 자신의 도구를 갖고 오지 않아서 컴퓨터를 고칠 수 없었다.
④ Keilen이 자신의 도구를 갖고 왔다면 컴퓨터를 고칠 수 있었을 텐데.

* 직설법 과거는 가정법 과거완료로 나타낸다.

19 나는 그녀의 휴대전화번호를 모르기 때문에 지금 그녀에게 전화할 수 없다.
④ 내가 그녀의 휴대전화 번호를 안다면 지금 그녀에게 전화할 텐데.

* 직설법 현재는 가정법 과거로 바꿔 쓸 수 있다.

20 A: 이번 겨울방학에 뭐할 거야?
B: 무얼 할지 잘 모르겠어.
A: 내가 너라면 나는 학교에서 겨울학기 수업을 들을 텐데.

* 조건절이 가정법 과거이므로 주절은 〈주어 + 조동사의 과거형 + 동사원형〉이 와야 한다.

21 * 학창시절은 과거이고 지금은 현재이므로 혼합가정법으로 나타낸다. 즉, 조건절은 가정법 과거완료, 주절은 가정법 과거로 쓴다.

22 (a) 현대의 사람들은 TV를 보지 않는다면 견딜 수 없을 텐데.
(b) 부모님의 지원이 없었다면 나는 그 비싼 학교에 다닐 수 없었을 텐데.

* '~이 없다면' 혹은 '~이 없었다면'이라는 뜻은 without이나 but for로 나타낸다.

23 나는 노트북 컴퓨터가 없기 때문에 너에게 빌려줄 수 없다.
→ 내가 노트북 컴퓨터가 있다면 너에게 빌려줄 텐데.

* 직설법 현재는 가정법 과거로 바꿔 쓸 수 있다. 직설법 현재와 반대되는 내용이므로 직설법 부정은 가정법 긍정으로 표현한다.

24 ① Victor는 학교에 갈 수 있으면 좋겠다고 생각한다.
→ Victor는 학교에 갈 수 없어서 유감이다.
② 그는 내 선생님처럼 말한다.
→ 사실, 그는 나의 선생님이 아니다.
③ 그들이 기름 값을 올린다면 큰 문제가 될 텐데.
→ 그들이 기름 값을 올리지 않아서 그것은 큰 문제가 되지 않을 것이다.
④ 그가 충분한 경험을 갖고 있었다면 그들은 그를 고용했을 텐데.
→ 그가 충분한 경험이 있었기(→ 없었기) 때문에 그들은 그를 고용했다(→ 고용하지 않았다).
⑤ Hank가 KTX를 타고 갔다면 많은 시간을 절약했을 텐데.
→ Hank는 KTX를 타고 가지 않았기 때문에 많은 시간을 절약할 수 없었다.

* [had → didn't have / would → would not] 가정법이 긍정이면 직설법은 부정이 되어야 한다.

25 Thomas Edison은 전깃불의 발명과 함께 세계를 밝혔다. 그가 있었다면(→ 없었다면) 세계는 여전히 어두울 텐데. 그러나 놀랍게도 전깃불은 오직 그만의 발명품이 아니었다.

* 의미상 '그가 없었다면'이 되어야 한다.

26 ① 내가 어렸을 때 너를 만났으면 좋았을 텐데.
② 그녀의 기술이 없었다면 그는 죽었을 텐데.
③ 그는 마치 그 분야에서 전문가였던 것처럼 얘기했다.
④ Jane이 더 나은 시대에 태어났다면 유명해졌을 텐데.
⑤ 그가 의사의 충고를 받아들였다면 지금 건강할 텐데.

* [met → had met] when I was young이라는 과거를 나타내는 말이 있으므로 가정법 과거완료가 와야 한다.

27 Amy가 매우 바쁘기 때문에 그 문제에 대하여 말하기 위해 여기에 오지 않을 것이다.

* 직설법 현재는 가정법 과거로 바꿔 쓸 수 있다. 가정법 과거는 현재 사실에 대한 반대를 가정하는 것이므로 직설법 부정은 가정법 긍정으로, 직설법 긍정은 가정법 부정으로 나타낸다.

28 (a) 너는 지금 떠나지 않으면 직장에 늦을 것이다.
(b) 날씨가 좋았다면 우리는 야구 경기를 했을 텐데.

* (a) 가정법 현재(단순 조건문)의 조건절은 현재 시제를 사용하고, 주절은 미래 시제를 사용한다.
(b) 주절에 〈조동사의 과거형 + have + 과거분사〉가 왔으므로 가정법 과거완료이다.

29 * 과거의 일을 가정한 것이므로 가정법 과거완료로 나타낸다. 조건절의 if가 생략되면 주어와 동사가 도치된다.

30 A: 너는 지난밤에 가족들과 외식했니?
B: 아니, 갈 수 없었어. 내가 나의 가족들과 함께 그곳에 있었다면 즐거운 시간을 보냈을 텐데.
A: 너는 왜 가족들과 함께 저녁을 먹지 않았니?
B: 내 일 때문에. 내 일이 없었다면 나는 그곳에서 맛있는 음식을 많이 먹을 수 있었을 텐데.
A: 알잖아, 네 동생이 그곳에서 그렇게 많이 먹지 않았다면 그는 지금 배가 아프지 않을 거야.

* [would not have had → would not have] 조건절은 과거의 일이고 주절은 현재의 일이므로 혼합가정법 문장이다. 혼합가정법은 〈If + 주어 + had + 과거분사 ~, 주어 + 조동사의 과거형 + 동사원형 ...〉으로 쓴다.

Sentence Writing

▶ 본문 212쪽

Part A
1 were, could not register
2 without, couldn't have graduated
3 donated

Part B
1 I wish Cathy had kept her promise.
2 If I lived in Italy, I would like spaghetti.
3 If you had told me about the problem, I would have helped you.
4 He spent money as if he were rich.

Part A

몇 십 년 동안 많은 대학들은 성공적인 재정 도움 프로그램을 운영해 왔다.

Unit 12 일치, 화법

DAY 23 일치

2교시 In - Class Questions ▸ 본문 217쪽

STEP A	1 student 2 is 3 keeps
STEP B	1 are[were] 2 are[were] 3 is 4 ended
STEP C	1 went → goes 2 were → was 3 is → are 4 has → have
STEP D	1 had, already, sent 2 told, is 3 are 4 is

STEP A
1 교실의 모든 학생은 이 책을 받을 것이다.
2 당뇨병은 요즘 심각하고 위험한 병이다.
3 신생아의 수는 계속 증가하고 있다.

STEP B
1 Jane도 그녀의 친구들도 더 이상 학생이 아니다/아니었다.
2 그 건물에 있는 경찰들은 지원 병력을 기다리고 있다/있었다.
3 몇몇 사람들이 태양은 둥글고 뜨겁다고 말했다.
4 우리는 한국전쟁이 1953년에 끝났다고 배웠다.

STEP C
1 Nancy는 매주 일요일에 교회에 간다고 나에게 말했다.
2 Brian이 했던 것은 전혀 도움이 안 되었다.
3 그녀의 이야기 중 3분의 2가 파리의 패션에 관한 것이다.
4 가난한 사람들은 부자보다 훨씬 다른 관점을 갖고 있다.

3교시 After - Class Questions ▸ 본문 218 - 221쪽

01 ① 02 ③ 03 ⑤ 04 ③ 05 ② 06 ⑤ 07 ④ 08 ① 09 ④ 10 ② 11 ⑤ 12 ① 13 are → is 14 ② 15 ④ 16 ① 17 ② 18 was 19 are 20 ④ 21 ③ 22 ④ 23 ①, ②, ④ 24 ③, ⑤ 25 They, he, are

01 내가 알고 싶은 것은 그것이 얼마나 오래 걸릴 것인지 이다.
* 주어로 쓰인 절은 항상 단수 취급하므로 단수 동사가 온다.

02 그녀의 교수님은 Columbus가 1492년에 미국을 발견했다고 말씀하셨다.
* 역사적 사실은 언제나 과거시제로 쓴다.

03 내 수업의 각 남자아이들은 나에게 그들의 열정을 보여준다.
* each는 단수 취급하므로 단수 동사가 오며, 단수형 소유대명사로 받는다.

04 * 주절은 과거시제일지라도 종속절이 과학적 사실을 나타내기 때문에 현재시제를 써야 한다.

05 * 시간은 복수형으로 쓰이지만 하나의 단위로 쓰일 경우 단수 취급하여 뒤에 단수 동사가 온다.

06 ① 각 남자아이는 다른 선호하는 게임이 있다.
② 너뿐만 아니라 대부분의 학생들이 시험을 준비한다.
③ 그 마을에서 태어난 아이들의 수는 증가하지 않는다.
④ 수학은 숫자와 공식의 문제를 다룬다.
⑤ 이 이야기의 3분의 2는 캐나다에서의 실제 사고에 대한 것이었다.
* [were → was] 분수의 경우 뒤에 오는 명사에 따라 수가 결정된다. this story는 단수 명사이므로 단수 동사가 와야 한다.

07 ① Brown 선생님은 전에 Jacky를 만난 적이 있다고 말했다.
② Jason은 그녀의 여동생이 열심히 공부할 것이라고 믿었다.
③ 나의 선생님은 정직이 최상의 정책이라고 말씀하신다.
④ 그들은 빛은 소리보다 더 빠르게 전해진다는 것을 알지 못했다.
⑤ 엄마는 그녀의 아버지가 매일 아침 일찍 일어나신다고 나에게 말씀하셨다.
* [traveled → travels] 과학적 사실은 항상 현재시제로 쓴다.

08 ① 오늘의 뉴스는 우리에게 충격적이었다.
② 1 더하기 2는 합이 3이다.
③ 당뇨는 매우 심각한 병이다.
④ 시인이자 소설가인 사람이 내 이웃이다.
⑤ 버터를 바른 빵이 나의 점심이다.
* [were → was] news는 단수 명사이므로 단수 동사가 와야 한다.
② 수학공식은 단수 취급한다.
③ 질병 이름은 단수 취급한다.
④ and로 연결되었지만 동일인을 지칭하면 단수 취급한다.
⑤ bread and butter는 '버터 바른 빵'이라는 뜻으로 단수 취급한다.

09 ① 나무들 아래 소떼가 있었다.
② 네덜란드는 꽃으로 잘 알려져 있다.
③ 부자들이 항상 그들의 삶에 만족하는 것은 아니다.
④ 영어와 수학을 함께 공부하는 것은 힘들다.
⑤ 잘 먹고 잘 자는 것은 나에게 가장 중요한 일이다.
* [are → is] 동명사가 주어이므로 단수 동사가 와야 한다.
① cattle은 '소 떼'라는 뜻으로 항상 복수 취급한다.
② the Netherlands는 복수형 나라 이름이지만 단수 취급한다.
③ 〈the + 형용사〉는 복수 보통명사를 의미하며 복수 취급한다. the rich는 '부자들'이라는 뜻이다.
⑤ to부정사가 주어로 쓰이면 단수 취급한다.

10 몇몇 선생님들은 Catherine에게 대부분의 학생들이 다음 주 금요일에 박물관을 방문할 것이라고 말했다. 그 이유는 그들이 프로젝트를 끝내야 하기 때문이었다. 그래서 그녀는 선생님들에게 그들과 함께 갈 수 있는지를 물어보았다.
* [will → would] 주절의 시제가 과거이므로 종속절의 시제도 과거시제가 와야 한다.

11 나의 학기말 발표에 10명의 교수님이 계신다. 그들 중에서 나는 이미 다섯 분의 교수님들 수업을 수강했었다. 그래서 그분들 중 다섯 분은 친근하다. 하지만 다른 분들은 낯설다. 나는 매우 초초하다. 내 생각에는 내 방 친구들이나 Thomas가 그분들의 수업을 듣는 것 같다.
* [take → takes] 상관접속사 〈either A or B〉는 B에 따라 동사의 수가 결정된다.

12 (a) Kelly는 그녀의 친구가 직업을 ____________ 믿는다.
② 가졌다고 ③ 가지고 있다고 ④ 가질 것이라고
(b) 나는 그 여자배우가 상을 ____________ 알았다.
② 받는다는 것을 ⑤ 받았다는 것을
* (a) 주절의 동사가 현재시제이므로 종속절에는 현재, 과거, 미래가 올 수 있다. 단, her friend가 3인칭 단수이므로 get은 올 수 없다.
(b) 주절의 동사가 과거시제이므로 종속절에는 과거, 과거완료만 올 수 있다.

13 그 돈의 절반은 너의 것이 아니라 너의 부모님의 것이다.
* half는 다음에 나오는 명사로 동사의 수를 결정한다. the money는 단수 취급하므로 단수 동사가 와야 한다.

14 A: 일요일에 몇 명의 친구들이 이 파티에 올 예정이니?
B: 나의 많은 친구들이 올 것이고 카드게임을 할거야. 너도 꼭 와!
A: 미안하지만 못 갈 것 같아. 나의 집에서 너무 멀어. 50분은 나에겐 긴 시간이야.
* 문맥상 '많은 친구들'이라는 표현이 와야 하므로 〈a number of + 복수명사〉가 와야 한다. 〈the number of + 복수명사〉는 '~의 수'라는 뜻이다. 시간은 복수로 쓰이지만 하나의 단위로 쓰일 경우 단수 취급하므로 단수 동사가 온다.

15 (a) 아버지가 돌아가신 지 5년이 지났다.
(b) 5년은 그렇게 긴 기간이 아니다.
* (a) 5년이 한 단위가 아닌 개별적인 단위로 세는 경우이므로 복수 취급한다.
(b) 5년이라는 기간을 한 단위를 말할 경우이므로 단수 취급한다.

16 (a) 내 돈의 나머지는 엄마에게 드렸다.
(b) 그 동물들의 절반은 중국에서 왔다.
* (a) 〈the rest of + 단수 명사〉는 단수 취급하므로 단수 동사가 와야 한다.
(b) 〈the half of + 복수 명사〉는 복수 취급하므로 복수 동사가 와야 한다.

17 (a) 나의 선생님은 캐나다가 세계에서 두 번째로 큰 나라라고 말씀하셨다.
(b) 나의 선생님은 1차 세계대전이 1918년에 끝났다고 말씀하셨다.
* (a) 현재의 사실을 말하는 것은 항상 현재시제로 쓴다.
(b) 역사적 사실은 항상 과거시제로 쓴다.

18 우리는 홍콩이 한 때 영국의 영토였다는 것을 몰랐다.
* 과거의 역사적 사실은 항상 과거시제로 쓴다.

19 나의 아들은 박쥐가 날 수 있는 유일한 포유류라는 것을 배웠다.
* 일반적인 사실은 항상 현재시제로 쓴다.

20 ① 그를 제외하고 모두가 나를 좋아한다.
② 그의 행동 때문에 아무도 그를 좋아하지 않는다.
③ 각 소녀가 그 남자아이로부터 사탕을 받았다.
④ 모든 남녀가 그 뉴스에 놀랐다.
⑤ 영화를 보는 것과 음악을 듣는 것은 내가 가장 좋아하는 두 가지이다.
* [were → was] 주어로 every와 each가 포함된 경우에는 단수 취급하므로 단수 동사를 쓴다.
① everyone, ② no one, ③ each는 단수 취급한다.
⑤ 동명사 주어는 단수 취급하지만 and로 연결되어 두 가지 일을 말하는 것이므로 복수 취급한다.

21 ① 그 귤의 절반이 신선하지 않다.
② 네덜란드는 풍차로 유명하다.
③ 5킬로미터는 여기서 멀지 않다.
④ 나는 경제학이 배우기 어려운 과목이라고 생각한다.
⑤ 그 돈의 일부가 그에 의해서 그 고아원에 보내졌다.
* [are → is] 거리가 하나의 단위로 쓰이면 단수 취급한다.
① 〈half of + 복수 명사〉는 복수 취급, ② 복수형 나라이름은 단수 취급,
④ 학과명은 단수 취급, ⑤ 〈some of + 단수 명사〉는 단수 취급

22 ① Tom과 Jane은 좋은 친구들이다.
② 선생님이자 시인은 내 사촌이다.
③ 나는 그녀의 가족들이 모두 행복하고 친절하다는 걸 알고 있다.
④ 그 사람들은 가끔씩 그 유명한 장소를 방문한다.
⑤ 식탁 위의 카레라이스는 나의 아빠를 위해 준비되었다.
* [visits → visit] people은 복수 취급하므로 복수 동사가 와야 한다.
① 명사가 and로 연결되어 두 사람을 말하는 것이므로 복수 취급한다.
② and로 연결된 주어가 한 사람을 나타낼 때는 단수 취급한다.
③ family가 집단 자체를 의미할 때는 단수, 구성원을 의미할 때는 복수 취급한다.
이 문장에서는 그녀의 가족 전체를 의미하므로 단수 취급한다.
⑤ A and B가 하나의 사물을 나타낼 때는 단수 취급한다.

23 ① 어제 많은 가구가 팔렸다.
② 이 딸기의 3분의 2가 썩었다.
③ 줄이 있는 시계가 책상 위에서 발견되었다.
④ 불법 이민자의 수가 급속히 증가하고 있다.
⑤ 휴일임에도 불구하고 많은 슈퍼마켓이 오늘 문을 열었다.
* ① [were → was], ② [is → are] 분수, plenty of는 뒤따라오는 명사의 수에 따라 수를 결정한다.
④ [are → is] 〈the number of + 복수 명사〉는 단수 취급하며 '~의 수'라는 뜻이다.
③ a watch and chain은 '줄이 있는 시계'라는 뜻으로 하나의 물건을 뜻한다.
⑤ 〈a number of + 복수 동사〉는 복수 취급하며 '많은 ~'라는 뜻이다.

24 ① 10년은 긴 시간이 아니다.
② 내 친구 중에 한 명은 일본어를 매우 잘한다.
③ 일찍 자고 일찍 일어나는 것은 나를 건강하게 한다.
④ 많은 아이들이 스마트폰에 의해 잘못되고 있다.
⑤ 필리핀은 많은 섬을 가진 나라이다.
* ③ and로 연결된 말이 하나의 개념을 의미할 때는 단수 취급한다.
⑤ 복수 국가명은 형태는 복수지만 단수 취급한다.
① [are → is] 시간이 하나의 개념을 의미할 때는 단수 취급.
② [speak → speaks] 〈one of + 복수 명사〉는 단수 취급.
④ [have → has] 〈many a + 단수 명사〉는 단수 취급

25 그뿐만 아니라 그들도 지난주에 일어났던 그 일에 책임이 있다.
* not only A but also B = B as well as A로 쓰며, 둘 다 동사는 B에 맞춘다.

24 화법 전환

2교시 In - Class Questions
▶ 본문 223쪽

STEP A 1 asked, if, could 2 had bought
3 what, she wanted

STEP B 1 that he would behave himself
2 when he wanted to leave
3 not to drink beer anymore
4 whether I would go or stay there

STEP C 1 told → asked 2 met → had met
3 you were my → I was your

STEP D 1 James asked his wife where she had gotten that bag.
2 I told my mother that I was totally exhausted and starving.
3 My daughter advised me not to use my smartphone while I was driving.

STEP A
1 그 노부인은 나에게 "나를 도와줄 수 있니?"라고 말했다.
→ 그 노부인은 내가 그녀를 도와줄 수 있는지 물었다.
2 그는 "나는 이 손목시계를 지난주에 샀어."라고 말했다.
→ 그는 전 주에 저 손목시계를 구입했다고 말했다.
3 나는 나의 여자 친구에게 "너는 어떤 종류의 음료수를 마시고 싶니?"라고 말했다.
→ 나는 나의 여자 친구에게 어떤 종류의 음료수를 마시고 싶은지 물었다.

STEP B
1 Wayne은 "나는 얌전히 굴게."라고 약속했다.
→ Wayne은 얌전히 굴겠다고 약속했다.
2 June은 그에게 "너는 언제 떠나고 싶니?"라고 물었다.
→ June은 그에게 언제 떠나기를 원하는지 물었다.
3 나의 아내는 나에게 "맥주를 더 이상 마시지 말아요."라고 말했다.
→ 나의 아내는 나에게 맥주를 더 이상 마시지 말라고 충고했다.
4 그녀는 나에게 "너는 갈거니 여기에 머물거니?"라고 말했다.
→ 그녀는 나에게 갈 건지 그곳에 머무를 건지 물었다.

STEP C
1 Joan은 나에게 "너는 돈이 좀 있니?"라고 말했다.
→ Joan은 나에게 돈이 좀 있는지 물었다.
2 Audrey는 "너는 Ralph를 전에 만난 적이 있니?"라고 말했다.
→ Audrey는 나에게 Ralph를 전에 만난 적이 있는지 물었다.
3 너는 나에게 "너는 나의 가장 친한 친구야."라고 말했다.
→ 너는 나에게 내가 너의 가장 친한 친구라고 말했다.

STEP D
1 James는 그의 아내에게 "당신 이 가방을 어디에서 샀어요?"라고 말했다.
2 나는 나의 어머니에게 "저는 완전히 피곤하고 배가 고파요."라고 말했다.
3 내 딸은 나에게 "운전하는 동안 스마트폰을 사용하지 마세요."라고 말했다.

3교시 After - Class Questions
▶ 본문 224 - 227쪽

01 ⑤ **02** ② **03** ④ **04** ④ **05** ④ **06** ⑤ **07** ④ **08** ③ **09** had, met, there **10** if, everything, was **11** ② **12** did I need → I needed **13** ④ **14** ③ **15** ② **16** ⑤ **17** ⑤ **18** ② **19** James advised[told] me to go on a diet. **20** Ben told me that he had been to Australia. **21** (1) Andrew said to Belle, "I went to the movie theater with her yesterday." (2) Andrew told Belle that he had gone to the movie theater with her the day before. **22** (1) The gentleman sitting next to me asked me, "How old are you?" (2) The gentleman sitting next to me asked me how old I was. **23** ④ **24** ③ moved → moves **25** she told me that she would make a delicious dinner for me.

01 * [the day after → the day before]

02 그녀의 의사는 "당신은 빨리 좋아질 거예요."라고 말했다.
→ 그녀의 의사는 그녀가 빨리 좋아질 것이라고 말했다.
* 전달동사 said는 그대로 쓰고, that절의 시제는 전달동사의 시제와 일치시켜야 하

므로 will → would로 바꿔야 한다.

03 Thomas는 "나는 이번 해에 파리를 방문하고 싶어."라고 나에게 말했다.
→ Thomas는 그 해에 파리를 방문하고 싶다고 나에게 말했다.
* 전달동사 told는 그대로 쓰고, that절의 시제는 전달동사의 시제와 일치시켜야 하므로 want → wanted로 바꿔야 한다. 부사의 경우 화법 전환 시 this → that로 바꾼다.

04 나의 엄마는 나에게 "나는 내일 너에게 책들을 사줄 게."라고 말씀하셨다.
→ 나의 엄마는 나에게 다음날 책들을 사주겠다고 말씀하셨다.
* 전달동사는 said to → told로 바꾸고, that절의 시제는 전달동사의 시제와 일치시켜야 하므로 will → would로 바꿔야 한다. 대명사 you → me로, 부사 tomorrow → the next day 혹은 the following day로 바꾼다.

05 Bobby는 그녀에게 어디 출신인지 물어봤다.
→ Bobby는 그녀에게 "너는 어디 출신이니?"라고 말했다.
* 간접화법에서 〈의문사(where) + 주어(she) + 동사(was)〉는 직접화법으로 바꿀 때 〈의문사(where) +동사(are) + 주어(you) ~?〉의 어순이 된다.

06 Jake는 그녀에게 여름보다 가을이 더 좋은지 물었다.
* 의문사가 없는 의문문을 간접화법으로 나타낼 때 피전달문에 쓰이는 접속사는 if 또는 whether로 쓴다.

07 사람들은 호준이에게 저 MP3가 얼마인지 물었다.
* 문맥상 〈의문사(how much) + 주어(that MP3) + 동사(cost)〉의 어순으로 써야 한다. 전달동사가 과거이므로 피전달문의 동사도 과거형인 cost가 와야 한다.

08 ① 그녀는 나에게 "무엇을 하고 싶니?"라고 말했다.
→ 그녀는 나에게 무엇을 하고 싶은지 물었다.
② Lucy는 "나는 오늘 그 자전거를 고칠 수 있어."라고 말했다.
→ Lucy는 그날 그 자전거를 고칠 수 있다고 말했다.
③ 내 친구는 Ken에게 "그만 말해."라고 말했다.
→ 내 친구는 Ken에게 그만 말하라고 말했다.
④ 그는 그들에게 "나는 지금 TV를 보고 있어."라고 말했다.
→ 그는 그때 TV를 보고 있었다고 그들에게 말했다.
⑤ Anne은 그에게 "너는 이 소설들을 읽은 적이 있니?"라고 말했다.
→ Anne은 그에게 저 소설들을 읽은 적이 있었는지를 물었다.
* [said to → told] 명령문의 화법 전환 시 전달동사 said to는 내용에 따라 told, asked, ordered, advised로 바꿔야 한다.

09 Charlie는 나에게 "나는 여기에서 Anne을 만났어."라고 말했다.
→ Charlie는 나에게 거기에서 Anne을 만났었다고 말했다.
* 전달동사가 과거시제(told)이므로 피전달문의 동사도 이에 맞게 과거시제로 바꾼다. 부사도 here → there로 바꿔야 한다.

10 너는 나에게 "모든 게 잘 되니?"라고 말했다.
→ 너는 나에게 모든 게 잘 되는지 물었다.
* 전달동사가 과거시제(asked)이므로 피전달문의 동사도 이에 맞게 과거시제로 바꾼다. 의문사가 없는 의문문은 〈if + 주어 + 동사〉로 나타낸다.

11 **보기** 그의 오빠는 나에게 "이 문제에 대해서는 걱정하지 마."라고 말했다.
→ 그의 오빠는 나에게 그 문제에 대해서는 걱정하지 말라고 말했다/요청했다/명령했다/충고했다.
* [to not → not to] 직접화법의 부정 명령문을 간접화법으로 바꿀 경우 전달동사를 tell, ask, order, advise로 바꾸고 〈not + to부정사〉로 연결해야 한다.

12 한 공무원은 나에게 "도움이 필요하신가요?"라고 말했다.
→ 한 공무원이 나에게 도움이 필요한지 물었다.
* 의문사가 없는 의문문을 간접화법으로 바꿀 때 〈if[whether] + 주어 + 동사〉의 어순으로 써야 한다.

13 ① 아무도 "너는 무엇을 제일 좋아하니?"라고 말하지 않는다.
② 그는 나에게 이 선생님을 잘 아는지 물었다.
③ 나는 그들에게 "너희들은 어디에 있니?"라고 말하지 않았다.
④ 너는 나에게 그들이 언제 행복했었는지 말했다.
⑤ 그는 내가 그것을 어떻게 해결했는지 물었다.
* 전달동사의 시제인 과거(나에게 말했던) 시점보다 피전달문이 앞선 시제이므로 대과거로 썼다.
① [you → do you], ② [know → knew], ③ [tell → say], ⑤ [can I → I could]

14 Sean은 "나는 보통 나의 약속을 지킨다."라고 말했다.
→ Sean은 보통 자신의 약속을 지킨다고 말했다.
* 피전달문의 내용이 현재의 습관적인 일을 말할 때는 항상 현재형으로 써야 한다. 따라서 동사는 keep → keeps로 바꿔야 한다. 피전달문에서 I → he로, my → his로 바꿔야 한다.

15 나의 여동생은 그에게 "당신은 회의에 참석했나요?"라고 말했다.
→ 나의 여동생은 그가 회의에 참석했었는지를 물었다.
* 전달동사가 과거시제이므로 피전달문의 동사는 그보다 하나 앞선 대과거로 써야 한다. 의문사가 없는 의문문은 〈if/whether + 주어 + 동사〉로 나타낸다.

16 David는 나에게 "너는 나를 위해 노래 부르고 춤을 출 수 있니?"라고 말했다.
→ David는 나에게 그를 위해 노래 부르고 춤을 출 수 있는지 물었다.
* 전달동사가 과거시제이므로 피전달문의 동사도 이에 맞게 과거시제로 바꾼다. 의문사가 없는 의문문은 〈if + 주어 + 동사〉로 나타내고, 대명사는 me → him으로 바꾼다.

17 ① Miranda는 그녀가 시카고에서 일한다고 말했다.
② 나의 아들들은 4 곱하기 5가 20이라고 말했다.
③ 그 선생님은 일본이 1909년에 한국을 식민지화했다고 말씀하셨다.
④ 우리는 우리의 부모님들이 그 회의에 오실 수 있다는 것을 알았다.
⑤ 그는 우리에게 우리가 물 없이는 살 수 없다고 말했다.
* [could → can] '물 없이 살 수 없다'는 것은 과학적인 사실이므로 항상 현재형으로 써야 한다.
① 현재도 일하고 있는 사실이므로 현재시제로 썼다. ② 수학 공식은 항상 현재시제로 쓴다. ③ 역사적 사실은 항상 과거시제로 쓴다. ④ 주절이 과거시제이므로 종속절에도 과거시제가 쓰였다.

18 * [that day → today]로 바꿔야 한다.

19 James는 나에게 "다이어트를 해."라고 조언했다.
* 긍정 명령문이므로 전달동사를 told, advised, ordered, asked로 바꾸고, 피전달문은 to부정사로 나타낸다.

20 Ben은 나에게 "나는 호주에 갔다 온 적이 있어."라고 말했다.
* 평서문이므로 전달동사는 say to → tell로 바꾸고, 피전달문의 인칭대명사는 I → he로 바꾸고 시제도 전달문의 시제보다 앞선 대과거로 쓴다.

21 * 평서문이므로 직접화법을 간접화법으로 바꿔 쓸 때 전달동사는 say to → tell로 바꾸고, 피전달문의 인칭대명사 I → he, 부사 yesterday → the day before로 바꾸고 시제는 전달동사보다 하나 앞선 대과거 시제로 바꾼다.

22 * 의문사가 있는 의문문이므로 직접화법을 간접화법으로 바꿔 쓸 때 피전달문은 〈의문사 + 주어 +동사〉의 어순으로 쓰고, 전달동사의 시제에 맞게 피전달문의 동사도 과거시제로 바꾼다.

23 나의 엄마는 나에게 "너는 어디에서 저녁을 먹었니?"라고 물으셨다.
* My mom asked me where I had had supper.에서 일곱 번째 말은 had이다.

24 Edward 선생님은 지난 수업에서 지구는 둥글고 태양 주변을 돈다. 그래서 태양은 동쪽에서 떠서 서쪽으로 진다고 말씀하셨다.
* 화법 전환에서 불변의 진리는 항상 현재시제를 사용한다.

25 A: Billy, 퇴근 후에 무슨 계획이 있어요?
B: 네. 나의 아내가 나에게 전화해서 그녀는 나에게 "내가 당신을 위해 맛있는 저녁을 만들어줄게요."라고 말했어요.
A: 당신은 퇴근하고 바로 집에 가는 게 좋겠어요.
B: 그러고 싶지만 저는 일을 끝내는 데 시간이 더 필요해요. 일을 끝내고 바로 집에 갈 거예요.
A: 걱정하지 마요. 제가 도와줄게요.
* 직접화법을 간접화법으로 바꿔 쓸 때 전달동사 said to → told로 바꾸고, 피전달문에서 주어는 I → she로 바꾸고 시제를 전달동사의 시제와 같은 과거시제로 바꾼다.

Final Test

▶ 본문 228 - 231쪽

01 ④ **02** ③ **03** ⑤ **04** ③ **05** went → goes **06** ③ **07** ④ **08** ④ **09** ④ **10** ① **11** what he was doing then **12** (1) asks, if he knows me (2) asked, he had met **13** ① **14** ⑤ **15** if he could ask, his, to visit, that day **16** ④ **17** ⑤ **18** ②, ⑤ **19** Not only she but also I have difficulty speaking English. **20** ① **21** ① **22** to, bring **23** ③ **24** ①, ⑤ **25** ③ **26** ④ **27** ⑤ **28** ③ **29** knew, had, been **30** ④

01 A: 너의 동아리에 얼마나 많은 사람이 있니?
B: 내가 추측하기론 우리 동아리 사람들의 수는 100명이 넘어.
* 사람들의 수를 묻고 있으므로 the number of ~가 와야 하고, the number of 다음에는 단수 동사가 온다.

02 (a) 시인이자 가수인 Bella는 새로운 식당을 열 것이다.
(b) 경찰은 많은 나라에서 매우 인기 있다.
(c) 우리는 어렸을 때 1 더하기 1은 2라고 배웠다.
* (a) the poet and singer는 한 사람(Bella)을 의미하므로 단수 취급한다.
(b) The police는 항상 복수 취급한다.
(c) 과거를 나타내는 부사구 When we were young이 있으므로 주절에도 과거시제가 와야 한다. 주절 안의 종속절은 수학 규칙이므로 현재시제를 쓴다.

03 ① 이 감자의 4분의 3은 상했다.
② Gary가 아니라 Lisa가 이번 달에 파산했다.
③ 그들 각각은 그들의 부모와 함께 여행한다.
④ 모든 학생은 정보를 얻기 위해 취업박람회에 간다.
⑤ 내 모자도 바지도 모두 이 긴 재킷과 어울리지 않는다.
* [goes → go] neither A nor B는 B에 수를 일치시킨다. B가 my pants로 복수이므로 go가 들어가야 한다.

04 * '~의 수'는 〈the number of + 복수 동사〉로 나타내며 단수 취급을 한다. '줄어들고 있다'는 진행시제로 나타낸다.

05 Kelly는 Henry를 만나서 그에게 회의할 날을 결정할 것을 요청했다. 그녀는 일요일을 제안했다. 하지만 그는 일요일마다 교회에 간다고 그녀에게 말했다.
* 매주 일요일에 가는 습관적인 일이므로 현재시제로 써야 한다.

06 Walter는 나에게 "당신은 나와 함께 거기에 갈 수 있나요?"라고 말했다.
→ Walter는 나에게 자기와 함께 거기에 갈 수 있는지 물었다.
* 전달동사가 과거이므로 시제 일치 때문에 피전달문에 can은 들어갈 수 없다.

07 A: 무슨 일이야, Andy? Cathy는 네가 딩황한 것처럼 보인다고 나에게 얘기하던데. 무슨 일이 있었니?
B: 흠... 내 아들 Eric과 관련된 일이 있었어.
A: Eric? 그 아이한테 무슨 일이 있었는데?
B: 어제 그와 함께 집에 있었는데 그가 나에게 여자 친구랑 영화를 볼 것이라고 말했어.
A: 정말? 이상하네. 그가 나에게는 "전 여자 친구가 있었던 적이 결코 없어요."라고 말했는데.
* [will → would] 전달동사가 과거(said)이므로 피전달문의 시제도 과거가 되어야 한다.

08 그 선생님은 우리에게 "이 프로젝트를 지금 끝내라."라고 말씀하셨다.
④ 그 선생님은 우리에게 그 프로젝트를 그때 끝내라고 말씀하셨다.
* 전달동사는 said to → told로 바꾸고, 명령문을 간접화법으로 바꿀 경우 to부정사로 쓴다. 부사 now → then으로 바꾼다.

09 여준이는 스스로에게 "나는 어디로 가고 있을까?"라고 말했다.
→ 여준이는 어디로 가고 있었는지를 스스로에게 물었다.
* 전달동사는 said to → asked로 바꾸고, 피전달문에서 주어 I → he, 동사 am → was로 바꾼다. 의문사 있는 의문문은 간접화법으로 바꿀 때 〈의문사 + 주어 + 동사〉의 어순으로 쓴다.

10 Parker 교수님은 나에게 "누가 네 발표를 도와주었니?"라고 말씀하셨다.
→ Parker 교수님은 나에게 누가 나의 발표를 도와주었는지 물으셨다.
* 의문사 who가 주어로 쓰였으므로 〈의문사 + 동사〉의 어순으로 써야 한다. 전달문의 시제가 과거시제이므로 피전달문은 이보다 앞선 대과거시제가 되어야 한다.

11 * 직접화법으로는 The policeman said to the thief, "What are you doing now?"인데 이것을 간접화법으로 바꾸면 〈의문사(what) + 주어(you) + 동사(were doing) + 부사(then)〉의 어순이 된다.

12 (1) 준모는 나에게 "너는 나를 아니?"라고 말한다.
→ 준모는 나에게 그가 나를 아는지 물어본다.
(2) 명이는 그녀에게 "내가 너를 언제 만났지?"라고 말했다.
→ 명이는 그녀에게 언제 그가 그녀를 만났었는지를 물어봤다.
* (1) 피전달문에 현재시제가 오면 주절과 같은 시제가 와야 한다. 의문사 없는 의문문은 간접화법으로 바꿀 때 if[whether]와 함께 쓴다. (2) 전달동사가 과거시제이므로 피전달문의 시제는 대과거(had + 과거분사)로 써야 한다.

13 Mike는 내가 그 전날에 그녀와 함께 저녁을 먹었는지를 물었다.
① MIke는 나에게 "너는 어제 그녀와 함께 저녁을 먹었니?"라고 말했다.
* 전달동사는 asked → said to로 바꾸고, if가 사용되었으므로 의문사가 없는 의문문으로 바꿔야 한다. 대과거(had + 과거분사)가 있는 것으로 보아 과거시제 의문문이 와야 한다.

14 Brown씨는 그녀에게 자신은 다음 날 집에 돌아갈 거라고 말했다.
→ Brown씨는 그녀에게 "나는 내일 집에 돌아갈 거야."라고 말했다.
* 전달동사는 told → said to로 바꾸고, 피전달문의 주어는 he → I, 시제는 would → will, 부사어는 the next day → tomorrow로 바꾼다.

15 Morris: 제 과제에 대해 몇 가지 질문을 해도 될까요?
Cindy: 물론이지. 오늘 내 사무실에 와도 돼.
Morris: 정말 감사합니다.
→ Morris는 Cindy에게 그의 과제에 대해 몇 가지 질문을 할 수 있는지를 물어보았다. Cindy는 동의했고, 그에게 그날 그녀의 사무실로 방문하라고 말했다.
* 의문사 없는 의문문을 간접화법으로 바꿀 때 〈if[whether] + 주어 + 동사〉의 어순으로 쓴다.

16 (a) 김 선생님은 그녀를 3일 전에 만났었다고 말했다.
(b) 우리는 그녀에게 그날 밤 화가 났었는지 물었다.
* 직접화법에서 간접화법으로 바꿀 때 ago → before, tonight → that night으로 쓴다.

17 ① 그 가위는 다 팔렸다.
② 모든 여자아이는 자신만의 방이 필요하다.
③ 절반의 일이 5시간 만에 완료되었다.
④ 많은 사람들이 그 손님을 기다리고 있다.
⑤ 40달러는 너의 아들에게 주기에 너무 많은 돈이다.
* 40달러라는 돈을 하나의 단위로 볼 경우 단수 취급해야 한다.

18 (a) 말하기나 쓰기 둘 중 하나는 재미있다.
(b) 듣기와 읽기 둘 다 재미있지 않다.
(c) 사람뿐만 아니라 돈도 중요하다.
* either A or B(A와 B 둘 중 하나), neither A nor B(A와 B 둘 다 아닌), B as well as A(B뿐만 아니라 A도)는 모두 B에 동사의 수를 일치시킨다. (b)는 빈칸에 nor와 is가 와야 한다.

19 * not only A but also B(A뿐만 아니라 B도 역시)는 B에 동사의 수를 일치시킨다.

20 (a) 그 셔츠의 일부는 일본에서 만든다/만들어졌다.
(b) 내 강의의 3분의 1은 과학에 관한 것이다/것이었다.
(c) 동물들을 연구하는 것은 매우 재미있다/재미있었다.
(d) 나의 아버지는 인생은 짧다고 말씀하셨다.
(e) Dana가 아니라 네가 그때 나의 반 친구였다.
(f) 물리학은 여자아이들에게 가장 어려운 과목 중 하나이다/하나였다.
* (a) are/were, (b) is/was, (c) is/was, (d) is(격언은 항상 현재형), (e) were(you에 시제 일치, then이 있으므로 과거형), (f) is/was(과목명은 항상 단수)가 들어간다.

21 해양들을 연구하는 것은 많은 유용한 정보를 준다. 사람들에게 해산물은 단백질의 공급원이다. 태국과 일본을 포함한 많은 나라들은 해양 관광 활동에 의존을 하고 있다. 게다가, 세계 인구의 약 50퍼센트가 바다 가까이에 살고 있다. 그래서 바다가 한 번 오염되면 사람들에게 금전적으로 부정적인 타격을 많이 준다.
* [give → gives] to부정사가 주어로 쓰였을 때는 단수 취급하므로 단수 동사가 온다.

22 나는 비행기 승무원에게 "저에게 담요를 갖다 주세요."라고 말했다.
→ 나는 비행기 승무원에게 담요를 갖다 달라고 요청했다.
* 명령문의 화법 전환에서 피전달문의 동사원형 → to부정사로 바꾼다.

23 ① 식당종업원은 "그밖에 더 필요한 것이 있으세요?"라고 말했다.
→ 식당종업원은 내게 그밖에 더 필요한 게 있는지 물었다.
② 한 학생은 "제가 지금 교실을 나가도 될까요?"라고 말했다.
→ 한 학생은 교실을 그때 나가도 되는지 물었다.
③ Owen은 나에게 "너는 나의 보살핌을 정말로 원하니?"라고 말했다.
→ Owen은 나에게 그의 보살핌을 정말로 원하는지 물었다.
④ 내 친구 Jack은 "너는 어디에 가고 있니?"라고 말했다.
→ 내 친구 Jack은 나에게 어디를 가고 있는지 물었다.
⑤ 그녀는 나에게 "너는 내 생일 파티에 올 수 있니?"라고 말했다.
→ 그녀는 나에게 그녀의 생일 파티에 올 수 있는지 물었다.
* [you → I] 화법 전환을 할 때 피전달문의 대명사는 화자의 입장에 맞게 바꿔야 한다.

24 ① 나의 선생님은 물이 100℃에 끓는다고 말했다.
② 그녀는 나에게 SNS를 사용하는지 물었다.
③ Emily는 그녀의 휴대전화 번호를 바꿨다고 말했다.
④ 그는 나에게 놀이공원에 가기를 원하는지 물었다.
⑤ 그녀는 나에게 저 가방을 어디에서 구입했는지 물었다.
* ① [boiled → boils] 과학적 사실은 항상 과거시제로 나타낸다.
⑤ [did I purchase → I purchased] 의문사가 있는 의문문의 경우 〈의문사 + 주어 + 동사〉의 어순으로 쓴다.

25 ① Jay는 Emma에게 자신은 그녀를 무척 사랑한다고 말했다.
② Mika는 얇은 크러스트 피자와 크림 스파게티를 먹고 싶다고 말했다.
③ Blair는 나에게 자신은 중국에 여러 번 갔었다고 말했다.
④ Tom은 Abigail에게 자신은 수업에 올 수 있다고 말했다.
⑤ 그는 나에게 자신이 학교에서 반장이라고 말했다.
* [said to → told] 직접화법을 간접화법으로 고칠 때 전달동사 said to는 told로 바꿔야 한다.

26 ① 그가 나를 사랑한다는 그 사실이 믿기지 않는다.
② 독서는 내가 가장 좋아하는 취미이다.
③ 계속 연습하는 것이 너를 성공하게 할 것이다.
④ 현금 대신 신용카드를 사용하는 것은 돈을 절약하는 좋은 방법이 아니다.
⑤ 꼭대기로 통하는 계단은 다소 위험하다.
* [are → is] 주어가 동명사이므로 단수 동사가 와야 한다. 주어를 수식하여 주어가 길어진 경우 동사에 가까이 있는 명사를 주어로 혼동하지 않도록 수의한다.
①⑤ 동격의 that절이나 관계대명사절이 주어를 수식해서 주어가 길어지는 경우도 동사와 가까이 있는 명사를 주어로 착각하지 않는다. ②③ 동명사나 to부정사가 주어로 쓰일 때는 단수 취급한다.

27 ① 그는 신제품 카메라를 사겠다고 말했다.
② 김 선생님은 나에게 실패는 단지 성공을 향한 발판일 뿐이라고 말씀하셨다.
③ 그녀는 매일 아침 6시에 일어나서 7시 30분에 학교에 간다고 말했다.
④ 나는 한국전쟁이 1950년에 일어났다는 걸 알고 있다.
⑤ 그 당시 사람들은 지구가 둥글다는 사실을 믿지 않았다.
* [was → is] 변함없는 과학적 사실은 현재시제로 쓴다.

28 ① 이 통계 수치들은 2013년에 인구 1,000명당 사망자 수를 보여준다.
② 총 300명의 중국인들이 차이나타운에 살고 있다.
③ 경찰들이 그 무자비한 살인범들을 찾고 있다.
④ 하루 중 이맘때면 이 지역은 언제나 교통량이 많다.
⑤ 몇몇 소방관들은 한 사람 이상이 그 화재에 대한 책임이 있다고 믿는다.
* [is → are] the police는 모양은 단수이지만 복수 취급하므로 뒤에 복수 명사가 나와야 한다.
② a total of는 '~의 총합계'라는 의미로 단수 취급한다.

29 나의 아버지는 내가 만화를 그리는 것에 흥미가 있다는 사실을 아신다.
→ 나의 아버지는 내가 만화를 그리는 것에 흥미가 있었다는 사실을 알았다.
* 주절의 시제가 현재 → 과거로 바뀌면 종속절의 시제는 현재완료 → 과거완료로 바뀌어야 한다.

30 나는 어렸을 때 베른이 스위스의 수도라는 것을 몰랐다.
* 일반적인 사실은 항상 현재시제를 쓴다.

Sentence Writing

▶ 본문 232쪽

Part A
1 would not get along with her friend
2 My daughter's English is much better than, said, her son was more handsome
3 not to talk with Joe

Part B
1 He said to me, "I will buy you this house."
2 My brother asked me to wake him up at six o'clock.
3 Dad told me not to go out.
4 Helen asked Hank whether[if] that was an essay or a poem.

Part A
1 Amy는 나에게 그녀의 친구 Joe와 어울리지 않을 것이라고 말했다.
2 지난 금요일, 그들은 대학교 동창회에 갔다. Joe는 Amy에게 "내 딸 영어실력이 네 딸보다 훨씬 낫더라."라고 말했다. 그리고 또한 그녀의 아들이 Amy의 아들보다 더 잘생겼다고 그녀에게 말했다.
3 마침내, Amy는 나에게 Joe와 더 이상 이야기하지 않겠다고 말했다.

Unit 13 특수구문

DAY 25 강조, 부정

2교시 In - Class Questions

▶ 본문 237쪽

STEP A 1 the very 2 did 3 on earth 4 at all

STEP B 1 It was many grammar mistakes that John made in his writing.
2 It was the day before yesterday when I used her computer.
3 She did work at a hospital for 20 years.

STEP C 1 don't, always 2 Neither, of, them
3 Not, all, live

STEP D 1 Jisu doesn't know anything about the accident at all.
2 I couldn't understand in the least what my professor said.
3 It was in front of my house where Yunho picked up my wallet.

STEP A
1 Keilen은 모든 사람들이 만나고 싶어 하는 바로 그 여자이다.
2 그 새 커플은 그때 매우 행복하게 보이기를 정말로 원했다.
3 학교를 전학 가는 데 도대체 뭐가 문제니?
4 지금 나는 비싼 프린터를 살 필요가 전혀 없다.

STEP B
1 John은 그의 글쓰기에서 많은 문법 실수를 했다.
→ John이 그의 글쓰기에서 했던 것은 바로 매우 많은 문법 실수였다.
2 나는 그저께 그녀의 컴퓨터를 사용했다.
→ 내가 그녀의 컴퓨터를 사용한 것은 바로 그저께이다.
3 그녀는 20년 동안 병원에서 일했다.
→ 그녀는 20년 동안 병원에서 정말 일했다.

3교시 After - Class Questions

▶ 본문 238 - 241쪽

01 not always **02** Neither Dad nor my brother **03** ② **04** ④ **05** ③ **06** ⑤ **07** ④ **08** ④ **09** (a) at the last → in the least **10** ② **11** ③ **12** ② **13** ③ **14** ⑤ **15** (1) doesn't have all (2) doesn't have any **16** It was Paul and her who you saw in the hospital. **17** ② **18** (1) in Iowa (2) you and me **19** ④ **20** in, the, world **21** It, was **22** ② **23** ⑤ **24** ⑤ **25** until

01 사람들은 대개 그들의 삶에 만족하지만 가끔씩은 만족하지 않는다.
→ 사람들에게 삶은 항상 만족스러운 것은 아니다.
* '항상 ~한 것은 아니다'의 부분부정 표현이 알맞다.

02 아빠는 쇼핑하는 것을 좋아하지 않는다. 내 남동생도 또한 쇼핑하러 가는 것을 좋아하지 않는다.
→ 아빠도 내 남동생도 둘 다 쇼핑하러 가는 것을 좋아하지 않는다.
* 'A와 B 둘 다 아닌'의 전체부정 표현이 알맞다.

03 ① Ken은 그것에 대해 거의 의심을 하지 않는다.

② 그들 중 아무도 가난한 사람들을 돕기 위해 오지 않았다.
③ 내 여자 친구는 나에게 전화를 거의 하지 않는다.
④ 많은 십대들은 거의 소설과 시를 읽지 않는다.
⑤ 두 개념의 차이를 이해하는 사람은 거의 없다.
* ②의 none은 전체부정을 나타내는 말이며, 나머지는 '거의 ~아니다'라는 의미의 준부정 문장이다.

04 새로운 영화가 개봉된 것은 바로 어제였다.
* 강조하는 말(yesterday)이 시간을 나타내므로 that을 when으로 바꿀 수 있다.

05 ① 나를 온종일 매료시킨 것은 바로 그녀의 목소리였다.
② Sally가 그녀의 선생님을 만난 것은 강당에서였다.
③ 그 가게가 일요일에 문을 닫는다는 것은 사실이다.
④ Hank와 Nick과 함께 학교를 간 것은 Jane이다.
⑤ 잡지에서 내가 읽은 것은 믿을 수 없는 이야기였다.
* ③은 가주어로 쓰인 It이고, 나머지는 강조구문에 쓰인 It이다.

06 * 명사(place)를 강조하는 것이므로 〈the very + 명사〉로 나타내야 한다.

07 한 의사는 작은 마을의 가난한 아이들을 도와주기 위해 노력한다.
④ 한 의사는 작은 마을에서 가난한 아이들을 도와주기 위해 정말로 노력한다.
* 주어가 3인칭 단수이므로 동사 강조의 〈does + 동사원형〉으로 나타내야 한다.

08 Victoria는 방콕 행 표를 예약했다.
④ Victoria가 예약한 것은 바로 방콕 행 비행기 표였다.
* 강조구문을 만들 때는 강조하는 말을 that 앞에 넣는다. 시제가 과거이므로 be동사도 과거시제로 써야 한다.

09 (a) Harry는 이 문제에 대해 전혀 걱정하지 않았다.
(b) Ron은 Brian이 말한 것을 전혀 이해하지 못한다.
* at the last는 '최후에는'의 뜻이다. 부정의 의미를 강조하는 표현은 in the least, at all이다.

10 Hank는 어제 서점에서 이 공책을 샀다.
* 〈It + be동사 ~ that ...〉 강조구문으로 동사는 강조할 수 없다. bought를 강조하기 위해서는 〈did + 동사원형〉을 사용해야 한다.

11 이 카레 식당에 줄서서 기다리는 사람들이 거의 없다. 고객 중 아무도 여기에 아직 도착하지 않았다.
* few people은 '사람들이 거의 없는'의 뜻이므로 '아무도 없는'이라는 의미의 none으로 표현할 수 없다.

12 나의 할머니는 내가 초등학교에 들어갔던 날을 전혀 기억하지 못하셨다. 나는 실망했지만 할머니에게 그것을 일깨워드리는 것을 절대 포기하지 않았다. 마침내, 그녀는 내가 다녔던 바로 그 학교를 언급하셨다.
* 문맥상 '전혀 기억하지 못 한다'라는 의미의 not ~ at all로 표현한다. 명사 school을 강조하는 말은 the very이다.

13 ① 사랑이는 그녀의 아버지를 잘 따른다.
② 너의 친구가 너에게 도대체 뭐라고 말했니?
③ Jeff는 너의 엄마에게 아무 것도 말하지 않을 것이다.
④ 그녀가 파스타에 필요로 했던 것은 바로 우유였다.
⑤ 윤 선생님은 내가 배우고 싶은 바로 그 선생님이다.
* 부정문을 강조하려면 not ~ at all로 표현해야 한다.
① 동사를 강조하는 does, ② 의문사를 강조하는 on earth, ④ 〈It ~ that ...〉 강조구문, ⑤ 명사를 강조하는 the very

14 ① Kelly는 조금도 영리하지 않다.
② 이 비싼 장치를 고친 것은 바로 나였다.
③ Jack은 자세한 정보를 전혀 주지 않았다.
④ 도대체 당신의 남동생은 문제가 뭡니까?
⑤ Sam과 Josh 둘 다 함께 숙제를 했다.
* 강조의 did가 아닌 do one's homework로 쓰인 본동사이다.
① 부정문을 강조하는 in the least, ② 〈It ~ that ...〉 강조구문, ③ 부정문을 강조하는 at all, ④ 의문문을 강조하는 on earth

15 * (1) 부분부정은 〈not + all〉로 표현한다.
(2) 전체부정은 〈not + any〉로 표현한다.

16 * It과 who 사이에 강조어구인 Paul and her를 넣어야 한다.

17 Brian은 아침 일찍 그의 아이들을 위해 점심을 쌌다.
① 아침 일찍 아이들을 위해 점심을 쌌던 사람은 Brian이었다.
③ Brian이 아이들을 위해 아침 일찍 쌌던 것은 점심이었다.
④ Brian이 아침 일찍 점심을 쌌던 것은 아이들을 위해서였다.
⑤ Brian이 아이들을 위해 점심을 쌌던 때는 아침 일찍이었다.
* [→ Brian did pack lunch for his kids early in the morning.] 동사의 강조는 〈It ~ that〉 강조구문으로 나타낼 수 없다.

18 (1) 내가 남편을 처음으로 만났던 곳은 아이오와에서였다.
(2) 그들이 그들의 연구소로 초대했던 것은 너와 나였다.
* (1) that 뒤의 문장이 완벽하므로 장소의 부사구가 강조된 것이다.
(2) 목적어가 강조되었으므로 목적격이 와야 한다.

19 ① 나의 부모님 두 분 다 돌아가신 건 아니다.
② 엄마조차도 스스로 모든 것을 다 할 수는 없다.
③ 모든 학생들이 선생님의 지도사항을 따랐던 것은 아니다.
④ 그는 그의 형제 중 누구와도 함께 노는 데 시간을 보내지 않았다.
⑤ 착해 보이는 사람이 항상 너에게 친절한 것은 아니다.
* ④는 전체부정이고, 나머지는 부분부정을 나타내는 문장이다.

20 너는 무엇을 하고 싶니?
→ 도대체 너는 무엇을 하고 싶니?
* 의문사를 강조할 때는 의문사 뒤에 on earth나 in the world를 쓴다.

21 Juliet은 그녀의 사촌 결혼식 날에 Romeo와 사랑에 빠졌다.
→ Juliet이 그녀의 사촌 결혼식 날에 사랑에 빠진 사람은 바로 Romeo였다.
* 강조하는 말 뒤에 who가 왔으므로 〈It + be동사 + who[that] ~〉 강조구문이다. who절의 시제가 과거이므로 It 다음의 be동사도 과거시제로 써야 한다.

22 ① 내가 실수한 것을 알게 되었던 것은 바로 어제 저녁이었다.
② 그녀가 두 번 결혼했다는 것은 사실이 아니다.
③ Sean에게 오늘 아침에 이메일을 썼던 사람은 바로 나였다.
④ 내가 오늘 점심에 길에서 만났던 것은 바로 너의 여자 친구였다.
⑤ Jim이 어제 100달러짜리 지폐를 주웠던 것은 바로 길에서였다.
* ②의 〈It ~ that ...〉은 가주어 · 진주어 구문이고, 나머지는 〈It ~ that ...〉 강조구문이다. ① 부사어 강조, ③ 주어 강조, ④ 목적어 강조, ⑤ 부사어 강조

23 ① 나는 내가 할 수 있는 모든 것을 했다.
② 나는 분명히 당신에게 미리 알려주었다.
③ 그들은 서로 분명히 만난다.
④ 너의 친한 친구들은 정말로 너를 걱정한다.
⑤ 내가 시키는 대로 해라.
* ⑤의 do는 '~하다'라는 본동사로 쓰였고, 나머지 일반동사를 강조하는 do/did로 쓰였다.

24 * 부분부정으로 나타내야 하고, 앞에 not이 있으므로 both가 알맞다.

25 * 'A하고 나서야 비로소 B하다'는 〈not A until B〉로 표현한다.

DAY 26 도치, 생략

2교시 In - Class Questions

▶ 본문 243쪽

STEP A 1 does she go 2 are two little girls
3 does Jennifer meet 4 did Lily

STEP B 1 ran, Jeongmin 2 he, drank
3 neither, does, he

STEP C 1 she 2 (to 다음의) go out 3 that 4 I was

STEP D 1 Not only does this food look good, but it is also delicious.
2 Not until we lose our health do we realize its importance.
3 Down the street walk people with gray hair.
4 Hardly did Susan dream that she would visit here.

STEP A 1 요즘 그녀는 절대 병원에 가지 않는다.
2 탁자 아래에 두 명의 작은 여자아이들이 있다.

3 Jennifer는 좀처럼 많은 사람을 만나지 않는다.
4 Keilen은 자격증을 따지 못했고, Lily 또한 따지 못했다.

STEP B
1 교실 안으로 정민이는 뛰어 들어갔다.
2 카페에서 그는 밀크티를 마셨다.
3 당신이 그것을 원하지 않고, 그도 역시 원하지 않는다.

STEP C
1 Jane은 지하철을 놓쳐서 버스를 탔다.
2 누군가 (가길) 원한다면 가도 좋다.
3 Frank는 곧 좋은 직업을 갖기를 희망한다.
4 나는 어렸을 때 많은 친구들과 놀기를 좋아했다.

STEP D
1 이 음식은 멋져 보일 뿐만 아니라 맛도 있다.
2 우리는 건강을 잃고서야 비로소 그것의 중요성을 깨닫는다.
3 길을 따라서 회색머리의 사람들이 걸어간다.
4 Susan은 자신이 여기를 방문하리라고 거의 꿈꾸지 못했다.

3교시 After - Class Questions ▶ 본문 244 - 247쪽

01 ⑤ **02** ② **03** ③ **04** ④ **05** ③ **06** ④ **07** ③ **08** ② **09** ⑤ **10** ③ **11** ⑤ **12** ③ **13** flows the Han River **14** ② **15** do the girls look, they also like **16** ⑤ **17** jumped a rabbit, flew an eagle **18** ⑤ **19** (1) either → neither (2) nor → so (3) so → and so **20** ⑤ **21** (두 번째) I like **22** did, I, tell **23** ①, ② **24** ②, ⑤ **25** ②

01 Brian은 이번 주말에 그의 숙제를 할 것이며, 나도 또한 그렇다.
* 긍정의 동의를 표현하는 '~도 또한 그렇다'는 ⟨so + 조동사(will) + 주어(I)⟩로 나타낼 수 있다.

02 나는 결코 길에 그렇게 많은 개와 고양이가 있는 것을 본 적이 없다.
* 부정어가 강조를 위해 문두에 오면 ⟨부정어 + 조동사(had) + 주어(I) + 본동사(seen)⟩의 어순이 된다.

03 너의 아빠는 너에게 돈을 주지 않으실 거야. 나도 역시 너에게 주지 않을 거고.
* 부정의 동의를 표현하는 '~도 또한 아니다'는 ⟨Neither + 조동사(will) + 주어(I)⟩로 나타낸다.

04 ① 네가 원한다면 집에 가도 좋다.
② 그들은 가능한 한 빠르게 걸었다.
③ 위험할 때는 나에게 전화해라.
④ 여기에 다섯 명의 여자아이들과 두 명의 남자아이들이 있다.
⑤ 민지는 콘서트에 갈 것이며, 나 또한 그렇다.
* [five girls and two boys are → are five girls and two boys] 장소부사구가 문두로 오면 ⟨Here + 동사 + 주어⟩의 어순이 된다.

05 ① 나는 네가 사과할 때까지 너를 용서하지 않을 것이다.
② 그녀는 그를 만나자마자 도망가 버렸다.
③ 지호는 저녁을 먹고 나서 바로 떠났고, 민수도 그랬다.
④ 그는 늦게 왔을 뿐만 아니라 숙제도 잊어버렸다.
⑤ 나는 숙제를 끝내기 전에는 집에서 컴퓨터게임을 결코 하지 않는다.
* [Minsu did → did Minsu] '~도 역시 그렇다'는 ⟨so + 동사 + 주어⟩의 어순으로 나타낸다.

06 ① 좀처럼 나는 학교에 지각한 적이 없다.
② 즉시 그녀는 창문을 열었다.
③ 나는 9월이 되어서야 비로소 휴가를 갖게 될 것이다.
④ 나는 그렇게 예쁜 소녀를 본 적이 없었다.
⑤ 엄마는 지난주부터 한 마디도 하지 않으셨다.
* [I have → have I] 부정어 never를 강조하기 위해서 문장 맨 앞에 쓰면 ⟨부정어 + 조동사 + 주어⟩의 어순이 된다.

07 Gary는 그가 최고의 비행기 조종사가 될 것이라고 꿈꾼 적이 거의 없었다.
* 부정어 little을 강조하여 문두로 오면 ⟨부정어(little) + 조동사(has) + 주어(Gary) + 본동사(dreamed)⟩의 어순이 된다.

08 토요일 아침에 내가 방에 있었을 때 나는 숙제를 하는 중이었다. 갑자기 초인종이 울렸다. 내가 문을 열려고 갔을 때 부모님으로부터 문을 열지 말라는 말을 들었다. 벨은 계속 울렸지만 나는 문을 열지 않았다.
* 시간 접속사 다음의 주어가 주절의 주어와 동일할 경우 ⟨주어(I) + be동사(was)⟩를 생략할 수 있다.

09 ① Nancy와 Rick 둘 다 어렸을 때 미술에 관심이 있었다.
② 이 사람은 내가 유치원 때 만났던 나의 가장 친한 친구이다.
③ 몇몇 사람들은 이 문제들이 풀기 어렵다고 생각했다.
④ Victoria는 Dan보다 에세이를 더 잘 쓴다.
⑤ Kevin은 매우 피곤했지만 그가 해야 할 모든 일을 끝냈다.
* 부사절의 주어와 주절의 주어가 일치하지 않으면 부사절의 ⟨주어(Kevin) + 동사(is)⟩를 생략할 수 없다.

10 A: 이 파일을 내 USB에 저장해도 괜찮을까?
B: 응, 만약 나의 언니가 네가 그렇게 하는 것을 허락한다면.
* to부정사의 동사가 반복되면 to만 쓰고 save this file in your USB를 생략할 수 있다.

11 A: 나는 역사 과제를 끝내지 못했어.
B: 나도 못 끝냈어.
* A의 말이 부정이기 때문에 '나도 또한 끝내지 못했어.'라는 말이 되려면 ⟨Neither + 조동사(did) + 주어(I)⟩로 표현해야 한다.

12 * 부정어가 강조되어 문두에 놓이면 ⟨부정문 + 동사 + 주어⟩의 어순으로 쓴다. '~해 본 적이 없다'는 의미는 현재완료로 표현한다.

13 * 장소부사구가 문두에 왔으므로 다음에는 ⟨동사(flows)+ 주어(the Han River)⟩의 어순으로 쓴다.

14 우리 비행기가 저 커다란 농장 위로 날아간다.
* 장소부사구를 강조하기 위해 문두로 나가면 다음에는 ⟨동사 + 주어⟩의 어순으로 쓴다.

15 그 여자아이들은 매우 비슷하게 생겼다. 그들은 또한 같은 음식을 좋아한다.
→ 그 여자아이들은 매우 비슷하게 생겼을 뿐만 아니라 똑같은 음식을 좋아한다.
* 부정어구 not only가 문두로 왔으므로 뒤에는 ⟨do + 주어 + 동사원형⟩의 어순으로 쓴다.

16 어제가 되어서야 비로소 엄마는 나의 텝스 시험 점수를 아셨다.
* not until이 문두로 나가면 다음에는 ⟨did + 주어 + 동사원형⟩의 어순이 된다.

17 * 장소의 부사가 문두로 나가면 조동사 do가 아닌 문장의 동사가 도치된다.

18 (a) 오직 그녀의 도움으로 나의 가족은 그 사실을 알았다.
(b) 매우 피곤했기 때문에 Mary는 바로 곯아 떨어졌다.
* [Mary was → was Mary] 부사구와 보어가 강조하기 위해 문두로 가면 다음에는 ⟨동사 + 주어⟩의 어순이 되어야 한다.

19 (1) 나의 중국어 실력은 좋지 않은데, 그의 실력도 마찬가지이다.
(2) 나는 스페인어를 말해서 기쁘고, 그녀도 마찬가지이다.
(3) 결국, 너는 상을 받았고, 나도 받았다.
* (1) 앞 문장이 부정문이므로 이에 대한 동의를 하려면 neither로 써야 한다.
(2) 앞 문장이 긍정문이므로 이에 대한 동의를 하려면 so로 써야 한다.
(3) so는 부사이고 접속사가 아니므로 and so로 써야 한다.

20 (a) 한 여자가 이 마을에 살았었다.
(b) 창문 옆 책상 위에 그녀의 램프가 놓여있었다.
(c) 너는 12살이 되어서야 피자를 먹었다.
(d) 그는 그 공고문을 거의 알아차리지 못했다.
(e) 이 교실로 그녀가 온다.
* (a) 유도부사로 쓰인 there 다음에는 주어와 동사가 도치된다.
(c) 부정어 not until이 문두로 오면 문장의 주어와 동사는 ⟨did + 주어 + 동사원형⟩의 어순이 된다.
(e) she는 대명사이므로 장소부사구가 문두로 왔지만 주어와 동사가 도치되지 않았다.
(b) [her lamp lay → lay her lamp], (d) [have → has]

21 나는 야구보다 농구를 더 좋아한다.
* 비교구문에서는 than 뒤의 반복되는 부분을 생략할 수 있다.

22 나는 그에게 어제 내가 누구를 만났는지 결코 말하지 않았다.
* 부정어가 문장의 맨 앞에 나올 경우 ⟨부정어 + do동사 + 주어 + 동사원형⟩의 어순으로 쓴다.

23 ① 그는 길을 따라 걸어 내려갔다.
② 몇 개의 접시를 나의 엄마가 또 깨셨다.
③ 봉투 안에 동봉된 것은 내 초대장이다.
④ 그녀는 어떤 흔적도 그 방에 남기지 않았다.

⑤ 다른 사람을 돕는 기쁨을 아는 사람들은 행복하다.

* ① [walked he → he walked] 장소를 나타내는 부사구가 문두로 나와도 주어가 대명사인 경우에는 주어와 동사가 도치되지 않는다.
② [broke my mom → my mom broke] 목적어가 문두로 나오는 경우에는 주어와 동사가 도치되지 않는다.

24 ① 그는 그의 집에서만 편안하고 행복하게 느낀다.
② 호텔에 돌아온 후에야 나는 쉴 수 있었다.
③ 내 친구들 몇 명만이 내가 새로 남자 친구를 사귀는 걸 알고 있다.
④ 내 여동생만 부모님과 함께 캐나다에 갔다 왔다.
⑤ 엄마는 지난주에서야 나의 담임선생님을 처음으로 만났다.

* ② [I could → could I] 부사절 Only after ~가 문두로 나왔으므로 다음에는 〈조동사 + 주어 + 동사원형〉의 어순이 되어야 한다.
⑤ [my mom met → did my mom meet] 부사구 Only last week가 문두로 나왔으므로 다음에는 〈do동사 + 주어 + 동사원형〉의 어순이 되어야 한다.
③④ Only는 주어인 a few my friends와 my little sister를 수식하고 있으므로 도치구문이 아니다.

25 ① 내 머리 위로 새 한 마리가 지나갔다.
② 꽃 위에 벌 몇 마리가 앉았다.
③ 부산에는 거의 눈이 내리지 않는다.
④ 그녀는 자기가 얼마나 예쁜지 알지 못한다.
⑤ 산꼭대기에 많은 나무들이 서있다.

* 부사구 on a flower를 강조하기 위해 문두로 나왔으므로 주어와 동사가 도치되었다.
① [a bird passed → passed a bird], ③ it snows → does it snow],
④ [she realizes → does she realize], ⑤ [many trees stood → stood many trees]

Final Test

▶ 본문 248 - 251쪽

01 ① **02** ⑤ **03** ④ **04** ② **05** ② **06** ④ **07** ③ **08** at 6 o'clock that[when] the box was delivered **09** ⑤ **10** (b), (c), (d) **11** ① **12** ⑤ **13** ① **14** (1) rarely do they fall asleep at night. (2) On the green grass are 100 sheep. **15** I didn't know he was my student until the boy left. **16** (1) Although I am invited to the party (2) If it is necessary **17** (1) neither (2) both (3) Neither, are, you, nor, do, you **18** ④ **19** ③ **20** (1) lay a mall (2) we are (3) we said (4) in Manhattan **21** (a) ② (b) ③ **22** (1) on earth (2) that (3) neither (4) did **23** It was last Sunday that[when] I played baseball with a famous player in this baseball park. **24** ② **25** ③ **26** ⑤ **27** ⑤ **28** will you find any stores **29** Here are you. → Here you are. **30** ④

01 ① 당신이 늦게까지 깨어있는 것은 쉬운 일이었다.
② 부모님이 집으로 돌아오시는 날은 바로 오늘이다.
③ 너를 매우 사랑하는 사람은 바로 Mike였다.
④ 그 눈이 쌓이는 곳은 바로 도로이다.
⑤ 모든 학생들이 보기를 원하는 사람은 바로 그 유명한 영화배우이다.

* ①의 It은 〈It ~ for + 목적격 + to부정사 ...〉의 가주어-진주어 구문에 쓰인 가주어 It이고, 나머지는 강조구문에 쓰인 It이다.

02 Eunice는 Anne이 미소를 지을 동안 사진을 찍었다.

* 동사를 강조할 수 있는 것은 do만 가능하다. 과거형(took)이므로 〈did + 동사원형(take)〉으로 쓴다.

03 * neither of us는 전체부정이므로 '우리들 중 누구도 그 수수께끼를 푸는 것에 대해 생각하지 않는다.'라는 의미이다.

04 ① 네가 원한다면 이 차를 살 수 있다.
② Eric은 모든 여자가 데이트하고 싶은 바로 그 남자이다.
③ Vicky는 춤을 잘 추는데, Micky도 또한 잘 춘다.
④ Cathy는 입학시험을 통과하지 못했다.
⑤ 새로운 컴퓨터를 사기로 결정한 것은 바로 Jane이었다.

* man을 강조하기 위해서는 the very man으로 표현해야 한다.

05 ① 그들은 늙었을 때 모든 일을 하는 것이 귀찮아진다.
② 지붕 위에 암탉 한마리가 서있다.
③ 그의 집에 많은 사람이 있다.
④ 많은 배심원단은 그가 무죄라는 것을 정말로 믿었다.
⑤ 바구니에는 작은 핀과 클립이 있었다.

* [a hen stood → stood a hen] 부사구 on the top of the roof가 문두에 왔으므로 다음에는 〈동사 + 주어〉의 어순이 되어야 한다.

06 ① 한국의 모든 학생들이 행복한 것은 아니다.
② 여기에는 그 남자가 있었고, 저기에는 그녀가 있었다.
③ 그 희생자들을 도와주는 사람이 바로 그 형사이다.
④ 그녀는 간호사이고, 나도 그러하다.
⑤ 나는 그의 미래에 관하여 조금도 고민하지 않는다.

* [do → am] 앞 문장의 동사가 be동사이므로 '나도 역시 그렇다'는 표현도 be동사로 나타내야 한다.

07 어제 나는 어떤 남자를 만났는데 그는 나와 함께 저녁을 먹고 싶어 했다. 우리는 식사를 했고 좋은 시간을 보냈다. 그는 멋진 남자였다. 그는 친절할 뿐만 아니라 좋은 매너도 갖고 있었다. 나는 그를 정말로 다시 만나고 싶다.

* 부정어 not only가 문두로 오면 다음에는 〈be동사(was) + 주어(he)〉의 어순이 된다.

08 * 6시를 강조하는 것이므로 〈It was + 강조할 말 + that ...〉으로 표현한다.

09 내 여동생들은 지난밤에 서로 싸움을 한 후 어떤 말도 하지 않았다.

* 부정어를 강조하기 위해 부정어를 문두에 두면 〈부정어 + 조동사 + 주어 + 동사원형〉의 어순으로 쓴다.

10 (a) Frank는 그 똑똑한 새가 그의 새장으로 다시 돌아가는 것을 보았다.
(b) 진석이는 집에 가서 컴퓨터게임을 했다.
(c) 우리는 이탈리아에 있는 동안 저 호텔에 머물러야 했다.
(d) Karen은 저 남자가 그 수업을 듣고 싶어 한다고 믿었다.

* (b) 접속사 and로 연결되어 반복되는 주어(Jinseok)가 생략되었다.
(c) 때를 나타내는 부사절의 주어가 주절의 주어와 동일할 경우 부사절의 〈주어(we) + be동사(were)〉는 생략할 수 있다.
(d) believe의 목적어 역할을 하는 명사절을 이끄는 접속사 that은 생략할 수 있다. that man에서의 that은 지시형용사로 '저 남자'의 뜻이다. 만약 that을 접속사로 본다면 man의 관사가 없어 비문이 된다.

11 Jane과 Dona는 교통체증에 있었는데, 그들의 남편들도 마찬가지였다.

* 내용상 '~도 역시 그렇다'의 의미가 알맞다. 긍정문에 대한 동의는 〈So + 동사 + 주어〉로 나타낸다.

12 ① Yuki는 Hunter보다 좀 더 조심스럽게 운전을 했다.
② Sunny는 발레를 전공하고 있는 댄서이다.
③ 민준이는 어려서 미식축구에 매우 열광했었다.
④ 가능하다면 나의 집에 잠깐 들러라.
⑤ 네가 집에 있는 동안 집배원이 문을 두드렸다.

* 주절의 주어와 부사절의 주어가 일치할 경우에만 부사절의 〈주어 + be동사〉를 생략할 수 있다. you와 the mailman은 다른 사람이기 때문에 생략할 수 없다.

13 A: 나는 러시아에 가는 것이 정말 걱정스러워. 왜냐하면 나는 러시아어와 영어 둘 다 못해.
B: 나도 마찬가지야. 하지만 그건 아무 문제가 안 돼. 너는 관광안내 센터에 가서 도움을 얻을 수 있어.

* 문맥상 '둘 다 할 수 없다'는 뜻이고 앞에 부정어(can't)가 있으므로 〈either A or B〉가 와야 한다. '나도 또한 못 해'라는 의미가 되려면 〈Neither + 조동사 + 주어〉로 나타낸다.

14 많은 사람들이 수면 장애에 시달리고 있다. 가장 흔한 증상은 그들이 밤에 거의 잠을 이루지 못한다는 것이다. 그래서 한국에서는 불면증에 시달리는 사람들이 양을 세기 시작한다. 100마리의 양이 푸른 잔디에 있다. 그것이 처음에 시작하는 것이다.

* (1) 부정어 강조는 〈부정어 + 조동사 + 주어 + 동사원형〉, (2) 장소부사구 강조는 〈장소부사구 + 동사 + 주어〉의 어순으로 쓴다.

15 나는 그 소년이 떠나고 나서야 비로소 그가 나의 학생이었음을 알았다.

* 〈not until A B〉 구문은 주절의 동사를 부정으로 바꾸고 until 뒤의 문장은 긍정으로 바꾼다.

16 (1) 나는 파티에 초대를 받았지만 가지 않을 것이다.
(2) 필요하다면 그는 너에게 도움을 요청할 것이다.

* (1) 주절의 주어와 부사절의 주어가 같은 경우에 생략된다는 점을 생각한다.
(2) if necessary는 사람이 주어가 될 수 없고 it is로 써야 한다.

17 * (1) 전체부정은 neither, (2) 부분부정은 both, (3) 'A도 B도 아닌'은 neither A nor B로 표현한다. 부정어가 도치되면 〈be동사 + 주어〉 혹은 〈do동사 + 주어〉의 어순이 된다.

18 ① 내가 그를 만났던 곳은 바로 도서관에서였다.
② 그에게 선물을 준 것은 바로 너와 그녀였다.
③ 우리가 파티를 한 때는 바로 어제이다.
④ 오늘 아침에서야 그가 그 답을 찾았다.
⑤ 그는 숙제를 거의 하지 않아서 문제가 생겼다.
* ① [the library → at the library], ② [her → she], ③ [where → when], ⑤ [he → he do]

19 ① 내가 그녀를 만난 곳은 바로 너의 집 앞이었다.
② 그는 전 세계를 여행하기를 정말 원한다.
③ 너의 선생님이 가르치는 것이 항상 옳기만 한 것은 아니다.
④ 내가 아이돌 그룹 EXO를 만날 것이라고는 꿈도 꾸지 못했다.
⑤ 어젯밤에 큰 문제를 일으켰던 사람은 바로 Jim이었다.
* '항상 ~인 것은 아니다'라는 의미의 부분부정 문장이다. ① [which → where 혹은 that], ② [do → does], ④ [dreamed I → did I dream], ⑤ [whom → who 혹은 that]

20 (1) 길 건너에 상점이 하나가 있었다.
(2) 우리 여기에 있어요.
(3) 우리가 말했던 어느 것도 사실이 아니었다.
(4) 지나가 공부를 했던 곳은 맨해튼에서였다.
* (1) 장소 부사구가 문두로 가면 주어와 동사가 도치되지만, (2) 주어가 대명사일 때는 도치될 수 없다. (3) nothing we said 자체가 주어이므로 도치될 수 없으며, (4) 강조되는 말이 in Manhattan이다. (Gina studied in Manhattan)

21 (a) 그 유명한 빵집은 이 동네 근처에 있었다.
(b) David는 공원에서 그의 자전거를 잃어버렸다.
* 장소의 부사구가 문두에 나올 경우, (a) 자동사는 주어와 동사가 도치되지만, (b) 타동사는 도치될 수 없다.

22 (1) 너는 도대체 무엇을 하려고 하는 거니?
(2) 나를 놀라게 했던 것은 바로 그가 Emma와 결혼한다는 소식이었다.
(3) 나의 아내는 나에게 화가 난 것 같다. 그녀는 오늘 아침 나에게 말을 하지도 않고 나를 쳐다보지도 않았다.
(4) 그 소방관은 희생자들의 생명을 살리기 위해 정말 열심히 노력했다.
* (1) 의문사를 강조할 수 있는 어구는 on earth이다. (2) 〈It ~ that ...〉 강조구문이다. (3) 전체 부정을 나타내는 것은 〈neither A nor B〉 구문이다. (4) 일반동사의 강조는 do동사를 사용한다.

23 나는 지난주 일요일에 이 야구장에서 유명한 야구선수와 같이 경기를 했다.
→ 내가 이 야구장에서 유명한 야구선수와 야구경기를 한 것은 바로 지난 주 일요일이었다.
* 강조구문은 〈It + be동사 + 강조하는 말 + that ~〉으로 나타낸다. 강조하는 말이 시간이므로 that 대신 when을 사용할 수 있다.

24 보기 나는 엊그제 백화점에서 Kenny를 정말 만났다.
① 그들은 그 경기에서 이기기 위해서 최선을 다했다.
② 그녀는 최근에 정말 행복해 보인다.
③ 그녀는 그녀의 과제를 하고 있니?
④ 엊그제 너는 뭐했니?
⑤ 그녀는 네가 도움을 요청하기를 원하지 않았니?
* 〈보기〉와 ②는 일반동사를 강조하는 do로 쓰였다. ①③ 본동사, ④⑤ 조동사

25 ① 내가 갖고 싶어 했던 것은 바로 이 장난감이었다.
② 빈민들을 보살폈던 것은 Teresa 수녀님이었다.
③ 그가 중간고사에서 100점을 받은 것은 사실이다.
④ 나의 가족이 낚시를 가기로 한 날은 바로 이번 주 토요일이다.
⑤ 잃어버린 아이가 발견된 장소는 바로 우체국 앞이었다.
* ③은 가주어 · 진주어 구문으로 쓰였고, 나머지는 강조구문으로 쓰였다.

26 A: ___________ / B: 나도 그래.
① 나는 영어를 좋아하지 않는다.
② 나는 토마토를 먹지 않는다.
③ 그는 공부를 열심히 하지 않는다.
④ 나는 그와 이야기할 기회가 없다.
⑤ 나의 아버지가 엄마에게 편지를 쓰셨다.
* Neither do I.는 부정문에 대한 동의의 표현이다. 긍정문에 동의할 때는 〈So + (조)동사 + 주어〉로 쓴다.

27 ① 수민이는 운전할 수 있고 나도 할 수 있다.
② 나는 키가 매우 작고 내 동생도 그렇다.
③ Jane은 하와이에 살고 있고 Bob도 그랬다.
④ 그녀는 등산을 갈 것이고 그 또한 그럴 것이다.
⑤ 내 여동생은 그녀의 숙제를 끝냈고 Hannah도 그렇다.
* 긍정문에 대해서 동의하는 말은 〈So + be동사/조동사 + 주어〉를 쓴다. 이 때 앞 문장에 쓰인 동사가 be동사면 be동사로, 일반동사면 do동사로, 조동사면 조동사로 써야 한다. ① [do → can], ② [does → is], ③ [do → does], ④ [does → will]

28 * 장소를 나타내는 부사(구)를 강조하기 위해서 문두에 올 경우 〈부사구 + (조)동사 + 주어〉의 어순으로 쓴다.

29 A: 밖에는 너무 춥네요. 무언가 뜨거운 마실 것을 주세요.
B: 알겠습니다. 잠시만 기다려 주세요. ... 여기 있습니다. 맛있게 드세요.
A: 감사합니다. 이게 뭔가요?
B: 생강차입니다. 그것은 당신의 혈액순환을 도와줄 거예요.
A: 오, 저는 이 차를 전에 맛본 적이 없습니다. 맛있네요.
* 주어가 대명사일 경우에는 〈Here + 주어 + 동사〉의 어순으로 쓴다.

30 ① 누가 너의 새로운 영어 선생님이니?
② 그녀는 13살짜리 아들이 있다.
③ 매우 아픈 사람들은 병원에 갈 필요가 있다.
④ 너는 저기서 John과 이야기하고 있는 여자아이를 알고 있니?
⑤ 매우 멋지고 친절한 그녀의 오빠는 종종 우리에게 음식을 사주었다.
* 〈관계대명사 + be동사〉 뒤에 분사가 나오면 〈관계대명사 + be동사〉를 생략할 수 있다.

Sentence Writing

▶ 본문 252쪽

Part A
1 are many [a lot of, lots of] trees and flowers
2 is a wooden bench
3 comes a woman
4 a principal, the woman is in this school

Part B
1 Jeff won't go there, and neither will I.
2 It is you that [who] the teacher likes (the) best of all of the students.
3 The chicken pox is the very disease that Edward had discovered before.
4 Over the hill started the sudden shower.

Part A
1 학교 운동장에는 많은 나무들과 꽃들이 있다.
2 큰 나무 아래에는 나무로 만들어진 벤치가 하나 있다. 한 남자아이와 여자아이가 거기에서 앉아 아이스크림을 먹고 있다.
3 큰 모자를 쓴 여자 한 분이 오고 있다.
4 그 여자분은 바로 이 학교의 교장선생님이다.

총정리 모의고사

1회

▶ 본문 256 - 259쪽

01 ④ 02 ⑤ 03 ② 04 ④ 05 ③ 06 used, to 07 enough, to, know 08 ② 09 ③ 10 are being taken care of 11 ④ 12 ④ 13 my, father's, shouting 14 ③ 15 ① 16 ① 17 ⑤ 18 ② 19 ④ 20 ① 21 ② 22 ⑤ 23 ③ 24 ② 25 ②

01 ① 그 사장은 그를 은퇴하게 했다.

② 그 사실은 그녀를 정말로 실망하게 했다.
③ 그 선생님은 그들에게 문제를 풀게 했다.
④ Jessica는 그에게 뭔가 맛있는 것을 만들어주었다.
⑤ 그녀의 충고는 내가 했었던 것을 후회하게 했다.
* ④는 4형식(주어 + 동사 + 간접목적어 + 직접목적어) 문장이고, 나머지는 5형식(주어 + 동사 + 목적어 + 목적격 보어) 문장이다.

02 * 기준 시점이 과거(arrived)이고 그때까지 계속되던 행위를 나타내야 하므로, 과거완료 진행시제로 쓴다.

03 * 주어(you and I)가 강조되는 것이므로 강조구문 〈It + be동사 + 강조어구 + that ~〉으로 나타낼 수 있다. 이때 주어 you and I는 두 명이므로 동사는 are to blame이 와야 한다.

04 * 〈look forward to -ing〉에서 to는 전치사이므로 to 다음에 동명사가 나와야 한다.

05 A: Jason, 너는 왜 방을 치우지 않았니?
B: 제가 들어갔을 때, 방이 치워져 있다는 것을 알았어요. 저는 엄마가 치우셨다고 생각했어요. 그래서 저는 아무 것도 할 게 없었어요.
* [has been cleaned → had been cleaned] 주절의 동사(found)가 과거시제이고 종속절의 내용(방을 치운 것)이 더 이전에 발생했으므로 과거완료시제(had been cleaned)로 써야 한다.

06 Harry는 그 아파트에 살았지만 지금은 거기서 살지 않는다.
→ Harry는 그 아파트에서 살았었다.
* 현재는 아닌 과거의 상태(~하곤 했다)를 나타낼 때는 〈used to + 동사원형〉으로 쓴다.

07 나의 남편은 매우 똑똑해서 모든 것을 안다.
* 〈so + 형용사 + that + 주어 + can ...〉 = 〈형용사 + enough to부정사 ...〉 '매우 ~해서 …할 수 있다'

08 A: 나는 오늘 오후의 시험을 통과하지 못했어. 그것은 너무 어려웠어.
B: 너는 지난밤에 더 열심히 공부했어야 했어. 하지만 넌 컴퓨터게임을 했잖아.
* 문맥상 '지난밤에 공부를 더 열심히 했어야 했는데 하지 않고 놀았다'는 표현이 되어야 하므로 〈should have + 과거분사〉로 나타낸다.

09 그들은 나에게 좋은 책 한 권을 선물로 줬다.
→ 좋은 책 한 권이 그들에 의해 나에게 선물로 주어졌다.
* 4형식 동사 give는 직접목적어를 주어로 한 수동태로 만들 경우 간접목적어 앞에 전치사 to가 와야 한다.

10 A: 누가 나이든 사람들을 돌보고 있나요?
B: 그들은 Catherine이라는 이름의 여성에 의해 보살핌을 받고 있어요.
* 진행형 수동태는 〈be being + 과거분사〉 형태로 쓰며, 구동사 take care of는 하나의 동사로 보아 함께 써야 한다.

11 외로운 사람들은 같이 놀 수 있는 친구들이 필요하다.
* '같이 놀 수 있는 친구(play with some friends)'라는 의미이므로 전치사 with가 와야 한다.

12 나는 카페에서 공부를 하고 있었을 때, Danny가 그의 여자 친구와 함께 거리를 건너서 편의점에 들어가는 것을 봤다.
* [to go → go] 〈지각동사(saw) + 목적어(Danny) + 동사원형(cross ~ and go ~)〉의 형태가 되어야 한다.

13 어제 나의 아버지가 나에게 크게 소리치셨다. 나는 그의 행동을 이해할 수 없었다.
→ 나는 어제 나의 아버지가 나에게 크게 소리친 것을 이해할 수 없었다.
* 문맥상 '나의 아버지가 소리치는 것을'이라는 의미가 들어가야 하므로, 동명사의 의미상 주어 〈my father's + 동명사 (shouting)〉로 나타낸다.

14 ① Diana는 TV를 켜둔 채로 잠이 들었다.
② 저 여자아이들은 머리를 묶지 않은 채로 주위를 뛰어다녔다.
③ 저 사람들 모두는 그들의 얼굴이 칠해진 채로 일했다.
④ 전화가 온종일 울리는 채로 바쁜 날이었다.
⑤ 그 커플은 개들이 그들을 쫓아오게 하면서 산책했다.
* [painting → painted] '얼굴이 칠해진' 수동 관계이므로 〈with + 명사 + 과거분사〉의 형태로 써야 한다.

15 * 분사구문의 주어와 주절의 주어가 다르고 시제가 같으므로 There being이 먼저 와야 한다. '먹을 것이 없다'는 표현은 nothing to eat으로 나타낸다.

16 내 집이 가장 편안한 장소이다.
→ 다른 어떤 장소도 내 집보다 더 편한 곳은 없다.
* 〈the + 최상급〉 = 〈no other + 단수 명사 + 비교급 + than ~〉

17 * 과거 사실에 대한 소망을 말하는 것이므로 〈I wish + 주어 + had + 과거분사〉로 나타낸다.

18 ① 유나는 그렇게 하는 것이 맞았는지 물었다.
② 내일 비가 내린다면 그는 집에 있을 것이다.
③ 우리 팀이 이길지 아닐지는 아무도 모른다.
④ 내가 거기에 제시간에 도착할 수 있을지 확실하지 않다.
⑤ 그가 아직 결정하지 못했는지 나에게 말하지 말라.
* ②는 if가 부사절(조건)을 이끄는 접속사로 쓰였고, 나머지는 명사절을 이끄는 접속사로 쓰였다. 부사절을 이끌 때는 '~라면', 명사절을 이끌 때는 '~인지 아닌지'라는 뜻이다.

19 네가 가장 필요한 것은 이 논술에 대한 너의 선생님의 논평이다.
* 명사절을 이끌고 선행사를 포함하여 '~하는 것'이라는 의미로 쓰이는 것은 관계대명사 What이다.

20 (a) 나는 같이 일했던 남자를 만났다.
(b) Andrew는 창문이 다 깨진 차를 보았다.
(c)(d) 여기는 Jack이 어렸을 때 살았던 집이다.
* (a) [who → whom] 〈전치사 + 목적격 관계대명사〉의 형태가 되어야 한다.
(c) [in that Jack lived → that Jack lived in] 목적격 관계대명사 that 앞에는 전치사를 쓸 수 없다.

21 ① 의사는 아픈 사람들을 사랑해야 한다.
② 로마는 하루 아침에 이루어지지 않았다.
③ Frank와 Sue는 같은 학교에 다닌다.
④ 너는 일주일에 두 번씩 이 방을 방문해야 한다.
⑤ 탁자 위의 그 책은 매우 재미있지 않다.
* [the → a] '하루 만에'라는 의미가 되려면 부정관사로 써야 한다.

22 ① Lucy는 다리가 좀 더 길었다면 더 빠르게 뛸 수 있을 텐데.
→ Lucy는 다리가 좀 더 길지 않아서 좀 더 빠르게 뛸 수 없다.
② 네가 내 충고를 들었더라면 더 나은 삶을 살고 있었을 텐데.
→ 너는 내 충고를 듣지 않았기 때문에 더 나은 삶을 살지 않았다.
③ 그녀는 심각한 허리통증을 갖고 있었던 것처럼 보인다.
→ 사실 그녀는 심각한 허리통증을 갖고 있지 않았다.
④ 내가 지난 학기에 모든 과목을 공부했으면 좋았을 텐데.
→ 나는 지난 학기에 모든 과목을 공부하지 않아서 유감이다.
⑤ 내가 몇 분 전에 점심을 먹었더라면 지금 배가 고프지 않을 텐데.
→ 나는 몇 분 전에 점심을 먹지 않았기 때문에 지금 배가 고프다.
* [was → am] 혼합가정법 문장을 직설법 문장으로 바꿔 쓸 때 if절은 과거시제로, 주절은 현재시제로 써야 한다.

23 A: Jack이 아직 도착하지 않았어. 그가 곧 여기에 올지 모르겠어. 내가 물어볼 게 있거든.
B: 그는 심한 감기에 걸렸어. 만약 그가 건강했다면 여기에 이미 왔을 텐데.
A: 진짜? 그걸 몰랐네. 그에게 전화해서 괜찮은지 물어봐야겠다.
* [would come → would have come] 앞 문장이 과거시제이고, 조건절도 가정법 과거완료이므로, 주절은 〈would have + 과거분사〉의 형태로 써야 한다.

24 A: 너는 신문을 확인해봤니? 나는 재미있는 기사를 읽었어.
B: 무엇에 관한 거? 실종된 아이들 말이니?
A: 응. 실종된 아이들의 수를 알지 못한다네.
B: 말도 안 돼. 경찰이나 정부 둘 중 하나는 그 수를 알아.
A: 불행히도, 둘 다 몰라. 그것이 충격적인 소식이지.
* [are → is] 〈the number of + 복수명사〉가 주어로 올 경우 '~의 수'라는 뜻으로 단수 취급하므로 단수 동사가 온다.

25 어느 비 오는 날 Kevin은 집에 강아지 한 마리를 데리고 와서 그의 아버지에게 애완동물로 키워도 되냐고 물어봤다. 그의 아버지는 "너는 두 가지를 약속을 하는 한 그것을 키울 수 있어. 첫 번째는 어떠한 문제도 일으키지 않겠다는 것이다. 두 번째는 네 스스로 강아지를 돌봐야 한다는 것이다."
* 전달동사는 asked나 told, said to로 바꿔 쓸 수 있다. 피전달문에서 주어 He → I로 바꾸고, 의문사가 없는 의문문이므로 현재시제의 조동사 can를 이용한 의문문으로 바꿔 쓴다.

2회

▶ 본문 260 - 263쪽

01 ② **02** ③ **03** (1) had to take care of (2) must have been tired **04** ⑤ **05** ③ **06** ② **07** ② **08** ③ **09** ③ **10** ③, ⑤ **11** ⑤ **12** ④ **13** ② **14** meeting **15** ① **16** ④ **17** ② than → to **18** ⑤ **19** (1) Needless to say (2) attending this lecture **20** (1) Without (2) If, it, had, not, been, for (3) Had, it, not, been, for **21** When have → When did **22** (1) attend (2) attend **23** (1) However (2) Whoever **24** ④ **25** to carry it → to carry

01 저희 비행기는 30분 후 인천국제 공항에 도착할 예정입니다.

* 비행 시간, 기차 시간 등의 정해진 시간을 표현할 때 in 30minutes(30분 후에)라는 미래를 나타내는 어구가 있어도 현재시제로 미래시제를 나타낸다.

02 한국 영화의 가치는 미국 영화의 가치만큼 높게 여겨진다.

* 〈as + 원급 + as〉 형태로 표현해야 하며, 비교되는 대상이 The value of Korean movies이므로 이를 받는 말도 that(value) of American movies가 되어야 한다.

03 * (1) '~해야 했다'는 의무를 나타내는 조동사 must의 과거형은 had to로 나타낸다.
(2) '~였음에 틀림없다'는 과거의 추측은 〈must have + 과거분사〉로 나타낸다.

04 ① Tom은 아팠다고 생각된다.
② 그 소문은 사실이었을 리가 없었다.
③ 나는 물이 0도에서 언다고 배웠다.
④ 내가 너라면, 나는 그녀를 외롭게 두지 않을 텐데.
⑤ 그 책은 급하게 쓰였기 때문에 주목을 받지 못했다.

* [Having written → Having been written] Having written은 능동형 완료 분사구문이다. 주어인 the book이 쓰이는 것이므로 수동형 완료 분사구문이 되어야 한다.

05 ① 모두는 그가 정직한 남자라고 생각한다.
② 나는 여태까지 그의 새 영화를 본 적이 없다.
③ 그의 남동생은 그때까지 우리 중 누구도 만난 적이 없었다.
④ 그 팀은 첫 번째 공연을 위해 연습하려고 노력했다.
⑤ 새미는 Lina를 격려해주기 위해서 그녀의 아파트를 방문했다.

* [didn't meet → hadn't met] until then이 있으므로 과거완료시제로 써야 한다.

06 (1) 나의 차는 지금 수리기사에 의해 수리되는 중이다.
(2) 그의 노트북 컴퓨터는 아직 수리되지 않았다.

* (1) now가 있으므로 현재진행 수동태가 와야 한다.
(2) yet(이미)으로 보아 부정형 현재완료 수동태가 와야 한다.

07 (a) James는 낯선 사람에 의해서 그의 차를 도둑맞았다.
(b) 천이는 나에게 아침을 요리하라고 시켰다.

* (a) 사역동사 have의 목적어와 목적격 보어의 관계가 수동이면 목적격 보어는 과거분사가 온다.
(b) '~이 …하도록 시키다'의 의미를 가진 동사 get의 목적어와 목적격 보어의 관계가 능동이면 목적격 보어는 to부정사가 온다.

08 (a) 그 여자는 마치 그녀가 최고의 선생님인 것처럼 이야기한다.
(b) 그 남자아이는 그 때 어떤 외국어라도 했으면 좋았을 것이라고 생각한다.

* (a) 〈as if + 가정법 과거〉로 쓰이면 동사의 과거형이 와야 한다. 가정법에 쓰인 be동사는 항상 were로 쓰인다.
(b) 과거를 나타내는 at that time이 있으므로 〈주어 + wish + 가정법 과거완료〉가 와야 한다.

09 (a) 그가 내일 집에 돌아올지 말해줘.
(b) 성우는 내년에 그의 약혼자와 결혼하면 하와이로 신혼여행을 갈 것이다.

* (a) if가 명사절을 이끄는 경우 미래시제는 will을 써서 나타낸다.
(b) if가 조건의 부사절을 이끄는 경우 현재시제가 미래시제를 대신한다.

10 (a) 송 선생님은 내가 그의 방갈로에 머무르는 것을 허락하셨다.
(b) 우리는 그 학생이 나무에서 떨어지는 것을 보았다.

* (a) allow는 목적격 보어로 to부정사를 취한다.
(b) 지각동사 see는 목적격 보어로 동사원형이나 현재분사를 취한다.

11 나는 소심한 여자아이이다. 나는 어렸을 때 사람들과 이야기를 하지 않았었다. 지금 나는 웅변수업을 듣는다. 그래서 사람들과 이야기하는 것에 점점 익숙해지고 있다.

* 문맥상 '사람들과 이야기하는 것에 익숙해지고 있다'라는 의미이므로 〈get used to -ing〉가 와야 한다.

12 나는 한 유명한 강연자가 우리 마을로 온다는 것을 들었다. 나는 그의 강의를 듣기 위해 등록을 했다. 불행히도 나는 매우 실망했다. 왜냐하면 그의 강의는 매우 지루했기 때문이다.

* '그의 연설이 지루한' 감정을 주는 것이므로 현재분사로 나타내야 한다.

13 나의 아들은 지금 문제가 있다. 그가 그의 반 친구를 괴롭혔다. 그 피해자의 부모는 용서해주지 않을 것 같다. 너는 그가 얼마나 실망스러운지 상상하지 못할 것이다.

* '그가 실망스러운' 감정을 받는 것이므로 과거분사가 와야 하고, 〈how + 형용사(과거분사) + 주어 + 동사〉의 어순으로 써야 한다.

14 Smith 선생님은 전에 노스트롬 몰에서 나의 엄마를 만났던 것을 잊으셨다.

* '(전에) ~했던 것을 잊다'는 표현이 되려면 〈forget + 동명사〉의 형태로 쓴다.

15 * '둘 다 ~는 아니다'라는 부분부정은 both ~ not으로 표현한다. 두 명이므로 All이 아니라 Both가 와야 한다.

16 지희가 그녀의 엄마를 도와주었다면 그녀의 엄마는 그녀의 학위를 끝마칠 수 있었을 텐데.

* 주절에 could have finished가 있으므로 가정법 과거완료문장이다. 따라서 조건절에는 〈If + 주어 + had + 과거분사〉가 와야 한다. 이때 If가 생략되면 〈Had + 주어+ 과거분사〉의 어순이 된다.

17 (a) 주민들은 공장을 짓는 것보다 체육관을 짓는 것을 선호한다.
(b) 그 어린아이들은 집에 있는 것보다는 차라리 친구들과 함께 논다.

* 라틴어 비교급인 prefer는 〈prefer A to B〉로 쓰며, 'A보다 B를 더 좋아하다'라는 뜻이다.

18 A: 당신은 왜 여기에 왔나요?
B: 제가 저기에서 얘기했던 첫 번째 남자가 당신 가게를 추천해줬어요.

* '여기에는 왜 왔나요?'라는 표현은 What makes ~?로 표현한다. 선행사에 the first가 있으므로 관계대명사 that만 올 수 있다.

19 * (1) '말할 필요도 없이'는 독립부정사로 needless to say로 나타낸다.
(2) 동명사의 관용표현으로 '~할 만한 가치가 있다'는 〈be worthy -ing〉로 나타낸다.

20 그 돈이 없었다면 나의 가족은 여름 방학에 외국을 갈 수 없었을 텐데.

* 〈but for + 가정법 과거완료〉 = 〈without + 가정법 과거완료〉 = if it had not been for = Had it not been for

21 A: Sera와 너는 언제 이 호텔에 도착했니?
B: 우리는 여기에 막 도착했어.

* When은 현재완료시제와 함께 사용할 수 없다.

22 (1) 많은 수의 사람들이 그의 수업에 참석한다.
(2) 그들 대부분은 프로젝트 회의에 참석한다.

* (1) 〈a number of + 복수 명사 + 복수 동사〉
(2) 〈most of + 복수 명사 + 복수 동사〉

23 (1) 밖이 아무리 더워도 우리는 수영하러 갈 것이다.
(2) 먼저 끝내는 사람은 누구든지 우승자가 될 것이다.

* (1) 문맥상 '아무리 ~하더라도'라는 의미가 되려면 〈however + 형용사 + 주어 + 동사〉로 나타낸다.
(2) 본동사가 will be이고 문맥상 '~하는 누구든지'라는 의미가 되려면 whoever가 알맞다.

24 ① 나의 계획은 더 나은 점수를 받는 것이었다.
② 네가 나의 의자를 가져다 준 것은 친절하다.
③ 새 단어를 찾아보는 것이 나의 공부 습관이다.
④ 나는 산꼭대기까지 도달하는 목표가 있다.
⑤ 나는 4시에 너의 사무실에 들를 것을 잊지 않을 것이다.

* ④는 형용사적 용법으로 쓰여 앞의 명사 a goal을 수식한다. 나머지는 명사적 용법으로 쓰였다. ① 보어 역할, ② 진주어 역할, ③ 주어 역할, ⑤ 목적어 역할

25 이 상자는 너무 무거워서 내가 그것을 나를 수 없다.

* to부정사의 목적어와 문장의 주어가 같으면 중복해서 사용하지 않는다.

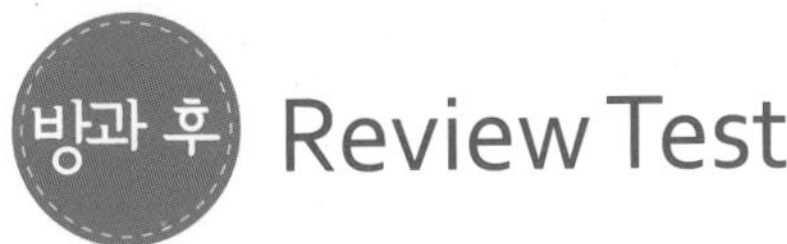

DAY 01 5형식 문장 ▶ 본문 266쪽

A 1 to work 2 sing 3 wash 4 to speak

B 1 played → play[playing] 2 making → make[to make]
3 to buy → buy 4 OK

C 1 I found it difficult to be a good teacher.
2 Thomas thinks of himself as a pretty smart boy.

DAY 02 현재완료시제, 과거완료시제 ▶ 본문 267쪽

A 1 before 2 How long 3 had bought 4 was

B 1 have → did
2 don't find → haven't found 혹은 didn't find
3 has → 삭제
4 He raises → He has raised

C 1 My computer has been broken since last night.
2 I have never been abroad in my life.

DAY 03 미래완료시제, 완료진행시제 ▶ 본문 268쪽

A 1 had been going 2 have drunk 3 had been playing

B 1 OK 2 has → had 3 will know → will have known

C 1 Ethan has been talking to his girlfriend on the phone for half an hour.
2 My sister has been learning Chinese for several years.
3 When I phoned my friend, she had been singing songs.

DAY 04 will/would, can/could ▶ 본문 269쪽

A 1 Will 2 cannot have finished 3 will /be going to
4 Could 5 would rather

B 1 may not → cannot 2 to go → go 3 must → cannot
4 can be going to → will be able to

C 1 Abigail cannot have made such a big mistake.
2 I could have bought a better computer, but I didn't have enough money.

DAY 05 may/might, must/have to ▶ 본문 270쪽

A 1 must have been 2 might have been
3 had to 4 must 5 may as well

B 1 went → have gone 2 buy → bought
3 win → have won

C 1 His opinion may not be true.
2 I will have to submit my report by next Monday.

DAY 06 should, had better, used to ▶ 본문 271쪽

A 1 need 2 used to buy 3 had better 4 dare not

B 1 shouldn't → should 2 has → had 3 would → used to

C 1 Did you use to play that computer game?
2 He would often go to an Internet cafe when he was young.
3 You should study harder to enter university.

DAY 07 4, 5형식 문장의 수동태 ▶ 본문 272쪽

A 1 to cross 2 to feel 3 for 4 given

B 1 for → to 2 stealed → stolen 3 OK 4 drive → to drive

C 1 I was told to come back home by 9 o'clock.
2 I was given a bouquet of flowers for our wedding anniversary by my husband.

DAY 08 주의해야 할 수동태 ▶ 본문 273쪽

A 1 was run over by 2 is believed
3 costs 4 been closed

B 1 serve → served 2 taught → been taught
3 care → care of 4 preparing → prepared 혹은 by → to

C 1 This matter must be handled as soon as possible.
2 We are asked to submit our term papers by next Friday.

DAY 09 to부정사의 명사적 용법 ▶ 본문 274쪽

A 1 crying 2 throw 3 to do 4 for

B 1 comes → come
2 who should we → who we should 혹은 who to
3 for the young → the young
4 to repair → repair

C 1 Mom will allow me to play computer games with my friends.
2 When I was in L.A., I felt the apartment shaking.

DAY 10 to부정사의 형용사적, 부사적 용법 ▶ 본문 275쪽

A 1 big enough 2 couldn't 3 only to 4 to increase

B 1 swim → swim in 2 for breaking → to break
3 not → not to 4 so → too

C 1 My mother used a coupon to get a discount at the department store.
2 Do you need someone to help you with your presentation?

DAY 11 to부정사의 기타 용법 ▶ 본문 276쪽

A 1 to have 2 to 3 to be invited 4 to have stayed

B 1 to have forgotten 2 seems, my computer is
3 seemed to be 4 seems, he was

C 1 I like baseball, not to mention soccer.
2 I was lost. To make matters worse, it began to rain.

DAY 12 동명사의 용법, 시제, 능동과 수동 ▶ 본문 277쪽

A **1** changing **2** having made **3** being promoted
4 students' **5** Helping

B **1** Following not → Not following
2 swim → swimming
3 telling → being told

C **1** It is no use crying over spilt milk.
2 Ben got used to walking to work.

DAY 13 동사에 따른 목적어의 형태, 관용표현 ▶ 본문 278쪽

A **1** eating **2** passing **3** worrying **4** giving **5** working

B **1** go → going **2** to share → sharing
3 to have → having **4** to drive → driving

C **1** Some students start learning Japanese in high school.
2 I am looking forward to you(r) visiting my blog.

DAY 14 분사, 분사구문 ▶ 본문 279쪽

A **1** occurring **2** Being located **3** turned
4 Not having **5** cut

B **1** played → playing **2** tiring → tired **3** broke → broken

C **1** Many people interested in losing weight were excited by the news.
2 She concentrated on listening to music with her eyes closed.

DAY 15 분사구문의 시제와 수동태 ▶ 본문 280쪽

A **1** Being **2** Having spent **3** There being
4 Frankly speaking **5** Impressed

B **1** Be → Having been **2** Don't finished → Not Finishing
3 Injuring → Having been injured

C **1** Frankly speaking, Emma is not that beautiful.
2 Not knowing how to solve the problem, he decided to give up on it.

DAY 16 비교급, 최상급 ▶ 본문 281쪽

A **1** the most romantic **2** any other **3** as **4** far

B **1** better → 삭제 **2** doctors → doctor
3 could → can **4** more → 삭제

C **1** Ellen speaks Korean much more fluently than Jonathan.
2 The more you study for the final exam, the better grade you can get.

DAY 17 관계대명사 ▶ 본문 282쪽

A **1** who **2** whose **3** with whom **4** which

B **1** whom → who[that] **2** that → whose
3 who → whom **4** of → 삭제

C **1** This is my diary which I have written since I was a child.
2 I looked for the man whose credit card had been lost.

DAY 18 주의해야 할 관계대명사 ▶ 본문 283쪽

A **1** that **2** what **3** whom **4** with which

B **1** which → that **2** that → what
3 that → who **4** who → that

C **1** Mr. Bossman gave me this English grammar book, which was very helpful.
2 Dora lost the prettiest doll (that) she had.

DAY 19 관계부사, 복합관계사 ▶ 본문 284쪽

A **1** how **2** whatever **3** however **4** anything that

B **1** Whatever → However **2** OK
3 OK **4** where → which

C **1** Do you know how your mother folded the paper cranes?
2 Whoever wants to take the lesson will be welcomed.

DAY 20 관사의 의미와 용법 (심화) ▶ 본문 285쪽

A **1** × **2** the **3** the

B **1** the front → front **2** a → the
3 names → the names **4** OK

C **1** is an officer in the ROK Air force
2 a cell phone on the street. And the phone suddenly rang

DAY 21 가정법 과거, 과거완료, 혼합가정법 ▶ 본문 286쪽

A **1** had known **2** be **3** walk **4** have done

B **1** feel → have felt **2** was → were
3 had → 삭제 **4** didn't study → hadn't studied

C **1** If I had gone back to university, I might have become a surgeon.
2 If I weren't busy, I could meet you now.

DAY 22 기타 가정법 ▶ 본문 287쪽

A **1** were **2** had **3** had not been **4** had been

B **1** was → were **2** I had → Had I **3** saw → had seen

C **1** But for the Internet, we could not find this valuable information.
2 Isabella acts as if she had completed the presentation by herself.

DAY 23 일치 ▶ 본문 288쪽

A **1** broke **2** is **3** had studied **4** were

B **1** have → has **2** want → wants **3** OK **4** is → are

C **1** My mother said that she never puts sugar and cream in her coffee.
2 Every student studies hard on the final exam.

DAY 24 화법 전환

▶ 본문 289쪽

A **1** my favorite food was **2** said to
3 the previous day **4** not to touch

B **1** told → asked **2** to not → not to
3 did he leave → he left

C **1** My mother told me not to go to the movies.
2 The secretary asked me if I had liked coffee before.

DAY 25 강조, 부정

▶ 본문 290쪽

A **1** the very **2** does **3** None **4** on earth

B **1** on → in **2** him → he **3** wasn't → was

C **1** I don't know how to play the guitar at all.
2 It was at the park where I came across Jim.

DAY 26 도치, 생략

▶ 본문 291쪽

A **1** it passed **2** was her son tired
3 So have **4** Neither did

B **1** she gave → did she give **2** you are → it is
3 the bus is → is the bus **4** neither → and neither

C **1** Some students like math, and others (like) English.
2 Little did I dream that I would meet her again.